# Getting Started with Python

Understand key data structures and use Python in
object-oriented programming

**Fabrizio Romano**
**Benjamin Baka**
**Dusty Phillips**

BIRMINGHAM - MUMBAI

# Getting Started with Python

First published: February 2019

Production reference: 1270219

Published by Packt Publishing Ltd.
Livery Place
35 Livery Street
Birmingham
B3 2PB, UK.

ISBN 978-1-83855-191-9

www.packtpub.com

`mapt.io`

Mapt is an online digital library that gives you full access to over 5,000 books and videos, as well as industry leading tools to help you plan your personal development and advance your career. For more information, please visit our website.

## Why subscribe?

- Spend less time learning and more time coding with practical eBooks and Videos from over 4,000 industry professionals

- Improve your learning with Skill Plans built especially for you

- Get a free eBook or video every month

- Mapt is fully searchable

- Copy and paste, print, and bookmark content

## Packt.com

Did you know that Packt offers eBook versions of every book published, with PDF and ePub files available? You can upgrade to the eBook version at `www.packt.com` and as a print book customer, you are entitled to a discount on the eBook copy. Get in touch with us at `customercare@packtpub.com` for more details.

At `www.packt.com`, you can also read a collection of free technical articles, sign up for a range of free newsletters, and receive exclusive discounts and offers on Packt books and eBooks.

# Contributors

## About the authors

**Fabrizio Romano** holds a master's degree in computer science engineering from the University of Padova. He is also a certified scrum master, Reiki master and teacher, and a member of CNHC. He moved to London in 2011 to work for companies, such as Glasses Direct and TBG/Sprinklr. He now works at Sohonet as a principal engineer/team lead. He has given talks on Teaching Python and TDD at two editions of EuroPython, and at Skillsmatter and ProgSCon in London.

**Benjamin Baka** works as a software developer and considers himself to be language agnostic and seeks out the elegant solutions which his toolset of C, Java, Python, Ruby, and other languages can enable him to accomplish. With a huge interest in algorithms, he seeks to always write code that borrows from Dr. Knuth's words, both simple and elegant. He also enjoys playing the bass guitar and listening to silence. He currently works with mPedigree Network.

**Dusty Phillips** is a software developer and author currently living in New Brunswick. He has been active in the open source community for two decades and has been programming in Python for nearly as long. He holds a master's degree in computer science and has worked for Facebook, the United Nations, and several start-ups. He's currently researching privacy-preserving technology at beanstalk.network. *Python 3 Object-Oriented Programming* is his first book. He has also written *Creating Apps in Kivy*, and self-published *Hacking Happy*, a journey to mental wellness for the technically inclined. A work of fiction is coming as well, so stay tuned!

# Packt is searching for authors like you

If you're interested in becoming an author for Packt, please visit `authors.packtpub.com` and apply today. We have worked with thousands of developers and tech professionals, just like you, to help them share their insight with the global tech community. You can make a general application, apply for a specific hot topic that we are recruiting an author for, or submit your own idea.

# Table of Contents

# Preface

This learning path helps you get comfortable in the world of Python. It starts with a thorough and practical introduction to Python. You'll quickly start writing programs in the first part of the learning path. With the power of linked lists, binary searches, and sorting algorithms, you'll easily create complex data structures, such as graphs, stacks, and queues. After understanding cooperative inheritance, you'll expertly raise, handle, and manipulate exceptions. You will effortlessly integrate the object-oriented and not-so-object-oriented aspects of Python, and create maintainable applications using higher level design patterns. Once you've covered the core topics, you'll understand the joy of unit testing and just how easy it is to create unit tests.

By the end of this learning path, you will have built components that are easy to understand, debug, and can be used across different applications.

This learning path includes content from the following Packt products:

- Learn Python Programming – Second Edition by Fabrizio Romano
- Python Data Structures and Algorithms by Benjamin Baka
- Python 3 Object-Oriented Programming by Dusty Phillips

## Who this book is for

If you are relatively new to coding and want to write scripts or programs to accomplish tasks using Python, or if you are an object-oriented programmer for other languages and seeking a leg up in the world of Python, then this learning path is for you. Though not essential, it will help you to have basic knowledge of programming and OOP.

## What this book covers

Chapter 1, *A Gentle Introduction to Python*, introduces you to fundamental programming concepts. It guides you through getting Python up and running on your computer and introduces you to some of its constructs.

Chapter 2, *Built-in Data Types*, introduces you to Python built-in data types. Python has a very rich set of native data types, and this chapter will give you a description and a short example for each of them.

Chapter 3, *Iterating and Making Decisions*, teaches you how to control the flow of your code by inspecting conditions, applying logic, and performing loops.

Chapter 4, *Functions, the Building Blocks of Code*, teaches you how to write functions. Functions are the keys to reusing code, to reducing debugging time, and, in general, to writing better code.

Chapter 5, *Files and Data Persistence*, teaches you how to deal with files, streams, data interchange formats, and databases, among other things.

Chapter 6, *Principles of Algorithm Design*, covers how we can build structures with specific capabilities using the existing Python data structures. In general, the data structures we create need to conform to a number of principles. These principles include robustness, adaptability, reusability, and separating the structure from a function. We look at the role iteration plays and introduce recursive data structures.

Chapter 7, *Lists and Pointer Structures*, covers linked lists, which are one of the most common data structures and are often used to implement other structures, such as stacks and queues. In this chapter, we describe their operation and implementation. We compare their behavior to arrays and discuss the relative advantages and disadvantages of each.

Chapter 8, *Stacks and Queues*, discusses the behavior and demonstrates some implementations of these linear data structures. We give examples of typical applications.

Chapter 9, *Trees*, will look at how to implement a binary tree. Trees form the basis of many of the most important advanced data structures. We will examine how to traverse trees and retrieve and insert values. We will also look at how to create structures such as heaps.

Chapter 10, *Hashing and Symbol Tables*, describes symbol tables, gives some typical implementations, and discusses various applications. We will look at the process of hashing, give an implementation of a hash table, and discuss the various design considerations.

Chapter 11, *Graphs and Other Algorithms*, looks at some of the more specialized structures, including graphs and spatial structures. Representing data as a set of nodes and vertices is convenient in a number of applications, and from this, we can create structures such as directed and undirected graphs. We will also introduce some other structures and concepts such as priority queues, heaps, and selection algorithms.

Chapter 12, *Searching*, discusses the most common searching algorithms and gives examples of their use for various data structures. Searching a data structure is a fundamental task and there are a number of approaches.

Chapter 13, *Sorting*, looks at the most common approaches to sorting. This will include bubble sort, insertion sort, and selection sort.

Chapter 14, *Selection Algorithms*, covers algorithms that involve finding statistics, such as the minimum, maximum, or median elements in a list. There are a number of approaches and one of the most common approaches is to first apply a sort operation. Other approaches include partition and linear selection.

Chapter 15, *Object-Oriented Design*, covers important object-oriented concepts. It deals mainly with terminology such as abstraction, classes, encapsulation, and inheritance. We also briefly look at UML to model our classes and objects.

Chapter 16, *Objects in Python*, discusses classes and objects as they are used in Python. We will learn about attributes and behaviors of Python objects, and the organization of classes into packages and modules. Lastly, we will see how to protect our data.

Chapter 17, *When Objects Are Alike*, gives us a more in-depth look into inheritance. It covers multiple inheritance and shows us how to extend built-in. This chapter also covers how polymorphism and duck typing work in Python.

Chapter 18, *Expecting the Unexpected*, looks into exceptions and exception handling. We will learn how to create our own exceptions and how to use exceptions for program flow control.

Chapter 19, *When to Use Object-Oriented Programming*, deals with creating and using objects. We will see how to wrap data using properties and restrict data access. This chapter also discusses the DRY principle and how not to repeat code.

Chapter 20, *Python Object-Oriented Shortcuts*, as the name suggests, deals with time-savers in Python. We will look at many useful built-in functions, such as method overloading using default arguments. We'll also see that functions themselves are objects and how this is useful.

Chapter 21, *The Iterator Pattern*, introduces the concept of design patterns and covers Python's iconic implementation of the iterator pattern. We'll learn about list, set, and dictionary comprehensions. We'll also demystify generators and coroutines.

Chapter 22, *Python Design Patterns I*, covers several design patterns, including the decorator, observer, strategy, state, singleton, and template patterns. Each pattern is discussed with suitable examples and programs implemented in Python.

Chapter 23, *Python Design Patterns II*, wraps up our discussion of design patterns with coverage of the adapter, facade, flyweight, command, abstract, and composite patterns. More examples of how idiomatic Python code differs from canonical implementations are provided.

Chapter 24, *Testing Object-Oriented Programs*, opens with why testing is so important in Python applications. It focuses on test-driven development and introduces two different testing suites: unittest and py.test. Finally, it discusses mocking test objects and code coverage.

# To get the most out of this book

The code in this book will require you to run Python 2.7.x or higher. Python's default interactive environment can also be used to run the snippets of code.

Some of the examples in this book rely on third-party libraries that do not ship with Python. They are introduced within the book at the time they are used, so you do not need to install them in advance.

# Download the example code files

You can download the example code files for this book from your account at www.packt.com. If you purchased this book elsewhere, you can visit www.packt.com/support and register to have the files emailed directly to you.

You can download the code files by following these steps:

1. Log in or register at www.packt.com.
2. Select the **SUPPORT** tab.
3. Click on **Code Downloads & Errata**.
4. Enter the name of the book in the **Search** box and follow the onscreen instructions.

Once the file is downloaded, please make sure that you unzip or extract the folder using the latest version of:

- WinRAR/7-Zip for Windows
- Zipeg/iZip/UnRarX for Mac
- 7-Zip/PeaZip for Linux

The code bundle for the book is also hosted on GitHub at https://github.com/ PacktPublishing/Getting-Started-with-Python. In case there's an update to the code, it will be updated on the existing GitHub repository.

We also have other code bundles from our rich catalog of books and videos available at https://github.com/PacktPublishing/. Check them out!

# Conventions used

There are a number of text conventions used throughout this book.

`CodeInText`: Indicates code words in text, database table names, folder names, filenames, file extensions, pathnames, dummy URLs, user input, and Twitter handles. Here is an example: "The `if`, `else`, and `elif` statements control the conditional execution of statements."

A block of code is set as follows:

```
a=10; b=20
def my_function():
```

When we wish to draw your attention to a particular part of a code block, the relevant lines or items are set in bold:

```
if "WARNING" in l:
    yield l.replace("\tWARNING", "")
```

Any command-line input or output is written as follows:

```
>>> print(warnings_filter([]))
```

**Bold**: Indicates a new term, an important word, or words that you see onscreen. For example, words in menus or dialog boxes appear in the text like this. Here is an example: "Then you have to manually click **Yes** or **No** if the label matches the color."

Warnings or important notes appear like this.

Tips and tricks appear like this.

# Get in touch

Feedback from our readers is always welcome.

**General feedback**: If you have questions about any aspect of this book, mention the book title in the subject of your message and email us at customercare@packtpub.com.

**Errata**: Although we have taken every care to ensure the accuracy of our content, mistakes do happen. If you have found a mistake in this book, we would be grateful if you would report this to us. Please visit www.packt.com/submit-errata, selecting your book, clicking on the Errata Submission Form link, and entering the details.

**Piracy**: If you come across any illegal copies of our works in any form on the Internet, we would be grateful if you would provide us with the location address or website name. Please contact us at copyright@packt.com with a link to the material.

**If you are interested in becoming an author**: If there is a topic that you have expertise in and you are interested in either writing or contributing to a book, please visit authors.packtpub.com.

# Reviews

Please leave a review. Once you have read and used this book, why not leave a review on the site that you purchased it from? Potential readers can then see and use your unbiased opinion to make purchase decisions, we at Packt can understand what you think about our products, and our authors can see your feedback on their book. Thank you!

For more information about Packt, please visit packt.com.

# A Gentle Introduction to Python

**1**

*"Give a man a fish and you feed him for a day. Teach a man to fish and you feed him for a lifetime."*

*– Chinese proverb*

According to Wikipedia, **computer programming** is:

*"...a process that leads from an original formulation of a computing problem to executable computer programs. Programming involves activities such as analysis, developing understanding, generating algorithms, verification of requirements of algorithms including their correctness and resources consumption, and implementation (commonly referred to as coding) of algorithms in a target programming language."*

In a nutshell, coding is telling a computer to do something using a language it understands.

Computers are very powerful tools, but unfortunately, they can't think for themselves. They need to be told everything: how to perform a task, how to evaluate a condition to decide which path to follow, how to handle data that comes from a device, such as the network or a disk, and how to react when something unforeseen happens, say, something is broken or missing.

You can code in many different styles and languages. Is it hard? I would say *yes* and *no*. It's a bit like writing. Everybody can learn how to write, and you can too. But, what if you wanted to become a poet? Then writing alone is not enough. You have to acquire a whole other set of skills and this will take a longer and greater effort.

In the end, it all comes down to how far you want to go down the road. Coding is not just putting together some instructions that work. It is so much more!

Good code is short, fast, elegant, easy to read and understand, simple, easy to modify and extend, easy to scale and refactor, and easy to test. It takes time to be able to write code that has all these qualities at the same time, but the good news is that you're taking the first step towards it at this very moment by reading this book. And I have no doubt you can do it. Anyone can; in fact, we all program all the time, only we aren't aware of it.

Would you like an example?

Say you want to make instant coffee. You have to get a mug, the instant coffee jar, a teaspoon, water, and the kettle. Even if you're not aware of it, you're evaluating a lot of data. You're making sure that there is water in the kettle and that the kettle is plugged in, that the mug is clean, and that there is enough coffee in the jar. Then, you boil the water and maybe, in the meantime, you put some coffee in the mug. When the water is ready, you pour it into the cup, and stir.

So, how is this programming?

Well, we gathered resources (the kettle, coffee, water, teaspoon, and mug) and we verified some conditions concerning them (the kettle is plugged in, the mug is clean, and there is enough coffee). Then we started two actions (boiling the water and putting coffee in the mug), and when both of them were completed, we finally ended the procedure by pouring water in to the mug and stirring.

Can you see it? I have just described the high-level functionality of a coffee program. It wasn't that hard because this is what the brain does all day long: evaluate conditions, decide to take actions, carry out tasks, repeat some of them, and stop at some point. Clean objects, put them back, and so on.

All you need now is to learn how to deconstruct all those actions you do automatically in real life so that a computer can actually make some sense of them. And you need to learn a language as well, to instruct it.

So this is what this book is for. I'll tell you how to do it and I'll try to do that by means of many simple but focused examples (my favorite kind).

In this chapter, we are going to cover the following:

- Python's characteristics and ecosystem
- Guidelines on how to get up and running with Python and virtual environments

- How to run Python programs
- How to organize Python code and Python's execution model

# A proper introduction

I love to make references to the real world when I teach coding; I believe they help people retain the concepts better. However, now is the time to be a bit more rigorous and see what coding is from a more technical perspective.

When we write code, we're instructing a computer about the things it has to do. Where does the action happen? In many places: the computer memory, hard drives, network cables, the CPU, and so on. It's a whole *world*, which most of the time is the representation of a subset of the real world.

If you write a piece of software that allows people to buy clothes online, you will have to represent real people, real clothes, real brands, sizes, and so on and so forth, within the boundaries of a program.

In order to do so, you will need to create and handle objects in the program you're writing. A person can be an object. A car is an object. A pair of socks is an object. Luckily, Python understands objects very well.

The two main features any object has are properties and methods. Let's take a person object as an example. Typically in a computer program, you'll represent people as customers or employees. The properties that you store against them are things like the name, the SSN, the age, if they have a driving license, their email, gender, and so on. In a computer program, you store all the data you need in order to use an object for the purpose you're serving. If you are coding a website to sell clothes, you probably want to store the heights and weights as well as other measures of your customers so that you can suggest the appropriate clothes for them. So, properties are characteristics of an object. We use them all the time: *Could you pass me that pen?—Which one?—The black one*. Here, we used the *black* property of a pen to identify it (most likely among a blue and a red one).

Methods are things that an object can do. As a person, I have methods such as *speak, walk, sleep, wake up, eat, dream, write, read,* and so on. All the things that I can do could be seen as methods of the objects that represent me.

So, now that you know what objects are and that they expose methods that you can run and properties that you can inspect, you're ready to start coding. Coding in fact is simply about managing those objects that live in the subset of the world that we're reproducing in our software. You can create, use, reuse, and delete objects as you please.

According to the *Data Model* chapter on the official Python documentation (`https://docs.python.org/3/reference/datamodel.html`):

> *"Objects are Python's abstraction for data. All data in a Python program is represented by objects or by relations between objects."*

We'll take a closer look at Python objects in later chapters. For now, all we need to know is that every object in Python has an ID (or identity), a type, and a value.

Once created, the ID of an object is never changed. It's a unique identifier for it, and it's used behind the scenes by Python to retrieve the object when we want to use it.

The type, as well, never changes. The type tells what operations are supported by the object and the possible values that can be assigned to it.

We'll see Python's most important data types in `Chapter 2`, *Built-in Data Types*.

The value can either change or not. If it can, the object is said to be **mutable**, while when it cannot, the object is said to be **immutable**.

How do we use an object? We give it a name, of course! When you give an object a name, then you can use the name to retrieve the object and use it.

In a more generic sense, objects such as numbers, strings (text), collections, and so on are associated with a name. Usually, we say that this name is the name of a variable. You can see the variable as being like a box, which you can use to hold data.

So, you have all the objects you need; what now? Well, we need to use them, right? We may want to send them over a network connection or store them in a database. Maybe display them on a web page or write them into a file. In order to do so, we need to react to a user filling in a form, or pressing a button, or opening a web page and performing a search. We react by running our code, evaluating conditions to choose which parts to execute, how many times, and under which circumstances.

And to do all this, basically we need a language. That's what Python is for. Python is the language we'll use together throughout this book to instruct the computer to do something for us.

Now, enough of this theoretical stuff; let's get started.

# Enter the Python

Python is the marvelous creation of Guido Van Rossum, a Dutch computer scientist and mathematician who decided to gift the world with a project he was playing around with over Christmas 1989. The language appeared to the public somewhere around 1991, and since then has evolved to be one of the leading programming languages used worldwide today.

I started programming when I was 7 years old, on a Commodore VIC-20, which was later replaced by its bigger brother, the Commodore 64. Its language was *BASIC*. Later on, I landed on Pascal, Assembly, C, C++, Java, JavaScript, Visual Basic, PHP, ASP, ASP .NET, C#, and other minor languages I cannot even remember, but only when I landed on Python did I finally have that feeling that you have when you find the right couch in the shop. When all of your body parts are yelling, *Buy this one! This one is perfect for us!*

It took me about a day to get used to it. Its syntax is a bit different from what I was used to, but after getting past that initial feeling of discomfort (like having new shoes), I just fell in love with it. Deeply. Let's see why.

# About Python

Before we get into the gory details, let's get a sense of why someone would want to use Python (I would recommend you to read the Python page on Wikipedia to get a more detailed introduction).

To my mind, Python epitomizes the following qualities.

# Portability

Python runs everywhere, and porting a program from Linux to Windows or Mac is usually just a matter of fixing paths and settings. Python is designed for portability and it takes care of specific **operating system** (**OS**) quirks behind interfaces that shield you from the pain of having to write code tailored to a specific platform.

# Coherence

Python is extremely logical and coherent. You can see it was designed by a brilliant computer scientist. Most of the time, you can just guess how a method is called, if you don't know it.

You may not realize how important this is right now, especially if you are at the beginning, but this is a major feature. It means less cluttering in your head, as well as less skimming through the documentation, and less need for mappings in your brain when you code.

# Developer productivity

According to Mark Lutz (*Learning Python, 5th Edition, O'Reilly Media*), a Python program is typically one-fifth to one-third the size of equivalent Java or C++ code. This means the job gets done faster. And faster is good. Faster means a faster response on the market. Less code not only means less code to write, but also less code to read (and professional coders read much more than they write), less code to maintain, to debug, and to refactor.

Another important aspect is that Python runs without the need for lengthy and time-consuming compilation and linkage steps, so you don't have to wait to see the results of your work.

# An extensive library

Python has an incredibly wide standard library (it's said to come with *batteries included*). If that wasn't enough, the Python community all over the world maintains a body of third-party libraries, tailored to specific needs, which you can access freely at the **Python Package Index** (**PyPI**). When you code Python and you realize that you need a certain feature, in most cases, there is at least one library where that feature has already been implemented for you.

# Software quality

Python is heavily focused on readability, coherence, and quality. The language uniformity allows for high readability and this is crucial nowadays where coding is more of a collective effort than a solo endeavor. Another important aspect of Python is its intrinsic multiparadigm nature. You can use it as a scripting language, but you also can exploit object-oriented, imperative, and functional programming styles. It is versatile.

# Software integration

Another important aspect is that Python can be extended and integrated with many other languages, which means that even when a company is using a different language as their mainstream tool, Python can come in and act as a glue agent between complex applications that need to talk to each other in some way. This is kind of an advanced topic, but in the real world, this feature is very important.

# Satisfaction and enjoyment

Last, but not least, there is the fun of it! Working with Python is fun. I can code for 8 hours and leave the office happy and satisfied, alien to the struggle other coders have to endure because they use languages that don't provide them with the same amount of well-designed data structures and constructs. Python makes coding fun, no doubt about it. And fun promotes motivation and productivity.

# What are the drawbacks?

Probably, the only drawback that one could find in Python, which is not due to personal preferences, is its *execution speed*. Typically, Python is slower than its compiled brothers. The standard implementation of Python produces, when you run an application, a compiled version of the source code called byte code (with the extension `.pyc`), which is then run by the Python interpreter. The advantage of this approach is portability, which we pay for with a slowdown due to the fact that Python is not compiled down to machine level as are other languages.

However, Python speed is rarely a problem today, hence its wide use regardless of this suboptimal feature. What happens is that, in real life, hardware cost is no longer a problem, and usually it's easy enough to gain speed by parallelizing tasks. Moreover, many programs spend a great proportion of the time waiting for IO operations to complete; therefore, the raw execution speed is often a secondary factor to the overall performance. When it comes to number crunching though, one can switch to faster Python implementations, such as PyPy, which provides an average five-fold speedup by implementing advanced compilation techniques (check `http://pypy.org/` for reference).

When doing data science, you'll most likely find that the libraries that you use with Python, such as **Pandas** and **NumPy**, achieve native speed due to the way they are implemented.

If that wasn't a good-enough argument, you can always consider that Python has been used to drive the backend of services such as Spotify and Instagram, where performance is a concern. Nonetheless, Python has done its job perfectly adequately.

# Who is using Python today?

Not yet convinced? Let's take a very brief look at the companies that are using Python today: Google, YouTube, Dropbox, Yahoo!, Zope Corporation, Industrial Light & Magic, Walt Disney Feature Animation, Blender 3D, Pixar, NASA, the NSA, Red Hat, Nokia, IBM, Netflix, Yelp, Intel, Cisco, HP, Qualcomm, and JPMorgan Chase, to name just a few.

Even games such as *Battlefield 2, Civilization IV,* and *QuArK* are implemented using Python.

Python is used in many different contexts, such as system programming, web programming, GUI applications, gaming and robotics, rapid prototyping, system integration, data science, database applications, and much more. Several prestigious universities have also adopted Python as their main language in computer science courses.

# Setting up the environment

Before we talk about installing Python on your system, let me tell you about which Python version I'll be using in this book.

# Python 2 versus Python 3

Python comes in two main versions: Python 2, which is the past, and Python 3, which is the present. The two versions, though very similar, are incompatible in some respects.

In the real world, Python 2 is actually quite far from being the past. In short, even though Python 3 has been out since 2008, the transition phase from Version 2 is still far from being over. This is mostly due to the fact that Python 2 is widely used in the industry, and of course, companies aren't so keen on updating their systems just for the sake of updating them, following the *if it ain't broke, don't fix it* philosophy. You can read all about the transition between the two versions on the web.

Another issue that has hindered the transition is the availability of third-party libraries. Usually, a Python project relies on tens of external libraries, and of course, when you start a new project, you need to be sure that there is already a Version-3-compatible library for any business requirement that may come up. If that's not the case, starting a brand-new project in Python 3 means introducing a potential risk, which many companies are not happy to take.

At the time of writing, though, the majority of the most widely used libraries have been ported to Python 3, and it's quite safe to start a project in Python 3 for most cases. Many of the libraries have been rewritten so that they are compatible with both versions, mostly harnessing the power of the `six` library (the name comes from the multiplication 2 x 3, due to the porting from Version 2 to 3), which helps introspecting and adapting the behavior according to the version used. According to PEP 373 (`https://legacy.python.org/dev/peps/pep-0373/`), the **end of life** (**EOL**) of Python 2.7 has been set to 2020, and there won't be a Python 2.8, so this is the time when companies that have projects running in Python 2 need to start devising an upgrade strategy to move to Python 3 before it's too late.

On my box (MacBook Pro), this is the latest Python version I have:

```
>>> import sys
>>> print(sys.version)
3.7.0a3 (default, Jan 27 2018, 00:46:45)
[Clang 9.0.0 (clang-900.0.39.2)]
```

So you can see that the version is an alpha release of Python 3.7, which will be released in June 2018. The preceding text is a little bit of Python code that I typed into my console. We'll talk about it in a moment.

All the examples in this book will be run using Python 3.7. Even though at the moment the final version might still be slightly different than what I have, I will make sure that all the code and examples are up to date with 3.7 by the time the book is published.

Some of the code can also run in Python 2.7, either as it is or with minor tweaks, but at this point in time, I think it's better to learn Python 3, and then, if you need to, learn the differences it has with Python 2, rather than going the other way around.

Don't worry about this version thing though; it's not that big an issue in practice.

# Installing Python

I never really got the point of having a *setup* section in a book, regardless of what it is that you have to set up. Most of the time, between the time the author writes the instructions and the time you actually try them out, months have passed. That is, if you're lucky. One version change and things may not work in the way that is described in the book. Luckily, we have the web now, so in order to help you get up and running, I'll just give you pointers and objectives.

I am conscious that the majority of readers would probably have preferred to have guidelines in the book. I doubt it would have made their life much easier, as I strongly believe that if you want to get started with Python you have to put in that initial effort in order to get familiar with the ecosystem. It is very important, and it will boost your confidence to face the material in the chapters ahead. If you get stuck, remember that Google is your friend.

# Setting up the Python interpreter

First of all, let's talk about your OS. Python is fully integrated and most likely already installed in basically almost every Linux distribution. If you have a macOS, it's likely that Python is already there as well (however, possibly only Python 2.7), whereas if you're using Windows, you probably need to install it.

Getting Python and the libraries you need up and running requires a bit of handiwork. Linux and macOS seem to be the most user-friendly OSes for Python programmers; Windows, on the other hand, is the one that requires the biggest effort.

My current system is a MacBook Pro, and this is what I will use throughout the book, along with Python 3.7.

The place you want to start is the official Python website: `https://www.python.org`. This website hosts the official Python documentation and many other resources that you will find very useful. Take the time to explore it.

> Another excellent, resourceful website on Python and its ecosystem is `http://docs.python-guide.org`. You can find instructions to set up Python on different operating systems, using different methods.

Find the download section and choose the installer for your OS. If you are on Windows, make sure that when you run the installer, you check the option `install pip` (actually, I would suggest to make a complete installation, just to be safe, of all the components the installer holds). We'll talk about `pip` later.

Now that Python is installed in your system, the objective is to be able to open a console and run the Python interactive shell by typing `python`.

> Please note that I usually refer to the **Python interactive shell** simply as the **Python console**.

To open the console in Windows, go to the **Start** menu, choose **Run**, and type `cmd`. If you encounter anything that looks like a permission problem while working on the examples in this book, please make sure you are running the console with administrator rights.

On the macOS X, you can start a Terminal by going to **Applications | Utilities | Terminal**.

If you are on Linux, you know all that there is to know about the console.

I will use the term *console* interchangeably to indicate the Linux console, the Windows Command Prompt, and the Macintosh Terminal. I will also indicate the command-line prompt with the Linux default format, like this:

```
$ sudo apt-get update
```

If you're not familiar with that, please take some time to learn the basics on how a console works. In a nutshell, after the `$` sign, you normally find an instruction that you have to type. Pay attention to capitalization and spaces, as they are very important.

Whatever console you open, type `python` at the prompt, and make sure the Python interactive shell shows up. Type `exit()` to quit. Keep in mind that you may have to specify `python3` if your OS comes with Python 2.* preinstalled.

This is roughly what you should see when you run Python (it will change in some details according to the version and OS):

```
$ python3.7
Python 3.7.0a3 (default, Jan 27 2018, 00:46:45)
[Clang 9.0.0 (clang-900.0.39.2)] on darwin
Type "help", "copyright", "credits" or "license" for more information.
>>>
```

Now that Python is set up and you can run it, it's time to make sure you have the other tool that will be indispensable to follow the examples in the book: virtualenv.

# About virtualenv

As you probably have guessed by its name, **virtualenv** is all about virtual environments. Let me explain what they are and why we need them and let me do it by means of a simple example.

You install Python on your system and you start working on a website for Client X. You create a project folder and start coding. Along the way, you also install some libraries; for example, the Django framework. Let's say the Django version you install for Project X is 1.7.1.

Now, your website is so good that you get another client, Y. She wants you to build another website, so you start Project Y and, along the way, you need to install Django again. The only issue is that now the Django version is 1.8 and you cannot install it on your system because this would replace the version you installed for Project X. You don't want to risk introducing incompatibility issues, so you have two choices: either you stick with the version you have currently on your machine, or you upgrade it and make sure the first project is still fully working correctly with the new version.

Let's be honest, neither of these options is very appealing, right? Definitely not. So, here's the solution: virtualenv!

virtualenv is a tool that allows you to create a virtual environment. In other words, it is a tool to create isolated Python environments, each of which is a folder that contains all the necessary executables to use the packages that a Python project would need (think of packages as libraries for the time being).

So you create a virtual environment for Project X, install all the dependencies, and then you create a virtual environment for Project Y, installing all its dependencies without the slightest worry because every library you install ends up within the boundaries of the appropriate virtual environment. In our example, Project X will hold Django 1.7.1, while Project Y will hold Django 1.8.

It is of vital importance that you never install libraries directly at the system level. Linux, for example, relies on Python for many different tasks and operations, and if you fiddle with the system installation of Python, you risk compromising the integrity of the whole system (guess to whom this happened...). So take this as a rule, such as brushing your teeth before going to bed: *always, always create a virtual environment when you start a new project.*

To install virtualenv on your system, there are a few different ways. On a Debian-based distribution of Linux, for example, you can install it with the following command:

```
$ sudo apt-get install python-virtualenv
```

Probably, the easiest way is to follow the instructions you can find on the virtualenv official website: https://virtualenv.pypa.io.

You will find that one of the most common ways to install virtualenv is by using pip, a package management system used to install and manage software packages written in Python.

As of Python 3.5, the suggested way to create a virtual environment is to use the venv module. Please see the official documentation for further information. However, at the time of writing, virtualenv is still by far the tool most used for creating virtual environments.

# Your first virtual environment

It is very easy to create a virtual environment, but according to how your system is configured and which Python version you want the virtual environment to run, you need to run the command properly. Another thing you will need to do with virtualenv, when you want to work with it, is to activate it. Activating virtualenv basically produces some path juggling behind the scenes so that when you call the Python interpreter, you're actually calling the active virtual environment one, instead of the mere system one.

I'll show you a full example on my Macintosh console. We will:

1. Create a folder named `learn.pp` under your project root (which in my case is a folder called `srv`, in my home folder). Please adapt the paths according to the setup you fancy on your box.
2. Within the `learn.pp` folder, we will create a virtual environment called `learnpp`.

 Some developers prefer to call all virtual environments using the same name (for example, `.venv`). This way they can run scripts against any virtualenv by just knowing the name of the project they dwell in. The dot in `.venv` is there because in Linux/macOS prepending a name with a dot makes that file or folder invisible.

3. After creating the virtual environment, we will activate it. The methods are slightly different between Linux, macOS, and Windows.
4. Then, we'll make sure that we are running the desired Python version (3.7.*) by running the Python interactive shell.
5. Finally, we will deactivate the virtual environment using the `deactivate` command.

These five simple steps will show you all you have to do to start and use a project.

Here's an example of how those steps might look (note that you might get a slightly different result, according to your OS, Python version, and so on) on the macOS (commands that start with a # are comments, spaces have been introduced for readability, and ⋯→ indicates where the line has wrapped around due to lack of space):

```
fabmp:srv fab$ # step 1 - create folder
fabmp:srv fab$ mkdir learn.pp
fabmp:srv fab$ cd learn.pp

fabmp:learn.pp fab$ # step 2 - create virtual environment
fabmp:learn.pp fab$ which python3.7
/Users/fab/.pyenv/shims/python3.7
fabmp:learn.pp fab$ virtualenv -p
⋯→ /Users/fab/.pyenv/shims/python3.7 learnpp
Running virtualenv with interpreter /Users/fab/.pyenv/shims/python3.7
Using base prefix '/Users/fab/.pyenv/versions/3.7.0a3'
New python executable in /Users/fab/srv/learn.pp/learnpp/bin/python3.7
Also creating executable in /Users/fab/srv/learn.pp/learnpp/bin/python
Installing setuptools, pip, wheel...done.

fabmp:learn.pp fab$ # step 3 - activate virtual environment
```

```
fabmp:learn.pp fab$ source learnpp/bin/activate

(learnpp) fabmp:learn.pp fab$ # step 4 - verify which python
(learnpp) fabmp:learn.pp fab$ which python
/Users/fab/srv/learn.pp/learnpp/bin/python

(learnpp) fabmp:learn.pp fab$ python
Python 3.7.0a3 (default, Jan 27 2018, 00:46:45)
[Clang 9.0.0 (clang-900.0.39.2)] on darwin
Type "help", "copyright", "credits" or "license" for more information.
>>> exit()

(learnpp) fabmp:learn.pp fab$ # step 5 - deactivate
(learnpp) fabmp:learn.pp fab$ deactivate
fabmp:learn.pp fab$
```

Notice that I had to tell virtualenv explicitly to use the Python 3.7 interpreter because on my box Python 2.7 is the default one. Had I not done that, I would have had a virtual environment with Python 2.7 instead of Python 3.7.

You can combine the two instructions for step 2 in one single command like this:

```
$ virtualenv -p $( which python3.7 ) learnpp
```

I chose to be explicitly verbose in this instance, to help you understand each bit of the procedure.

Another thing to notice is that in order to activate a virtual environment, we need to run the /bin/activate script, which needs to be sourced. When a script is **sourced**, it means that it is executed in the current shell, and therefore its effects last after the execution. This is very important. Also notice how the prompt changes after we activate the virtual environment, showing its name on the left (and how it disappears when we deactivate it). On Linux, the steps are the same so I won't repeat them here. On Windows, things change slightly, but the concepts are the same. Please refer to the official virtualenv website for guidance.

At this point, you should be able to create and activate a virtual environment. Please try and create another one without me guiding you. Get acquainted with this procedure because it's something that you will always be doing: **we never work system-wide with Python**, remember? It's extremely important.

So, with the scaffolding out of the way, we're ready to talk a bit more about Python and how you can use it. Before we do that though, allow me to speak a few words about the console.

# Your friend, the console

In this era of GUIs and touchscreen devices, it seems a little ridiculous to have to resort to a tool such as the console, when everything is just about one click away.

But the truth is every time you remove your right hand from the keyboard (or the left one, if you're a lefty) to grab your mouse and move the cursor over to the spot you want to click on, you're losing time. Getting things done with the console, counter-intuitive as it may be, results in higher productivity and speed. I know, you have to trust me on this.

Speed and productivity are important and, personally, I have nothing against the mouse, but there is another very good reason for which you may want to get well-acquainted with the console: when you develop code that ends up on some server, the console might be the only available tool. If you make friends with it, I promise you, you will never get lost when it's of utmost importance that you don't (typically, when the website is down and you have to investigate very quickly what's going on).

So it's really up to you. If you're undecided, please grant me the benefit of the doubt and give it a try. It's easier than you think, and you'll never regret it. There is nothing more pitiful than a good developer who gets lost within an SSH connection to a server because they are used to their own custom set of tools, and only to that.

Now, let's get back to Python.

# How you can run a Python program

There are a few different ways in which you can run a Python program.

# Running Python scripts

Python can be used as a scripting language. In fact, it always proves itself very useful. Scripts are files (usually of small dimensions) that you normally execute to do something like a task. Many developers end up having their own arsenal of tools that they fire when they need to perform a task. For example, you can have scripts to parse data in a format and render it into another different format. Or you can use a script to work with files and folders. You can create or modify configuration files, and much more. Technically, there is not much that cannot be done in a script.

It's quite common to have scripts running at a precise time on a server. For example, if your website database needs cleaning every 24 hours (for example, the table that stores the user sessions, which expire pretty quickly but aren't cleaned automatically), you could set up a Cron job that fires your script at 3:00 A.M. every day.

 According to Wikipedia, the software utility Cron is a time-based job scheduler in Unix-like computer operating systems. People who set up and maintain software environments use Cron to schedule jobs (commands or shell scripts) to run periodically at fixed times, dates, or intervals.

# Running the Python interactive shell

Another way of running Python is by calling the interactive shell. This is something we already saw when we typed `python` on the command line of our console.

So, open a console, activate your virtual environment (which by now should be second nature to you, right?), and type `python`. You will be presented with a couple of lines that should look like this:

```
$ python
Python 3.7.0a3 (default, Jan 27 2018, 00:46:45)
[Clang 9.0.0 (clang-900.0.39.2)] on darwin
Type "help", "copyright", "credits" or "license" for more information.
>>>
```

Those >>> are the prompt of the shell. They tell you that Python is waiting for you to type something. If you type a simple instruction, something that fits in one line, that's all you'll see. However, if you type something that requires more than one line of code, the shell will change the prompt to . . ., giving you a visual clue that you're typing a multiline statement (or anything that would require more than one line of code).

Go on, try it out; let's do some basic math:

```
>>> 2 + 4
6
>>> 10 / 4
2.5
>>> 2 ** 1024
```

```
1797693134862315907729305190789024733617976978942306572734300811577326
7580550096313270847732240753602112011387987139335765878976881441662249
2847430639474124377767893424865485276302219601246094119453082952085005
7688381506823424628814739131105408272371633505106845862982399472459384
7971630483535632962422413721
```

The last operation is showing you something incredible. We raise 2 to the power of 1024, and Python is handling this task with no trouble at all. Try to do it in Java, C++, or C#. It won't work, unless you use special libraries to handle such big numbers.

I use the interactive shell every day. It's extremely useful to debug very quickly, for example, to check if a data structure supports an operation. Or maybe to inspect or run a piece of code.

When you use Django (a web framework), the interactive shell is coupled with it and allows you to work your way through the framework tools, to inspect the data in the database, and many more things. You will find that the interactive shell will soon become one of your dearest friends on the journey you are embarking on.

Another solution, which comes in a much nicer graphic layout, is to use **Integrated DeveLopment Environment (IDLE)**. It's quite a simple IDE, which is intended mostly for beginners. It has a slightly larger set of capabilities than the naked interactive shell you get in the console, so you may want to explore it. It comes for free in the Windows Python installer and you can easily install it in any other system. You can find information about it on the Python website.

Guido Van Rossum named Python after the British comedy group, Monty Python, so it's rumored that the name IDLE has been chosen in honor of Eric Idle, one of Monty Python's founding members.

# Running Python as a service

Apart from being run as a script, and within the boundaries of a shell, Python can be coded and run as an application. We'll see many examples throughout the book about this mode. And we'll understand more about it in a moment, when we'll talk about how Python code is organized and run.

# Running Python as a GUI application

Python can also be run as a **graphical user interface** (**GUI**). There are several frameworks available, some of which are cross-platform and some others are platform-specific.

Among the other GUI frameworks, we find that the following are the most widely used:

- PyQt
- Tkinter
- wxPython
- PyGTK

Describing them in detail is outside the scope of this book, but you can find all the information you need on the Python website (`https://docs.python.org/3/faq/gui.html`) in the *What platform-independent GUI toolkits exist for Python?* section. If GUIs are what you're looking for, remember to choose the one you want according to some principles. Make sure they:

- Offer all the features you may need to develop your project
- Run on all the platforms you may need to support
- Rely on a community that is as wide and active as possible
- Wrap graphic drivers/tools that you can easily install/access

# How is Python code organized?

Let's talk a little bit about how Python code is organized. In this section, we'll start going down the rabbit hole a little bit more and introduce more technical names and concepts.

Starting with the basics, how is Python code organized? Of course, you write your code into files. When you save a file with the extension `.py`, that file is said to be a Python module.

 If you're on Windows or macOS that typically hide file extensions from the user, please make sure you change the configuration so that you can see the complete names of the files. This is not strictly a requirement, but a suggestion.

It would be impractical to save all the code that it is required for software to work within one single file. That solution works for scripts, which are usually not longer than a few hundred lines (and often they are quite shorter than that).

A complete Python application can be made of hundreds of thousands of lines of code, so you will have to scatter it through different modules, which is better, but not nearly good enough. It turns out that even like this, it would still be impractical to work with the code. So Python gives you another structure, called **package**, which allows you to group modules together. A package is nothing more than a folder, which must contain a special file, `__init__.py`, that doesn't need to hold any code but whose presence is required to tell Python that the folder is not just some folder, but it's actually a package (note that as of Python 3.3, the `__init__.py` module is not strictly required any more).

As always, an example will make all of this much clearer. I have created an example structure in my book project, and when I type in my console:

```
$ tree -v example
```

I get a tree representation of the contents of the `ch1/example` folder, which holds the code for the examples of this chapter. Here's what the structure of a really simple application could look like:

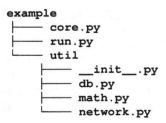

```
example
├── core.py
├── run.py
└── util
    ├── __init__.py
    ├── db.py
    ├── math.py
    └── network.py
```

You can see that within the root of this example, we have two modules, `core.py` and `run.py`, and one package: util. Within `core.py`, there may be the core logic of our application. On the other hand, within the `run.py` module, we can probably find the logic to start the application. Within the `util` package, I expect to find various utility tools, and in fact, we can guess that the modules there are named based on the types of tools they hold: `db.py` would hold tools to work with databases, `math.py` would, of course, hold mathematical tools (maybe our application deals with financial data), and `network.py` would probably hold tools to send/receive data on networks.

As explained before, the __init__.py file is there just to tell Python that `util` is a package and not just a mere folder.

Had this software been organized within modules only, it would have been harder to infer its structure. I put a *module only* example under the `ch1/files_only` folder; see it for yourself:

```
$ tree -v files_only
```

This shows us a completely different picture:

```
files_only/
├──── core.py
├──── db.py
├──── math.py
├──── network.py
└──── run.py
```

It is a little harder to guess what each module does, right? Now, consider that this is just a simple example, so you can guess how much harder it would be to understand a real application if we couldn't organize the code in packages and modules.

# How do we use modules and packages?

When a developer is writing an application, it is likely that they will need to apply the same piece of logic in different parts of it. For example, when writing a parser for the data that comes from a form that a user can fill in a web page, the application will have to validate whether a certain field is holding a number or not. Regardless of how the logic for this kind of validation is written, it's likely that it will be needed in more than one place.

For example, in a poll application, where the user is asked many questions, it's likely that several of them will require a numeric answer. For example:

- What is your age?
- How many pets do you own?
- How many children do you have?
- How many times have you been married?

It would be very bad practice to copy/paste (or, more properly said: duplicate) the validation logic in every place where we expect a numeric answer. This would violate the **don't repeat yourself** (**DRY**) principle, which states that you should never repeat the same piece of code more than once in your application. I feel the need to stress the importance of this principle: *you should never repeat the same piece of code more than once in your application* (pun intended).

There are several reasons why repeating the same piece of logic can be very bad, the most important ones being:

- There could be a bug in the logic, and therefore, you would have to correct it in every place that the logic is applied.
- You may want to amend the way you carry out the validation, and again you would have to change it in every place it is applied.
- You may forget to fix/amend a piece of logic because you missed it when searching for all its occurrences. This would leave wrong/inconsistent behavior in your application.
- Your code would be longer than needed, for no good reason.

Python is a wonderful language and provides you with all the tools you need to apply all the coding best practices. For this particular example, we need to be able to reuse a piece of code. To be able to reuse a piece of code, we need to have a construct that will hold the code for us so that we can call that construct every time we need to repeat the logic inside it. That construct exists, and it's called a **function**.

I'm not going too deep into the specifics here, so please just remember that a function is a block of organized, reusable code that is used to perform a task. Functions can assume many forms and names, according to what kind of environment they belong to, but for now this is not important. We'll see the details when we are able to appreciate them, later on, in the book. Functions are the building blocks of modularity in your application, and they are almost indispensable. Unless you're writing a super-simple script, you'll use functions all the time. We'll explore functions in `Chapter 4`, *Functions, the Building Blocks of Code*.

Python comes with a very extensive library, as I have already said a few pages ago. Now, maybe it's a good time to define what a library is: a **library** is a collection of functions and objects that provide functionalities that enrich the abilities of a language.

For example, within Python's `math` library, we can find a plethora of functions, one of which is the `factorial` function, which of course calculates the factorial of a number.

In mathematics, the **factorial** of a non-negative integer number $N$, denoted as $N!$, is defined as the product of all positive integers less than or equal to $N$. For example, the factorial of 5 is calculated as:
`5! = 5 * 4 * 3 * 2 * 1 = 120`
The factorial of 0 is `0! = 1`, to respect the convention for an empty product.

So, if you wanted to use this function in your code, all you would have to do is to import it and call it with the right input values. Don't worry too much if input values and the concept of calling is not very clear for now; please just concentrate on the import part. We use a library by importing what we need from it, and then we use it.

In Python, to calculate the factorial of number 5, we just need the following code:

```
>>> from math import factorial
>>> factorial(5)
120
```

Whatever we type in the shell, if it has a printable representation, will be printed on the console for us (in this case, the result of the function call: `120`).

So, let's go back to our example, the one with `core.py`, `run.py`, `util`, and so on.

In our example, the package `util` is our utility library. Our custom utility belt that holds all those reusable tools (that is, functions), which we need in our application. Some of them will deal with databases (`db.py`), some with the network (`network.py`), and some will perform mathematical calculations (`math.py`) that are outside the scope of Python's standard `math` library and, therefore, we have to code them for ourselves.

We will see in detail how to import functions and use them in their dedicated chapter. Let's now talk about another very important concept: *Python's execution model.*

# Python's execution model

In this section, I would like to introduce you to a few very important concepts, such as scope, names, and namespaces. You can read all about Python's execution model in the official language reference, of course, but I would argue that it is quite technical and abstract, so let me give you a less formal explanation first.

## Names and namespaces

Say you are looking for a book, so you go to the library and ask someone for the book you want to fetch. They tell you something like *Second Floor, Section X, Row Three*. So you go up the stairs, look for Section X, and so on.

It would be very different to enter a library where all the books are piled together in random order in one big room. No floors, no sections, no rows, no order. Fetching a book would be extremely hard.

When we write code, we have the same issue: we have to try and organize it so that it will be easy for someone who has no prior knowledge about it to find what they're looking for. When software is structured correctly, it also promotes code reuse. On the other hand, disorganized software is more likely to expose scattered pieces of duplicated logic.

First of all, let's start with the book. We refer to a book by its title and in Python lingo, that would be a name. Python names are the closest abstraction to what other languages call variables. Names basically refer to objects and are introduced by name-binding operations. Let's make a quick example (notice that anything that follows a # is a comment):

```
>>> n = 3  # integer number
>>> address = "221b Baker Street, NW1 6XE, London"  # Sherlock Holmes'
address
>>> employee = {
...      'age': 45,
...      'role': 'CTO',
...      'SSN': 'AB1234567',
... }
>>> # let's print them
>>> n
3
>>> address
'221b Baker Street, NW1 6XE, London'
>>> employee
```

```
{'age': 45, 'role': 'CTO', 'SSN': 'AB1234567'}
>>> other_name
Traceback (most recent call last):
  File "<stdin>", line 1, in <module>
NameError: name 'other_name' is not defined
```

We defined three objects in the preceding code (do you remember what are the three features every Python object has?):

- An integer number n (type: `int`, value: `3`)
- A string `address` (type: `str`, value: Sherlock Holmes' address)
- A dictionary `employee` (type: `dict`, value: a dictionary that holds three key/value pairs)

Don't worry, I know you're not supposed to know what a dictionary is. We'll see in Chapter 2, *Built-in Data Types*, that it's the king of Python data structures.

 Have you noticed that the prompt changed from >>> to ... when I typed in the definition of employee? That's because the definition spans over multiple lines.

So, what are n, `address`, and `employee`? They are **names**. Names that we can use to retrieve data within our code. They need to be kept somewhere so that whenever we need to retrieve those objects, we can use their names to fetch them. We need some space to hold them, hence: namespaces!

A **namespace** is therefore a mapping from names to objects. Examples are the set of built-in names (containing functions that are always accessible in any Python program), the global names in a module, and the local names in a function. Even the set of attributes of an object can be considered a namespace.

The beauty of namespaces is that they allow you to define and organize your names with clarity, without overlapping or interference. For example, the namespace associated with that book we were looking for in the library can be used to import the book itself, like this:

```
from library.second_floor.section_x.row_three import book
```

We start from the `library` namespace, and by means of the dot (`.`) operator, we walk into that namespace. Within this namespace, we look for `second_floor`, and again we walk into it with the . operator. We then walk into `section_x`, and finally within the last namespace, `row_three`, we find the name we were looking for: `book`.

Walking through a namespace will be clearer when we'll be dealing with real code examples. For now, just keep in mind that namespaces are places where names are associated with objects.

There is another concept, which is closely related to that of a namespace, which I'd like to briefly talk about: the **scope**.

# Scopes

According to Python's documentation:

> *" A scope is a textual region of a Python program, where a namespace is directly accessible. "*

Directly accessible means that when you're looking for an unqualified reference to a name, Python tries to find it in the namespace.

Scopes are determined statically, but actually, during runtime, they are used dynamically. This means that by inspecting the source code, you can tell what the scope of an object is, but this doesn't prevent the software from altering that during runtime. There are four different scopes that Python makes accessible (not necessarily all of them are present at the same time, of course):

- The **local** scope, which is the innermost one and contains the local names.
- The **enclosing** scope, that is, the scope of any enclosing function. It contains non-local names and also non-global names.
- The **global** scope contains the global names.
- The **built-in** scope contains the built-in names. Python comes with a set of functions that you can use in an off-the-shelf fashion, such as `print`, `all`, `abs`, and so on. They live in the built-in scope.

The rule is the following: when we refer to a name, Python starts looking for it in the current namespace. If the name is not found, Python continues the search to the enclosing scope and this continues until the built-in scope is searched. If a name hasn't been found after searching the built-in scope, then Python raises a `NameError` **exception**, which basically means that the name hasn't been defined (you saw this in the preceding example).

The order in which the namespaces are scanned when looking for a name is therefore: **local, enclosing, global, built-in (LEGB)**.

This is all very theoretical, so let's see an example. In order to show you local and enclosing namespaces, I will have to define a few functions. Don't worry if you are not familiar with their syntax for the moment. We'll study functions in Chapter 4, *Functions, the Building Blocks of Code*. Just remember that in the following code, when you see def, it means I'm defining a function:

```python
# scopes1.py
# Local versus Global

# we define a function, called local
def local():
    m = 7
    print(m)

m = 5
print(m)

# we call, or `execute` the function local
local()
```

In the preceding example, we define the same name m, both in the global scope and in the local one (the one defined by the local function). When we execute this program with the following command (have you activated your virtualenv?):

```
$ python scopes1.py
```

We see two numbers printed on the console: 5 and 7.

What happens is that the Python interpreter parses the file, top to bottom. First, it finds a couple of comment lines, which are skipped, then it parses the definition of the function local. When called, this function does two things: it sets up a name to an object representing number 7 and prints it. The Python interpreter keeps going and it finds another name binding. This time the binding happens in the global scope and the value is 5. The next line is a call to the print function, which is executed (and so we get the first value printed on the console: 5).

After this, there is a call to the function local. At this point, Python executes the function, so at this time, the binding m = 7 happens and it's printed.

One very important thing to notice is that the part of the code that belongs to the definition of the `local` function is indented by four spaces on the right. Python, in fact, defines scopes by indenting the code. You walk into a scope by indenting, and walk out of it by unindenting. Some coders use two spaces, others three, but the suggested number of spaces to use is four. It's a good measure to maximize readability. We'll talk more about all the conventions you should embrace when writing Python code later.

What would happen if we removed that m = 7 line? Remember the LEGB rule. Python would start looking for m in the local scope (function `local`), and, not finding it, it would go to the next enclosing scope. The next one, in this case, is the global one because there is no enclosing function wrapped around `local`. Therefore, we would see two numbers 5 printed on the console. Let's actually see what the code would look like:

```
# scopes2.py
# Local versus Global

def local():
    # m doesn't belong to the scope defined by the local function
    # so Python will keep looking into the next enclosing scope.
    # m is finally found in the global scope
    print(m, 'printing from the local scope')

m = 5
print(m, 'printing from the global scope')

local()
```

Running `scopes2.py` will print this:

```
$ python scopes2.py
5 printing from the global scope
5 printing from the local scope
```

As expected, Python prints m the first time, then when the function `local` is called, m isn't found in its scope, so Python looks for it following the LEGB chain until m is found in the global scope.

Let's see an example with an extra layer, the enclosing scope:

```
# scopes3.py
# Local, Enclosing and Global

def enclosing_func():
    m = 13
```

```
def local():
    # m doesn't belong to the scope defined by the local
    # function so Python will keep looking into the next
    # enclosing scope. This time m is found in the enclosing
    # scope
    print(m, 'printing from the local scope')

# calling the function local
local()

m = 5
print(m, 'printing from the global scope')

enclosing_func()
```

Running `scopes3.py` will print on the console:

```
$ python scopes3.py
(5, 'printing from the global scope')
(13, 'printing from the local scope')
```

As you can see, the `print` instruction from the function `local` is referring to `m` as before. `m` is still not defined within the function itself, so Python starts walking scopes following the LEGB order. This time `m` is found in the enclosing scope.

Don't worry if this is still not perfectly clear for now. It will come to you as we go through the examples in the book. The *Classes* section of the Python tutorial (`https://docs.python.org/3/tutorial/classes.html`) has an interesting paragraph about scopes and namespaces. Make sure you read it at some point if you want a deeper understanding of the subject.

Before we finish off this chapter, I would like to talk a bit more about objects. After all, basically everything in Python is an object, so I think they deserve a bit more attention.

# Objects and classes

When I introduced objects previously in the *A proper introduction* section of the chapter, I said that we use them to represent real-life objects. For example, we sell goods of any kind on the web nowadays and we need to be able to handle, store, and represent them properly. But objects are actually so much more than that. Most of what you will ever do, in Python, has to do with manipulating objects.

So, without going into too much detail (we'll do that in later chapters), I want to give you the *in a nutshell* kind of explanation about classes and objects.

We've already seen that objects are Python's abstraction for data. In fact, everything in Python is an object, infact numbers, strings (data structures that hold text), containers, collections, even functions. You can think of them as if they were boxes with at least three features: an ID (unique), a type, and a value.

But how do they come to life? How do we create them? How do we write our own custom objects? The answer lies in one simple word: **classes**.

Objects are, in fact, instances of classes. The beauty of Python is that classes are objects themselves, but let's not go down this road. It leads to one of the most advanced concepts of this language: **metaclasses**. For now, the best way for you to get the difference between classes and objects is by means of an example.

Say a friend tells you, *I bought a new bike!* You immediately understand what she's talking about. Have you seen the bike? No. Do you know what color it is? Nope. The brand? Nope. Do you know anything about it? Nope. But at the same time, you know everything you need in order to understand what your friend meant when she told you she bought a new bike. You know that a bike has two wheels attached to a frame, a saddle, pedals, handlebars, brakes, and so on. In other words, even if you haven't seen the bike itself, you know the concept of *bike*. An abstract set of features and characteristics that together form something called *bike*.

In computer programming, that is called a **class**. It's that simple. Classes are used to create objects. In fact, objects are said to be **instances of classes**.

In other words, we all know what a bike is; we know the class. But then I have my own bike, which is an instance of the bike class. And my bike is an object with its own characteristics and methods. You have your own bike. Same class, but different instance. Every bike ever created in the world is an instance of the bike class.

Let's see an example. We will write a class that defines a bike and then we'll create two bikes, one red and one blue. I'll keep the code very simple, but don't fret if you don't understand everything about it; all you need to care about at this moment is to understand the difference between a class and an object (or instance of a class):

```python
# bike.py
# let's define the class Bike
class Bike:

    def __init__(self, colour, frame_material):
        self.colour = colour
```

```
        self.frame_material = frame_material

    def brake(self):
        print("Braking!")

# let's create a couple of instances
red_bike = Bike('Red', 'Carbon fiber')
blue_bike = Bike('Blue', 'Steel')

# let's inspect the objects we have, instances of the Bike class.
print(red_bike.colour)  # prints: Red
print(red_bike.frame_material)  # prints: Carbon fiber
print(blue_bike.colour)  # prints: Blue
print(blue_bike.frame_material)  # prints: Steel

# let's brake!
red_bike.brake()  # prints: Braking!
```

 I hope by now I don't need to tell you to run the file every time, right? The filename is indicated in the first line of the code block. Just run $ `python filename`, and you'll be fine. But remember to have your virtualenv activated!

So many interesting things to notice here. First things first; the definition of a class happens with the `class` statement. Whatever code comes after the `class` statement, and is indented, is called the body of the class. In our case, the last line that belongs to the class definition is the `print("Braking!")` one.

After having defined the class, we're ready to create instances. You can see that the class body hosts the definition of two methods. A method is basically (and simplistically) a function that belongs to a class.

The first method, \_\_init\_\_, is an **initializer**. It uses some Python magic to set up the objects with the values we pass when we create it.

 Every method that has leading and trailing double underscores, in Python, is called a **magic method**. Magic methods are used by Python for a multitude of different purposes; hence it's never a good idea to name a custom method using two leading and trailing underscores. This naming convention is best left to Python.

The other method we defined, `brake`, is just an example of an additional method that we could call if we wanted to brake the bike. It contains just a `print` statement, of course; it's an example.

We created two bikes then. One has red color and a carbon fiber frame, and the other one has blue color and a steel frame. We pass those values upon creation. After creation, we print out the color property and frame type of the red bike, and the frame type of the blue one just as an example. We also call the `brake` method of the `red_bike`.

One last thing to notice. You remember I told you that the set of attributes of an object is considered to be a namespace? I hope it's clearer what I meant now. You see that by getting to the `frame_type` property through different namespaces (`red_bike`, `blue_bike`), we obtain different values. No overlapping, no confusion.

The dot (`.`) operator is of course the means we use to walk into a namespace, in the case of objects as well.

# Guidelines on how to write good code

Writing good code is not as easy as it seems. As I already said before, good code exposes a long list of qualities that is quite hard to put together. Writing good code is, to some extent, an art. Regardless of where on the path you will be happy to settle, there is something that you can embrace which will make your code instantly better: **PEP 8**.

According to Wikipedia:

> *"Python's development is conducted largely through the Python Enhancement Proposal (PEP) process. The PEP process is the primary mechanism for proposing major new features, for collecting community input on an issue, and for documenting the design decisions that have gone into Python."*

PEP 8 is perhaps the most famous of all PEPs. It lays out a simple but effective set of guidelines to define Python aesthetics so that we write beautiful Python code. If you take one suggestion out of this chapter, please let it be this: use it. Embrace it. You will thank me later.

Coding today is no longer a check-in/check-out business. Rather, it's more of a social effort. Several developers collaborate on a piece of code through tools such as Git and Mercurial, and the result is code that is fathered by many different hands.

 Git and Mercurial are probably the distributed revision control systems that are most used today. They are essential tools designed to help teams of developers collaborate on the same software.

These days, more than ever, we need to have a consistent way of writing code, so that readability is maximized. When all developers of a company abide by PEP 8, it's not uncommon for any of them landing on a piece of code to think they wrote it themselves. It actually happens to me all the time (I always forget the code I write).

This has a tremendous advantage: when you read code that you could have written yourself, you read it easily. Without a convention, every coder would structure the code the way they like most, or simply the way they were taught or are used to, and this would mean having to interpret every line according to someone else's style. It would mean having to lose much more time just trying to understand it. Thanks to PEP 8, we can avoid this. I'm such a fan of it that I won't sign off a code review if the code doesn't respect it. So, please take the time to study it; it's very important.

In the examples in this book, I will try to respect it as much as I can. Unfortunately, I don't have the luxury of 79 characters (which is the maximum line length suggested by PEP 8), and I will have to cut down on blank lines and other things, but I promise you I'll try to lay out my code so that it's as readable as possible.

# The Python culture

Python has been adopted widely in all coding industries. It's used by many different companies for many different purposes, and it's also used in education (it's an excellent language for that purpose, because of its many qualities and the fact that it's easy to learn).

One of the reasons Python is so popular today is that the community around it is vast, vibrant, and full of brilliant people. Many events are organized all over the world, mostly either around Python or its main web framework, Django.

Python is open, and very often so are the minds of those who embrace it. Check out the community page on the Python website for more information and get involved!

There is another aspect to Python which revolves around the notion of being **Pythonic**. It has to do with the fact that Python allows you to use some idioms that aren't found elsewhere, at least not in the same form or as easy to use (I feel quite claustrophobic when I have to code in a language which is not Python now).

Anyway, over the years, this concept of being Pythonic has emerged and, the way I understand it, is something along the lines of *doing things the way they are supposed to be done in Python.*

To help you understand a little bit more about Python's culture and about being Pythonic, I will show you the *Zen of Python*. A lovely Easter egg that is very popular. Open up a Python console and type `import this`. What follows is the result of this line:

```
>>> import this
The Zen of Python, by Tim Peters

Beautiful is better than ugly.
Explicit is better than implicit.
Simple is better than complex.
Complex is better than complicated.
Flat is better than nested.
Sparse is better than dense.
Readability counts.
Special cases aren't special enough to break the rules.
Although practicality beats purity.
Errors should never pass silently.
Unless explicitly silenced.
In the face of ambiguity, refuse the temptation to guess.
There should be one-- and preferably only one --obvious way to do it.
Although that way may not be obvious at first unless you're Dutch.
Now is better than never.
Although never is often better than *right* now.
If the implementation is hard to explain, it's a bad idea.
If the implementation is easy to explain, it may be a good idea.
Namespaces are one honking great idea -- let's do more of those!
```

There are two levels of reading here. One is to consider it as a set of guidelines that have been put down in a fun way. The other one is to keep it in mind, and maybe read it once in a while, trying to understand how it refers to something deeper: some Python characteristics that you will have to understand deeply in order to write Python the way it's supposed to be written. Start with the fun level, and then dig deeper. Always dig deeper.

# A note on IDEs

Just a few words about IDEs. To follow the examples in this book, you don't need one; any text editor will do fine. If you want to have more advanced features, such as syntax coloring and auto completion, you will have to fetch yourself an IDE. You can find a comprehensive list of open source IDEs (just Google Python IDEs) on the Python website. I personally use Sublime Text editor. It's free to try out and it costs just a few dollars. I have tried many IDEs in my life, but this is the one that makes me most productive.

Two important pieces of advice:

- Whatever IDE you choose to use, try to learn it well so that you can exploit its strengths, but *don't depend on it*. Exercise yourself to work with VIM (or any other text editor) once in a while; learn to be able to do some work on any platform, with any set of tools.
- Whatever text editor/IDE you use, when it comes to writing Python, *indentation is four spaces*. Don't use tabs, don't mix them with spaces. Use four spaces, not two, not three, not five. Just use four. The whole world works like that, and you don't want to become an outcast because you were fond of the three-space layout.

# Summary

In this chapter, we started to explore the world of programming and that of Python. We've barely scratched the surface, just a little, touching concepts that will be discussed later on in the book in greater detail.

We talked about Python's main features, who is using it and for what, and what are the different ways in which we can write a Python program.

In the last part of the chapter, we flew over the fundamental notions of namespaces, scopes, classes, and objects. We also saw how Python code can be organized using modules and packages.

On a practical level, we learned how to install Python on our system, how to make sure we have the tools we need, `pip` and virtualenv, and we also created and activated our first virtual environment. This will allow us to work in a self-contained environment without the risk of compromising the Python system installation.

Now you're ready to start this journey with me. All you need is enthusiasm, an activated virtual environment, this book, your fingers, and some coffee.

Try to follow the examples; I'll keep them simple and short. If you put them under your fingertips, you will retain them much better than if you just read them.

In the next chapter, we will explore Python's rich set of built-in data types. There's much to cover and much to learn!

# Built-in Data Types

2

*"Data! Data! Data!" he cried impatiently. "I can't make bricks without clay."*

*– Sherlock Holmes – The Adventure of the Copper Beeches*

Everything you do with a computer is managing data. Data comes in many different shapes and flavors. It's the music you listen to, the movies you stream, the PDFs you open. Even the source of the chapter you're reading at this very moment is just a file, which is data.

Data can be simple, an integer number to represent an age, or complex, like an order placed on a website. It can be about a single object or about a collection of them. Data can even be about data, that is, metadata. Data that describes the design of other data structures or data that describes application data or its context. In Python, *objects are abstraction for data*, and Python has an amazing variety of data structures that you can use to represent data, or combine them to create your own custom data.

In this chapter, we are going to cover the following:

- Python objects' structures
- Mutability and immutability
- Built-in data types: numbers, strings, sequences, collections, and mapping types
- The collections module
- Enumerations

# Everything is an object

Before we delve into the specifics, I want you to be very clear about objects in Python, so let's talk a little bit more about them. As we already said, everything in Python is an object. But what really happens when you type an instruction like age = 42 in a Python module?

If you go to http://pythontutor.com/, you can type that instruction into a text box and get its visual representation. Keep this website in mind; it's very useful to consolidate your understanding of what goes on behind the scenes.

So, what happens is that an object is created. It gets an id, the type is set to int (integer number), and the value to 42. A name age is placed in the global namespace, pointing to that object. Therefore, whenever we are in the global namespace, after the execution of that line, we can retrieve that object by simply accessing it through its name: age.

If you were to move house, you would put all the knives, forks, and spoons in a box and label it *cutlery*. Can you see it's exactly the same concept? Here's a screenshot of what it may look like (you may have to tweak the settings to get to the same view):

So, for the rest of this chapter, whenever you read something such as name = some_value, think of a name placed in the namespace that is tied to the scope in which the instruction was written, with a nice arrow pointing to an object that has an id, a type, and a value. There is a little bit more to say about this mechanism, but it's much easier to talk about it over an example, so we'll get back to this later.

# Mutable or immutable? That is the question

A first fundamental distinction that Python makes on data is about whether or not the value of an object changes. If the value can change, the object is called **mutable**, while if the value cannot change, the object is called **immutable**.

It is very important that you understand the distinction between mutable and immutable because it affects the code you write, so here's a question:

```
>>> age = 42
>>> age
42
>>> age = 43    #A
>>> age
43
```

In the preceding code, on the line #A, have I changed the value of age? Well, no. But now it's 43 (I hear you say...). Yes, it's 43, but 42 was an integer number, of the type int, which is immutable. So, what happened is really that on the first line, age is a name that is set to point to an int object, whose value is 42. When we type age = 43, what happens is that another object is created, of the type int and value 43 (also, the id will be different), and the name age is set to point to it. So, we didn't change that 42 to 43. We actually just pointed age to a different location: the new int object whose value is 43. Let's see the same code also printing the IDs:

```
>>> age = 42
>>> id(age)
4377553168
>>> age = 43
>>> id(age)
4377553200
```

Notice that we print the IDs by calling the built-in id function. As you can see, they are different, as expected. Bear in mind that age points to one object at a time: 42 first, then 43. Never together.

Now, let's see the same example using a mutable object. For this example, let's just use a Person object, that has a property age (don't worry about the class declaration for now; it's there only for completeness):

```
>>> class Person():
...     def __init__(self, age):
...         self.age = age
```

```
...
>>> fab = Person(age=42)
>>> fab.age
42
>>> id(fab)
4380878496
>>> id(fab.age)
4377553168
>>> fab.age = 25  # I wish!
>>> id(fab)   # will be the same
4380878496
>>> id(fab.age)   # will be different
4377552624
```

In this case, I set up an object `fab` whose `type` is `Person` (a custom class). On creation, the object is given the `age` of 42. I'm printing it, along with the object `id`, and the ID of `age` as well. Notice that, even after I change `age` to be 25, the ID of `fab` stays the same (while the ID of `age` has changed, of course). Custom objects in Python are mutable (unless you code them not to be). Keep this concept in mind; it's very important. I'll remind you about it throughout the rest of the chapter.

# Numbers

Let's start by exploring Python's built-in data types for numbers. Python was designed by a man with a master's degree in mathematics and computer science, so it's only logical that it has amazing support for numbers.

Numbers are immutable objects.

## Integers

Python integers have an unlimited range, subject only to the available virtual memory. This means that it doesn't really matter how big a number you want to store is: as long as it can fit in your computer's memory, Python will take care of it. Integer numbers can be positive, negative, and 0 (zero). They support all the basic mathematical operations, as shown in the following example:

```
>>> a = 14
>>> b = 3
>>> a + b  # addition
17
>>> a - b  # subtraction
```

```
11
>>> a * b  # multiplication
42
>>> a / b  # true division
4.666666666666667
>>> a // b  # integer division
4
>>> a % b  # modulo operation (reminder of division)
2
>>> a ** b  # power operation
2744
```

The preceding code should be easy to understand. Just notice one important thing: Python has two division operators, one performs the so-called **true division** (/), which returns the quotient of the operands, and the other one, the so-called **integer division** (//), which returns the *floored* quotient of the operands. It might be worth noting that in Python 2 the division operator / behaves differently than in Python 3. See how that is different for positive and negative numbers:

```
>>> 7 / 4  # true division
1.75
>>> 7 // 4  # integer division, truncation returns 1
1
>>> -7 / 4  # true division again, result is opposite of previous
-1.75
>>> -7 // 4  # integer div., result not the opposite of previous
-2
```

This is an interesting example. If you were expecting a −1 on the last line, don't feel bad, it's just the way Python works. The result of an integer division in Python is always rounded towards minus infinity. If, instead of flooring, you want to truncate a number to an integer, you can use the built-in int function, as shown in the following example:

```
>>> int(1.75)
1
>>> int(-1.75)
-1
```

Notice that the truncation is done toward 0.

There is also an operator to calculate the remainder of a division. It's called a modulo operator, and it's represented by a percentage (%):

```
>>> 10 % 3  # remainder of the division 10 // 3
1
```

```
>>> 10 % 4  # remainder of the division 10 // 4
2
```

One nice feature introduced in Python 3.6 is the ability to add underscores within number literals (between digits or base specifiers, but not leading or trailing). The purpose is to help make some numbers more readable, like for example 1_000_000_000:

```
>>> n = 1_024
>>> n
1024
>>> hex_n = 0x_4_0_0  # 0x400 == 1024
>>> hex_n
1024
```

# Booleans

Boolean algebra is that subset of algebra in which the values of the variables are the truth values: true and false. In Python, True and False are two keywords that are used to represent truth values. Booleans are a subclass of integers, and behave respectively like 1 and 0. The equivalent of the int class for Booleans is the bool class, which returns either True or False. Every built-in Python object has a value in the Boolean context, which means they basically evaluate to either True or False when fed to the bool function. We'll see all about this in Chapter 3, *Iterating and Making Decisions*.

Boolean values can be combined in Boolean expressions using the logical operators and, or, and not. Again, we'll see them in full in the next chapter, so for now let's just see a simple example:

```
>>> int(True)  # True behaves like 1
1
>>> int(False)  # False behaves like 0
0
>>> bool(1)  # 1 evaluates to True in a boolean context
True
>>> bool(-42)  # and so does every non-zero number
True
>>> bool(0)  # 0 evaluates to False
False
>>> # quick peak at the operators (and, or, not)
>>> not True
False
>>> not False
```

```
True
>>> True and True
True
>>> False or True
True
```

You can see that `True` and `False` are subclasses of integers when you try to add them. Python upcasts them to integers and performs the addition:

```
>>> 1 + True
2
>>> False + 42
42
>>> 7 - True
6
```

> **Upcasting** is a type conversion operation that goes from a subclass to its parent. In the example presented here, `True` and `False`, which belong to a class derived from the integer class, are converted back to integers when needed.

# Real numbers

Real numbers, or floating point numbers, are represented in Python according to the IEEE 754 double-precision binary floating-point format, which is stored in 64 bits of information divided into three sections: sign, exponent, and mantissa.

> Quench your thirst for knowledge about this format on Wikipedia: http://en.wikipedia.org/wiki/Double-precision_floating-point_format.

Usually, programming languages give coders two different formats: single and double precision. The former takes up 32 bits of memory, and the latter 64. Python supports only the double format. Let's see a simple example:

```
>>> pi = 3.1415926536  # how many digits of PI can you remember?
>>> radius = 4.5
>>> area = pi * (radius ** 2)
>>> area
63.617251235400005
```

In the calculation of the area, I wrapped the `radius ** 2` within braces. Even though that wasn't necessary because the power operator has higher precedence than the multiplication one, I think the formula reads more easily like that. Moreover, should you get a slightly different result for the area, don't worry. It might depend on your OS, how Python was compiled, and so on. As long as the first few decimal digits are correct, you know it's a correct result.

The `sys.float_info` struct sequence holds information about how floating point numbers will behave on your system. This is what I see on my box:

```
>>> import sys
>>> sys.float_info
sys.float_info(max=1.7976931348623157e+308, max_exp=1024,
max_10_exp=308, min=2.2250738585072014e-308, min_exp=-1021,
min_10_exp=-307, dig=15, mant_dig=53, epsilon=2.220446049250313e-16,
radix=2, rounds=1)
```

Let's make a few considerations here: we have 64 bits to represent float numbers. This means we can represent at most `2 ** 64 == 18,446,744,073,709,551,616` numbers with that amount of bits. Take a look at the `max` and `epsilon` values for the float numbers, and you'll realize it's impossible to represent them all. There is just not enough space, so they are approximated to the closest representable number. You probably think that only extremely big or extremely small numbers suffer from this issue. Well, think again and try the following in your console:

```
>>> 0.3 - 0.1 * 3  # this should be 0!!!
-5.551115123125783e-17
```

What does this tell you? It tells you that double precision numbers suffer from approximation issues even when it comes to simple numbers like `0.1` or `0.3`. Why is this important? It can be a big problem if you're handling prices, or financial calculations, or any kind of data that needs not to be approximated. Don't worry, Python gives you the **decimal** type, which doesn't suffer from these issues; we'll see them in a moment.

# Complex numbers

Python gives you complex numbers support out of the box. If you don't know what complex numbers are, they are numbers that can be expressed in the form *a* + *ib* where *a* and *b* are real numbers, and *i* (or *j* if you're an engineer) is the imaginary unit, that is, the square root of *-1*. *a* and *b* are called, respectively, the *real* and *imaginary* part of the number.

It's actually unlikely you'll be using them, unless you're coding something scientific. Let's see a small example:

```
>>> c = 3.14 + 2.73j
>>> c.real  # real part
3.14
>>> c.imag  # imaginary part
2.73
>>> c.conjugate()  # conjugate of A + Bj is A - Bj
(3.14-2.73j)
>>> c * 2  # multiplication is allowed
(6.28+5.46j)
>>> c ** 2  # power operation as well
(2.4067000000000007+17.1444j)
>>> d = 1 + 1j  # addition and subtraction as well
>>> c - d
(2.14+1.73j)
```

# Fractions and decimals

Let's finish the tour of the number department with a look at fractions and decimals. Fractions hold a rational numerator and denominator in their lowest forms. Let's see a quick example:

```
>>> from fractions import Fraction
>>> Fraction(10, 6)  # mad hatter?
Fraction(5, 3)  # notice it's been simplified
>>> Fraction(1, 3) + Fraction(2, 3)  # 1/3 + 2/3 == 3/3 == 1/1
Fraction(1, 1)
>>> f = Fraction(10, 6)
>>> f.numerator
5
>>> f.denominator
3
```

Although they can be very useful at times, it's not that common to spot them in commercial software. Much easier instead, is to see decimal numbers being used in all those contexts where precision is everything; for example, in scientific and financial calculations.

It's important to remember that arbitrary precision decimal numbers come at a price in performance, of course. The amount of data to be stored for each number is far greater than it is for fractions or floats as well as the way they are handled, which causes the Python interpreter much more work behind the scenes. Another interesting thing to note is that you can get and set the precision by accessing `decimal.getcontext().prec`.

Let's see a quick example with decimal numbers:

```
>>> from decimal import Decimal as D  # rename for brevity
>>> D(3.14)  # pi, from float, so approximation issues
Decimal('3.140000000000000124344978758017532527446746826171875')
>>> D('3.14')  # pi, from a string, so no approximation issues
Decimal('3.14')
>>> D(0.1) * D(3) - D(0.3)  # from float, we still have the issue
Decimal('2.775557561565156540423631668E-17')
>>> D('0.1') * D(3) - D('0.3')  # from string, all perfect
Decimal('0.0')
>>> D('1.4').as_integer_ratio()  # 7/5 = 1.4 (isn't this cool?!)
(7, 5)
```

Notice that when we construct a `Decimal` number from a `float`, it takes on all the approximation issues `float` may come from. On the other hand, when the `Decimal` has no approximation issues (for example, when we feed an `int` or a `string` representation to the constructor), then the calculation has no quirky behavior. When it comes to money, use decimals.

This concludes our introduction to built-in numeric types. Let's now look at sequences.

# Immutable sequences

Let's start with immutable sequences: strings, tuples, and bytes.

# Strings and bytes

Textual data in Python is handled with `str` objects, more commonly known as **strings**. They are immutable sequences of **Unicode code points**. Unicode code points can represent a character, but can also have other meanings, such as formatting data, for example. Python, unlike other languages, doesn't have a `char` type, so a single character is rendered simply by a string of length `1`.

Unicode is an excellent way to handle data, and should be used for the internals of any application. When it comes to storing textual data though, or sending it on the network, you may want to encode it, using an appropriate encoding for the medium you're using. The result of an encoding produces a `bytes` object, whose syntax and behavior is similar to that of strings. String literals are written in Python using single, double, or triple quotes (both single or double). If built with triple quotes, a string can span on multiple lines. An example will clarify this:

```
>>> # 4 ways to make a string
>>> str1 = 'This is a string. We built it with single quotes.'
>>> str2 = "This is also a string, but built with double quotes."
>>> str3 = '''This is built using triple quotes,
... so it can span multiple lines.'''
>>> str4 = """This too
... is a multiline one
... built with triple double-quotes."""
>>> str4  #A
'This too\nis a multiline one\nbuilt with triple double-quotes.'
>>> print(str4)  #B
This too
is a multiline one
built with triple double-quotes.
```

In #A and #B, we print `str4`, first implicitly, and then explicitly, using the `print` function. A nice exercise would be to find out why they are different. Are you up to the challenge? (hint: look up the `str` function.)

Strings, like any sequence, have a length. You can get this by calling the `len` function:

```
>>> len(str1)
49
```

# Encoding and decoding strings

Using the `encode`/`decode` methods, we can encode Unicode strings and decode bytes objects. **UTF-8** is a variable length character encoding, capable of encoding all possible Unicode code points. It is the dominant encoding for the web. Notice also that by adding a literal b in front of a string declaration, we're creating a *bytes* object:

```
>>> s = "This is üņíc0de"  # unicode string: code points
>>> type(s)
<class 'str'>
>>> encoded_s = s.encode('utf-8')  # utf-8 encoded version of s
>>> encoded_s
b'This is \xc3\xbc\xc5\x8b\xc3\xadc0de'  # result: bytes object
>>> type(encoded_s)  # another way to verify it
<class 'bytes'>
>>> encoded_s.decode('utf-8')  # let's revert to the original
'This is üņíc0de'
>>> bytes_obj = b"A bytes object"  # a bytes object
>>> type(bytes_obj)
<class 'bytes'>
```

# Indexing and slicing strings

When manipulating sequences, it's very common to have to access them at one precise position (indexing), or to get a subsequence out of them (slicing). When dealing with immutable sequences, both operations are read-only.

While indexing comes in one form, a zero-based access to any position within the sequence, slicing comes in different forms. When you get a slice of a sequence, you can specify the `start` and `stop` positions, and the `step`. They are separated with a colon (`:`) like this: `my_sequence[start:stop:step]`. All the arguments are optional, `start` is inclusive, and `stop` is exclusive. It's much easier to show an example, rather than explain them further in words:

```
>>> s = "The trouble is you think you have time."
>>> s[0]  # indexing at position 0, which is the first char
'T'
>>> s[5]  # indexing at position 5, which is the sixth char
'r'
>>> s[:4]  # slicing, we specify only the stop position
'The '
>>> s[4:]  # slicing, we specify only the start position
'trouble is you think you have time.'
>>> s[2:14]  # slicing, both start and stop positions
'e trouble is'
```

```
>>> s[2:14:3]  # slicing, start, stop and step (every 3 chars)
'erb '
>>> s[:]  # quick way of making a copy
'The trouble is you think you have time.'
```

Of all the lines, the last one is probably the most interesting. If you don't specify a parameter, Python will fill in the default for you. In this case, start will be the start of the string, stop will be the end of the string, and step will be the default 1. This is an easy and quick way of obtaining a copy of the string s (same value, but different object). Can you find a way to get the reversed copy of a string using slicing (don't look it up; find it for yourself)?

# String formatting

One of the features strings have is the ability to be used as a template. There are several different ways of formatting a string, and for the full list of possibilities, I encourage you to look up the documentation. Here are some common examples:

```
>>> greet_old = 'Hello %s!'
>>> greet_old % 'Fabrizio'
'Hello Fabrizio!'

>>> greet_positional = 'Hello {} {}!'
>>> greet_positional.format('Fabrizio', 'Romano')
'Hello Fabrizio Romano!'

>>> greet_positional_idx = 'This is {0}! {1} loves {0}!'
>>> greet_positional_idx.format('Python', 'Fabrizio')
'This is Python! Fabrizio loves Python!'
>>> greet_positional_idx.format('Coffee', 'Fab')
'This is Coffee! Fab loves Coffee!'

>>> keyword = 'Hello, my name is {name} {last_name}'
>>> keyword.format(name='Fabrizio', last_name='Romano')
'Hello, my name is Fabrizio Romano'
```

In the previous example, you can see four different ways of formatting stings. The first one, which relies on the % operator, is deprecated and shouldn't be used any more. The current, modern way to format a string is by using the `format` string method. You can see, from the different examples, that a pair of curly braces acts as a placeholder within the string. When we call `format`, we feed it data that replaces the placeholders. We can specify indexes (and much more) within the curly braces, and even names, which implies we'll have to call `format` using keyword arguments instead of positional ones.

Notice how `greet_positional_idx` is rendered differently by feeding different data to the call to `format`. Apparently, I'm into Python and coffee... big surprise!

One last feature I want to show you is a relatively new addition to Python (Version 3.6) and it's called **formatted string literals**. This feature is quite cool: strings are prefixed with `f`, and contain replacement fields surrounded by curly braces. Replacement fields are expressions evaluated at runtime, and then formatted using the `format` protocol:

```
>>> name = 'Fab'
>>> age = 42
>>> f"Hello! My name is {name} and I'm {age}"
"Hello! My name is Fab and I'm 42"
>>> from math import pi
>>> f"No arguing with {pi}, it's irrational..."
"No arguing with 3.141592653589793, it's irrational..."
```

Check out the official documentation to learn everything about string formatting and how powerful it can be.

# Tuples

The last immutable sequence type we're going to see is the tuple. A **tuple** is a sequence of arbitrary Python objects. In a tuple, items are separated by commas. They are used everywhere in Python, because they allow for patterns that are hard to reproduce in other languages. Sometimes tuples are used implicitly; for example, to set up multiple variables on one line, or to allow a function to return multiple different objects (usually a function returns one object only, in many other languages), and even in the Python console, you can use tuples implicitly to print multiple elements with one single instruction. We'll see examples for all these cases:

```
>>> t = ()  # empty tuple
>>> type(t)
<class 'tuple'>
```

```
>>> one_element_tuple = (42, )  # you need the comma!
>>> three_elements_tuple = (1, 3, 5)  # braces are optional here
>>> a, b, c = 1, 2, 3  # tuple for multiple assignment
>>> a, b, c  # implicit tuple to print with one instruction
(1, 2, 3)
>>> 3 in three_elements_tuple  # membership test
True
```

Notice that the membership operator `in` can also be used with lists, strings, dictionaries, and, in general, with collection and sequence objects.

Notice that to create a tuple with one item, we need to put that comma after the item. The reason is that without the comma that item is just itself wrapped in braces, kind of in a redundant mathematical expression. Notice also that on assignment, braces are optional so `my_tuple = 1, 2, 3` is the same as `my_tuple = (1, 2, 3)`.

One thing that tuple assignment allows us to do, is *one-line swaps*, with no need for a third temporary variable. Let's see first a more traditional way of doing it:

```
>>> a, b = 1, 2
>>> c = a  # we need three lines and a temporary var c
>>> a = b
>>> b = c
>>> a, b  # a and b have been swapped
(2, 1)
```

And now let's see how we would do it in Python:

```
>>> a, b = 0, 1
>>> a, b = b, a  # this is the Pythonic way to do it
>>> a, b
(1, 0)
```

Take a look at the line that shows you the Pythonic way of swapping two values. Do you remember what I wrote in `Chapter 1`, *A Gentle Introduction to Python*? A Python program is typically one-fifth to one-third the size of equivalent Java or C++ code, and features like one-line swaps contribute to this. Python is elegant, where elegance in this context also means economy.

Because they are immutable, tuples can be used as keys for dictionaries (we'll see this shortly). To me, tuples are Python's built-in data that most closely represent a mathematical vector. This doesn't mean that this was the reason for which they were created though. Tuples usually contain an heterogeneous sequence of elements, while on the other hand, lists are most of the times homogeneous. Moreover, tuples are normally accessed via unpacking or indexing, while lists are usually iterated over.

# Mutable sequences

Mutable sequences differ from their immutable sisters in that they can be changed after creation. There are two mutable sequence types in Python: lists and byte arrays. I said before that the dictionary is the king of data structures in Python. I guess this makes the list its rightful queen.

# Lists

Python lists are mutable sequences. They are very similar to tuples, but they don't have the restrictions of immutability. Lists are commonly used to storing collections of homogeneous objects, but there is nothing preventing you from store heterogeneous collections as well. Lists can be created in many different ways. Let's see an example:

```
>>> []   # empty list
[]
>>> list()   # same as []
[]
>>> [1, 2, 3]   # as with tuples, items are comma separated
[1, 2, 3]
>>> [x + 5 for x in [2, 3, 4]]   # Python is magic
[7, 8, 9]
>>> list((1, 3, 5, 7, 9))   # list from a tuple
[1, 3, 5, 7, 9]
>>> list('hello')   # list from a string
['h', 'e', 'l', 'l', 'o']
```

In the previous example, I showed you how to create a list using different techniques. I would like you to take a good look at the line that says `Python is magic`, which I am not expecting you to fully understand at this point (unless you cheated and you're not a novice!). That is called a **list comprehension**, a very powerful functional feature of Python.

Creating lists is good, but the real fun comes when we use them, so let's see the main methods they gift us with:

```
>>> a = [1, 2, 1, 3]
>>> a.append(13)   # we can append anything at the end
>>> a
[1, 2, 1, 3, 13]
>>> a.count(1)   # how many `1` are there in the list?
2
>>> a.extend([5, 7])   # extend the list by another (or sequence)
>>> a
[1, 2, 1, 3, 13, 5, 7]
>>> a.index(13)   # position of `13` in the list (0-based indexing)
4
>>> a.insert(0, 17)   # insert `17` at position 0
>>> a
[17, 1, 2, 1, 3, 13, 5, 7]
>>> a.pop()   # pop (remove and return) last element
7
>>> a.pop(3)   # pop element at position 3
1
>>> a
[17, 1, 2, 3, 13, 5]
>>> a.remove(17)   # remove `17` from the list
>>> a
[1, 2, 3, 13, 5]
>>> a.reverse()   # reverse the order of the elements in the list
>>> a
[5, 13, 3, 2, 1]
>>> a.sort()   # sort the list
>>> a
[1, 2, 3, 5, 13]
>>> a.clear()   # remove all elements from the list
>>> a
[]
```

The preceding code gives you a roundup of a list's main methods. I want to show you how powerful they are, using `extend` as an example. You can extend lists using any sequence type:

```
>>> a = list('hello')  # makes a list from a string
>>> a
['h', 'e', 'l', 'l', 'o']
>>> a.append(100)  # append 100, heterogeneous type
>>> a
['h', 'e', 'l', 'l', 'o', 100]
>>> a.extend((1, 2, 3))  # extend using tuple
>>> a
['h', 'e', 'l', 'l', 'o', 100, 1, 2, 3]
>>> a.extend('...')  # extend using string
>>> a
['h', 'e', 'l', 'l', 'o', 100, 1, 2, 3, '.', '.', '.']
```

Now, let's see what are the most common operations you can do with lists:

```
>>> a = [1, 3, 5, 7]
>>> min(a)  # minimum value in the list
1
>>> max(a)  # maximum value in the list
7
>>> sum(a)  # sum of all values in the list
16
>>> len(a)  # number of elements in the list
4
>>> b = [6, 7, 8]
>>> a + b  # `+` with list means concatenation
[1, 3, 5, 7, 6, 7, 8]
>>> a * 2  # `*` has also a special meaning
[1, 3, 5, 7, 1, 3, 5, 7]
```

The last two lines in the preceding code are quite interesting because they introduce us to a concept called **operator overloading**. In short, it means that operators such as +, -. *, %, and so on, may represent different operations according to the context they are used in. It doesn't make any sense to sum two lists, right? Therefore, the + sign is used to concatenate them. Hence, the * sign is used to concatenate the list to itself according to the right operand.

Now, let's take a step further and see something a little more interesting. I want to show you how powerful the `sorted` method can be and how easy it is in Python to achieve results that require a great deal of effort in other languages:

```
>>> from operator import itemgetter
>>> a = [(5, 3), (1, 3), (1, 2), (2, -1), (4, 9)]
```

```
>>> sorted(a)
[(1, 2), (1, 3), (2, -1), (4, 9), (5, 3)]
>>> sorted(a, key=itemgetter(0))
[(1, 3), (1, 2), (2, -1), (4, 9), (5, 3)]
>>> sorted(a, key=itemgetter(0, 1))
[(1, 2), (1, 3), (2, -1), (4, 9), (5, 3)]
>>> sorted(a, key=itemgetter(1))
[(2, -1), (1, 2), (5, 3), (1, 3), (4, 9)]
>>> sorted(a, key=itemgetter(1), reverse=True)
[(4, 9), (5, 3), (1, 3), (1, 2), (2, -1)]
```

The preceding code deserves a little explanation. First of all, a is a list of tuples. This means each element in a is a tuple (a 2-tuple, to be precise). When we call sorted(some_list), we get a sorted version of some_list. In this case, the sorting on a 2-tuple works by sorting them on the first item in the tuple, and on the second when the first one is the same. You can see this behavior in the result of sorted(a), which yields [(1, 2), (1, 3), ...]. Python also gives us the ability to control which element(s) of the tuple the sorting must be run against. Notice that when we instruct the sorted function to work on the first element of each tuple (by key=itemgetter(0)), the result is different: [(1, 3), (1, 2), ...]. The sorting is done only on the first element of each tuple (which is the one at position 0). If we want to replicate the default behavior of a simple sorted(a) call, we need to use key=itemgetter(0, 1), which tells Python to sort first on the elements at position 0 within the tuples, and then on those at position 1. Compare the results and you'll see they match.

For completeness, I included an example of sorting only on the elements at position 1, and the same but in reverse order. If you have ever seen sorting in Java, I expect you to be quite impressed at this moment.

The Python sorting algorithm is very powerful, and it was written by Tim Peters (we've already seen this name, can you recall when?). It is aptly named **Timsort**, and it is a blend between **merge** and **insertion sort** and has better time performances than most other algorithms used for mainstream programming languages. Timsort is a stable sorting algorithm, which means that when multiple records have the same key, their original order is preserved. We've seen this in the result of sorted(a, key=itemgetter(0)), which has yielded [(1, 3), (1, 2), ...], in which the order of those two tuples has been preserved because they have the same value at position 0.

# Byte arrays

To conclude our overview of mutable sequence types, let's spend a couple of minutes on the `bytearray` type. Basically, they represent the mutable version of `bytes` objects. They expose most of the usual methods of mutable sequences as well as most of the methods of the `bytes` type. Items are integers in the range [0, 256).

> When it comes to intervals, I'm going to use the standard notation for open/closed ranges. A square bracket on one end means that the value is included, while a round brace means it's excluded. The granularity is usually inferred by the type of the edge elements so, for example, the interval [3, 7] means all integers between 3 and 7, inclusive. On the other hand, (3, 7) means all integers between 3 and 7 exclusive (hence 4, 5, and 6). Items in a `bytearray` type are integers between 0 and 256; 0 is included, 256 is not. One reason intervals are often expressed like this is to ease coding. If we break a range $[a, b)$ into $N$ consecutive ranges, we can easily represent the original one as a concatenation like this:
> $[a,k_1)+[k_1,k_2)+[k_2,k_3)+...+[k_{N-1},b)$
> The middle points ($k_i$) being excluded on one end, and included on the other end, allow for easy concatenation and splitting when intervals are handled in the code.

Let's see a quick example with the `bytearray` type:

```
>>> bytearray()   # empty bytearray object
bytearray(b'')
>>> bytearray(10)   # zero-filled instance with given length
bytearray(b'\x00\x00\x00\x00\x00\x00\x00\x00\x00\x00')
>>> bytearray(range(5)) # bytearray from iterable of integers
bytearray(b'\x00\x01\x02\x03\x04')
>>> name = bytearray(b'Lina')   #A - bytearray from bytes
>>> name.replace(b'L', b'l')
bytearray(b'lina')
>>> name.endswith(b'na')
True
>>> name.upper()
bytearray(b'LINA')
>>> name.count(b'L')
1
```

As you can see in the preceding code, there are a few ways to create a `bytearray` object. They can be useful in many situations; for example, when receiving data through a socket, they eliminate the need to concatenate data while polling, hence they can prove to be very handy. On the line `#A`, I created a `bytearray` named as `name` from the bytes literal `b'Lina'` to show you how the `bytearray` object exposes methods from both sequences and strings, which is extremely handy. If you think about it, they can be considered as mutable strings.

# Set types

Python also provides two set types, `set` and `frozenset`. The `set` type is mutable, while `frozenset` is immutable. They are unordered collections of immutable objects. **Hashability** is a characteristic that allows an object to be used as a set member as well as a key for a dictionary, as we'll see very soon.

 From the official documentation: *An object is hashable if it has a hash value which never changes during its lifetime, and can be compared to other objects. Hashability makes an object usable as a dictionary key and a set member, because these data structures use the hash value internally. All of Python's immutable built-in objects are hashable while mutable containers are not.*

Objects that compare equally must have the same hash value. Sets are very commonly used to test for membership, so let's introduce the `in` operator in the following example:

```
>>> small_primes = set()  # empty set
>>> small_primes.add(2)   # adding one element at a time
>>> small_primes.add(3)
>>> small_primes.add(5)
>>> small_primes
{2, 3, 5}
>>> small_primes.add(1)   # Look what I've done, 1 is not a prime!
>>> small_primes
{1, 2, 3, 5}
>>> small_primes.remove(1)   # so let's remove it
>>> 3 in small_primes # membership test
True
>>> 4 in small_primes
False
>>> 4 not in small_primes  # negated membership test
True
>>> small_primes.add(3)   # trying to add 3 again
```

```
>>> small_primes
{2, 3, 5}  # no change, duplication is not allowed
>>> bigger_primes = set([5, 7, 11, 13])  # faster creation
>>> small_primes | bigger_primes # union operator `|`
{2, 3, 5, 7, 11, 13}
>>> small_primes & bigger_primes  # intersection operator `&`
{5}
>>> small_primes - bigger_primes  # difference operator `-`
{2, 3}
```

In the preceding code, you can see two different ways to create a set. One creates an empty set and then adds elements one at a time. The other creates the set using a list of numbers as an argument to the constructor, which does all the work for us. Of course, you can create a set from a list or tuple (or any iterable) and then you can add and remove members from the set as you please.

We'll look at iterable objects and iteration in the next chapter. For now, just know that iterable objects are objects you can iterate on in a direction.

Another way of creating a set is by simply using the curly braces notation, like this:

```
>>> small_primes = {2, 3, 5, 5, 3}
>>> small_primes
{2, 3, 5}
```

Notice I added some duplication to emphasize that the resulting set won't have any. Let's see an example about the immutable counterpart of the set type, `frozenset`:

```
>>> small_primes = frozenset([2, 3, 5, 7])
>>> bigger_primes = frozenset([5, 7, 11])
>>> small_primes.add(11)   # we cannot add to a frozenset
Traceback (most recent call last):
  File "<stdin>", line 1, in <module>
AttributeError: 'frozenset' object has no attribute 'add'
>>> small_primes.remove(2)   # neither we can remove
Traceback (most recent call last):
  File "<stdin>", line 1, in <module>
AttributeError: 'frozenset' object has no attribute 'remove'
>>> small_primes & bigger_primes  # intersect, union, etc. allowed
frozenset({5, 7})
```

As you can see, `frozenset` objects are quite limited in respect of their mutable counterpart. They still prove very effective for membership test, union, intersection, and difference operations, and for performance reasons.

# Mapping types – dictionaries

Of all the built-in Python data types, the dictionary is easily the most interesting one. It's the only standard mapping type, and it is the backbone of every Python object.

A dictionary maps keys to values. Keys need to be hashable objects, while values can be of any arbitrary type. Dictionaries are mutable objects. There are quite a few different ways to create a dictionary, so let me give you a simple example of how to create a dictionary equal to `{'A': 1, 'Z': -1}` in five different ways:

```
>>> a = dict(A=1, Z=-1)
>>> b = {'A': 1, 'Z': -1}
>>> c = dict(zip(['A', 'Z'], [1, -1]))
>>> d = dict([('A', 1), ('Z', -1)])
>>> e = dict({'Z': -1, 'A': 1})
>>> a == b == c == d == e  # are they all the same?
True  # They are indeed
```

Have you noticed those double equals? Assignment is done with one equal, while to check whether an object is the same as another one (or five in one go, in this case), we use double equals. There is also another way to compare objects, which involves the `is` operator, and checks whether the two objects are the same (if they have the same ID, not just the value), but unless you have a good reason to use it, you should use the double equals instead. In the preceding code, I also used one nice function: `zip`. It is named after the real-life zip, which glues together two things taking one element from each at a time. Let me show you an example:

```
>>> list(zip(['h', 'e', 'l', 'l', 'o'], [1, 2, 3, 4, 5]))
[('h', 1), ('e', 2), ('l', 3), ('l', 4), ('o', 5)]
>>> list(zip('hello', range(1, 6)))  # equivalent, more Pythonic
[('h', 1), ('e', 2), ('l', 3), ('l', 4), ('o', 5)]
```

In the preceding example, I have created the same list in two different ways, one more explicit, and the other a little bit more Pythonic. Forget for a moment that I had to wrap the `list` constructor around the `zip` call (the reason is because `zip` returns an iterator, not a `list`, so if I want to see the result I need to exhaust that iterator into something—a list in this case), and concentrate on the result. See how `zip` has coupled the first elements of its two arguments together, then the second ones, then the third ones, and so on and so forth? Take a look at your pants (or at your purse, if you're a lady) and you'll see the same behavior in your actual zip. But let's go back to dictionaries and see how many wonderful methods they expose for allowing us to manipulate them as we want.

Let's start with the basic operations:

```
>>> d = {}
>>> d['a'] = 1  # let's set a couple of (key, value) pairs
>>> d['b'] = 2
>>> len(d)  # how many pairs?
2
>>> d['a']  # what is the value of 'a'?
1
>>> d  # how does `d` look now?
{'a': 1, 'b': 2}
>>> del d['a']  # let's remove `a`
>>> d
{'b': 2}
>>> d['c'] = 3  # let's add 'c': 3
>>> 'c' in d  # membership is checked against the keys
True
>>> 3 in d  # not the values
False
>>> 'e' in d
False
>>> d.clear()  # let's clean everything from this dictionary
>>> d
{}
```

Notice how accessing keys of a dictionary, regardless of the type of operation we're performing, is done through square brackets. Do you remember strings, lists, and tuples? We were accessing elements at some position through square brackets as well, which is yet another example of Python's consistency.

Let's see now three special objects called dictionary views: `keys`, `values`, and `items`. These objects provide a dynamic view of the dictionary entries and they change when the dictionary changes. `keys()` returns all the keys in the dictionary, `values()` returns all the values in the dictionary, and `items()` returns all the *(key, value)* pairs in the dictionary.

According to the Python documentation: "*Keys and values are iterated over in an arbitrary order which is non-random, varies across Python implementations, and depends on the dictionary's history of insertions and deletions. If keys, values and items views are iterated over with no intervening modifications to the dictionary, the order of items will directly correspond.*"

Enough with this chatter; let's put all this down into code:

```
>>> d = dict(zip('hello', range(5)))
>>> d
{'h': 0, 'e': 1, 'l': 3, 'o': 4}
>>> d.keys()
dict_keys(['h', 'e', 'l', 'o'])
>>> d.values()
dict_values([0, 1, 3, 4])
>>> d.items()
dict_items([('h', 0), ('e', 1), ('l', 3), ('o', 4)])
>>> 3 in d.values()
True
>>> ('o', 4) in d.items()
True
```

There are a few things to notice in the preceding code. First, notice how we're creating a dictionary by iterating over the zipped version of the string `'hello'` and the list `[0, 1, 2, 3, 4]`. The string `'hello'` has two `'l'` characters inside, and they are paired up with the values 2 and 3 by the `zip` function. Notice how in the dictionary, the second occurrence of the `'l'` key (the one with value 3), overwrites the first one (the one with value 2). Another thing to notice is that when asking for any view, the original order is now preserved, while before Version 3.6 there was no guarantee of that.

As of Python 3.6, the `dict` type has been reimplemented to use a more compact representation. This resulted in dictionaries using 20% to 25% less memory when compared to Python 3.5. Moreover, in Python 3.6, as a side effect, dictionaries are natively ordered. This feature has received such a welcome from the community that in 3.7 it has become a legit feature of the language rather than an implementation side effect. A `dict` is ordered if it remembers the order in which keys were first inserted.

We'll see how these views are fundamental tools when we talk about iterating over collections. Let's take a look now at some other methods exposed by Python's dictionaries; there's plenty of them and they are very useful:

```
>>> d
{'e': 1, 'h': 0, 'o': 4, 'l': 3}
>>> d.popitem()  # removes a random item (useful in algorithms)
('o', 4)
>>> d
{'h': 0, 'e': 1, 'l': 3}
>>> d.pop('l')  # remove item with key `l`
```

```
3
>>> d.pop('not-a-key')  # remove a key not in dictionary: KeyError
Traceback (most recent call last):
  File "<stdin>", line 1, in <module>
KeyError: 'not-a-key'
>>> d.pop('not-a-key', 'default-value')  # with a default value?
'default-value'  # we get the default value
>>> d.update({'another': 'value'})  # we can update dict this way
>>> d.update(a=13)  # or this way (like a function call)
>>> d
{'h': 0, 'e': 1, 'another': 'value', 'a': 13}
>>> d.get('a')  # same as d['a'] but if key is missing no KeyError
13
>>> d.get('a', 177)  # default value used if key is missing
13
>>> d.get('b', 177)  # like in this case
177
>>> d.get('b')  # key is not there, so None is returned
```

All these methods are quite simple to understand, but it's worth talking about that None, for a moment. Every function in Python returns None, unless the return statement is explicitly used to return something else, but we'll see this when we explore functions. None is frequently used to represent the absence of a value, and it is quite commonly used as a default value for arguments in function declaration. Some inexperienced coders sometimes write code that returns either False or None. Both False and None evaluate to False in a Boolean context so it may seem there is not much difference between them. But actually, I would argue there is quite an important difference: False means that we have information, and the information we have is False. None means *no information*. And no information is very different from information that is False. In layman's terms, if you ask your mechanic, *Is my car ready?*, there is a big difference between the answer, *No, it's not* (False) and, *I have no idea* (None).

One last method I really like about dictionaries is setdefault. It behaves like get, but also sets the key with the given value if it is not there. Let's see an example:

```
>>> d = {}
>>> d.setdefault('a', 1)  # 'a' is missing, we get default value
1
>>> d
{'a': 1}  # also, the key/value pair ('a', 1) has now been added
>>> d.setdefault('a', 5)  # let's try to override the value
1
>>> d
{'a': 1}  # no override, as expected
```

So, we're now at the end of this tour. Test your knowledge about dictionaries by trying to foresee what d looks like after this line:

```
>>> d = {}
>>> d.setdefault('a', {}).setdefault('b', []).append(1)
```

Don't worry if you don't get it immediately. I just wanted to encourage you to experiment with dictionaries.

This concludes our tour of built-in data types. Before I discuss some considerations about what we've seen in this chapter, I want to take a peek briefly at the collections module.

# The collections module

When Python general purpose built-in containers (tuple, list, set, and dict) aren't enough, we can find specialized container datatypes in the collections module. They are:

| Data type | Description |
|---|---|
| namedtuple() | Factory function for creating tuple subclasses with named fields |
| deque | List-like container with fast appends and pops on either end |
| ChainMap | Dictionary-like class for creating a single view of multiple mappings |
| Counter | Dictionary subclass for counting hashable objects |
| OrderedDict | Dictionary subclass that remembers the order entries were added |
| defaultdict | Dictionary subclass that calls a factory function to supply missing values |
| UserDict | Wrapper around dictionary objects for easier dictionary subclassing |
| UserList | Wrapper around list objects for easier list subclassing |
| UserString | Wrapper around string objects for easier string subclassing |

We don't have the room to cover all of them, but you can find plenty of examples in the official documentation, so here I'll just give a small example to show you namedtuple, defaultdict, and ChainMap.

# namedtuple

A `namedtuple` is a tuple-like object that has fields accessible by attribute lookup as well as being indexable and iterable (it's actually a subclass of `tuple`). This is sort of a compromise between a full-fledged object and a tuple, and it can be useful in those cases where you don't need the full power of a custom object, but you want your code to be more readable by avoiding weird indexing. Another use case is when there is a chance that items in the tuple need to change their position after refactoring, forcing the coder to refactor also all the logic involved, which can be very tricky. As usual, an example is better than a thousand words (or was it a picture?). Say we are handling data about the left and right eyes of a patient. We save one value for the left eye (position 0) and one for the right eye (position 1) in a regular tuple. Here's how that might be:

```
>>> vision = (9.5, 8.8)
>>> vision
(9.5, 8.8)
>>> vision[0]  # left eye (implicit positional reference)
9.5
>>> vision[1]  # right eye (implicit positional reference)
8.8
```

Now let's pretend we handle `vision` objects all the time, and at some point the designer decides to enhance them by adding information for the combined vision, so that a `vision` object stores data in this format: *(left eye, combined, right eye)*.

Do you see the trouble we're in now? We may have a lot of code that depends on `vision[0]` being the left eye information (which it still is) and `vision[1]` being the right eye information (which is no longer the case). We have to refactor our code wherever we handle these objects, changing `vision[1]` to `vision[2]`, and it can be painful. We could have probably approached this a bit better from the beginning, by using a `namedtuple`. Let me show you what I mean:

```
>>> from collections import namedtuple
>>> Vision = namedtuple('Vision', ['left', 'right'])
>>> vision = Vision(9.5, 8.8)
>>> vision[0]
9.5
>>> vision.left  # same as vision[0], but explicit
9.5
>>> vision.right  # same as vision[1], but explicit
8.8
```

If within our code, we refer to the left and right eyes using `vision.left` and `vision.right`, all we need to do to fix the new design issue is to change our factory and the way we create instances. The rest of the code won't need to change:

```
>>> Vision = namedtuple('Vision', ['left', 'combined', 'right'])
>>> vision = Vision(9.5, 9.2, 8.8)
>>> vision.left   # still correct
9.5
>>> vision.right  # still correct (though now is vision[2])
8.8
>>> vision.combined  # the new vision[1]
9.2
```

You can see how convenient it is to refer to those values by name rather than by position. After all, a wise man once wrote, *Explicit is better than implicit* (can you recall where? Think *Zen* if you can't...). This example may be a little extreme; of course, it's not likely that our code designer will go for a change like this, but you'd be amazed to see how frequently issues similar to this one happen in a professional environment, and how painful it is to refactor them.

# defaultdict

The `defaultdict` data type is one of my favorites. It allows you to avoid checking if a key is in a dictionary by simply inserting it for you on your first access attempt, with a default value whose type you pass on creation. In some cases, this tool can be very handy and shorten your code a little. Let's see a quick example. Say we are updating the value of `age`, by adding one year. If `age` is not there, we assume it was 0 and we update it to 1:

```
>>> d = {}
>>> d['age'] = d.get('age', 0) + 1  # age not there, we get 0 + 1
>>> d
{'age': 1}
>>> d = {'age': 39}
>>> d['age'] = d.get('age', 0) + 1  # age is there, we get 40
>>> d
{'age': 40}
```

Now let's see how it would work with a `defaultdict` data type. The second line is actually the short version of a four-lines-long `if` clause that we would have to write if dictionaries didn't have the `get` method (we'll see all about `if` clauses in Chapter 3, *Iterating and Making Decisions*):

```
>>> from collections import defaultdict
>>> dd = defaultdict(int)  # int is the default type (0 the value)
>>> dd['age'] += 1  # short for dd['age'] = dd['age'] + 1
>>> dd
defaultdict(<class 'int'>, {'age': 1})  # 1, as expected
```

Notice how we just need to instruct the `defaultdict` factory that we want an `int` number to be used in case the key is missing (we'll get 0, which is the default for the `int` type). Also, notice that even though in this example there is no gain on the number of lines, there is definitely a gain in readability, which is very important. You can also use a different technique to instantiate a `defaultdict` data type, which involves creating a factory object. To dig deeper, please refer to the official documentation.

# ChainMap

`ChainMap` is an extremely nice data type which was introduced in Python 3.3. It behaves like a normal dictionary but according to the Python documentation: *"is provided for quickly linking a number of mappings so they can be treated as a single unit"*. This is usually much faster than creating one dictionary and running multiple update calls on it. `ChainMap` can be used to simulate nested scopes and is useful in templating. The underlying mappings are stored in a list. That list is public and can be accessed or updated using the maps attribute. Lookups search the underlying mappings successively until a key is found. By contrast, writes, updates, and deletions only operate on the first mapping.

A very common use case is providing defaults, so let's see an example:

```
>>> from collections import ChainMap
>>> default_connection = {'host': 'localhost', 'port': 4567}
>>> connection = {'port': 5678}
>>> conn = ChainMap(connection, default_connection)  # map creation
>>> conn['port']  # port is found in the first dictionary
5678
>>> conn['host']  # host is fetched from the second dictionary
'localhost'
>>> conn.maps  # we can see the mapping objects
[{'port': 5678}, {'host': 'localhost', 'port': 4567}]
```

```
>>> conn['host'] = 'packtpub.com'  # let's add host
>>> conn.maps
[{'port': 5678, 'host': 'packtpub.com'},
 {'host': 'localhost', 'port': 4567}]
>>> del conn['port']  # let's remove the port information
>>> conn.maps
[{'host': 'packtpub.com'}, {'host': 'localhost', 'port': 4567}]
>>> conn['port']  # now port is fetched from the second dictionary
4567
>>> dict(conn)  # easy to merge and convert to regular dictionary
{'host': 'packtpub.com', 'port': 4567}
```

I just love how Python makes your life easy. You work on a `ChainMap` object, configure the first mapping as you want, and when you need a complete dictionary with all the defaults as well as the customized items, you just feed the `ChainMap` object to a `dict` constructor. If you have never coded in other languages, such as Java or C++, you probably won't be able to appreciate fully how precious this is, and how Python makes your life so much easier. I do, I feel claustrophobic every time I have to code in some other language.

# Enums

Technically not a built-in data type, as you have to import them from the `enum` module, but definitely worth mentioning, are enumerations. They were introduced in Python 3.4, and though it is not that common to see them in professional code (yet), I thought I'd give you an example anyway.

The official definition goes like this: "*An enumeration is a set of symbolic names (members) bound to unique, constant values. Within an enumeration, the members can be compared by identity, and the enumeration itself can be iterated over.*"

Say you need to represent traffic lights. In your code, you might resort to doing this:

```
>>> GREEN = 1
>>> YELLOW = 2
>>> RED = 4
>>> TRAFFIC_LIGHTS = (GREEN, YELLOW, RED)
>>> # or with a dict
>>> traffic_lights = {'GREEN': 1, 'YELLOW': 2, 'RED': 4}
```

There's nothing special about the preceding code. It's something, in fact, that is very common to find. But, consider doing this instead:

```
>>> from enum import Enum
>>> class TrafficLight(Enum):
...         GREEN = 1
...         YELLOW = 2
...         RED = 4
...
>>> TrafficLight.GREEN
<TrafficLight.GREEN: 1>
>>> TrafficLight.GREEN.name
'GREEN'
>>> TrafficLight.GREEN.value
1
>>> TrafficLight(1)
<TrafficLight.GREEN: 1>
>>> TrafficLight(4)
<TrafficLight.RED: 4>
```

Ignoring for a moment the (relative) complexity of a class definition, you can appreciate how this might be more advantageous. The data structure is much cleaner, and the API it provides is much more powerful. I encourage you to check out the official documentation to explore all the great features you can find in the `enum` module. I think it's worth exploring, at least once.

# Final considerations

That's it. Now you have seen a very good proportion of the data structures that you will use in Python. I encourage you to take a dive into the Python documentation and experiment further with each and every data type we've seen in this chapter. It's worth it, believe me. Everything you'll write will be about handling data, so make sure your knowledge about it is rock solid.

Before we leap into Chapter 3, *Iterating and Making Decisions*, I'd like to share some final considerations about different aspects that to my mind are important and not to be neglected.

# Small values caching

When we discussed objects at the beginning of this chapter, we saw that when we assigned a name to an object, Python creates the object, sets its value, and then points the name to it. We can assign different names to the same value and we expect different objects to be created, like this:

```
>>> a = 1000000
>>> b = 1000000
>>> id(a) == id(b)
False
```

In the preceding example, a and b are assigned to two int objects, which have the same value but they are not the same object, as you can see, their id is not the same. So let's do it again:

```
>>> a = 5
>>> b = 5
>>> id(a) == id(b)
True
```

Oh, oh! Is Python broken? Why are the two objects the same now? We didn't do a = b = 5, we set them up separately. Well, the answer is performances. Python caches short strings and small numbers, to avoid having many copies of them clogging up the system memory. Everything is handled properly under the hood so you don't need to worry a bit, but make sure that you remember this behavior should your code ever need to fiddle with IDs.

# How to choose data structures

As we've seen, Python provides you with several built-in data types and sometimes, if you're not that experienced, choosing the one that serves you best can be tricky, especially when it comes to collections. For example, say you have many dictionaries to store, each of which represents a customer. Within each customer dictionary, there's an 'id': 'code' unique identification code. In what kind of collection would you place them? Well, unless I know more about these customers, it's very hard to answer. What kind of access will I need? What sort of operations will I have to perform on each of them, and how many times? Will the collection change over time? Will I need to modify the customer dictionaries in any way? What is going to be the most frequent operation I will have to perform on the collection?

If you can answer the preceding questions, then you will know what to choose. If the collection never shrinks or grows (in other words, it won't need to add/delete any customer object after creation) or shuffles, then tuples are a possible choice. Otherwise, lists are a good candidate. Every customer dictionary has a unique identifier though, so even a dictionary could work. Let me draft these options for you:

```
# example customer objects
customer1 = {'id': 'abc123', 'full_name': 'Master Yoda'}
customer2 = {'id': 'def456', 'full_name': 'Obi-Wan Kenobi'}
customer3 = {'id': 'ghi789', 'full_name': 'Anakin Skywalker'}
# collect them in a tuple
customers = (customer1, customer2, customer3)
# or collect them in a list
customers = [customer1, customer2, customer3]
# or maybe within a dictionary, they have a unique id after all
customers = {
    'abc123': customer1,
    'def456': customer2,
    'ghi789': customer3,
}
```

Some customers we have there, right? I probably wouldn't go with the tuple option, unless I wanted to highlight that the collection is not going to change. I'd say usually a list is better, as it allows for more flexibility.

Another factor to keep in mind is that tuples and lists are ordered collections. If you use a dictionary (prior to Python 3.6) or a set, you lose the ordering, so you need to know if ordering is important in your application.

What about performances? For example, in a list, operations such as insertion and membership can take $O(n)$, while they are $O(1)$ for a dictionary. It's not always possible to use dictionaries though, if we don't have the guarantee that we can uniquely identify each item of the collection by means of one of its properties, and that the property in question is hashable (so it can be a key in `dict`).

If you're wondering what *O(n)* and *O(1)* mean, please Google `big O notation`. In this context, let's just say that if performing an operation *Op* on a data structure takes *O(f(n))*, it would mean that *Op* takes at most a time $t \leq c * f(n)$ to complete, where *c* is some positive constant, *n* is the size of the input, and *f* is some function. So, think of *O(...)* as an upper bound for the running time of an operation (it can be used also to size other measurable quantities, of course).

Another way of understanding if you have chosen the right data structure is by looking at the code you have to write in order to manipulate it. If everything comes easily and flows naturally, then you probably have chosen correctly, but if you find yourself thinking your code is getting unnecessarily complicated, then you probably should try and decide whether you need to reconsider your choices. It's quite hard to give advice without a practical case though, so when you choose a data structure for your data, try to keep ease of use and performance in mind and give precedence to what matters most in the context you are in.

# About indexing and slicing

At the beginning of this chapter, we saw slicing applied on strings. Slicing, in general, applies to a sequence: tuples, lists, strings, and so on. With lists, slicing can also be used for assignment. I've almost never seen this used in professional code, but still, you know you can. Could you slice dictionaries or sets? I hear you scream, *Of course not!*. Excellent; I see we're on the same page here, so let's talk about indexing.

There is one characteristic about Python indexing I haven't mentioned before. I'll show you by way of an example. How do you address the last element of a collection? Let's see:

```
>>> a = list(range(10))  # `a` has 10 elements. Last one is 9.
>>> a
[0, 1, 2, 3, 4, 5, 6, 7, 8, 9]
>>> len(a)  # its length is 10 elements
10
>>> a[len(a) - 1]  # position of last one is len(a) - 1
9
>>> a[-1]  # but we don't need len(a)! Python rocks!
9
>>> a[-2]  # equivalent to len(a) - 2
```

```
8
>>> a[-3]    # equivalent to len(a) - 3
7
```

If the list a has 10 elements, because of the 0-index positioning system of Python, the first one is at position 0 and the last one is at position 9. In the preceding example, the elements are conveniently placed in a position equal to their value: 0 is at position 0, 1 at position 1, and so on.

So, in order to fetch the last element, we need to know the length of the whole list (or tuple, or string, and so on) and then subtract 1. Hence: len(a) - 1. This is so common an operation that Python provides you with a way to retrieve elements using **negative indexing**. This proves very useful when you do data manipulation. Here's a nice diagram about how indexing works on the string "HelloThere" (which is Obi-Wan Kenobi sarcastically greeting General Grievous):

| Positive Indexing | | | | | | | | | |
|---|---|---|---|---|---|---|---|---|---|
| 0 | 1 | 2 | 3 | 4 | 5 | 6 | 7 | 8 | 9 |
| H | e | l | l | o | T | h | e | r | e |
| -10 | -9 | -8 | -7 | -6 | -5 | -4 | -3 | -2 | -1 |
| Negative Indexing | | | | | | | | | |

Trying to address indexes greater than **9** or smaller than **-10** will raise an IndexError, as expected.

# About the names

You may have noticed that, in order to keep the examples as short as possible, I have called many objects using simple letters, like a, b, c, d, and so on. This is perfectly OK when you debug on the console or when you show that a + b == 7, but it's bad practice when it comes to professional coding (or any type of coding, for that matter). I hope you will indulge me if I sometimes do it; the reason is to present the code in a more compact way.

In a real environment though, when you choose names for your data, you should choose them carefully and they should reflect what the data is about. So, if you have a collection of `Customer` objects, `customers` is a perfectly good name for it. Would `customers_list`, `customers_tuple`, or `customers_collection` work as well? Think about it for a second. Is it good to tie the name of the collection to the datatype? I don't think so, at least in most cases. So I'd say if you have an excellent reason to do so, go ahead; otherwise, don't. The reason is, once that `customers_tuple` starts being used in different places of your code, and you realize you actually want to use a list instead of a tuple, you're up for some fun refactoring (also known as **wasted time**). Names for data should be nouns, and names for functions should be verbs. Names should be as expressive as possible. Python is actually a very good example when it comes to names. Most of the time you can just guess what a function is called if you know what it does. Crazy, huh?

*Chapter 2* of *Meaningful Names* of *Clean Code, Robert C. Martin, Prentice Hall* is entirely dedicated to names. It's an amazing book that helped me improve my coding style in many different ways, and is a must-read if you want to take your coding to the next level.

# Summary

In this chapter, we've explored the built-in data types of Python. We've seen how many there are and how much can be achieved by just using them in different combinations.

We've seen number types, sequences, sets, mappings, collections (and a special guest appearance by `Enum`), we've seen that everything is an object, we've learned the difference between mutable and immutable, and we've also learned about slicing and indexing (and, proudly, negative indexing as well).

We've presented simple examples, but there's much more that you can learn about this subject, so stick your nose into the official documentation and explore.

Most of all, I encourage you to try out all the exercises by yourself, get your fingers using that code, build some muscle memory, and experiment, experiment, experiment. Learn what happens when you divide by zero, when you combine different number types into a single expression, when you manage strings. Play with all data types. Exercise them, break them, discover all their methods, enjoy them, and learn them very, very well.

If your foundation is not rock solid, how good can your code be? And data is the foundation for everything. Data shapes what dances around it.

The more you progress with the book, the more it's likely that you will find some discrepancies or maybe a small typo here and there in my code (or yours). You will get an error message, something will break. That's wonderful! When you code, things break all the time, you debug and fix all the time, so consider errors as useful exercises to learn something new about the language you're using, and not as failures or problems. Errors will keep coming up until your very last line of code, that's for sure, so you may as well start making your peace with them now.

The next chapter is about iterating and making decisions. We'll see how actually to put those collections to use, and take decisions based on the data we're presented with. We'll start to go a little faster now that your knowledge is building up, so make sure you're comfortable with the contents of this chapter before you move to the next one. Once more, have fun, explore, break things. It's a very good way to learn.

# 3
# Iterating and Making Decisions

*"Insanity: doing the same thing over and over again and expecting different results."*

– *Albert Einstein*

In the previous chapter, we looked at Python's built-in data types. Now that you're familiar with data in its many forms and shapes, it's time to start looking at how a program can use it.

According to Wikipedia:

> *In computer science, control flow (or alternatively, flow of control) refers to the specification of the order in which the individual statements, instructions or function calls of an imperative program are executed or evaluated.*

In order to control the flow of a program, we have two main weapons: **conditional programming** (also known as **branching**) and **looping**. We can use them in many different combinations and variations, but in this chapter, instead of going through all the possible forms of those two constructs in a *documentation* fashion, I'd rather give you the basics and then I'll write a couple of small scripts with you. In the first one, we'll see how to create a rudimentary prime-number generator, while in the second one, we'll see how to apply discounts to customers based on coupons. This way, you should get a better feeling for how conditional programming and looping can be used.

In this chapter, we are going to cover the following:

- Conditional programming
- Looping in Python
- A quick peek at the itertools module

# Conditional programming

Conditional programming, or branching, is something you do every day, every moment. It's about evaluating conditions: *if the light is green, then I can cross; if it's raining, then I'm taking the umbrella;* and *if I'm late for work, then I'll call my manager.*

The main tool is the `if` statement, which comes in different forms and colors, but basically it evaluates an expression and, based on the result, chooses which part of the code to execute. As usual, let's look at an example:

```
# conditional.1.py
late = True
if late:
    print('I need to call my manager!')
```

This is possibly the simplest example: when fed to the `if` statement, `late` acts as a conditional expression, which is evaluated in a Boolean context (exactly like if we were calling `bool(late)`). If the result of the evaluation is `True`, then we enter the body of the code immediately after the `if` statement. Notice that the `print` instruction is indented: this means it belongs to a scope defined by the `if` clause. Execution of this code yields:

```
$ python conditional.1.py
I need to call my manager!
```

Since `late` is `True`, the `print` statement was executed. Let's expand on this example:

```
# conditional.2.py
late = False
if late:
    print('I need to call my manager!')   #1
else:
    print('no need to call my manager...')   #2
```

This time I set `late = False`, so when I execute the code, the result is different:

```
$ python conditional.2.py
no need to call my manager...
```

Depending on the result of evaluating the `late` expression, we can either enter block #1 or block #2, *but not both*. Block #1 is executed when `late` evaluates to `True`, while block #2 is executed when `late` evaluates to `False`. Try assigning `False`/`True` values to the `late` name, and see how the output for this code changes accordingly.

The preceding example also introduces the `else` clause, which becomes very handy when we want to provide an alternative set of instructions to be executed when an expression evaluates to `False` within an `if` clause. The else clause is optional, as is evident by comparing the preceding two examples.

# A specialized else – elif

Sometimes all you need is to do something if a condition is met (a simple `if` clause). At other times, you need to provide an alternative, in case the condition is `False` (`if`/`else` clause), but there are situations where you may have more than two paths to choose from, so, since calling the manager (or not calling them) is kind of a binary type of example (either you call or you don't), let's change the type of example and keep expanding. This time, we decide on tax percentages. If my income is less than $10,000, I won't pay any taxes. If it is between $10,000 and $30,000, I'll pay 20% in taxes. If it is between $30,000 and $100,000, I'll pay 35% in taxes, and if it's over $100,000, I'll (gladly) pay 45% in taxes. Let's put this all down into beautiful Python code:

```
# taxes.py
income = 15000
if income < 10000:
    tax_coefficient = 0.0    #1
elif income < 30000:
    tax_coefficient = 0.2    #2
elif income < 100000:
    tax_coefficient = 0.35   #3
else:
    tax_coefficient = 0.45   #4

print('I will pay:', income * tax_coefficient, 'in taxes')
```

Executing the preceding code yields:

```
$ python taxes.py
I will pay: 3000.0 in taxes
```

Let's go through the example line by line: we start by setting up the income value. In the example, my income is $15,000. We enter the `if` clause. Notice that this time we also introduced the `elif` clause, which is a contraction of `else-if`, and it's different from a bare `else` clause in that it also has its own condition. So, the `if` expression of `income < 10000` evaluates to `False`, therefore block #1 is not executed.

The control passes to the next condition evaluator: `elif income < 30000`. This one evaluates to `True`, therefore block #2 is executed, and because of this, Python then resumes execution after the whole `if/elif/elif/else` clause (which we can just call the `if` clause from now on). There is only one instruction after the `if` clause, the `print` call, which tells us I will pay `3000.0` in taxes this year (*15,000 \* 20%*). Notice that the order is mandatory: `if` comes first, then (optionally) as many `elif` clauses as you need, and then (optionally) an `else` clause.

Interesting, right? No matter how many lines of code you may have within each block, when one of the conditions evaluates to `True`, the associated block is executed and then execution resumes after the whole clause. If none of the conditions evaluates to `True` (for example, `income = 200000`), then the body of the `else` clause would be executed (block #4). This example expands our understanding of the behavior of the `else` clause. Its block of code is executed when none of the preceding `if/elif/.../elif` expressions has evaluated to `True`.

Try to modify the value of `income` until you can comfortably execute all blocks at will (one per execution, of course). And then try the **boundaries**. This is crucial, whenever you have conditions expressed as **equalities** or **inequalities** (==, !=, <, >, <=, >=), those numbers represent boundaries. It is essential to test boundaries thoroughly. Should I allow you to drive at 18 or 17? Am I checking your age with `age < 18`, or `age <= 18`? You can't imagine how many times I've had to fix subtle bugs that stemmed from using the wrong operator, so go ahead and experiment with the preceding code. Change some < to <= and set income to be one of the boundary values (10,000, 30,000, 100,000) as well as any value in between. See how the result changes, and get a good understanding of it before proceeding.

Let's now see another example that shows us how to nest `if` clauses. Say your program encounters an error. If the alert system is the console, we print the error. If the alert system is an email, we send it according to the severity of the error. If the alert system is anything other than console or email, we don't know what to do, therefore we do nothing. Let's put this into code:

```
# errorsalert.py
alert_system = 'console'  # other value can be 'email'
error_severity = 'critical'  # other values: 'medium' or 'low'
error_message = 'OMG! Something terrible happened!'

if alert_system == 'console':
    print(error_message)  #1
elif alert_system == 'email':
    if error_severity == 'critical':
        send_email('admin@example.com', error_message)  #2
    elif error_severity == 'medium':
        send_email('support.1@example.com', error_message)  #3
    else:
        send_email('support.2@example.com', error_message)  #4
```

The preceding example is quite interesting, because of its silliness. It shows us two nested `if` clauses (**outer** and **inner**). It also shows us that the outer `if` clause doesn't have any `else`, while the inner one does. Notice how indentation is what allows us to nest one clause within another one.

If `alert_system == 'console'`, body #1 is executed, and nothing else happens. On the other hand, if `alert_system == 'email'`, then we enter into another `if` clause, which we called inner. In the inner `if` clause, according to `error_severity`, we send an email to either an admin, first-level support, or second-level support (blocks #2, #3, and #4). The `send_email` function is not defined in this example, therefore trying to run it would give you an error. In the source code of the book, which you can download from the website, I included a trick to redirect that call to a regular `print` function, just so you can experiment on the console without actually sending an email. Try changing the values and see how it all works.

# The ternary operator

One last thing I would like to show you, before moving on to the next subject, is the **ternary operator** or, in layman's terms, the short version of an if/else clause. When the value of a name is to be assigned according to some condition, sometimes it's easier and more readable to use the ternary operator instead of a proper if clause. In the following example, the two code blocks do exactly the same thing:

```
# ternary.py
order_total = 247  # GBP

# classic if/else form
if order_total > 100:
    discount = 25  # GBP
else:
    discount = 0  # GBP
print(order_total, discount)

# ternary operator
discount = 25 if order_total > 100 else 0
print(order_total, discount)
```

For simple cases like this, I find it very nice to be able to express that logic in one line instead of four. Remember, as a coder, you spend much more time reading code than writing it, so Python's conciseness is invaluable.

Are you clear on how the ternary operator works? Basically, name = something if condition else something-else. So name is assigned something if condition evaluates to True, and something-else if condition evaluates to False.

Now that you know everything about controlling the path of the code, let's move on to the next subject: *looping*.

# Looping

If you have any experience with looping in other programming languages, you will find Python's way of looping a bit different. First of all, what is looping? **Looping** means being able to repeat the execution of a code block more than once, according to the loop parameters we're given. There are different looping constructs, which serve different purposes, and Python has distilled all of them down to just two, which you can use to achieve everything you need. These are the for and while statements.

While it's definitely possible to do everything you need using either of them, they serve different purposes and therefore they're usually used in different contexts. We'll explore this difference thoroughly in this chapter.

# The for loop

The `for` loop is used when looping over a sequence, such as a list, tuple, or a collection of objects. Let's start with a simple example and expand on the concept to see what the Python syntax allows us to do:

```
# simple.for.py
for number in [0, 1, 2, 3, 4]:
    print(number)
```

This simple snippet of code, when executed, prints all numbers from 0 to 4. The `for` loop is fed the list [0, 1, 2, 3, 4] and at each iteration, `number` is given a value from the sequence (which is iterated sequentially, in order), then the body of the loop is executed (the print line). The `number` value changes at every iteration, according to which value is coming next from the sequence. When the sequence is exhausted, the `for` loop terminates, and the execution of the code resumes normally with the code after the loop.

# Iterating over a range

Sometimes we need to iterate over a range of numbers, and it would be quite unpleasant to have to do so by hardcoding the list somewhere. In such cases, the `range` function comes to the rescue. Let's see the equivalent of the previous snippet of code:

```
# simple.for.py
for number in range(5):
    print(number)
```

The `range` function is used extensively in Python programs when it comes to creating sequences: you can call it by passing one value, which acts as `stop` (counting from `0`), or you can pass two values (`start` and `stop`), or even three (`start`, `stop`, and `step`). Check out the following example:

```
>>> list(range(10))   # one value: from 0 to value (excluded)
[0, 1, 2, 3, 4, 5, 6, 7, 8, 9]
>>> list(range(3, 8))   # two values: from start to stop (excluded)
[3, 4, 5, 6, 7]
>>> list(range(-10, 10, 4))   # three values: step is added
[-10, -6, -2, 2, 6]
```

For the moment, ignore that we need to wrap `range(...)` within a `list`. The `range` object is a little bit special, but in this case, we're just interested in understanding what values it will return to us. You can see that the deal is the same with slicing: `start` is included, `stop` excluded, and optionally you can add a `step` parameter, which by default is `1`.

Try modifying the parameters of the `range()` call in our `simple.for.py` code and see what it prints. Get comfortable with it.

## Iterating over a sequence

Now we have all the tools to iterate over a sequence, so let's build on that example:

```
# simple.for.2.py
surnames = ['Rivest', 'Shamir', 'Adleman']
for position in range(len(surnames)):
    print(position, surnames[position])
```

The preceding code adds a little bit of complexity to the game. Execution will show this result:

```
$ python simple.for.2.py
0 Rivest
1 Shamir
2 Adleman
```

Let's use the **inside-out** technique to break it down, OK? We start from the innermost part of what we're trying to understand, and we expand outward. So, `len(surnames)` is the length of the surnames list: 3. Therefore, `range(len(surnames))` is actually transformed into `range(3)`. This gives us the range [0, 3), which is basically a sequence (0, 1, 2). This means that the `for` loop will run three iterations. In the first one, `position` will take value 0, while in the second one, it will take value 1, and finally value 2 in the third and last iteration. What is (0, 1, 2), if not the possible indexing positions for the `surnames` list? At position 0, we find `'Rivest'`, at position 1, `'Shamir'`, and at position 2, `'Adleman'`. If you are curious about what these three men created together, change `print(position, surnames[position])` to `print(surnames[position][0], end='')`, add a final `print()` outside of the loop, and run the code again.

Now, this style of looping is actually much closer to languages such as Java or C++. In Python, it's quite rare to see code like this. You can just iterate over any sequence or collection, so there is no need to get the list of positions and retrieve elements out of a sequence at each iteration. It's expensive, needlessly expensive. Let's change the example into a more Pythonic form:

```
# simple.for.3.py
surnames = ['Rivest', 'Shamir', 'Adleman']
for surname in surnames:
    print(surname)
```

Now that's something! It's practically English. The `for` loop can iterate over the `surnames` list, and it gives back each element in order at each interaction. Running this code will print the three surnames, one at a time. It's much easier to read, right?

What if you wanted to print the position as well though? Or what if you actually needed it? Should you go back to the `range(len(...))` form? No. You can use the `enumerate` built-in function, like this:

```
# simple.for.4.py
surnames = ['Rivest', 'Shamir', 'Adleman']
for position, surname in enumerate(surnames):
    print(position, surname)
```

This code is very interesting as well. Notice that enumerate gives back a two-tuple (position, surname) at each iteration, but still, it's much more readable (and more efficient) than the range(len(...)) example. You can call enumerate with a start parameter, such as enumerate(iterable, start), and it will start from start, rather than 0. Just another little thing that shows you how much thought has been given in designing Python so that it makes your life easier.

You can use a for loop to iterate over lists, tuples, and in general anything that Python calls iterable. This is a very important concept, so let's talk about it a bit more.

# Iterators and iterables

According to the Python documentation (https://docs.python.org/3/glossary. html), an iterable is:

> *An object capable of returning its members one at a time. Examples of iterables include all sequence types (such as list, str, and tuple) and some non-sequence types like dict, file objects, and objects of any classes you define with an __iter__() or __getitem__() method. Iterables can be used in a for loop and in many other places where a sequence is needed (zip(), map(), ...). When an iterable object is passed as an argument to the built-in function iter(), it returns an iterator for the object. This iterator is good for one pass over the set of values. When using iterables, it is usually not necessary to call iter() or deal with iterator objects yourself. The for statement does that automatically for you, creating a temporary unnamed variable to hold the iterator for the duration of the loop.*

Simply put, what happens when you write for k in sequence: ... body ..., is that the for loop asks sequence for the next element, it gets something back, it calls that something k, and then executes its body. Then, once again, the for loop asks sequence for the next element, it calls it k again, and executes the body again, and so on and so forth, until the sequence is exhausted. Empty sequences will result in zero executions of the body.

Some data structures, when iterated over, produce their elements in order, such as lists, tuples, and strings, while some others don't, such as sets and dictionaries (prior to Python 3.6). Python gives us the ability to iterate over iterables, using a type of object called an **iterator**.

According to the official documentation (`https://docs.python.org/3/glossary.html`), an iterator is:

> *An object representing a stream of data. Repeated calls to the iterator's __next__() method (or passing it to the built-in function next()) return successive items in the stream. When no more data are available a StopIteration exception is raised instead. At this point, the iterator object is exhausted and any further calls to its __next__() method just raise StopIteration again. Iterators are required to have an __iter__() method that returns the iterator object itself so every iterator is also iterable and may be used in most places where other iterables are accepted. One notable exception is code which attempts multiple iteration passes. A container object (such as a list) produces a fresh new iterator each time you pass it to the iter() function or use it in a for loop. Attempting this with an iterator will just return the same exhausted iterator object used in the previous iteration pass, making it appear like an empty container.*

Don't worry if you don't fully understand all the preceding legalese, you will in due time. I put it here as a handy reference for the future.

In practice, the whole iterable/iterator mechanism is somewhat hidden behind the code. Unless you need to code your own iterable or iterator for some reason, you won't have to worry about this too much. But it's very important to understand how Python handles this key aspect of control flow because it will shape the way you will write your code.

# Iterating over multiple sequences

Let's see another example of how to iterate over two sequences of the same length, in order to work on their respective elements in pairs. Say we have a list of people and a list of numbers representing the age of the people in the first list. We want to print a pair person/age on one line for all of them. Let's start with an example and let's refine it gradually:

```python
# multiple.sequences.py
people = ['Conrad', 'Deepak', 'Heinrich', 'Tom']
ages = [29, 30, 34, 36]
for position in range(len(people)):
    person = people[position]
    age = ages[position]
    print(person, age)
```

By now, this code should be pretty straightforward for you to understand. We need to iterate over the list of positions (0, 1, 2, 3) because we want to retrieve elements from two different lists. Executing it we get the following:

```
$ python multiple.sequences.py
Conrad 29
Deepak 30
Heinrich 34
Tom 36
```

This code is both inefficient and not Pythonic. It's inefficient because retrieving an element given the position can be an expensive operation, and we're doing it from scratch at each iteration. The postal worker doesn't go back to the beginning of the road each time they deliver a letter, right? They move from house to house. From one to the next one. Let's try to make it better using `enumerate`:

```python
# multiple.sequences.enumerate.py
people = ['Conrad', 'Deepak', 'Heinrich', 'Tom']
ages = [29, 30, 34, 36]
for position, person in enumerate(people):
    age = ages[position]
    print(person, age)
```

That's better, but still not perfect. And it's still a bit ugly. We're iterating properly on `people`, but we're still fetching `age` using positional indexing, which we want to lose as well. Well, no worries, Python gives you the `zip` function, remember? Let's use it:

```python
# multiple.sequences.zip.py
people = ['Conrad', 'Deepak', 'Heinrich', 'Tom']
ages = [29, 30, 34, 36]
for person, age in zip(people, ages):
    print(person, age)
```

Ah! So much better! Once again, compare the preceding code with the first example and admire Python's elegance. The reason I wanted to show this example is twofold. On the one hand, I wanted to give you an idea of how shorter code in Python can be compared to other languages where the syntax doesn't allow you to iterate over sequences or collections as easily. And on the other hand, and much more importantly, notice that when the `for` loop asks `zip(sequenceA, sequenceB)` for the next element, it gets back a tuple, not just a single object. It gets back a tuple with as many elements as the number of sequences we feed to the `zip` function. Let's expand a little on the previous example in two ways, using explicit and implicit assignment:

```python
# multiple.sequences.explicit.py
```

```
people = ['Conrad', 'Deepak', 'Heinrich', 'Tom']
ages = [29, 30, 34, 36]
nationalities = ['Poland', 'India', 'South Africa', 'England']
for person, age, nationality in zip(people, ages, nationalities):
    print(person, age, nationality)
```

In the preceding code, we added the nationalities list. Now that we feed three sequences to the zip function, the for loop gets back a *three-tuple* at each iteration. Notice that the position of the elements in the tuple respects the position of the sequences in the zip call. Executing the code will yield the following result:

```
$ python multiple.sequences.explicit.py
Conrad 29 Poland
Deepak 30 India
Heinrich 34 South Africa
Tom 36 England
```

Sometimes, for reasons that may not be clear in a simple example such as the preceding one, you may want to explode the tuple within the body of the for loop. If that is your desire, it's perfectly possible to do so:

```
# multiple.sequences.implicit.py
people = ['Conrad', 'Deepak', 'Heinrich', 'Tom']
ages = [29, 30, 34, 36]
nationalities = ['Poland', 'India', 'South Africa', 'England']
for data in zip(people, ages, nationalities):
    person, age, nationality = data
    print(person, age, nationality)
```

It's basically doing what the for loop does automatically for you, but in some cases you may want to do it yourself. Here, the three-tuple data that comes from zip(...) is exploded within the body of the for loop into three variables: person, age, and nationality.

# The while loop

In the preceding pages, we saw the for loop in action. It's incredibly useful when you need to loop over a sequence or a collection. The key point to keep in mind, when you need to be able to discriminate which looping construct to use, is that the for loop rocks when you have to iterate over a finite amount of elements. It can be a huge amount, but still, something that ends at some point.

There are other cases though, when you just need to loop until some condition is satisfied, or even loop indefinitely until the application is stopped, such as cases where we don't really have something to iterate on, and therefore the for loop would be a poor choice. But fear not, for these cases, Python provides us with the while loop.

The while loop is similar to the for loop, in that they both loop, and at each iteration they execute a body of instructions. What is different between them is that the while loop doesn't loop over a sequence (it can, but you have to write the logic manually and it wouldn't make any sense, you would just want to use a for loop), rather, it loops as long as a certain condition is satisfied. When the condition is no longer satisfied, the loop ends.

As usual, let's see an example that will clarify everything for us. We want to print the binary representation of a positive number. In order to do so, we can use a simple algorithm that collects the remainders of division by 2 (in reverse order), and that turns out to be the binary representation of the number itself:

```
6 / 2 = 3 (remainder: 0)
3 / 2 = 1 (remainder: 1)
1 / 2 = 0 (remainder: 1)
List of remainders: 0, 1, 1.
Inverse is 1, 1, 0, which is also the binary representation of 6: 110
```

Let's write some code to calculate the binary representation for the number 39: $100111_2$:

```python
# binary.py
n = 39
remainders = []
while n > 0:
    remainder = n % 2  # remainder of division by 2
    remainders.insert(0, remainder)  # we keep track of remainders
    n //= 2  # we divide n by 2

print(remainders)
```

In the preceding code, I highlighted n > 0, which is the condition to keep looping. We can make the code a little shorter (and more Pythonic), by using the divmod function, which is called with a number and a divisor, and returns a tuple with the result of the integer division and its remainder. For example, divmod(13, 5) would return (2, 3), and indeed $5 * 2 + 3 = 13$:

```python
# binary.2.py
n = 39
```

```
remainders = []
while n > 0:
    n, remainder = divmod(n, 2)
    remainders.insert(0, remainder)

print(remainders)
```

In the preceding code, we have reassigned n to the result of the division by 2, and the remainder, in one single line.

Notice that the condition in a `while` loop is a condition to continue looping. If it evaluates to `True`, then the body is executed and then another evaluation follows, and so on, until the condition evaluates to `False`. When that happens, the loop is exited immediately without executing its body.

If the condition never evaluates to `False`, the loop becomes a so-called **infinite loop**. Infinite loops are used, for example, when polling from network devices: you ask the socket whether there is any data, you do something with it if there is any, then you sleep for a small amount of time, and then you ask the socket again, over and over again, without ever stopping.

Having the ability to loop over a condition, or to loop indefinitely, is the reason why the `for` loop alone is not enough, and therefore Python provides the `while` loop.

By the way, if you need the binary representation of a number, check out the `bin` function.

Just for fun, let's adapt one of the examples (`multiple.sequences.py`) using the while logic:

```
# multiple.sequences.while.py
people = ['Conrad', 'Deepak', 'Heinrich', 'Tom']
ages = [29, 30, 34, 36]
position = 0
while position < len(people):
    person = people[position]
    age = ages[position]
    print(person, age)
    position += 1
```

In the preceding code, I have highlighted the *initialization, condition,* and *update* of the `position` variable, which makes it possible to simulate the equivalent `for` loop code by handling the iteration variable manually. Everything that can be done with a `for` loop can also be done with a `while` loop, even though you can see there's a bit of boilerplate you have to go through in order to achieve the same result. The opposite is also true, but unless you have a reason to do so, you ought to use the right tool for the job, and 99.9% of the time you'll be fine.

So, to recap, use a `for` loop when you need to iterate over an iterable, and a `while` loop when you need to loop according to a condition being satisfied or not. If you keep in mind the difference between the two purposes, you will never choose the wrong looping construct.

Let's now see how to alter the normal flow of a loop.

# The break and continue statements

According to the task at hand, sometimes you will need to alter the regular flow of a loop. You can either skip a single iteration (as many times as you want), or you can break out of the loop entirely. A common use case for skipping iterations is, for example, when you're iterating over a list of items and you need to work on each of them only if some condition is verified. On the other hand, if you're iterating over a collection of items, and you have found one of them that satisfies some need you have, you may decide not to continue the loop entirely and therefore break out of it. There are countless possible scenarios, so it's better to see a couple of examples.

Let's say you want to apply a 20% discount to all products in a basket list for those that have an expiration date of today. The way you achieve this is to use the `continue` statement, which tells the looping construct (`for` or `while`) to stop execution of the body immediately and go to the next iteration, if any. This example will take us a little deeper down the rabbit hole, so be ready to jump:

```python
# discount.py
from datetime import date, timedelta

today = date.today()
tomorrow = today + timedelta(days=1)  # today + 1 day is tomorrow
products = [
    {'sku': '1', 'expiration_date': today, 'price': 100.0},
    {'sku': '2', 'expiration_date': tomorrow, 'price': 50},
    {'sku': '3', 'expiration_date': today, 'price': 20},
]
```

```
for product in products:
    if product['expiration_date'] != today:
        continue
    product['price'] *= 0.8  # equivalent to applying 20% discount
    print(
        'Price for sku', product['sku'],
        'is now', product['price'])
```

We start by importing the `date` and `timedelta` objects, then we set up our products. Those with `sku` as 1 and 3 have an expiration date of `today`, which means we want to apply a 20% discount on them. We loop over each `product` and we inspect the expiration date. If it is not (inequality operator, `!=`) `today`, we don't want to execute the rest of the body suite, so we `continue`.

Notice that it is not important where in the body suite you place the `continue` statement (you can even use it more than once). When you reach it, execution stops and goes back to the next iteration. If we run the `discount.py` module, this is the output:

```
$ python discount.py
Price for sku 1 is now 80.0
Price for sku 3 is now 16.0
```

This shows you that the last two lines of the body haven't been executed for `sku` number 2.

Let's now see an example of breaking out of a loop. Say we want to tell whether at least one of the elements in a list evaluates to `True` when fed to the `bool` function. Given that we need to know whether there is at least one, when we find it, we don't need to keep scanning the list any further. In Python code, this translates to using the `break` statement. Let's write this down into code:

```
# any.py
items = [0, None, 0.0, True, 0, 7]  # True and 7 evaluate to True

found = False  # this is called "flag"
for item in items:
    print('scanning item', item)
    if item:
        found = True  # we update the flag
        break

if found:  # we inspect the flag
    print('At least one item evaluates to True')
else:
    print('All items evaluate to False')
```

The preceding code is such a common pattern in programming, you will see it a lot. When you inspect items this way, basically what you do is to set up a `flag` variable, then start the inspection. If you find one element that matches your criteria (in this example, that evaluates to `True`), then you update the flag and stop iterating. After iteration, you inspect the flag and take action accordingly. Execution yields:

```
$ python any.py
scanning item 0
scanning item None
scanning item 0.0
scanning item True
At least one item evaluates to True
```

See how execution stopped after `True` was found? The `break` statement acts exactly like the `continue` one, in that it stops executing the body of the loop immediately, but also, prevents any other iteration from running, effectively breaking out of the loop. The `continue` and `break` statements can be used together with no limitation in their numbers, both in the `for` and `while` looping constructs.

 By the way, there is no need to write code to detect whether there is at least one element in a sequence that evaluates to `True`. Just check out the built-in `any` function.

# A special else clause

One of the features I've seen only in the Python language is the ability to have `else` clauses after `while` and `for` loops. It's very rarely used, but it's definitely nice to have. In short, you can have an `else` suite after a `for` or `while` loop. If the loop ends normally, because of exhaustion of the iterator (`for` loop) or because the condition is finally not met (`while` loop), then the `else` suite (if present) is executed. In case execution is interrupted by a `break` statement, the `else` clause is not executed. Let's take an example of a `for` loop that iterates over a group of items, looking for one that would match some condition. In case we don't find at least one that satisfies the condition, we want to raise an **exception**. This means we want to arrest the regular execution of the program and signal that there was an error, or exception, that we cannot deal with. Exceptions will be the subject of a later chapter, so don't worry if you don't fully understand them now. Just bear in mind that they will alter the regular flow of the code.

Let me now show you two examples that do exactly the same thing, but one of them is using the special for...else syntax. Say that we want to find, among a collection of people, one that could drive a car:

```python
# for.no.else.py
class DriverException(Exception):
    pass

people = [('James', 17), ('Kirk', 9), ('Lars', 13), ('Robert', 8)]
driver = None
for person, age in people:
    if age >= 18:
        driver = (person, age)
        break

if driver is None:
    raise DriverException('Driver not found.')
```

Notice the flag pattern again. We set the driver to be None, then if we find one, we update the driver flag, and then, at the end of the loop, we inspect it to see whether one was found. I kind of have the feeling that those kids would drive a very *metallic* car, but anyway, notice that if a driver is not found, DriverException is raised, signaling to the program that execution cannot continue (we're lacking the driver).

The same functionality can be rewritten a bit more elegantly using the following code:

```python
# for.else.py
class DriverException(Exception):
    pass

people = [('James', 17), ('Kirk', 9), ('Lars', 13), ('Robert', 8)]
for person, age in people:
    if age >= 18:
        driver = (person, age)
        break
else:
    raise DriverException('Driver not found.')
```

Notice that we aren't forced to use the flag pattern any more. The exception is raised as part of the for loop logic, which makes good sense because the for loop is checking on some condition. All we need is to set up a driver object in case we find one, because the rest of the code is going to use that information somewhere. Notice the code is shorter and more elegant, because the logic is now correctly grouped together where it belongs.

In the *Transforming Code into Beautiful, Idiomatic Python* video, Raymond Hettinger suggests a much better name for the `else` statement associated with a for loop: `nobreak`. If you struggle remembering how the `else` works for a `for` loop, simply remembering this fact should help you.

# Putting all this together

Now that you have seen all there is to see about conditionals and loops, it's time to spice things up a little, and look at those two examples I anticipated at the beginning of this chapter. We'll mix and match here, so you can see how you can use all these concepts together. Let's start by writing some code to generate a list of prime numbers up to some limit. Please bear in mind that I'm going to write a very inefficient and rudimentary algorithm to detect primes. The important thing for you is to concentrate on those bits in the code that belong to this chapter's subject.

## A prime generator

According to Wikipedia:

> *A prime number (or a prime) is a natural number greater than 1 that has no positive divisors other than 1 and itself. A natural number greater than 1 that is not a prime number is called a composite number.*

Based on this definition, if we consider the first 10 natural numbers, we can see that 2, 3, 5, and 7 are primes, while 1, 4, 6, 8, 9, and 10 are not. In order to have a computer tell you whether a number, *N*, is prime, you can divide that number by all natural numbers in the range [2, *N*). If any of those divisions yields zero as a remainder, then the number is not a prime. Enough chatter, let's get down to business. I'll write two versions of this, the second of which will exploit the `for...else` syntax:

```
# primes.py
primes = []  # this will contain the primes in the end
upto = 100  # the limit, inclusive
for n in range(2, upto + 1):
    is_prime = True  # flag, new at each iteration of outer for
    for divisor in range(2, n):
        if n % divisor == 0:
            is_prime = False
            break
```

```
    if is_prime:  # check on flag
        primes.append(n)
print(primes)
```

There are a lot of things to notice in the preceding code. First of all, we set up an empty `primes` list, which will contain the primes at the end. The limit is `100`, and you can see it's inclusive in the way we call `range()` in the outer loop. If we wrote `range(2, upto)` that would be *[2, upto)*, right? Therefore `range(2, upto + 1)` gives us *[2, upto + 1) == [2, upto]*.

So, there are two `for` loops. In the outer one, we loop over the candidate primes, that is, all natural numbers from 2 to `upto`. Inside each iteration of this outer loop, we set up a flag (which is set to `True` at each iteration), and then start dividing the current n by all numbers from 2 to n – 1. If we find a proper divisor for n, it means n is composite, and therefore we set the flag to `False` and break the loop. Notice that when we break the inner one, the outer one keeps on going normally. The reason why we break after having found a proper divisor for n is that we don't need any further information to be able to tell that n is not a prime.

When we check on the `is_prime` flag, if it is still `True`, it means we couldn't find any number in [2, *n*) that is a proper divisor for n, therefore n is a prime. We append n to the `primes` list, and hop! Another iteration proceeds, until n equals `100`.

Running this code yields:

```
$ python primes.py
[2, 3, 5, 7, 11, 13, 17, 19, 23, 29, 31, 37, 41, 43, 47, 53, 59, 61,
67, 71, 73, 79, 83, 89, 97]
```

Before we proceed, one question: of all the iterations of the outer loop, one of them is different from all the others. Could you tell which one, and why? Think about it for a second, go back to the code, try to figure it out for yourself, and then keep reading on.

Did you figure it out? If not, don't feel bad, it's perfectly normal. I asked you to do it as a small exercise because it's what coders do all the time. The skill to understand what the code does by simply looking at it is something you build over time. It's very important, so try to exercise it whenever you can. I'll tell you the answer now: the iteration that behaves differently from all others is the first one. The reason is because in the first iteration, n is 2. Therefore the innermost `for` loop won't even run, because it's a `for` loop that iterates over `range(2, 2)`, and what is that if not [2, 2)? Try it out for yourself, write a simple `for` loop with that iterable, put a `print` in the body suite, and see whether anything happens (it won't...).

Now, from an algorithmic point of view, this code is inefficient, so let's at least make it more beautiful:

```python
# primes.else.py
primes = []
upto = 100
for n in range(2, upto + 1):
    for divisor in range(2, n):
        if n % divisor == 0:
            break
    else:
        primes.append(n)
print(primes)
```

Much nicer, right? The `is_prime` flag is gone, and we append `n` to the `primes` list when we know the inner `for` loop hasn't encountered any `break` statements. See how the code looks cleaner and reads better?

# Applying discounts

In this example, I want to show you a technique I like a lot. In many programming languages, other than the `if/elif/else` constructs, in whatever form or syntax they may come, you can find another statement, usually called `switch/case`, that in Python is missing. It is the equivalent of a cascade of `if/elif/.../elif/else` clauses, with a syntax similar to this (warning! JavaScript code!):

```javascript
/* switch.js */
switch (day_number) {
    case 1:
    case 2:
    case 3:
    case 4:
    case 5:
        day = "Weekday";
        break;
    case 6:
        day = "Saturday";
        break;
    case 0:
        day = "Sunday";
        break;
    default:
        day = "";
```

```
        alert(day_number + ' is not a valid day number.')
    }
```

In the preceding code, we `switch` on a variable called `day_number`. This means we get its value and then we decide what case it fits in (if any). From 1 to 5 there is a cascade, which means no matter the number, [1, 5] all go down to the bit of logic that sets `day` as `"Weekday"`. Then we have single cases for 0 and 6, and a `default` case to prevent errors, which alerts the system that `day_number` is not a valid day number, that is, not in [0, 6]. Python is perfectly capable of realizing such logic using `if/elif/else` statements:

```python
# switch.py
if 1 <= day_number <= 5:
    day = 'Weekday'
elif day_number == 6:
    day = 'Saturday'
elif day_number == 0:
    day = 'Sunday'
else:
    day = ''
    raise ValueError(
        str(day_number) + ' is not a valid day number.')
```

In the preceding code, we reproduce the same logic of the JavaScript snippet in Python, using `if/elif/else` statements. I raised the `ValueError` exception just as an example at the end, if `day_number` is not in [0, 6]. This is one possible way of translating the `switch/case` logic, but there is also another one, sometimes called dispatching, which I will show you in the last version of the next example.

 By the way, did you notice the first line of the previous snippet? Have you noticed that Python can make double (actually, even multiple) comparisons? It's just wonderful!

Let's start the new example by simply writing some code that assigns a discount to customers based on their coupon value. I'll keep the logic down to a minimum here, remember that all we really care about is understanding conditionals and loops:

```python
# coupons.py
customers = [
    dict(id=1, total=200, coupon_code='F20'),   # F20: fixed, £20
    dict(id=2, total=150, coupon_code='P30'),   # P30: percent, 30%
    dict(id=3, total=100, coupon_code='P50'),   # P50: percent, 50%
    dict(id=4, total=110, coupon_code='F15'),   # F15: fixed, £15
]
```

```
for customer in customers:
    code = customer['coupon_code']
    if code == 'F20':
        customer['discount'] = 20.0
    elif code == 'F15':
        customer['discount'] = 15.0
    elif code == 'P30':
        customer['discount'] = customer['total'] * 0.3
    elif code == 'P50':
        customer['discount'] = customer['total'] * 0.5
    else:
        customer['discount'] = 0.0

for customer in customers:
    print(customer['id'], customer['total'], customer['discount'])
```

We start by setting up some customers. They have an order total, a coupon code, and an ID. I made up four different types of coupons, two are fixed and two are percentage-based. You can see that in the if/elif/else cascade I apply the discount accordingly, and I set it as a 'discount' key in the customer dictionary.

At the end, I just print out part of the data to see whether my code is working properly:

```
$ python coupons.py
1 200 20.0
2 150 45.0
3 100 50.0
4 110 15.0
```

This code is simple to understand, but all those clauses are kind of cluttering the logic. It's not easy to see what's going on at a first glance, and I don't like it. In cases like this, you can exploit a dictionary to your advantage, like this:

```
# coupons.dict.py
customers = [
    dict(id=1, total=200, coupon_code='F20'),   # F20: fixed, £20
    dict(id=2, total=150, coupon_code='P30'),   # P30: percent, 30%
    dict(id=3, total=100, coupon_code='P50'),   # P50: percent, 50%
    dict(id=4, total=110, coupon_code='F15'),   # F15: fixed, £15
]
discounts = {
    'F20': (0.0, 20.0),   # each value is (percent, fixed)
    'P30': (0.3, 0.0),
    'P50': (0.5, 0.0),
    'F15': (0.0, 15.0),
}
```

```
for customer in customers:
    code = customer['coupon_code']
    percent, fixed = discounts.get(code, (0.0, 0.0))
    customer['discount'] = percent * customer['total'] + fixed

for customer in customers:
    print(customer['id'], customer['total'], customer['discount'])
```

Running the preceding code yields exactly the same result we had from the snippet before it. We spared two lines, but more importantly, we gained a lot in readability, as the body of the `for` loop now is just three lines long, and very easy to understand. The concept here is to use a dictionary as a **dispatcher**. In other words, we try to fetch something from the dictionary based on a code (our `coupon_code`), and by using `dict.get(key, default)`, we make sure we also cater for when the `code` is not in the dictionary and we need a default value.

Notice that I had to apply some very simple linear algebra in order to calculate the discount properly. Each discount has a percentage and fixed part in the dictionary, represented by a two-tuple. By applying `percent * total + fixed`, we get the correct discount. When `percent` is 0, the formula just gives the fixed amount, and it gives `percent * total` when fixed is 0.

This technique is important because it is also used in other contexts, with functions, where it actually becomes much more powerful than what we've seen in the preceding snippet. Another advantage of using it is that you can code it in such a way that the keys and values of the `discounts` dictionary are fetched dynamically (for example, from a database). This will allow the code to adapt to whatever discounts and conditions you have, without having to modify anything.

If it's not completely clear to you how it works, I suggest you take your time and experiment with it. Change values and add print statements to see what's going on while the program is running.

# A quick peek at the itertools module

A chapter about iterables, iterators, conditional logic, and looping wouldn't be complete without a few words about the `itertools` module. If you are into iterating, this is a kind of heaven.

According to the Python official documentation (`https://docs.python.org/2/library/itertools.html`), the `itertools` module is:

> *This module which implements a number of iterator building blocks inspired by constructs from APL, Haskell, and SML. Each has been recast in a form suitable for Python. The module standardizes a core set of fast, memory efficient tools that are useful by themselves or in combination. Together, they form an "iterator algebra" making it possible to construct specialized tools succinctly and efficiently in pure Python.*

By no means do I have the room here to show you all the goodies you can find in this module, so I encourage you to go check it out for yourself, I promise you'll enjoy it. In a nutshell, it provides you with three broad categories of iterators. I will give you a very small example of one iterator taken from each one of them, just to make your mouth water a little.

## Infinite iterators

Infinite iterators allow you to work with a `for` loop in a different fashion, such as if it were a `while` loop:

```
# infinite.py
from itertools import count

for n in count(5, 3):
    if n > 20:
        break
    print(n, end=', ') # instead of newline, comma and space
```

Running the code gives this:

```
$ python infinite.py
5, 8, 11, 14, 17, 20,
```

The `count` factory class makes an iterator that just goes on and on counting. It starts from 5 and keeps adding 3 to it. We need to break it manually if we don't want to get stuck in an infinite loop.

# Iterators terminating on the shortest input sequence

This category is very interesting. It allows you to create an iterator based on multiple iterators, combining their values according to some logic. The key point here is that among those iterators, in case any of them are shorter than the rest, the resulting iterator won't break, it will simply stop as soon as the shortest iterator is exhausted. This is very theoretical, I know, so let me give you an example using compress. This iterator gives you back the data according to a corresponding item in a selector being True or False:

compress('ABC', (1, 0, 1)) would give back 'A' and 'C', because they correspond to 1. Let's see a simple example:

```
# compress.py
from itertools import compress
data = range(10)
even_selector = [1, 0] * 10
odd_selector = [0, 1] * 10

even_numbers = list(compress(data, even_selector))
odd_numbers = list(compress(data, odd_selector))

print(odd_selector)
print(list(data))
print(even_numbers)
print(odd_numbers)
```

Notice that odd_selector and even_selector are 20 elements long, while data is just 10 elements long. compress will stop as soon as data has yielded its last element. Running this code produces the following:

```
$ python compress.py
[0, 1, 0, 1, 0, 1, 0, 1, 0, 1, 0, 1, 0, 1, 0, 1, 0, 1, 0, 1]
[0, 1, 2, 3, 4, 5, 6, 7, 8, 9]
[0, 2, 4, 6, 8]
[1, 3, 5, 7, 9]
```

It's a very fast and nice way of selecting elements out of an iterable. The code is very simple, just notice that instead of using a for loop to iterate over each value that is given back by the compress calls, we used list(), which does the same, but instead of executing a body of instructions, puts all the values into a list and returns it.

# Combinatoric generators

Last but not least, combinatoric generators. These are really fun, if you are into this kind of thing. Let's just see a simple example on permutations.

According to Wolfram Mathworld:

> *A permutation, also called an "arrangement number" or "order", is a rearrangement of the elements of an ordered list S into a one-to-one correspondence with S itself.*

For example, there are six permutations of ABC: ABC, ACB, BAC, BCA, CAB, and CBA.

If a set has $N$ elements, then the number of permutations of them is $N!$ ($N$ factorial). For the ABC string, the permutations are $3! = 3 * 2 * 1 = 6$. Let's do it in Python:

```
# permutations.py
from itertools import permutations
print(list(permutations('ABC')))
```

This very short snippet of code produces the following result:

```
$ python permutations.py
[('A', 'B', 'C'), ('A', 'C', 'B'), ('B', 'A', 'C'), ('B', 'C', 'A'),
('C', 'A', 'B'), ('C', 'B', 'A')]
```

Be very careful when you play with permutations. Their number grows at a rate that is proportional to the factorial of the number of the elements you're permuting, and that number can get really big, really fast.

# Summary

In this chapter, we've taken another step toward expanding our coding vocabulary. We've seen how to drive the execution of the code by evaluating conditions, and we've seen how to loop and iterate over sequences and collections of objects. This gives us the power to control what happens when our code is run, which means we are getting an idea of how to shape it so that it does what we want and it reacts to data that changes dynamically.

We've also seen how to combine everything together in a couple of simple examples, and in the end, we took a brief look at the `itertools` module, which is full of interesting iterators that can enrich our abilities with Python even more.

Now it's time to switch gears, take another step forward, and talk about functions. The next chapter is all about them because they are extremely important. Make sure you're comfortable with what has been covered up to now. I want to provide you with interesting examples, so I'll have to go a little faster. Ready? Turn the page.

# 4
# Functions, the Building Blocks of Code

*To create architecture is to put in order. Put what in order? Functions and objects."*

*– Le Corbusier*

In the previous chapters, we have seen that everything is an object in Python, and functions are no exception. But, what exactly is a function? A **function** is a sequence of instructions that perform a task, bundled as a unit. This unit can then be imported and used wherever it's needed. There are many advantages to using functions in your code, as we'll see shortly.

In this chapter, we are going to cover the following:

- Functions—what they are and why we should use them
- Scopes and name resolution
- Function signatures—input parameters and return values
- Recursive and anonymous functions
- Importing objects for code reuse

I believe the saying, *a picture is worth one thousand words,* is particularly true when explaining functions to someone who is new to this concept, so please take a look at the following diagram:

As you can see, a function is a block of instructions, packaged as a whole, like a box. Functions can accept input arguments and produce output values. Both of these are optional, as we'll see in the examples in this chapter.

A function in Python is defined by using the def keyword, after which the name of the function follows, terminated by a pair of parentheses (which may or may not contain input parameters), and a colon (:) signals the end of the function definition line. Immediately afterwards, indented by four spaces, we find the body of the function, which is the set of instructions that the function will execute when called.

 Note that the indentation by four spaces is not mandatory, but it is the amount of spaces suggested by **PEP 8**, and, in practice, it is the most widely used spacing measure.

A function may or may not return an output. If a function wants to return an output, it does so by using the return keyword, followed by the desired output. If you have an eagle eye, you may have noticed the little **\*** after **Optional** in the output section of the preceding diagram. This is because a function always returns something in Python, even if you don't explicitly use the return clause. If the function has no return statement in its body, or no value is given to the return statement itself, the function returns None. The reasons behind this design choice are outside the scope of an introductory chapter, so all you need to know is that this behavior will make your life easier. As always, thank you, Python.

# Why use functions?

Functions are among the most important concepts and constructs of any language, so let me give you a few reasons why we need them:

- They reduce code duplication in a program. By having a specific task taken care of by a nice block of packaged code that we can import and call whenever we want, we don't need to duplicate its implementation.
- They help in splitting a complex task or procedure into smaller blocks, each of which becomes a function.
- They hide the implementation details from their users.
- They improve traceability.
- They improve readability.

Let's look at a few examples to get a better understanding of each point.

# Reducing code duplication

Imagine that you are writing a piece of scientific software, and you need to calculate primes up to a limit, as we did in the previous chapter. You have a nice algorithm to calculate them, so you copy and paste it to wherever you need. One day, though, your friend, *B. Riemann*, gives you a better algorithm to calculate primes, which will save you a lot of time. At this point, you need to go over your whole code base and replace the old code with the new one.

This is actually a bad way to go about it. It's error-prone, you never know what lines you are chopping out or leaving in by mistake, when you cut and paste code into other code, and you may also risk missing one of the places where prime calculation is done, leaving your software in an inconsistent state where the same action is performed in different places in different ways. What if, instead of replacing code with a better version of it, you need to fix a bug, and you miss one of the places? That would be even worse.

So, what should you do? Simple! You write a function, `get_prime_numbers(upto)`, and use it anywhere you need a list of primes. When *B. Riemann* comes to you and gives you the new code, all you have to do is replace the body of that function with the new implementation, and you're done! The rest of the software will automatically adapt, since it's just calling the function.

Your code will be shorter, it will not suffer from inconsistencies between old and new ways of performing a task, or undetected bugs due to copy-and-paste failures or oversights. Use functions, and you'll only gain from it, I promise.

# Splitting a complex task

Functions are also very useful for splitting long or complex tasks into smaller ones. The end result is that the code benefits from it in several ways, for example, readability, testability, and reuse. To give you a simple example, imagine that you're preparing a report. Your code needs to fetch data from a data source, parse it, filter it, polish it, and then a whole series of algorithms needs to be run against it, in order to produce the results that will feed the `Report` class. It's not uncommon to read procedures like this that are just one big `do_report(data_source)` function. There are tens or hundreds of lines of code that end with `return report`.

These situations are slightly more common in scientific code, which tend to be brilliant from an algorithmic point of view, but sometimes lack the touch of experienced programmers when it comes to the style in which they are written. Now, picture a few hundred lines of code. It's very hard to follow through, to find the places where things are changing context (such as finishing one task and starting the next one). Do you have the picture in your mind? Good. Don't do it! Instead, look at this code:

```python
# data.science.example.py
def do_report(data_source):
    # fetch and prepare data
    data = fetch_data(data_source)
    parsed_data = parse_data(data)
    filtered_data = filter_data(parsed_data)
    polished_data = polish_data(filtered_data)

    # run algorithms on data
    final_data = analyse(polished_data)

    # create and return report
    report = Report(final_data)
    return report
```

The previous example is fictitious, of course, but can you see how easy it would be to go through the code? If the end result looks wrong, it would be very easy to debug each of the single data outputs in the `do_report` function. Moreover, it's even easier to exclude part of the process temporarily from the whole procedure (you just need to comment out the parts you need to suspend). Code like this is easier to deal with.

# Hiding implementation details

Let's stay with the preceding example to talk about this point as well. You can see that, by going through the code of the `do_report` function, you can get a pretty good understanding without reading one single line of implementation. This is because functions hide the implementation details. This feature means that, if you don't need to delve into the details, you are not forced to, in the way you would if `do_report` was just one big, fat function. In order to understand what was going on, you would have to read every single line of code. With functions, you don't need to. This reduces the time you spend reading the code and since, in a professional environment, reading code takes much more time than actually writing it, it's very important to reduce it by as much as we can.

# Improving readability

Coders sometimes don't see the point in writing a function with a body of one or two lines of code, so let's look at an example that shows you why you should do it.

Imagine that you need to multiply two matrices:

$$\begin{pmatrix} 1 & 2 \\ 3 & 4 \end{pmatrix} \cdot \begin{pmatrix} 5 & 1 \\ 2 & 1 \end{pmatrix} = \begin{pmatrix} 9 & 3 \\ 23 & 7 \end{pmatrix}$$

Would you prefer to have to read this code:

```
# matrix.multiplication.nofunc.py
a = [[1, 2], [3, 4]]
b = [[5, 1], [2, 1]]

c = [[sum(i * j for i, j in zip(r, c)) for c in zip(*b)]
        for r in a]
```

Or would you prefer this one:

```
# matrix.multiplication.func.py
# this function could also be defined in another module
def matrix_mul(a, b):
    return [[sum(i * j for i, j in zip(r, c)) for c in zip(*b)]
            for r in a]

a = [[1, 2], [3, 4]]
b = [[5, 1], [2, 1]]
c = matrix_mul(a, b)
```

It's much easier to understand that c is the result of the multiplication between a and b in the second example. It's much easier to read through the code and, if you don't need to modify that multiplication logic, you don't even need to go into the implementation details. Therefore, readability is improved here while, in the first snippet, you would have to spend time trying to understand what that complicated list comprehension is doing.

# Improving traceability

Imagine that you have written an e-commerce website. You have displayed the product prices all over the pages. Imagine that the prices in your database are stored with no VAT (sales tax), but you want to display them on the website with VAT at 20%. Here's a few ways of calculating the VAT-inclusive price from the VAT-exclusive price:

```
# vat.py
price = 100   # GBP, no VAT
final_price1 = price * 1.2
final_price2 = price + price / 5.0
final_price3 = price * (100 + 20) / 100.0
final_price4 = price + price * 0.2
```

All these four different ways of calculating a VAT-inclusive price are perfectly acceptable, and I promise you I have found them all in my colleagues' code, over the years. Now, imagine that you have started selling your products in different countries and some of them have different VAT rates, so you need to refactor your code (throughout the website) in order to make that VAT calculation dynamic.

How do you trace all the places in which you are performing a VAT calculation? Coding today is a collaborative task and you cannot be sure that the VAT has been calculated using only one of those forms. It's going to be hell, believe me.

So, let's write a function that takes the input values, `vat` and `price` (VAT-exclusive), and returns a VAT-inclusive price:

```
# vat.function.py
def calculate_price_with_vat(price, vat):
    return price * (100 + vat) / 100
```

Now you can import that function and use it in any place in your website where you need to calculate a VAT-inclusive price, and when you need to trace those calls, you can search for `calculate_price_with_vat`.

 Note that, in the preceding example, `price` is assumed to be VAT-exclusive, and `vat` is a percentage value (for example, 19, 20, or 23).

# Scopes and name resolution

Do you remember when we talked about scopes and namespaces in Chapter 1, *A Gentle Introduction to Python*? We're going to expand on that concept now. Finally, we can talk about functions and this will make everything easier to understand. Let's start with a very simple example:

```python
# scoping.level.1.py
def my_function():
    test = 1  # this is defined in the local scope of the function
    print('my_function:', test)

test = 0  # this is defined in the global scope
my_function()
print('global:', test)
```

I have defined the test name in two different places in the previous example. It is actually in two different scopes. One is the global scope (test = 0), and the other is the local scope of the my_function function (test = 1). If you execute the code, you'll see this:

```
$ python scoping.level.1.py
my_function: 1
global: 0
```

It's clear that test = 1 shadows the test = 0 assignment in my_function. In the global context, test is still 0, as you can see from the output of the program, but we define the test name again in the function body, and we set it to point to an integer of value 1. Both the two test names therefore exist, one in the global scope, pointing to an int object with a value of 0, the other in the my_function scope, pointing to an int object with a value of 1. Let's comment out the line with test = 1. Python searches for the test name in the next enclosing namespace (recall the **LEGB** rule: **local, enclosing, global, built-in** described in Chapter 1, *A Gentle Introduction to Python*) and, in this case, we will see the value 0 printed twice. Try it in your code.

Now, let's raise the stakes here and level up:

```python
# scoping.level.2.py
def outer():
    test = 1  # outer scope
    def inner():
        test = 2  # inner scope
        print('inner:', test)

    inner()
```

```
        print('outer:', test)

    test = 0   # global scope
    outer()
    print('global:', test)
```

In the preceding code, we have two levels of shadowing. One level is in the function `outer`, and the other one is in the function `inner`. It is far from rocket science, but it can be tricky. If we run the code, we get:

```
$ python scoping.level.2.py
inner: 2
outer: 1
global: 0
```

Try commenting out the `test = 1` line. Can you figure out what the result will be? Well, when reaching the `print('outer:', test)` line, Python will have to look for `test` in the next enclosing scope, therefore it will find and print 0, instead of 1. Make sure you comment out `test = 2` as well, to see whether you understand what happens, and whether the LEGB rule is clear, before proceeding.

Another thing to note is that Python gives you the ability to define a function in another function. The inner function's name is defined within the namespace of the outer function, exactly as would happen with any other name.

# The global and nonlocal statements

Going back to the preceding example, we can alter what happens to the shadowing of the test name by using one of these two special statements: `global` and `nonlocal`. As you can see from the previous example, when we define `test = 2` in the `inner` function, we overwrite `test` neither in the `outer` function nor in the global scope. We can get read access to those names if we use them in a nested scope that doesn't define them, but we cannot modify them because, when we write an assignment instruction, we're actually defining a new name in the current scope.

How do we change this behavior? Well, we can use the `nonlocal` statement. According to the official documentation:

> "The nonlocal statement causes the listed identifiers to refer to previously bound variables in the nearest enclosing scope excluding globals."

Let's introduce it in the `inner` function, and see what happens:

```
# scoping.level.2.nonlocal.py
def outer():
    test = 1  # outer scope
    def inner():
        nonlocal test
        test = 2  # nearest enclosing scope (which is 'outer')
        print('inner:', test)

    inner()
    print('outer:', test)

test = 0  # global scope
outer()
print('global:', test)
```

Notice how in the body of the `inner` function, I have declared the `test` name to be `nonlocal`. Running this code produces the following result:

```
$ python scoping.level.2.nonlocal.py
inner: 2
outer: 2
global: 0
```

Wow, look at that result! It means that, by declaring `test` to be `nonlocal` in the `inner` function, we actually get to bind the `test` name to the one declared in the `outer` function. If we removed the `nonlocal test` line from the `inner` function and tried the same trick in the `outer` function, we would get a `SyntaxError`, because the `nonlocal` statement works on enclosing scopes excluding the global one.

Is there a way to get to that `test = 0` in the global namespace then? Of course, we just need to use the `global` statement:

```
# scoping.level.2.global.py
def outer():
    test = 1  # outer scope
    def inner():
        global test
        test = 2  # global scope
        print('inner:', test)

    inner()
    print('outer:', test)

test = 0  # global scope
outer()
```

```
print('global:', test)
```

Note that we have now declared the `test` name to be `global`, which will basically bind it to the one we defined in the global namespace (`test = 0`). Run the code and you should get the following:

```
$ python scoping.level.2.global.py
inner: 2
outer: 1
global: 2
```

This shows that the name affected by the `test = 2` assignment is now the `global` one. This trick would also work in the `outer` function because, in this case, we're referring to the global scope. Try it for yourself and see what changes, get comfortable with scopes and name resolution, it's very important. Also, could you tell what happens if you defined `inner` outside `outer` in the preceding examples?

# Input parameters

At the beginning of this chapter, we saw that a function can take input parameters. Before we delve into all possible type of parameters, let's make sure you have a clear understanding of what passing a parameter to a function means. There are three key points to keep in mind:

- Argument passing is nothing more than assigning an object to a local variable name
- Assigning an object to an argument name inside a function doesn't affect the caller
- Changing a mutable object argument in a function affects the caller

Let's look at an example for each of these points.

# Argument passing

Take a look at the following code. We declare a name, x, in the global scope, then we declare a function, `func(y)`, and finally we call it, passing x:

```
# key.points.argument.passing.py
x = 3
```

```
def func(y):
    print(y)
func(x)   # prints: 3
```

When `func` is called with x, within its local scope, a name, y, is created, and it's pointed to the same object x is pointing to. This is better clarified by the following figure (don't worry about **Python 3.3**, this is a feature that hasn't changed):

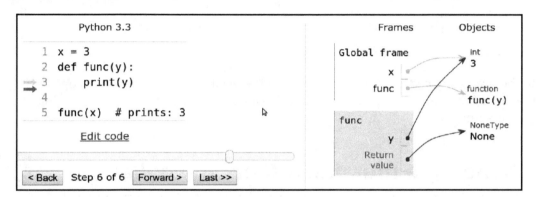

The right part of the preceding figure depicts the state of the program when execution has reached the end, after `func` has returned (`None`). Take a look at the **Frames** column, and note that we have two names, x and `func`, in the global namespace **(Global frame)**, pointing to an `int` (with a value of **3**) and to a `function` object, respectively. Right beneath it, in the rectangle titled `func`, we can see the function's local namespace, in which only one name has been defined: y. Because we have called `func` with x (line **5** in the left part of the figure), y is pointing to the same object that x is pointing to. This is what happens under the hood when an argument is passed to a function. If we had used the name x instead of y in the function definition, things would have been exactly the same (only maybe a bit confusing at first), there would be a local x in the function, and a global x outside, as we saw in the *Scopes and name resolution* section previously in this chapter.

So, in a nutshell, what really happens is that the function creates, in its local scope, the names defined as arguments and, when we call it, we basically tell Python which objects those names must be pointed toward.

# Assignment to argument names doesn't affect the caller

This is something that can be tricky to understand at first, so let's look at an example:

```
# key.points.assignment.py
x = 3
def func(x):
    x = 7  # defining a local x, not changing the global one
func(x)
print(x)  # prints: 3
```

In the preceding code, when the x = 7 line is executed, within the local scope of the func function, the name, x, is pointed to an integer with a value of 7, leaving the global x unaltered.

# Changing a mutable affects the caller

This is the final point, and it's very important because Python apparently behaves differently with mutables (just apparently, though). Let's look at an example:

```
# key.points.mutable.py
x = [1, 2, 3]
def func(x):
    x[1] = 42  # this affects the caller!

func(x)
print(x)  # prints: [1, 42, 3]
```

Wow, we actually changed the original object! If you think about it, there is nothing weird in this behavior. The x name in the function is set to point to the caller object by the function call and within the body of the function, we're not changing x, in that we're not changing its reference, or, in other words, we are not changing the object x is pointing to. We're accessing that object's element at position 1, and changing its value.

Remember point #2 under the *Input parameters* section: *Assigning an object to an argument name within a function doesn't affect the caller*. If that is clear to you, the following code should not be surprising:

```
# key.points.mutable.assignment.py
x = [1, 2, 3]
def func(x):
```

```
    x[1] = 42   # this changes the caller!
    x = 'something else'  # this points x to a new string object

func(x)
print(x)  # still prints: [1, 42, 3]
```

Take a look at the two lines I have highlighted. At first, like before, we just access the caller object again, at position 1, and change its value to number 42. Then, we reassign x to point to the 'something else' string. This leaves the caller unaltered and, in fact, the output is the same as that of the previous snippet.

Take your time to play around with this concept, and experiment with prints and calls to the id function until everything is clear in your mind. This is one of the key aspects of Python and it must be very clear, otherwise you risk introducing subtle bugs into your code. Once again, the Python Tutor website (http://www. pythontutor.com/) will help you a lot by giving you a visual representation of these concepts.

Now that we have a good understanding of input parameters and how they behave, let's see how we can specify them.

# How to specify input parameters

There are five different ways of specifying input parameters:

- Positional arguments
- Keyword arguments
- Variable positional arguments
- Variable keyword arguments
- Keyword-only arguments

Let's look at them one by one.

## Positional arguments

Positional arguments are read from left to right and they are the most common type of arguments:

```
# arguments.positional.py
def func(a, b, c):
    print(a, b, c)
func(1, 2, 3)  # prints: 1 2 3
```

There is not much else to say. They can be as numerous as you want and they are assigned by position. In the function call, 1 comes first, 2 comes second, and 3 comes third, therefore they are assigned to a, b, and c, respectively.

# Keyword arguments and default values

**Keyword arguments** are assigned by keyword using the name=value syntax:

```
# arguments.keyword.py
def func(a, b, c):
    print(a, b, c)
func(a=1, c=2, b=3)  # prints: 1 3 2
```

Keyword arguments are matched by name, even when they don't respect the definition's original position (we'll see that there is a limitation to this behavior later, when we mix and match different types of arguments).

The counterpart of keyword arguments, on the definition side, is **default values**. The syntax is the same, name=value, and allows us to not have to provide an argument if we are happy with the given default:

```
# arguments.default.py
def func(a, b=4, c=88):
    print(a, b, c)

func(1)  # prints: 1 4 88
func(b=5, a=7, c=9)  # prints: 7 5 9
func(42, c=9)  # prints: 42 4 9
func(42, 43, 44)   # prints: 42, 43, 44
```

The are two things to notice, which are very important. First of all, you cannot specify a default argument on the left of a positional one. Second, note how in the examples, when an argument is passed without using the argument_name=value syntax, it must be the first one in the list, and it is always assigned to a. Notice also that passing values in a positional fashion still works, and follows the function signature order (last line of the example).

Try and scramble those arguments and see what happens. Python error messages are very good at telling you what's wrong. So, for example, if you tried something such as this:

```
# arguments.default.error.py
def func(a, b=4, c=88):
    print(a, b, c)
func(b=1, c=2, 42)  # positional argument after keyword one
```

You would get the following error:

```
$ python arguments.default.error.py
  File "arguments.default.error.py", line 4
    func(b=1, c=2, 42) # positional argument after keyword one
                   ^
SyntaxError: positional argument follows keyword argument
```

This informs you that you've called the function incorrectly.

# Variable positional arguments

Sometimes you may want to pass a variable number of positional arguments to a function, and Python provides you with the ability to do it. Let's look at a very common use case, the `minimum` function. This is a function that calculates the minimum of its input values:

```
# arguments.variable.positional.py
def minimum(*n):
    # print(type(n))  # n is a tuple
    if n:  # explained after the code
        mn = n[0]
        for value in n[1:]:
            if value < mn:
                mn = value
        print(mn)

minimum(1, 3, -7, 9)  # n = (1, 3, -7, 9) - prints: -7
minimum()             # n = () - prints: nothing
```

As you can see, when we specify a parameter prepending a `*` to its name, we are telling Python that that parameter will be collecting a variable number of positional arguments, according to how the function is called. Within the function, n is a tuple. Uncomment `print(type(n))` to see for yourself and play around with it for a bit.

Have you noticed how we checked whether n wasn't empty with a simple `if n:`? This is because collection objects evaluate to `True` when non-empty, and otherwise `False` in Python. This is true for tuples, sets, lists, dictionaries, and so on.
One other thing to note is that we may want to throw an error when we call the function with no arguments, instead of silently doing nothing. In this context, we're not concerned about making this function robust, but in understanding variable positional arguments.

Let's make another example to show you two things that, in my experience, are confusing to those who are new to this:

```python
# arguments.variable.positional.unpacking.py
def func(*args):
    print(args)

values = (1, 3, -7, 9)
func(values)    # equivalent to: func((1, 3, -7, 9))
func(*values)   # equivalent to: func(1, 3, -7, 9)
```

Take a good look at the last two lines of the preceding example. In the first one, we call `func` with one argument, a four-elements tuple. In the second example, by using the `*` syntax, we're doing something called **unpacking**, which means that the four-elements tuple is unpacked, and the function is called with four arguments: `1, 3, -7, 9`.

This behavior is part of the magic Python does to allow you to do amazing things when calling functions dynamically.

## Variable keyword arguments

Variable keyword arguments are very similar to variable positional arguments. The only difference is the syntax (`**` instead of `*`) and that they are collected in a dictionary. Collection and unpacking work in the same way, so let's look at an example:

```python
# arguments.variable.keyword.py
def func(**kwargs):
    print(kwargs)

# All calls equivalent. They print: {'a': 1, 'b': 42}
func(a=1, b=42)
func(**{'a': 1, 'b': 42})
func(**dict(a=1, b=42))
```

All the calls are equivalent in the preceding example. You can see that adding a `**` in front of the parameter name in the function definition tells Python to use that name to collect a variable number of keyword parameters. On the other hand, when we call the function, we can either pass `name=value` arguments explicitly, or unpack a dictionary using the same `**` syntax.

The reason why being able to pass a variable number of keyword parameters is so important may not be evident at the moment, so, how about a more realistic example? Let's define a function that connects to a database. We want to connect to a default database by simply calling this function with no parameters. We also want to connect to any other database by passing the function the appropriate arguments. Before you read on, try to spend a couple of minutes figuring out a solution by yourself:

```
# arguments.variable.db.py
def connect(**options):
    conn_params = {
        'host': options.get('host', '127.0.0.1'),
        'port': options.get('port', 5432),
        'user': options.get('user', ''),
        'pwd': options.get('pwd', ''),
    }
    print(conn_params)
    # we then connect to the db (commented out)
    # db.connect(**conn_params)

connect()
connect(host='127.0.0.42', port=5433)
connect(port=5431, user='fab', pwd='gandalf')
```

Note that in the function, we can prepare a dictionary of connection parameters (conn_params) using default values as fallbacks, allowing them to be overwritten if they are provided in the function call. There are better ways to do this with fewer lines of code, but we're not concerned with that right now. Running the preceding code yields the following result:

```
$ python arguments.variable.db.py
{'host': '127.0.0.1', 'port': 5432, 'user': '', 'pwd': ''}
{'host': '127.0.0.42', 'port': 5433, 'user': '', 'pwd': ''}
{'host': '127.0.0.1', 'port': 5431, 'user': 'fab', 'pwd': 'gandalf'}
```

Note the correspondence between the function calls and the output. Notice how default values are overridden according to what was passed to the function.

# Keyword-only arguments

Python 3 allows for a new type of parameter: the **keyword-only** parameter. We are going to study them only briefly as their use cases are not that frequent. There are two ways of specifying them, either after the variable positional arguments, or after a bare *. Let's see an example of both:

```python
# arguments.keyword.only.py
def kwo(*a, c):
    print(a, c)

kwo(1, 2, 3, c=7)  # prints: (1, 2, 3) 7
kwo(c=4)  # prints: () 4
# kwo(1, 2)  # breaks, invalid syntax, with the following error
# TypeError: kwo() missing 1 required keyword-only argument: 'c'

def kwo2(a, b=42, *, c):
    print(a, b, c)

kwo2(3, b=7, c=99)  # prints: 3 7 99
kwo2(3, c=13)  # prints: 3 42 13
# kwo2(3, 23)  # breaks, invalid syntax, with the following error
# TypeError: kwo2() missing 1 required keyword-only argument: 'c'
```

As anticipated, the function, `kwo`, takes a variable number of positional arguments (`a`) and a keyword-only one, `c`. The results of the calls are straightforward and you can uncomment the third call to see what error Python returns.

The same applies to the function, `kwo2`, which differs from `kwo` in that it takes a positional argument, `a`, a keyword argument, `b`, and then a keyword-only one, `c`. You can uncomment the third call to see the error.

Now that you know how to specify different types of input parameters, let's see how you can combine them in function definitions.

# Combining input parameters

You can combine input parameters, as long as you follow these ordering rules:

- When defining a function, normal positional arguments come first (`name`), then any default arguments (`name=value`), then the variable positional arguments (`*name` or simply `*`), then any keyword-only arguments (either `name` or `name=value` form is good), and then any variable keyword arguments (`**name`).

- On the other hand, when calling a function, arguments must be given in the following order: positional arguments first (`value`), then any combination of keyword arguments (`name=value`), variable positional arguments (`*name`), and then variable keyword arguments (`**name`).

Since this can be a bit tricky when left hanging in the theoretical world, let's look at a couple of quick examples:

```
# arguments.all.py
def func(a, b, c=7, *args, **kwargs):
    print('a, b, c:', a, b, c)
    print('args:', args)
    print('kwargs:', kwargs)

func(1, 2, 3, *(5, 7, 9), **{'A': 'a', 'B': 'b'})
func(1, 2, 3, 5, 7, 9, A='a', B='b')  # same as previous one
```

Note the order of the parameters in the function definition, and that the two calls are equivalent. In the first one, we're using the unpacking operators for iterables and dictionaries, while in the second one we're using a more explicit syntax. The execution of this yields the following (I printed only the result of one call, the other one being the same):

```
$ python arguments.all.py
a, b, c: 1 2 3
args: (5, 7, 9)
kwargs: {'A': 'a', 'B': 'b'}
```

Let's now look at an example with keyword-only arguments:

```
# arguments.all.kwonly.py
def func_with_kwonly(a, b=42, *args, c, d=256, **kwargs):
    print('a, b:', a, b)
    print('c, d:', c, d)
    print('args:', args)
    print('kwargs:', kwargs)

# both calls equivalent
func_with_kwonly(3, 42, c=0, d=1, *(7, 9, 11), e='E', f='F')
func_with_kwonly(3, 42, *(7, 9, 11), c=0, d=1, e='E', f='F')
```

Note that I have highlighted the keyword-only arguments in the function declaration. They come after the `*args` variable positional argument, and it would be the same if they came right after a single `*` (in which case there wouldn't be a variable positional argument).

The execution of this yields the following (I printed only the result of one call):

```
$ python arguments.all.kwonly.py
a, b: 3 42
c, d: 0 1
args: (7, 9, 11)
kwargs: {'e': 'E', 'f': 'F'}
```

One other thing to note is the names I gave to the variable positional and keyword arguments. You're free to choose differently, but be aware that `args` and `kwargs` are the conventional names given to these parameters, at least generically.

## Additional unpacking generalizations

One of the recent new features, introduced in Python 3.5, is the ability to extend the iterable (`*`) and dictionary (`**`) unpacking operators to allow unpacking in more positions, an arbitrary number of times, and in additional circumstances. I'll present you with an example concerning function calls:

```
# additional.unpacking.py
def additional(*args, **kwargs):
    print(args)
    print(kwargs)

args1 = (1, 2, 3)
args2 = [4, 5]
kwargs1 = dict(option1=10, option2=20)
kwargs2 = {'option3': 30}
additional(*args1, *args2, **kwargs1, **kwargs2)
```

In the previous example, we defined a simple function that prints its input arguments, `args` and `kwargs`. The new feature lies in the way we call this function. Notice how we can unpack multiple iterables and dictionaries, and they are correctly coalesced under `args` and `kwargs`. The reason why this feature is important is that it allows us not to have to merge `args1` with `args2`, and `kwargs1` with `kwargs2` in the code. Running the code produces:

```
$ python additional.unpacking.py
(1, 2, 3, 4, 5)
{'option1': 10, 'option2': 20, 'option3': 30}
```

Please refer to PEP 448 (`https://www.python.org/dev/peps/pep-0448/`) to learn the full extent of this new feature and see further examples.

# Avoid the trap! Mutable defaults

One thing to be very aware of with Python is that default values are created at `def`
time, therefore, subsequent calls to the same function will possibly behave differently
according to the mutability of their default values. Let's look at an example:

```
# arguments.defaults.mutable.py
def func(a=[], b={}):
    print(a)
    print(b)
    print('#' * 12)
    a.append(len(a))  # this will affect a's default value
    b[len(a)] = len(a)  # and this will affect b's one

func()
func()
func()
```

Both parameters have mutable default values. This means that, if you affect those
objects, any modification will stick around in subsequent function calls. See if you can
understand the output of those calls:

```
$ python arguments.defaults.mutable.py
[]
{}
############
[0]
{1: 1}
############
[0, 1]
{1: 1, 2: 2}
############
```

It's interesting, isn't it? While this behavior may seem very weird at first, it actually
makes sense, and it's very handy, for example, when using memoization techniques
(Google an example of that, if you're interested). Even more interesting is what
happens when, between the calls, we introduce one that doesn't use defaults, such as
this:

```
# arguments.defaults.mutable.intermediate.call.py
func()
func(a=[1, 2, 3], b={'B': 1})
func()
```

When we run this code, this is the output:

```
$ python arguments.defaults.mutable.intermediate.call.py
[]
{}
###########
[1, 2, 3]
{'B': 1}
###########
[0]
{1: 1}
###########
```

This output shows us that the defaults are retained even if we call the function with other values. One question that comes to mind is, how do I get a fresh empty value every time? Well, the convention is the following:

```
# arguments.defaults.mutable.no.trap.py
def func(a=None):
    if a is None:
        a = []
    # do whatever you want with `a` ...
```

Note that, by using the preceding technique, if `a` isn't passed when calling the function, you always get a brand new, empty list.

Okay, enough with the input, let's look at the other side of the coin, the output.

# Return values

The return values of functions are one of those things where Python is ahead of most other languages. Functions are usually allowed to return one object (one value) but, in Python, you can return a tuple, and this implies that you can return whatever you want. This feature allows a coder to write software that would be much harder to write in any other language, or certainly more tedious. We've already said that to return something from a function we need to use the `return` statement, followed by what we want to return. There can be as many return statements as needed in the body of a function.

On the other hand, if within the body of a function we don't return anything, or we invoke a bare `return` statement, the function will return `None`. This behavior is harmless and, even though I don't have the room here to go into detail explaining why Python was designed like this, let me just tell you that this feature allows for several interesting patterns, and confirms Python as a very consistent language.

I say it's harmless because you are never forced to collect the result of a function call. I'll show you what I mean with an example:

```
# return.none.py
def func():
    pass
func()  # the return of this call won't be collected. It's lost.
a = func()  # the return of this one instead is collected into `a`
print(a)  # prints: None
```

Note that the whole body of the function is composed only of the `pass` statement. As the official documentation tells us, `pass` is a null operation. When it is executed, nothing happens. It is useful as a placeholder when a statement is required syntactically, but no code needs to be executed. In other languages, we would probably just indicate that with a pair of curly brackets ({ }), which define an *empty scope*, but in Python, a scope is defined by indenting code, therefore a statement such as `pass` is necessary.

Notice also that the first call of the `func` function returns a value (None) which we don't collect. As I said before, collecting the return value of a function call is not mandatory.

Now, that's good but not very interesting so, how about we write an interesting function? Remember that in `Chapter 1`, *A Gentle Introduction to Python*, we talked about the factorial of a function. Let's write our own here (for simplicity, I will assume the function is always called correctly with appropriate values so I won't sanity-check the input argument):

```
# return.single.value.py
def factorial(n):
    if n in (0, 1):
        return 1
    result = n
    for k in range(2, n):
        result *= k
    return result

f5 = factorial(5)  # f5 = 120
```

Note that we have two points of return. If `n` is either 0 or 1 (in Python it's common to use the `in` type of check, as I did instead of the more verbose if n == 0 or n == 1:), we return 1. Otherwise, we perform the required calculation and we return `result`. Let's try to write this function a little bit more succinctly:

```
# return.single.value.2.py
```

```
from functools import reduce
from operator import mul

def factorial(n):
    return reduce(mul, range(1, n + 1), 1)

f5 = factorial(5)   # f5 = 120
```

I know what you're thinking: one line? Python is elegant, and concise! I think this function is readable even if you have never seen `reduce` or `mul`, but if you can't read it or understand it, set aside a few minutes and do some research on the Python documentation until its behavior is clear to you. Being able to look up functions in the documentation and understand code written by someone else is a task every developer needs to be able to perform, so take this as a challenge.

 To this end, make sure you look up the `help` function, which proves quite helpful when exploring with the console.

# Returning multiple values

Unlike in most other languages, in Python it's very easy to return multiple objects from a function. This feature opens up a whole world of possibilities and allows you to code in a style that is hard to reproduce with other languages. Our thinking is limited by the tools we use, therefore when Python gives you more freedom than other languages, it is actually boosting your own creativity as well. To return multiple values is very easy, you just use tuples (either explicitly or implicitly). Let's look at a simple example that mimics the `divmod` built-in function:

```
# return.multiple.py
def moddiv(a, b):
    return a // b, a % b

print(moddiv(20, 7))   # prints (2, 6)
```

I could have wrapped the highlighted part in the preceding code in brackets, making it an explicit tuple, but there's no need for that. The preceding function returns both the result and the remainder of the division, at the same time.

In the source code for this example, I have left a simple example of a test function to make sure my code is doing the correct calculation.

# A few useful tips

When writing functions, it's very useful to follow guidelines so that you write them well. I'll quickly point some of them out:

- **Functions should do one thing**: Functions that do one thing are easy to describe in one short sentence. Functions that do multiple things can be split into smaller functions that do one thing. These smaller functions are usually easier to read and understand. Remember the data science example we saw a few pages ago.
- **Functions should be small**: The smaller they are, the easier it is to test them and to write them so that they do one thing.
- **The fewer input parameters, the better**: Functions that take a lot of arguments quickly become harder to manage (among other issues).
- **Functions should be consistent in their return values**: Returning `False` or `None` is not the same thing, even if within a Boolean context they both evaluate to `False`. `False` means that we have information (`False`), while `None` means that there is no information. Try writing functions that return in a consistent way, no matter what happens in their body.
- **Functions shouldn't have side effects**: In other words, functions should not affect the values you call them with. This is probably the hardest statement to understand at this point, so I'll give you an example using lists. In the following code, note how `numbers` is not sorted by the `sorted` function, which actually returns a sorted copy of `numbers`. Conversely, the `list.sort()` method is acting on the `numbers` object itself, and that is fine because it is a method (a function that belongs to an object and therefore has the rights to modify it):

```
>>> numbers = [4, 1, 7, 5]
>>> sorted(numbers)  # won't sort the original `numbers` list
[1, 4, 5, 7]
>>> numbers  # let's verify
[4, 1, 7, 5]  # good, untouched
```

```
>>> numbers.sort()   # this will act on the list
>>> numbers
[1, 4, 5, 7]
```

Follow these guidelines and you'll write better functions, which will serve you well.

# Recursive functions

When a function calls itself to produce a result, it is said to be **recursive**. Sometimes recursive functions are very useful in that they make it easier to write code. Some algorithms are very easy to write using the recursive paradigm, while others are not. There is no recursive function that cannot be rewritten in an iterative fashion, so it's usually up to the programmer to choose the best approach for the case at hand.

The body of a recursive function usually has two sections: one where the return value depends on a subsequent call to itself, and one where it doesn't (called a base case).

As an example, we can consider the (hopefully familiar by now) `factorial` function, *N!*. The base case is when *N* is either `0` or `1`. The function returns `1` with no need for further calculation. On the other hand, in the general case, *N!* returns the product *1 \* 2 \* ... \* (N-1) \* N*. If you think about it, *N!* can be rewritten like this: *N! = (N-1)! \* N*. As a practical example, consider *5! = 1 \* 2 \* 3 \* 4 \* 5 = (1 \* 2 \* 3 \* 4) \* 5 = 4! \* 5*.

Let's write this down in code:

```
# recursive.factorial.py
def factorial(n):
    if n in (0, 1):  # base case
        return 1
    return factorial(n - 1) * n  # recursive case
```

 When writing recursive functions, always consider how many nested calls you make, since there is a limit. For further information on this, check out `sys.getrecursionlimit()` and `sys.setrecursionlimit()`.

Recursive functions are used a lot when writing algorithms and they can be really fun to write. As an exercise, try to solve a couple of simple problems using both a recursive and an iterative approach.

# Anonymous functions

One last type of functions that I want to talk about are **anonymous** functions. These functions, which are called **lambdas** in Python, are usually used when a fully-fledged function with its own name would be overkill, and all we want is a quick, simple one-liner that does the job.

Imagine that you want a list of all the numbers up to *N* that are multiples of five. Imagine that you want to filter those out using the `filter` function, which takes a function and an iterable and constructs a filter object that you can iterate on, from those elements of iterables for which the function returns `True`. Without using an anonymous function, you would do something like this:

```python
# filter.regular.py
def is_multiple_of_five(n):
    return not n % 5

def get_multiples_of_five(n):
    return list(filter(is_multiple_of_five, range(n)))
```

Note how we use `is_multiple_of_five` to filter the first n natural numbers. This seems a bit excessive, the task is simple and we don't need to keep the `is_multiple_of_five` function around for anything else. Let's rewrite it using a lambda function:

```python
# filter.lambda.py
def get_multiples_of_five(n):
    return list(filter(lambda k: not k % 5, range(n)))
```

The logic is exactly the same but the filtering function is now a lambda. Defining a lambda is very easy and follows this form: `func_name = lambda [parameter_list]: expression`. A function object is returned, which is equivalent to this: `def func_name([parameter_list]): return expression`.

 Note that optional parameters are indicated following the common syntax of wrapping them in square brackets.

Let's look at another couple of examples of equivalent functions defined in the two forms:

```
# lambda.explained.py
# example 1: adder
def adder(a, b):
    return a + b

# is equivalent to:
adder_lambda = lambda a, b: a + b

# example 2: to uppercase
def to_upper(s):
    return s.upper()

# is equivalent to:
to_upper_lambda = lambda s: s.upper()
```

The preceding examples are very simple. The first one adds two numbers, and the second one produces the uppercase version of a string. Note that I assigned what is returned by the `lambda` expressions to a name (`adder_lambda`, `to_upper_lambda`), but there is no need for that when you use lambdas in the way we did in the `filter` example.

# Function attributes

Every function is a fully-fledged object and, as such, they have many attributes. Some of them are special and can be used in an introspective way to inspect the function object at runtime. The following script is an example that shows a part of them and how to display their value for an example function:

```python
# func.attributes.py
def multiplication(a, b=1):
    """Return a multiplied by b. """
    return a * b

special_attributes = [
    "__doc__", "__name__", "__qualname__", "__module__",
    "__defaults__", "__code__", "__globals__", "__dict__",
    "__closure__", "__annotations__", "__kwdefaults__",
]

for attribute in special_attributes:
    print(attribute, '->', getattr(multiplication, attribute))
```

I used the built-in `getattr` function to get the value of those attributes. `getattr(obj, attribute)` is equivalent to `obj.attribute` and comes in handy when we need to get an attribute at runtime using its string name. Running this script yields:

```
$ python func.attributes.py
__doc__ -> Return a multiplied by b.
__name__ -> multiplication
__qualname__ -> multiplication
__module__ -> __main__
__defaults__ -> (1,)
__code__ -> <code object multiplication at 0x10caf7660, file
"func.attributes.py", line 1>
__globals__ -> {...omitted...}
__dict__ -> {}
```

```
__closure__  -> None
__annotations__  -> {}
__kwdefaults__  -> None
```

I have omitted the value of the __globals__ attribute, as it was too big. An explanation of the meaning of this attribute can be found in the *Callable types* section of the *Python Data Model* documentation page (https://docs.python.org/3/reference/datamodel.html#the-standard-type-hierarchy). Should you want to see all the attributes of an object, just call dir(object_name) and you'll be given the list of all of its attributes.

# Built-in functions

Python comes with a lot of built-in functions. They are available anywhere and you can get a list of them by inspecting the builtins module with dir(__builtins__), or by going to the official Python documentation. Unfortunately, I don't have the room to go through all of them here. We've already seen some of them, such as any, bin, bool, divmod, filter, float, getattr, id, int, len, list, min, print, set, tuple, type, and zip, but there are many more, which you should read at least once. Get familiar with them, experiment, write a small piece of code for each of them, and make sure you have them at your finger tips so that you can use them when you need them.

# One final example

Before we finish off this chapter, how about one last example? I was thinking we could write a function to generate a list of prime numbers up to a limit. We've already seen the code for this so let's make it a function and, to keep it interesting, let's optimize it a bit.

It turns out that you don't need to divide it by all numbers from 2 to $N$-1 to decide whether a number, $N$, is prime. You can stop at $\sqrt{N}$. Moreover, you don't need to test the division for all numbers from 2 to $\sqrt{N}$, you can just use the primes in that range. I'll leave it to you to figure out why this works, if you're interested. Let's see how the code changes:

```
# primes.py
from math import sqrt, ceil

def get_primes(n):
```

```
"""Calculate a list of primes up to n (included). """
primelist = []
for candidate in range(2, n + 1):
    is_prime = True
    root = ceil(sqrt(candidate))  # division limit
    for prime in primelist:  # we try only the primes
        if prime > root:  # no need to check any further
            break
        if candidate % prime == 0:
            is_prime = False
            break
    if is_prime:
        primelist.append(candidate)
return primelist
```

The code is the same as in the previous chapter. We have changed the division algorithm so that we only test divisibility using the previously calculated primes and we stopped once the testing divisor was greater than the root of the candidate. We used the `primelist` result list to get the primes for the division. We calculated the root value using a fancy formula, the integer value of the ceiling of the root of the candidate. While a simple `int(k ** 0.5) + 1` would have served our purpose as well, the formula I chose is cleaner and requires me to use a couple of imports, which I wanted to show you. Check out the functions in the `math` module, they are very interesting!

# Documenting your code

I'm a big fan of code that doesn't need documentation. When you program correctly, choose the right names and take care of the details, your code should come out as self-explanatory and documentation should not be needed. Sometimes a comment is very useful though, and so is some documentation. You can find the guidelines for documenting Python in *PEP 257 - Docstring conventions* (https://www.python.org/dev/peps/pep-0257/), but I'll show you the basics here.

Python is documented with strings, which are aptly called **docstrings**. Any object can be documented, and you can use either one-line or multiline docstrings. One-liners are very simple. They should not provide another signature for the function, but clearly state its purpose:

```
# docstrings.py
def square(n):
    """Return the square of a number n. """
    return n ** 2
```

```
def get_username(userid):
    """Return the username of a user given their id. """
    return db.get(user_id=userid).username
```

Using triple double-quoted strings allows you to expand easily later on. Use sentences that end in a period, and don't leave blank lines before or after.

Multiline comments are structured in a similar way. There should be a one-liner that briefly gives you the gist of what the object is about, and then a more verbose description. As an example, I have documented a fictitious `connect` function, using the Sphinx notation, in the following example:

```
def connect(host, port, user, password):
    """Connect to a database.

    Connect to a PostgreSQL database directly, using the given
    parameters.

    :param host: The host IP.
    :param port: The desired port.
    :param user: The connection username.
    :param password: The connection password.
    :return: The connection object.
    """
    # body of the function here...
    return connection
```

 **Sphinx** is probably the most widely used tool for creating Python documentation. In fact, the official Python documentation was written with it. It's definitely worth spending some time checking it out.

# Importing objects

Now that you know a lot about functions, let's look at how to use them. The whole point of writing functions is to be able to reuse them later, and in Python, this translates to importing them into the namespace where you need them. There are many different ways to import objects into a namespace, but the most common ones are `import module_name` and `from module_name import function_name`. Of course, these are quite simplistic examples, but bear with me for the time being.

The `import module_name` form finds the `module_name` module and defines a name for it in the local namespace where the `import` statement is executed. The `from module_name import identifier` form is a little bit more complicated than that, but basically does the same thing. It finds `module_name` and searches for an attribute (or a submodule) and stores a reference to `identifier` in the local namespace.

Both forms have the option to change the name of the imported object using the `as` clause:

```
from mymodule import myfunc as better_named_func
```

Just to give you a flavor of what importing looks like, here's an example from a test module of one of my projects (notice that the blank lines between blocks of imports follow the guidelines from PEP 8 at `https://www.python.org/dev/peps/pep-0008/#imports`: standard library, third party, and local code):

```
from datetime import datetime, timezone  # two imports on the same
line
from unittest.mock import patch  # single import

import pytest  # third party library

from core.models import (  # multiline import
    Exam,
    Exercise,
    Solution,
)
```

When you have a structure of files starting in the root of your project, you can use the dot notation to get to the object you want to import into your current namespace, be it a package, a module, a class, a function, or anything else. The `from module import` syntax also allows a catch-all clause, `from module import *`, which is sometimes used to get all the names from a module into the current namespace at once, but it's frowned upon for several reasons, such as performance and the risk of silently shadowing other names. You can read all that there is to know about imports in the official Python documentation but, before we leave the subject, let me give you a better example.

Imagine that you have defined a couple of functions: square(n) and cube(n) in a module, funcdef.py, which is in the lib folder. You want to use them in a couple of modules that are at the same level of the lib folder, called func_import.py and func_from.py. Showing the tree structure of that project produces something like this:

```
├──── func_from.py
├──── func_import.py
├──── lib
    ├──── funcdef.py
    └──── __init__.py
```

Before I show you the code of each module, please remember that in order to tell Python that it is actually a package, we need to put a __init__.py module in it.

 There are two things to note about the __init__.py file. First of all, it is a fully-fledged Python module so you can put code into it as you would with any other module. Second, as of Python 3.3, its presence is no longer required to make a folder be interpreted as a Python package.

The code is as follows:

```python
# funcdef.py
def square(n):
    return n ** 2
def cube(n):
    return n ** 3

# func_import.py
import lib.funcdef
print(lib.funcdef.square(10))
print(lib.funcdef.cube(10))

# func_from.py
from lib.funcdef import square, cube
print(square(10))
print(cube(10))
```

Both these files, when executed, print 100 and 1000. You can see how differently we then access the square and cube functions, according to how and what we imported in the current scope.

# Relative imports

The imports we've seen so far are called **absolute**, that is, they define the whole path of the module that we want to import, or from which we want to import an object. There is another way of importing objects into Python, which is called a **relative import**. It's helpful in situations where we want to rearrange the structure of large packages without having to edit sub-packages, or when we want to make a module inside a package able to import itself. Relative imports are done by adding as many leading dots in front of the module as the number of folders we need to backtrack, in order to find what we're searching for. Simply put, it is something such as this:

```
from .mymodule import myfunc
```

For a complete explanation of relative imports, refer to PEP 328 (`https://www.python.org/dev/peps/pep-0328/`).

# Summary

In this chapter, we explored the world of functions. They are extremely important and, from now on, we'll use them basically everywhere. We talked about the main reasons for using them, the most important of which are code reuse and implementation hiding.

We saw that a function object is like a box that takes optional inputs and produces outputs. We can feed input values to a function in many different ways, using positional and keyword arguments, and using variable syntax for both types.

Now you should know how to write a function, document it, import it into your code, and call it.

In the next chapter, we're going to see how to deal with files and how to persist data in several different ways and formats.

# Files and Data Persistence

**5**

*"Persistence is the key to the adventure we call life."*

*– Torsten Alexander Lange*

In the previous chapters, we have explored several different aspects of Python. As the examples have a didactic purpose, we've run them in a simple Python shell, or in the form of a Python module. They ran, maybe printed something on the console, and then they terminated, leaving no trace of their brief existence.

Real-world applications though are generally much different. Naturally, they still run in memory, but they interact with networks, disks, and databases. They also exchange information with other applications and devices, using formats that are suitable for the situation.

In this chapter, we are going to start closing in to the real world by exploring the following:

- Files and directories
- Compression
- Networks and streams
- The JSON data-interchange format
- Data persistence with pickle and shelve, from the standard library
- Data persistence with SQLAlchemy

As usual, I will try to balance breadth and depth, so that by the end of the chapter, you will have a solid grasp of the fundamentals and will know how to fetch further information on the web.

# Working with files and directories

When it comes to files and directories, Python offers plenty of useful tools. In particular, in the following examples, we will leverage the os and shutil modules. As we'll be reading and writing on the disk, I will be using a file, fear.txt, which contains an excerpt from *Fear*, by Thich Nhat Hanh, as a guinea pig for some of our examples.

# Opening files

Opening a file in Python is very simple and intuitive. In fact, we just need to use the open function. Let's see a quick example:

```
# files/open_try.py
fh = open('fear.txt', 'rt')  # r: read, t: text

for line in fh.readlines():
    print(line.strip())  # remove whitespace and print

fh.close()
```

The previous code is very simple. We call open, passing the filename, and telling open that we want to read it in text mode. There is no path information before the filename; therefore, open will assume the file is in the same folder the script is run from. This means that if we run this script from outside the files folder, then fear.txt won't be found.

Once the file has been opened, we obtain a file object back, fh, which we can use to work on the content of the file. In this case, we use the readlines() method to iterate over all the lines in the file, and print them. We call strip() on each line to get rid of any extra spaces around the content, including the line termination character at the end, since print will already add one for us. This is a quick and dirty solution that works in this example, but should the content of the file contain meaningful spaces that need to be preserved, you will have to be slightly more careful in how you sanitize the data. At the end of the script, we flush and close the stream.

Closing a file is very important, as we don't want to risk failing to release the handle we have on it. Therefore, we need to apply some precaution, and wrap the previous logic in a try/finally block. This has the effect that, whatever error might occur while we try to open and read the file, we can rest assured that close() will be called:

```
# files/open_try.py
try:
    fh = open('fear.txt', 'rt')
    for line in fh.readlines():
        print(line.strip())
finally:
    fh.close()
```

The logic is exactly the same, but now it is also safe.

 Don't worry if you don't understand `try/finally` for now. We will explore how to deal with exceptions in a later chapter. For now, suffice to say that putting code within the body of a `try` block adds a mechanism around that code that allows us to detect errors (which are called *exceptions*) and decide what to do if they happen. In this case, we don't really do anything in case of errors, but by closing the file within the `finally` block, we make sure that line is executed whether or not any error has happened.

We can simplify the previous example this way:

```
# files/open_try.py
try:
    fh = open('fear.txt')  # rt is default
    for line in fh:  # we can iterate directly on fh
        print(line.strip())
finally:
    fh.close()
```

As you can see, `rt` is the default mode for opening files, so we don't need to specify it. Moreover, we can simply iterate on `fh`, without explicitly calling `readlines()` on it. Python is very nice and gives us shorthands to make our code shorter and simpler to read.

All the previous examples produce a print of the file on the console (check out the source code to read the whole content):

```
An excerpt from Fear - By Thich Nhat Hanh

The Present Is Free from Fear

When we are not fully present, we are not really living. We're not
really there, either for our loved ones or for ourselves. If we're not
there, then where are we? We are running, running, running, even
during our sleep. We run because we're trying to escape from our fear.
...
```

## Using a context manager to open a file

Let's admit it: the prospect of having to disseminate our code with `try/finally` blocks is not one of the best. As usual, Python gives us a much nicer way to open a file in a secure fashion: by using a *context manager*. Let's see the code first:

```
# files/open_with.py
with open('fear.txt') as fh:
    for line in fh:
        print(line.strip())
```

The previous example is equivalent to the one before it, but reads so much better. The `with` statement supports the concept of a runtime context defined by a context manager. This is implemented using a pair of methods, `__enter__` and `__exit__`, that allow user-defined classes to define a runtime context that is entered before the statement body is executed and exited when the statement ends. The `open` function is capable of producing a file object when invoked by a context manager, but the true beauty of it lies in the fact that `fh.close()` will be called automatically for us, even in case of errors.

Context managers are used in several different scenarios, such as thread synchronization, closure of files or other objects, and management of network and database connections. You can find information about them in the `contextlib` documentation page (`https://docs.python.org/3.7/library/contextlib.html`).

## Reading and writing to a file

Now that we know how to open a file, let's see a couple of different ways that we have to read and write to it:

```
# files/print_file.py
with open('print_example.txt', 'w') as fw:
    print('Hey I am printing into a file!!!', file=fw)
```

A first approach uses the `print` function, which you've seen plenty of times in the previous chapters. After obtaining a file object, this time specifying that we intend to write to it ("w"), we can tell the call to `print` to direct its effects on the file, instead of the default `sys.stdout`, which, when executed on a console, is mapped to it.

The previous code has the effect of creating the `print_example.txt` file if it doesn't exist, or truncate it in case it does, and writes the line `Hey I am printing into a file!!!` to it.

This is all nice and easy, but not what we typically do when we want to write to a file. Let's see a much more common approach:

```
# files/read_write.py
with open('fear.txt') as f:
    lines = [line.rstrip() for line in f]

with open('fear_copy.txt', 'w') as fw:
    fw.write('\n'.join(lines))
```

In the previous example, we first open fear.txt and collect its content into a list, line by line. Notice that this time, I'm calling a more precise method, rstrip(), as an example, to make sure I only strip the whitespace on the right-hand side of every line.

In the second part of the snippet, we create a new file, fear_copy.txt, and we write to it all the lines from the original file, joined by a newline, \n. Python is gracious and works by default with *universal newlines*, which means that even though the original file might have a newline that is different than \n, it will be translated automatically for us before the line is returned. This behavior is, of course, customizable, but normally it is exactly what you want. Speaking of newlines, can you think of one of them that might be missing in the copy?

# Reading and writing in binary mode

Notice that by opening a file passing t in the options (or omitting it, as it is the default), we're opening the file in text mode. This means that the content of the file is treated and interpreted as text. If you wish to write bytes to a file, you can open it in binary mode. This is a common requirement when you deal with files that don't just contain raw text, such as images, audio/video, and, in general, any other proprietary format.

In order to handle files in binary mode, simply specify the b flag when opening them, as in the following example:

```
# files/read_write_bin.py
with open('example.bin', 'wb') as fw:
    fw.write(b'This is binary data...')

with open('example.bin', 'rb') as f:
    print(f.read())  # prints: b'This is binary data...'
```

In this example, I'm still using text as binary data, but it could be anything you want. You can see it's treated as a binary by the fact that you get the b'This ...' prefix in the output.

## Protecting against overriding an existing file

Python gives us the ability to open files for writing. By using the w flag, we open a file and truncate its content. This means the file is overwritten with an empty file, and the original content is lost. If you wish to only open a file for writing in case it doesn't exist, you can use the x flag instead, in the following example:

```
# files/write_not_exists.py
with open('write_x.txt', 'x') as fw:
    fw.write('Writing line 1')  # this succeeds

with open('write_x.txt', 'x') as fw:
    fw.write('Writing line 2')  # this fails
```

If you run the previous snippet, you will find a file called write_x.txt in your directory, containing only one line of text. The second part of the snippet, in fact, fails to execute. This is the output I get on my console:

```
$ python write_not_exists.py
Traceback (most recent call last):
  File "write_not_exists.py", line 6, in <module>
    with open('write_x.txt', 'x') as fw:
FileExistsError: [Errno 17] File exists: 'write_x.txt'
```

# Checking for file and directory existence

If you want to make sure a file or directory exists (or it doesn't), the os.path module is what you need. Let's see a small example:

```
# files/existence.py
import os

filename = 'fear.txt'
path = os.path.dirname(os.path.abspath(filename))

print(os.path.isfile(filename))  # True
print(os.path.isdir(path))  # True
print(path)  # /Users/fab/srv/lpp/ch5/files
```

The preceding snippet is quite interesting. After declaring the filename with a relative reference (in that it is missing the path information), we use `abspath` to calculate the full, absolute path of the file. Then, we get the path information (by removing the filename at the end) by calling `dirname` on it. The result, as you can see, is printed on the last line. Notice also how we check for existence, both for a file and a directory, by calling `isfile` and `isdir`. In the `os.path` module, you find all the functions you need to work with pathnames.

 Should you ever need to work with paths in a different way, you can check out `pathlib`. While `os.path` works with strings, `pathlib` offers classes representing filesystem paths with semantics appropriate for different operating systems. It is beyond the scope of this chapter, but if you're interested, check out PEP428 (`https://www.python.org/dev/peps/pep-0428/`), and its page in the standard library.

# Manipulating files and directories

Let's see a couple of quick examples on how to manipulate files and directories. The first example manipulates the content:

```python
# files/manipulation.py
from collections import Counter
from string import ascii_letters

chars = ascii_letters + ' '

def sanitize(s, chars):
    return ''.join(c for c in s if c in chars)

def reverse(s):
    return s[::-1]

with open('fear.txt') as stream:
    lines = [line.rstrip() for line in stream]

with open('raef.txt', 'w') as stream:
    stream.write('\n'.join(reverse(line) for line in lines))

# now we can calculate some statistics
lines = [sanitize(line, chars) for line in lines]
whole = ' '.join(lines)
cnt = Counter(whole.lower().split())
print(cnt.most_common(3))
```

The previous example defines two functions: sanitize and reverse. They are simple functions whose purpose is to remove anything that is not a letter or space from a string, and produce the reversed copy of a string, respectively.

We open fear.txt and we read its content into a list. Then we create a new file, raef.txt, which will contain the horizontally-mirrored version of the original one. We write all the content of lines with a single operation, using join on a new line character. Maybe more interesting, is the bit in the end. First, we reassign lines to a sanitized version of itself, by means of list comprehension. Then we put them together in the whole string, and finally, we pass the result to Counter. Notice that we split the string and put it in lowercase. This way, each word will be counted correctly, regardless of its case, and, thanks to split, we don't need to worry about extra spaces anywhere. When we print the three most common words, we realize that truly Thich Nhat Hanh's focus is on others, as we is the most common word in the text:

```
$ python manipulation.py
[('we', 17), ('the', 13), ('were', 7)]
```

Let's now see an example of manipulation more oriented to disk operations, in which we put the shutil module to use:

```
# files/ops_create.py
import shutil
import os

BASE_PATH = 'ops_example'  # this will be our base path
os.mkdir(BASE_PATH)

path_b = os.path.join(BASE_PATH, 'A', 'B')
path_c = os.path.join(BASE_PATH, 'A', 'C')
path_d = os.path.join(BASE_PATH, 'A', 'D')

os.makedirs(path_b)
os.makedirs(path_c)

for filename in ('ex1.txt', 'ex2.txt', 'ex3.txt'):
    with open(os.path.join(path_b, filename), 'w') as stream:
        stream.write(f'Some content here in {filename}\n')

shutil.move(path_b, path_d)

shutil.move(
    os.path.join(path_d, 'ex1.txt'),
```

```
        os.path.join(path_d, 'ex1d.txt')
    )
```

In the previous code, we start by declaring a base path, which will safely contain all the files and folders we're going to create. We then use `makedirs` to create two directories: `ops_example/A/B` and `ops_example/A/C`. (Can you think of a way of creating the two directories by using `map`?).

We use `os.path.join` to concatenate directory names, as using / would specialize the code to run on a platform where the directory separator is /, but then the code would fail on platforms with a different separator. Let's delegate to `join` the task to figure out which is the appropriate separator.

After creating the directories, within a simple `for` loop, we put some code that creates three files in directory B. Then, we move the folder B and its content to a different name: D. And finally, we rename `ex1.txt` to `ex1d.txt`. If you open that file, you'll see it still contains the original text from the `for` loop. Calling `tree` on the result produces the following:

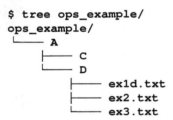

```
$ tree ops_example/
ops_example/
└── A
    ├── C
    └── D
        ├── ex1d.txt
        ├── ex2.txt
        └── ex3.txt
```

# Manipulating pathnames

Let's explore a little more the abilities of `os.path` by means of a simple example:

```
# files/paths.py
import os

filename = 'fear.txt'
path = os.path.abspath(filename)

print(path)
print(os.path.basename(path))
print(os.path.dirname(path))
print(os.path.splitext(path))
print(os.path.split(path))

readme_path = os.path.join(
```

```
        os.path.dirname(path), '..', '..', 'README.rst')

print(readme_path)
print(os.path.normpath(readme_path))
```

Reading the result is probably a good enough explanation for this simple example:

```
/Users/fab/srv/lpp/ch5/files/fear.txt              # path
fear.txt                                           # basename
/Users/fab/srv/lpp/ch5/files                       # dirname
('/Users/fab/srv/lpp/ch5/files/fear', '.txt')      # splitext
('/Users/fab/srv/lpp/ch5/files', 'fear.txt')       # split
/Users/fab/srv/lpp/ch5/files/../../README.rst      # readme_path
/Users/fab/srv/lpp/README.rst                      # normalized
```

# Temporary files and directories

Sometimes, it's very useful to be able to create a temporary directory or file when running some code. For example, when writing tests that affect the disk, you can use temporary files and directories to run your logic and assert that it's correct, and to be sure that at the end of the test run, the test folder has no leftovers. Let's see how you do it in Python:

```python
# files/tmp.py
import os
from tempfile import NamedTemporaryFile, TemporaryDirectory

with TemporaryDirectory(dir='.') as td:
    print('Temp directory:', td)
    with NamedTemporaryFile(dir=td) as t:
        name = t.name
        print(os.path.abspath(name))
```

The preceding example is quite straightforward: we create a temporary directory in the current one ("."), and we create a named temporary file in it. We print the filename, as well as its full path:

```
$ python tmp.py
Temp directory: ./tmpwa9bdwgo
/Users/fab/srv/lpp/ch5/files/tmpwa9bdwgo/tmp3d45hm46
```

Running this script will produce a different result every time. After all, it's a temporary random name we're creating here, right?

# Directory content

With Python, you can also inspect the content of a directory. I'll show you two ways of doing this:

```
# files/listing.py
import os

with os.scandir('.') as it:
    for entry in it:
        print(
            entry.name, entry.path,
            'File' if entry.is_file() else 'Folder'
        )
```

This snippet uses `os.scandir`, called on the current directory. We iterate on the results, each of which is an instance of `os.DirEntry`, a nice class that exposes useful properties and methods. In the code, we access a subset of those: `name`, `path`, and `is_file()`. Running the code yields the following (I omitted a few results for brevity):

```
$ python listing.py
fixed_amount.py ./fixed_amount.py File
existence.py ./existence.py File
...
ops_example ./ops_example Folder
...
```

A more powerful way to scan a directory tree is given to us by `os.walk`. Let's see an example:

```
# files/walking.py
import os

for root, dirs, files in os.walk('.'):
    print(os.path.abspath(root))
    if dirs:
        print('Directories:')
        for dir_ in dirs:
            print(dir_)
        print()
    if files:
        print('Files:')
        for filename in files:
            print(filename)
        print()
```

Running the preceding snippet will produce a list of all files and directories in the current one, and it will do the same for each sub-directory.

# File and directory compression

Before we leave this section, let me give you an example of how to create a compressed file. In the source code of the book, I have two examples: one creates a ZIP file, while the other one creates a `tar.gz` file. Python allows you to create compressed files in several different ways and formats. Here, I am going to show you how to create the most common one, ZIP:

```
# files/compression/zip.py
from zipfile import ZipFile

with ZipFile('example.zip', 'w') as zp:
    zp.write('content1.txt')
    zp.write('content2.txt')
    zp.write('subfolder/content3.txt')
    zp.write('subfolder/content4.txt')

with ZipFile('example.zip') as zp:
    zp.extract('content1.txt', 'extract_zip')
    zp.extract('subfolder/content3.txt', 'extract_zip')
```

In the preceding code, we import `ZipFile`, and then, within a context manager, we write into it four dummy context files (two of which are in a sub-folder, to show ZIP preserves the full path). Afterwards, as an example, we open the compressed file and extract a couple of files from it, into the `extract_zip` directory. If you are interested in learning more about data compression, make sure you check out the *Data Compression and Archiving* section on the standard library (`https://docs.python.org/3.7/library/archiving.html`), where you'll be able to learn all about this topic.

# Data interchange formats

Modern software architecture tends to split an application into several components. Whether you embrace the service-oriented architecture paradigm, or you push it even further into the microservices realm, these components will have to exchange data. But even if you are coding a monolithic application, whose code base is contained in one project, chances are that you have to still exchange data with APIs, other programs, or simply handle the data flow between the frontend and the backend part of your website, which very likely won't speak the same language.

Choosing the right format in which to exchange information is crucial. A language-specific format has the advantage that the language itself is very likely to provide you with all the tools to make serialization and deserialization a breeze. However, you will lose the ability to talk to other components that have been written in different versions of the same language, or in different languages altogether. Regardless of what the future looks like, going with a language-specific format should only be done if it is the only possible choice for the given situation.

A much better approach is to choose a format that is language agnostic, and can be spoken by all (or at least most) languages. In the team I lead, we have people from England, Poland, South Africa, Spain, Greece, India, Italy, to mention just a few. We all speak English, so regardless of our native tongue, we can all understand each other (well... mostly!).

In the software world, some popular formats have become the de facto standard over recent years. The most famous ones probably are XML, YAML, and JSON. The Python standard library features the `xml` and `json` modules, and, on PyPI (`https://docs.python.org/3.7/library/archiving.html`), you can find a few different packages to work with YAML.

In the Python environment, JSON is probably the most commonly used one. It wins over the other two because of being part of the standard library, and for its simplicity. If you have ever worked with XML, you know what a nightmare it can be.

# Working with JSON

**JSON** is the acronym of **JavaScript Object Notation**, and it is a subset of the JavaScript language. It has been there for almost two decades now, so it is well known and widely adopted by basically all languages, even though it is actually language independent. You can read all about it on its website (`https://www.json.org/`), but I'm going to give you a quick introduction to it now.

JSON is based on two structures: a collection of name/value pairs, and an ordered list of values. You will immediately realize that these two objects map to the dictionary and list data types in Python, respectively. As data types, it offers strings, numbers, objects, and values, such as true, false, and null. Let's see a quick example to get us started:

```
# json_examples/json_basic.py
import sys
import json
```

```
data = {
    'big_number': 2 ** 3141,
    'max_float': sys.float_info.max,
    'a_list': [2, 3, 5, 7],
}

json_data = json.dumps(data)
data_out = json.loads(json_data)
assert data == data_out  # json and back, data matches
```

We begin by importing the `sys` and `json` modules. Then we create a simple dictionary with some numbers inside and a list. I wanted to test serializing and deserializing using very big numbers, both `int` and `float`, so I put $2^{3141}$ and whatever is the biggest floating point number my system can handle.

We serialize with `json.dumps`, which takes data and converts it into a JSON formatted string. That data is then fed into `json.loads`, which does the opposite: from a JSON formatted string, it reconstructs the data into Python. On the last line, we make sure that the original data and the result of the serialization/deserialization through JSON match.

Let's see, in the next example, what JSON data would look like if we printed it:

```
# json_examples/json_basic.py
import json

info = {
    'full_name': 'Sherlock Holmes',
    'address': {
        'street': '221B Baker St',
        'zip': 'NW1 6XE',
        'city': 'London',
        'country': 'UK',
    }
}

print(json.dumps(info, indent=2, sort_keys=True))
```

In this example, we create a dictionary with Sherlock Holmes' data in it. If, like me, you're a fan of Sherlock Holmes, and are in London, you'll find his museum at that address (which I recommend visiting, it's small but very nice).

Notice how we call `json.dumps`, though. We have told it to indent with two spaces, and sort keys alphabetically. The result is this:

```
$ python json_basic.py
{
  "address": {
    "city": "London",
    "country": "UK",
    "street": "221B Baker St",
    "zip": "NW1 6XE"
  },
  "full_name": "Sherlock Holmes"
}
```

The similarity with Python is huge. The one difference is that if you place a comma on the last element in a dictionary, like I've done in Python (as it is customary), JSON will complain.

Let me show you something interesting:

```python
# json_examples/json_tuple.py
import json

data_in = {
    'a_tuple': (1, 2, 3, 4, 5),
}

json_data = json.dumps(data_in)
print(json_data)  # {"a_tuple": [1, 2, 3, 4, 5]}
data_out = json.loads(json_data)
print(data_out)  # {'a_tuple': [1, 2, 3, 4, 5]}
```

In this example, we have put a tuple, instead of a list. The interesting bit is that, conceptually, a tuple is also an ordered list of items. It doesn't have the flexibility of a list, but still, it is considered the same from the perspective of JSON. Therefore, as you can see by the first `print`, in JSON a tuple is transformed into a list. Naturally then, the information that it was a tuple is lost, and when deserialization happens, what we have in `data_out`, `a_tuple` is actually a list. It is important that you keep this in mind when dealing with data, as going through a transformation process that involves a format that only comprises a subset of the data structures you can use implies there will be information loss. In this case, we lost the information about the type (tuple versus list).

This is actually a common problem. For example, you can't serialize all Python objects to JSON, as it is not clear if JSON should revert that (or how). Think about `datetime`, for example. An instance of that class is a Python object that JSON won't allow serializing. If we transform it into a string such as `2018-03-04T12:00:30Z`, which is the ISO 8601 representation of a date with time and time zone information, what should JSON do when deserializing? Should it say *this is actually deserializable into a datetime object, so I'd better do it,* or should it simply consider it as a string and leave it as it is? What about data types that can be interpreted in more than one way?

The answer is that when dealing with data interchange, we often need to transform our objects into a simpler format prior to serializing them with JSON. This way, we will know how to reconstruct them correctly when we deserialize them.

In some cases, though, and mostly for internal use, it is useful to be able to serialize custom objects, so, just for fun, I'm going to show you how with two examples: complex numbers (because I love math) and *datetime* objects.

# Custom encoding/decoding with JSON

In the JSON world, we can consider terms like encoding/decoding as synonyms to serializing/deserializing. They basically all mean transforming to and back from JSON. In the following example, I'm going to show you how to encode complex numbers:

```python
# json_examples/json_cplx.py
import json

class ComplexEncoder(json.JSONEncoder):
    def default(self, obj):
        if isinstance(obj, complex):
            return {
                '_meta': '_complex',
                'num': [obj.real, obj.imag],
            }
        return json.JSONEncoder.default(self, obj)

data = {
    'an_int': 42,
    'a_float': 3.14159265,
    'a_complex': 3 + 4j,
}

json_data = json.dumps(data, cls=ComplexEncoder)
print(json_data)
```

```
def object_hook(obj):
    try:
        if obj['_meta'] == '_complex':
            return complex(*obj['num'])
    except (KeyError, TypeError):
        return obj

data_out = json.loads(json_data, object_hook=object_hook)
print(data_out)
```

We start by defining a `ComplexEncoder` class, which needs to implement the `default` method. This method is passed to all the objects that have to be serialized, one at a time, in the `obj` variable. At some point, `obj` will be our complex number, *3+4j*. When that is true, we return a dictionary with some custom meta information, and a list that contains both the real and the imaginary part of the number. That is all we need to do to avoid losing information for a complex number.

We then call `json.dumps`, but this time we use the `cls` argument to specify our custom encoder. The result is printed:

```
{"an_int": 42, "a_float": 3.14159265, "a_complex": {"_meta":
"_complex", "num": [3.0, 4.0]}}
```

Half the job is done. For the deserialization part, we could have written another class that would inherit from `JSONDecoder`, but, just for fun, I've used a different technique that is simpler and uses a small function: `object_hook`.

Within the body of `object_hook`, we find another `try` block. The important part is the two lines within the body of the `try` block itself. The function receives an object (notice, the function is only called when `obj` is a dictionary), and if the metadata matches our convention for complex numbers, we pass the real and imaginary parts to the `complex` function. The `try/except` block is there only to prevent malformed JSON from ruining the party (and if that happens, we simply return the object as it is).

The last print returns:

```
{'an_int': 42, 'a_float': 3.14159265, 'a_complex': (3+4j)}
```

You can see that `a_complex` has been correctly deserialized.

Let's see a slightly more complex (no pun intended) example now: dealing with `datetime` objects. I'm going to split the code into two blocks, the serializing part, and the deserializing afterwards:

```
# json_examples/json_datetime.py
import json
from datetime import datetime, timedelta, timezone

now = datetime.now()
now_tz = datetime.now(tz=timezone(timedelta(hours=1)))

class DatetimeEncoder(json.JSONEncoder):
    def default(self, obj):
        if isinstance(obj, datetime):
            try:
                off = obj.utcoffset().seconds
            except AttributeError:
                off = None

            return {
                '_meta': '_datetime',
                'data': obj.timetuple()[:6] + (obj.microsecond, ),
                'utcoffset': off,
            }
        return json.JSONEncoder.default(self, obj)

data = {
    'an_int': 42,
    'a_float': 3.14159265,
    'a_datetime': now,
    'a_datetime_tz': now_tz,
}

json_data = json.dumps(data, cls=DatetimeEncoder)
print(json_data)
```

The reason why this example is slightly more complex lies in the fact that datetime objects in Python can be time zone aware or not; therefore, we need to be more careful. The flow is basically the same as before, only it is dealing with a different data type. We start by getting the current date and time information, and we do it both without (now) and with (now_tz) time zone awareness, just to make sure our script works. We then proceed to define a custom encoder as before, and we implement once again the default method. The important bits in that method are how we get the time zone offset (off) information, in seconds, and how we structure the dictionary that returns the data. This time, the metadata says it's a *datetime* information, and then we save the first six items in the time tuple (year, month, day, hour, minute, and second), plus the microseconds in the data key, and the offset after that. Could you tell that the value of data is a concatenation of tuples? Good job if you could!

When we have our custom encoder, we proceed to create some data, and then we serialize. The print statement returns (after I've done some prettifying):

```
{
  "a_datetime": {
    "_meta": "_datetime",
    "data": [2018, 3, 18, 17, 57, 27, 438792],
    "utcoffset": null
  },
  "a_datetime_tz": {
    "_meta": "_datetime",
    "data": [2018, 3, 18, 18, 57, 27, 438810],
    "utcoffset": 3600
  },
  "a_float": 3.14159265,
  "an_int": 42
}
```

Interestingly, we find out that None is translated to null, its JavaScript equivalent. Moreover, we can see our data seems to have been encoded properly. Let's proceed to the second part of the script:

```python
# json_examples/json_datetime.py
def object_hook(obj):
    try:
        if obj['_meta'] == '_datetime':
            if obj['utcoffset'] is None:
                tz = None
            else:
                tz = timezone(timedelta(seconds=obj['utcoffset']))
            return datetime(*obj['data'], tzinfo=tz)
    except (KeyError, TypeError):
        return obj

data_out = json.loads(json_data, object_hook=object_hook)
```

Once again, we first verify that the metadata is telling us it's a datetime, and then we proceed to fetch the time zone information. Once we have that, we pass the 7-tuple (using * to unpack its values in the call) and the time zone information to the datetime call, getting back our original object. Let's verify it by printing data_out:

```python
{
  'a_datetime': datetime.datetime(2018, 3, 18, 18, 1, 46, 54693),
  'a_datetime_tz': datetime.datetime(
    2018, 3, 18, 19, 1, 46, 54711,
    tzinfo=datetime.timezone(datetime.timedelta(seconds=3600))),
  'a_float': 3.14159265,
  'an_int': 42
}
```

As you can see, we got everything back correctly. As an exercise, I'd like to challenge you to write the same logic, but for a date object, which should be simpler.

Before we move on to the next topic, a word of caution. Perhaps it is counter-intuitive, but working with `datetime` objects can be one of the trickiest things to do, so, although I'm pretty sure this code is doing what it is supposed to do, I want to stress that I only tested it very lightly. So if you intend to grab it and use it, please do test it thoroughly. Test for different time zones, test for daylight saving time being on and off, test for dates before the epoch, and so on. You might find that the code in this section then would need some modifications to suit your cases.

Let's now move to the next topic, IO.

# IO, streams, and requests

**IO** stands for **input/output**, and it broadly refers to the communication between a computer and the outside world. There are several different types of IO, and it is outside the scope of this chapter to explain all of them, but I still want to offer you a couple of examples.

## Using an in-memory stream

The first will show you the `io.StringIO` class, which is an in-memory stream for text IO. The second one instead will escape the locality of our computer, and show you how to perform an HTTP request. Let's see the first example:

```python
# io_examples/string_io.py
import io

stream = io.StringIO()
stream.write('Learning Python Programming.\n')
print('Become a Python ninja!', file=stream)

contents = stream.getvalue()
print(contents)

stream.close()
```

In the preceding code snippet, we import the `io` module from the standard library. This is a very interesting module that features many tools related to streams and IO. One of them is `StringIO`, which is an in-memory buffer in which we're going to write two sentences, using two different methods, as we did with files in the first examples of this chapter. We can both call `StringIO.write` or we can use `print`, and tell it to direct the data to our stream.

By calling `getvalue`, we can get the content of the stream (and print it), and finally we close it. The call to `close` causes the text buffer to be immediately discarded.

There is a more elegant way to write the previous code (can you guess it, before you look?):

```
# io_examples/string_io.py
with io.StringIO() as stream:
    stream.write('Learning Python Programming.\n')
    print('Become a Python ninja!', file=stream)
    contents = stream.getvalue()
    print(contents)
```

Yes, it is again a context manager. Like `open`, `io.StringIO` works well within a context manager block. Notice the similarity with `open`: in this case too, we don't need to manually close the stream.

In-memory objects can be useful in a multitude of situations. Memory is much faster than a disk and, for small amounts of data, can be the perfect choice.

When running the script, the output is:

```
$ python string_io.py
Learning Python Programming.
Become a Python ninja!
```

# Making HTTP requests

Let's now explore a couple of examples on HTTP requests. I will use the `requests` library for these examples, which you can install with `pip`. We're going to perform HTTP requests against the `httpbin.org` API, which, interestingly, was developed by Kenneth Reitz, the creator of the `requests` library itself. This library is amongst the most widely adopted all over the world:

```
import requests

urls = {
    'get': 'https://httpbin.org/get?title=learn+python+programming',
    'headers': 'https://httpbin.org/headers',
    'ip': 'https://httpbin.org/ip',
    'now': 'https://now.httpbin.org/',
    'user-agent': 'https://httpbin.org/user-agent',
    'UUID': 'https://httpbin.org/uuid',
}
```

```
def get_content(title, url):
    resp = requests.get(url)
    print(f'Response for {title}')
    print(resp.json())

for title, url in urls.items():
    get_content(title, url)
    print('-' * 40)
```

The preceding snippet should be simple to understand. I declare a dictionary of URLs against which I want to perform `requests`. I have encapsulated the code that performs the request into a tiny function: `get_content`. As you can see, very simply, we perform a GET request (by using `requests.get`), and we print the title and the JSON decoded version of the body of the response. Let me spend a word about this last bit.

When we perform a request to a website, or API, we get back a response object, which is, very simply, what was returned by the server we performed the request against. The body of all responses from `httpbin.org` happens to be JSON encoded, so instead of getting the body as it is (by getting `resp.text`) and manually decoding it, calling `json.loads` on it, we simply combine the two by leveraging the `json` method on the response object. There are plenty of reasons why the `requests` package has become so widely adopted, and one of them is definitely its ease of use.

Now, when you perform a request in your application, you will want to have a much more robust approach in dealing with errors and so on, but for this chapter, a simple example will do.

Going back to our code, in the end, we run a `for` loop and get all the URLs. When you run it, you will see the result of each call printed on your console, like this (prettified and trimmed for brevity):

```
$ python reqs.py
Response for get
{
  "args": {
    "title": "learn python programming"
  },
  "headers": {
    "Accept": "*/*",
    "Accept-Encoding": "gzip, deflate",
    "Connection": "close",
    "Host": "httpbin.org",
    "User-Agent": "python-requests/2.19.0"
  },
```

```
    "origin": "82.47.175.158",
    "url": "https://httpbin.org/get?title=learn+python+programming"
}
... rest of the output omitted ...
```

Notice that you might get a slightly different output in terms of version numbers and IPs, which is fine. Now, GET is only one of the HTTP verbs, and it is definitely the most commonly used. The second one is the ubiquitous POST, which is the type of request you make when you need to send data to the server. Every time you submit a form on the web, you're basically making a POST request. So, let's try to make one programmatically:

```python
# io_examples/reqs_post.py
import requests

url = 'https://httpbin.org/post'
data = dict(title='Learn Python Programming')

resp = requests.post(url, data=data)
print('Response for POST')
print(resp.json())
```

The previous code is very similar to the one we saw before, only this time we don't call `get`, but `post`, and because we want to send some data, we specify that in the call. The `requests` library offers much, much more than this, and it has been praised by the community for the beautiful API it exposes. It is a project that I encourage you to check out and explore, as you will end up using it all the time, anyway.

Running the previous script (and applying some prettifying magic to the output) yields the following:

```
$ python reqs_post.py
Response for POST
{ 'args': {},
  'data': '',
  'files': {},
  'form': {'title': 'Learn Python Programming'},
  'headers': { 'Accept': '*/*',
               'Accept-Encoding': 'gzip, deflate',
               'Connection': 'close',
               'Content-Length': '30',
               'Content-Type': 'application/x-www-form-urlencoded',
               'Host': 'httpbin.org',
               'User-Agent': 'python-requests/2.7.0 CPython/3.7.0b2 '
                             'Darwin/17.4.0'},
  'json': None,
```

```
'origin': '82.45.123.178',
'url': 'https://httpbin.org/post'}
```

Notice how the headers are now different, and we find the data we sent in the `form` key/value pair of the response body.

I hope these short examples are enough to get you started, especially with requests. The web changes every day, so it's worth learning the basics and then brush up every now and then.

Let's now move on to the last topic of this chapter: persisting data on disk in different formats.

# Persisting data on disk

In the last section of this chapter, we're exploring how to persist data on disk in three different formats. We will explore `pickle`, `shelve`, and a short example that will involve accessing a database using SQLAlchemy, the most widely adopted ORM library in the Python ecosystem.

## Serializing data with pickle

The `pickle` module, from the Python standard library, offers tools to convert Python objects into byte streams, and vice versa. Even though there is a partial overlap in the API that `pickle` and `json` expose, the two are quite different. As we have seen previously in this chapter, JSON is a text format, human readable, language independent, and supports only a restricted subset of Python data types. The `pickle` module, on the other hand, is not human readable, translates to bytes, is Python specific, and, thanks to the wonderful Python introspection capabilities, it supports an extremely large amount of data types.

Regardless of these differences, though, which you should know when you consider whether to use one or the other, I think that the most important concern regarding `pickle` lies in the security threats you are exposed to when you use it. *Unpickling* erroneous or malicious data from an untrusted source can be very dangerous, so if you decide to adopt it in your application, you need to be extra careful.

That said, let's see it in action, by means of a simple example:

```python
# persistence/pickler.py
import pickle
from dataclasses import dataclass

@dataclass
class Person:
    first_name: str
    last_name: str
    id: int

    def greet(self):
        print(f'Hi, I am {self.first_name} {self.last_name}'
              f' and my ID is {self.id}'
        )

people = [
    Person('Obi-Wan', 'Kenobi', 123),
    Person('Anakin', 'Skywalker', 456),
]

# save data in binary format to a file
with open('data.pickle', 'wb') as stream:
    pickle.dump(people, stream)

# load data from a file
with open('data.pickle', 'rb') as stream:
    peeps = pickle.load(stream)

for person in peeps:
    person.greet()
```

In the previous example, we create a `Person` class using the `dataclass` decorator (we will cover how to do this in later chapters). The only reason I wrote this example with a data class is to show you how effortlessly `pickle` deals with it, with no need for us to do anything we wouldn't do for a simpler data type.

The class has three attributes: `first_name`, `last_name`, and `id`. It also exposes a `greet` method, which simply prints a hello message with the data.

We create a list of instances, and then we save it to a file. In order to do so, we use `pickle.dump`, to which we feed the content to be *pickled*, and the stream to which we want to write. Immediately after that, we read from that same file, and by using `pickle.load`, we convert back into Python the whole content of that stream. Just to make sure that the objects have been converted correctly, we call the `greet` method on both of them. The result is the following:

```
$ python pickler.py
Hi, I am Obi-Wan Kenobi and my ID is 123
Hi, I am Anakin Skywalker and my ID is 456
```

The `pickle` module also allows you to convert to (and from) byte objects, by means of the `dumps` and `loads` functions (note the s at the end of both names). In day-to-day applications, `pickle` is usually used when we need to persist Python data that is not supposed to be exchanged with another application. One example I stumbled upon recently was the session management in a `flask` plugin, which pickles the session object before sending it to Redis. In practice, though, you are unlikely to have to deal with this library very often.

Another tool that is possibly used even less, but that proves to be very useful when you are short of resources, is `shelve`.

# Saving data with shelve

A `shelf`, is a persistent dictionary-like object. The beauty of it is that the values you save into a `shelf` can be any object you can `pickle`, so you're not restricted like you would be if you were using a database. Albeit interesting and useful, the `shelve` module is used quite rarely in practice. Just for completeness, let's see a quick example of how it works:

```
# persistence/shelf.py
import shelve

class Person:
    def __init__(self, name, id):
        self.name = name
        self.id = id

with shelve.open('shelf1.shelve') as db:
    db['obi1'] = Person('Obi-Wan', 123)
    db['ani'] = Person('Anakin', 456)
    db['a_list'] = [2, 3, 5]
    db['delete_me'] = 'we will have to delete this one...'
```

```
print(list(db.keys()))  # ['ani', 'a_list', 'delete_me', 'obi1']

del db['delete_me']  # gone!

print(list(db.keys()))  # ['ani', 'a_list', 'obi1']

print('delete_me' in db)  # False
print('ani' in db)  # True

a_list = db['a_list']
a_list.append(7)
db['a_list'] = a_list
print(db['a_list'])  # [2, 3, 5, 7]
```

Apart from the wiring and the boilerplate around it, the previous example resembles an exercise with dictionaries. We create a simple `Person` class and then we open a `shelve` file within a context manager. As you can see, we use the dictionary syntax to store four objects: two `Person` instances, a list, and a string. If we print the `keys`, we get a list containing the four keys we used. Immediately after printing it, we delete the (aptly named) `delete_me` key/value pair from shelf. Printing the `keys` again shows the deletion has succeeded. We then test a couple of keys for membership, and finally, we append number 7 to `a_list`. Notice how we have to extract the list from the shelf, modify it, and save it again.

In case this behavior is undesired, there is something we can do:

```
# persistence/shelf.py
with shelve.open('shelf2.shelve', writeback=True) as db:
    db['a_list'] = [11, 13, 17]
    db['a_list'].append(19)  # in-place append!
    print(db['a_list'])  # [11, 13, 17, 19]
```

By opening the shelf with `writeback=True`, we enable the `writeback` feature, which allows us to simply append to `a_list` as if it actually was a value within a regular dictionary. The reason why this feature is not active by default is that it comes with a price that you pay in terms of memory consumption and slower closing of the shelf.

Now that we have paid homage to the standard library modules related to data persistence, let's take a look at the most widely adopted ORM in the Python ecosystem: *SQLAlchemy*.

# Saving data to a database

For this example, we are going to work with an in-memory database, which will make things simpler for us. In the source code of the book, I have left a couple of comments to show you how to generate a SQLite file, so I hope you'll explore that option as well.

 You can find a free database browser for SQLite at `sqlitebrowser.org`. If you are not satisfied with it, you will be able to find a wide range of tools, some free, some not free, that you can use to access and manipulate a database file.

Before we dive into the code, allow me to briefly introduce the concept of a relational database.

A relational database is a database that allows you to save data following the **relational model**, invented in 1969 by Edgar F. Codd. In this model, data is stored in one or more tables. Each table has rows (also known as **records**, or **tuples**), each of which represents an entry in the table. Tables also have columns (also known as **attributes**), each of which represents an attribute of the records. Each record is identified through a unique key, more commonly known as the **primary key**, which is the union of one or more columns in the table. To give you an example: imagine a table called `Users`, with columns `id`, `username`, `password`, `name`, and `surname`. Such a table would be perfect to contain users of our system. Each row would represent a different user. For example, a row with the values `3`, `gianchub`, `my_wonderful_pwd`, `Fabrizio`, and `Romano`, would represent my user in the system.

The reason why the model is called **relational** is because you can establish relations between tables. For example, if you added a table called `PhoneNumbers` to our fictitious database, you could insert phone numbers into it, and then, through a relation, establish which phone number belongs to which user.

In order to query a relational database, we need a special language. The main standard is called **SQL**, which stands for **Structured Query Language**. It is born out of something called **relational algebra**, which is a very nice family of algebras used to model data stored according to the relational model, and performing queries on it. The most common operations you can perform usually involve filtering on the rows or columns, joining tables, aggregating the results according to some criteria, and so on. To give you an example in English, a query on our imaginary database could be: *Fetch all users (username, name, surname) whose username starts with "m", who have at most one phone number*. In this query, we are asking for a subset of the columns in the User table. We are filtering on users by taking only those whose username starts with the letter *m*, and even further, only those who have at most one phone number.

 Back in the days when I was a student in Padova, I spent a whole semester learning both the relational algebra semantics, and the standard SQL (amongst other things). If it wasn't for a major bicycle accident I had the day of the exam, I would say that this was one of the most fun exams I ever had to prepare.

Now, each database comes with its own *flavor* of SQL. They all respect the standard to some extent, but none fully does, and they are all different from one another in some respects. This poses an issue in modern software development. If our application contains SQL code, it is quite likely that if we decided to use a different database engine, or maybe a different version of the same engine, we would find our SQL code needs amending.

This can be quite painful, especially since SQL queries can become very, very complicated quite quickly. In order to alleviate this pain a little, computer scientists (*bless them*) have created code that maps objects of a particular language to tables of a relational database. Unsurprisingly, the name of such tools is **Object-Relational Mapping (ORMs)**.

In modern application development, you would normally start interacting with a database by using an ORM, and should you find yourself in a situation where you can't perform a query you need to perform, through the ORM, you would then resort to using SQL directly. This is a good compromise between having no SQL at all, and using no ORM, which ultimately means specializing the code that interacts with the database, with the aforementioned disadvantages.

In this section, I'd like to show an example that leverages SQLAlchemy, the most popular Python ORM. We are going to define two models (Person and Address) which map to a table each, and then we're going to populate the database and perform a few queries on it.

Let's start with the model declarations:

```
# persistence/alchemy_models.py
from sqlalchemy.ext.declarative import declarative_base
from sqlalchemy import (
    Column, Integer, String, ForeignKey, create_engine)
from sqlalchemy.orm import relationship
```

At the beginning, we import some functions and types. The first thing we need to do then is to create an engine. This engine tells SQLAlchemy about the type of database we have chosen for our example:

```
# persistence/alchemy_models.py
engine = create_engine('sqlite:///:memory:')
Base = declarative_base()

class Person(Base):
    __tablename__ = 'person'

    id = Column(Integer, primary_key=True)
    name = Column(String)
    age = Column(Integer)

    addresses = relationship(
        'Address',
        back_populates='person',
        order_by='Address.email',
        cascade='all, delete-orphan'
    )

    def __repr__(self):
        return f'{self.name}(id={self.id})'

class Address(Base):
    __tablename__ = 'address'

    id = Column(Integer, primary_key=True)
    email = Column(String)
    person_id = Column(ForeignKey('person.id'))
    person = relationship('Person', back_populates='addresses')

    def __str__(self):
```

```
        return self.email
    __repr__ = __str__

Base.metadata.create_all(engine)
```

Each model then inherits from the `Base` table, which in this example consists of the mere default, returned by `declarative_base()`. We define `Person`, which maps to a table called `person`, and exposes the attributes `id`, `name`, and `age`. We also declare a relationship with the `Address` model, by stating that accessing the `addresses` attribute will fetch all the entries in the `address` table that are related to the particular `Person` instance we're dealing with. The `cascade` option affects how creation and deletion work, but it is a more advanced concept, so I'd suggest you glide on it for now and maybe investigate more later on.

The last thing we declare is the `__repr__` method, which provides us with the official string representation of an object. This is supposed to be a representation that can be used to completely reconstruct the object, but in this example, I simply use it to provide something in output. Python redirects `repr(obj)` to a call to `obj.__repr__()`.

We also declare the `Address` model, which will contain email addresses, and a reference to the person they belong to. You can see the `person_id` and `person` attributes are both about setting a relation between the `Address` and `Person` instances. Note how I declared the `__str__` method on `Address`, and then assigned an alias to it, called `__repr__`. This means that calling both `repr` and `str` on `Address` objects will ultimately result in calling the `__str__` method. This is quite a common technique in Python, so I took the opportunity to show it to you here.

On the last line, we tell the engine to create tables in the database according to our models.

A deeper understanding of this code would require much more space than I can afford, so I encourage you to read up on **database management systems (DBMS)**, SQL, Relational Algebra, and SQLAlchemy.

Now that we have our models, let's use them to persist some data!

Let's take a look at the following example:

```python
# persistence/alchemy.py
from alchemy_models import Person, Address, engine
from sqlalchemy.orm import sessionmaker

Session = sessionmaker(bind=engine)
session = Session()
```

First we create `session`, which is the object we use to manage the database. Next, we proceed by creating two people:

```python
anakin = Person(name='Anakin Skywalker', age=32)
obi1 = Person(name='Obi-Wan Kenobi', age=40)
```

We then add email addresses to both of them, using two different techniques. One assigns them to a list, and the other one simply appends them:

```python
obi1.addresses = [
    Address(email='obi1@example.com'),
    Address(email='wanwan@example.com'),
]

anakin.addresses.append(Address(email='ani@example.com'))
anakin.addresses.append(Address(email='evil.dart@example.com'))
anakin.addresses.append(Address(email='vader@example.com'))
```

We haven't touched the database yet. It's only when we use the session object that something actually happens in it:

```python
session.add(anakin)
session.add(obi1)
session.commit()
```

Adding the two `Person` instances is enough to also add their addresses (this is thanks to the cascading effect). Calling `commit` is what actually tells SQLAlchemy to commit the transaction and save the data in the database. A transaction is an operation that provides something like a sandbox, but in a database context. As long as the transaction hasn't been committed, we can roll back any modification we have done to the database, and by so doing, revert to the state we were before starting the transaction itself. SQLAlchemy offers more complex and granular ways to deal with transactions, which you can study in its official documentation, as it is quite an advanced topic.

We now query for all the people whose name starts with Obi by using like, which hooks to the LIKE operator in SQL:

```
obi1 = session.query(Person).filter(
    Person.name.like('Obi%')
).first()
print(obi1, obi1.addresses)
```

We take the first result of that query (we know we only have Obi-Wan anyway), and print it. We then fetch anakin, by using an exact match on his name (just to show you a different way of filtering):

```
anakin = session.query(Person).filter(
    Person.name=='Anakin Skywalker'
).first()
print(anakin, anakin.addresses)
```

We then capture Anakin's ID, and delete the anakin object from the global frame:

```
anakin_id = anakin.id
del anakin
```

The reason we do this is because I want to show you how to fetch an object by its ID. Before we do that, we write the display_info function, which we will use to display the full content of the database (fetched starting from the addresses, in order to demonstrate how to fetch objects by using a relation attribute in SQLAlchemy):

```
def display_info():
    # get all addresses first
    addresses = session.query(Address).all()

    # display results
    for address in addresses:
        print(f'{address.person.name} <{address.email}>')

    # display how many objects we have in total
    print('people: {}, addresses: {}'.format(
        session.query(Person).count(),
        session.query(Address).count())
    )
```

The `display_info` function prints all the addresses, along with the respective person's name, and, at the end, produces a final piece of information regarding the number of objects in the database. We call the function, then we fetch and delete `anakin` (think about *Darth Vader* and you won't be sad about deleting him), and then we display the info again, to verify he's actually disappeared from the database:

```
display_info()

anakin = session.query(Person).get(anakin_id)
session.delete(anakin)
session.commit()

display_info()
```

The output of all these snippets run together is the following (for your convenience, I have separated the output into four blocks, to reflect the four blocks of code that actually produce that output):

```
$ python alchemy.py
Obi-Wan Kenobi(id=2) [obi1@example.com, wanwan@example.com]

Anakin Skywalker(id=1) [ani@example.com, evil.dart@example.com,
vader@example.com]

Anakin Skywalker <ani@example.com>
Anakin Skywalker <evil.dart@example.com>
Anakin Skywalker <vader@example.com>
Obi-Wan Kenobi <obi1@example.com>
Obi-Wan Kenobi <wanwan@example.com>
people: 2, addresses: 5

Obi-Wan Kenobi <obi1@example.com>
Obi-Wan Kenobi <wanwan@example.com>
people: 1, addresses: 2
```

As you can see from the last two blocks, deleting `anakin` has deleted one `Person` object, and the three addresses associated with it. Again, this is due to the fact that cascading took place when we deleted `anakin`.

This concludes our brief introduction to data persistence. It is a vast and, at times, complex domain, which I encourage you to explore learning as much theory as possible. Lack of knowledge or proper understanding, when it comes to database systems, can really bite.

# Summary

In this chapter, we have explored working with files and directories. We have learned how to open files for reading and writing and how to do that more elegantly by using context managers. We also explored directories: how to list their content, both recursively and not. We also learned about pathnames, which are the gateway to accessing both files and directories.

We then briefly saw how to create a ZIP archive, and extract its content. The source code of the book also contains an example with a different compression format: `tar.gz`.

We talked about data interchange formats, and have explored JSON in some depth. We had some fun writing custom encoders and decoders for specific Python data types.

Then we explored IO, both with in-memory streams and HTTP requests.

And finally, we saw how to persist data using `pickle`, `shelve`, and the SQLAlchemy ORM library.

You should now have a pretty good idea of how to deal with files and data persistence, and I hope you will take the time to explore these topics in much more depth by yourself.

From the next chapter, we will begin our journey into data structures and algorithms, beginning with the principles of algorithm design.

# 6
# Principles of Algorithm Design

Why do we want to study algorithm design? There are of course many reasons, and our motivation for learning something is very much dependent on our own circumstances. There are without doubt important professional reasons for being interested in algorithm design. Algorithms are the foundations of all computing. We think of a computer as being a piece of hardware, a hard drive, memory chips, processors, and so on. However, the essential component, the thing that, if missing, would render modern technology impossible, is algorithms.

The theoretical foundation of algorithms, in the form of the Turing machine, was established several decades before digital logic circuits could actually implement such a machine. The Turing machine is essentially a mathematical model that, using a predefined set of rules, translates a set of inputs into a set of outputs. The first implementations of Turing machines were mechanical and the next generation may likely see digital logic circuits replaced by quantum circuits or something similar. Regardless of the platform, algorithms play a central predominant role.

Another aspect is the effect algorithms have in technological innovation. As an obvious example, consider the page rank search algorithm, a variation of which the Google search engine is based on. Using this and similar algorithms allows researchers, scientists, technicians, and others to quickly search through vast amounts of information extremely quickly. This has a massive effect on the rate at which new research can be carried out, new discoveries made, and new innovative technologies developed.

The study of algorithms is also important because it trains us to think very specifically about certain problems. It can serve to increase our mental and problem solving abilities by helping us isolate the components of a problem and define relationships between these components. In summary, there are four broad reasons for studying algorithms:

1. They are essential for computer science and *intelligent* systems.
2. They are important in many other domains (computational biology, economics, ecology, communications, ecology, physics, and so on).
3. They play a role in technology innovation.
4. They improve problem solving and analytical thinking.

Algorithms, in their simplest form, are just a sequence of actions, a list of instructions. It may just be a linear construct of the form do $x$, then do $y$, then do $z$, then finish. However, to make things more useful we add clauses to the effect of, $x$ then do $y$, in Python the `if-else` statements. Here, the future course of action is dependent on some conditions; say the state of a data structure. To this we also add the operation, iteration, the while, and for statements. Expanding our algorithmic literacy further we add recursion. Recursion can often achieve the same result as iteration, however, they are fundamentally different. A recursive function calls itself, applying the same function to progressively smaller inputs. The input of any recursive step is the output of the previous recursive step.

Essentially, we can say that algorithms are composed of the following four elements:

- Sequential operations
- Actions based on the state of a data structure
- Iteration, repeating an action a number of times
- Recursion, calling itself on a subset of inputs

# Algorithm design paradigms

In general, we can discern three broad approaches to algorithm design. They are:

- Divide and conquer
- Greedy algorithms
- Dynamic programming

As the name suggests, the divide and conquer paradigm involves breaking a problem into smaller sub problems, and then in some way combining the results to obtain a global solution. This is a very common and natural problem solving technique, and is, arguably, the most commonly used approach to algorithm design.

Greedy algorithms often involve optimization and combinatorial problems; the classic example is applying it to the traveling salesperson problem, where a greedy approach always chooses the closest destination first. This shortest path strategy involves finding the best solution to a local problem in the hope that this will lead to a global solution.

The dynamic programming approach is useful when our sub problems overlap. This is different from divide and conquer. Rather than break our problem into independent sub problems, with dynamic programming, intermediate results are cached and can be used in subsequent operations. Like divide and conquer it uses recursion; however, dynamic programming allows us to compare results at different stages. This can have a performance advantage over divide and conquer for some problems because it is often quicker to retrieve a previously calculated result from memory rather than having to recalculate it.

# Recursion and backtracking

Recursion is particularly useful for divide and conquer problems; however, it can be difficult to understand exactly what is happening, since each recursive call is itself spinning off other recursive calls. At the core of a recursive function are two types of cases: base cases, which tell the recursion when to terminate, and recursive cases that call the function they are in. A simple problem that naturally lends itself to a recursive solution is calculating factorials. The recursive factorial algorithm defines two cases: the base case when *n* is zero, and the recursive case when *n* is greater than zero. A typical implementation is the following:

```
def factorial(n):
    #test for a base case
    if n==0:
        return 1
        # make a calculation and a recursive call
        f= n*factorial(n-1)
    print(f)
    return(f)
    factorial(4)
```

This code prints out the digits 1, 2, 4, 24. To calculate 4 requires four recursive calls plus the initial parent call. On each recursion, a copy of the methods variables is stored in memory. Once the method returns it is removed from memory. The following is a way we can visualize this process:

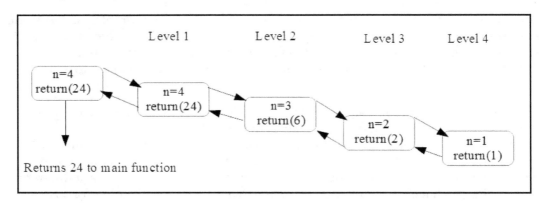

It may not necessarily be clear if recursion or iteration is a better solution to a particular problem; after all they both repeat a series of operations and both are very well suited to divide and conquer approaches to algorithm design. Iteration churns away until the problem is done. Recursion breaks the problem down into smaller and smaller chunks and then combines the results. Iteration is often easier for programmers, because control stays local to a loop, whereas recursion can more closely represent mathematical concepts such as factorials. Recursive calls are stored in memory, whereas iterations are not. This creates a trade off between processor cycles and memory usage, so choosing which one to use may depend on whether the task is processor or memory intensive. The following table outlines the key differences between recursion and iteration:

| Recursion | Iteration |
|---|---|
| Terminates when a base case is reached | Terminates when a defined condition is met |
| Each recursive call requires space in memory | Each iteration is not stored in memory |
| An infinite recursion results in a stack overflow error | An infinite iteration will run while the hardware is powered |
| Some problems are naturally better suited to recursive solutions | Iterative solutions may not always be obvious |

# Backtracking

Backtracking is a form of recursion that is particularly useful for types of problems such as traversing tree structures, where we are presented with a number of options at each node, from which we must choose one. Subsequently we are presented with a different set of options, and depending on the series of choices made either a goal state or a dead end is reached. If it is the latter, we must backtrack to a previous node and traverse a different branch. Backtracking is a divide and conquer method for exhaustive search. Importantly backtracking **prunes** branches that cannot give a result.

An example of back tracking is given in the following example. Here, we have used a recursive approach to generating all the possible permutations of a given string, *s*, of a given length *n*:

```
def bitStr(n, s):

    if n == 1: return s
    return [ digit + bits for digit in bitStr(1,s)for bits in
bitStr(n - 1,s)]

    print (bitStr(3,'abc'))
```

This generates the following output:

```
['aaa', 'aab', 'aac', 'aba', 'abb', 'abc', 'aca', 'acb', 'acc', 'baa', 'bab', 'bac', 'bba',
'bbb', 'bbc', 'bca', 'bcb', 'bcc', 'caa', 'cab', 'cac', 'cba', 'cbb', 'cbc', 'cca', 'ccb', 'ccc']
```

Notice the double list compression and the two recursive calls within this comprehension. This recursively concatenates each element of the initial sequence, returned when *n* = 1, with each element of the string generated in the previous recursive call. In this sense it is *backtracking* to uncover previously ingenerated combinations. The final string that is returned is all *n* letter combinations of the initial string.

# Divide and conquer - long multiplication

For recursion to be more than just a clever trick, we need to understand how to compare it to other approaches, such as iteration, and to understand when its use will lead to a faster algorithm. An iterative algorithm that we are all familiar with is the procedure we learned in primary math classes, used to multiply two large numbers. That is, long multiplication. If you remember, long multiplication involved iterative multiplying and carry operations followed by a shifting and addition operation.

Our aim here is to examine ways to measure how efficient this procedure is and attempt to answer the question; is this the most efficient procedure we can use for multiplying two large numbers together?

In the following figure, we can see that multiplying two 4 digit numbers together requires 16 multiplication operations, and we can generalize to say that an $n$ digit number requires, approximately, $n^2$ multiplication operations:

```
              1   2   3   4
              3   4   5   6   x
         ─────────────────────
              7   4   0   4
          6   1   7   0   0
      4   9   3   6   0   0      ≈ n²operations
    3 7   0   2   0   0   0
    4 2   6   4   7   0   4
```

$\approx n^2 operations$

This method of analyzing algorithms, in terms of the number of computational primitives such as multiplication and addition, is important because it gives us a way to understand the relationship between the time it takes to complete a certain computation and the size of the input to that computation. In particular, we want to know what happens when the input, the number of digits, n, is very large. This topic, called asymptotic analysis, or time complexity, is essential to our study of algorithms and we will revisit it often during this chapter and the rest of this book.

# Can we do better? A recursive approach

It turns out that in the case of long multiplication the answer is yes, there are in fact several algorithms for multiplying large numbers that require less operations. One of the most well-known alternatives to long multiplication is the **Karatsuba algorithm**, first published in 1962. This takes a fundamentally different approach: rather than iteratively multiplying single digit numbers, it recursively carries out multiplication operations on progressively smaller inputs. Recursive programs call themselves on smaller subsets of the input. The first step in building a recursive algorithm is to decompose a large number into several smaller numbers. The most natural way to do this is to simply split the number in to two halves, the first half of most significant digits, and a second half of least significant digits. For example, our four-digit number, 2345, becomes a pair of two-digit numbers, 23 and 45. We can write a more general decomposition of any $2n$ digit numbers, $x$ and $y$ using the following, where $m$ is any positive integer less than $n$:

$$x = 10^m a + b$$

$$y = 10^m c + d$$

So now we can rewrite our multiplication problem $x, y$ as follows:

$$(10^m a + b)(10^m c + d)$$

When we expand and gather like terms we get the following:

$$10^m ac + 10^{2m}(ad + bc) + bd$$

More conveniently, we can write it like this:

$$10^{2m} z_2 + 10^m z_1 + z_0$$

Where:

$$z_2 = ac \quad ; \quad z_1 = ad + bc \quad ; \quad z_0 = bd$$

It should be pointed out that this suggests a recursive approach to multiplying two numbers since this procedure does itself involve multiplication. Specifically, the products *ac, ad, bc,* and *bd* all involve numbers smaller than the input number and so it is conceivable that we could apply the same operation as a partial solution to the overall problem. This algorithm, so far, consists of four recursive multiplication steps and it is not immediately clear if it will be faster than the classic long multiplication approach.

What we have discussed so far in regards to the recursive approach to multiplication, has been well known to mathematicians since the late 19th century. The Karatsuba algorithm improves on this is by making the following observation. We really only need to know three quantities: $z_2 = ac$ ; $z_1 = ad + bc$, and $z_0 = bd$ to solve equation 3.1. We need to know the values of *a, b, c, d* only in so far as they contribute to the overall sum and products involved in calculating the quantities $z_2$, $z_1$, and $z_0$. This suggests the possibility that perhaps we can reduce the number of recursive steps. It turns out that this is indeed the situation.

Since the products *ac* and *bd* are already in their simplest form, it seems unlikely that we can eliminate these calculations. We can however make the following observation:

$$(a + b)(c + d) = ac + bd + ad + bc$$

When we subtract the quantities *ac* and *bd*, which we have calculated in the previous recursive step, we get the quantity we need, namely (*ad* + *bc*):

$$ac + bd + ad + bc - ac - bd = ad + bc$$

This shows that we can indeed compute the sum of *ad* + *bc* without separately computing each of the individual quantities. In summary, we can improve on equation 3.1 by reducing from four recursive steps to three. These three steps are as follows:

1. Recursively calculate *ac*.
2. Recursively calculate *bd*.
3. Recursively calculate (*a* + *b*)(*c* + *d*) and subtract *ac* and *bd*.

The following example shows a Python implementation of the Karatsuba algorithm:

```
from math import log10
def karatsuba(x,y):

    # The base case for recursion
    if x < 10 or y < 10:
        return x*y

    #sets n, the number of digits in the highest input number
    n = max(int(log10(x)+1), int(log10(y)+1))

    # rounds up n/2
    n_2 = int(math.ceil(n / 2.0))
    #adds 1 if n is uneven
    n = n if n % 2 == 0 else n + 1

    #splits the input numbers
    a, b = divmod(x, 10**n_2)
    c, d = divmod(y, 10**n_2)

    #applies the three recursive steps
    ac = karatsuba(a,c)
    bd = karatsuba(b,d)
    ad_bc = karatsuba((a+b),(c+d)) - ac - bd

    #performs the multiplication
    return (((10**n)*ac) + bd + ((10**n_2)*(ad_bc)))
```

To satisfy ourselves that this does indeed work, we can run the following test function:

```
import random
def test():
        for i in range(1000):
            x = random.randint(1,10**5)
            y = random.randint(1,10**5)
            expected = x * y
            result = karatsuba(x, y)
            if result != expected:
                return("failed")
        return('ok')
```

# Runtime analysis

It should be becoming clear that an important aspect to algorithm design is gauging the efficiency both in terms of space (memory) and time (number of operations). This second measure, called runtime performance, is the subject of this section. It should be mentioned that an identical metric is used to measure an algorithm's memory performance. There are a number of ways we could, conceivably, measure run time and probably the most obvious is simply to measure the time the algorithm takes to complete. The major problem with this approach is that the time it takes for an algorithm to run is very much dependent on the hardware it is run on. A platform-independent way to gauge an algorithm's runtime is to count the number of operations involved. However, this is also problematic in that there is no definitive way to quantify an operation. This is dependent on the programming language, the coding style, and how we decide to count operations. We can use this idea, though, of counting operations, if we combine it with the expectation that as the size of the input increases the runtime will increase in a specific way. That is, there is a mathematical relationship between $n$, the size of the input, and the time it takes for the algorithm to run.

Much of the discussion that follows will be framed by the following three guiding principles. The rational and importance of these principles should become clearer as we proceed. These principles are as follows:

- Worst case analysis. Make no assumptions on the input data.
- Ignore or suppress constant factors and lower order terms. At large inputs higher order terms dominate.
- Focus on problems with large input sizes.

Worst case analysis is useful because it gives us a tight upper bound that our algorithm is guaranteed not to exceed. Ignoring small constant factors, and lower order terms is really just about ignoring the things that, at large values of the input size, $n$, do not contribute, in a large degree, to the overall run time. Not only does it make our work mathematically easier, it also allows us to focus on the things that are having the most impact on performance.

We saw with the Karatsuba algorithm that the number of multiplication operations increased to the square of the size, $n$, of the input. If we have a four-digit number the number of multiplication operations is 16; an eight-digit number requires 64 operations. Typically, though, we are not really interested in the behavior of an algorithm at small values of $n$, so we most often ignore factors that increase at slower rates, say linearly with $n$. This is because at high values of $n$, the operations that increase the fastest as we increase $n$, will dominate.

We will explain this in more detail with an example, the merge sort algorithm. Sorting is the subject of Chapter 13, *Sorting*, however, as a precursor and as a useful way to learn about runtime performance, we will introduce merge sort here.

The merge sort algorithm is a classic algorithm developed over 60 years ago. It is still used widely in many of the most popular sorting libraries. It is relatively simple and efficient. It is a recursive algorithm that uses a divide and conquer approach. This involves breaking the problem into smaller sub problems, recursively solving them, and then somehow combining the results. Merge sort is one of the most obvious demonstrations of the divide and conquer paradigm.

The merge sort algorithm consists of three simple steps:

1. Recursively sort the left half of the input array.
2. Recursively sort the right half of the input array.
3. Merge two sorted sub arrays into one.

A typical problem is sorting a list of numbers into a numerical order. Merge sort works by splitting the input into two halves and working on each half in parallel. We can illustrate this process schematically with the following diagram:

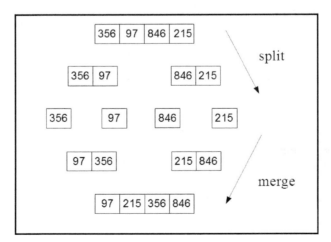

Here is the Python code for the merge sort algorithm:

```python
def mergeSort(A):
    #base case if the input array is one or zero just return.
    if len(A) > 1:
        # splitting input array
        print('splitting ', A )
        mid = len(A)//2
        left = A[:mid]
        right = A[mid:]
        #recursive calls to mergeSort for left and right sub
arrays
        mergeSort(left)
        mergeSort(right)
        #initalizes pointers for left (i) right (j) and output
array (k)
    # 3 initalization operations
        i = j = k = 0
        #Traverse and merges the sorted arrays
        while i <len(left) and j<len(right):
    # if left < right comparison operation
            if left[i] < right[j]:
    # if left < right Assignment operation
                A[k]=left[i]
                i=i+1
            else:
    #if right <= left assignment
                A[k]= right[j]
                j=j+1
            k=k+1

        while i<len(left):
    #Assignment operation
            A[k]=left[i]
            i=i+1
            k=k+1

        while j<len(right):
    #Assignment operation
            A[k]=right[j]
            j=j+1
            k=k+1
    print('merging ', A)
    return(A)
```

We run this program for the following results:

```
In [2]: mergeSort([356,97,846,215])
splitting  [356, 97, 846, 215]
splitting  [356, 97]
merging  [356]
merging  [97]
merging  [97, 356]
splitting  [846, 215]
merging  [846]
merging  [215]
merging  [215, 846]
merging  [97, 215, 356, 846]
Out[2]: [97, 215, 356, 846]
```

The problem that we are interested in is how we determine the running time performance, that is, what is the rate of growth in the time it takes for the algorithm to complete relative to the size of *n*. To understand this a bit better, we can map each recursive call onto a tree structure.

Each node in the tree is a recursive call working on progressively smaller sub problems:

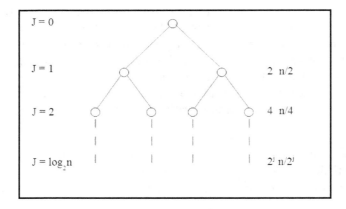

Each invocation of merge-sort subsequently creates two recursive calls, so we can represent this with a binary tree. Each of the child nodes receives a sub set of the input. Ultimately we want to know the total time it takes for the algorithm to complete relative to the size of *n*. To begin with we can calculate the amount of work and the number of operations at each level of the tree.

Focusing on the runtime analysis, at level 1, the problem is split into two $n/2$ sub problems, at level 2 there is four $n/4$ sub problems, and so on. The question is when does the recursion bottom out, that is, when does it reach its base case. This is simply when the array is either zero or one.

The number of recursive levels is exactly the number of times you need to divide $n$ by 2 until you get a number that is at most 1. This is precisely the definition of log2. Since we are counting the initial recursive call as level 0, the total number of levels is $\log_2 n + 1$.

Let's just pause to refine our definitions. So far we have been describing the number of elements in our input by the letter $n$. This refers to the number of elements in the first level of the recursion, that is, the length of the initial input. We are going to need to differentiate between the size of the input at subsequent recursive levels. For this we will use the letter $m$ or specifically $m_j$ for the length of the input at recursive level $j$.

Also there are a few details we have overlooked, and I am sure you are beginning to wonder about. For example, what happens when $m/2$ is not an integer, or when we have duplicates in our input array. It turns out that this does not have an important impact on our analysis here.

The advantage of using a recursion tree to analyze algorithms is that we can calculate the work done at each level of the recursion. How to define this work is simply as the total number of operations and this of course is related to the size of the input. It is important to measure and compare the performance of algorithms in a platform independent way. The actual run time will of course be dependent on the hardware on which it is run. Counting the number of operations is important because it gives us a metric that is directly related to an algorithm's performance, independent of the platform.

In general, since each invocation of merge sort is making two recursive calls, the number of calls is doubling at each level. At the same time each of these calls is working on an input that is half of its parents. We can formalize this and say that:

 For level j , where $j$ is an integer 0, 1, 2 ... $\log_2 n$, there are two $^j$ sub problems each of size $n/2^j$.

To calculate the total number of operations, we need to know the number of operations encompassed by a single merge of two sub arrays. Let's count the number of operations in the previous Python code. What we are interested in is all the code after the two recursive calls have been made. Firstly, we have the three assignment operations. This is followed by three while loops. In the first loop we have an if else statement and within each of are two operations, a comparison followed by an assignment. Since there are only one of these sets of operations within the if else statements, we can count this block of code as two operations carried out $m$ times. This is followed by two while loops with an assignment operation each. This makes a total of $4m + 3$ operations for each recursion of merge sort.

Since $m$ must be at least 1, the upper bound for the number of operations is $7m$. It has to be said that this has no pretense at being an exact number. We could of course decide to count operations in a different way. We have not counted the increment operations or any of the housekeeping operations; however, this is not so important as we are more concerned with the rate of growth of the runtime with respect to $n$ at high values of $n$.

This may seem a little daunting since each call of a recursive call itself spins off more recursive calls, and seemingly explodes exponentially. The key fact that makes this manageable is that as the number of recursive calls doubles, the size of each sub problem halves. These two opposing forces cancel out nicely as we can demonstrate.

To calculate the maximum number of operations at each level of the recursion tree we simply multiply the number of sub problems by the number of operations in each sub problem as follows:

$$2^j \times 7(n/2^j) = 7n$$

Importantly this shows that, because the $2^j$ cancels out the number of operations at each level is independent of the level. This gives us an upper bound to the number of operations carried out on each level, in this example, $7n$. It should be pointed out that this includes the number of operations performed by each recursive call on that level, not the recursive calls made on subsequent levels. This shows that the work done, as the number of recursive calls doubles with each level, is exactly counter balanced by the fact that the input size for each sub problem is halved.

To find the total number of operations for a complete merge sort we simply multiply the number of operations on each level by the number of levels. This gives us the following:

$$7\,n(\log_2 n + 1)$$

When we expand this out, we get the following:

$$7\,n\log_2 n + 7$$

The key point to take from this is that there is a logarithmic component to the relationship between the size of the input and the total running time. If you remember from school mathematics, the distinguishing characteristic of the logarithm function is that it flattens off very quickly. As an input variable, $x$, increases in size, the output variable, $y$ increases by smaller and smaller amounts. For example, compare the log function to a linear function:

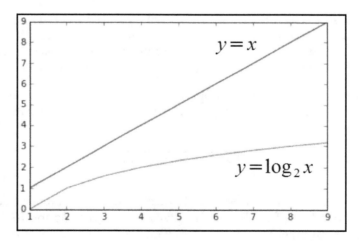

In the previous example, multiplying the $n\log_2 n$ component and comparing it to $n^2$.

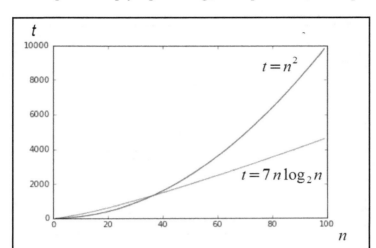

Notice how for very low values of $n$, the time to complete, $t$, is actually lower for an algorithm that runs in $n^2$ time. However, for values above about 40, the log function begins to dominate, flattening the output until at the comparatively moderate size $n$ = 100, the performance is more than twice than that of an algorithm running in $n^2$ time. Notice also that the disappearance of the constant factor, + 7 is irrelevant at high values of $n$.

The code used to generate these graphs is as follows:

```
import matplotlib.pyplot as plt
import math
x=list(range(1,100))
l =[]; l2=[]; a = 1
plt.plot(x , [y * y for y in x] )
plt.plot(x, [(7 *y )* math.log(y, 2) for y in x])
plt.show()
```

You will need to install the matplotlib library, if it is not installed already, for this to work. Details can be found at the following address; I encourage you to experiment with this list comprehension expression used to generate the plots. For example, adding the following plot statement:

```
plt.plot(x, [(6 *y )* math.log(y, 2) for y in x])
```

Gives the following output:

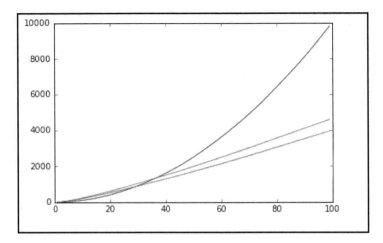

The preceding graph shows the difference between counting six operations or seven operations. We can see how the two cases diverge, and this is important when we are talking about the specifics of an application. However, what we are more interested in here is a way to characterize growth rates. We are not so much concerned with the absolute values, but how these values change as we increase $n$. In this way we can see that the two lower curves have similar growth rates, when compared to the top ($x^2$) curve. We say that these two lower curves have the same **complexity class**. This is a way to understand and describe different runtime behaviors. We will formalize this performance metric in the next section.

# Asymptotic analysis

There are essentially three things that characterize an algorithm's runtime performance. They are:

- Worst case - Use an input that gives the slowest performance
- Best case - Use an input that give, the best results
- Average case - Assumes the input is random

To calculate each of these, we need to know the upper and lower bounds. We have seen a way to represent an algorithm's runtime using mathematical expressions, essentially adding and multiplying operations. To use asymptotic analyses, we simply create two expressions, one each for the best and worst cases.

# Big O notation

The letter "O" in big $O$ notation stands for order, in recognition that rates of growth are defined as the order of a function. We say that one function $T(n)$ is a big O of another function, $F(n)$, and we define this as follows:

$$T(n) = O(F(n)) \text{ iff there exists constants, } n_0 \text{ and } C \text{ such that:}$$
$$T(n) \leq C(F(n)) \text{ for all } n \geq n_0$$

The function, $g(n)$, of the input size, $n$, is based on the observation that for all sufficiently large values of $n$, $g(n)$ is bounded above by a constant multiple of $f(n)$. The objective is to find the smallest rate of growth that is less than or equal to $f(n)$. We only care what happens at higher values of $n$. The variable $n_0$ represents the threshold below which the rate of growth is not important, The function T(n) represents the **tight upper bound** F(n). In the following plot we see that $T(n) = n^2 + 500 = O(n^2)$ with $C = 2$ and $n_0$ is approximately 23:

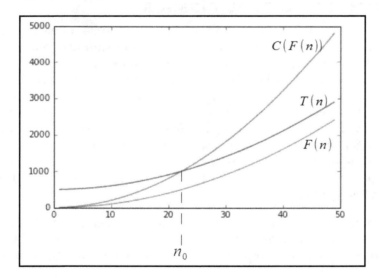

You will also see the notation $f(n) = O(g(n))$. This describes the fact that $O(g(n))$ is really a set of functions that include all functions with the same or smaller rates of growth than $f$(n). For example, $O(n^2)$ also includes the functions $O(n)$, $O(n\log n)$, and so on.

In the following table, we list the most common growth rates in order from lowest to highest. We sometimes call these growth rates the **time complexity** of a function, or the complexity class of a function:

| Complexity Class | Name | Example operations |
|---|---|---|
| $O(1)$ | Constant | append, get item, set item. |
| $O(\log n)$ | Logarithmic | Finding an element in a sorted array. |
| $O(n)$ | Linear | copy, insert, delete, iteration. |
| $n \log n$ | Linear-Logarithmic | Sort a list, merge - sort. |
| $n^2$ | Quadratic | Find the shortest path between two nodes in a graph. Nested loops. |
| $n^3$ | Cubic | Matrix multiplication. |
| $2^n$ | Exponential | 'Towers of Hanoi' problem, backtracking. |

# Composing complexity classes

Normally, we need to find the total running time of a number of basic operations. It turns out that we can combine the complexity classes of simple operations to find the complexity class of more complex, combined operations. The goal is to analyze the combined statements in a function or method to understand the total time complexity of executing several operations. The simplest way to combine two complexity classes is to add them. This occurs when we have two sequential operations. For example, consider the two operations of inserting an element into a list and then sorting that list. We can see that inserting an item occurs in $O(n)$ time and sorting is $O(n\log n)$ time. We can write the total time complexity as $O(n + n\log n)$, that is, we bring the two functions inside the $O(...)$. We are only interested in the highest order term, so this leaves us with just $O(n\log n)$.

If we repeat an operation, for example, in a while loop, then we multiply the complexity class by the number of times the operation is carried out. If an operation with time complexity $O(f(n))$ is repeated $O(n)$ times then we multiply the two complexities:

$O(f(n) * O(n)) = O(nf(n))$.

For example, suppose the function f(...) has a time complexity of $O(n^2)$ and it is executed $n$ times in a while loop as follows:

```
for i n range(n):
    f(...)
```

The time complexity of this loop then becomes $O(n^2) * O(n) = O(n * n^2) = O(n^3)$. Here we are simply multiplying the time complexity of the operation with the number of times this operation executes. The running time of a loop is at most the running time of the statements inside the loop multiplied by the number of iterations. A single nested loop, that is, one loop nested inside another loop, will run in $n^2$ time assuming both loops run $n$ times. For example:

```
for i in range(0,n):
    for j in range(0,n)
        #statements
```

Each statement is a constant, c, executed $nn$ times, so we can express the running time as ; $cn\ n = cn^2 = O(n2)$.

For consecutive statements within nested loops we add the time complexities of each statement and multiply by the number of times the statement executed. For example:

```
n = 500      #c0
#executes n times
for i in range(0,n):
    print(i)     #c1
#executes n times
for i in range(0,n):
    #executes n times
    for j in range(0,n):
    print(j)    #c2
```

This can be written as $c_0 + c_1 n + cn^2 = O(n^2)$.

We can define (base 2) logarithmic complexity, reducing the size of the problem by ½, in constant time. For example, consider the following snippet:

```
i = 1
while i <= n:
    i=i * 2
    print(i)
```

Notice that i is doubling on each iteration, if we run this with $n = 10$ we see that it prints out four numbers; 2, 4, 8, and 16. If we double $n$ we see it prints out five numbers. With each subsequent doubling of n the number of iterations is only increased by 1. If we assume $k$ iterations, we can write this as follows:

$$\log_2(2^k) = \log_2 n$$
$$k\log_2 = \log_2 n$$
$$k = \log n$$

From this we can conclude that the total time = $\mathbf{O}(log(n))$.

Although Big O is the most used notation involved in asymptotic analysis, there are two other related notations that should be briefly mentioned. They are Omega notation and Theta notation.

## Omega notation ($\Omega$)

In a similar way that Big O notation describes the upper bound, Omega notation describes a **tight lower bound**. The definition is as follows:

$$T(n) = \Omega(F(n)) \text{ iff there exists positive constants, } n_0 \text{ and } C \text{ such that:}$$
$$0 \le C(F(n)) \le T(n) \text{ for all } n \ge n_0$$

The objective is to give the largest rate of growth that is equal to or less than the given algorithms, T($n$), rate of growth.

# Theta notation (Θ)

It is often the case where both the upper and lower bounds of a given function are the same and the purpose of Theta notation is to determine if this is the case. The definition is as follows:

$$T(n) = \Theta(F(n)) \text{ iff there exists positive constants, } n_0, C_1 \text{ and } C_2 \text{ such that:}$$
$$0 \leq C_1(F(n)) \leq T(n) \leq C_2(F(n)) \text{ for all } n \geq n_0$$

Although Omega and Theta notations are required to completely describe growth rates, the most practically useful is Big O notation and this is the one you will see most often.

# Amortized analysis

Often we are not so interested in the time complexity of individual operations, but rather the time averaged running time of sequences of operations. This is called amortized analysis. It is different from average case analysis, which we will discuss shortly, in that it makes no assumptions regarding the data distribution of input values. It does, however, take into account the state change of data structures. For example, if a list is sorted it should make any subsequent find operations quicker. Amortized analysis can take into account the state change of data structures because it analyzes sequences of operations, rather then simply aggregating single operations.

Amortized analysis finds an upper bound on runtime by imposing an artificial cost on each operation in a sequence of operations, and then combining each of these costs. The artificial cost of a sequence takes in to account that the initial expensive operations can make subsequent operations cheaper.

When we have a small number of expensive operations, such as sorting, and lots of cheaper operations such as lookups, standard worst case analysis can lead to overly pessimistic results, since it assumes that each lookup must compare each element in the list until a match is found. We should take into account that once we sort the list we can make subsequent find operations cheaper.

So far in our runtime analysis we have assumed that the input data was completely random and have only looked at the effect the size of the input has on the runtime. There are two other common approaches to algorithm analysis; they are:

- Average case analysis
- Benchmarking

Average case analysis finds the average running time based on some assumptions regarding the relative frequencies of various input values. Using real-world data, or data that replicates the distribution of real-world data, is many times on a particular data distribution and the average running time is calculated.

Benchmarking is simply having an agreed set of typical inputs that are used to measure performance. Both benchmarking and average time analysis rely on having some domain knowledge. We need to know what the typical or expected datasets are. Ultimately we will try to find ways to improve performance by fine-tuning to a very specific application setting.

Let's look at a straightforward way to benchmark an algorithm's runtime performance. This can be done by simply timing how long the algorithm takes to complete given various input sizes. As we mentioned earlier, this way of measuring runtime performance is dependent on the hardware that it is run on. Obviously faster processors will give better results, however, the relative growth rates as we increase the input size will retain characteristics of the algorithm itself rather than the hardware it is run on. The absolute time values will differ between hardware (and software) platforms; however, their relative growth will still be bound by the time complexity of the algorithm.

Let's take a simple example of a nested loop. It should be fairly obvious that the time complexity of this algorithm is $O(n^2)$ since for each n iterations in the outer loop there are also n iterations in the inter loop. For example, our simple nested for loop consists of a simple statement executed on the inner loop:

```
def nest(n):
    for i in range(n):
        for j in range(n):
            i+j
```

The following code is a simple test function that runs the nest function with increasing values of n. With each iteration we calculate the time this function takes to complete using the `timeit.timeit` function. The `timeit` function, in this example, takes three arguments, a string representation of the function to be timed, a setup function that imports the nest function, and an `int` parameter that indicates the number of times to execute the main statement. Since we are interested in the time the nest function takes to complete relative to the input size, n, it is sufficient, for our purposes, to call the nest function once on each iteration. The following function returns a list of the calculated runtimes for each value of n:

```
import timeit
def test2(n):
    ls=[]
    for n in range(n):
        t=timeit.timeit("nest(" + str(n) +")", setup="from
__main__ import nest", number = 1)
        ls.append(t)
    return ls
```

In the following code we run the test2 function and graph the results, together with the appropriately scaled $n^2$ function for comparison, represented by the dashed line:

```
import matplotlib.pyplot as plt
n=1000
plt.plot(test2(n))
plt.plot([x*x/10000000 for x in range(n)])
```

This gives the following results:

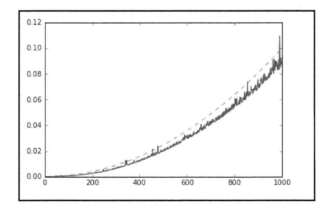

As we can see, this gives us pretty much what we expect. It should be remembered that this represents both the performance of the algorithm itself as well as the behavior of underlying software and hardware platforms, as indicated by both the variability in the measured runtime and the relative magnitude of the runtime. Obviously a faster processor will result in faster runtimes, and also performance will be affected by other running processes, memory constraints, clock speed, and so on.

# Summary

In this chapter, we have taken a general overview of algorithm design. Importantly, we saw a platform independent way to measure an algorithm's performance. We looked at some different approaches to algorithmic problems. We looked at a way to recursively multiply large numbers and also a recursive approach for merge sort. We saw how to use backtracking for exhaustive search and generating strings. We also introduced the idea of benchmarking and a simple platform-dependent way to measure runtime. In the following chapters, we will revisit many of these ideas with reference to specific data structures. In the next chapter, we will discuss linked lists and other pointer structures.

# Lists and Pointer Structures

# 7

You will have already seen lists in Python. They are convenient and powerful. Normally, any time you need to store something in a list, you use python's built-in list implementation. In this chapter, however, we are more interested in understanding how lists work. So we are going to study list internals. As you will notice, there are different types of lists.

Python's list implementation is designed to be powerful and to encompass several different use cases. We are going to be a bit more strict in our definition of what a list is. The concept of a node is very important to lists. We shall discuss them in this chapter, but this concept will, in different forms, come back throughout the rest of the book.

The focus of this chapter will be the following:

- Understand pointers in Python
- Treating the concept of nodes
- Implementing singly, doubly, and circularly linked lists

In this chapter, we are going to deal quite a bit with pointers. So it may be useful to remind ourselves what these are. To begin with, imagine that you have a house that you want to sell. Lacking time, you contact an agent to find interested buyers. So you pick up your house and take it over to the agent, who will in turn carry the house to anybody who may want to buy it. Ludicrous, you say? Now imagine that you have a few Python functions that work with images. So you pass high-resolution image data between your functions.

Of course, you don't carry your house around. What you would do is write the address of the house down on a piece of scrap paper and hand it over to the agent. The house remains where it is, but the note containing the directions to the house is passed around. You might even write it down on several pieces of paper. Each one is small enough to fit in your wallet, but they all point to the same house.

As it turns out, things are not very different in Python land. Those large image files remain in one single place in memory. What you do is create variables that hold the locations of those images in memory. These variables are small and can easily be passed around between different functions.

That is the big benefit of pointers: they allow you to point to a potentially large segment of memory with just a simple memory address.

Support for pointers exists in your computer's hardware, where it is known as indirect addressing.

In Python, you don't manipulate pointers directly, unlike in some other languages, such as C or Pascal. This has led some people to think that pointers aren't used in Python. Nothing could be further from the truth. Consider this assignment in the Python interactive shell:

```
>>> s = set()
```

We would normally say that s is a variable of the type set. That is, s is a set. This is not strictly true, however. The variable s is rather a reference (a "safe" pointer) to a set. The set constructor creates a set somewhere in memory and returns the memory location where that set starts. This is what gets stored in s.

Python hides this complexity from us. We can safely assume that s is a set and that everything works fine.

# Arrays

An array is a sequential list of data. Being sequential means that each element is stored right after the previous one in memory. If your array is really big and you are low on memory, it could be impossible to find large enough storage to fit your entire array. This will lead to problems.

Of course, the flip side of the coin is that arrays are very fast. Since each element follows from the previous one in memory, there is no need to jump around between different memory locations. This can be a very important point to take into consideration when choosing between a list and an array in your own real-world applications.

# Pointer structures

Contrary to arrays, pointer structures are lists of items that can be spread out in memory. This is because each item contains one or more links to other items in the structure. What type of links these are dependent on the type of structure we have. If we are dealing with linked lists, then we will have links to the next (and possibly previous) items in the structure. In the case of a tree, we have parent-child links as well as sibling links. In a tile-based game where the game map is built up of hexes, each node will have links to up to six adjacent map cells.

There are several benefits with pointer structures. First of all, they don't require sequential storage space. Second, they can start small and grow arbitrarily as you add more nodes to the structure.

This, however, comes at a cost. If you have a list of integers, each node is going to take up the space of an integer, as well as an additional integer for storing the pointer to the next node.

# Nodes

At the heart of lists (and several other data structures) is the concept of a node. Before we go any further, let us consider this idea for a while.

To begin with, we shall create a few strings:

```
>>> a = "eggs"
>>> b = "ham"
>>> c = "spam"
```

Now you have three variables, each with a unique name, a type, and a value. What we do not have is a way of saying in which way the variables relate to each other. Nodes allow us to do this. A node is a container of data, together with one or more links to other nodes. A link is a pointer.

A simple type of node is one that only has a link to the next node.

Of course, knowing what we do about pointers, we realize that this is not entirely true. The string is not really stored in the node, but is rather a pointer to the actual string:

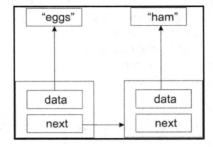

Thus the storage requirement for this simple node is two memory addresses. The data attribute of the nodes are pointers to the strings eggs and ham.

# Finding endpoints

We have created three nodes: one containing **eggs**, one **ham**, and another **spam**. The **eggs** node points to the **ham** node, which in turn points to the **spam** node. But what does the **spam** node point to? Since this is the last element in the list, we need to make sure its next member has a value that makes this clear.

If we make the last element point to nothing then we make this fact clear. In python, we will use the special value None to denote nothing:

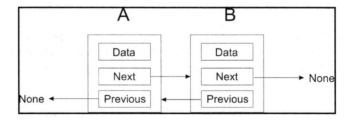

The last node has its next point pointing to None. As such it is the last node in the chain of nodes.

# Node

Here is a simple node implementation of what we have discussed so far:

```
class Node:
    def __init__(self, data=None):
        self.data = data
        self.next = None
```

 Do not confuse the concept of a node with Node.js, a server-side technology implemented in JavaScript.

The `next` pointer is initialized to `None`, meaning that unless you change the value of `next`, the node is going to be an end-point. This is a good idea, so that we do not forget to terminate the list properly.

You can add other things to the `node` class as you see fit. Just make sure that you keep in mind the distinction between node and data. If your node is going to contain customer data, then create a `Customer` class and put all the data there.

One thing you may want to do is implement the __str__ method so that it calls the __str__ method of the contained object is called when the node object is passed to print:

```
def __str__(self):
    return str(data)
```

# Other node types

We have assumed nodes that have a pointer to the next node. This is probably the simplest type of node. However, depending on our requirements, we can create a number of other types of nodes.

Sometimes we want to go from A to B, but at the same time from B to A. In that case, we add a previous pointer in addition to the next pointer:

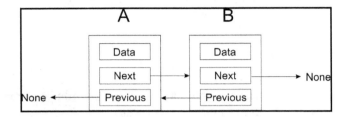

As you can see from the figure, we let both the last and the first nodes point to `None`, to indicate that we have reached they form the boundary of our list end-point. The first node's previous pointer points to None since it has no predecessor, just as the last item's next pointer points to `None` because it no successor node.

You might also be creating tiles for a tile-based game. In such a case, instead of previous and next, you might use north, south, east, and west. There are more types of pointers, but the principle is the same. Tiles at the end of the map will point to `None`:

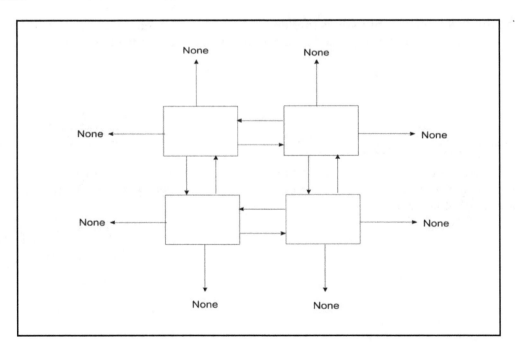

You can take this as far as you need to. If you need to be able to move north-west, north-east, south-east, and south-west as well, all you have to do is add these pointers to your node class.

# Singly linked lists

A singly linked list is a list with only one pointer between two successive nodes. It can only be traversed in a single direction, that is, you can go from the first node in the list to the last node, but you cannot move from the last node to the first node.

We can actually use the node class that we created earlier to implement a very simple singly linked list:

```
>>> n1 = Node('eggs')
>>> n2 = Node('ham')
>>> n3 = Node('spam')
```

Next we link the nodes together so that they form a *chain*:

```
>>> n1.next = n2
>>> n2.next = n3
```

To traverse the list, you could do something like the following. We start by setting the variable current to the first item in the list:

```
current = n1
while current:
    print(current.data)
    current = current.next
```

In the loop we print out the current element after which we set current to point to the next element in the list. We keep doing this until we have reached the end of the list.

There are, however, several problems with this simplistic list implementation:

- It requires too much manual work by the programmer
- It is too error-prone (this is a consequence of the first point)
- Too much of the inner workings of the list is exposed to the programmer

We are going to address all these issues in the following sections.

# Singly linked list class

A list is clearly a separate concept from a node. So we start by creating a very simple class to hold our list. We will start with a constructor that holds a reference to the very first node in the list. Since this list is initially empty, we will start by setting this reference to None:

```
class SinglyLinkedList:
    def __init__(self):
        self.tail = None
```

# Append operation

The first operation that we need to perform is to append items to the list. This operation is sometimes called an insert operation. Here we get a chance to hide away the Node class. The user of our list class should really never have to interact with Node objects. These are purely for internal use.

A first shot at an append() method may look like this:

```
class SinglyLinkedList:
    # ...

    def append(self, data):
        # Encapsulate the data in a Node
        node = Node(data)

        if self.tail == None:
            self.tail = node
        else:
            current = self.tail
            while current.next:
                current = current.next
            current.next = node
```

We encapsulate data in a node, so that it now has the next pointer attribute. From here we check if there are any existing nodes in the list (that is, does self.tail point to a Node). If there is none, we make the new node the first node of the list; otherwise, find the insertion point by traversing the list to the last node, updating the next pointer of the last node to the new node.

We can append a few items:

```
>>> words = SinglyLinkedList()
 >>> words.append('egg')
 >>> words.append('ham')
 >>> words.append('spam')
```

List traversal will work more or less like before. You will get the first element of the list from the list itself:

```
>>> current = words.tail
>>> while current:
        print(current.data)
        current = current.next
```

# A faster append operation

There is a big problem with the append method in the previous section: it has to traverse the entire list to find the insertion point. This may not be a problem when there are just a few items in the list, but wait until you need to add thousands of items. Each append will be slightly slower than the previous one. A **O**(n) goes to prove how slow our current implementation of the append method will actually be.

To fix this, we will store, not only a reference to the first node in the list, but also a reference to the last node. That way, we can quickly append a new node at the end of the list. The worst case running time of the append operation is now reduced from **O**(n) to **O**(1). All we have to do is make sure the previous last node points to the new node, that is about to be appended to the list. Here is our updated code:

```
class SinglyLinkedList:
    def __init__(self):
        # ...
        self.tail = None

    def append(self, data):
        node = Node(data)
        if self.head:
            self.head.next = node
            self.head = node
        else:
            self.tail = node
            self.head = node
```

Take note of the convention being used. The point at which we append new nodes is through `self.head`. The `self.tail` variable points to the first node in the list.

# Getting the size of the list

We would like to be able to get the size of the list by counting the number of nodes. One way we could do this is by traversing the entire list and increasing a counter as we go along:

```
def size(self):
    count = 0
    current = self.tail
    while current:
        count += 1
        current = current.next
    return count
```

This works, but list traversal is potentially an expensive operation that we should avoid when we can. So instead, we shall opt for another rewrite of the method. We add a size member to the `SinglyLinkedList` class, initializing it to 0 in the constructor. Then we increment size by one in the `append` method:

```
class SinglyLinkedList:
    def __init__(self):
        # ...
        self.size = 0

    def append(self, data):
        # ...
        self.size += 1
```

Because we are now only reading the size attribute of the node object, and not using a loop to count the number of nodes in the list, we get to reduce the worst case running time from $O(n)$ to $O(1)$.

# Improving list traversal

If you notice how we traverse our list. That one place where we are still exposed to the node class. We need to use `node.data` to get the contents of the node and `node.next` to get the next node. But we mentioned earlier that client code should never need to interact with Node objects. We can achieve this by creating a method that returns a generator. It looks as follows:

```
def iter(self):
    current = self.tail
    while current:
        val = current.data
        current = current.next
        yield val
```

Now list traversal is much simpler and looks a lot better as well. We can completely ignore the fact that there is anything called a Node outside of the list:

```
for word in words.iter():
    print(word)
```

Notice that since the `iter()` method yields the data member of the node, our client code doesn't need to worry about that at all.

# Deleting nodes

Another common operation that you would need to be able to do on a list is to delete nodes. This may seem simple, but we'd first have to decide how to select a node for deletion. Is it going to be by an index number or by the data the node contains? Here we will choose to delete a node by the data it contains.

The following is a figure of a special case considered when deleting a node from the list:

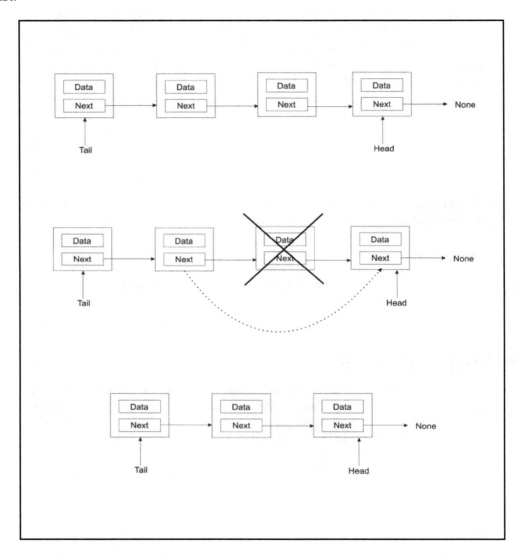

When we want to delete a node that is between two other nodes, all we have to do is make the previous node directly to the successor of its next node. That is, we simply cut the node to be deleted out of the chain as in the preceding image.

Here is the implementation of the `delete()` method may look like:

```
def delete(self, data):
    current = self.tail
    prev = self.tail
    while current:
        if current.data == data:
            if current == self.tail:
                self.tail = current.next
            else:
                prev.next = current.next
            self.size -= 1
            return
        prev = current
        current = current.next
```

It should take a **O**(n) to delete a node.

# List search

We may also need a way to check whether a list contains an item. This method is fairly easy to implement thanks to the `iter()` method we previously wrote. Each pass of the loop compares the current data to the data being searched for. If a match is found, `True` is returned, or else `False` is returned:

```
def search(self, data):
    for node in self.iter():
        if data == node:
            return True
    return False
```

# Clearing a list

We may want a quick way to clear a list. Fortunately for us, this is very simple. All we do is clear the pointers `head` and `tail` by setting them to `None`:

```
def clear(self):
    """ Clear the entire list. """
    self.tail = None
    self.head = None
```

In one fell swoop, we orphan all the nodes at the `tail` and `head` pointers of the list. This has a ripple effect of orphaning all the nodes in between.

# Doubly linked lists

Now that we have a solid grounding on what a singly linked list is and the kind of operations that can be performed on it, we shall now turn our focus one notch higher to the topic of doubly linked lists.

A doubly linked list is somehow similar to a singly linked list in that we make use of the same fundamental idea of stringing nodes together. In a Singly linked list, there exists one link between each successive node. A node in a doubly linked list has two pointers: a pointer to the next node and a pointer to the previous node:

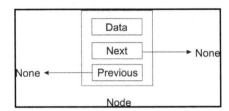

A node in a singly linked list can only determine the next node associated with it. But the referenced node or next node has no way of telling who is doing the referencing. The flow of direction is **only one way**.

In a doubly linked list, we add to each node the ability to not only reference the next node but also the previous node.

Let's examine the nature of the linkages that exist between two successive nodes for better understanding:

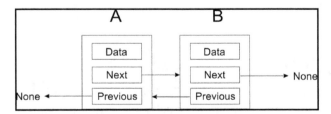

With the existence of two pointers that point to the next and previous nodes, doubly linked lists become equipped with certain capabilities.

Doubly linked lists can be traversed in any direction. Depending on the operation being performed, a node within a doubly linked list can easily refer to its previous node where necessary without having to designate a variable to keep track of that node. Because a Singly linked list can only be traversed in one direction it may sometimes mean moving to the start or beginning of the list in order to effect certain changes buried within the list.

Since there is immediate access to both next and previous nodes, deletion operations are much easier to perform, as you will see later on in this chapter.

# A doubly linked list node

The Python code that creates a class to capture what a doubly linked list node is includes in its initializing method, the `prev`, `next`, and `data` instance variables. When a node is newly created, all these variables default to `None`:

```python
class Node(object):
    def __init__(self, data=None, next=None, prev=None):
        self.data = data
        self.next = next
        self.prev = prev
```

The `prev` variable holds a reference to the previous node, while the `next` variable continues to hold a reference to the next node.

# Doubly linked list

It is still important to create a class that captures the data that our functions will be operating on:

```python
class DoublyLinkedList(object):
    def __init__(self):
        self.head = None
        self.tail = None
        self.count = 0
```

For the purposes of enhancing the `size` method, we also set the `count` instance variable to 0. `head` and `tail` will point to the head and tail of the list when we begin to insert nodes into the list.

We adopt a new convention where `self.head` points to the beginner node of the list and `self.tail` points to the latest node added to the list. This is contrary to the convention we used in the singly linked list. There are no fixed rules as to the naming of the head and tail node pointers.

Doubly linked lists also need to provide functions that return the size of the list, inserts into the list, and also deletes nodes from the list. We will be examining some of the code to do this. Let's commence with the `append` operation.

# Append operation

During an `append` operation, it is important to check whether the `head` is `None`. If it is `None`, it means that the list is empty and should have the `head` set pointing to the just-created node. The `tail` of the list is also pointed at the new node through the head. By the end of these series of steps, `head` and `tail` will now be pointing to the same node:

```
def append(self, data):
    """ Append an item to the list. """

    new_node = Node(data, None, None)
    if self.head is None:
        self.head = new_node
        self.tail = self.head
    else:
        new_node.prev = self.tail
        self.tail.next = new_node
        self.tail = new_node

    self.count += 1
```

The following diagram illustrates the head and tail pointers of the doubly linked list when a new node is added to an empty list.

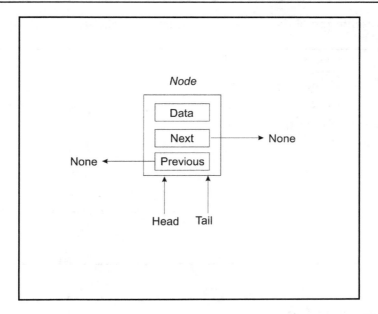

The `else` part of the algorithm is only executed if the list is not empty. The new node's previous variable is set to the tail of the list:

```
new_node.prev = self.tail
```

The tail's next pointer (or variable) is set to the new node:

```
self.tail.next = new_node
```

Lastly, we update the tail pointer to point to the new node:

```
self.tail = new_node
```

Since an `append` operation increases the number of nodes by one, we increase the counter by one:

```
self.count += 1
```

A visual representation of the append operation is as follows:

# Delete operation

Unlike the singly linked list, where we needed to keep track of the previously encountered node anytime we traversed the whole length of the list, the doubly linked list avoids that whole step. This is made possible by the use of the previous pointer.

The algorithm for removing nodes from a doubly linked list caters for basically four scenarios before deletion of a node is completed. These are:

- When the search item is not found at all
- When the search item is found at the very beginning of the list
- When the search item is found at the tail end of the list
- When the search item is found somewhere in the middle of the list

The node to be removed is identified when its data instance variable matches the data that is passed to the method to be used in the search for the node. If a matching node is found and subsequently removed, the variable node_deleted is set to True. Any other outcome results in node_deleted being set to False:

```
def delete(self, data):
    current = self.head
    node_deleted = False
    ...
```

In the `delete` method, the `current` variable is set to the head of the list (that is, it points to the `self.head` of the list). A set of `if...else` statements are then used to search the various parts of the list to find the node with the specified data.

The `head` node is searched first. Since `current` is pointing at `head`, if `current` is None, it is presumed that the list has no nodes for a search to even begin to find the node to be removed:

```
if current is None:
    node_deleted = False
```

However, if `current` (which now points to head) contains the very data being searched for, then `self.head` is set to point to the `current` next node. Since there is no node behind head now, `self.head.prev` is set to None:

```
elif current.data == data:
    self.head = current.next
    self.head.prev = None
    node_deleted = True
```

A similar strategy is adopted if the node to be removed is located at the tail end of the list. This is the third statement that searches for the possibility that the node to be removed might be located at the end of the list:

```
elif self.tail.data == data:
    self.tail = self.tail.prev
    self.tail.next = None
    node_deleted = True
```

Lastly, the algorithm to find and remove a node loops through the list of nodes. If a matching node is found, `current`'s previous node is connected to current's next node. After that step, `current`'s next node is connected to previous node of `current`:

```
else
    while current:
        if current.data == data:
            current.prev.next = current.next
            current.next.prev = current.prev
            node_deleted = True
        current = current.next
```

The `node_delete` variable is then checked after all the `if-else` statements has been evaluated. If any of the `if-else` statements changed this variable, then it means a node has been deleted from the list. The count variable is therefore decremented by 1:

```
if node_deleted:
    self.count -= 1
```

As an example of deleting a node that is buried within a list, assume the existence of three nodes, A, B, and C. To delete node B in the middle of the list, we will essentially make A point to C as its next node, while making C point to A as its previous node:

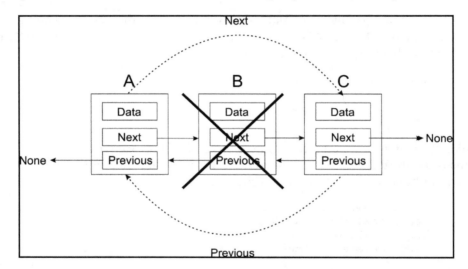

After such an operation, we end up with the following list:

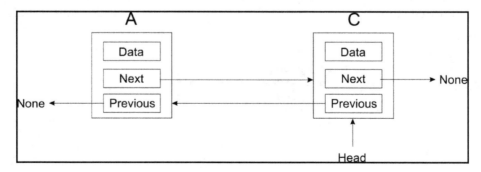

# List search

The search algorithm is similar to that of the `search` method in a singly linked list. We call the internal method `iter()` to return the data in all the nodes. As we loop through the data, each is matched against the data passed into the `contain` method. If there is a match, we return `True`, or else we return `False` to symbolize that no match was found:

```
def contain(self, data):
    for node_data in self.iter():
        if data == node_data:
            return True
        return False
```

Our doubly linked list has a **O**(1) for the `append` operation and **O**(n) for the `delete` operation.

# Circular lists

A circular list is a special case of a linked list. It is a list where the endpoints are connected. That is, the last node in the list points back to the first node. Circular lists can be based on both singly and doubly linked lists. In the case of a doubly linked circular list, the first node also needs to point to the last node.

Here we are going to look at an implementation of a singly linked circular list. It should be straightforward to implement a doubly linked circular list, once you have grasped the basic concepts.

We can reuse the `node` class that we created in the section on singly linked lists. As a matter of fact, we can reuse most parts of the `SinglyLinkedList` class as well. So we are going to focus on the methods where the circular list implementation differs from the normal singly linked list.

# Appending elements

When we append an element to the circular list, we need to make sure that the new node points back to the tail node. This is demonstrated in the following code. There is one extra line as compared to the singly linked list implementation:

```
def append(self, data):
    node = Node(data)
```

```
    if self.head:
        self.head.next = node
        self.head = node
    else:
        self.head = node
        self.tail = node
    self.head.next = self.tail
    self.size += 1
```

# Deleting an element

We may think that we can follow the same principle as for append and simply make sure the head points to the tail. This would give us the following implementation:

```
def delete(self, data):
    current = self.tail
    prev = self.tail
    while current:
        if current.data == data:
            if current == self.tail:
                self.tail = current.next
                self.head.next = self.tail
            else:
                prev.next = current.next
            self.size -= 1
            return
        prev = current
        current = current.next
```

As previously, there is just a single line that needs to change. It is only when we remove the tail node that we need to make sure that the head node is updated to point to the new tail node.

However, there is a serious problem with this code. In the case of a circular list, we cannot loop until current becomes None, since that will never happen. If you delete an existing node, you wouldn't see this, but try deleting a nonexistent node and you will get stuck in an indefinite loop.

We thus need to find a different way to control the `while` loop. We cannot check whether current has reached head, because then it will never check the last node. But we could use `prev`, since it lags behind current by one node. There is a special case, however. The very first loop iteration, `current` and `prev`, will point to the same node, namely the tail node. We want to ensure that the loop does run here, since we need to take the one node list into consideration. The updated `delete` method now looks as follows:

```
def delete(self, data):
    current = self.tail
    prev = self.tail
    while prev == current or prev != self.head:
        if current.data == data:
            if current == self.tail:
                self.tail = current.next
                self.head.next = self.tail
            else:
                prev.next = current.next
            self.size -= 1
            return
        prev = current
        current = current.next
```

# Iterating through a circular list

You do not need to modify the `iter()` method. It will work perfectly well for our circular list. But you do need to put in an exit condition when you are iterating through the circular list, otherwise your program will get stuck in a loop. Here is a way you could do this, by using a counter variable:

```
words = CircularList()
words.append('eggs')
words.append('ham')
words.append('spam')

counter = 0
for word in words.iter():
    print(word)
    counter += 1
    if counter > 1000:
        break
```

Once we have printed out 1,000 elements, we break out of the loop.

# Summary

In this chapter, we have looked at linked lists. We have studied the concepts that underlie lists, such as nodes and pointers to other nodes. We implemented the major operations that occur on these types of list and saw how their worst case running times compare.

In the next chapter, we are going to look at two other data structures that are usually implemented using lists: stacks and queues.

# 8
# Stacks and Queues

In this chapter, we are going to build upon the skills we learned in the last chapter in order to create special list implementations. We are still sticking to linear structures. We will get to more complex data structures in the coming chapters.

In this chapter, we are going to look at the following:

- Implementing stacks and queues
- Some applications of stacks and queues

## Stacks

A stack is a data structure that is often likened to a stack of plates. If you have just washed a plate, you put it on top of the stack. When you need a plate, you take it off the top of the stack. So the last plate to be added to the stack will be the first to be removed from the stack. Thus, a stack is a **last in, first out** (**LIFO**) structure:

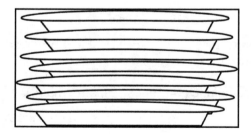

The preceding figure depicts a stack of plates. Adding a plate to the pile is only possible by leaving that plate on top of the pile. To remove a plate from the pile of plates means to remove the plate that is on top of the pile.

There are two primary operations that are done on stacks: push and pop. When an element is added to the top of the stack, it is pushed onto the stack. When an element is taken off the top of the stack, it is popped off the stack. Another operation which is used sometimes is peek, which makes it possible to see the element on the stack without popping it off.

Stacks are used for a number of things. One very common usage for stacks is to keep track of the return address during function calls. Let's imagine that we have the following little program:

```
def b():
    print('b')

def a():
    b()

a()
print("done")
```

When the program execution gets to the call to a(), it first pushes the address of the following instruction onto the stack, then jumps to a. Inside a, b() is called, but before that, the return address is pushed onto the stack. Once in b() and the function is done, the return address is popped off the stack, which takes us back to a(). When a has completed, the return address is popped off the stack, which takes us back to the print statement.

Stacks are actually also used to pass data between functions. Say you have the following function call somewhere in your code:

```
somefunc(14, 'eggs', 'ham', 'spam')
```

What is going to happen is that 14, 'eggs', 'ham' and 'spam' will be pushed onto the stack, one at a time:

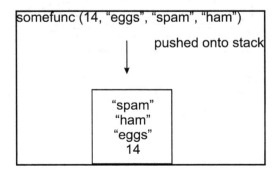

When the code jumps into the function, the values for a, b, c, d will be popped off the stack. The spam element will be popped off first and assigned to d, then "ham" will be assigned to c, and so on:

```
def somefunc(a, b, c, d):
    print("function executed")
```

# Stack implementation

Now let us study an implementation of a stack in Python. We start off by creating a node class, just as we did in the previous chapter with lists:

```
class Node:
    def __init__(self, data=None):
        self.data = data
        self.next = None
```

This should be familiar to you by now: a node holds data and a reference to the next item in a list. We are going to implement a stack instead of a list, but the same principle of nodes linked together still applies.

Now let us look at the stack class. It starts off similar to a singly linked list. We need to know the node at the top of the stack. We would also like to keep track of the number of nodes in the stack. So we will add these fields to our class:

```
class Stack:
    def __init__(self):
        self.top = None
        self.size = 0
```

# Push operation

The push operation is used to add an element to the top of the stack. Here is an implementation:

```
def push(self, data):
    node = Node(data)
    if self.top:
        node.next = self.top
        self.top = node
    else:
        self.top = node
    self.size += 1
```

In the following figure, there is no existing node after creating our new node. Thus `self.top` will point to this new node. The else part of the `if` statement guarantees that this happens:

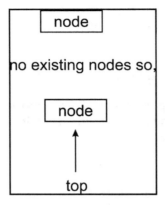

In a scenario where we have an existing stack, we move `self.top` so that it points to the newly created node. The newly created node must have its **next** pointer, pointing to the node that used to be the top node on the stack:

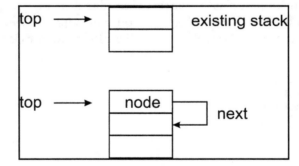

# Pop operation

Now we need a `pop` method to remove the top element from the stack. As we do so, we need to return the topmost element as well. We will make the stack return `None` if there are no more elements:

```python
def pop(self):
    if self.top:
        data = self.top.data
```

```
        self.size -= 1
        if self.top.next:
            self.top = self.top.next
        else:
            self.top = None
        return data
    else:
        return None
```

The thing to pay attention to here is the inner `if` statement. If the top node has its **next** attribute pointing to another node, then we must set the top of the stack to now point to that node:

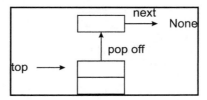

When there is only one node in the stack, the `pop` operation will proceed as follows:

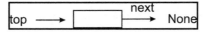

Removing such a node results in `self.top` pointing to `None`:

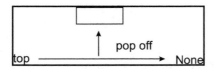

# Peek

As we said earlier, we could also add a `peek` method. This will just return the top of the stack without removing it from the stack, allowing us to look at the top element without changing the stack itself. This operation is very straightforward. If there is a top element, return its data, otherwise return `None` (so that the behavior of `peek` matches that of `pop`):

```
def peek(self):
    if self.top:
        return self.top.data
```

```
        else:
            return None
```

# Bracket-matching application

Now let us look at an example of how we can use our stack implementation. We are going to write a little function that will verify whether a statement containing brackets--(, [, or {--is balanced, that is, whether the number of closing brackets matches the number of opening brackets. It will also ensure that one pair of brackets really is contained in another:

```
def check_brackets(statement):
    stack = Stack()
    for ch in statement:
        if ch in ('{', '[', '('):
            stack.push(ch)
        if ch in ('}', ']', ')'):
            last = stack.pop()
        if last is '{' and ch is '}':
            continue
        elif last is '[' and ch is ']':
            continue
        elif last is '(' and ch is ')':
            continue
        else:
            return False
if stack.size > 0:
    return False
else:
    return True
```

Our function parses each character in the statement passed to it. If it gets an open bracket, it pushes it onto the stack. If it gets a closing bracket, it pops the top element off the stack and compares the two brackets to make sure their types match: ( should match ), [ should match ], and { should match }. If they don't, we return `False`, otherwise we continue parsing.

Once we have got to the end of the statement, we need to do one last check. If the stack is empty, then we are fine and we can return `True`. But if the stack is not empty, then we have some opening bracket which does not have a matching closing bracket and we shall return `False`. We can test the bracket-matcher with the following little code:

```
sl = (
    "{(foo)(bar)}[hello](((this)is)a)test",
    "{(foo)(bar)}[hello](((this)is)atest",
    "{(foo)(bar)}[hello](((this)is)a)test))"
)
for s in sl:
    m = check_brackets(s)
    print("{}: {}".format(s, m))
```

Only the first of the three statements should match. And when we run the code, we get the following output:

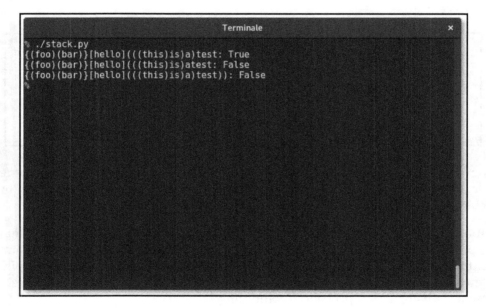

`True`, `False`, `False`. The code works. In summary, the `push` and `pop` operations of the stack data structure attract a **O**(*1*). The stack data structure is simply enough but is used to implement a whole range of functionality in the real world. The back and forward buttons on the browser are made possible by stacks. To be able to have undo and redo functionality in word processors, stacks are also used.

# Queues

Another special type of list is the queue data structure. This data structure is no different from the regular queue you are accustomed to in real life. If you have stood in line at an airport or to be served your favorite burger at your neighborhood shop, then you should know how things work in a queue.

Queues are also a very fundamental and important concept to grasp since many other data structures are built on them.

The way a queue works is that the first person to join the queue usually gets served first, all things being equal. The acronym FIFO best explains this. **FIFO** stands for **first in, first out**. When people are standing in a queue waiting for their turn to be served, service is only rendered at the front of the queue. The only time people exit the queue is when they have been served, which only occurs at the very front of the queue. By strict definition, it is illegal for people to join the queue at the front where people are being served:

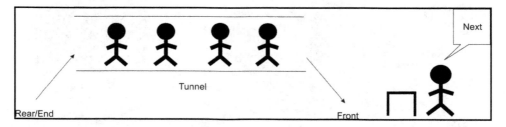

To join the queue, participants must first move behind the last person in the queue. The length of the queue does not matter. This is the only legal or permitted way by which the queue accepts new entrants.

As human as we are, the queues that we form do not conform to strict rules. It may have people who are already in the queue deciding to fall out or even have others substituting for them. It is not our intent to model all the dynamics that happen in a real queue. Abstracting what a queue is and how it behaves enables us to solve a plethora of challenges, especially in computing.

We shall provide various implementations of a queue but all will revolve around the same idea of FIFO. We shall call the operation to add an element to the queue enqueue. To remove an element from the queue, we will create a `dequeue` operation. Anytime an element is enqueued, the length or size of the queue increases by one. Conversely, dequeuing items reduce the number of elements in the queue by one.

To demonstrate the two operations, the following table shows the effect of adding and removing elements from a queue:

| Queue operation | Size | Contents | Operation results |
|---|---|---|---|
| Queue() | 0 | [] | Queue object created |
| Enqueue "Mark" | 1 | ['mark'] | Mark added to queue |
| Enqueue "John" | 2 | ['mark','john'] | John added to queue |
| Size() | 2 | ['mark','john'] | Number of items in queue returned |
| Dequeue() | 1 | ['mark'] | John is dequeued and returned |
| Dequeue() | 0 | [] | Mark is dequeued and returned |

# List-based queue

To put into code everything discussed about queues to this point, let's go ahead and implement a very simple queue using Python's list class. This is to help us develop quickly and learn about queues. The operations that must be performed on the queue are encapsulated in the ListQueue class:

```
class ListQueue:
    def __init__(self):
        self.items = []
        self.size = 0
```

In the initialization method __init__, the items instance variable is set to [], which means the queue is empty when created. The size of the queue is also set to zero. The more interesting methods are the enqueue and dequeue methods.

# Enqueue operation

The enqueue operation or method uses the insert method of the list class to insert items (or data) at the front of the list:

```
def enqueue(self, data):
    self.items.insert(0, data)
    self.size += 1
```

Do note how we implement insertions to the end of the queue. Index 0 is the first position in any list or array. However, in our implementation of a queue using a Python list, the array index 0 is the only place where new data elements are inserted into the queue. The `insert` operation will shift existing data elements in the list by one position up and then insert the new data in the space created at index 0. The following figure visualizes this process:

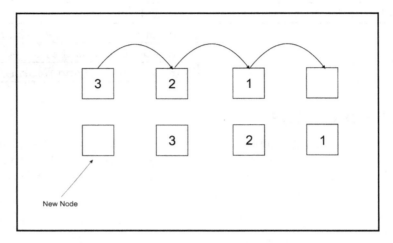

To make our queue reflect the addition of the new element, the size is increased by one:

```
self.size += 1
```

We could have used Python's `shift` method on the list as another way of implementing the "insert at 0". At the end of the day, an implementation is the overall objective of the exercise.

## Dequeue operation

The `dequeue` operation is used to remove items from the queue. With reference to the introduction to the topic of queues, this operation captures the point where we serve the customer who joined the queue first and also waited the longest:

```python
def dequeue(self):
    data = self.items.pop()
    self.size -= 1
    return data
```

The Python `list` class has a method called `pop()`. The `pop` method does the following:

1. Removes the last item from the list.
2. Returns the removed item from the list back to the user or code that called it.

The last item in the list is popped and saved in the `data` variable. In the last line of the method, the data is returned.

Consider the tunnel in the following figure as our queue. To perform a `dequeue` operation, the node with data 1 is removed from the front of the queue:

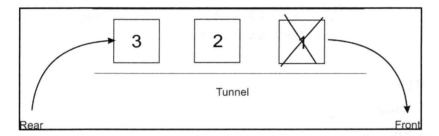

The resulting elements in the queue are as shown as follows:

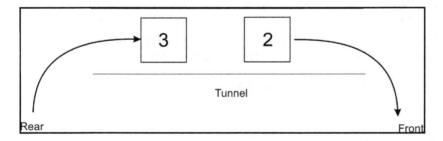

 What can we say about the `enqueue` operation? It is highly inefficient in more than one way. The method has to first shift all the elements by one space. Imagine when there are 1 million elements in a list which need to be shifted around anytime a new element is being added to the queue. This will generally make the enqueue process very slow for large lists.

# Stack-based queue

Yet another implementation of a queue is to use two stacks. Once more, the Python `list` class will be used to simulate a stack:

```python
class Queue:
    def __init__(self):
        self.inbound_stack = []
        self.outbound_stack = []
```

The preceding `queue` class sets the two instance variables to empty lists upon initialization. These are the stacks that will help us implement a queue. The stacks in this case are simply Python lists that allow us to call `push` and `pop` methods on them.

The `inbound_stack` is only used to store elements that are added to the queue. No other operation can be performed on this stack.

## Enqueue operation

The `enqueue` method is what adds elements to the queue:

```python
def enqueue(self, data):
    self.inbound_stack.append(data)
```

The method is a simple one that only receives the `data` the client wants to append to the queue. This data is then passed to the `append` method of the `inbound_stack` in the `queue` class. Furthermore, the `append` method is used to mimic the `push` operation, which pushes elements to the top of the stack.

To `enqueue` data onto the `inbound_stack`, the following code does justice:

```python
queue = Queue()
queue.enqueue(5)
queue.enqueue(6)
queue.enqueue(7)
print(queue.inbound_stack)
```

A command-line output of the `inbound_stack` inside the queue is as follows:

```
[5, 6, 7]
```

# Dequeue operation

The dequeue operation is a little more involved than its enqueue counterpart operation. New elements added to our queue end up in the inbound_stack. Instead of removing elements from the inbound_stack, we shift our attention to the outbound_stack. As we said, elements can be deleted from our queue only through the outbound_stack:

```
if not self.outbound_stack:
    while self.inbound_stack:
        self.outbound_stack.append(self.inbound_stack.pop())
return self.outbound_stack.pop()
```

The if statement first checks whether the outbound_stack is empty or not. If it is not empty, we proceed to remove the element at the front of the queue by doing the following:

```
return self.outbound_stack.pop()
```

If the outbound_stack is empty instead, all the elements in the inbound_stack are moved to the outbound_stack before the front element in the queue is popped out:

```
while self.inbound_stack:
    self.outbound_stack.append(self.inbound_stack.pop())
```

The while loop will continue to be executed as long as there are elements in the inbound_stack.

The statement self.inbound_stack.pop() will remove the latest element that was added to the inbound_stack and immediately pass the popped data to the self.outbound_stack.append() method call.

Initially, our inbound_stack was filled with the elements **5**, **6** and **7**:

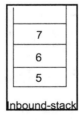

After executing the body of the `while` loop, the `outbound_stack` looks like this:

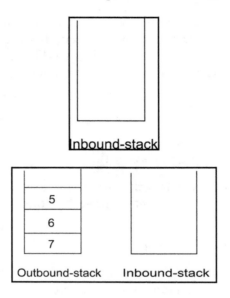

The last line in the `dequeue` method will return 5 as the result of the `pop` operation on the `outbound_stack`:

```
return self.outbound_stack.pop()
```

This leaves the `outbound_stack` with only two elements:

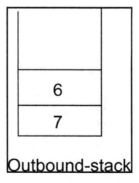

The next time the `dequeue` operation is called, the `while` loop will not be executed because there are no elements in the `outbound_stack`, which makes the outer `if` statement fail.

The `pop` operation is called right away in that case so that only the element in the queue that has waited the longest is returned.

A typical run of code to use this queue implementation is as follows:

```
queue = Queue()
queue.enqueue(5)
queue.enqueue(6)
queue.enqueue(7)
print(queue.inbound_stack)
queue.dequeue()
print(queue.inbound_stack)
print(queue.outbound_stack)
queue.dequeue()
print(queue.outbound_stack)
```

The output for the preceding code is as follows:

```
[5, 6, 7]
[]
[7, 6]
[7]
```

The code sample adds elements to a queue and prints out the elements within the queue. The `dequeue` method is called, after which a change in the number of elements is observed when the queue is printed out again.

 Implementing a queue with two stacks is a popular question posed during interviews.

# Node-based queue

Using a Python list to implement a queue is a good starter to get the feel of how queues work. It is completely possible for us to implement our own queue data structure by utilizing our knowledge of pointer structures.

A queue can be implemented using a doubly linked list, and `insertion` and `deletion` operations on this data structure have a time complexity of **O**(*1*).

The definition for the `node` class remains the same as the `Node` we defined when we touched on doubly linked list, The doubly linked list can be treated as a queue if it enables a FIFO kind of data access, where the first element added to the list is the first to be removed.

# Queue class

The `queue` class is very similar to that of the doubly linked `list` class:

```
class Queue:
def __init__(self):
        self.head = None
        self.tail = None
        self.count = 0
```

`self.head` and `self.tail` pointers are set to `None` upon creation of an instance of the `queue` class. To keep a count of the number of nodes in `Queue`, the `count` instance variable is maintained here too and set to `0`.

# Enqueue operation

Elements are added to a `Queue` object via the `enqueue` method. The elements in this case are the nodes:

```
def enqueue(self, data):
    new_node = Node(data, None, None)
    if self.head is None:
        self.head = new_node
        self.tail = self.head
    else:
        new_node.prev = self.tail
        self.tail.next = new_node
        self.tail = new_node

    self.count += 1
```

The `enqueue` method code is the same code already explained in the `append` operation of the doubly linked list. It creates a node from the data passed to it and appends it to the tail of the queue, or points both `self.head` and `self.tail` to the newly created node if the queue is empty. The total count of elements in the queue is increased by the line `self.count += 1`.

# Dequeue operation

The other operation that makes our doubly linked list behave as a queue is the dequeue method. This method is what removes the node at the front of the queue.

To remove the first element pointed to by self.head, an if statement is used:

```
def dequeue(self):
current = self.head
        if self.count == 1:
            self.count -= 1
            self.head = None
            self.tail = None
        elif self.count > 1:
            self.head = self.head.next
            self.head.prev = None
            self.count -= 1
```

current is initialized by pointing it to self.head. If self.count is 1, then it means only one node is in the list and invariably the queue. Thus, to remove the associated node (pointed to by self.head), the self.head and self.tail variables are set to None.

If, on the other hand, the queue has many nodes, then the head pointer is shifted to point to self.head's next node.

After the if statement is run, the method returns the node that was pointed to by head. self.count is decremented by one in either way the if statement execution path flows.

Equipped with these methods, we have successfully implemented a queue, borrowing heavily from the idea of a doubly linked list.

Remember also that the only things transforming our doubly linked list into a queue are the two methods, namely enqueue and dequeue.

# Application of queues

Queues are used to implement a variety of functionalities in computer land. For instance, instead of providing each computer on a network with its own printer, a network of computers can be made to share one printer by queuing what each printer wants to print. When the printer is ready to print, it will pick one of the items (usually called jobs) in the queue to print out.

Operating systems also queue processes to be executed by the CPU. Let's create an application that makes use of a queue to create a bare-bones media player.

# Media player queue

Most music player software allows users the chance to add songs to a playlist. Upon hitting the play button, all the songs in the main playlist are played one after the other. The sequential playing of the songs can be implemented with queues because the first song to be queued is the first song that is played. This aligns with the FIFO acronym. We shall implement our own playlist queue that plays songs in the FIFO manner.

Basically, our media player queue will only allow for the addition of tracks and a way to play all the tracks in the queue. In a full-blown music player, threads would be used to improve how the queue is interacted with, while the music player continues to be used to select the next song to be played, paused, or even stopped.

The track class will simulate a musical track:

```
from random import randint
class Track:

    def __init__(self, title=None):
        self.title = title
        self.length = randint(5, 10)
```

Each track holds a reference to the title of the song and also the length of the song. The length is a random number between 5 and 10. The random module provides the randint method to enable us generate the random numbers. The class represents any MP3 track or file that contains music. The random length of a track is used to simulate the number of seconds it takes to play a song or track.

To create a few tracks and print out their lengths, we do the following:

```
track1 = Track("white whistle")
track2 = Track("butter butter")
print(track1.length)
print(track2.length)
```

The output of the preceding code is as follows:

```
6
7
```

Your output may be different depending on the random length generated for the two tracks.

Now, let's create our queue. Using inheritance, we simply inherit from the queue class:

```
import time
class MediaPlayerQueue(Queue):

    def __init__(self):
        super(MediaPlayerQueue, self).__init__()
```

A call is made to properly initialize the queue by making a call to super. This class is essentially a queue that holds a number of track objects in a queue. To add tracks to the queue, an add_track method is created:

```
    def add_track(self, track):
        self.enqueue(track)
```

The method passes a track object to the enqueue method of the queue super class. This will, in effect, create a Node using the track object (as the node's data) and point either the tail, if the queue is not empty, or both head and tail, if the queue is empty, to this new node.

Assuming the tracks in the queue are played sequentially from the first track added to the last (FIFO), then the play function has to loop through the elements in the queue:

```
def play(self):
        while self.count > 0:
            current_track_node = self.dequeue()
            print("Now playing
{}".format(current_track_node.data.title))
            time.sleep(current_track_node.data.length)
```

self.count keeps count of when a track is added to our queue and when tracks have been dequeued. If the queue is not empty, a call to the dequeue method will return the node (which houses the track object) at the front of the queue. The print statement then accesses the title of the track through the data attribute of the node. To further simulate the playing of a track, the time.sleep() method halts program execution till the number of seconds of the track has elapsed:

```
    time.sleep(current_track_node.data.length)
```

The media player queue is made up of nodes. When a track is added to the queue, the track is hidden in a newly created node and associated with the data attribute of the node. That explains why we access a node's `track` object through the data property of the node which is returned by the call to `dequeue`:

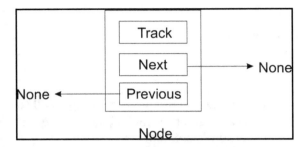

You can see, instead of our `node` object just storing just any data, it stores tracks in this case.

Let's take our music player for a spin:

```
track1 = Track("white whistle")
track2 = Track("butter butter")
track3 = Track("Oh black star")
track4 = Track("Watch that chicken")
track5 = Track("Don't go")
```

We create five track objects with random words as titles:

```
print(track1.length)
print(track2.length)
>> 8
>> 9
```

The output should be different from what you get on your machine due to the random length.

Next, an instance of the `MediaPlayerQueue` class is created:

```
media_player = MediaPlayerQueue()
```

The tracks will be added and the output of the `play` function should print out the tracks being played in the same order in which we queued them:

```
media_player.add_track(track1)
media_player.add_track(track2)
media_player.add_track(track3)
media_player.add_track(track4)
media_player.add_track(track5)
media_player.play()
```

The output of the preceding code is as follows:

```
>>Now playing white whistle
>>Now playing butter butter
>>Now playing Oh black star
>>Now playing Watch that chicken
>>Now playing Don't go
```

Upon execution of the program, it can be seen that the tracks are played in the order in which they were queued. When playing the track, the system also pauses for the number of seconds equal to that of the length of the track.

# Summary

In this chapter, we used our knowledge of linking nodes together to create other data structures, namely stacks and queues. We have seen how these data structures closely mimic stacks and queues in the real world. Concrete implementations, together with their varying types, have been shown. We later applied the concept of stacks and queues to write real-life programs.

We shall consider trees in the next chapter. The major operations on a tree will be discussed, likewise the different spheres in which to apply the data structure.

# 9
## Trees

A tree is a hierarchical form of data structure. When we dealt with lists, queues, and stacks, items followed each other. But in a tree, there is a *parent-child* relationship between items.

To visualize what trees look like, imagine a tree growing up from the ground. Now remove that image from your mind. Trees are normally drawn downward, so you would be better off imagining the root structure of the tree growing downward.

At the top of every tree is the so-called *root node*. This is the ancestor of all other nodes in the tree.

Trees are used for a number of things, such as parsing expressions, and searches. Certain document types, such as XML and HTML, can also be represented in a tree form. We shall look at some of the uses of trees in this chapter.

In this chapter, we will cover the following areas:

- Terms and definitions of trees
- Binary trees and binary search trees
- Tree traversal

# Terminology

Let's consider some terms associated with trees.

To understand trees, we need to first understand the basic ideas on which they rest. The following figure contains a typical tree consisting of character nodes lettered **A** through to **M**.

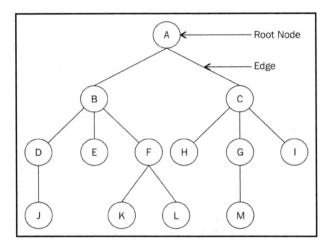

Here is a list of terms associated with a Tree:

- **Node**: Each circled alphabet represents a node. A node is any structure that holds data.
- **Root node**: The root node is the only node from which all other nodes come. A tree with an undistinguishable root node cannot be considered as a tree. The root node in our tree is the node A.
- **Sub-tree**: A sub-tree of a tree is a tree with its nodes being a descendant of some other tree. Nodes F, K, and L form a sub-tree of the original tree consisting of all the nodes.
- **Degree**: The number of sub-trees of a given node. A tree consisting of only one node has a degree of 0. This one tree node is also considered as a tree by all standards. The degree of node A is 2.
- **Leaf node**: This is a node with a degree of 0. Nodes J, E, K, L, H, M, and I are all leaf nodes.
- **Edge**: The connection between two nodes. An edge can sometimes connect a node to itself, making the edge appear as a loop.

- **Parent**: A node in the tree with other connecting nodes is the parent of those nodes. Node B is the parent of nodes D, E, and F.
- **Child**: This is a node connected to its parent. Nodes B and C are children of node A, the parent and root node.
- **Sibling**: All nodes with the same parent are siblings. This makes the nodes B and C siblings.
- **Level**: The level of a node is the number of connections from the root node. The root node is at level 0. Nodes B and C are at level 1.
- **Height of a tree**: This is the number of levels in a tree. Our tree has a height of 4.
- **Depth**: The depth of a node is the number of edges from the root of the tree to that node. The depth of node H is 2.

We shall begin our treatment of trees by considering the node in a tree and abstracting a class.

# Tree nodes

Just as was the case with other data structures that we encountered, such as lists and stacks, trees are built up of nodes. But the nodes that make up a tree need to contain data about the parent-child relationship that we mentioned earlier.

Let us now look at how to build a binary tree `node` class in Python:

```python
class Node:
    def __init__(self, data):
        self.data = data
        self.right_child = None
        self.left_child = None
```

Just like in our previous implementations, a node is a container for data and holds references to other nodes. Being a binary tree node, these references are to the left and the right children.

To test this class out, we first create a few nodes:

```python
n1 = Node("root node")
n2 = Node("left child node")
n3 = Node("right child node")
n4 = Node("left grandchild node")
```

Next, we connect the nodes to each other. We let n1 be the root node with n2 and n3 as its children. Finally, we hook n4 as the left child to n2, so that we get a few iterations when we traverse the left sub-tree:

```
n1.left_child = n2
n1.right_child = n3
n2.left_child = n4
```

Once we have our tree structure set up, we are ready to traverse it. As mentioned previously, we shall traverse the left sub-tree. We print out the node and move down the tree to the next left node. We keep doing this until we have reached the end of the left sub-tree:

```
current = n1
while current:
    print(current.data)
    current = current.left_child
```

As you will probably have noticed, this requires quite a bit of work in the client code, as you have to manually build up the tree structure.

# Binary trees

A binary tree is one in which each node has a maximum of two children. Binary trees are very common and we shall use them to build up a BST implementation in Python.

The following figure is an example of a binary tree with 5 being the root node:

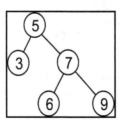

Each child is identified as being the right or left child of its parent. Since the parent node is also a node by itself, each node will hold a reference to a right and left node even if the nodes do not exist.

A regular binary tree has no rules as to how elements are arranged in the tree. It only satisfies the condition that each node should have a maximum of two children.

# Binary search trees

A **binary search tree** (**BST**) is a special kind of a binary tree. That is, it is a tree that is structurally a binary tree. Functionally, it is a tree that stores its nodes in such a way to be able to search through the tree efficiently.

There is a structure to a BST. For a given node with a value, all the nodes in the left sub-tree are less than or equal to the value of that node. Also, all the nodes in the right sub-tree of this node are greater than that of the parent node. As an example, consider the following tree:

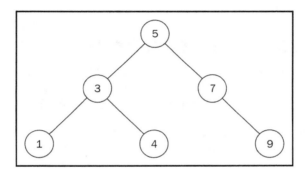

This is an example of a BST. Testing our tree for the properties of a BST, you realize that all the nodes in the left sub-tree of the root node have a value less than 5. Likewise, all the nodes in the right sub-tree have a value that is greater than 5. This property applies to all the nodes in a BST, with no exceptions:

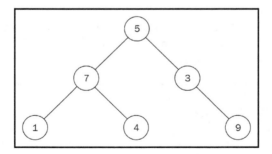

Despite the fact that the preceding figure looks similar to the previous figure, it does not qualify as a BST. Node 7 is greater than the root node 5; however, it is located to the left of the root node. Node 4 is to the right sub-tree of its parent node 7, which is incorrect.

# Binary search tree implementation

Let us begin our implementation of a BST. We will want the tree to hold a reference to its own root node:

```
class Tree:
    def __init__(self):
        self.root_node = None
```

That's all that is needed to maintain the state of a tree. Let's examine the main operations on the tree in the next section.

# Binary search tree operations

There are essentially two operations that are needful for having a usable BST. These are the `insert` and `remove` operations. These operations must occur with the one rule that they must maintain the principle that gives the BST its structure.

Before we tackle the insertion and removal of nodes, let's discuss some equally important operations that will help us better understand the `insert` and `remove` operations.

# Finding the minimum and maximum nodes

The structure of the BST makes looking for the node with the maximum and minimum values very easy.

To find the node with smallest value, we start our traversal from the root of the tree and visit the left node each time we reach a sub-tree. We do the opposite to find the node with the biggest value in the tree:

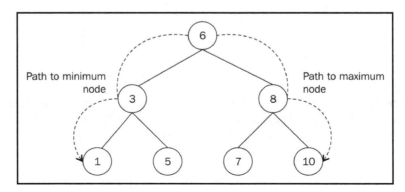

We move down from node 6 to 3 to 1 to get to the node with smallest value. Likewise, we go down 6, 8 to node 10, which is the node with the largest value.

This same means of finding the minimum and maximum nodes applies to sub-trees too. The minimum node in the sub-tree with root node 8 is 7. The node within that sub-tree with the maximum value is 10.

The method that returns the minimum node is as follows:

```
def find_min(self):
    current = self.root_node
    while current.left_child:
        current = current.left_child

    return current
```

The `while` loop continues to get the left node and visits it until the last left node points to `None`. It is a very simple method. The method to return the maximum node does the opposite, where `current.left_child` now becomes `current.right_child`.

It takes **O**(*h*) to find the minimum or maximum value in a BST, where *h* is the height of the tree.

# Inserting nodes

One of the operations on a BST is the need to insert data as nodes. Whereas in our first implementation, we had to insert the nodes ourselves, here we are going to let the tree be in charge of storing its data.

In order to make a search possible, the nodes must be stored in a specific way. For each given node, its left child node will hold data that is less than its own value, as already discussed. That node's right child node will hold data greater than that of its parent node.

We are going to create a new BST of integers by starting with the data 5. To do this, we will create a node with its data attribute set to 5.

Now, to add the second node with value 3, 3 is compared with 5, the root node:

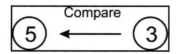

Since 5 is greater than 3, it will be put in the left sub-tree of node 5. Our BST will look as follows:

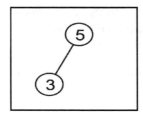

The tree satisfies the BST rule, where all the nodes in the left sub-tree are less than its parent.

To add another node of value 7 to the tree, we start from the root node with value 5 and do a comparison:

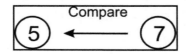

Since 7 is greater than 5, the node with value 7 is situated to the right of this root.

What happens when we want to add a node that is equal to an existing node? We will simply add it as a left node and maintain this rule throughout the structure.

If a node already has a child in the place where the new node goes, then we have to move down the tree and attach it.

Let's add another node with value 1. Starting from the root of the tree, we do a comparison between 1 and 5:

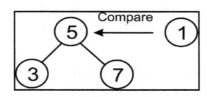

The comparison reveals that 1 is less than 5, so we move our attention to the left node of 5, which is the node with value 3:

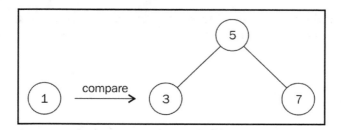

We compare 1 with 3 and since 1 is less than 3, we move a level below node 3 and to its left. But there is no node there. Therefore, we create a node with the value 1 and associate it with the left pointer of node 3 to obtain the following structure:

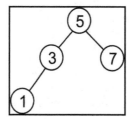

So far, we have been dealing only with nodes that contain only integers or numbers. For numbers, the idea of greater than and lesser than are clearly defined. Strings would be compared alphabetically, so there are no major problems there either. But if you want to store your own custom data types inside a BST, you would have to make sure that your class supports ordering.

Let's now create a function that enables us to add data as nodes to the BST. We begin with a function declaration:

```
def insert(self, data):
```

By now, you will be used to the fact that we encapsulate the data in a node. This way, we hide away the node class from the client code, who only needs to deal with the tree:

```
node = Node(data)
```

A first check will be to find out whether we have a root node. If we don't, the new node becomes the root node (we cannot have a tree without a root node):

```
if self.root_node is None:
    self.root_node = node
else:
```

As we walk down the tree, we need to keep track of the current node we are working on, as well as its parent. The variable `current` is always used for this purpose:

```
current = self.root_node
parent = None
while True:
    parent = current
```

Here we must perform a comparison. If the data held in the new node is less than the data held in the current node, then we check whether the current node has a left child node. If it doesn't, this is where we insert the new node. Otherwise, we keep traversing:

```
if node.data < current.data:
    current = current.left_child
    if current is None:
        parent.left_child = node
        return
```

Now we take care of the greater than or equal case. If the current node doesn't have a right child node, then the new node is inserted as the right child node. Otherwise, we move down and continue looking for an insertion point:

```
else:
    current = current.right_child
    if current is None:
        parent.right_child = node
        return
```

Insertion of a node in a BST takes **O**(*h*), where h is the height of the tree.


# Deleting nodes

Another important operation on a BST is the `deletion` or `removal` of nodes. There are three scenarios that we need to cater for during this process. The node that we want to remove might have the following:

- No children
- One child
- Two children

The first scenario is the easiest to handle. If the node about to be removed has no children, we simply detach it from its parent:

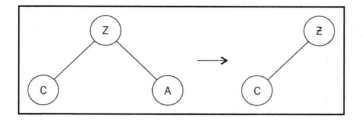

Because node A has no children, we will simply dissociate it from its parent, node Z.

On the other hand, when the node we want to remove has one child, the parent of that node is made to point to the child of that particular node:

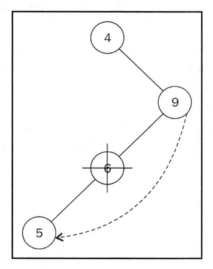

In order to remove node 6, which has as its only child, node 5, we point the left pointer of node 9 to node 5. The relationship between the parent node and child has to be preserved. That is why we need to take note of how the child node is connected to its parent (which is the node about to be deleted). The child node of the deleted node is stored. Then we connect the parent of the deleted node to that child node.

A more complex scenario arises when the node we want to delete has two children:

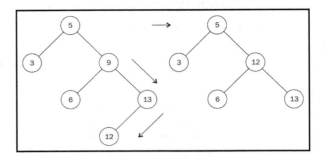

We cannot simply replace node 9 with either node 6 or 13. What we need to do is to find the next biggest descendant of node 9. This is node 12. To get to node 12, we move to the right node of node 9. And then move left to find the leftmost node. Node 12 is called the in-order successor of node 9. The second step resembles the move to find the maximum node in a sub-tree.

We replace the value of node 9 with the value 12 and remove node 12. In removing node 12, we end up with a simpler form of node removal that has been addressed previously. Node 12 has no children, so we apply the rule for removing nodes without children accordingly.

Our node class does not have reference to a parent. As such, we need to use a helper method to search for and return the node with its parent node. This method is similar to the search method:

```
def get_node_with_parent(self, data):
    parent = None
    current = self.root_node
    if current is None:
        return (parent, None)
    while True:
        if current.data == data:
            return (parent, current)
        elif current.data > data:
            parent = current
            current = current.left_child
        else:
            parent = current
            current = current.right_child

    return (parent, current)
```

The only difference is that before we update the current variable inside the loop, we store its parent with `parent = current`. The method to do the actual removal of a node begins with this search:

```
def remove(self, data):
    parent, node = self.get_node_with_parent(data)

    if parent is None and node is None:
        return False

    # Get children count
    children_count = 0

    if node.left_child and node.right_child:
        children_count = 2
    elif (node.left_child is None) and (node.right_child is None):
        children_count = 0
    else:
        children_count = 1
```

We pass the parent and the found node to `parent` and `node` respectively with the line `parent, node = self.get_node_with_parent(data)`. It is helpful to know the number of children that the node we want to delete has. That is the purpose of the `if` statement.

After this, we need to begin handling the various conditions under which a node can be deleted. The first part of the `if` statement handles the case where the node has no children:

```
if children_count == 0:
    if parent:
        if parent.right_child is node:
            parent.right_child = None
        else:
            parent.left_child = None
    else:
        self.root_node = None
```

`if parent:` is used to handle cases where there is a BST that has only one node in the whole of the three.

In the case where the node about to be deleted has only one child, the `elif` part of the `if` statement does the following:

```
elif children_count == 1:
    next_node = None
```

```
        if node.left_child:
            next_node = node.left_child
        else:
            next_node = node.right_child

        if parent:
            if parent.left_child is node:
                parent.left_child = next_node
            else:
                parent.right_child = next_node
        else:
            self.root_node = next_node
```

`next_node` is used to keep track of where the single node pointed to by the node we want to delete is. We then connect `parent.left_child` or `parent.right_child` to `next_node`.

Lastly, we handle the condition where the node we want to delete has two children:

```
        ...
        else:
            parent_of_leftmost_node = node
            leftmost_node = node.right_child
            while leftmost_node.left_child:
                parent_of_leftmost_node = leftmost_node
                leftmost_node = leftmost_node.left_child

            node.data = leftmost_node.data
```

In finding the in-order successor, we move to the right node with `leftmost_node = node.right_child`. As long as there exists a left node, `leftmost_node.left_child` will evaluate to `True` and the `while` loop will run. When we get to the leftmost node, it will either be a leaf node (meaning that it will have no child node) or have a right child.

We update the node about to be removed with the value of the in-order successor with `node.data = leftmost_node.data`:

```
        if parent_of_leftmost_node.left_child == leftmost_node:
            parent_of_leftmost_node.left_child = leftmost_node.right_child
        else:
            parent_of_leftmost_node.right_child = leftmost_node.right_child
```

The preceding statement allows us to properly attach the parent of the leftmost node with any child node. Observe how the right-hand side of the equals sign stays unchanged. That is because the in-order successor can only have a right child as its only child.

The `remove` operation takes **O**(*h*), where h is the height of the tree.

# Searching the tree

Since the `insert` method organizes data in a specific way, we will follow the same procedure to find the data. In this implementation, we will simply return the data if it was found or `None` if the data wasn't found:

```
def search(self, data):
```

We need to start searching at the very top, that is, at the root node:

```
current = self.root_node
while True:
```

We may have passed a leaf node, in which case the data doesn't exist in the tree and we return `None` to the client code:

```
if current is None:
    return None
```

We might also have found the data, in which case we return it:

```
elif current.data is data:
    return data
```

As per the rules for how data is stored in the BST, if the data we are searching for is less than that of the current node, we need to go down the tree to the left:

```
elif current.data > data:
    current = current.left_child
```

Now we only have one option left: the data we are looking for is greater than the data held in the current node, which means we go down the tree to the right:

```
else:
    current = current.right_child
```

Finally, we can write some client code to test how the BST works. We create a tree and insert a few numbers between 1 and 10. Then we search for all the numbers in that range. The ones that exist in the tree get printed:

```
tree = Tree()
tree.insert(5)
tree.insert(2)
tree.insert(7)
tree.insert(9)
tree.insert(1)

for i in range(1, 10):
    found = tree.search(i)
    print("{}: {}".format(i, found))
```

# Tree traversal

Visiting all the nodes in a tree can be done depth first or breadth first. These modes of traversal are not peculiar to only binary search trees but trees in general.

# Depth-first traversal

In this traversal mode, we follow a branch (or edge) to its limit before recoiling upwards to continue traversal. We will be using the recursive approach for the traversal. There are three forms of depth-first traversal, namely `in-order`, `pre-order`, and `post-order`.

### In-order traversal and infix notation

Most of us are probably used to this way of representing an arithmetic expression, since this is the way we are normally taught in schools. The operator is inserted (infixed) between the operands, as in `3 + 4`. When necessary, parentheses can be used to build a more complex expression: `(4 + 5) * (5 - 3)`.

In this mode of traversal, you would visit the left sub-tree, the parent node, and finally the right sub-tree.

The recursive function to return an in-order listing of nodes in a tree is as follows:

```
def inorder(self, root_node):
    current = root_node
    if current is None:
        return
    self.inorder(current.left_child)
    print(current.data)
    self.inorder(current.right_child)
```

We visit the node by printing the node and making two recursive calls with `current.left_child` and `current.right_child`.

## Pre-order traversal and prefix notation

Prefix notation is commonly referred to as Polish notation. Here, the operator comes before its operands, as in + 3 4. Since there is no ambiguity of precedence, parentheses are not required: * + 4 5 - 5 3.

To traverse a tree in pre-order mode, you would visit the node, the left sub-tree, and the right sub-tree node, in that order.

Prefix notation is well known to LISP programmers.

The recursive function for this traversal is as follows:

```
def preorder(self, root_node):
    current = root_node
    if current is None:
        return
    print(current.data)
    self.preorder(current.left_child)
    self.preorder(current.right_child)
```

Note the order in which the recursive call is made.

## Post-order traversal and postfix notation.

Postfix or **reverse Polish notation** (RPN) places the operator after its operands, as in 3 4 +. As is the case with Polish notation, there is never any confusion over the precedence of operators, so parentheses are never needed: 4 5 + 5 3 - *.

In this mode of traversal, you would visit the left sub-tree, the right sub-tree, and lastly the root node.

The `post-order` method is as follows:

```
def postorder(self, root_node):
    current = root_node
    if current is None:
        return
    self.postorder(current.left_child)
    self.postorder(current.right_child)

    print(current.data)
```

## Breadth-first traversal

This kind of traversal starts from the root of a tree and visits the node from one level of the tree to the other:

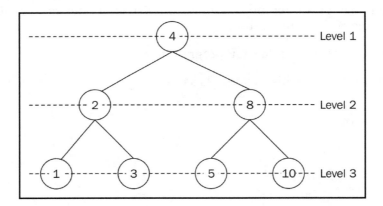

The node at level 1 is node 4. We visit this node by printing out its value. Next, we move to level 2 and visit the nodes on that level, which are nodes 2 and 8. On the last level, level 3, we visit nodes 1, 3, 5, and 10.

The complete output of such a traversal is 4, 2, 8, 1, 3, 5, and 10.

This mode of traversal is made possible by using a queue data structure. Starting with the root node, we push it into a queue. The node at the front of the queue is accessed (dequeued) and either printed and stored for later use. The left node is added to the queue followed by the right node. Since the queue is not empty, we repeat the process.

A dry run of the algorithm will enqueue the root node 4, dequeue, and access, or visit the node. Nodes 2 and 8 are enqueued as they are the left and right nodes respectively. Node 2 is dequeued in order to be visited. Its left and right nodes, 1 and 3, are enqueued. At this point, the node at the front of the queue is 8. We dequeue and visit node 8, after which we enqueue its left and right nodes. So the process continues until the queue is empty.

The algorithm is as follows:

```
from collections import deque
class Tree:
    def breadth_first_traversal(self):
        list_of_nodes = []
        traversal_queue = deque([self.root_node])
```

We enqueue the root node and keep a list of the visited nodes in the list_of_nodes list. The dequeue class is used to maintain a queue:

```
while len(traversal_queue) > 0:
    node = traversal_queue.popleft()
    list_of_nodes.append(node.data)

    if node.left_child:
        traversal_queue.append(node.left_child)

    if node.right_child:
        traversal_queue.append(node.right_child)
return list_of_nodes
```

If the number of elements in the traversal_queue is greater than zero, the body of the loop is executed. The node at the front of the queue is popped off and appended to the list_of_nodes list. The first if statement will enqueue the left child node of the node provided a left node exists. The second if statement does the same for the right child node.

The list_of_nodes is returned in the last statement.

# Benefits of a binary search tree

We shall now briefly look at what makes a BST a better idea than using a list for data that needs to be searched. Let us assume that we have the following dataset: 5, 3, 7, 1, 4, 6, and 9. Using a list, the worst-case scenario would require you to search through the entire list of seven elements before finding the search term:

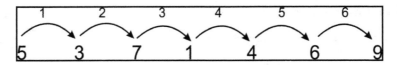

Searching for 9 requires six jumps.

With a tree, the worst-case scenario is three comparisons:

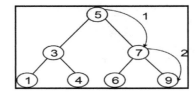

Searching for 9 requires two steps.

Notice, however, that if you insert the elements into the tree in the order 1, 2, 3, 5, 6, 7, 9, then the tree would not be more efficient than the list. We would have to balance the tree first:

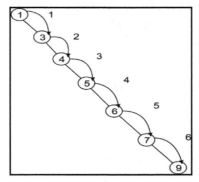

So not only is it important to use a BST but choosing a self-balancing tree helps to improve the `search` operation.

# Expression trees

The tree structure is also used to parse arithmetic and Boolean expressions. For example, the expression tree for 3 + 4 would look as follows:

For a slightly more complex expression, `(4 + 5)` * `(5-3)`, we would get the following:

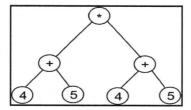

# Parsing a reverse Polish expression

Now we are going to build up a tree for an expression written in postfix notation. Then we will calculate the result. We will use a simple tree implementation. To keep it really simple, since we are going to grow the tree by merging smaller trees, we only need a tree node implementation:

```
class TreeNode:
    def __init__(self, data=None):
        self.data = data
        self.right = None
        self.left = None
```

In order to build the tree, we are going to enlist the help of a stack. You will see why soon. But for the time being, let us just create an arithmetic expression and set up our stack:

```
expr = "4 5 + 5 3 - *".split()
stack = Stack()
```

Since Python is a language that tries hard to have sensible defaults, its split() method splits on whitespace by default. (If you think about it, this is most likely what you would expect as well.) The result is going to be that expr is a list with the values 4, 5, +, 5, 3, - and *.

Each element of the expr list is going to be either an operator or an operand. If we get an operand then we embed it in a tree node and push it onto the stack. If we get an operator, on the other hand, then we embed the operator into a tree node and pop its two operands into the node's left and right children. Here we have to take care to ensure that the first pop goes into the right child, otherwise we will have problems with subtraction and division.

Here is the code to build the tree:

```
for term in expr:
    if term in "+-*/":
        node = TreeNode(term)
        node.right = stack.pop()
        node.left = stack.pop()
    else:
        node = TreeNode(int(term))
    stack.push(node)
```

Notice that we perform a conversion from string to int in the case of an operand. You could use float() instead, if you wanted to support floating point operands.

At the end of this operation, we should have one single element in the stack, and that holds the full tree.

We may now want to be able to evaluate the expression. We build the following little function to help us:

```
def calc(node):
    if node.data is "+":
        return calc(node.left) + calc(node.right)
    elif node.data is "-":
        return calc(node.left) - calc(node.right)
    elif node.data is "*":
        return calc(node.left) * calc(node.right)
```

```
elif node.data is "/":
    return calc(node.left) / calc(node.right)
else:
    return node.data
```

This function is very simple. We pass in a node. If the node contains an operand, then we simply return that value. If we get an operator, however, then we perform the operation that the operator represents, on the node's two children. However, since one or more of the children could also contain either operators or operands, we call the `calc()` function recursively on the two child nodes (bearing in mind that all the children of every node are also nodes).

Now we just need to pop the root node off the stack and pass it into the `calc()` function and we should have the result of the calculation:

```
root = stack.pop()
result = calc(root)
print(result)
```

Running this program should yield the result 18, which is the result of `(4 + 5) * (5 - 3)`.

# Balancing trees

Earlier, we mentioned that if nodes are inserted into the tree in a sequential order, then the tree behaves more or less like a list, that is, each node has exactly one child node. We normally would like to reduce the height of the tree as much as possible, by filling up each row in the tree. This process is called balancing the tree.

There are a number of types of self-balancing trees, such as red-black trees, AA trees, and scapegoat trees. These balance the tree during each operation that modifies the tree, such as insert or delete.

There are also external algorithms that balance a tree. The benefit of these is that you wouldn't need to balance the tree on every single operation, but could rather leave balancing to the point when you need it.

# Heaps

At this point, we shall briefly introduce the heap data structure. A heap is a specialization of a tree in which the nodes are ordered in a specific way. Heaps are divided into max and min heaps. In a max heap, each parent node must always be greater than or equal to its children. It follows that the root node must be the greatest value in the tree. A min heap is the opposite. Each parent node must be less than or equal to both its children. As a consequence, the root node holds the lowest value.

Heaps are used for a number of different things. For one, they are used to implement priority queues. There is also a very efficient sorting algorithm, called heap sort, that uses heaps. We are going to study these in depth in subsequent chapters.

# Summary

In this chapter, we have looked at tree structures and some example uses of them. We studied binary trees in particular, which is a subtype of trees where each node has at most two children.

We looked at how a binary tree can be used as a searchable data structure with a BST. We saw that, in most cases, finding data in a BST is faster than in a linked list, although this is not the case if the data is inserted sequentially, unless of course the tree is balanced.

The breadth- and depth-first search traversal modes were also implemented using queue recursion.

We also looked at how a binary tree can be used to represent an arithmetic or a Boolean expression. We built up an expression tree to represent an arithmetic expression. We showed how to use a stack to parse an expression written in RPN, build up the expression tree, and finally traverse it to get the result of the arithmetic expression.

Finally, we mentioned heaps, a specialization of a tree structure. We have tried to at least lay down the theoretical foundation for the heap in this chapter, so that we can go on to implement heaps for different purposes in upcoming chapters.

# Hashing and Symbol Tables

**10**

We have previously looked at lists, where items are stored in sequence and accessed by index number. Index numbers work well for computers. They are integers so they are fast and easy to manipulate. However, they don't always work so well for us. If we have an address book entry, for example, with index number 56, that number doesn't tell us much. There is nothing to link a particular contact with number 56. It just happens to be the next available position in the list.

In this chapter, we are going to look at a similar structure: a dictionary. A dictionary uses a keyword instead of an index number. So, if that contact was called *James*, we would probably use the keyword *James* to locate the contact. That is, instead of accessing the contact by calling *contacts [56]*, we would use *contacts ["james"]*.

Dictionaries are often built using hash tables. As the name suggests, hash tables rely on a concept called **hashing**. That is where we are going to begin our discussion.

We will cover the following topics in this chapter:

- Hashing
- Hash tables
- Different functions with elements

## Hashing

Hashing is the concept of converting data of arbitrary size into data of fixed size. A little bit more specifically, we are going to use this to turn strings (or possibly other data types) into integers. This possibly sounds more complex than it is so let's look at an example. We want to hash the expression `hello world`, that is, we want to get a numeric value that we could say *represents* the string.

By using the `ord()` function, we can get the ordinal value of any character. For example, the `ord('f')` function gives 102. To get the hash of the whole string, we could just sum the ordinal numbers of each character in the string:

```
>>> sum(map(ord, 'hello world'))
1116
```

| h | e | l | l | o | | w | o | r | l | d | |
|---|---|---|---|---|---|---|---|---|---|---|---|
| 104 | 101 | 108 | 108 | 111 | 32 | 119 | 111 | 114 | 108 | 100 | = 1116 |

This works fine. However, note that we could change the order of the characters in the string and get the same hash:

```
>>> sum(map(ord, 'world hello'))
1116
```

And the sum of the ordinal values of the characters would be the same for the string `gello xorld` as well, since g has an ordinal value which is one less than that of h, and x has an ordinal value that is one greater than that of w, hence:

```
>>> sum(map(ord, 'gello xorld'))
1116
```

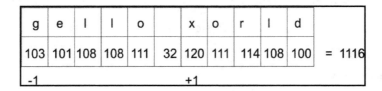

# Perfect hashing functions

A perfect hashing function is one in which each string (as we are limiting the discussion to strings for now) is guaranteed to be unique. In practice, hashing functions normally need to be very fast, so trying to create a function that will give each string a unique hash value is normally not possible. Instead, we live with the fact that we sometimes get collisions (two or more strings having the same hash value), and when that happens, we come up with a strategy for resolving them.

In the meantime, we can at least come up with a way to avoid some of the collisions. We could, for example, add a multiplier, so that the hash value for each character becomes the multiplier value, multiplied by the ordinal value of the character. The multiplier then increases as we progress through the string. This is shown in the following function:

```python
def myhash(s):
    mult = 1
    hv = 0
    for ch in s:
        hv += mult * ord(ch)
        mult += 1
    return hv
```

We can test this function on the strings that we used earlier:

```python
for item in ('hello world', 'world hello', 'gello xorld'):
    print("{}: {}".format(item, myhash(item)))
```

Running the program, we get the following output:

```
% python hashtest.py

hello world: 6736
world hello: 6616
gello xorld: 6742
```

| h | e | l | l | o | | w | o | r | l | d | | |
|---|---|---|---|---|---|---|---|---|---|---|---|---|
| 104 | 101 | 108 | 108 | 111 | 32 | 119 | 111 | 114 | 108 | 100 | = | 1116 |
| 1 | 2 | 3 | 4 | 5 | 6 | 7 | 8 | 9 | 10 | 11 | | |
| 104 | 202 | 324 | 432 | 555 | 192 | 833 | 888 | 1026 | 1080 | 1100 | = | 6736 |

Note that the last row is the result of multiplying the values in rows 2 and 3 such that 104 x 1 equals 104, as an example.

This time we get different hash values for our strings. Of course, this doesn't mean that we have a perfect hash. Let us try the strings ad and ga:

```
% python hashtest.py

ad: 297
ga: 297
```

There we still get the same hash value for two different strings. As we have said before, this doesn't have to be a problem, but we need to devise a strategy for resolving collisions. We shall look at that shortly, but first we will study an implementation of a hash table.

# Hash table

A **hash table** is a form of list where elements are accessed by a keyword rather than an index number. At least, this is how the client code will see it. Internally, it will use a slightly modified version of our hashing function in order to find the index position in which the element should be inserted. This gives us fast lookups, since we are using an index number which corresponds to the hash value of the key.

We start by creating a class to hold hash table items. These need to have a key and a value, since our hash table is a key-value store:

```
class HashItem:
    def __init__(self, key, value):
        self.key = key
        self.value = value
```

This gives us a very simple way to store items. Next, we start working on the hash table class itself. As usual, we start off with a constructor:

```
class HashTable:
    def __init__(self):
        self.size = 256
        self.slots = [None for i in range(self.size)]
        self.count = 0
```

The hash table uses a standard Python list to store its elements. We could equally well have used the linked list that we developed previously, but right now our focus is on understanding the hash table, so we shall use what is at our disposal.

We set the size of the hash table to 256 elements to start with. Later, we will look at strategies for how to grow the table as we begin filling it up. We now initialize a list containing 256 elements. These elements are often referred to as slots or buckets. Finally, we add a counter for the number of actual hash table elements we have:

| 0 | 1 | 2 | ...... | 255 |
|-------|-------|-------|--------|-------|
| empty | empty | empty | ...... | empty |
| used slots = 0 | | | | |

It is important to notice the difference between the size and count of a table. Size of a table refers to the total number of slots in the table (used or unused). Count of the table, on the other hand, simply refers to the number of slots that are filled, or put another way, the number of actual key-value pairs we have added to the table.

Now, we are going to add our hashing function to the table. It will be similar to what we evolved in the section on hashing functions, but with a slight difference: we need to ensure that our hashing function returns a value between 1 and 256 (the size of the table). A good way of doing so is to return the remainder of dividing the hash by the size of the table, since the remainder is always going to be an integer value between 0 and 255.

As the hashing function is only meant to be used internally by the class, we put an underscore(_) at the beginning of the name to indicate this. This is a normal Python convention for indicating that something is meant for internal use:

```
def _hash(self, key):
    mult = 1
    hv = 0
    for ch in key:
        hv += mult * ord(ch)
        mult += 1
    return hv % self.size
```

For the time being, we are going to assume that keys are strings. We shall discuss how one can use non-string keys later. For now, just bear in mind that the _hash() function is going to generate the hash value of a string.

# Putting elements

We add elements to the hash with the put() function and retrieve with the get() function. First, we will look at the implementation of the put() function. We start by embedding the key and the value into the HashItem class and computing the hash of the key:

```
def put(self, key, value):
    item = HashItem(key, value)
    h = self._hash(key)
```

Now we need to find an empty slot. We start at the slot that corresponds to the hash value of the key. If that slot is empty, we insert our item there.

However, if the slot is not empty and the key of the item is not the same as our current key, then we have a collision. This is where we need to figure out a way to handle a conflict. We are going to do this by adding one to the previous hash value we had and getting the remainder of dividing this value by the size of the hash table. This is a linear way of resolving collisions and it is quite simple:

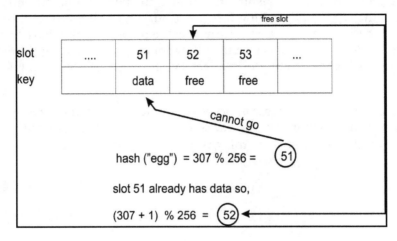

```
while self.slots[h] is not None:
    if self.slots[h].key is key:
        break
    h = (h + 1) % self.size
```

We have found our insertion point. If this is a new element (that is, it contained None previously), then we increase the count by one. Finally, we insert the item into the list at the required position:

```
if self.slots[h] is None:
    self.count += 1
self.slots[h] = item
```

# Getting elements

The implementation of the get() method should return the value that corresponds to a key. We also have to decide what to do in the event that the key does not exist in the table. We start by calculating the hash of the key:

```
def get(self, key):
    h = self._hash(key)
```

Now, we simply start looking through the list for an element that has the key we are searching for, starting at the element which has the hash value of the key that was passed in. If the current element is not the correct one, then, just like in the put() method, we add one to the previous hash value and get the remainder of dividing this value by the size of the list. This becomes our new index. If we find an element that contains None, we stop looking. If we find our key, we return the value:

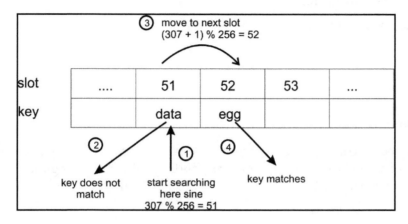

```
while self.slots[h] is not None:
    if self.slots[h].key is key:
        return self.slots[h].value
    h = (h+ 1) % self.size
```

Finally, we decide what to do if the key was not found in the table. Here we will choose to return None. Another good alternative may be to raise an exception:

```
return None
```

# Testing the hash table

To test our hash table, we create a HashTable, put a few elements in it, then try to retrieve these. We will also try to get() a key that does not exist. Remember the two strings ad and ga which returned the same hash value by our hashing function? For good measure, we throw those in as well, just to see that the collision is properly resolved:

```
ht = HashTable()
ht.put("good", "eggs")
ht.put("better", "ham")
ht.put("best", "spam")
```

```
ht.put("ad", "do not")
ht.put("ga", "collide")

for key in ("good", "better", "best", "worst", "ad", "ga"):
    v = ht.get(key)
    print(v)
```

Running this returns the following:

```
% python hashtable.py

eggs
ham
spam
None
do not
collide
```

As you can see, looking up the key worst returns None, since the key does not exist. The keys ad and ga also return their corresponding values, showing that the collision between them is dealt with.

# Using [] with the hash table

Using the put() and get() methods doesn't look very good, however. We want to be able to treat our hash table as a list, that is, we would like to be able to use ht["good"] instead of ht.get("good"). This is easily done with the special methods __setitem__() and __getitem__():

```
def __setitem__(self, key, value):
    self.put(key, value)

def __getitem__(self, key):
    return self.get(key)
```

Our test code can now look like this instead:

```
ht = HashTable()
ht["good"] = "eggs"
ht["better"] = "ham"
ht["best"] = "spam"
ht["ad"] = "do not"
ht["ga"] = "collide"
```

```
for key in ("good", "better", "best", "worst", "ad", "ga"):
    v = ht[key]
    print(v)

print("The number of elements is: {}".format(ht.count))
```

Notice that we also print the number of elements in the hash table. This is useful for our next discussion.

# Non-string keys

In most cases, it makes more sense to just use strings for the keys. However, if necessary, you could use any other Python type. If you create your own class that you want to use as a key, you will probably want to override the special __hash__() function for that class, so that you get reliable hash values.

Note that you would still have to calculate the modulo (%) of the hash value and the size of the hash table to get the slot. That calculation should happen in the hash table and not in the key class, since the table knows its own size (the key class should not know anything about the table that it belongs to).

# Growing a hash table

In our example, the hash table's size was set to 256. Obviously, as we add elements to the list, we begin to fill up the empty slots. At some point, all the slots will be filled up and the table will be full. To avoid this, we can grow the table when it is getting full.

To do this, we compare the size and the count. Remember that `size` held the total number of slots and `count` the number of those slots that contained elements? Well, if `count` equals `size` then we have filled up the table.

The hash table's load factor gives us an indication of how large a portion of the available slots are being used. It is defined as follows:

$$\text{load factor} = \frac{n}{k}$$

**n** is the number of used slots
**k** is the total number of slots

As the load factor approaches 1, we need to grow the table. In fact, we should do it before it gets there in order to avoid gets becoming too slow. A value of 0.75 may be a good value in which to grow the table.

The next question is how much to grow the table by. One strategy would be to simply double the size of the table.

# Open addressing

The collision resolution mechanism we used in our example, linear probing, is an example of an open addressing strategy. Linear probing is really simple since we use a fixed interval between our probes. There are other open addressing strategies as well but they all share the idea that there is an array of slots. When we want to insert a key, we check whether the slot already has an item or not. If it does, we look for the next available slot.

If we have a hash table that contains 256 slots, then 256 is the maximum number of elements in that hash. Moreover, as the load factor increases, it will take longer to find the insertion point for the new element.

Because of these limitations, we may prefer to use a different strategy to resolve collisions, such as chaining.

## Chaining

Chaining is a strategy for resolving conflicts and avoiding the limit to the number of elements in a hash table. In chaining, the slots in the hash table are initialized with empty lists:

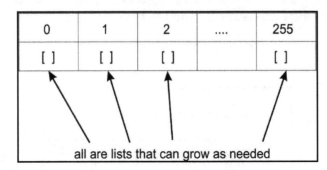

When an element is inserted, it will be appended to the list that corresponds to that element's hash value. That is, if you have two elements that both have the hash value 1167, these two elements will both be added to the list that exists in slot 1167 of the hash table:

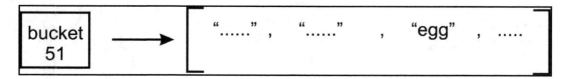

The preceding diagram shows a list of entries with hash value 51.

Chaining then avoids conflict by allowing multiple elements to have the same hash value. It also avoids the problem of insertions as the load factor increases, since we don't have to look for a slot. Moreover, the hash table can hold more values than the number of available slots, since each slot holds a list that can grow.

Of course, if a particular slot has many items, searching them can get very slow, since we have to do a linear search through the list until we find the element that has the key we want. This can slow down retrieval, which is not good, since hash tables are meant to be efficient:

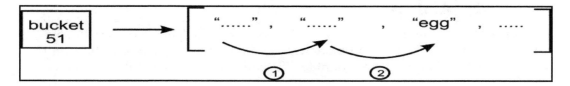

The preceding diagram demonstrates a linear search through list items until we find a match.

Instead of using lists in the table slots, we could use another structure that allows for fast searching. We have already looked at **binary search trees (BSTs)**. We could simply put an (initially empty) BST in each slot:

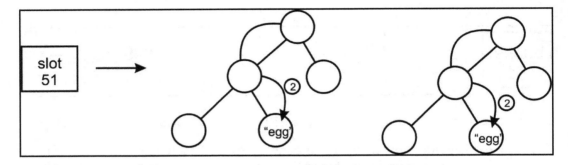

Slot 51 holds a BST which we search for the key. But we would still have a potential problem: depending on the order in which the items were added to the BST, we could end up with a search tree that is as inefficient as a list. That is, each node in the tree has exactly one child. To avoid this, we would need to ensure that our BST is self-balancing.

# Symbol tables

Symbol tables are used by compilers and interpreters to keep track of the symbols that have been declared and information about them. Symbol tables are often built using hash tables, since it is important to efficiently retrieve a symbol in the table.

Let us look at an example. Suppose we have the following Python code:

```
name = "Joe"
age = 27
```

Here we have two symbols, name and age. They belong to a namespace, which could be __main__, but it could also be the name of a module if you placed it there. Each symbol has a value; name has the value Joe and age has the value 27. A symbol table allows the compiler or the interpreter to look these values up. The symbols name and age become the keys in our hash table. All the other information associated with it, such as the value, become part of the value of the symbol table entry.

Not only variables are symbols, but functions and classes as well. They will all be added to our symbol table, so that when any one of them needs to be accessed, they are accessible from the symbol table:

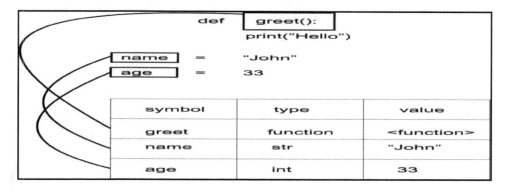

In Python, each module that is loaded has its own symbol table. The symbol table is given the name of that module. This way, modules act as namespaces. We can have multiple symbols called age, as long as they exist in different symbol tables. To access either one, we access it through the appropriate symbol table:

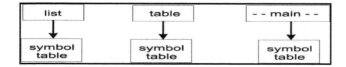

# Summary

In this chapter, we have looked at hash tables. We looked at how to write a hashing function to turn string data into integer data. Then we looked at how we can use hashed keys to quickly and efficiently look up the value that corresponds to a key.

We also noticed how hashing functions are not perfect and that several strings can end up having the same hash value. This led us to look at collision resolution strategies.

We looked at growing a hash table and how to look at the load factor of the table in order to determine exactly when to grow the hash.

In the last section of the chapter, we studied symbol tables, which often are built using hash tables. Symbol tables allow a compiler or an interpreter to look up a symbol (variable, function, class, and so on) that has been defined and retrieve all information about it.

In the next chapter, we will talk about graphs and other algorithms.

# Graphs and Other Algorithms

# 11

In this chapter, we are going to talk about graphs. This is a concept that comes from the branch of mathematics called graph theory.

Graphs are used to solve a number of computing problems. They also have much less structure than other data structures we have looked at and things like traversal can be much more unconventional, as we shall see.

By the end of this chapter, you should be able to do the following:

- Understand what graphs are
- Know the types of graphs and their constituents
- Know how to represent a graph and traverse it
- Get a fundamental idea of what priority queues are
- Be able to implement a priority queue
- Be able to determine the ith smallest element in a list

## Graphs

A graph is a set of vertices and edges that form connections between the vertices. In a more formal approach, a graph G is an ordered pair of a set V of vertices and a set E of edges given as `G = (V, E)` in formal mathematical notation.

An example of a graph is given here:

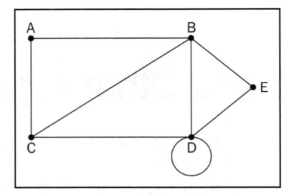

Let's now go through some definitions of a graph:

- **Node or vertex**: A point, usually represented by a dot in a graph. The vertices or nodes are A, B, C, D, and E.
- **Edge**: This is a connection between two vertices. The line connecting A and B is an example of an edge.
- **Loop**: When an edge from a node is incident on itself, that edge forms a loop.
- **Degree of a vertex**: This is the number of vertices that are incident on a given vertex. The degree of vertex B is 4.
- **Adjacency**: This refers to the connection(s) between a node and its neighbor. The node C is adjacent to node A because there is an edge between them.
- **Path**: A sequence of vertices where each adjacent pair is connected by an edge.

# Directed and undirected graphs

Graphs can be classified based on whether they are undirected or directed. An undirected graph simply represents edges as lines between the nodes. There is no additional information about the relationship between the nodes than the fact that they are connected:

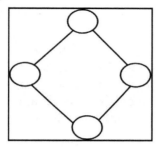

In a directed graph, the edges provide orientation in addition to connecting nodes. That is, the edges, which will be drawn as lines with an arrow, will point in which direction the edge connects the two nodes:

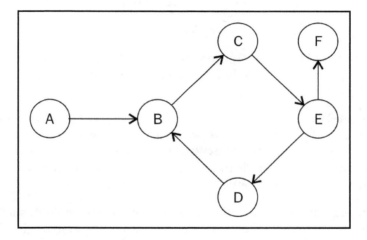

The arrow of an edge determines the flow of direction. One can only move from **A** to **B** in the preceding diagram. Not **B** to **A**.

# Weighted graphs

A weighted graph adds a bit of extra information to the edges. This can be a numerical value that indicates something. Let's say, for example, that the following graph indicates different ways to get from point **A** to point **D**. You can either go straight from **A** to **D**, or choose to pass through **B** and **C**. Associated with each edge is the amount of time in minutes the journey to the next node will take:

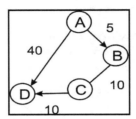

Perhaps the journey **AD** would require you to ride a bike (or walk). **B** and **C** might represent bus stops. At **B** you would have to change to a different bus. Finally, **CD** may be a short walk to reach **D**.

In this example, **AD** and **ABCD** represent two different paths. A path is simply a sequence of edges that you *pass through* between two nodes. Following these paths, you see that the total journey **AD** takes **40** minutes, whereas the journey **ABCD** takes **25** minutes. If your only concern is time, you would be better off traveling along **ABCD**, even with the added inconvenience of changing buses.

The fact that edges can be directed and may hold other information, such as time taken or whatever other value the move along a path is associated with, indicates something interesting. In previous data structures that we have worked with, the *lines* we have drawn between nodes have simply been connectors. Even when they had arrows pointing from a node to another, that was easy to represent in the node class by using `next` or `previous`, `parent` or `child`.

With graphs, it makes sense to see edges as objects just as much as nodes. Just like nodes, edges can contain extra information that is necessary to follow a particular path.

# Graph representation

Graphs can be represented in two main forms. One way is to use an adjacency matrix and the other is to use an adjacency list.

We shall be working with the following figure to develop both types of representation for graphs:

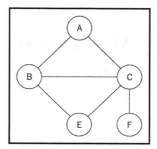

# Adjacency list

A simple list can be used to present a graph. The indices of the list will represent the nodes or vertices in the graph. At each index, the adjacent nodes to that vertex can be stored:

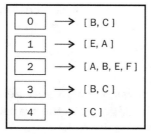

The numbers in the box represent the vertices. Index **0** represents vertex **A**, with its adjacent nodes being **B** and **C**.

Using a list for the representation is quite restrictive because we lack the ability to directly use the vertex labels. A dictionary is therefore more suited. To represent the graph in the diagram, we can use the following statements:

```
graph = dict()
graph['A'] = ['B', 'C']
graph['B'] = ['E','A']
graph['C'] = ['A', 'B', 'E','F']
graph['E'] = ['B', 'C']
graph['F'] = ['C']
```

Now we easy establish that vertex **A** has the adjacent vertices **B** and **C**. Vertex F has vertex **C** as its only neighbor.

## Adjacency matrix

Another approach by which a graph can be represented is by using an adjacency matrix. A matrix is a two-dimensional array. The idea here is to represent the cells with a 1 or 0 depending on whether two vertices are connected by an edge.

Given an adjacency list, it should be possible to create an adjacency matrix. A sorted list of keys of graph is required:

```
matrix_elements = sorted(graph.keys())
cols = rows = len(matrix_elements)
```

The length of the keys is used to provide the dimensions of the matrix which are stored in `cols` and `rows`. These values in `cols` and `rows` are equal:

```
adjacency_matrix = [[0 for x in range(rows)] for y in range(cols)]
edges_list = []
```

We then set up a `cols` by `rows` array, filling it with zeros. The `edges_list` variable will store the tuples that form the edges of in the graph. For example, an edge between node A and B will be stored as (A, B).

The multidimensional array is filled using a nested for loop:

```
for key in matrix_elements:
    for neighbor in graph[key]:
        edges_list.append((key,neighbor))
```

The neighbors of a vertex are obtained by `graph[key]`. The key in combination with the `neighbor` is then used to create the tuple stored in `edges_list`.

The output of the iteration is as follows:

```
>>> [('A', 'B'), ('A', 'C'), ('B', 'E'), ('B', 'A'), ('C', 'A'),
    ('C', 'B'), ('C', 'E'), ('C', 'F'), ('E', 'B'), ('E', 'C'),
    ('F', 'C')]
```

What needs to be done now is to fill the our multidimensional array by using 1 to mark the presence of an edge with the line `adjacency_matrix[index_of_first_vertex][index_of_second_vertex] = 1`:

```
for edge in edges_list:
    index_of_first_vertex = matrix_elements.index(edge[0])
    index_of_second_vertex = matrix_elements.index(edge[1])
    adjacecy_matrix[index_of_first_vertex][index_of_second_vertex]
= 1
```

The `matrix_elements` array has its `rows` and `cols` starting from A through to E with the indices 0 through to 5. The `for` loop iterates through our list of tuples and uses the `index` method to get the corresponding index where an edge is to be stored.

The adjacency matrix produced looks like so:

```
>>>
[0, 1, 1, 0, 0]
[1, 0, 0, 1, 0]
[1, 1, 0, 1, 1]
[0, 1, 1, 0, 0]
[0, 0, 1, 0, 0]
```

At column 1 and row 1, the 0 there represents the absence of an edge between A and A. On column 2 and row 3, there is an edge between C and B.

# Graph traversal

Since graphs don't necessarily have an ordered structure, traversing a graph can be more involving. Traversal normally involves keeping track of which nodes or vertices have already been visited and which ones have not. A common strategy is to follow a path until a dead end is reached, then walking back up until there is a point where there is an alternative path. We can also iteratively move from one node to another in order to traverse the full graph or part of it. In the next section, we will discuss breadth and depth-first search algorithms for graph traversal.

# Breadth-first search

The breadth-first search algorithm starts at a node, chooses that node or vertex as its root node, and visits the neighboring nodes, after which it explores neighbors on the next level of the graph.

Consider the following diagram as a graph:

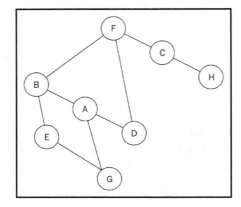

The diagram is an example of an undirected graph. We continue to use this type of graph to help make explanation easy without being too verbose.

The adjacency list for the graph is as follows:

```
graph = dict()
graph['A'] = ['B', 'G', 'D']
graph['B'] = ['A', 'F', 'E']
graph['C'] = ['F', 'H']
graph['D'] = ['F', 'A']
graph['E'] = ['B', 'G']
graph['F'] = ['B', 'D', 'C']
graph['G'] = ['A', 'E']
graph['H'] = ['C']
```

In trying to traverse this graph breadth first, we will employ the use of a queue. The algorithm creates a list to store the nodes that have been visited as the traversal process proceeds. We shall start our traversal from node A.

Node A is queued and added to the list of visited nodes. Afterward, we use a `while` loop to effect traversal of the graph. In the `while` loop, node A is dequeued. Its unvisited adjacent nodes B, G, and D are sorted in alphabetical order and queued up. The queue will now contain the nodes B, D, and G. These nodes are also added to the list of visited nodes. At this point, we start another iteration of the `while` loop because the queue is not empty, which also means we are not really done with the traversal.

Node B is dequeued. Out of its adjacent nodes A, F, and E, node A has already been visited. Therefore, we only enqueue the nodes E and F in alphabetical order. Nodes E and F are then added to the list of visited nodes.

Our queue now holds the following nodes at this point: D, G, E, and F. The list of visited nodes contains A, B, D, G, E, F.

Node D is dequeued but all of its adjacent nodes have been visited so we simply dequeue it. The next node at the front of the queue is G. We dequeue node G but we also find out that all its adjacent nodes have been visited because they are in the list of visited nodes. Node G is also dequeued. We dequeue node E too because all of its nodes have been visited. The only node in the queue now is node F.

Node F is dequeued and we realize that out of its adjacent nodes B, D, and C, only node C has not been visited. We then enqueue node C and add it to the list of visited nodes. Node C is dequeued. Node C has the adjacent nodes F and H but F has already been visited, leaving node H. Node H is enqueued and added to the list of visited nodes.

Finally, the last iteration of the `while` loop will lead to node H being dequeued. Its only adjacent node C has already been visited. Once the queue is completely empty, the loop breaks.

The output of the traversing the graph in the diagram is A, B, D, G, E, F, C, H.

The code for a breadth-first search is given as follows:

```
from collections import deque

def breadth_first_search(graph, root):
    visited_vertices = list()
    graph_queue = deque([root])
    visited_vertices.append(root)
    node = root

    while len(graph_queue) > 0:
        node = graph_queue.popleft()
```

```
    adj_nodes = graph[node]

    remaining_elements =
        set(adj_nodes).difference(set(visited_vertices))
    if len(remaining_elements) > 0:
        for elem in sorted(remaining_elements):
            visited_vertices.append(elem)
            graph_queue.append(elem)

return visited_vertices
```

 When we want to find out whether a set of nodes are in the list of visited nodes, we use the statement `remaining_elements = set(adj_nodes).difference(set(visited_vertices))`. This uses the set object's difference method to find the nodes that are in `adj_nodes` but not in `visited_vertices`.

In the worst-case scenario, each vertex or node and edge will be traversed, thus the time complexity of the algorithm is `O(|V| + |E|)`, where `|V|` is the number of vertices or nodes while `|E|` is the number of edges in the graph.

# Depth-first search

As the name suggests, this algorithm traverses the depth of any particular path in the graph before traversing its breadth. As such, child nodes are visited first before sibling nodes. It works on finite graphs and requires the use of a stack to maintain the state of the algorithm:

```
def depth_first_search(graph, root):
    visited_vertices = list()
    graph_stack = list()

    graph_stack.append(root)
    node = root
```

The algorithm begins by creating a list to store the visited nodes. The `graph_stack` stack variable is used to aid the traversal process. For continuity's sake, we are using a regular Python list as a stack.

The starting node, called `root`, is passed with the graph's adjacency matrix, graph. `root` is pushed onto the stack. `node = root` holds the first node in the stack:

```
while len(graph_stack) > 0:

    if node not in visited_vertices:
        visited_vertices.append(node)

    adj_nodes = graph[node]

    if set(adj_nodes).issubset(set(visited_vertices)):
        graph_stack.pop()
    if len(graph_stack) > 0:
        node = graph_stack[-1]
        continue
    else:
        remaining_elements =
        set(adj_nodes).difference(set(visited_vertices))

    first_adj_node = sorted(remaining_elements)[0]
    graph_stack.append(first_adj_node)
    node = first_adj_node
        return visited_vertices
```

The body of the `while` loop will be executed provided the stack is not empty. If `node` is not in the list of visited nodes, we add it. All adjacent nodes to `node` are collected by `adj_nodes = graph[node]`. If all the adjacent nodes have been visited, we pop that node from the stack and set `node` to `graph_stack[-1]`. `graph_stack[-1]` is the top node on the stack. The `continue` statement jumps back to the beginning of the while loop's test condition.

If, on the other hand, not all the adjacent nodes have been visited, the nodes that are yet to be visited are obtained by finding the difference between the `adj_nodes` and `visited_vertices` with the statement `remaining_elements = set(adj_nodes).difference(set(visited_vertices))`.

The first item within `sorted(remaining_elements)` is assigned to `first_adj_node`, and pushed onto the stack. We then point the top of the stack to this node.

When the `while` loop exists, we will return the `visited_vertices`.

Dry running the algorithm will prove useful. Consider the following graph:

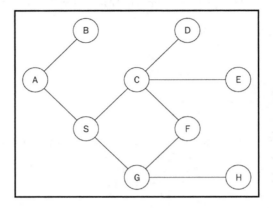

The adjacency list of such a graph is given as follows:

```
graph = dict()
graph['A'] = ['B', 'S']
graph['B'] = ['A']
graph['S'] = ['A','G','C']
graph['D'] = ['C']
graph['G'] = ['S','F','H']
graph['H'] = ['G','E']
graph['E'] = ['C','H']
graph['F'] = ['C','G']
graph['C'] = ['D','S','E','F']
```

Node A is chosen as our beginning node. Node A is pushed onto the stack and added to the `visisted_vertices` list. In doing so, we mark it as having been visited. The stack `graph_stack` is implemented with a simple Python list. Our stack now has A as its only element. We examine node A's adjacent nodes B and S. To test whether all the adjacent nodes of A have been visited, we use the if statement:

```
if set(adj_nodes).issubset(set(visited_vertices)):
    graph_stack.pop()
    if len(graph_stack) > 0:
        node = graph_stack[-1]
    continue
```

If all the nodes have been visited, we pop the top of the stack. If the stack `graph_stack` is not empty, we assign the node on top of the stack to `node` and start the beginning of another execution of the body of the `while` loop. The statement `set(adj_nodes).issubset(set(visited_vertices))` will evaluate to `True` if all the nodes in `adj_nodes` are a subset of `visited_vertices`. If the if statement fails, it means that some nodes remain to be visited. We obtain that list of nodes with `remaining_elements =` `set(adj_nodes).difference(set(visited_vertices))`.

From the diagram, nodes **B** and **S** will be stored in `remaining_elements`. We will access the list in alphabetical order:

```
first_adj_node = sorted(remaining_elements)[0]
graph_stack.append(first_adj_node)
node = first_adj_node
```

We sort `remaining_elements` and return the first node to `first_adj_node`. This will return B. We push node B onto the stack by appending it to the `graph_stack`. We prepare node B for access by assigning it to `node`.

On the next iteration of the `while` loop, we add node B to the list of `visited nodes`. We discover that the only adjacent node to B, which is A, has already been visited. Because all the adjacent nodes of B have been visited, we pop it off the stack, leaving node A as the only element on the stack. We return to node A and examine whether all of its adjacent nodes have been visited. The node A now has S as the only unvisited node. We push S to the stack and begin the whole process again.

The output of the traversal is A-B-S-C-D-E-H-G-F.

Depth-first searches find application in solving maze problems, finding connected components, and finding the bridges of a graph, among others.

# Other useful graph methods

Very often, you are concerned with finding a path between two nodes. You may also want to find all the paths between nodes. Another useful method would be to find the shortest path between nodes. In an unweighted graph, this would simply be the path with the lowest number of edges between them. In a weighted graph, as you have seen, this could involve calculating the total weight of passing through a set of edges.

Of course, in a different situation, you may want to find the longest or shortest path.

# Priority queues and heaps

A priority queue is basically a type of queue that will always return items in order of priority. This priority could be, for example, that the lowest item is always popped off first. Although it is called a queue, priority queues are often implemented using a heap, since it is very efficient for this purpose.

Consider that, in a store, customers queue in a line where service is only rendered at the front of the queue. Each customer will spend some time in the queue to get served. If the waiting times for the customers in the queue are 4, 30, 2, and 1, then the average time spent in the queue becomes `(4 + 34 + 36 + 37)/4`, which is `27.75`. However, if we change the order of service such that customers with the least amount of waiting time are served first, then we obtain a different average waiting time. In doing so, we calculate our new average waiting time by `(1 + 3 + 7 + 37)/4`, which now equals `12`, a better average waiting time. Clearly, there is merit to serving the customers from the least waiting time upward. This method of selecting the next item by priority or some other criterion is the basis for creating priority queues.

A heap is a data structure that satisfies the heap property. The heap property states that there must be a certain relationship between a parent node and its child nodes. This property must apply through the entire heap.

In a min heap, the relationship between parent and children is that the parent must always be less than or equal to its children. As a consequence of this, the lowest element in the heap must be the root node.

In a max heap, on the other hand, the parent is greater than or equal to its child or its children. It follows from this that the largest value makes up the root node.

As you can see from what we just mentioned, heaps are trees and, to be more specific, binary trees.

Although we are going to use a binary tree, we will actually use a list to represent it. This is possible because the heap will store a complete binary tree. A complete binary tree is one in which each row must be fully filled before starting to fill the next row:

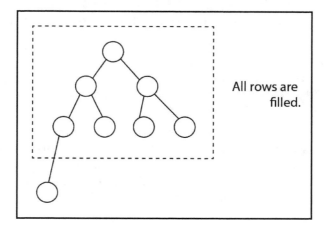

All rows are filled.

To make the math with indexes easier, we are going to leave the first item in the list (index 0) empty. After that, we place the tree nodes into the list, from top to bottom, left to right:

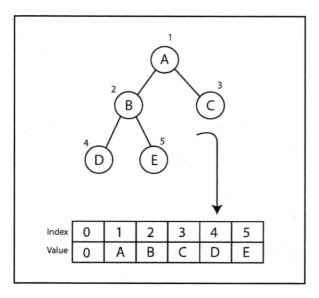

If you observe carefully, you will notice that you can retrieve the children of any node n very easily. The left child is located at $2n$ and the right child is located at $2n + 1$. This will always hold true.

We are going to look at a min heap implementation. It shouldn't be difficult to reverse the logic in order to get a max heap:

```
class Heap:
    def __init__(self):
        self.heap = [0]
        self.size = 0
```

We initialize our heap list with a zero to represent the dummy first element (remember that we are only doing this to make the math simpler). We also create a variable to hold the size of the heap. This would not be necessary as such, since we could check the size of the list, but we would always have to remember to reduce it by one. So we chose to keep a separate variable instead.

## Inserting

Inserting an item is very simple in itself. We add the new element to the end of the list (which we understand to be the bottom of the tree). Then we increment the size of the heap by one.

But after each insert, we need to float the new element up if needed. Bear in mind that the lowest element in the min heap needs to be the root element. We first create a helper method called `float` that takes care of this. Let us look at how it is meant to behave. Imagine that we have the following heap and want to insert the value 2:

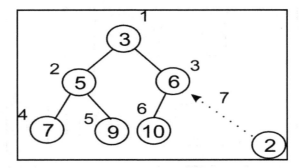

The new element has occupied the last slot in the third row or level. Its index value is 7. Now we compare that value with its parent. The parent is at index 7/2 = 3 (integer division). That element holds **6** so we swap the **2**:

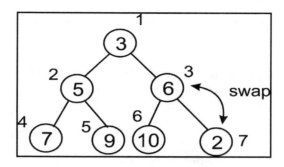

Our new element has been swapped and moved up to index **3**. We have not reached the top of the heap yet (3 / 2 > 0), so we continue. The new parent of our element is at index 3/2 = 1. So we compare and, if necessary, swap again:

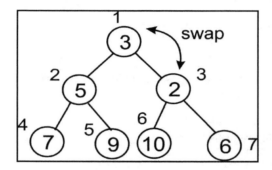

After the final swap, we are left with the heap looking as follows. Notice how it adheres to the definition of a heap:

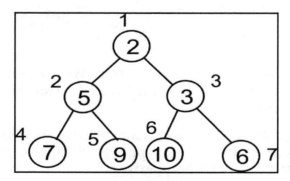

Here follows an implementation of what we have just described:

```
def float(self, k):
```

We are going to loop until we have reached the root node so that we can keep floating the element up as high as it needs to go. Since we are using integer division, as soon as we get below 2, the loop will break out:

```
while k // 2 > 0:
```

Compare parent and child. If the parent is greater than the child, swap the two values:

```
if self.heap[k] < self.heap[k//2]:
    self.heap[k], self.heap[k//2] = self.heap[k//2],
    self.heap[k]
```

Finally, let's not forget to move up the tree:

```
k //= 2
```

This method ensures that the elements are ordered properly. Now we just need to call this from our `insert` method:

```
def insert(self, item):
    self.heap.append(item)
    self.size += 1
    self.float(self.size)
```

Notice the last line in insert calls the `float()` method to reorganize the heap as necessary.

# Pop

Just like insert, `pop()` is by itself a simple operation. We remove the root node and decrement the size of the heap by one. However, once the root has been popped off, we need a new root node.

To make this as simple as possible, we just take the last item in the list and make it the new root. That is, we move it to the beginning of the list. But now we might not have the lowest element at the top of the heap, so we perform the opposite of the float operation: we let the new root node sink down as required.

As we did with insert, let us have a look at how the whole operation is meant to work on an existing heap. Imagine the following heap. We pop off the `root` element, leaving the heap temporarily rootless:

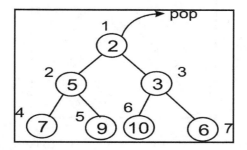

Since we cannot have a rootless heap, we need to fill this slot with something. If we choose to move up one of the children, we will have to figure out how to rebalance the entire tree structure. So instead, we do something really interesting. We move up the very last element in the list to fill the position of the `root` element:

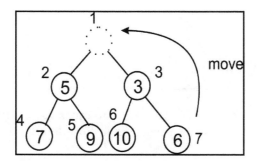

Now this element clearly is not the lowest in the heap. This is where we begin to sink it down. First we need to determine where to sink it down. We compare the two children, so that the lowest element will be the one to float up as the root sinks down:

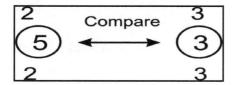

The right child is clearly less. Its index is **3**, which represents the root index `*  2  +  1`. We go ahead and compare our new root node with the value at this index:

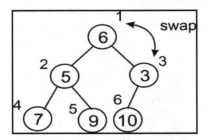

Now our node has jumped down to index **3**. We need to compare it to the lesser of its children. However, now we only have one child, so we don't need to worry about which child to compare against (for a min heap, it is always the lesser child):

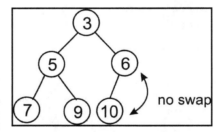

There is no need to swap here. Since there are no more rows either, we are done. Notice again how, after the `sink()` operation is completed, our heap adheres to the definition of a heap.

Now we can begin implementing this. Before we do the `sink()` method itself, notice how we need to determine which of the children to compare our parent node against. Well, let us put that selection in its own little method, just to make the code look a little simpler:

```
def minindex(self, k):
```

We may get beyond the end of the list, in which case we return the index of the left child:

```
if k * 2 + 1 > self.size:
    return k * 2
```

Otherwise, we simply return the index of the lesser of the two children:

```
elif self.heap[k*2] < self.heap[k*2+1]:
    return k * 2
else:
    return k * 2 + 1
```

Now we can create the `sink` function:

```
def sink(self, k):
```

As before, we are going to loop so that we can sink our element down as far as is needed:

```
while k * 2 <= self.size:
```

Next we need to know which of the left or the right child to compare against. This is where we make use of the `minindex()` function:

```
mi = self.minindex(k)
```

As we did in the `float()` method, we compare parent and child to see whether we need to swap:

```
if self.heap[k] > self.heap[mi]:
    self.heap[k], self.heap[mi] = self.heap[mi],
    self.heap[k]
```

And we need to make sure that we move down the tree so that we don't get stuck in a loop:

```
k = mi
```

The only thing remaining now is to implement `pop()` itself. This is very straightforward as the grunt work is performed by the `sink()` method:

```
def pop(self):
    item = self.heap[1]
    self.heap[1] = self.heap[self.size]
    self.size -= 1
    self.heap.pop()
    self.sink(1)
    return item
```

# Testing the heap

Now we just need some code to test the heap. We begin by creating our heap and inserting some data:

```
h = Heap()
for i in (4, 8, 7, 2, 9, 10, 5, 1, 3, 6):
    h.insert(i)
```

We can print the heap list, just to inspect how the elements are ordered. If you redraw this as a tree structure, you should notice that it meets the required properties of a heap:

```
print(h.heap)
```

Now we will pop off the items, one at a time. Notice how the items come out in a sorted order, from lowest to highest. Also notice how the heap list changes after each pop. It is a good idea to take out a pen and paper and to redraw this list as a tree after each pop, to fully understand how the `sink()` method works:

```
for i in range(10):
    n = h.pop()
    print(n)
    print(h.heap)
```

In the chapter on sorting algorithms, we will reorganize the code for the heap sort algorithm.

Once you have the min heap working properly and understand how it works, it should be a simple task to implement a max heap. All you have to do is to reverse the logic.

# Selection algorithms

Selection algorithms fall under a class of algorithms that seek to answer the problem of finding the ith-smallest element in a list. When a list is sorted in ascending order, the first element in the list will be the smallest item in the list. The second element in the list will be the second-smallest element in the list. The last element in the list will be the last-smallest element in the list but that will also qualify as the largest element in the list.

In creating the heap data structure, we have come to the understanding that a call to the pop method will return the smallest element in the heap. The first element to pop off a min heap is the first-smallest element in the list. Similarly, the seventh element to be popped off the min heap will be the seventh-smallest element in the list. Therefore, to find the ith-smallest element in a list will require us to pop the heap *i* number of times. That is a very simple and efficient way of finding the ith-smallest element in a list.

But in Chapter 14, *Selection Algorithms*, we will study another approach by which we can find the ith-smallest element in a list.

Selection algorithms have applications in filtering out noisy data, finding the median, smallest, and largest elements in a list, and can even be applied in computer chess programs.

# Summary

Graphs and heaps have been treated in this chapter. We looked at ways to represent a graph in Python using lists and dictionaries. In order to traverse the graph, we looked at breadth-first searches and depth-first searches.

We then switched our attention to heaps and priority queues to understand their implementation. The chapter ended with using the concept of a heap to find the ith-smallest element in a list.

The subject of graphs is very complicated and just one chapter will not do justice to it. The journey with nodes will end with this chapter. The next chapter will usher us into the arena of searching and the various means by which we can efficiently search for items in lists.

# 12
# Searching

With the data structures that have been developed in the preceding chapters, one critical operation performed on all of them is searching. In this chapter, we shall explore the different strategies that can be used to find elements in a collection of items.

One other important operation that makes use of searching is sorting. It is virtually impossible to sort without some variant of a search operation. The "how of searching" is also important as it has a bearing on how quick a sorting algorithm ends up performing.

Searching algorithms are categorized under two broad types. One category assumes that the list of items to apply the searching operation on, has already been sorted whiles the other does not.

The performance of a search operation is heavily influenced by whether the items about to be searched have already been sorted or not as we will see in the subsequent topics too.

## Linear Search

Let us focus our discussions on linear search, performed on a typical Python list.

| 60 | 1 | 88 | 10 | 11 | 100 |
|----|----|----|----|----|----|
| [0] | [1] | [2] | [3] | [4] | [5] |

The preceding list has elements that are accessible through the list index. To find an element in the list we employ the linear searching technique. This technique traverses the list of elements, by using the index to move from the beginning of the list to the end. Each element is examined and if it does not match the search item, the next item is examined. By hopping from one item to its next, the list is traversed sequentially.

 In treating the sections in this chapter and others, we use a list with integers to enhance our understanding since integers lend themselves to easy comparison.

# Unordered linear search

A list containing elements **60**, **1**, **88**, **10**, and **100** is an example of an unordered list. The items in the list have no order by magnitude. To perform a search operation on such a list, one proceeds from the very first item, compares that with the search item. If a match is not made the next element in the list is examined. This continues till we reach the last element in the list or until a match is made.

```
def search(unordered_list, term):
    unordered_list_size = len(unordered_list)
    for i in range(unordered_list_size):
        if term == unordered_list[i]:
            return i

    return None
```

The `search` function takes as parameters, the list that houses our data and the item that we are looking for called the **search term**.

The size of the array is obtained and determines the number of times the `for` loop is executed.

```
if term == unordered_list[i]:
    . . .
```

On every pass of the `for` loop, we test if the search term is equal to the item that the index points to. If true, then there is no need to proceed with the search. We return the position where the match occurred.

If the loop runs to the end of the list with no match being made, `None` is returned to signify that there is no such item in the list.

In an unordered list of items, there is no guiding rule for how elements are inserted. This therefore impacts the way the search is done. The lack of order means that we cannot rely on any rule to perform the search. As such, we must visit the items in the list one after the other. As can be seen in the following image, the search for the term **66**, starts from the first element and moves to next element in the list. Thus **60** compared with **66** and if it is not equal, we compare **66** with **1, 88** and so on till we find the search term in the list.

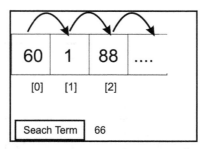

The unordered linear search has a worst case running time of O(n). All the elements may need to be visited before finding the search term. This will be the case if the search term is located at the last position of the list.

# Ordered linear search

In the case where the elements of a list have been already sorted, our search algorithm can be improved. Assuming the elements have been sorted in ascending order, the search operation can take advantage of the ordered nature of the list to make search more efficient.

The algorithm is reduced to the following steps:

1. Move through the list sequentially.
2. If a search item is greater than the object or item currently under inspection in the loop, then quit and return None.

In the process of iterating through the list, if the search term is greater than the current item, then there is no need to continue with the search.

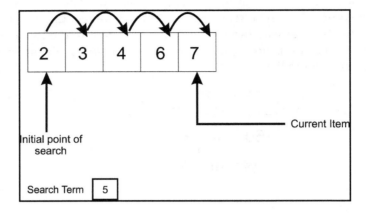

When the search operation starts and the first element is compared with (**5**), no match is made. But because there are more elements in the list the search operation moves on to examine the next element. A more compelling reason to move on is that we know the search item may match any of the elements greater than **2**.

After the 4th comparison, we come to the conclusion that the search term, can not be found in any position above where **6** is located. In other words, if the current item is greater than the search term, then it means there is no need to further search the list.

```python
def search(ordered_list, term):
    ordered_list_size = len(ordered_list)
    for i in range(ordered_list_size):
        if term == ordered_list[i]:
            return i
        elif ordered_list[i] > term:
            return None

    return None
```

The `if` statement now caters for this check. The `elif` portion tests the condition where `ordered_list[i] > term`. The method returns `None` if the comparison evaluates to `True`.

The last line in the method returns `None` because the loop may go through the list and still not find any element matching the search term.

The worst case time complexity of an ordered linear search is $O(n)$. In general, this kind of search is considered inefficient especially when dealing with large data sets.

# Binary search

A binary search is a search strategy used to find elements within a list by consistently reducing the amount of data to be searched and thereby increasing the rate at which the search term is found.

To use a binary search algorithm, the list to be operated on must have already been sorted.

The *binary* term carries a number of meanings and helps us put our minds in the right frame to understand the algorithm.

A binary decision has to be made at each attempt to find an item in the list. One critical decision is to guess which part of the list is likely to house the item we are looking for. Would the search term be in the first half of second half of the list, that is, if we always perceive the list as being comprised of two parts?

Instead of moving from one cell of the list to the other, if we employ the use of an educated guessing strategy, we are likely to arrive at the position where the item will be found much faster.

As an example, lets take it that we want to find the middle page of a 1000 page book. We already know that every book has its pages numbered sequentially from 1 upwards. So it figures that the 500th page should be found right at the middle of the book, instead of moving and flipping from page 1, 2 to reach the 500th page. Let's say we decide to now look for the page 250. We can still use our strategy to find the page easily. We guess that page 500 cuts the book in half. Page 250, will lay to the left of the book. No need to worry about whether we can find 250th page between page 500 and 1000 because it can never be found there. So using page 500 as reference, we can open to about half of the pages that lay between the 1st and 500th page. That brings us closer to finding the 250th page.

The following is the algorithm for conducting a binary search on an ordered list of items:

```python
def binary_search(ordered_list, term):

    size_of_list = len(ordered_list) - 1

    index_of_first_element = 0
```

```
index_of_last_element = size_of_list

while index_of_first_element <= index_of_last_element:
    mid_point = (index_of_first_element + index_of_last_element)/2

    if ordered_list[mid_point] == term:
        return mid_point

    if term > ordered_list[mid_point]:
        index_of_first_element = mid_point + 1
    else:
        index_of_last_element = mid_point - 1

if index_of_first_element > index_of_last_element:
    return None
```

Let's assume we have to find the position where the item **10** is located in the list as follows:

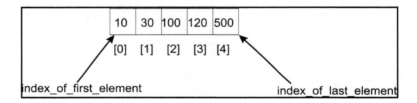

The algorithm uses a `while` loop to iteratively adjust the limits in the list within which to find a search term. So far as the difference between the starting index, `index_of_first_element` and the `index_of_last_element` index is positive, the `while` loop will run.

The algorithm first finds the mid point of the list by adding the index of the first element (**0**) to that of the last (**4**) and dividing it by **2** to find the middle index, `mid_point`.

```
mid_point = (index_of_first_element + index_of_last_element)/2
```

In this case, **10** is not found at the middle position or index in the list. If we were searching for **120**, we would have had to adjust the `index_of_first_element` to `mid_point` +1. But because **10** lies on the other side of the list, we adjust `index_of_last_element` to `mid_point-1`:

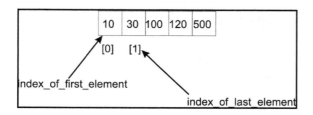

With our new index of `index_of_first_element` and `index_of_last_element` now being **0** and **1** respectively, we compute the mid `(0 + 1)/2`, which equals `0`. The new midpoint is **0**, We find the middle item and compare with the search item, `ordered_list[0]` which yields the value **10**. Voila! Our search term is found.

This reduction of our list size by half, by re-adjusting the index of the `index_of_first_element` and `index_of_last_element` continues as long as `index_of_first_element` is less than `index_of_last_element`. When this fails to be the case it is most likely that our search term is not in the list.

The implementation here is an iterative one. We can also develop a recursive variant of the algorithm by applying the same principle of shifting the pointers that mark the beginning and ending of the search list.

```python
def binary_search(ordered_list, first_element_index,
last_element_index, term):

    if (last_element_index < first_element_index):
        return None
    else:
        mid_point = first_element_index + ((last_element_index -
first_element_index) / 2)

        if ordered_list[mid_point] > term:
            return binary_search(ordered_list, first_element_index,
mid_point-1,term)
        elif ordered_list[mid_point] < term:
            return binary_search(ordered_list, mid_point+1,
last_element_index, term)
        else:
            return mid_point
```

A call to this recursive implementation of the binary search algorithm and its output is as follows:

```
store = [2, 4, 5, 12, 43, 54, 60, 77]
print(binary_search(store, 0, 7, 2))
```

**Output:**
```
>> 0
```

There only distinction between the recursive binary search and the iterative binary search is the function definition and also the way in which `mid_point` is calculated. The calculation for the `mid_point` after the `((last_element_index - first_element_index) / 2)` operation must add its result to `first_element_index`. That way we define the portion of the list to attempt the search.

The binary search algorithm has a worst time complexity of `O(log n)`. The half-ing of the list on each iteration follows a log n of the number of elements progression.

 It goes without saying that in `log x` is assumed to be referring to log base 2.

# Interpolation search

There is another variant of the binary search algorithm that may closely be said to mimic more, how humans perform search on any list of items. It is still based off trying to make a good guess of where in a sorted list of items, a search item is likely to be found.

Examine the following list of items for example:

| 44 | 60 | 75 | 100 | 120 | 230 | 250 |
|----|----|----|-----|-----|-----|-----|
| [0] | [1] | [2] | [3] | [4] | [5] | [6] |

To find **120**, we know to look at the right hand portion of the list. Our initial treatment of binary search would typically examine the middle element first in order to determine if it matches the search term.

A more human thing would be to pick a middle element in a such a way as to not only split the array in half but to get as close as possible to the search term. The middle position was calculated for using the following rule:

```
mid_point = (index_of_first_element + index_of_last_element)/2
```

We shall replace this formula with a better one that brings us close to the search term. mid_point will receive the return value of the nearest_mid function.

```
def nearest_mid(input_list, lower_bound_index, upper_bound_index,
search_value):
    return lower_bound_index + (( upper_bound_index -
lower_bound_index)/ (input_list[upper_bound_index] -
input_list[lower_bound_index])) * (search_value -
input_list[lower_bound_index])
```

The nearest_mid function takes as arguments, the list on which to perform the search. The lower_bound_index and upper_bound_index parameters represent the bounds in the list within which we are hoping to find the search term. search_value represents the value being searched for.

These are used in the formula:

```
lower_bound_index + (( upper_bound_index - lower_bound_index)/
(input_list[upper_bound_index] - input_list[lower_bound_index])) *
(search_value - input_list[lower_bound_index])
```

Given our search list, **44**, **60**, **75**, **100**, **120**, **230** and **250**, the nearest_mid will be computed with the following values:

```
lower_bound_index = 0
upper_bound_index = 6
input_list[upper_bound_index] = 250
input_list[lower_bound_index] = 44
search_value = 230
```

It can now be seen that, the mid_point will receive the value **5**, which is the index of the location of our search term. A binary search would have chosen **100** as the mid which will require another run of the algorithm.

A more visual illustration of how a typical binary search differs from an interpolation is given as follows. For a typical binary search finds the midpoint like so:

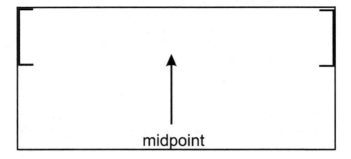

One can see that the midpoint is actually standing approximately in the middle of the preceding list. This is as a result of dividing by list 2.

An interpolation search on the other hand would move like so:

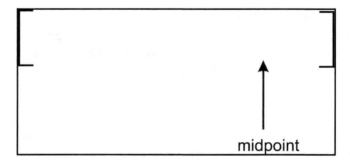

In interpolation search, our midpoint is swayed more to the left or right. This is caused by the effect of the multiplier used when dividing to obtain the midpoint. From the preceding image, our midpoint has been skewed to the right.

The remainder of the interpolation algorithm remains the same as that of the binary search except for the way the mid position is calculated for.

```
def interpolation_search(ordered_list, term):

    size_of_list = len(ordered_list) - 1

    index_of_first_element = 0
    index_of_last_element = size_of_list

    while index_of_first_element <= index_of_last_element:
```

```
        mid_point = nearest_mid(ordered_list, index_of_first_element,
index_of_last_element, term)

        if mid_point > index_of_last_element or mid_point <
index_of_first_element:
            return None

        if ordered_list[mid_point] == term:
            return mid_point

        if term > ordered_list[mid_point]:
            index_of_first_element = mid_point + 1
        else:
            index_of_last_element = mid_point - 1

    if index_of_first_element > index_of_last_element:
        return None
```

The nearest_mid function makes use of a multiplication operation. This can produce values that are greater than the upper_bound_index or lower than the lower_bound_index. When this occurs, it means the search term, term, is not in the list. None is therefore returned to represent this.

So what happens when ordered_list[mid_point] does not equal the search them? Well, we must now re-adjust the index_of_first_element and index_of_last_element such that the algorithm will focus on the part of the array that is likely to contain the search term. This is like exactly what we did in the binary search.

```
if term > ordered_list[mid_point]:
index_of_first_element = mid_point + 1
```

If the search term is greater than the value stored at ordered_list[mid_point], then we only adjust the index_of_first_element variable to point to the index mid_point + 1.

The following image shows how the adjustment occurs. The `index_of_first_element` is adjusted and pointed to the index of `mid_point+1`.

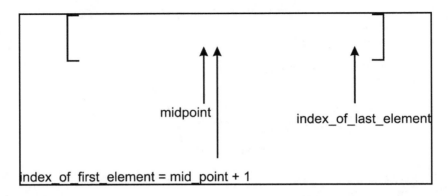

 The image only illustrates the adjustment of the midpoint. In interpolation rarely does the midpoint divide the list in 2 equal halves.

On the other hand, if the search term is lesser than the value stored at `ordered_list[mid_point]`, then we only adjust the `index_of_last_element` variable to point to the index `mid_point - 1`. This logic is captured in the else part of the if statement `index_of_last_element = mid_point - 1`.

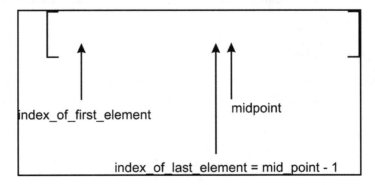

The image shows the effect of the recalculation of `index_of_last_element` on the position of the midpoint.

Let's use a more practical example to understand the inner workings of both the binary search and interpolation algorithms.

Take the list with elements:

```
[ 2, 4, 5, 12, 43, 54, 60, 77]
```

At index 0 is stored 2 and at index 7 is found the value 77. Now, assume that we want to find the element 2 in the list. How will the two different algorithms go about it?

If we pass this list to the interpolation `search` function, the `nearest_mid` function will return a value equal to 0. Just by one comparison, we would have found the search term.

On the other hand, the binary search algorithm would need three comparisons to arrive at the search term as illustrated in the following image:

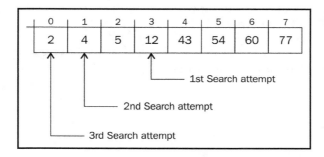

The first `mid_point` calculated is 3. The second `mid_point` is 1 and the last `mid_point` where the search term is found is 0.

# Choosing a search algorithm

The binary search and interpolation search operations are better in performance than both ordered and unordered linear search functions. Because of the sequential probing of elements in the list to find the search term, ordered and unordered linear search have a time complexity of `O(n)`. This gives very poor performance when the list is large.

The binary search operation on the other hand, slices the list in two, anytime a search is attempted. On each iteration, we approach the search term much faster than in a linear strategy. The time complexity yields `O(log n)`. Despite the speed gain in using binary search, it is most it can not be used on an unsorted list of items neither is it advised to be used for list of small sizes.

The ability to get to the portion of the list that houses a search term determines to a large extent, how well a search algorithm will perform. In the interpolation search algorithm, the mid is calculated for which gives a higher probability of obtaining our search term. The time complexity of the interpolation search is `O( log ( log n))`. This gives rise to a faster search compared to its variant, binary search.

# Summary

In this chapter, we have examined two breeds of search algorithms. The implementation of both linear and binary search algorithms have been discussed and their comparisons drawn. The binary search variant, interpolation search has also been treated in this section. Knowing which kind of search operation to use will be relevant in subsequent chapters.

In our next chapter, we shall use the knowledge that we have gained to enable us perform sorting operations on a list of items.

# 13
## Sorting

Whenever data is collected, there comes a time when it becomes necessary to sort the data. The sorting operation is common to all datasets, be it a collection of names, telephone numbers, or items on a simple to-do list.

In this chapter, we'll study a few sorting techniques, including the following:

- Bubble sort
- Insertion sort
- Selection sort
- Quick sort
- Heap sort

In our treatment of these sorting algorithms, we will take into consideration their asymptotic behavior. Some of the algorithms are relatively easy to develop but may perform poorly. Other algorithms that are a little complex to write will show impressive performance.

After sorting, it becomes much easier to conduct search operations on a collection of items. We'll start with the simplest of all sorting algorithms--the bubble sort algorithm.

## Sorting algorithms

In this chapter, we will go through a number of sorting algorithms that have varying levels of difficulty of implementation. Sorting algorithms are categorized by their memory usage, complexity, recursion, whether they are comparison-based among other considerations.

Some of the algorithms use more CPU cycles and as such have bad asymptotic values. Others chew on more memory and other computing resources as they sort a number of values. Another consideration is how sorting algorithms lend themselves to being expressed recursively or iteratively or both. There are algorithms that use comparison as the basis for sorting elements. An example of this is the bubble sort algorithm. Examples of a non-comparison sorting algorithm are the buck sort and pigeonhole sort.

# Bubble sort

The idea behind a bubble sort algorithm is very simple. Given an unordered list, we compare adjacent elements in the list, each time, putting in the right order of magnitude, only two elements. The algorithm hinges on a swap procedure.

Take a list with only two elements:

To sort this list, simply swap them into the right position with **2** occupying index **0** and **5** occupying index **1**. To effectively swap these elements, we need to have a temporary storage area:

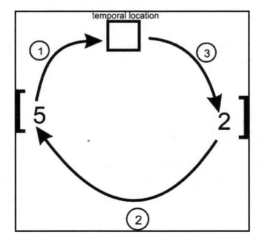

Implementation of the bubble sort algorithm starts with the swap method, illustrated in the preceding image. First, element **5** will be copied to a temporary location, `temp`. Then element **2** will be moved to index **0**. Finally, **5** will be moved from temp to index **1**. At the end of it all, the elements will have been swapped. The list will now contain the element: `[2, 5]`. The following code will swap the elements of `unordered_list[j]` with `unordered_list[j+1]` if they are not in the right order:

```
temp = unordered_list[j]
unordered_list[j] = unordered_list[j+1]
unordered_list[j+1] = temp
```

Now that we have been able to swap a two-element array, it should be simple to use this same idea to sort a whole list.

We'll run this swap operation in a double-nested loop. The inner loop is as follows:

```
for j in range(iteration_number):
    if unordered_list[j] > unordered_list[j+1]:
        temp = unordered_list[j]
        unordered_list[j] = unordered_list[j+1]
        unordered_list[j+1] = temp
```

Knowing how many times to swap is important when implementing a bubble sort algorithm. To sort a list of numbers such as `[3, 2, 1]`, we need to swap the elements a maximum of twice. This is equal to the length of the list minus 1, `iteration_number = len(unordered_list) -1`. We subtract 1 because it gives us exactly the maximum number of iterations to run:

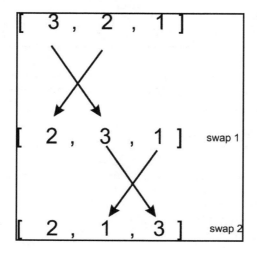

By swapping the adjacent elements in exactly two iterations, the largest number ends up at the last position on the list.

The `if` statement makes sure that no needless swaps occur if two adjacent elements are already in the right order. The inner `for` loop only causes the swapping of adjacent elements to occur exactly twice in our list.

However, you'll realize that the running of the `for` loop for the first time does not entirely sort our list. How many times does this swapping operation have to occur in order for the entire list to be sorted? If we repeat the whole process of swapping the adjacent elements a number of times, the list will be sorted. An outer loop is used to make this happen. The swapping of elements in the list results in the following dynamics:

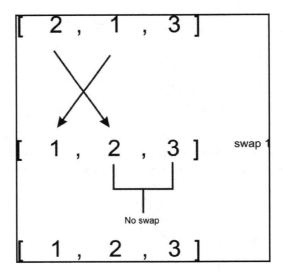

We recognize that a total of four comparisons at most were needed to get our list sorted. Therefore, both inner and outer loops have to run `len(unordered_list)-1` times for all elements to be sorted:

```
iteration_number = len(unordered_list)-1
    for i in range(iteration_number):
        for j in range(iteration_number):
            if unordered_list[j] > unordered_list[j+1]:
                temp = unordered_list[j]
                unordered_list[j] = unordered_list[j+1]
                unordered_list[j+1] = temp
```

The same principle is used even if the list contains many elements. There are a lot of variations of the bubble sort too that minimize the number of iterations and comparisons.

The bubble sort is a highly inefficient sorting algorithm with a time complexity of O(n2) and best case of O(n). Generally, the bubble sort algorithm should not be used to sort large lists. However, on relatively small lists, it performs fairly well.

There is a variant of the bubble sort algorithm where if there is no comparison within the inner loop, we simply quit the entire sorting process. The absence of the need to swap elements in the inner loop suggests the list has already been sorted. In a way, this can help speed up the generally considered slow algorithm.

# Insertion sort

The idea of swapping adjacent elements to sort a list of items can also be used to implement the insertion sort. In the insertion sort algorithm, we assume that a certain portion of the list has already been sorted, while the other portion remains unsorted. With this assumption, we move through the unsorted portion of the list, picking one element at a time. With this element, we go through the sorted portion of the list and insert it in the right order so that the sorted portion of the list remains sorted. That is a lot of grammar. Let's walk through the explanation with an example.

Consider the following array:

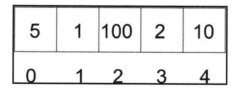

The algorithm starts by using a `for` loop to run between the indexes **1** and **4**. We start from index **1** because we assume the sub-array with index **0** to already be in the sorted order:

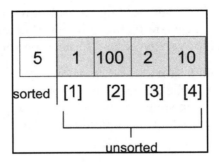

At the start of the execution of the loop, we have the following:

```
for index in range(1, len(unsorted_list)):
    search_index = index
    insert_value = unsorted_list[index]
```

At the beginning of the execution of each run of the `for` loop, the element at `unsorted_list[index]` is stored in the `insert_value` variable. Later, when we find the appropriate position in the sorted portion of the list, `insert_value` will be stored at that index or location:

```
for index in range(1, len(unsorted_list)):
    search_index = index
    insert_value = unsorted_list[index]

    while search_index > 0 and unsorted_list[search_index-1] >
            insert_value :
        unsorted_list[search_index] =
unsorted_list[search_index-1]
        search_index -= 1

    unsorted_list[search_index] = insert_value
```

The `search_index` is used to provide information to the `while` loop--exactly where to find the next element that needs to be inserted in the sorted portion of the list.

The `while` loop traverses the list backwards, guided by two conditions: first, if `search_index > 0`, then it means that there are more elements in the sorted portion of the list; second, for the `while` loop to run, `unsorted_list[search_index-1]` must be greater than the `insert_value`.

The `unsorted_list[search_index-1]` array will do either of the following things:

- Point to the element just before the `unsorted_list[search_index]` before the `while` loop is executed the first time
- Point to one element before `unsorted_list[search_index-1]` after the `while` loop has been run the first time

In our list example, the `while` loop will be executed because 5 > 1. In the body of the while loop, the element at `unsorted_list[search_index-1]` is stored at `unsorted_list[search_index]`. `search_index -= 1` moves the list traversal backwards till it bears the value 0.

Our list now looks like this:

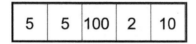

After the `while` loop exits, the last known position of `search_index` (which in this case is 0) now helps us to know where to insert `insert_value`:

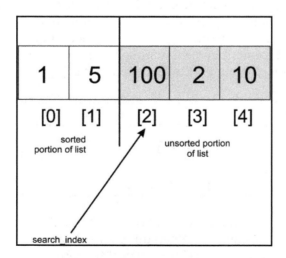

On the second iteration of the `for` loop, `search_index` will have the value **2**, which is the index of the third element in the array. At this point, we start our comparison in the direction to the left (towards index 0). **100** will be compared with **5** but because **100** is greater than **5**, the while loop will not be executed. **100** will be replaced by itself because the `search_index` variable never got decremented. As such, `unsorted_list[search_index] = insert_value` will have no effect.

When `search_index` is pointing at index **3**, we compare **2** with **100** and move **100** to where **2** is stored. We then compare **2** with **5** and move **5** to where **100** was initially stored. At this point, the `while` loop will break and **2** will be stored in index **1**. The array will be partially sorted with the values `[1, 2, 5, 100, 10]`.

The preceding step will occur one last time for the list to be sorted.

The insertion sort algorithm is considered stable in that it does not change the relative order of elements that have equal keys. It also only requires no more memory than what is consumed by the list because it does the swapping in-place.

Its worst case value is $O(n^2)$ and its best case is $O(n)$.

# Selection sort

Another popular sorting algorithm is the selection sort. This sorting algorithm is simple to understand, yet also inefficient, with its worst and best asymptotic values being $O(n^2)$. It begins by finding the smallest element in an array and interchanging it with data at, for instance, array index **[0]**. The same operation is done a second time; however, the smallest element in the remainder of the list after finding the first smallest element is interchanged with the data at index **[1]**.

In a bid to throw more light on how the algorithm works, lets sort a list of numbers:

| 5 | 2 | 65 | 10 | |
|---|---|----|----|--|
| 0 | 1 | 2 | 3 | |

Starting at index **0**, we search for the smallest item in the list that exists between index **1** and the index of the last element. When this element has been found, it is exchanged with the data found at index **0**. We simply repeat this process until the list becomes sorted.

Searching for the smallest item within the list is an incremental process:

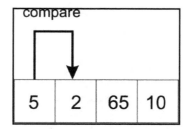

A comparison of elements **2** and **5** selects **2** as the lesser of the two. The two elements are swapped.

After the swap operation, the array looks like this:

| 2 | 5 | 65 | 10 |

Still at index **0**, we compare **2** with **65**:

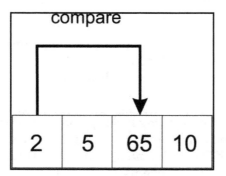

Since **65** is greater than **2**, the two elements are not swapped. A further comparison is made between the element at index **0**, which is **2**, with element at index **3**, which is **10**. No swap takes place. When we get to the last element in the list, we will have the smallest element occupying index **0**.

A new set of comparisons will begin, but this time, from index **1**. We repeat the whole process of comparing the element stored there with all the elements between index **2** through to the last index.

The first step of the second iteration will look like this:

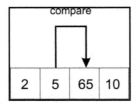

The following is an implementation of the selection sort algorithm. The argument to the function is the unsorted list of items we want to put in ascending order of magnitude:

```
def selection_sort(unsorted_list):

    size_of_list = len(unsorted_list)

    for i in range(size_of_list):
        for j in range(i+1, size_of_list):

            if unsorted_list[j] < unsorted_list[i]:
                temp = unsorted_list[i]
                unsorted_list[i] = unsorted_list[j]
                unsorted_list[j] = temp
```

The algorithm begins by using the outer `for` loop to go through the list, `size_of_list`, a number of times. Because we pass `size_of_list` to the `range` method, it will produce a sequence from **0** through to `size_of_list-1`. It is a subtle note.

The inner loop is responsible for going through the list and making the necessary swap any time that we encounter an element less than the element pointed to by `unsorted_list[i]`. Notice that the inner loop begins from `i+1` up to `size_of_list-1`. The inner loop begins its search for the smallest element between `i+1` but uses the `j` index:

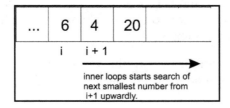

The preceding diagram shows the direction in which the algorithm searches for the next smallest item.

# Quick sort

The quick sort algorithm falls under the divide and conquer class of algorithms, where we break (divide) a problem into smaller chunks that are much simpler to solve (conquer). In this case, an unsorted array is broken into sub-arrays that are partially sorted, until all elements in the list are in the right position, by which time our unsorted list will have become sorted.

## List partitioning

Before we divide the list into smaller chunks, we have to partition it. This is the heart of the quick sort algorithm. To partition the array, we must first select a pivot. All the elements in the array will be compared with this pivot. At the end of the partitioning process, all elements that are less than the pivot will be to the left of the pivot, while all elements greater than the pivot will lie to the right of the pivot in the array.

## Pivot selection

For the sake of simplicity, we'll take the first element in any array as the pivot. This kind of pivot selection degrades in performance, especially when sorting an already sorted list. Randomly picking the middle or last element in the array as the pivot does not improve the situation any further. In the next chapter, we will adopt a better approach to selecting the pivot in order to help us find the smallest element in a list.

## Implementation

Before we delve into the code, let's run through the sorting of a list using the quick sort algorithm. The partitioning step is very important to understand so we'll tackle that operation first.

Consider the following list of integers. We shall partition this list using the partition function below:

```
43 , 3 , 20 , 89 , 4 , 77
```

```
def partition(unsorted_array, first_index, last_index):

    pivot = unsorted_array[first_index]
    pivot_index = first_index
    index_of_last_element = last_index

    less_than_pivot_index = index_of_last_element
    greater_than_pivot_index = first_index + 1
    ...
```

The partition function receives the array that we need to partition as its parameters: the index of its first element and the index of its last element.

The value of the pivot is stored in the `pivot` variable, while its index is stored in `pivot_index`. We are not using `unsorted_array[0]` because when the unsorted array parameter is called with a segment of an array, index 0 will not necessarily point to the first element in that array. The index of the next element to the pivot, `first_index + 1`, marks the position where we begin to look for the element in the array that is greater than the `pivot, greater_than_pivot_index = first_index + 1`.

`less_than_pivot_index = index_of_last_element` marks the position of the last element in the list which is, where we begin the search for the element that is less than the pivot:

```
while True:

    while unsorted_array[greater_than_pivot_index] < pivot and
          greater_than_pivot_index < last_index:
        greater_than_pivot_index += 1

    while unsorted_array[less_than_pivot_index] > pivot and
          less_than_pivot_index >= first_index:
        less_than_pivot_index -= 1
```

At the beginning of the execution of the main `while` loop the array looks like this:

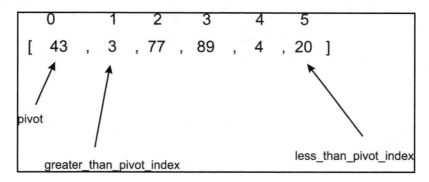

The first inner `while` loop moves one index to the right until it lands on index **2**, because the value at that index is greater than **43**. At this point, the first `while` loop breaks and does not continue. At each test of the condition in the first `while` loop, `greater_than_pivot_index += 1` is evaluated only if the `while` loop's test condition evaluates to `True`. This makes the search for the element greater than the pivot progress to the next element on the right.

The second inner `while` loop moves one index at a time to the left, until it lands on index **5**, whose value, **20**, is less than **43**:

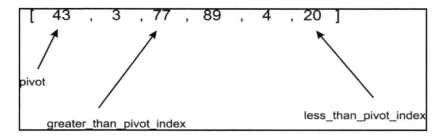

At this point, neither inner `while` loop can be executed any further:

```
if greater_than_pivot_index < less_than_pivot_index:
    temp = unsorted_array[greater_than_pivot_index]
        unsorted_array[greater_than_pivot_index] =
            unsorted_array[less_than_pivot_index]
        unsorted_array[less_than_pivot_index] = temp
else:
    break
```

Since `greater_than_pivot_index` < `less_than_pivot_index`, the body of the if statement swaps the element at those indexes. The else condition breaks the infinite loop any time `greater_than_pivot_index` becomes greater than `less_than_pivot_index`. In such a condition, it means that `greater_than_pivot_index` and `less_than_pivot_index` have crossed over each other.

Our array now looks like this:

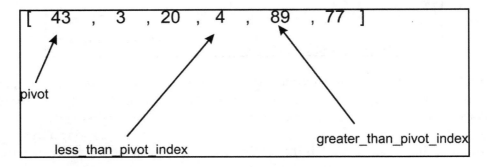

The break statement is executed when `less_than_pivot_index` is equal to 3 and `greater_than_pivot_index` is equal to 4.

As soon as we exit the `while` loop, we interchange the element at `unsorted_array[less_than_pivot_index]` with that of `less_than_pivot_index`, which is returned as the index of the pivot:

```
unsorted_array[pivot_index]=unsorted_array[less_than_pivot_index]
unsorted_array[less_than_pivot_index]=pivot
return less_than_pivot_index
```

The image below shows how the code interchanges 4 with 43 as the last step in the partitioning process:

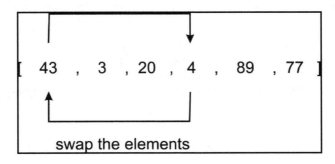

To recap, the first time the quick sort function was called, it was partitioned about the element at index **0**. After the return of the partitioning function, we obtain the array [4, 3, 20, 43, 89, 77].

As you can see, all elements to the right of element **43** are greater, while those to the left are smaller. The partitioning is complete.

Using the split point 43 with index 3, we will recursively sort the two sub-arrays [4, 30, 20] and [89, 77] using the same process we just went through.

The body of the main `quick sort` function is as follows:

```
def quick_sort(unsorted_array, first, last):
    if last - first <= 0:
        return
else:
    partition_point = partition(unsorted_array, first, last)
    quick_sort(unsorted_array, first, partition_point-1)
    quick_sort(unsorted_array, partition_point+1, last)
```

The `quick sort` function is a very simple method, no more than 6 lines of code. The heavy lifting is done by the `partition` function. When the `partition` method is called it returns the partition point. This is the point in the `unsorted_array` where all elements to the left are less than the pivot and all elements to its right are greater than it.

When we print the state of `unsorted_array` immediately after the partition progress, we see clearly how the partitioning is happening:

```
Output:
[43, 3, 20, 89, 4, 77]
[4, 3, 20, 43, 89, 77]
[3, 4, 20, 43, 89, 77]
[3, 4, 20, 43, 77, 89]
[3, 4, 20, 43, 77, 89]
```

Taking a step back, let's sort the first sub array after the first partition has happened. The partitioning of the [4, 3, 20] sub array will stop when `greater_than_pivot_index` is at index 2 and `less_than_pivot_index` is at index 1. At that point, the two markers are said to have crossed. Because `greater_than_pivot_index` is greater than `less_than_pivot_index`, further execution of the `while` loop will cease. Pivot 4 will be exchanged with 3, while index 1 is returned as the partition point.

The quick sort algorithm has a $O(n^2)$ worst case complexity, but it is efficient when sorting large amounts of data.

# Heap sort

In Chapter 11, *Graphs and Other Algorithms*, we implemented the (binary) heap data structure. Our implementation always made sure that after an element has been removed or added to a heap, the heap order property is maintained by using the sink and float helper methods.

The heap data structure can be used to implement the sorting algorithm called the heap sort. As a recap, let's create a simple heap with the following items:

```
h = Heap()
unsorted_list = [4, 8, 7, 2, 9, 10, 5, 1, 3, 6]
for i in unsorted_list:
    h.insert(i)
print("Unsorted list: {}".format(unsorted_list))
```

The heap, h, is created and the elements in the unsorted_list are inserted. After each method call to insert, the heap order property is restored by the subsequent call to the float method. After loop has terminated, at the top of our heap will be element 4.

The number of elements in our heap is 10. If we call the pop method on the heap object h, 10 times and store the actual elements being popped, we end up with a sorted list. After each pop operation, the heap is readjusted to maintain the heap order property.

The heap_sort method is as follows:

```
class Heap:
    ...
    def heap_sort(self):
        sorted_list = []
        for node in range(self.size):
            n = self.pop()
            sorted_list.append(n)

        return sorted_list
```

The for loop simply calls the pop method self.size number of times. sorted_list will contain a sorted list of items after the loop terminates.

The `insert` method is called *n* number of times. Together with the `float` method, the `insert` operation takes a worst case runtime of **O**(*n log n*), as does the `pop` method. As such, this sorting algorithm incurs a worst case runtime of **O**(*n log n*).

# Summary

In this chapter, we have explored a number of sorting algorithms. Quick sort performs much better than the other sorting algorithms. Of all the algorithms discussed, quick sort preserves the index of the list that it sorts. We'll use this property in the next chapter as we explore the selection algorithms.

# 14
# Selection Algorithms

One interesting set of algorithms related to finding elements in an unordered list of items is selection algorithms. In doing so, we shall be answering questions that have to do with selecting the median of a set of numbers and selecting the ith-smallest or -largest element in a list, among other things.

In this chapter, we will cover the following topics:

- Selection by sorting
- Randomized selection
- Deterministic selection

## Selection by sorting

Items in a list may undergo statistical enquiries such as finding the mean, median, and mode values. Finding the mean and mode values do not require the list to be ordered. However, to find the median in a list of numbers, the list must first be ordered. Finding the median requires one to find the element in the middle position of the ordered list. But what if we want to find the last-smallest item in the list or the first-smallest item in the list?

To find the ith-smallest number in an unordered list of items, the index of where that item occurs is important to obtain. But because the elements have not been sorted, it is difficult to know whether the element at index 0 in a list is really the first-smallest number.

A pragmatic and obvious thing to do when dealing with unordered lists is to first sort the list. Once the list is sorted, one is assured that the zeroth element in the list will house the first-smallest element in the list. Likewise, the last element in the list will house the last-smallest element in the list.

Assume that perhaps the luxury of sorting before performing the search cannot be afforded. Is it possible to find the ith-smallest element without having to sort the list in the first place?

# Randomized selection

In the previous chapter, we examined the quick sort algorithm. The quick sort algorithm allows us to sort an unordered list of items but has a way of preserving the index of elements as the sorting algorithm runs. Generally speaking, the quick sort algorithm does the following:

1. Selects a pivot.
2. Partitions the unsorted list around the pivot.
3. Recursively sorts the two halves of the partitioned list using *step 1* and *step 2*.

One interesting and important fact is that after every partitioning step, the index of the pivot will not change even after the list has become sorted. It is this property that enables us to be able to work with a not-so-fully sorted list to obtain the ith-smallest number. Because randomized selection is based on the quick sort algorithm, it is generally referred to as quick select.

# Quick select

The quick select algorithm is used to obtain the ith-smallest element in an unordered list of items, in this case, numbers. We declare the main method of the algorithm as follows:

```python
def quick_select(array_list, left, right, k):

    split = partition(array_list, left, right)

    if split == k:
        return array_list[split]
    elif split < k:
        return quick_select(array_list, split + 1, right, k)
    else:
        return quick_select(array_list, left, split-1, k)
```

The `quick_select` function takes as parameters the index of the first element in the list as well as the last. The ith element is specified by the third parameter k. Values greater or equal to zero (0) are allowed in such a way that when k is 0, we know to search for the first-smallest item in the list. Others like to treat the k parameter so that it maps directly with the index that the user is searching for, so that the first-smallest number maps to the 0 index of a sorted list. It's all a matter of preference.

A method call to the partition function, split = partition(array_list, left, right), returns the split index. This index of split array is the position in the unordered list where all elements between right to split-1 are less than the element contained in the array split, while all elements between split+1 to left are greater.

When the partition function returns the split value, we compare it with k to find out if the split corresponds to the kth items.

If split is less than k, then it means that the kth-smallest item should exist or be found between split+1 and right:

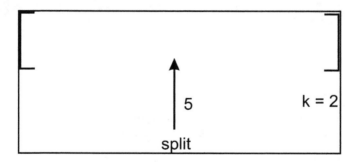

In the preceding example, a split within an imaginary unordered list occurs at index 5, while we are searching for the second-smallest number. Since 5<2 yields false, a recursive call to return quick_select(array_list, left, split-1, k) is made so that the other half of the list is searched:

If the `split` index was less than `k`, then we would make a call to `quick_select` like this:

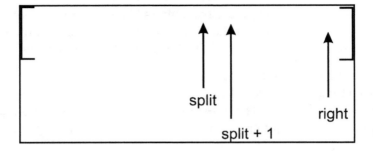

## Partition step

The partition step is exactly like we had in the quick sort algorithm. There are a couple of things worthy of note:

```
def partition(unsorted_array, first_index, last_index):
    if first_index == last_index:
        return first_index

    pivot = unsorted_array[first_index]
    pivot_index = first_index
    index_of_last_element = last_index

    less_than_pivot_index = index_of_last_element
    greater_than_pivot_index = first_index + 1

    while True:

        while unsorted_array[greater_than_pivot_index] < pivot and
            greater_than_pivot_index < last_index:
            greater_than_pivot_index += 1
        while unsorted_array[less_than_pivot_index] > pivot and
            less_than_pivot_index >= first_index:
            less_than_pivot_index -= 1

        if greater_than_pivot_index < less_than_pivot_index:
            temp = unsorted_array[greater_than_pivot_index]
            unsorted_array[greater_than_pivot_index] =
                unsorted_array[less_than_pivot_index]
            unsorted_array[less_than_pivot_index] = temp
        else:
            break
```

```
unsorted_array[pivot_index] =
    unsorted_array[less_than_pivot_index]
unsorted_array[less_than_pivot_index] = pivot

return less_than_pivot_index
```

An if statement has been inserted at the beginning of the function definition to cater for situations where `first_index` is equal to `last_index`. In such cases, it means there is only one element in our sublist. We therefore simply return any of the function parameters, in this case, `first_index`.

The first element is always chosen as the pivot. This choice to make the first element the pivot is a random decision. It often does not yield a good split and subsequently a good partition. However, the ith element will eventually be found even though the pivot is chosen at random.

The `partition` function returns the pivot index pointed to by `less_than_pivot_index`, as we saw in the preceding chapter.

From this point on, you will need to follow the program execution with a pencil and paper to get a better feel of how the split variable is being used to determine the section of the list to search for the ith-smallest item.

# Deterministic selection

The worst-case performance of a randomized selection algorithm is $O(n^2)$. It is possible to improve on a section of the randomized selection algorithm to obtain a worst-case performance of $O(n)$. This kind of algorithm is called **deterministic selection**.

The general approach to the deterministic algorithm is listed here:

1. Select a pivot:
    1. Split a list of unordered items into groups of five elements each.
    2. Sort and find the median of all the groups.
    3. Repeat *step 1* and *step 2* recursively to obtain the true median of the list.
2. Use the true median to partition the list of unordered items.
3. Recurse into the part of the partitioned list that may contain the ith-smallest element.

# Pivot selection

Previously, in the random selection algorithm, we selected the first element as the pivot. We shall replace that step with a sequence of steps that enables us to obtain the true or approximate median. This will improve the partitioning of the list about the pivot:

```
def partition(unsorted_array, first_index, last_index):

    if first_index == last_index:
        return first_index
    else:
        nearest_median =
        median_of_medians(unsorted_array[first_index:last_index])

    index_of_nearest_median =
        get_index_of_nearest_median(unsorted_array, first_index,
                                    last_index, nearest_median)

    swap(unsorted_array, first_index, index_of_nearest_median)

    pivot = unsorted_array[first_index]
    pivot_index = first_index
    index_of_last_element = last_index

    less_than_pivot_index = index_of_last_element
    greater_than_pivot_index = first_index + 1
```

Let's now study the code for the partition function. The `nearest_median` variable stores the true or approximate median of a given list:

```
def partition(unsorted_array, first_index, last_index):

    if first_index == last_index:
        return first_index
    else:
        nearest_median =
        median_of_medians(unsorted_array[first_index:last_index])
    ....
```

If the `unsorted_array` parameter has only one element, `first_index` and `last_index` will be equal. `first_index` is therefore returned anyway.

However, if the list size is greater than one, we call the `median_of_medians` function with the section of the array, demarcated by `first_index` and `last_index`. The return value is yet again stored in `nearest_median`.

# Median of medians

The `median_of_medians` function is responsible for finding the approximate median of any given list of items. The function uses recursion to return the true median:

```
def median_of_medians(elems):

    sublists = [elems[j:j+5] for j in range(0, len(elems), 5)]

    medians = []
    for sublist in sublists:
        medians.append(sorted(sublist)[len(sublist)/2])

    if len(medians) <= 5:
        return sorted(medians)[len(medians)/2]
    else:
        return median_of_medians(medians)
```

The function begins by splitting the list, `elems`, into groups of five elements each. This means that if `elems` contains 100 items, there will be 20 groups created by the statement `sublists = [elems[j:j+5] for j in range(0, len(elems), 5)]`, with each containing exactly five elements or fewer:

```
medians = []
    for sublist in sublists:
        medians.append(sorted(sublist)[len(sublist)/2])
```

An empty array is created and assigned to `medians,` which stores the medians in each of the five element arrays assigned to `sublists`.

The for loop iterates over the list of lists inside `sublists`. Each sublist is sorted, the median found, and stored in the `medians` list.

The `medians.append(sorted(sublist)[len(sublist)/2])` statement will sort the list and obtain the element stored in its middle index. This becomes the median of the five-element list. The use of an existing sorting function will not impact the performance of the algorithm due to the list's small size.

We understood from the outset that we would not sort the list in order to find the ith-smallest element, so why employ Python's sorted method? Well, since we are sorting a very small list of five elements or fewer, the impact of that operation on the overall performance of the algorithm is considered negligible.

Thereafter, if the list now contains five or fewer elements, we shall sort the `medians` list and return the element located in its middle index:

```
if len(medians) <= 5:
        return sorted(medians)[len(medians)/2]
```

If, on the other hand, the size of the list is greater than five, we recursively call the `median_of_medians` function again, supplying it with the list of the medians stored in `medians`.

Take, for instance, the following list of numbers:

*[2, 3, 5, 4, 1, 12, 11, 13, 16, 7, 8, 6, 10, 9, 17, 15, 19, 20, 18, 23, 21, 22, 25, 24, 14]*

We can break this list into groups of five elements each with the code statement `sublists = [elems[j:j+5] for j in range(0, len(elems), 5)]`, to obtain the following list:

*[[2, 3, 5, 4, 1], [12, 11, 13, 16, 7], [8, 6, 10, 9, 17], [15, 19, 20, 18, 23], [21, 22, 25, 24, 14]]*

Sorting each of the five-element lists and obtaining their medians produces the following list:

*[3, 12, 9, 19, 22]*

Since the list is five elements in size, we only return the median of the sorted list, or we would have made another call to the `median_of_median` function.

# Partitioning step

Now that we have obtained the approximate median, the `get_index_of_nearest_median` function takes the bounds of the list indicated by the `first` and `last` parameters:

```
    def get_index_of_nearest_median(array_list, first, second,
median):
        if first == second:
            return first
        else:
            return first + array_list[first:second].index(median)
```

Once again, we only return the first index if there is only one element in the list. The `arraylist[first:second]` returns an array with index 0 up to the size of the `list` −1. When we find the index of the median, we lose the portion in the list where it occurs because of the new range indexing the `[first:second]` code returns. Therefore, we must add whatever index is returned by `arraylist[first:second]` to `first` to obtain the true index where the median was found:

```
swap(unsorted_array, first_index, index_of_nearest_median)
```

We then swap the first element in `unsorted_array` with `index_of_nearest_median`, using the swap function.

The utility function to swap two array elements is shown here:

```
def swap(array_list, first, second):
    temp = array_list[first]
    array_list[first] = array_list[second]
    array_list[second] = temp
```

Our approximate median is now stored at `first_index` of the unsorted list.

The partition function continues as it would in the code of the quick select algorithm. After the partitioning step, the array looks like this:

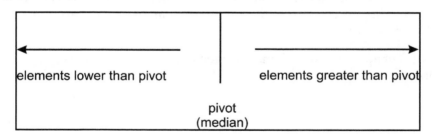

```
def deterministic_select(array_list, left, right, k):

    split = partition(array_list, left, right)


    if split == k:
        return array_list[split]
    elif split < k :
        return deterministic_select(array_list, split + 1, right,
k)
    else:
        return deterministic_select(array_list, left, split-1, k)
```

As you will have already observed, the main function of the deterministic selection algorithm looks exactly the same as its random selection counterpart. After the initial `array_list` has been partitioned about the approximate median, a comparison with the kth element is made.

If `split` is less than `k`, then a recursive call to `deterministic_select(array_list, split + 1, right, k)` is made. This will look for the kth element in that half of the array. Otherwise the function call to `deterministic_select(array_list, left, split-1, k)` is made.

# Summary

This chapter has examined ways to answer the question of how to find the ith-smallest element in a list. The trivial solution of simply sorting a list to perform the operation of finding the ith-smallest has been explored.

There is also the possibility of not necessarily sorting the list before we can determine the ith-smallest element. The random selection algorithm allows us to modify the quick sort algorithm to determine the ith-smallest element.

To further improve upon the random selection algorithm so that we can obtain a time complexity of $O(n)$, we embark on finding the median of medians to enable us find a good split during partitioning.

From the next chapter, we will change our focus and take a deep dive into Python's OOP concepts.

# 15
# Object-Oriented Design

In software development, design is often considered as the step done *before* programming. This isn't true; in reality, analysis, programming, and design tend to overlap, combine, and interweave. In this chapter, we will cover the following topics:

- What object-oriented means
- The difference between object-oriented design and object-oriented programming
- The basic principles of object-oriented design
- Basic **Unified Modeling Language** (**UML**) and when it isn't evil

## Introducing object-oriented

Everyone knows what an object is: a tangible thing that we can sense, feel, and manipulate. The earliest objects we interact with are typically baby toys. Wooden blocks, plastic shapes, and over-sized puzzle pieces are common first objects. Babies learn quickly that certain objects do certain things: bells ring, buttons are pressed, and levers are pulled.

The definition of an object in software development is not terribly different. Software objects may not be tangible things that you can pick up, sense, or feel, but they are models of something that can do certain things and have certain things done to them. Formally, an object is a collection of **data** and associated **behaviors**.

So, knowing what an object is, what does it mean to be object-oriented? In the dictionary, *oriented* means *directed toward*. So object-oriented means functionally directed toward modeling objects. This is one of many techniques used for modeling complex systems. It is defined by describing a collection of interacting objects via their data and behavior.

If you've read any hype, you've probably come across the terms *object-oriented analysis, object-oriented design, object-oriented analysis and design,* and *object-oriented programming*. These are all highly related concepts under the general *object-oriented* umbrella.

In fact, analysis, design, and programming are all stages of software development. Calling them object-oriented simply specifies what level of software development is being pursued.

**Object-oriented analysis (OOA)** is the process of looking at a problem, system, or task (that somebody wants to turn into an application) and identifying the objects and interactions between those objects. The analysis stage is all about *what* needs to be done.

The output of the analysis stage is a set of requirements. If we were to complete the analysis stage in one step, we would have turned a task, such as *I need a website*, into a set of requirements. As an example, here or some requirements as to what a website visitor might need to do (*italic* represents actions, **bold** represents objects):

- *Review* our **history**
- *Apply* for **jobs**
- *Browse, compare,* and *order* **products**

In some ways, *analysis* is a misnomer. The baby we discussed earlier doesn't analyze the blocks and puzzle pieces. Instead, she explores her environment, manipulates shapes, and sees where they might fit. A better turn of phrase might be *object-oriented exploration*. In software development, the initial stages of analysis include interviewing customers, studying their processes, and eliminating possibilities.

**Object-oriented design (OOD)** is the process of converting such requirements into an implementation specification. The designer must name the objects, define the behaviors, and formally specify which objects can activate specific behaviors on other objects. The design stage is all about *how* things should be done.

The output of the design stage is an implementation specification. If we were to complete the design stage in a single step, we would have turned the requirements defined during object-oriented analysis into a set of classes and interfaces that could be implemented in (ideally) any object-oriented programming language.

**Object-oriented programming (OOP)** is the process of converting this perfectly-defined design into a working program that does exactly what the CEO originally requested.

Yeah, right! It would be lovely if the world met this ideal and we could follow these stages one by one, in perfect order, like all the old textbooks told us to. As usual, the real world is much murkier. No matter how hard we try to separate these stages, we'll always find things that need further analysis while we're designing. When we're programming, we find features that need clarification in the design.

Most twenty-first century development happens in an iterative development model. In iterative development, a small part of the task is modeled, designed, and programmed, and then the program is reviewed and expanded to improve each feature and include new features in a series of short development cycles.

The rest of this book is about object-oriented programming, but in this chapter, we will cover the basic object-oriented principles in the context of design. This allows us to understand these (rather simple) concepts without having to argue with software syntax or Python tracebacks.

# Objects and classes

So, an object is a collection of data with associated behaviors. How do we differentiate between types of objects? Apples and oranges are both objects, but it is a common adage that they cannot be compared. Apples and oranges aren't modeled very often in computer programming, but let's pretend we're doing an inventory application for a fruit farm. To facilitate the example, we can assume that apples go in barrels and oranges go in baskets.

Now, we have four kinds of objects: apples, oranges, baskets, and barrels. In object-oriented modeling, the term used for a *kind of object* is **class**. So, in technical terms, we now have four classes of objects.

It's important to understand the difference between an object and a class. Classes describe objects. They are like blueprints for creating an object. You might have three oranges sitting on the table in front of you. Each orange is a distinct object, but all three have the attributes and behaviors associated with one class: the general class of oranges.

The relationship between the four classes of objects in our inventory system can be described using a **Unified Modeling Language** (invariably referred to as **UML**, because three-letter acronyms never go out of style) class diagram. Here is our first class diagram:

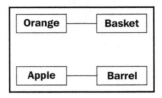

This diagram shows that an **Orange** is somehow associated with a **Basket** and that an **Apple** is also somehow associated with a **Barrel**. *Association* is the most basic way for two classes to be related.

UML is very popular among managers, and occasionally disparaged by programmers. The syntax of a UML diagram is generally pretty obvious; you don't have to read a tutorial to (mostly) understand what is going on when you see one. UML is also fairly easy to draw, and quite intuitive. After all, many people, when describing classes and their relationships, will naturally draw boxes with lines between them. Having a standard based on these intuitive diagrams makes it easy for programmers to communicate with designers, managers, and each other.

However, some programmers think UML is a waste of time. Citing iterative development, they will argue that formal specifications done up in fancy UML diagrams are going to be redundant before they're implemented, and that maintaining these formal diagrams will only waste time and not benefit anyone.

Depending on the corporate structure involved, this may or may not be true. However, every programming team consisting of more than one person will occasionally have to sit down and hash out the details of the subsystem it is currently working on. UML is extremely useful in these brainstorming sessions for quick and easy communication. Even those organizations that scoff at formal class diagrams tend to use some informal version of UML in their design meetings or team discussions.

Furthermore, the most important person you will ever have to communicate with is yourself. We all think we can remember the design decisions we've made, but there will always be the *Why did I do that?* moments hiding in our future. If we keep the scraps of papers we did our initial diagramming on when we started a design, we'll eventually find them a useful reference.

This chapter, however, is not meant to be a tutorial on UML. There are many of those available on the internet, as well as numerous books on the topic. UML covers far more than class and object diagrams; it also has a syntax for use cases, deployment, state changes, and activities. We'll be dealing with some common class diagram syntax in this discussion of object-oriented design. You can pick up the structure by example, and you'll subconsciously choose the UML-inspired syntax in your own team or personal design sessions.

Our initial diagram, while correct, does not remind us that apples go in barrels or how many barrels a single apple can go in. It only tells us that apples are somehow associated with barrels. The association between classes is often obvious and needs no further explanation, but we have the option to add further clarification as needed.

The beauty of UML is that most things are optional. We only need to specify as much information in a diagram as makes sense for the current situation. In a quick whiteboard session, we might just quickly draw lines between boxes. In a formal document, we might go into more detail. In the case of apples and barrels, we can be fairly confident that the association is **many apples go in one barrel**, but just to make sure nobody confuses it with **one apple spoils one barrel**, we can enhance the diagram as shown:

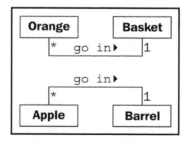

This diagram tells us that oranges **go in** baskets, with a little arrow showing what goes in what. It also tells us the number of that object that can be used in the association on both sides of the relationship. One **Basket** can hold many (represented by a \*) **Orange** objects. Any one **Orange** can go in exactly one **Basket**. This number is referred to as the *multiplicity* of the object. You may also hear it described as the *cardinality*. These are actually slightly distinct terms. Cardinality refers to the actual number of items in the set, whereas multiplicity specifies how small or how large the set could be.

I sometimes forget which end of the relationship line is supposed to have which multiplicity number. The multiplicity nearest to a class is the number of objects of that class that can be associated with any one object at the other end of the association. For the apple goes in barrel association, reading from left to right, many instances of the **Apple** class (that is many **Apple** objects) can go in any one **Barrel**. Reading from right to left, exactly one **Barrel** can be associated with any one **Apple**.

# Specifying attributes and behaviors

We now have a grasp of some basic object-oriented terminology. Objects are instances of classes that can be associated with each other. An object instance is a specific object with its own set of data and behaviors; a specific orange on the table in front of us is said to be an instance of the general class of oranges. That's simple enough, but let's dive into the meaning of those two words, *data* and *behaviors*.

## Data describes objects

Let's start with data. Data represents the individual characteristics of a certain object. A class can define specific sets of characteristics that are shared by all objects from that class. Any specific object can have different data values for the given characteristics. For example, the three oranges on our table (if we haven't eaten any) could each weigh a different amount. The orange class could have a weight attribute to represent that datum. All instances of the orange class have a weight attribute, but each orange has a different value for this attribute. Attributes don't have to be unique, though; any two oranges may weigh the same amount. As a more realistic example, two objects representing different customers might have the same value for a first name attribute.

Attributes are frequently referred to as **members** or **properties**. Some authors suggest that the terms have different meanings, usually that attributes are settable, while properties are read-only. In Python, the concept of *read-only* is rather pointless, so throughout this book, we'll see the two terms used interchangeably. In addition, as we'll discuss in Chapter 19, *When to Use Object-Oriented Programming*, the property keyword has a special meaning in Python for a particular kind of attribute.

In our fruit inventory application, the fruit farmer may want to know what orchard the orange came from, when it was picked, and how much it weighs. They might also want to keep track of where each **Basket** is stored. Apples might have a color attribute, and barrels might come in different sizes. Some of these properties may also belong to multiple classes (we may want to know when apples are picked, too), but for this first example, let's just add a few different attributes to our class diagram:

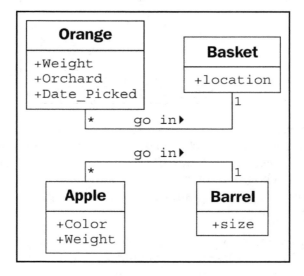

Depending on how detailed our design needs to be, we can also specify the type for each attribute. Attribute types are often primitives that are standard to most programming languages, such as integer, floating-point number, string, byte, or Boolean. However, they can also represent data structures such as lists, trees, or graphs, or most notably, other classes. This is one area where the design stage can overlap with the programming stage. The various primitives or objects available in one programming language may be different from what is available in another:

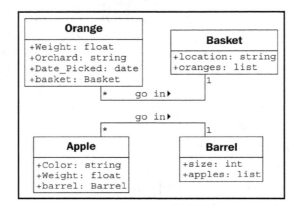

Usually, we don't need to be overly concerned with data types at the design stage, as implementation-specific details are chosen during the programming stage. Generic names are normally sufficient for design. If our design calls for a list container type, Java programmers can choose to use a `LinkedList` or an `ArrayList` when implementing it, while Python programmers (that's us!) might choose between the `list` built-in and a `tuple`.

In our fruit-farming example so far, our attributes are all basic primitives. However, there are some implicit attributes that we can make explicit—the associations. For a given orange, we might have an attribute referring to the basket that holds that orange.

# Behaviors are actions

Now that we know what data is, the last undefined term is *behaviors*. Behaviors are actions that can occur on an object. The behaviors that can be performed on a specific class of object are called **methods**. At the programming level, methods are like functions in structured programming, but they *magically* have access to all the data associated with this object. Like functions, methods can also accept **parameters** and return **values**.

A method's parameters are provided to it as a list of objects that need to be **passed** into that method. The actual object instances that are passed into a method during a specific invocation are usually referred to as **arguments**. These objects are used by the method to perform whatever behavior or task it is meant to do. Returned values are the results of that task.

We've stretched our *comparing apples and oranges* example into a basic (if far-fetched) inventory application. Let's stretch it a little further and see whether it breaks. One action that can be associated with oranges is the **pick** action. If you think about implementation, **pick** would need to do two things:

- Place the orange in a basket by updating the **Basket** attribute of the orange
- Add the orange to the **Orange** list on the given **Basket**.

So, **pick** needs to know what basket it is dealing with. We do this by giving the **pick** method a **Basket** parameter. Since our fruit farmer also sells juice, we can add a **squeeze** method to the **Orange** class. When called, the **squeeze** method might return the amount of juice retrieved, while also removing the **Orange** from the **Basket** it was in.

The class **Basket** can have a **sell** action. When a basket is sold, our inventory system might update some data on as-yet unspecified objects for accounting and profit calculations. Alternatively, our basket of oranges might go bad before we can sell them, so we add a **discard** method. Let's add these methods to our diagram:

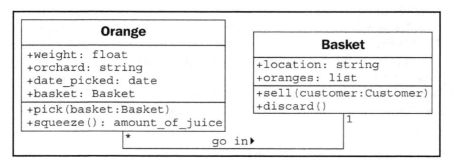

Adding attributes and methods to individual objects allows us to create a **system** of interacting objects. Each object in the system is a member of a certain class. These classes specify what types of data the object can hold and what methods can be invoked on it. The data in each object can be in a different state from other instances of the same class; each object may react to method calls differently because of the differences in state.

Object-oriented analysis and design is all about figuring out what those objects are and how they should interact. The next section describes principles that can be used to make those interactions as simple and intuitive as possible.

# Hiding details and creating the public interface

The key purpose of modeling an object in object-oriented design is to determine what the public **interface** of that object will be. The interface is the collection of attributes and methods that other objects can access to interact with that object. They do not need, and are often not allowed, to access the internal workings of the object.

A common real-world example is the television. Our interface to the television is the remote control. Each button on the remote control represents a method that can be called on the television object. When we, as the calling object, access these methods, we do not know or care if the television is getting its signal from a cable connection, a satellite dish, or an internet-enabled device. We don't care what electronic signals are being sent to adjust the volume, or whether the sound is destined for speakers or headphones. If we open the television to access the internal workings, for example, to split the output signal to both external speakers and a set of headphones, we will void the warranty.

This process of hiding the implementation of an object is suitably called **information hiding**. It is also sometimes referred to as **encapsulation**, but encapsulation is actually a more all-encompassing term. Encapsulated data is not necessarily hidden. Encapsulation is, literally, creating a capsule (think of creating a time capsule). If you put a bunch of information into a time capsule, and lock and bury it, it is both encapsulated and the information is hidden. On the other hand, if the time capsule, has not been buried and is unlocked or made of clear plastic, the items inside it are still encapsulated, but there is no information hiding.

The distinction between encapsulation and information hiding is largely irrelevant, especially at the design level. Many practical references use these terms interchangeably. As Python programmers, we don't actually have or need true information hiding (we'll discuss the reasons for this in Chapter 16, *Objects in Python*), so the more encompassing definition for encapsulation is suitable.

The public interface, however, is very important. It needs to be carefully designed as it is difficult to change it in the future. Changing the interface will break any client objects that are accessing it. We can change the internals all we like, for example, to make it more efficient, or to access data over the network as well as locally, and the client objects will still be able to talk to it, unmodified, using the public interface. On the other hand, if we alter the interface by changing publicly accessed attribute names or the order or types of arguments that a method can accept, all client classes will also have to be modified. When designing public interfaces, keep it simple. Always design the interface of an object based on how easy it is to use, not how hard it is to code (this advice applies to user interfaces as well).

Remember, program objects may represent real objects, but that does not make them real objects. They are models. One of the greatest gifts of modeling is the ability to ignore irrelevant details. The model car I built as a child looked like a real 1956 Thunderbird on the outside, but it obviously doesn't run. When I was too young to drive, these details were overly complex and irrelevant. The model is an **abstraction** of a real concept.

**Abstraction** is another object-oriented term related to encapsulation and information hiding. Abstraction means dealing with the level of detail that is most appropriate to a given task. It is the process of extracting a public interface from the inner details. A car's driver needs to interact with the steering, accelerator, and brakes. The workings of the motor, drive train, and brake subsystem don't matter to the driver. A mechanic, on the other hand, works at a different level of abstraction, tuning the engine and bleeding the brakes. Here's an example of two abstraction levels for a car:

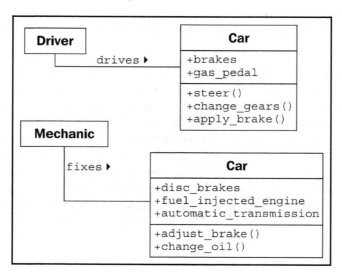

Now, we have several new terms that refer to similar concepts. Let's summarize all this jargon in a couple of sentences: abstraction is the process of encapsulating information with separate public and private interfaces. The private interfaces can be subject to information hiding.

The important lesson to take from all these definitions is to make our models understandable to other objects that have to interact with them. This means paying careful attention to small details. Ensure methods and properties have sensible names. When analyzing a system, objects typically represent nouns in the original problem, while methods are normally verbs. Attributes may show up as adjectives or more nouns. Name your classes, attributes, and methods accordingly.

When designing the interface, imagine you are the object and that you have a very strong preference for privacy. Don't let other objects have access to data about you unless you feel it is in your best interest for them to have it. Don't give them an interface to force you to perform a specific task unless you are certain you want them to be able to do that to you.

# Composition

So far, we have learned to design systems as a group of interacting objects, where each interaction involves viewing objects at an appropriate level of abstraction. But we don't know yet how to create these levels of abstraction. There are a variety of ways to do this; we'll discuss some advanced design patterns in Chapter 21, *The Iterator Pattern*. But even most design patterns rely on two basic object-oriented principles known as **composition** and **inheritance**. Composition is simpler, so let's start with it.

Composition is the act of collecting several objects together to create a new one. Composition is usually a good choice when one object is part of another object. We've already seen a first hint of composition in the mechanic example. A fossil-fueled car is composed of an engine, transmission, starter, headlights, and windshield, among numerous other parts. The engine, in turn, is composed of pistons, a crank shaft, and valves. In this example, composition is a good way to provide levels of abstraction. The **Car** object can provide the interface required by a driver, while also giving access to its component parts, which offers the deeper level of abstraction suitable for a mechanic. Those component parts can, of course, be further broken down if the mechanic needs more information to diagnose a problem or tune the engine.

A car is a common introductory example of composition, but it's not overly useful when it comes to designing computer systems. Physical objects are easy to break into component objects. People have been doing this at least since the ancient Greeks originally postulated that atoms were the smallest units of matter (they, of course, didn't have access to particle accelerators). Computer systems are generally less complicated than physical objects, yet identifying the component objects in such systems does not happen as naturally.

The objects in an object-oriented system occasionally represent physical objects such as people, books, or telephones. More often, however, they represent abstract ideas. People have names, books have titles, and telephones are used to make calls. Calls, titles, accounts, names, appointments, and payments are not usually considered objects in the physical world, but they are all frequently-modeled components in computer systems.

Let's try modeling a more computer-oriented example to see composition in action. We'll be looking at the design of a computerized chess game. This was a very popular pastime among academics in the 80s and 90s. People were predicting that computers would one day be able to defeat a human chess master. When this happened in 1997 (IBM's Deep Blue defeated world chess champion, Gary Kasparov), interest in the problem waned. Nowadays, the computer always wins.

As a basic, high-level analysis, a *game* of chess is **played** between two *players*, using a chess set featuring a *board* containing sixty-four *positions* in an 8x8 grid. The board can have two sets of sixteen *pieces* that can be **moved**, in alternating *turns* by the two players in different ways. Each piece can **take** other pieces. The board will be required to **draw** itself on the computer *screen* after each turn.

I've identified some of the possible objects in the description using *italics*, and a few key methods using **bold**. This is a common first step in turning an object-oriented analysis into a design. At this point, to emphasize composition, we'll focus on the board, without worrying too much about the players or the different types of pieces.

Let's start at the highest level of abstraction possible. We have two players interacting with a **Chess Set** by taking turns making moves:

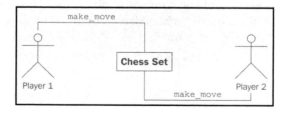

This doesn't quite look like our earlier class diagrams, which is a good thing since it isn't one! This is an **object diagram**, also called an **instance diagram**. It describes the system at a specific state in time, and is describing specific instances of objects, not the interaction between classes. Remember, both players are members of the same class, so the class diagram looks a little different:

The diagram shows that exactly two players can interact with one chess set. This also indicates that any one player can be playing with only one **Chess Set** at a time.

However, we're discussing composition, not UML, so let's think about what the **Chess Set** is composed of. We don't care what the player is composed of at this time. We can assume that the player has a heart and brain, among other organs, but these are irrelevant to our model. Indeed, there is nothing stopping said player from being Deep Blue itself, which has neither a heart nor a brain.

The chess set, then, is composed of a board and 32 pieces. The board further comprises 64 positions. You could argue that pieces are not part of the chess set because you could replace the pieces in a chess set with a different set of pieces. While this is unlikely or impossible in a computerized version of chess, it introduces us to **aggregation**.

Aggregation is almost exactly like composition. The difference is that aggregate objects can exist independently. It would be impossible for a position to be associated with a different chess board, so we say the board is composed of positions. But the pieces, which might exist independently of the chess set, are said to be in an aggregate relationship with that set.

Another way to differentiate between aggregation and composition is to think about the lifespan of the object. If the composite (outside) object controls when the related (inside) objects are created and destroyed, composition is most suitable. If the related object is created independently of the composite object, or can outlast that object, an aggregate relationship makes more sense. Also, keep in mind that composition is aggregation; aggregation is simply a more general form of composition. Any composite relationship is also an aggregate relationship, but not vice versa.

Let's describe our current **Chess Set** composition and add some attributes to the objects to hold the composite relationships:

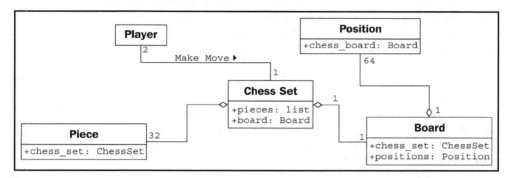

The composition relationship is represented in UML as a solid diamond. The hollow diamond represents the aggregate relationship. You'll notice that the board and pieces are stored as part of the **Chess Set** in exactly the same way a reference to them is stored as an attribute on the chess set. This shows that, once again, in practice, the distinction between aggregation and composition is often irrelevant once you get past the design stage. When implemented, they behave in much the same way. However, it can help to differentiate between the two when your team is discussing how the different objects interact. Often, you can treat them as the same thing, but when you need to distinguish between them (usually when talking about how long related objects exist), it's great to know the difference.

# Inheritance

We discussed three types of relationships between objects: association, composition, and aggregation. However, we have not fully specified our chess set, and these tools don't seem to give us all the power we need. We discussed the possibility that a player might be a human or it might be a piece of software featuring artificial intelligence. It doesn't seem right to say that a player is *associated* with a human, or that the artificial intelligence implementation is *part of* the player object. What we really need is the ability to say that *Deep Blue is a player*, or that *Gary Kasparov is a player*.

The *is a* relationship is formed by **inheritance**. Inheritance is the most famous, well-known, and over-used relationship in object-oriented programming. Inheritance is sort of like a family tree. My grandfather's last name was Phillips and my father inherited that name. I inherited it from him. In object-oriented programming, instead of inheriting features and behaviors from a person, one class can inherit attributes and methods from another class.

For example, there are 32 chess pieces in our chess set, but there are only six different types of pieces (pawns, rooks, bishops, knights, king, and queen), each of which behaves differently when it is moved. All of these classes of piece have properties, such as color and the chess set they are part of, but they also have unique shapes when drawn on the chess board, and make different moves. Let's see how the six types of pieces can inherit from a **Piece** class:

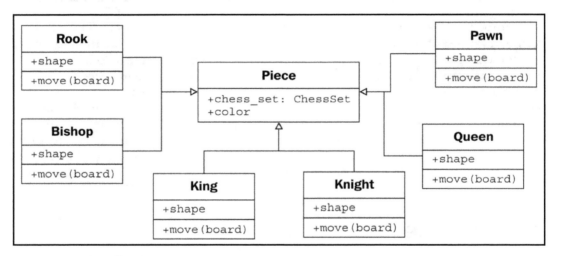

The hollow arrows indicate that the individual classes of pieces inherit from the **Piece** class. All the child classes automatically have a **chess_set** and **color** attribute inherited from the base class. Each piece provides a different shape property (to be drawn on the screen when rendering the board), and a different **move** method to move the piece to a new position on the board at each turn.

We actually know that all subclasses of the **Piece** class need to have a **move** method; otherwise, when the board tries to move the piece, it will get confused. It is possible that we would want to create a new version of the game of chess that has one additional piece (the wizard). Our current design will allow us to design this piece without giving it a **move** method. The board would then choke when it asked the piece to move itself.

We can fix this by creating a dummy move method on the **Piece** class. The subclasses can then **override** this method with a more specific implementation. The default implementation might, for example, pop up an error message that says **That piece cannot be moved**.

Overriding methods in subclasses allows very powerful object-oriented systems to be developed. For example, if we wanted to implement a **Player** class with artificial intelligence, we might provide a `calculate_move` method that takes a **Board** object and decides which piece to move where. A very basic class might randomly choose a piece and direction and move it accordingly. We could then override this method in a subclass with the Deep Blue implementation. The first class would be suitable for play against a raw beginner; the latter would challenge a grand master. The important thing is that other methods in the class, such as the ones that inform the board as to which move was chosen, need not be changed; this implementation can be shared between the two classes.

In the case of chess pieces, it doesn't really make sense to provide a default implementation of the move method. All we need to do is specify that the move method is required in any subclasses. This can be done by making **Piece** an **abstract class** with the move method declared **abstract**. Abstract methods basically say this:

> *We demand this method exist in any non-abstract subclass, but we are declining to specify an implementation in this class.*

Indeed, it is possible to make a class that does not implement any methods at all. Such a class would simply tell us what the class should do, but provides absolutely no advice on how to do it. In object-oriented parlance, such classes are called **interfaces**.

# Inheritance provides abstraction

Let's explore the longest word in object-oriented argot. **Polymorphism** is the ability to treat a class differently, depending on which subclass is implemented. We've already seen it in action with the pieces system we've described. If we took the design a bit further, we'd probably see that the **Board** object can accept a move from the player and call the **move** function on the piece. The board need not ever know what type of piece it is dealing with. All it has to do is call the **move** method, and the proper subclass will take care of moving it as a **Knight** or a **Pawn**.

Polymorphism is pretty cool, but it is a word that is rarely used in Python programming. Python goes an extra step past allowing a subclass of an object to be treated like a parent class. A board implemented in Python could take any object that has a **move** method, whether it is a bishop piece, a car, or a duck. When **move** is called, the **Bishop** will move diagonally on the board, the car will drive someplace, and the duck will swim or fly, depending on its mood.

This sort of polymorphism in Python is typically referred to as **duck typing**: *if it walks like a duck or swims like a duck, it's a duck*. We don't care if it really *is a* duck (*is a* being a cornerstone of inheritance), only that it swims or walks. Geese and swans might easily be able to provide the duck-like behavior we are looking for. This allows future designers to create new types of birds without actually specifying an inheritance hierarchy for aquatic birds. It also allows them to create completely different drop-in behaviors that the original designers never planned for. For example, future designers might be able to make a walking, swimming penguin that works with the same interface without ever suggesting that penguins are ducks.

# Multiple inheritance

When we think of inheritance in our own family tree, we can see that we inherit features from more than just one parent. When strangers tell a proud mother that her son has *his father's eyes*, she will typically respond along the lines of, *yes, but he got my nose*.

Object-oriented design can also feature such **multiple inheritance**, which allows a subclass to inherit functionality from multiple parent classes. In practice, multiple inheritance can be a tricky business, and some programming languages (most famously, Java) strictly prohibit it. However, multiple inheritance can have its uses. Most often, it can be used to create objects that have two distinct sets of behaviors. For example, an object designed to connect to a scanner and send a fax of the scanned document might be created by inheriting from two separate `scanner` and `faxer` objects.

As long as two classes have distinct interfaces, it is not normally harmful for a subclass to inherit from both of them. However, it gets messy if we inherit from two classes that provide overlapping interfaces. For example, if we have a motorcycle class that has a `move` method, and a boat class also featuring a `move` method, and we want to merge them into the ultimate amphibious vehicle, how does the resulting class know what to do when we call `move`? At the design level, this needs to be explained, and, at the implementation level, each programming language has different ways of deciding which parent class's method is called, or in what order.

Often, the best way to deal with it is to avoid it. If you have a design showing up like this, you're *probably* doing it wrong. Take a step back, analyze the system again, and see if you can remove the multiple inheritance relationship in favor of some other association or composite design.

Inheritance is a very powerful tool for extending behavior. It is also one of the most marketable advancements of object-oriented design over earlier paradigms. Therefore, it is often the first tool that object-oriented programmers reach for. However, it is important to recognize that owning a hammer does not turn screws into nails. Inheritance is the perfect solution for obvious *is a* relationships, but it can be abused. Programmers often use inheritance to share code between two kinds of objects that are only distantly related, with no *is a* relationship in sight. While this is not necessarily a bad design, it is a terrific opportunity to ask just why they decided to design it that way, and whether a different relationship or design pattern would have been more suitable.

# Case study

Let's tie all our new object-oriented knowledge together by going through a few iterations of object-oriented design on a somewhat real-world example. The system we'll be modeling is a library catalog. Libraries have been tracking their inventory for centuries, originally using card catalogs, and more recently, electronic inventories. Modern libraries have web-based catalogs that we can query from our homes.

Let's start with an analysis. The local librarian has asked us to write a new card catalog program because their ancient Windows XP-based program is ugly and out of date. That doesn't give us much detail, but before we start asking for more information, let's consider what we already know about library catalogs.

Catalogs contain lists of books. People search them to find books on certain subjects, with specific titles, or by a particular author. Books can be uniquely identified by an **International Standard Book Number (ISBN)**. Each book has a **Dewey Decimal System (DDS)** number assigned to help find it on a particular shelf.

This simple analysis tells us some of the obvious objects in the system. We quickly identify **Book** as the most important object, with several attributes already mentioned, such as author, title, subject, ISBN, and DDS number, and catalog as a sort of manager for books.

We also notice a few other objects that may or may not need to be modeled in the system. For cataloging purposes, all we need to search a book by author is an `author_name` attribute on the book. However, authors are also objects, and we might want to store some other data about the author. As we ponder this, we might remember that some books have multiple authors. Suddenly, the idea of having a single `author_name` attribute on objects seems a bit silly. A list of authors associated with each book is clearly a better idea.

The relationship between author and book is clearly association, since you would never say *a book is an author* (it's not inheritance), and saying *a book has an author*, though grammatically correct, does not imply that authors are part of books (it's not aggregation). Indeed, any one author may be associated with multiple books.

We should also pay attention to the noun (nouns are always good candidates for objects) *shelf*. Is a shelf an object that needs to be modeled in a cataloging system? How do we identify an individual shelf? What happens if a book is stored at the end of one shelf, and later moved to the beginning of the next shelf because a new book was inserted in the previous shelf?

DDS was designed to help locate physical books in a library. As such, storing a DDS attribute with the book should be enough to locate it, regardless of which shelf it is stored on. So we can, at least for the moment, remove shelf from our list of contending objects.

Another questionable object in the system is the user. Do we need to know anything about a specific user, such as their name, address, or list of overdue books? So far, the librarian has told us only that they want a catalog; they said nothing about tracking subscriptions or overdue notices. In the back of our minds, we also note that authors and users are both specific kinds of people; there might be a useful inheritance relationship here in the future.

For cataloging purposes, we decide we don't need to identify the user for now. We can assume that a user will be searching the catalog, but we don't have to actively model them in the system, beyond providing an interface that allows them to search.

We have identified a few attributes on the book, but what properties does a catalog have? Does any one library have more than one catalog? Do we need to uniquely identify them? Obviously, the catalog has to have a collection of the books it contains, somehow, but this list is probably not part of the public interface.

What about behaviors? The catalog clearly needs a search method, possibly separate ones for authors, titles, and subjects. Are there any behaviors on books? Would it need a preview method? Or could preview be identified by a first page attribute instead of a method?

The questions in the preceding discussion are all part of the object-oriented analysis phase. But intermixed with the questions, we have already identified a few key objects that are part of the design. Indeed, what you have just seen are several microiterations between analysis and design.

Likely, these iterations would all occur in an initial meeting with the librarian. Before this meeting, however, we can already sketch out a most basic design for the objects we have concretely identified, as follows:

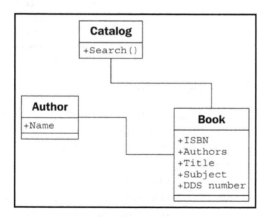

Armed with this basic diagram and a pencil to interactively improve it, we meet up with the librarian. They tell us that this is a good start, but libraries don't serve only books; they also have DVDs, magazines, and CDs, none of which have an ISBN or DDS number. All of these types of items can be uniquely identified by a UPC number, though. We remind the librarian that they have to find the items on the shelf, and these items probably aren't organized by UPC.

The librarian explains that each type is organized in a different way. The CDs are mostly audio books, and they only have two dozen in stock, so they are organized by the author's last name. DVDs are divided into genre and further organized by title. Magazines are organized by title and then refined by the volume and issue number. Books are, as we had guessed, organized by the DDS number.

With no previous object-oriented design experience, we might consider adding separate lists of DVDs, CDs, magazines, and books to our catalog, and search each one in turn. The trouble is, except for certain extended attributes, and identifying the physical location of the item, these items all behave much the same. This is a job for inheritance! We quickly update our UML diagram as follows:

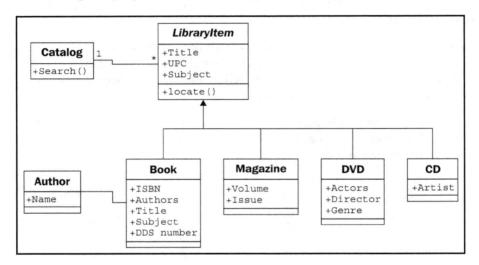

The librarian understands the gist of our sketched diagram, but is a bit confused by the **locate** functionality. We explain using a specific use case where the user is searching for the word *bunnies*. The user first sends a search request to the catalog. The catalog queries its internal list of items and finds a book and a DVD with *bunnies* in the title. At this point, the catalog doesn't care whether it is holding a DVD, book, CD, or magazine; all items are the same, as far as the catalog is concerned. However, the user wants to know how to find the physical items, so the catalog would be remiss if it simply returned a list of titles. So, it calls the **locate** method on the two items it has uncovered. The book's **locate** method returns a DDS number that can be used to find the shelf holding the book. The DVD is located by returning the genre and title of the DVD. The user can then visit the DVD section, find the section containing that genre, and find the specific DVD as sorted by the titles.

As we explain, we sketch a UML **sequence diagram**, explaining how the various objects are communicating:

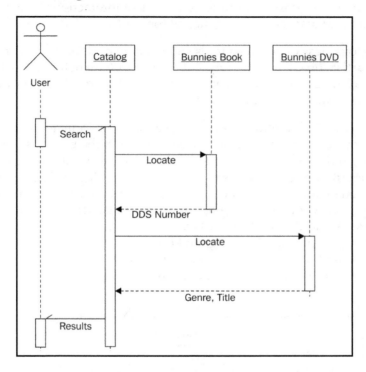

While class diagrams describe the relationships between classes, sequence diagrams describe specific sequences of messages passed between objects. The dashed line hanging from each object is a **lifeline** describing the lifetime of the object. The wider boxes on each lifeline represent active processing in that object (where there's no box, the object is basically sitting idle, waiting for something to happen). The horizontal arrows between the lifelines indicate specific messages. The solid arrows represent methods being called, while the dashed arrows with solid heads represent the method return values.

The half arrowheads indicate asynchronous messages sent to or from an object. An asynchronous message typically means the first object calls a method on the second object, which returns immediately. After some processing, the second object calls a method on the first object to give it a value. This is in contrast to normal method calls, which do the processing in the method, and return a value immediately.

Sequence diagrams, like all UML diagrams, are best used only when they are needed. There is no point in drawing a UML diagram for the sake of drawing a diagram. However, when you need to communicate a series of interactions between two objects, the sequence diagram is a very useful tool.

Unfortunately, our class diagram so far is still a messy design. We notice that actors on DVDs and artists on CDs are all types of people, but are being treated differently from the book authors. The librarian also reminds us that most of their CDs are audio books, which have authors instead of artists.

How can we deal with different kinds of people that contribute to a title? One obvious implementation is to create a `Person` class with the person's name and other relevant details, and then create subclasses of this for the artists, authors, and actors. However, is inheritance really necessary here? For searching and cataloging purposes, we don't really care that acting and writing are two very different activities. If we were doing an economic simulation, it would make sense to give separate actor and author classes, and different `calculate_income` and `perform_job` methods, but for cataloging purposes, it is enough to know how the person contributed to the item. Having thought this through, we recognize that all items have one or more `Contributor` objects, so we move the author relationship from the book to its parent class:

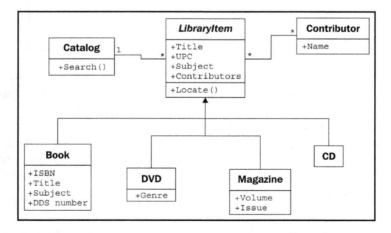

The multiplicity of the **Contributor/LibraryItem** relationship is **many-to-many**, as indicated by the * character at both ends of one relationship. Any one library item might have more than one contributor (for example, several actors and a director on a DVD). And many authors write many books, so they be attached to multiple library items.

This little change, while it looks a bit cleaner and simpler, has lost some vital information. We can still tell who contributed to a specific library item, but we don't know how they contributed. Were they the director or an actor? Did they write the audio book, or were they the voice that narrated the book?

It would be nice if we could just add a `contributor_type` attribute on the **Contributor** class, but this will fall apart when dealing with multi-talented people who have both authored books and directed movies.

One option is to add attributes to each of our **LibraryItem** subclasses to hold the information we need, such as **Author** on **Book**, or **Artist** on **CD**, and then make the relationship to those properties all point to the **Contributor** class. The problem with this is that we lose a lot of polymorphic elegance. If we want to list the contributors to an item, we have to look for specific attributes on that item, such as **Authors** or **Actors**. We can solve this by adding a **GetContributors** method on the **LibraryItem** class that subclasses can override. Then the catalog never has to know what attributes the objects are querying; we've abstracted the public interface:

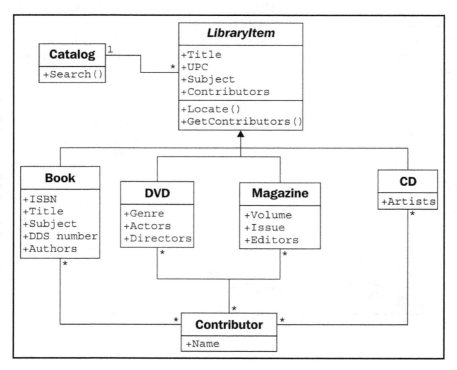

Just looking at this class diagram, it feels like we are doing something wrong. It is bulky and fragile. It may do everything we need, but it feels like it will be hard to maintain or extend. There are too many relationships, and too many classes would be affected by modifications to any one class. It looks like spaghetti and meatballs.

Now that we've explored inheritance as an option, and found it wanting, we might look back at our previous composition-based diagram, where **Contributor** was attached directly to **LibraryItem**. With some thought, we can see that we actually only need to add one more relationship to a brand-new class to identify the type of contributor. This is an important step in object-oriented design. We are now adding a class to the design that is intended to *support* the other objects, rather than modeling any part of the initial requirements. We are **refactoring** the design to facilitate the objects in the system, rather than objects in real life. Refactoring is an essential process in the maintenance of a program or design. The goal of refactoring is to improve the design by moving code around, removing duplicate code or complex relationships in favor of simpler, more elegant designs.

This new class is composed of a **Contributor** and an extra attribute identifying the type of contribution the person has made to the given **LibraryItem**. There can be many such contributions to a particular **LibraryItem**, and one contributor can contribute in the same way to different items. The following diagram communicates this design very well:

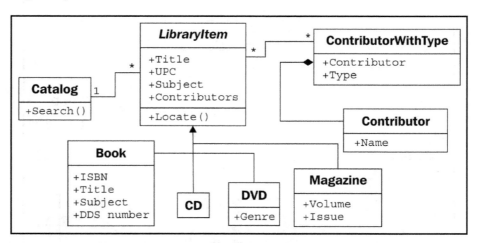

At first, this composition relationship looks less natural than the inheritance-based relationships. However, it has the advantage of allowing us to add new types of contributions without adding a new class to the design. Inheritance is most useful when the subclasses have some kind of **specialization**. Specialization is creating or changing attributes or behaviors on the subclass to make it somehow different from the parent class. It seems silly to create a bunch of empty classes solely for identifying different types of objects (this attitude is less prevalent among Java and other *everything is an object* programmers, but it is common among more pragmatic Python designers). If we look at the inheritance version of the diagram, we can see a bunch of subclasses that don't actually do anything:

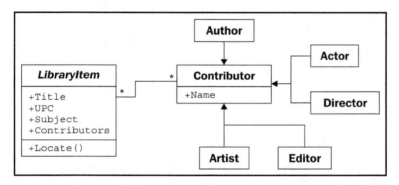

Sometimes, it is important to recognize when not to use object-oriented principles. This example of when not to use inheritance is a good reminder that objects are just tools, and not rules.

# Exercises

This is a practical book, not a textbook. As such, I'm not assigning a bunch of fake object-oriented analysis problems to create designs for you to analyze and design. Instead, I want to give you some ideas that you can apply to your own projects. If you have previous object-oriented experience, you won't need to put much effort into this chapter. However, they are useful mental exercises if you've been using Python for a while, but have never really cared about all that class stuff.

First, think about a recent programming project you've completed. Identify the most prominent object in the design. Try to think of as many attributes for this object as possible. Did it have the following: Color? Weight? Size? Profit? Cost? Name? ID number? Price? Style?

Think about the attribute types. Were they primitives or classes? Were some of those attributes actually behaviors in disguise? Sometimes, what looks like data is actually calculated from other data on the object, and you can use a method to do those calculations. What other methods or behaviors did the object have? Which objects called those methods? What kinds of relationships did they have with this object?

Now, think about an upcoming project. It doesn't matter what the project is; it might be a fun free-time project or a multi-million-dollar contract. It doesn't have to be a complete application; it could just be one subsystem. Perform a basic object-oriented analysis. Identify the requirements and the interacting objects. Sketch out a class diagram featuring the highest level of abstraction on that system. Identify the major interacting objects. Identify minor supporting objects. Go into detail for the attributes and methods of some of the most interesting ones. Take different objects to different levels of abstraction. Look for places where you can use inheritance or composition. Look for places where you should avoid inheritance.

The goal is not to design a system (although you're certainly welcome to do so if inclination meets both ambition and available time). The goal is to think about object-oriented design. Focusing on projects that you have worked on, or are expecting to work on in the future, simply makes it real.

Lastly, visit your favorite search engine and look up some tutorials on UML. There are dozens, so find one that suits your preferred method of study. Sketch some class diagrams or a sequence diagram for the objects you identified earlier. Don't get too hung up on memorizing the syntax (after all, if it is important, you can always look it up again); just get a feel for the language. Something will stay lodged in your brain, and it can make communicating a bit easier if you can quickly sketch a diagram for your next OOP discussion.

# Summary

In this chapter, we took a whirlwind tour through the terminology of the object-oriented paradigm, focusing on object-oriented design. We can separate different objects into a taxonomy of different classes and describe the attributes and behaviors of those objects via the class interface. Abstraction, encapsulation, and information hiding are highly-related concepts. There are many different kinds of relationships between objects, including association, composition, and inheritance. UML syntax can be useful for fun and communication.

In the next chapter, we'll explore how to implement classes and methods in Python.

# 16
# Objects in Python

So, we now have a design in hand and are ready to turn that design into a working program! Of course, it doesn't usually happen this way. We'll be seeing examples and hints for good software design throughout the book, but our focus is object-oriented programming. So, let's have a look at the Python syntax that allows us to create object-oriented software.

After completing this chapter, we will understand the following:

- How to create classes and instantiate objects in Python
- How to add attributes and behaviors to Python objects
- How to organize classes into packages and modules
- How to suggest that people don't clobber our data

## Creating Python classes

We don't have to write much Python code to realize that Python is a very *clean* language. When we want to do something, we can just do it, without having to set up a bunch of prerequisite code. The ubiquitous *hello world* in Python, as you've likely seen, is only one line.

Similarly, the simplest class in Python 3 looks like this:

```
class MyFirstClass:
    pass
```

There's our first object-oriented program! The class definition starts with the `class` keyword. This is followed by a name (of our choice) identifying the class, and is terminated with a colon.

 The class name must follow standard Python variable naming rules (it must start with a letter or underscore, and can only be comprised of letters, underscores, or numbers). In addition, the Python style guide (search the web for *PEP 8*) recommends that classes should be named using **CapWords** notation (start with a capital letter; any subsequent words should also start with a capital).

The class definition line is followed by the class contents, indented. As with other Python constructs, indentation is used to delimit the classes, rather than braces, keywords, or brackets, as many other languages use. Also in line with the style guide, use four spaces for indentation unless you have a compelling reason not to (such as fitting in with somebody else's code that uses tabs for indents).

Since our first class doesn't actually add any data or behaviors, we simply use the `pass` keyword on the second line to indicate that no further action needs to be taken.

We might think there isn't much we can do with this most basic class, but it does allow us to instantiate objects of that class. We can load the class into the Python 3 interpreter, so we can interactively play with it. To do this, save the class definition mentioned earlier in a file named `first_class.py` and then run the `python -i first_class.py` command. The `-i` argument tells Python to *run the code and then drop to the interactive interpreter*. The following interpreter session demonstrates a basic interaction with this class:

```
>>> a = MyFirstClass()
>>> b = MyFirstClass()
>>> print(a)
<__main__.MyFirstClass object at 0xb7b7faec>
>>> print(b)
<__main__.MyFirstClass object at 0xb7b7fbac>
>>>
```

This code instantiates two objects from the new class, named `a` and `b`. Creating an instance of a class is a simple matter of typing the class name, followed by a pair of parentheses. It looks much like a normal function call, but Python knows we're *calling* a class and not a function, so it understands that its job is to create a new object. When printed, the two objects tell us which class they are and what memory address they live at. Memory addresses aren't used much in Python code, but here, they demonstrate that there are two distinct objects involved.

# Adding attributes

Now, we have a basic class, but it's fairly useless. It doesn't contain any data, and it doesn't do anything. What do we have to do to assign an attribute to a given object?

In fact, we don't have to do anything special in the class definition. We can set arbitrary attributes on an instantiated object using dot notation:

```
class Point:
    pass

p1 = Point()
p2 = Point()

p1.x = 5
p1.y = 4

p2.x = 3
p2.y = 6

print(p1.x, p1.y)
print(p2.x, p2.y)
```

If we run this code, the two `print` statements at the end tell us the new attribute values on the two objects:

```
5 4
3 6
```

This code creates an empty `Point` class with no data or behaviors. Then, it creates two instances of that class and assigns each of those instances x and y coordinates to identify a point in two dimensions. All we need to do to assign a value to an attribute on an object is use the `<object>.<attribute> = <value>` syntax. This is sometimes referred to as **dot notation**. You have likely encountered this same notation before when reading attributes on objects provided by the standard library or a third-party library. The value can be anything: a Python primitive, a built-in data type, or another object. It can even be a function or another class!

# Making it do something

Now, having objects with attributes is great, but object-oriented programming is really about the interaction between objects. We're interested in invoking actions that cause things to happen to those attributes. We have data; now it's time to add behaviors to our classes.

Let's model a couple of actions on our `Point` class. We can start with a **method** called `reset`, which moves the point to the origin (the origin is the place where x and y are both zero). This is a good introductory action because it doesn't require any parameters:

```
class Point:
    def reset(self):
        self.x = 0
        self.y = 0

p = Point()
p.reset()
print(p.x, p.y)
```

This `print` statement shows us the two zeros on the attributes:

```
0 0
```

In Python, a method is formatted identically to a function. It starts with the `def` keyword , followed by a space, and the name of the method. This is followed by a set of parentheses containing the parameter list (we'll discuss that `self` parameter in just a moment), and terminated with a colon. The next line is indented to contain the statements inside the method. These statements can be arbitrary Python code operating on the object itself and any parameters passed in, as the method sees fit.

# Talking to yourself

The one difference, syntactically, between methods and normal functions is that all methods have one required argument. This argument is conventionally named `self`; I've never seen a Python programmer use any other name for this variable (convention is a very powerful thing). There's nothing stopping you, however, from calling it `this` or even `Martha`.

The `self` argument to a method is a reference to the object that the method is being invoked on. We can access attributes and methods of that object as if it were any another object. This is exactly what we do inside the `reset` method when we set the x and y attributes of the `self` object.

 Pay attention to the difference between a **class** and an **object** in this discussion. We can think of the **method** as a function attached to a class. The **self** parameter is a specific instance of that class. When you call the method on two different objects, you are calling the same method twice, but passing two different **objects** as the **self** parameter.

Notice that when we call the `p.reset()` method, we do not have to pass the `self` argument into it. Python automatically takes care of this part for us. It knows we're calling a method on the p object, so it automatically passes that object to the method.

However, the method really is just a function that happens to be on a class. Instead of calling the method on the object, we could invoke the function on the class, explicitly passing our object as the `self` argument:

```
>>> p = Point()
>>> Point.reset(p)
>>> print(p.x, p.y)
```

The output is the same as in the previous example because, internally, the exact same process has occurred.

What happens if we forget to include the `self` argument in our class definition? Python will bail with an error message, as follows:

```
>>> class Point:
... def reset():
... pass
...
>>> p = Point()
>>> p.reset()
Traceback (most recent call last):
  File "<stdin>", line 1, in <module>
TypeError: reset() takes 0 positional arguments but 1 was given
```

The error message is not as clear as it could be (Hey, silly, you forgot the `self` argument would be more informative). Just remember that when you see an error message that indicates missing arguments, the first thing to check is whether you forgot `self` in the method definition.

# More arguments

So, how do we pass multiple arguments to a method? Let's add a new method that allows us to move a point to an arbitrary position, not just to the origin. We can also include one that accepts another `Point` object as input and returns the distance between them:

```python
import math


class Point:
    def move(self, x, y):
        self.x = x
        self.y = y

    def reset(self):
        self.move(0, 0)

    def calculate_distance(self, other_point):
        return math.sqrt(
            (self.x - other_point.x) ** 2
            + (self.y - other_point.y) ** 2
        )


# how to use it:
point1 = Point()
point2 = Point()

point1.reset()
point2.move(5, 0)
print(point2.calculate_distance(point1))
assert point2.calculate_distance(point1) == point1.calculate_distance(
    point2
)
point1.move(3, 4)
print(point1.calculate_distance(point2))
print(point1.calculate_distance(point1))
```

The `print` statements at the end give us the following output:

```
5.0
4.47213595499958
0.0
```

A lot has happened here. The class now has three methods. The move method accepts two arguments, x and y, and sets the values on the self object, much like the old reset method from the previous example. The old reset method now calls move, since a reset is just a move to a specific known location.

The calculate_distance method uses the not-too-complex Pythagorean theorem to calculate the distance between two points. I hope you understand the math (**2 means squared, and math.sqrt calculates a square root), but it's not a requirement for our current focus, learning how to write methods.

The sample code at the end of the preceding example shows how to call a method with arguments: simply include the arguments inside the parentheses, and use the same dot notation to access the method. I just picked some random positions to test the methods. The test code calls each method and prints the results on the console. The assert function is a simple test tool; the program will bail if the statement after assert evaluates to False (or zero, empty, or None). In this case, we use it to ensure that the distance is the same regardless of which point called the other point's calculate_distance method.

# Initializing the object

If we don't explicitly set the x and y positions on our Point object, either using move or by accessing them directly, we have a broken point with no real position. What will happen when we try to access it?

Well, let's just try it and see. *Try it and see* is an extremely useful tool for Python study. Open up your interactive interpreter and type away. The following interactive session shows what happens if we try to access a missing attribute. If you saved the previous example as a file or are using the examples distributed with the book, you can load it into the Python interpreter with the python -i more_arguments.py command:

```
>>> point = Point()
>>> point.x = 5
>>> print(point.x)
5
>>> print(point.y)
Traceback (most recent call last):
  File "<stdin>", line 1, in <module>
AttributeError: 'Point' object has no attribute 'y'
```

Well, at least it threw a useful exception. We'll cover exceptions in detail in Chapter 18, *Expecting the Unexpected*. You've probably seen them before (especially the ubiquitous **SyntaxError**, which means you typed something incorrectly!). At this point, simply be aware that it means something went wrong.

The output is useful for debugging. In the interactive interpreter, it tells us the error occurred at **line 1**, which is only partially true (in an interactive session, only one line is executed at a time). If we were running a script in a file, it would tell us the exact line number, making it easy to find the offending code. In addition, it tells us that the error is an AttributeError, and gives a helpful message telling us what that error means.

We can catch and recover from this error, but in this case, it feels like we should have specified some sort of default value. Perhaps every new object should be reset() by default, or maybe it would be nice if we could force the user to tell us what those positions should be when they create the object.

Most object-oriented programming languages have the concept of a **constructor**, a special method that creates and initializes the object when it is created. Python is a little different; it has a constructor *and* an initializer. The constructor function is rarely used, unless you're doing something very exotic. So, we'll start our discussion with the much more common initialization method.

The Python initialization method is the same as any other method, except it has a special name, __init__. The leading and trailing double underscores mean this is a special method that the Python interpreter will treat as a special case.

 Never name a method of your own with leading and trailing double underscores. It may mean nothing to Python today, but there's always the possibility that the designers of Python will add a function that has a special purpose with that name in the future, and when they do, your code will break.

Let's add an initialization function on our Point class that requires the user to supply x and y coordinates when the Point object is instantiated:

```python
class Point:
    def __init__(self, x, y):
        self.move(x, y)

    def move(self, x, y):
        self.x = x
        self.y = y
```

```
def reset(self):
    self.move(0, 0)

# Constructing a Point
point = Point(3, 5)
print(point.x, point.y)
```

Now, our point can never go without a y coordinate! If we try to construct a point without including the proper initialization parameters, it will fail with a not enough arguments error similar to the one we received earlier when we forgot the self argument.

If we don't want to make the two arguments required, we can use the same syntax Python functions use to provide default arguments. The keyword argument syntax appends an equals sign after each variable name. If the calling object does not provide this argument, then the default argument is used instead. The variables will still be available to the function, but they will have the values specified in the argument list. Here's an example:

```
class Point:
    def __init__(self, x=0, y=0):
        self.move(x, y)
```

Most of the time, we put our initialization statements in an __init__ function. But as mentioned earlier, Python has a constructor in addition to its initialization function. You may never need to use the other Python constructor (in well over a decade of professional Python coding, I can only think of two cases where I've used it, and in one of them, I probably shouldn't have!), but it helps to know it exists, so we'll cover it briefly.

The constructor function is called __new__ as opposed to __init__, and accepts exactly one argument; the **class** that is being constructed (it is called *before* the object is constructed, so there is no self argument). It also has to return the newly created object. This has interesting possibilities when it comes to the complicated art of metaprogramming, but is not very useful in day-to-day Python. In practice, you will rarely, if ever, need to use __new__. The __init__ method will almost always be sufficient.

# Explaining yourself

Python is an extremely easy-to-read programming language; some might say it is self-documenting. However, when carrying out object-oriented programming, it is important to write API documentation that clearly summarizes what each object and method does. Keeping documentation up to date is difficult; the best way to do it is to write it right into our code.

Python supports this through the use of **docstrings**. Each class, function, or method header can have a standard Python string as the first line following the definition (the line that ends in a colon). This line should be indented the same as the code that follows it.

Docstrings are simply Python strings enclosed with apostrophes (') or quotation marks (") characters. Often, docstrings are quite long and span multiple lines (the style guide suggests that the line length should not exceed 80 characters), which can be formatted as multi-line strings, enclosed in matching triple apostrophe (''') or triple quote (""") characters.

A docstring should clearly and concisely summarize the purpose of the class or method it is describing. It should explain any parameters whose usage is not immediately obvious, and is also a good place to include short examples of how to use the API. Any caveats or problems an unsuspecting user of the API should be aware of should also be noted.

To illustrate the use of docstrings, we will end this section with our completely documented `Point` class:

```python
import math


class Point:
    "Represents a point in two-dimensional geometric coordinates"

    def __init__(self, x=0, y=0):
        """Initialize the position of a new point. The x and y
            coordinates can be specified. If they are not, the
            point defaults to the origin."""
        self.move(x, y)

    def move(self, x, y):
        "Move the point to a new location in 2D space."
        self.x = x
        self.y = y
```

```
    def reset(self):
        "Reset the point back to the geometric origin: 0, 0"
        self.move(0, 0)

    def calculate_distance(self, other_point):
        """Calculate the distance from this point to a second
        point passed as a parameter.

        This function uses the Pythagorean Theorem to calculate
        the distance between the two points. The distance is
        returned as a float."""

        return math.sqrt(
            (self.x - other_point.x) ** 2
            + (self.y - other_point.y) ** 2
        )
```

Try typing or loading (remember, it's `python -i point.py`) this file into the interactive interpreter. Then, enter `help(Point) <enter>` at the Python prompt.

You should see nicely formatted documentation for the class, as shown in the following screenshot:

# Modules and packages

Now we know how to create classes and instantiate objects. You don't need to write too many classes (or non-object-oriented code, for that matter) before you start to lose track of them. For small programs, we can just put all our classes into one file and add a little script at the end of the file to start them interacting. However, as our projects grow, it can become difficult to find the one class that needs to be edited among the many classes we've defined. This is where **modules** come in. Modules are simply Python files, nothing more. The single file in our small program is a module. Two Python files are two modules. If we have two files in the same folder, we can load a class from one module for use in the other module.

For example, if we are building an e-commerce system, we will likely be storing a lot of data in a database. We can put all the classes and functions related to database access into a separate file (we'll call it something sensible: database.py). Then, our other modules (for example, customer models, product information, and inventory) can import classes from that module in order to access the database.

The import statement is used for importing modules or specific classes or functions from modules. We've already seen an example of this in our Point class in the previous section. We used the import statement to get Python's built-in math module and use its sqrt function in the distance calculation.

Here's a concrete example. Assume we have a module called database.py, which contains a class called Database. A second module called products.py is responsible for product-related queries. At this point, we don't need to think too much about the contents of these files. What we know is that products.py needs to instantiate the Database class from database.py so that it can execute queries on the product table in the database.

There are several variations on the import statement syntax that can be used to access the class:

```
import database
db = database.Database()
# Do queries on db
```

This version imports the `database` module into the `products` namespace (the list of names currently accessible in a module or function), so any class or function in the `database` module can be accessed using the `database.<something>` notation. Alternatively, we can import just the one class we need using the `from...import` syntax:

```
from database import Database
db = Database()
# Do queries on db
```

If, for some reason, `products` already has a class called `Database`, and we don't want the two names to be confused, we can rename the class when used inside the `products` module:

```
from database import Database as DB
db = DB()
# Do queries on db
```

We can also import multiple items in one statement. If our `database` module also contains a `Query` class, we can import both classes using the following code:

```
from database import Database, Query
```

Some sources say that we can import all classes and functions from the `database` module using this syntax:

```
from database import *
```

**Don't do this.** Most experienced Python programmers will tell you that you should never use this syntax (a few will tell you there are some very specific situations where it is useful, but I disagree). They'll use obscure justifications such as *it clutters up the namespace*, which doesn't make much sense to beginners. One way to learn why to avoid this syntax is to use it and try to understand your code two years later. But we can save some time and two years of poorly written code with a quick explanation now!

When we explicitly import the `database` class at the top of our file using `from database import Database`, we can easily see where the `Database` class comes from. We might use `db = Database()` 400 lines later in the file, and we can quickly look at the imports to see where that `Database` class came from. Then, if we need clarification as to how to use the `Database` class, we can visit the original file (or import the module in the interactive interpreter and use the `help(database.Database)` command). However, if we use the `from database import *` syntax, it takes a lot longer to find where that class is located. Code maintenance becomes a nightmare.

In addition, most code editors are able to provide extra functionality, such as reliable code completion, the ability to jump to the definition of a class, or inline documentation, if normal imports are used. The `import *` syntax usually completely destroys their ability to do this reliably.

Finally, using the `import *` syntax can bring unexpected objects into our local namespace. Sure, it will import all the classes and functions defined in the module being imported from, but it will also import any classes or modules that were themselves imported into that file!

Every name used in a module should come from a well-specified place, whether it is defined in that module, or explicitly imported from another module. There should be no magic variables that seem to come out of thin air. We should *always* be able to immediately identify where the names in our current namespace originated. I promise that if you use this evil syntax, you will one day have extremely frustrating moments of *where on earth can this class be coming from?*

For fun, try typing `import this` into your interactive interpreter. It prints a nice poem (with a couple of inside jokes you can ignore) summarizing some of the idioms that Pythonistas tend to practice. Specific to this discussion, note the line *Explicit is better than implicit.* Explicitly importing names into your namespace makes your code much easier to navigate than the implicit `import *` syntax.

# Organizing modules

As a project grows into a collection of more and more modules, we may find that we want to add another level of abstraction, some kind of nested hierarchy on our modules' levels. However, we can't put modules inside modules; one file can hold only one file after all, and modules are just files.

Files, however, can go in folders, and so can modules. A **package** is a collection of modules in a folder. The name of the package is the name of the folder. We need to tell Python that a folder is a package to distinguish it from other folders in the directory. To do this, place a (normally empty) file in the folder named __init__.py. If we forget this file, we won't be able to import modules from that folder.

Let's put our modules inside an ecommerce package in our working folder, which will also contain a main.py file to start the program. Let's additionally add another package inside the ecommerce package for various payment options. The folder hierarchy will look like this:

```
parent_directory/
    main.py
    ecommerce/
        __init__.py
        database.py
        products.py
        payments/
            __init__.py
            square.py
            stripe.py
```

When importing modules or classes between packages, we have to be cautious about the syntax. In Python 3, there are two ways of importing modules: absolute imports and relative imports.

# Absolute imports

**Absolute imports** specify the complete path to the module, function, or class we want to import. If we need access to the `Product` class inside the `products` module, we could use any of these syntaxes to perform an absolute import:

```
import ecommerce.products
product = ecommerce.products.Product()

//or

from ecommerce.products import Product
product = Product()

//or

from ecommerce import products
product = products.Product()
```

The `import` statements use the period operator to separate packages or modules.

These statements will work from any module. We could instantiate a `Product` class using this syntax in `main.py`, in the `database` module, or in either of the two payment modules. Indeed, assuming the packages are available to Python, it will be able to import them. For example, the packages can also be installed in the Python site packages folder, or the `PYTHONPATH` environment variable could be customized to dynamically tell Python which folders to search for packages and modules it is going to import.

So, with these choices, which syntax do we choose? It depends on your personal taste and the application at hand. If there are dozens of classes and functions inside the `products` module that I want to use, I generally import the module name using the `from ecommerce import products` syntax, and then access the individual classes using `products.Product`. If I only need one or two classes from the `products` module, I can import them directly using the `from ecommerce.products import Product` syntax. I don't personally use the first syntax very often, unless I have some kind of name conflict (for example, I need to access two completely different modules called `products` and I need to separate them). Do whatever you think makes your code look more elegant.

# Relative imports

When working with related modules inside a package, it seems kind of redundant to specify the full path; we know what our parent module is named. This is where **relative imports** come in. Relative imports are basically a way of saying find a class, function, or module as it is positioned relative to the current module. For example, if we are working in the `products` module and we want to import the `Database` class from the `database` module next to it, we could use a relative import:

```
from .database import Database
```

The period in front of `database` says *use the database module inside the current package*. In this case, the current package is the package containing the `products.py` file we are currently editing, that is, the `ecommerce` package.

If we were editing the `paypal` module inside the `ecommerce.payments` package, we would want, for example, to *use the database package inside the parent package* instead. This is easily done with two periods, as shown here:

```
from ..database import Database
```

We can use more periods to go further up the hierarchy. Of course, we can also go down one side and back up the other. We don't have a deep enough example hierarchy to illustrate this properly, but the following would be a valid import if we had an `ecommerce.contact` package containing an `email` module and wanted to import the `send_mail` function into our `paypal` module:

```
from ..contact.email import send_mail
```

This import uses two periods indicating, *the parent of the payments package*, and then uses the normal `package.module` syntax to go back down into the contact package.

Finally, we can import code directly from packages, as opposed to just modules inside packages. In this example, we have an `ecommerce` package containing two modules named `database.py` and `products.py`. The database module contains a `db` variable that is accessed from a lot of places. Wouldn't it be convenient if this could be imported as `import ecommerce.db` instead of `import ecommerce.database.db`?

Remember the \_\_init\_\_.py file that defines a directory as a package? This file can contain any variable or class declarations we like, and they will be available as part of the package. In our example, if the ecommerce/\_\_init\_\_.py file contained the following line:

```
from .database import db
```

We could then access the db attribute from main.py or any other file using the following import:

```
from ecommerce import db
```

It might help to think of the \_\_init\_\_.py file as if it were an ecommerce.py file, if that file were a module instead of a package. This can also be useful if you put all your code in a single module and later decide to break it up into a package of modules. The \_\_init\_\_.py file for the new package can still be the main point of contact for other modules talking to it, but the code can be internally organized into several different modules or subpackages.

I recommend not putting much code in an \_\_init\_\_.py file, though. Programmers do not expect actual logic to happen in this file, and much like with from x import \*, it can trip them up if they are looking for the declaration of a particular piece of code and can't find it until they check \_\_init\_\_.py.

# Organizing module content

Inside any one module, we can specify variables, classes, or functions. They can be a handy way to store the global state without namespace conflicts. For example, we have been importing the Database class into various modules and then instantiating it, but it might make more sense to have only one database object globally available from the database module. The database module might look like this:

```
class Database:
    # the database implementation
    pass

database = Database()
```

Then we can use any of the import methods we've discussed to access the database object, for example:

```
from ecommerce.database import database
```

A problem with the preceding class is that the `database` object is created immediately when the module is first imported, which is usually when the program starts up. This isn't always ideal, since connecting to a database can take a while, slowing down startup, or the database connection information may not yet be available. We could delay creating the database until it is actually needed by calling an `initialize_database` function to create a module-level variable:

```
class Database:
    # the database implementation
    pass


database = None

def initialize_database():
    global database
    database = Database()
```

The `global` keyword tells Python that the database variable inside `initialize_database` is the module level one we just defined. If we had not specified the variable as global, Python would have created a new local variable that would be discarded when the method exits, leaving the module-level value unchanged.

As these two examples illustrate, all module-level code is executed immediately at the time it is imported. However, if it is inside a method or function, the function will be created, but its internal code will not be executed until the function is called. This can be a tricky thing for scripts that perform execution (such as the main script in our e-commerce example). Sometimes, we write a program that does something useful, and then later find that we want to import a function or class from that module into a different program. However, as soon as we import it, any code at the module level is immediately executed. If we are not careful, we can end up running the first program when we really only meant to access a couple of functions inside that module.

To solve this, we should always put our start up code in a function (conventionally, called `main`) and only execute that function when we know we are running the module as a script, but not when our code is being imported from a different script. We can do this by **guarding** the call to `main` inside a conditional statement, demonstrated as follows:

```
class UsefulClass:
    """This class might be useful to other modules."""

    pass
```

```
def main():
    """Creates a useful class and does something with it for our
module."""
    useful = UsefulClass()
    print(useful)


if __name__ == "__main__":
    main()
```

Every module has a __name__ special variable (remember, Python uses double underscores for special variables, such as a class's __init__ method) that specifies the name of the module when it was imported. When the module is executed directly with `python module.py`, it is never imported, so the __name__ is arbitrarily set to the "__main__" string. Make it a policy to wrap all your scripts in an if __name__ == "__main__": test, just in case you write a function that you may want to be imported by other code at some point in the future.

So, methods go in classes, which go in modules, which go in packages. Is that all there is to it?

Actually, no. This is the typical order of things in a Python program, but it's not the only possible layout. Classes can be defined anywhere. They are typically defined at the module level, but they can also be defined inside a function or method, like this:

```
def format_string(string, formatter=None):
    """Format a string using the formatter object, which
    is expected to have a format() method that accepts
    a string."""

    class DefaultFormatter:
        """Format a string in title case."""

        def format(self, string):
            return str(string).title()

    if not formatter:
        formatter = DefaultFormatter()

    return formatter.format(string)


hello_string = "hello world, how are you today?"
print(" input: " + hello_string)
print("output: " + format_string(hello_string))
```

The output would be as follows:

```
input: hello world, how are you today?
output: Hello World, How Are You Today?
```

The `format_string` function accepts a string and optional formatter object, and then applies the formatter to that string. If no formatter is supplied, it creates a formatter of its own as a local class and instantiates it. Since it is created inside the scope of the function, this class cannot be accessed from anywhere outside of that function. Similarly, functions can be defined inside other functions as well; in general, any Python statement can be executed at any time.

These inner classes and functions are occasionally useful for one-off items that don't require or deserve their own scope at the module level, or only make sense inside a single method. However, it is not common to see Python code that frequently uses this technique.

# Who can access my data?

Most object-oriented programming languages have a concept of **access control**. This is related to abstraction. Some attributes and methods on an object are marked private, meaning only that object can access them. Others are marked protected, meaning only that class and any subclasses have access. The rest are public, meaning any other object is allowed to access them.

Python doesn't do this. Python doesn't really believe in enforcing laws that might someday get in your way. Instead, it provides unenforced guidelines and best practices. Technically, all methods and attributes on a class are publicly available. If we want to suggest that a method should not be used publicly, we can put a note in docstrings indicating that the method is meant for internal use only (preferably, with an explanation of how the public-facing API works!).

By convention, we should also prefix an internal attribute or method with an underscore character, _. Python programmers will interpret this as *this is an internal variable, think three times before accessing it directly*. But there is nothing inside the interpreter to stop them from accessing it if they think it is in their best interest to do so. Because, if they think so, why should we stop them? We may not have any idea what future uses our classes may be put to.

There's another thing you can do to strongly suggest that outside objects don't access a property or method: prefix it with a double underscore, __. This will perform **name mangling** on the attribute in question. In essence, name mangling means that the method can still be called by outside objects if they really want to do so, but it requires extra work and is a strong indicator that you demand that your attribute remains **private**. Here is an example code snippet:

```
class SecretString:
    """A not-at-all secure way to store a secret string."""

    def __init__(self, plain_string, pass_phrase):
        self.__plain_string = plain_string
        self.__pass_phrase = pass_phrase

    def decrypt(self, pass_phrase):
        """Only show the string if the pass_phrase is correct."""
        if pass_phrase == self.__pass_phrase:
            return self.__plain_string
        else:
            return ""
```

If we load this class and test it in the interactive interpreter, we can see that it hides the plain text string from the outside world:

```
>>> secret_string = SecretString("ACME: Top Secret", "antwerp")
>>> print(secret_string.decrypt("antwerp"))
ACME: Top Secret
>>> print(secret_string.__plain_string)
Traceback (most recent call last):
  File "<stdin>", line 1, in <module>
AttributeError: 'SecretString' object has no attribute
'__plain_string'
```

It looks like it works; nobody can access our `plain_string` attribute without the passphrase, so it must be safe. Before we get too excited, though, let's see how easy it can be to hack our security:

```
>>> print(secret_string._SecretString__plain_string)
ACME: Top Secret
```

Oh no! Somebody has discovered our secret string. Good thing we checked.

This is Python name mangling at work. When we use a double underscore, the property is prefixed with _<classname>. When methods in the class internally access the variable, they are automatically unmangled. When external classes wish to access it, they have to do the name mangling themselves. So, name mangling does not guarantee privacy; it only strongly recommends it. Most Python programmers will not touch a double underscore variable on another object unless they have an extremely compelling reason to do so.

However, most Python programmers will not touch a single underscore variable without a compelling reason either. Therefore, there are very few good reasons to use a name-mangled variable in Python, and doing so can cause grief. For example, a name-mangled variable may be useful to an as-yet-unknown subclass, and it would have to do the mangling itself. Let other objects access your hidden information if they want to. Just let them know, using a single-underscore prefix or some clear docstrings, that you think this is not a good idea.

# Third-party libraries

Python ships with a lovely standard library, which is a collection of packages and modules that are available on every machine that runs Python. However, you'll soon find that it doesn't contain everything you need. When this happens, you have two options:

- Write a supporting package yourself
- Use somebody else's code

We won't be covering the details about turning your packages into libraries, but if you have a problem you need to solve and you don't feel like coding it (the best programmers are extremely lazy and prefer to reuse existing, proven code, rather than write their own), you can probably find the library you want on the **Python Package Index** (**PyPI**) at http://pypi.python.org/. Once you've identified a package that you want to install, you can use a tool called pip to install it. However, pip does not come with Python, but Python 3.4 and higher contain a useful tool called ensurepip. You can use this command to install it:

```
$python -m ensurepip
```

This may fail for you on Linux, macOS, or other Unix systems, in which case, you'll need to become a root user to make it work. On most modern Unix systems, this can be done with sudo python -m ensurepip.

If you are using an older version of Python than Python 3.4, you'll need to download and install `pip` yourself, since `ensurepip` isn't available. You can do this by following the instructions at: `http://pip.readthedocs.org/`.

Once `pip` is installed and you know the name of the package you want to install, you can install it using syntax such as the following:

```
$pip install requests
```

However, if you do this, you'll either be installing the third-party library directly into your system Python directory, or, more likely, will get an error that you don't have permission to do so. You could force the installation as an administrator, but common consensus in the Python community is that you should only use system installers to install the third-party library to your system Python directory.

Instead, Python 3.4 (and higher) supplies the `venv` tool. This utility basically gives you a mini Python installation called a *virtual environment* in your working directory. When you activate the mini Python, commands related to Python will work on that directory instead of the system directory. So, when you run `pip` or `python`, it won't touch the system Python at all. Here's how to use it:

```
cd project_directory
python -m venv env
source env/bin/activate    # on Linux or macOS
env/bin/activate.bat       # on Windows
```

Typically, you'll create a different virtual environment for each Python project you work on. You can store your virtual environments anywhere, but I traditionally keep mine in the same directory as the rest of my project files (but ignored in version control), so first we `cd` into that directory. Then, we run the `venv` utility to create a virtual environment named `env`. Finally, we use one of the last two lines (depending on the operating system, as indicated in the comments) to activate the environment. We'll need to execute this line each time we want to use that particular virtualenv, and then use the `deactivate` command when we are done working on this project.

Virtual environments are a terrific way to keep your third-party dependencies separate. It is common to have different projects that depend on different versions of a particular library (for example, an older website might run on Django 1.8, while newer versions run on Django 2.1). Keeping each project in separate virtualenvs makes it easy to work in either version of Django. Furthermore, it prevents conflicts between system-installed packages and `pip`-installed packages if you try to install the same package using different tools.

There are several third-party tools for managing virtual environments effectively. Some of these include `pyenv`, `virtualenvwrapper`, and `conda`. My personal preference at the time of writing is `pyenv`, but there is no clear winner here. Do a quick web search and see what works for you.

# Case study

To tie it all together, let's build a simple command-line notebook application. This is a fairly simple task, so we won't be experimenting with multiple packages. We will, however, see common usage of classes, functions, methods, and docstrings.

Let's start with a quick analysis: notes are short memos stored in a notebook. Each note should record the day it was written and can have tags added for easy querying. It should be possible to modify notes. We also need to be able to search for notes. All of these things should be done from the command line.

An obvious object is the `Note` object; a less obvious one is a `Notebook` container object. Tags and dates also seem to be objects, but we can use dates from Python's standard library and a comma-separated string for tags. To avoid complexity, in the prototype, we need not define separate classes for these objects.

`Note` objects have attributes for `memo` itself, `tags`, and `creation_date`. Each note will also need a unique integer `id` so that users can select them in a menu interface. Notes could have a method to modify note content and another for tags, or we could just let the notebook access those attributes directly. To make searching easier, we should put a `match` method on the `Note` object. This method will accept a string and can tell us whether a note matches the string without accessing the attributes directly. This way, if we want to modify the search parameters (to search tags instead of note contents, for example, or to make the search case-insensitive), we only have to do it in one place.

The `Notebook` object obviously has the list of notes as an attribute. It will also need a search method that returns a list of filtered notes.

But how do we interact with these objects? We've specified a command-line app, which can mean either that we run the program with different options to add or edit commands, or we have some kind of menu that allows us to pick different things to do to the notebook. We should try to design it such that either interface is supported and future interfaces, such as a GUI toolkit or web-based interface, could be added in the future.

As a design decision, we'll implement the menu interface now, but will keep the command-line options version in mind to ensure we design our `Notebook` class with extensibility in mind.

If we have two command-line interfaces, each interacting with the `Notebook` object, then `Notebook` will need some methods for those interfaces to interact with. We need to be able to `add` a new note, and `modify` an existing note by `id`, in addition to the `search` method we've already discussed. The interfaces will also need to be able to list all notes, but they can do that by accessing the `notes` list attribute directly.

We may be missing a few details, but we have a really good overview of the code we need to write. We can summarize all this analysis in a simple class diagram:

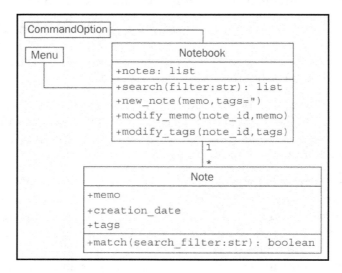

Before writing any code, let's define the folder structure for this project. The menu interface should clearly be in its own module, since it will be an executable script, and we may have other executable scripts accessing the notebook in the future. The `Notebook` and `Note` objects can live together in one module. These modules can both exist in the same top-level directory without having to put them in a package. An empty `command_option.py` module can help remind us in the future that we were planning to add new user interfaces:

```
parent_directory/
    notebook.py
    menu.py
    command_option.py
```

Now let's see some code. We start by defining the Note class, as it seems simplest. The following example presents Note in its entirety. Docstrings within the example explain how it all fits together, demonstrated as follows:

```python
import datetime

# Store the next available id for all new notes
last_id = 0


class Note:
    """Represent a note in the notebook. Match against a
    string in searches and store tags for each note."""

    def __init__(self, memo, tags=""):
        """initialize a note with memo and optional
        space-separated tags. Automatically set the note's
        creation date and a unique id."""
        self.memo = memo
        self.tags = tags
        self.creation_date = datetime.date.today()
        global last_id
        last_id += 1
        self.id = last_id

    def match(self, filter):
        """Determine if this note matches the filter
        text. Return True if it matches, False otherwise.

        Search is case sensitive and matches both text and
        tags."""
        return filter in self.memo or filter in self.tags
```

Before continuing, we should quickly fire up the interactive interpreter and test our code so far. Test frequently and often, because things never work the way you expect them to. Indeed, when I tested my first version of this example, I found out I had forgotten the self argument in the match function! We'll discuss automated testing in Chapter 24, *Testing Object-Oriented Programs*. For now, it suffices to check a few things using the interpreter:

```python
>>> from notebook import Note
>>> n1 = Note("hello first")
>>> n2 = Note("hello again")
>>> n1.id
1
>>> n2.id
2
```

```
>>> n1.match('hello')
True
>>> n2.match('second')
False
```

It looks like everything is behaving as expected. Let's create our notebook next:

```
class Notebook:
    """Represent a collection of notes that can be tagged,
    modified, and searched."""

    def __init__(self):
        """Initialize a notebook with an empty list."""
        self.notes = []

    def new_note(self, memo, tags=""):
        """Create a new note and add it to the list."""
        self.notes.append(Note(memo, tags))

    def modify_memo(self, note_id, memo):
        """Find the note with the given id and change its
        memo to the given value."""
        for note in self.notes:
            if note.id == note_id:
                note.memo = memo
                break

    def modify_tags(self, note_id, tags):
        """Find the note with the given id and change its
        tags to the given value."""
        for note in self.notes:
            if note.id == note_id:
                note.tags = tags
                break

    def search(self, filter):
        """Find all notes that match the given filter
        string."""
        return [note for note in self.notes if note.match(filter)]
```

We'll clean this up in a minute. First, let's test it to make sure it works:

```
>>> from notebook import Note, Notebook
>>> n = Notebook()
>>> n.new_note("hello world")
>>> n.new_note("hello again")
>>> n.notes
[<notebook.Note object at 0xb730a78c>, <notebook.Note object at
```

```
0xb73103ac>]
>>> n.notes[0].id
1
>>> n.notes[1].id
2
>>> n.notes[0].memo
'hello world'
>>> n.search("hello")
[<notebook.Note object at 0xb730a78c>, <notebook.Note object at
0xb73103ac>]
>>> n.search("world")
[<notebook.Note object at 0xb730a78c>]
>>> n.modify_memo(1, "hi world")
>>> n.notes[0].memo
'hi world'
```

It does work. The code is a little messy though; our `modify_tags` and `modify_memo` methods are almost identical. That's not good coding practice. Let's see how we can improve it.

Both methods are trying to identify the note with a given ID before doing something to that note. So, let's add a method to locate the note with a specific ID. We'll prefix the method name with an underscore to suggest that the method is for internal use only, but, of course, our menu interface can access the method if it wants to:

```
def _find_note(self, note_id):
    """Locate the note with the given id."""
    for note in self.notes:
        if note.id == note_id:
            return note
    return None

def modify_memo(self, note_id, memo):
    """Find the note with the given id and change its
    memo to the given value."""
    self._find_note(note_id).memo = memo

def modify_tags(self, note_id, tags):
    """Find the note with the given id and change its
    tags to the given value."""
    self._find_note(note_id).tags = tags
```

This should work for now. Let's have a look at the menu interface. The interface needs to present a menu and allow the user to input choices. Here's our first attempt:

```python
import sys
from notebook import Notebook


class Menu:
    """Display a menu and respond to choices when run."""

    def __init__(self):
        self.notebook = Notebook()
        self.choices = {
            "1": self.show_notes,
            "2": self.search_notes,
            "3": self.add_note,
            "4": self.modify_note,
            "5": self.quit,
        }

    def display_menu(self):
        print(
            """
Notebook Menu

1. Show all Notes
2. Search Notes
3. Add Note
4. Modify Note
5. Quit
"""
        )

    def run(self):
        """Display the menu and respond to choices."""
        while True:
            self.display_menu()
            choice = input("Enter an option: ")
            action = self.choices.get(choice)
            if action:
                action()
            else:
                print("{0} is not a valid choice".format(choice))

    def show_notes(self, notes=None):
        if not notes:
            notes = self.notebook.notes
        for note in notes:
```

```
                print("{0}: {1}\n{2}".format(note.id, note.tags,
    note.memo))

    def search_notes(self):
        filter = input("Search for: ")
        notes = self.notebook.search(filter)
        self.show_notes(notes)

    def add_note(self):
        memo = input("Enter a memo: ")
        self.notebook.new_note(memo)
        print("Your note has been added.")

    def modify_note(self):
        id = input("Enter a note id: ")
        memo = input("Enter a memo: ")
        tags = input("Enter tags: ")
        if memo:
            self.notebook.modify_memo(id, memo)
        if tags:
            self.notebook.modify_tags(id, tags)

    def quit(self):
        print("Thank you for using your notebook today.")
        sys.exit(0)


if __name__ == "__main__":
    Menu().run()
```

This code first imports the notebook objects using an absolute import. Relative imports wouldn't work because we haven't placed our code inside a package. The Menu class's run method repeatedly displays a menu and responds to choices by calling functions on the notebook. This is done using an idiom that is rather peculiar to Python; it is a lightweight version of the command pattern that we will discuss in Chapter 22, *Python Design Patterns I*. The choices entered by the user are strings. In the menu's __init__ method, we create a dictionary that maps strings to functions on the menu object itself. Then, when the user makes a choice, we retrieve the object from the dictionary. The action variable actually refers to a specific method, and is called by appending empty brackets (since none of the methods require parameters) to the variable. Of course, the user might have entered an inappropriate choice, so we check if the action really exists before calling it.

Each of the various methods request user input and call appropriate methods on the `Notebook` object associated with it. For the `search` implementation, we notice that after we've filtered the notes, we need to show them to the user, so we make the `show_notes` function serve double duty; it accepts an optional `notes` parameter. If it's supplied, it displays only the filtered notes, but if it's not, it displays all notes. Since the `notes` parameter is optional, `show_notes` can still be called with no parameters as an empty menu item.

If we test this code, we'll find that it fails if we try to modify a note. There are two bugs, namely:

- The notebook crashes when we enter a note ID that does not exist. We should never trust our users to enter correct data!
- Even if we enter a correct ID, it will crash because the note IDs are integers, but our menu is passing a string.

The latter bug can be solved by modifying the `Notebook` class's `_find_note` method to compare the values using strings instead of the integers stored in the note, as follows:

```python
def _find_note(self, note_id):
    """Locate the note with the given id."""
    for note in self.notes:
        if str(note.id) == str(note_id):
            return note
    return None
```

We simply convert both the input (`note_id`) and the note's ID to strings before comparing them. We could also convert the input to an integer, but then we'd have trouble if the user entered the letter `a` instead of the number `1`.

The problem with users entering note IDs that don't exist can be fixed by changing the two `modify` methods on the notebook to check whether `_find_note` returned a note or not, like this:

```python
def modify_memo(self, note_id, memo):
    """Find the note with the given id and change its
    memo to the given value."""
    note = self._find_note(note_id)
    if note:
        note.memo = memo
        return True
    return False
```

This method has been updated to return `True` or `False`, depending on whether a note has been found. The menu could use this return value to display an error if the user entered an invalid note.

> This code is a bit unwieldy. It would look a bit better if it raised an exception instead. We'll cover those in `Chapter 18`, *Expecting the Unexpected*.

# Exercises

Write some object-oriented code. The goal is to use the principles and syntax you learned in this chapter to ensure you understand the topics we've covered. If you've been working on a Python project, go back over it and see whether there are some objects you can create and add properties or methods to. If it's large, try dividing it into a few modules or even packages and play with the syntax.

If you don't have such a project, try starting a new one. It doesn't have to be something you intend to finish; just stub out some basic design parts. You don't need to fully implement everything; often, just a `print("this method will do something")` is all you need to get the overall design in place. This is called **top-down design**, in which you work out the different interactions and describe how they should work before actually implementing what they do. The converse, **bottom-up design**, implements details first and then ties them all together. Both patterns are useful at different times, but for understanding object-oriented principles, a top-down workflow is more suitable.

If you're having trouble coming up with ideas, try writing a to-do application. (Hint: it would be similar to the design of the notebook application, but with extra date management methods.) It can keep track of things you want to do each day, and allow you to mark them as completed.

Now try designing a bigger project. As before, it doesn't have to actually do anything, but make sure you experiment with the package and module-importing syntax. Add some functions in various modules and try importing them from other modules and packages. Use relative and absolute imports. See the difference, and try to imagine scenarios where you would want to use each one.

# Summary

In this chapter, we learned how simple it is to create classes and assign properties and methods in Python. Unlike many languages, Python differentiates between a constructor and an initializer. It has a relaxed attitude toward access control. There are many different levels of scope, including packages, modules, classes, and functions. We understood the difference between relative and absolute imports, and how to manage third-party packages that don't come with Python.

In the next chapter, we'll learn how to share implementation using inheritance.

# When Objects Are Alike

# 17

In the programming world, duplicate code is considered evil. We should not have multiple copies of the same, or similar, code in different places.

There are many ways to merge pieces of code or objects that have a similar functionality. In this chapter, we'll be covering the most famous object-oriented principle: inheritance. As discussed in `Chapter 15`, *Object-Oriented Design*, inheritance allows us to create is a relationships between two or more classes, abstracting common logic into superclasses and managing specific details in the subclass. In particular, we'll be covering the Python syntax and principles for the following:

- Basic inheritance
- Inheriting from built-in types
- Multiple inheritance
- Polymorphism and duck typing

## Basic inheritance

Technically, every class we create uses inheritance. All Python classes are subclasses of the special built-in class named `object`. This class provides very little in terms of data and behaviors (the behaviors it does provide are all double-underscore methods intended for internal use only), but it does allow Python to treat all objects in the same way.

If we don't explicitly inherit from a different class, our classes will automatically inherit from `object`. However, we can openly state that our class derives from `object` using the following syntax:

```
class MySubClass(object):
    pass
```

This is inheritance! This example is, technically, no different from our very first example in `Chapter 16`, *Objects in Python*, since Python 3 automatically inherits from `object` if we don't explicitly provide a different **superclass**. A superclass, or parent class, is a class that is being inherited from. A subclass is a class that is inheriting from a superclass. In this case, the superclass is `object`, and `MySubClass` is the subclass. A subclass is also said to be derived from its parent class or that the subclass extends the parent.

As you've probably figured out from the example, inheritance requires a minimal amount of extra syntax over a basic class definition. Simply include the name of the parent class inside parentheses between the class name and the colon that follows. This is all we have to do to tell Python that the new class should be derived from the given superclass.

How do we apply inheritance in practice? The simplest and most obvious use of inheritance is to add functionality to an existing class. Let's start with a simple contact manager that tracks the name and email address of several people. The `Contact` class is responsible for maintaining a list of all contacts in a class variable, and for initializing the name and address for an individual contact:

```
class Contact:
    all_contacts = []

    def __init__(self, name, email):
        self.name = name
        self.email = email
        Contact.all_contacts.append(self)
```

This example introduces us to **class variables**. The `all_contacts` list, because it is part of the class definition, is shared by all instances of this class. This means that there is only one `Contact.all_contacts` list. We can also access it as `self.all_contacts` from within any method on an instance of the `Contact` class. If a field can't be found on the object (via `self`), then it will be found on the class and will thus refer to the same single list.

Be careful with this syntax, for if you ever *set* the variable using `self.all_contacts`, you will actually be creating a **new** instance variable associated just with that object. The class variable will still be unchanged and accessible as `Contact.all_contacts`.

This is a simple class that allows us to track a couple of pieces of data about each contact. But what if some of our contacts are also suppliers that we need to order supplies from? We could add an `order` method to the `Contact` class, but that would allow people to accidentally order things from contacts who are customers or family friends. Instead, let's create a new `Supplier` class that acts like our `Contact` class, but has an additional `order` method:

```
class Supplier(Contact):
    def order(self, order):
        print(
            "If this were a real system we would send "
            f"'{order}' order to '{self.name}'"
        )
```

Now, if we test this class in our trusty interpreter, we see that all contacts, including suppliers, accept a name and email address in their \_\_init\_\_, but that only suppliers have a functional order method:

```
>>> c = Contact("Some Body", "somebody@example.net")
>>> s = Supplier("Sup Plier", "supplier@example.net")
>>> print(c.name, c.email, s.name, s.email)
Some Body somebody@example.net Sup Plier supplier@example.net
>>> c.all_contacts
[<__main__.Contact object at 0xb7375ecc>,
 <__main__.Supplier object at 0xb7375f8c>]
>>> c.order("I need pliers")
Traceback (most recent call last):
  File "<stdin>", line 1, in <module>
AttributeError: 'Contact' object has no attribute 'order'
>>> s.order("I need pliers")
If this were a real system we would send 'I need pliers' order to
'Sup Plier '
```

So, now our `Supplier` class can do everything a contact can do (including adding itself to the list of `all_contacts`) and all the special things it needs to handle as a supplier. This is the beauty of inheritance.

# Extending built-ins

One interesting use of this kind of inheritance is adding functionality to built-in classes. In the `Contact` class seen earlier, we are adding contacts to a list of all contacts. What if we also wanted to search that list by name? Well, we could add a method on the `Contact` class to search it, but it feels like this method actually belongs to the list itself. We can do this using inheritance:

```python
class ContactList(list):
    def search(self, name):
        """Return all contacts that contain the search value
        in their name."""
        matching_contacts = []
        for contact in self:
            if name in contact.name:
                matching_contacts.append(contact)
        return matching_contacts


class Contact:
    all_contacts = ContactList()

    def __init__(self, name, email):
        self.name = name
        self.email = email
        Contact.all_contacts.append(self)
```

Instead of instantiating a normal list as our class variable, we create a new `ContactList` class that extends the built-in `list` data type. Then, we instantiate this subclass as our `all_contacts` list. We can test the new search functionality as follows:

```python
>>> c1 = Contact("John A", "johna@example.net")
>>> c2 = Contact("John B", "johnb@example.net")
>>> c3 = Contact("Jenna C", "jennac@example.net")
>>> [c.name for c in Contact.all_contacts.search('John')]
['John A', 'John B']
```

Are you wondering how we changed the built-in syntax `[]` into something we can inherit from? Creating an empty list with `[]` is actually a shortcut for creating an empty list using `list()`; the two syntaxes behave identically:

```python
>>> [] == list()
True
```

In reality, the `[]` syntax is actually so-called **syntactic sugar** that calls the `list()` constructor under the hood. The `list` data type is a class that we can extend. In fact, the list itself extends the `object` class:

```
>>> isinstance([], object)
True
```

As a second example, we can extend the `dict` class, which is, similar to the list, the class that is constructed when using the `{}` syntax shorthand:

```
class LongNameDict(dict):
    def longest_key(self):
        longest = None
        for key in self:
            if not longest or len(key) > len(longest):
                longest = key
        return longest
```

This is easy to test in the interactive interpreter:

```
>>> longkeys = LongNameDict()
>>> longkeys['hello'] = 1
>>> longkeys['longest yet'] = 5
>>> longkeys['hello2'] = 'world'
>>> longkeys.longest_key()
'longest yet'
```

Most built-in types can be similarly extended. Commonly extended built-ins are `object`, `list`, `set`, `dict`, `file`, and `str`. Numerical types such as `int` and `float` are also occasionally inherited from.

# Overriding and super

So, inheritance is great for *adding* new behavior to existing classes, but what about *changing* behavior? Our `Contact` class allows only a name and an email address. This may be sufficient for most contacts, but what if we want to add a phone number for our close friends?

As we saw in Chapter 16, *Objects in Python*, we can do this easily by just setting a phone attribute on the contact after it is constructed. But if we want to make this third variable available on initialization, we have to override __init__. Overriding means altering or replacing a method of the superclass with a new method (with the same name) in the subclass. No special syntax is needed to do this; the subclass's newly created method is automatically called instead of the superclass's method. As shown in the following code:

```
class Friend(Contact):
    def __init__(self, name, email, phone):          self.name = name
        self.email = email
        self.phone = phone
```

Any method can be overridden, not just __init__. Before we go on, however, we need to address some problems in this example. Our Contact and Friend classes have duplicate code to set up the name and email properties; this can make code maintenance complicated, as we have to update the code in two or more places. More alarmingly, our Friend class is neglecting to add itself to the all_contacts list we have created on the Contact class.

What we really need is a way to execute the original __init__ method on the Contact class from inside our new class. This is what the super function does; it returns the object as an instance of the parent class, allowing us to call the parent method directly:

```
class Friend(Contact):
    def __init__(self, name, email, phone):
        super().__init__(name, email)
        self.phone = phone
```

This example first gets the instance of the parent object using super, and calls __init__ on that object, passing in the expected arguments. It then does its own initialization, namely, setting the phone attribute.

A super() call can be made inside any method. Therefore, all methods can be modified via overriding and calls to super. The call to super can also be made at any point in the method; we don't have to make the call as the first line. For example, we may need to manipulate or validate incoming parameters before forwarding them to the superclass.

# Multiple inheritance

Multiple inheritance is a touchy subject. In principle, it's simple: a subclass that inherits from more than one parent class is able to access functionality from both of them. In practice, this is less useful than it sounds and many expert programmers recommend against using it.

 As a humorous rule of thumb, if you think you need multiple inheritance, you're probably wrong, but if you know you need it, you might be right.

The simplest and most useful form of multiple inheritance is called a **mixin**. A mixin is a superclass that is not intended to exist on its own, but is meant to be inherited by some other class to provide extra functionality. For example, let's say we wanted to add functionality to our Contact class that allows sending an email to self.email. Sending email is a common task that we might want to use on many other classes. So, we can write a simple mixin class to do the emailing for us:

```
class MailSender:
    def send_mail(self, message):
        print("Sending mail to " + self.email)
        # Add e-mail logic here
```

For brevity, we won't include the actual email logic here; if you're interested in studying how it's done, see the smtplib module in the Python standard library.

This class doesn't do anything special (in fact, it can barely function as a standalone class), but it does allow us to define a new class that describes both a Contact and a MailSender, using multiple inheritance:

```
class EmailableContact(Contact, MailSender):
    pass
```

The syntax for multiple inheritance looks like a parameter list in the class definition. Instead of including one base class inside the parentheses, we include two (or more), separated by a comma. We can test this new hybrid to see the mixin at work:

```
>>> e = EmailableContact("John Smith", "jsmith@example.net")
>>> Contact.all_contacts
[<__main__.EmailableContact object at 0xb7205fac>]
>>> e.send_mail("Hello, test e-mail here")
Sending mail to jsmith@example.net
```

The `Contact` initializer is still adding the new contact to the `all_contacts` list, and the mixin is able to send mail to `self.email`, so we know that everything is working.

This wasn't so hard, and you're probably wondering what the dire warnings about multiple inheritance are. We'll get into the complexities in a minute, but let's consider some other options we had for this example, rather than using a mixin:

- We could have used single inheritance and added the `send_mail` function to the subclass. The disadvantage here is that the email functionality then has to be duplicated for any other classes that need an email.
- We can create a standalone Python function for sending an email, and just call that function with the correct email address supplied as a parameter when the email needs to be sent (this would be my choice).
- We could have explored a few ways of using composition instead of inheritance. For example, `EmailableContact` could have a `MailSender` object as a property instead of inheriting from it.
- We could monkey patch (we'll briefly cover monkey patching in Chapter 20, *Python Object-Oriented Shortcuts*) the `Contact` class to have a `send_mail` method after the class has been created. This is done by defining a function that accepts the `self` argument, and setting it as an attribute on an existing class.

Multiple inheritance works all right when mixing methods from different classes, but it gets very messy when we have to call methods on the superclass. There are multiple superclasses. How do we know which one to call? How do we know what order to call them in?

Let's explore these questions by adding a home address to our `Friend` class. There are a few approaches we might take. An address is a collection of strings representing the street, city, country, and other related details of the contact. We could pass each of these strings as a parameter into the `Friend` class's __init__ method. We could also store these strings in a tuple, dictionary, or dataclass and pass them into __init__ as a single argument. This is probably the best course of action if there are no methods that need to be added to the address.

Another option would be to create a new `Address` class to hold those strings together, and then pass an instance of this class into the __init__ method in our `Friend` class. The advantage of this solution is that we can add behavior (say, a method to give directions or to print a map) to the data instead of just storing it statically. This is an example of composition, as we discussed in Chapter 15, *Object-Oriented Design*. Composition is a perfectly viable solution to this problem and allows us to reuse `Address` classes in other entities, such as buildings, businesses, or organizations.

However, inheritance is also a viable solution, and that's what we want to explore. Let's add a new class that holds an address. We'll call this new class `AddressHolder` instead of `Address` because inheritance defines an is a relationship. It is not correct to say a `Friend` class is an `Address` class, but since a friend can have an `Address` class, we can argue that a `Friend` class is an `AddressHolder` class. Later, we could create other entities (companies, buildings) that also hold addresses. Then again, such convoluted naming is a decent indication we should be sticking with composition, rather than inheritance. But for pedagogical purposes, we'll stick with inheritance. Here's our `AddressHolder` class:

```
class AddressHolder:
    def __init__(self, street, city, state, code):
        self.street = street
        self.city = city
        self.state = state
        self.code = code
```

We just take all the data and toss it into instance variables upon initialization.

# The diamond problem

We can use multiple inheritance to add this new class as a parent of our existing `Friend` class. The tricky part is that we now have two parent __init__ methods, both of which need to be initialized. And they need to be initialized with different arguments. How do we do this? Well, we could start with a naive approach:

```
class Friend(Contact, AddressHolder):
    def __init__(
        self, name, email, phone, street, city, state, code):
        Contact.__init__(self, name, email)
        AddressHolder.__init__(self, street, city, state, code)
        self.phone = phone
```

In this example, we directly call the __init__ function on each of the superclasses and explicitly pass the self argument. This example technically works; we can access the different variables directly on the class. But there are a few problems.

First, it is possible for a superclass to go uninitialized if we neglect to explicitly call the initializer. That wouldn't break this example, but it could cause hard-to-debug program crashes in common scenarios. Imagine trying to insert data into a database that has not been connected to, for example.

A more insidious possibility is a superclass being called multiple times because of the organization of the class hierarchy. Look at this inheritance diagram:

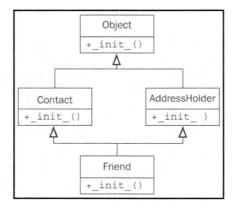

The __init__ method from the Friend class first calls __init__ on Contact, which implicitly initializes the object superclass (remember, all classes derive from object). Friend then calls __init__ on AddressHolder, which implicitly initializes the object superclass *again*. This means the parent class has been set up twice. With the object class, that's relatively harmless, but in some situations, it could spell disaster. Imagine trying to connect to a database twice for every request!

The base class should only be called once. Once, yes, but when? Do we call Friend, then Contact, then Object, and then AddressHolder? Or Friend, then Contact, then AddressHolder, and then Object?

The order in which methods can be called can be adapted on the fly by modifying the __mro__ (**Method Resolution Order**) attribute on the class. This is beyond the scope of this book. If you think you need to understand it, we recommend *Expert Python Programming, Tarek Ziadé, Packt Publishing*, or read the original documentation (beware, it's deep!) on the topic at

`http://www.python.org/download/releases/2.3/mro/`.

Let's look at a second contrived example, which illustrates this problem more clearly. Here, we have a base class that has a method named `call_me`. Two subclasses override that method, and then another subclass extends both of these using multiple inheritance. This is called diamond inheritance because of the diamond shape of the class diagram:

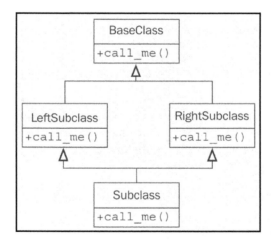

Let's convert this diagram to code; this example shows when the methods are called:

```
class BaseClass:
    num_base_calls = 0

    def call_me(self):
        print("Calling method on Base Class")
        self.num_base_calls += 1


class LeftSubclass(BaseClass):
    num_left_calls = 0

    def call_me(self):
        BaseClass.call_me(self)
```

```
        print("Calling method on Left Subclass")
        self.num_left_calls += 1


class RightSubclass(BaseClass):
    num_right_calls = 0

    def call_me(self):
        BaseClass.call_me(self)
        print("Calling method on Right Subclass")
        self.num_right_calls += 1


class Subclass(LeftSubclass, RightSubclass):
    num_sub_calls = 0

    def call_me(self):
        LeftSubclass.call_me(self)
        RightSubclass.call_me(self)
        print("Calling method on Subclass")
        self.num_sub_calls += 1
```

This example ensures that each overridden `call_me` method directly calls the parent method with the same name. It lets us know each time a method is called by printing the information to the screen. It also updates a static variable on the class to show how many times it has been called. If we instantiate one `Subclass` object and call the method on it once, we get the output:

```
>>> s = Subclass()
>>> s.call_me()
Calling method on Base Class
Calling method on Left Subclass
Calling method on Base Class
Calling method on Right Subclass
Calling method on Subclass
>>> print(
... s.num_sub_calls,
... s.num_left_calls,
... s.num_right_calls,
... s.num_base_calls)
1 1 1 2
```

Thus, we can clearly see the base class's `call_me` method being called twice. This could lead to some pernicious bugs if that method is doing actual work, such as depositing into a bank account, twice.

The thing to keep in mind with multiple inheritance is that we only want to call the next method in the class hierarchy, not the parent method. In fact, that next method may not be on a parent or ancestor of the current class. The super keyword comes to our rescue once again. Indeed, super was originally developed to make complicated forms of multiple inheritance possible. Here is the same code written using super:

```
class BaseClass:
    num_base_calls = 0

    def call_me(self):
        print("Calling method on Base Class")
        self.num_base_calls += 1


class LeftSubclass(BaseClass):
    num_left_calls = 0

    def call_me(self):
        super().call_me()
        print("Calling method on Left Subclass")
        self.num_left_calls += 1


class RightSubclass(BaseClass):
    num_right_calls = 0

    def call_me(self):
        super().call_me()
        print("Calling method on Right Subclass")
        self.num_right_calls += 1


class Subclass(LeftSubclass, RightSubclass):
    num_sub_calls = 0

    def call_me(self):
        super().call_me()
        print("Calling method on Subclass")
        self.num_sub_calls += 1
```

The change is pretty minor; we only replaced the naive direct calls with calls to super(), although the bottom subclass only calls super once rather than having to make the calls for both the left and right. The change is easy enough, but look at the difference when we execute it:

```
>>> s = Subclass()
>>> s.call_me()
```

```
Calling method on Base Class
Calling method on Right Subclass
Calling method on Left Subclass
Calling method on Subclass
>>> print(s.num_sub_calls, s.num_left_calls, s.num_right_calls,
s.num_base_calls)
1 1 1 1
```

Looks good; our base method is only being called once. But what is `super()` actually doing here? Since the `print` statements are executed after the `super` calls, the printed output is in the order each method is actually executed. Let's look at the output from back to front to see who is calling what.

First, `call_me` of `Subclass` calls `super().call_me()`, which happens to refer to `LeftSubclass.call_me()`. The `LeftSubclass.call_me()` method then calls `super().call_me()`, but in this case, `super()` is referring to `RightSubclass.call_me()`.

**Pay particular attention to this**: the `super` call is *not* calling the method on the superclass of `LeftSubclass` (which is `BaseClass`). Rather, it is calling `RightSubclass`, even though it is not a direct parent of `LeftSubclass`! This is the *next* method, not the parent method. `RightSubclass` then calls `BaseClass` and the `super` calls have ensured each method in the class hierarchy is executed once.

# Different sets of arguments

This is going to make things complicated as we return to our `Friend` multiple inheritance example. In the `__init__` method for `Friend`, we were originally calling `__init__` for both parent classes, *with different sets of arguments*:

```
Contact.__init__(self, name, email)
AddressHolder.__init__(self, street, city, state, code)
```

How can we manage different sets of arguments when using `super`? We don't necessarily know which class `super` is going to try to initialize first. Even if we did, we need a way to pass the `extra` arguments so that subsequent calls to `super`, on other subclasses, receive the right arguments.

Specifically, if the first call to `super` passes the `name` and `email` arguments to `Contact.__init__`, and `Contact.__init__` then calls `super`, it needs to be able to pass the address-related arguments to the `next` method, which is `AddressHolder.__init__`.

This problem manifests itself anytime we want to call superclass methods with the same name, but with different sets of arguments. Most often, the only time you would want to call a superclass with a completely different set of arguments is in __init__, as we're doing here. Even with regular methods, though, we may want to add optional parameters that only make sense to one subclass or set of subclasses.

Sadly, the only way to solve this problem is to plan for it from the beginning. We have to design our base class parameter lists to accept keyword arguments for any parameters that are not required by every subclass implementation. Finally, we must ensure the method freely accepts unexpected arguments and passes them on to its super call, in case they are necessary to later methods in the inheritance order.

Python's function parameter syntax provides all the tools we need to do this, but it makes the overall code look cumbersome. Have a look at the proper version of the Friend multiple inheritance code, as follows:

```python
class Contact:
    all_contacts = []

    def __init__(self, name="", email="", **kwargs):
        super().__init__(**kwargs)
        self.name = name
        self.email = email
        self.all_contacts.append(self)


class AddressHolder:
    def __init__(self, street="", city="", state="", code="",
**kwargs):
        super().__init__(**kwargs)
        self.street = street
        self.city = city
        self.state = state
        self.code = code


class Friend(Contact, AddressHolder):
    def __init__(self, phone="", **kwargs):
        super().__init__(**kwargs)
        self.phone = phone
```

We've changed all arguments to keyword arguments by giving them an empty string as a default value. We've also ensured that a `**kwargs` parameter is included to capture any additional parameters that our particular method doesn't know what to do with. It passes these parameters up to the next class with the `super` call.

> If you aren't familiar with the `**kwargs` syntax, it basically collects any keyword arguments passed into the method that were not explicitly listed in the parameter list. These arguments are stored in a dictionary named `kwargs` (we can call the variable whatever we like, but convention suggests `kw`, or `kwargs`). When we call a different method (for example, `super().__init__`) with a `**kwargs` syntax, it unpacks the dictionary and passes the results to the method as normal keyword arguments. We'll cover this in detail in `Chapter 20`, *Python Object-Oriented Shortcuts*.

The previous example does what it is supposed to do. But it's starting to look messy, and it is difficult to answer the question, *What arguments do we need to pass into* `Friend.__init__`? This is the foremost question for anyone planning to use the class, so a docstring should be added to the method to explain what is happening.

Furthermore, even this implementation is insufficient if we want to *reuse* variables in parent classes. When we pass the `**kwargs` variable to `super`, the dictionary does not include any of the variables that were included as explicit keyword arguments. For example, in `Friend.__init__`, the call to `super` does not have `phone` in the `kwargs` dictionary. If any of the other classes need the `phone` parameter, we need to ensure it is in the dictionary that is passed. Worse, if we forget to do this, it will be extremely frustrating to debug because the superclass will not complain, but will simply assign the default value (in this case, an empty string) to the variable.

There are a few ways to ensure that the variable is passed upward. Assume the `Contact` class does, for some reason, need to be initialized with a `phone` parameter, and the `Friend` class will also need access to it. We can do any of the following:

- Don't include `phone` as an explicit keyword argument. Instead, leave it in the `kwargs` dictionary. `Friend` can look it up using the `kwargs['phone']` syntax. When it passes `**kwargs` to the `super` call, `phone` will still be in the dictionary.

- Make `phone` an explicit keyword argument, but update the `kwargs` dictionary before passing it to `super`, using the standard dictionary `kwargs['phone'] = phone` syntax.
- Make `phone` an explicit keyword argument, but update the `kwargs` dictionary using the `kwargs.update` method. This is useful if you have several arguments to update. You can create the dictionary passed into `update` using either the `dict(phone=phone)` constructor, or the dictionary `{'phone': phone}` syntax.
- Make `phone` an explicit keyword argument, but pass it to the super call explicitly with the `super().__init__(phone=phone, **kwargs)` syntax.

We have covered many of the caveats involved with multiple inheritance in Python. When we need to account for all possible situations, we have to plan for them and our code will get messy. Basic multiple inheritance can be handy but, in many cases, we may want to choose a more transparent way of combining two disparate classes, usually using composition or one of the design patterns we'll be covering in `Chapter 22`, *Design Patterns I,* and `Chapter 23`, *Design Patterns II.*

 I have wasted entire days of my life trawling through complex multiple inheritance hierarchies trying to figure out what arguments I need to pass into one of the deeply nested subclasses. The author of the code tended not to document his classes and often passed the kwargs—Just in case they might be needed someday. This was a particularly bad example of using multiple inheritance when it was not needed. Multiple inheritance is a big fancy term that new coders like to show off, but I recommend avoiding it, even when you think it's a good choice. Your future self and other coders will be glad they understand your code when they have to read it later.

# Polymorphism

We were introduced to polymorphism in Chapter 15, *Object-Oriented Design*. It is a showy name describing a simple concept: different behaviors happen depending on which subclass is being used, without having to explicitly know what the subclass actually is. As an example, imagine a program that plays audio files. A media player might need to load an AudioFile object and then play it. We can put a play() method on the object, which is responsible for decompressing or extracting the audio and routing it to the sound card and speakers. The act of playing an AudioFile could feasibly be as simple as:

```
audio_file.play()
```

However, the process of decompressing and extracting an audio file is very different for different types of files. While .wav files are stored uncompressed, .mp3, .wma, and .ogg files all utilize totally different compression algorithms.

We can use inheritance with polymorphism to simplify the design. Each type of file can be represented by a different subclass of AudioFile, for example, WavFile and MP3File. Each of these would have a play() method that would be implemented differently for each file to ensure that the correct extraction procedure is followed. The media player object would never need to know which subclass of AudioFile it is referring to; it just calls play() and polymorphically lets the object take care of the actual details of playing. Let's look at a quick skeleton showing how this might look:

```python
class AudioFile:
    def __init__(self, filename):
        if not filename.endswith(self.ext):
            raise Exception("Invalid file format")

        self.filename = filename


class MP3File(AudioFile):
    ext = "mp3"

    def play(self):
        print("playing {} as mp3".format(self.filename))


class WavFile(AudioFile):
    ext = "wav"

    def play(self):
```

```
            print("playing {} as wav".format(self.filename))


class OggFile(AudioFile):
    ext = "ogg"

    def play(self):
        print("playing {} as ogg".format(self.filename))
```

All audio files check to ensure that a valid extension was given upon initialization. But did you notice how the __init__ method in the parent class is able to access the ext class variable from different subclasses? That's polymorphism at work. If the filename doesn't end with the correct name, it raises an exception (exceptions will be covered in detail in the next chapter). The fact that the AudioFile parent class doesn't actually store a reference to the ext variable doesn't stop it from being able to access it on the subclass.

In addition, each subclass of AudioFile implements play() in a different way (this example doesn't actually play the music; audio compression algorithms really deserve a separate book!). This is also polymorphism in action. The media player can use the exact same code to play a file, no matter what type it is; it doesn't care what subclass of AudioFile it is looking at. The details of decompressing the audio file are *encapsulated*. If we test this example, it works as we would hope:

```
>>> ogg = OggFile("myfile.ogg")
>>> ogg.play()
playing myfile.ogg as ogg
>>> mp3 = MP3File("myfile.mp3")
>>> mp3.play()
playing myfile.mp3 as mp3
>>> not_an_mp3 = MP3File("myfile.ogg")
Traceback (most recent call last):
  File "<stdin>", line 1, in <module>
  File "polymorphic_audio.py", line 4, in __init__
    raise Exception("Invalid file format")
Exception: Invalid file format
```

See how `AudioFile.__init__` is able to check the file type without actually knowing which subclass it is referring to?

Polymorphism is actually one of the coolest things about object-oriented programming, and it makes some programming designs obvious that weren't possible in earlier paradigms. However, Python makes polymorphism seem less awesome because of duck typing. Duck typing in Python allows us to use *any* object that provides the required behavior without forcing it to be a subclass. The dynamic nature of Python makes this trivial. The following example does not extend `AudioFile`, but it can be interacted with in Python using the exact same interface:

```python
class FlacFile:
    def __init__(self, filename):
        if not filename.endswith(".flac"):
            raise Exception("Invalid file format")

        self.filename = filename

    def play(self):
        print("playing {} as flac".format(self.filename))
```

Our media player can play this object just as easily as one that extends `AudioFile`.

Polymorphism is one of the most important reasons to use inheritance in many object-oriented contexts. Because any objects that supply the correct interface can be used interchangeably in Python, it reduces the need for polymorphic common superclasses. Inheritance can still be useful for sharing code, but if all that is being shared is the public interface, duck typing is all that is required. This reduced need for inheritance also reduces the need for multiple inheritance; often, when multiple inheritance appears to be a valid solution, we can just use duck typing to mimic one of the multiple superclasses.

Of course, just because an object satisfies a particular interface (by providing required methods or attributes) does not mean it will simply work in all situations. It has to fulfill that interface in a way that makes sense in the overall system. Just because an object provides a `play()` method does not mean it will automatically work with a media player. For example, our chess AI object from Chapter 15, *Object-Oriented Design*, may have a `play()` method that moves a chess piece. Even though it satisfies the interface, this class would likely break in spectacular ways if we tried to plug it into a media player!

Another useful feature of duck typing is that the duck-typed object only needs to provide those methods and attributes that are actually being accessed. For example, if we needed to create a fake file object to read data from, we can create a new object that has a read() method; we don't have to override the write method if the code that is going to interact with the fake object will not be calling it. More succinctly, duck typing doesn't need to provide the entire interface of an object that is available; it only needs to fulfill the interface that is actually accessed.

# Abstract base classes

While duck typing is useful, it is not always easy to tell in advance if a class is going to fulfill the protocol you require. Therefore, Python introduced the idea of **abstract base classes** (**ABC**s). Abstract base classes define a set of methods and properties that a class must implement in order to be considered a duck-type instance of that class. The class can extend the abstract base class itself in order to be used as an instance of that class, but it must supply all the appropriate methods.

In practice, it's rarely necessary to create new abstract base classes, but we may find occasions to implement instances of existing ABCs. We'll cover implementing ABCs first, and then briefly see how to create your own, should you ever need to.

# Using an abstract base class

Most of the abstract base classes that exist in the Python standard library live in the collections module. One of the simplest ones is the Container class. Let's inspect it in the Python interpreter to see what methods this class requires:

```
>>> from collections import Container
>>> Container.__abstractmethods__
frozenset(['__contains__'])
```

So, the Container class has exactly one abstract method that needs to be implemented, __contains__. You can issue help(Container.__contains__) to see what the function signature should look like:

```
Help on method __contains__ in module _abcoll:
 __contains__(self, x) unbound _abcoll.Container method
```

We can see that __contains__ needs to take a single argument. Unfortunately, the help file doesn't tell us much about what that argument should be, but it's pretty obvious from the name of the ABC and the single method it implements that this argument is the value the user is checking to see whether the container holds.

This method is implemented by list, str, and dict to indicate whether or not a given value is *in* that data structure. However, we can also define a silly container that tells us whether a given value is in the set of odd integers:

```
class OddContainer:
    def __contains__(self, x):
        if not isinstance(x, int) or not x % 2:
            return False
        return True
```

Here's the interesting part: we can instantiate an OddContainer object and determine that, even though we did not extend Container, the class is a Container object:

```
>>> from collections import Container
>>> odd_container = OddContainer()
>>> isinstance(odd_container, Container)
True
>>> issubclass(OddContainer, Container)
True
```

And that is why duck typing is way more awesome than classical polymorphism. We can create is a relationships without the overhead of writing the code to set up inheritance (or worse, multiple inheritance).

One cool thing about the Container ABC is that any class that implements it gets to use the in keyword for free. In fact, in is just syntax sugar that delegates to the __contains__ method. Any class that has a __contains__ method is a Container and can therefore be queried by the in keyword, for example:

```
>>> 1 in odd_container
True
>>> 2 in odd_container
False
>>> 3 in odd_container
True
>>> "a string" in odd_container
False
```

# Creating an abstract base class

As we saw earlier, it's not necessary to have an abstract base class to enable duck typing. However, imagine we were creating a media player with third-party plugins. It is advisable to create an abstract base class in this case to document what API the third-party plugins should provide (documentation is one of the stronger use cases for ABCs). The abc module provides the tools you need to do this, but I'll warn you in advance, this utilizes some of Python's most arcane concepts, as demonstrated in the following block of code::

```
import abc

class MediaLoader(metaclass=abc.ABCMeta):
    @abc.abstractmethod
    def play(self):
        pass

    @abc.abstractproperty
    def ext(self):
        pass

    @classmethod
    def __subclasshook__(cls, C):
        if cls is MediaLoader:
            attrs = set(dir(C))
            if set(cls.__abstractmethods__) <= attrs:
                return True

        return NotImplemented
```

This is a complicated example that includes several Python features that won't be explained until later in this book. It is included here for completeness, but you do not need to understand all of it to get the gist of how to create your own ABC.

The first weird thing is the metaclass keyword argument that is passed into the class where you would normally see the list of parent classes. This is a seldom-used construct from the mystic art of metaclass programming. We won't be covering metaclasses in this book, so all you need to know is that by assigning the ABCMeta metaclass, you are giving your class superhero (or at least superclass) abilities.

Next, we see the `@abc.abstractmethod` and `@abc.abstractproperty` constructs. These are Python decorators. We'll discuss those in `Chapter 22`, *Python Design Patterns I*. For now, just know that by marking a method or property as being abstract, you are stating that any subclass of this class must implement that method or supply that property in order to be considered a proper member of the class.

See what happens if you implement subclasses that do, or don't, supply those properties:

```
>>> class Wav(MediaLoader):
...     pass
...
>>> x = Wav()
Traceback (most recent call last):
  File "<stdin>", line 1, in <module>
TypeError: Can't instantiate abstract class Wav with abstract methods
ext, play
>>> class Ogg(MediaLoader):
...     ext = '.ogg'
...     def play(self):
...         pass
...
>>> o = Ogg()
```

Since the `Wav` class fails to implement the abstract attributes, it is not possible to instantiate that class. The class is still a legal abstract class, but you'd have to subclass it to actually do anything. The `Ogg` class supplies both attributes, so it instantiates cleanly.

Going back to the `MediaLoader` ABC, let's dissect that __subclasshook__ method. It is basically saying that any class that supplies concrete implementations of all the abstract attributes of this ABC should be considered a subclass of `MediaLoader`, even if it doesn't actually inherit from the `MediaLoader` class.

More common object-oriented languages have a clear separation between the interface and the implementation of a class. For example, some languages provide an explicit `interface` keyword that allows us to define the methods that a class must have without any implementation. In such an environment, an abstract class is one that provides both an interface and a concrete implementation of some, but not all, methods. Any class can explicitly state that it implements a given interface.

Python's ABCs help to supply the functionality of interfaces without compromising on the benefits of duck typing.

# Demystifying the magic

You can copy and paste the subclass code without understanding it if you want to make abstract classes that fulfill this particular contract. We'll cover most of the unusual syntaxes in the book, but let's go over it line by line to get an overview:

```
@classmethod
```

This decorator marks the method as a class method. It essentially says that the method can be called on a class instead of an instantiated object:

```
def __subclasshook__(cls, C):
```

This defines the __subclasshook__ class method. This special method is called by the Python interpreter to answer the question: Is the class C a subclass of this class?

```
if cls is MediaLoader:
```

We check to see whether the method was called specifically on this class, rather than, say, a subclass of this class. This prevents, for example, the Wav class from being thought of as a parent class of the Ogg class:

```
attrs = set(dir(C))
```

All this line does is get the set of methods and properties that the class has, including any parent classes in its class hierarchy:

```
if set(cls.__abstractmethods__) <= attrs:
```

This line uses set notation to see whether the set of abstract methods in this class has been supplied in the candidate class. Note that it doesn't check to see whether the methods have been implemented; just if they are there. Thus, it's possible for a class to be a subclass and yet still be an abstract class itself.

```
return True
```

If all the abstract methods have been supplied, then the candidate class is a subclass of this class and we return True. The method can legally return one of the three values: True, False, or NotImplemented. True and False indicate that the class is, or isn't, definitely a subclass of this class:

```
return NotImplemented
```

If any of the conditionals have not been met (that is, the class is not `MediaLoader` or not all abstract methods have been supplied), then return `NotImplemented`. This tells the Python machinery to use the default mechanism (does the candidate class explicitly extend this class?) for subclass detection.

In short, we can now define the `Ogg` class as a subclass of the `MediaLoader` class without actually extending the `MediaLoader` class:

```
>>> class Ogg(): ... ext = '.ogg' ... def play(self): ... print("this
will play an ogg file") ... >>> issubclass(Ogg, MediaLoader) True >>>
isinstance(Ogg(), MediaLoader) True
```

# Case study

Let's try to tie everything we've learned together with a larger example. We'll be developing an automated grading system for programming assignments, similar to that employed at Dataquest or Coursera. The system will need to provide a simple class-based interface for course writers to create their assignments and should give a useful error message if it does not fulfill that interface. The writers need to be able to supply their lesson content and to write custom answer checking code to make sure their students got the answer right. It will also be nice for them to have access to the students' names to make the content seem a little friendlier.

The grader itself will need to keep track of which assignment the student is currently working on. A student might make several attempts at an assignment before they get it right. We want to keep track of the number of attempts so the course authors can improve the content of the more difficult lessons.

Let's start by defining the interface that the course authors will need to use. Ideally, it will require the course authors to write a minimal amount of extra code besides their lesson content and answer checking code. Here is the simplest class I could come up with:

```
class IntroToPython:
    def lesson(self):
        return f"""
            Hello {self.student}. define two variables,
            an integer named a with value 1
            and a string named b with value 'hello'

        """
```

```
def check(self, code):
    return code == "a = 1\nb = 'hello'"
```

Admittedly, that particular course author may be a little naive in how they do their answer checking.

We can start with an abstract base class that defines this interface, as follows:

```
class Assignment(metaclass=abc.ABCMeta):
    @abc.abstractmethod
    def lesson(self, student):
        pass

    @abc.abstractmethod
    def check(self, code):
        pass

    @classmethod
    def __subclasshook__(cls, C):
        if cls is Assignment:
            attrs = set(dir(C))
            if set(cls.__abstractmethods__) <= attrs:
                return True

        return NotImplemented
```

This ABC defines the two required abstract methods and provides the magic __subclasshook__ method to allow a class to be perceived as a subclass without having to explicitly extend it (I usually just copy and paste this code. It isn't worth memorizing.)

We can confirm that the IntroToPython class fulfills this interface using issubclass(IntroToPython, Assignment), which should return True. Of course, we can explicitly extend the Assignment class if we prefer, as seen in this second assignment:

```
class Statistics(Assignment):
    def lesson(self):
        return (
            "Good work so far, "
            + self.student
            + ". Now calculate the average of the numbers "
            + " 1, 5, 18, -3 and assign to a variable named 'avg'"
        )

    def check(self, code):
        import statistics
```

```
            code = "import statistics\n" + code

            local_vars = {}
            global_vars = {}
            exec(code, global_vars, local_vars)

            return local_vars.get("avg") == statistics.mean([1, 5, 18,
    -3])
```

This course author, unfortunately, is also rather naive. The exec call will execute the student's code right inside the grading system, giving them access to the entire system. Obviously, the first thing they will do is hack the system to make their grades 100%. They probably think that's easier than doing the assignments correctly!

Next, we'll create a class that manages how many attempts the student has made at a given assignment:

```
class AssignmentGrader:
    def __init__(self, student, AssignmentClass):
        self.assignment = AssignmentClass()
        self.assignment.student = student
        self.attempts = 0
        self.correct_attempts = 0

    def check(self, code):
        self.attempts += 1
        result = self.assignment.check(code)
        if result:
            self.correct_attempts += 1

        return result

    def lesson(self):
        return self.assignment.lesson()
```

This class uses composition instead of inheritance. At first glance, it would make sense for these methods to exist on the Assignment superclass. That would eliminate the annoying lesson method, which just proxies through to the same method on the assignment object. It would certainly be possible to put all this logic directly on the Assignment abstract base class, or even to have the ABC inherit from this AssignmentGrader class. In fact, I would normally recommend that, but in this case, it would force all course authors to explicitly extend the class, which violates our request that content authoring be as simple as possible.

Finally, we can start to put together the `Grader` class, which is responsible for managing which assignments are available and which one each student is currently working on. The most interesting part is the register method:

```
import uuid

class Grader:
    def __init__(self):
        self.student_graders = {}
        self.assignment_classes = {}

    def register(self, assignment_class):
        if not issubclass(assignment_class, Assignment):
            raise RuntimeError(
                "Your class does not have the right methods"
            )

        id = uuid.uuid4()
        self.assignment_classes[id] = assignment_class
        return id
```

This code block includes the initializer, which includes two dictionaries we'll discuss in a minute. The `register` method is a bit complex, so we'll dissect it thoroughly.

The first odd thing is the parameter this method accepts: `assignment_class`. This parameter is intended to be an actual class, not an instance of the class. Remember, classes are objects, too, and can be passed around like other classes. Given the `IntroToPython` class we defined earlier, we might register it without instantiating it, as follows:

```
from grader import Grader
from lessons import IntroToPython, Statistics

grader = Grader()
itp_id = grader.register(IntroToPython)
```

The method first checks whether that class is a subclass of the `Assignment` class. Of course, we implemented a custom `__subclasshook__` method, so this includes classes that do not explicitly subclass `Assignment`. The naming is, perhaps, a bit deceitful! If it doesn't have the two required methods, it raises an exception. Exceptions are a topic we'll cover in detail in the next chapter; for now, just assume that it makes the program get angry and quit.

Then, we generate a random identifier to represent that specific assignment. We store the `assignment_class` in a dictionary indexed by that ID, and return the ID so that the calling code can look that assignment up in the future. Presumably, another object would then place that ID in a course syllabus of some sort so students do the assignments in order, but we won't be doing that for this part of the project.

> The `uuid` function returns a specially formatted string called a universally unique identifier, also known as a globally unique identifier. It essentially represents an extremely large random number that is almost, but not quite, impossible to conflict with another similarly generated identifier. It is a great, quick, and clean way to create an arbitrary ID to keep track of items.

Next up, we have the `start_assignment` function, which allows a student to start working on an assignment given the ID of that assignment. All it does is construct an instance of the `AssignmentGrader` class we defined earlier and plop it in a dictionary stored on the `Grader` class, as follows:

```python
def start_assignment(self, student, id):
    self.student_graders[student] = AssignmentGrader(
        student, self.assignment_classes[id]
    )
```

After that, we write a couple of proxy methods that get the lesson or check the code for whatever assignment the student is currently working on:

```python
def get_lesson(self, student):
    assignment = self.student_graders[student]
    return assignment.lesson()

def check_assignment(self, student, code):
    assignment = self.student_graders[student]
    return assignment.check(code)
```

Finally, we create a method that gives a summary of a student's current assignment progress. It looks up the assignment object and creates a formatted string with all the information we have about that student:

```python
def assignment_summary(self, student):
    grader = self.student_graders[student]
    return f"""
{student}'s attempts at
{grader.assignment.__class__.__name__}:

    attempts: {grader.attempts}
    correct: {grader.correct_attempts}
```

```
    passed: {grader.correct_attempts > 0}
    """
```

And that's it. You'll notice that this case study does not use a ton of inheritance, which may seem a bit odd given the topic of the chapter, but duck typing is very prevalent. It is quite common for Python programs to be designed with inheritance that gets simplified into more versatile constructs as it is iterated on. As another example, I originally defined the `AssignmentGrader` as an inheritance relationship, but realized halfway through that it would be better to use composition, for the reasons outlined previously.

Here's a bit of test code that shows all these objects connected together:

```
grader = Grader()
itp_id = grader.register(IntroToPython)
stat_id = grader.register(Statistics)

grader.start_assignment("Tammy", itp_id)
print("Tammy's Lesson:", grader.get_lesson("Tammy"))
print(
    "Tammy's check:",
    grader.check_assignment("Tammy", "a = 1 ; b = 'hello'"),
)
print(
    "Tammy's other check:",
    grader.check_assignment("Tammy", "a = 1\nb = 'hello'"),
)

print(grader.assignment_summary("Tammy"))

grader.start_assignment("Tammy", stat_id)
print("Tammy's Lesson:", grader.get_lesson("Tammy"))
print("Tammy's check:", grader.check_assignment("Tammy", "avg=5.25"))
print(
    "Tammy's other check:",
    grader.check_assignment(
        "Tammy", "avg = statistics.mean([1, 5, 18, -3])"
    ),
)

print(grader.assignment_summary("Tammy"))
```

# Exercises

Look around you at some of the physical objects in your workspace and see if you can describe them in an inheritance hierarchy. Humans have been dividing the world into taxonomies like this for centuries, so it shouldn't be difficult. Are there any non-obvious inheritance relationships between classes of objects? If you were to model these objects in a computer application, what properties and methods would they share? Which ones would have to be polymorphically overridden? What properties would be completely different between them?

Now write some code. No, not for the physical hierarchy; that's boring. Physical items have more properties than methods. Just think about a pet programming project you've wanted to tackle in the past year, but never gotten around to. For whatever problem you want to solve, try to think of some basic inheritance relationships and then implement them. Make sure that you also pay attention to the sorts of relationships that you actually don't need to use inheritance for. Are there any places where you might want to use multiple inheritance? Are you sure? Can you see any place where you would want to use a mixin? Try to knock together a quick prototype. It doesn't have to be useful or even partially working. You've seen how you can test code using `python -i` already; just write some code and test it in the interactive interpreter. If it works, write some more. If it doesn't, fix it!

Now, take a look at the student grader system in the case study. There is a lot missing from it, and not just decent course content! How do students get into the system? Is there a curriculum that defines which order they should study lessons in? What happens if you change the `AssignmentGrader` to use inheritance, rather than composition, on the `Assignment` objects?

Finally, try to come up with some good use cases for mixins, then experiment with them until you realize that there is probably a better design using composition!

# Summary

We've gone from simple inheritance, one of the most useful tools in the object-oriented programmer's toolbox, all the way through to multiple inheritance—One of the most complicated. Inheritance can be used to add functionality to existing classes and built-ins using inheritance. Abstracting similar code into a parent class can help increase maintainability. Methods on parent classes can be called using `super` and argument lists must be formatted safely for these calls to work when using multiple inheritance. Abstract base classes allow you to document what methods and properties a class must have to fulfill a particular interface, and even allow you to change the very definition of *subclass*.

In the next chapter, we'll cover the subtle art of handling exceptional circumstances.

# 18
# Expecting the Unexpected

Programs are very fragile. It would be ideal if code always returned a valid result, but sometimes a valid result can't be calculated. For example, it's not possible to divide by zero, or to access the eighth item in a five-item list.

In the old days, the only way around this was to rigorously check the inputs for every function to make sure they made sense. Typically, functions had special return values to indicate an error condition; for example, they could return a negative number to indicate that a positive value couldn't be calculated. Different numbers might mean different errors occurred. Any code that called this function would have to explicitly check for an error condition and act accordingly. A lot of developers didn't bother to do this, and programs simply crashed. However, in the object-oriented world, this is not the case.

In this chapter, we will study **exceptions**, special error objects that only need to be handled when it makes sense to handle them. In particular, we will cover the following:

- How to cause an exception to occur
- How to recover when an exception has occurred
- How to handle different exception types in different ways
- Cleaning up when an exception has occurred
- Creating new types of exception
- Using the exception syntax for flow control

# Raising exceptions

In principle, an exception is just an object. There are many different exception classes available, and we can easily define more of our own. The one thing they all have in common is that they inherit from a built-in class called `BaseException`. These exception objects become special when they are handled inside the program's flow of control. When an exception occurs, everything that was supposed to happen doesn't happen, unless it was supposed to happen when an exception occurred. Make sense? Don't worry, it will!

The easiest way to cause an exception to occur is to do something silly. Chances are you've done this already and seen the exception output. For example, any time Python encounters a line in your program that it can't understand, it bails with `SyntaxError`, which is a type of exception. Here's a common one:

```
>>> print "hello world"
  File "<stdin>", line 1
    print "hello world"
                      ^
SyntaxError: invalid syntax
```

This `print` statement was a valid command way back in the Python 2 and earlier days, but in Python 3, because `print` is a function, we have to enclose the arguments in parentheses. So, if we type the preceding command into a Python 3 interpreter, we get `SyntaxError`.

In addition to `SyntaxError`, some other common exceptions are shown in the following example:

```
>>> x = 5 / 0
Traceback (most recent call last):
  File "<stdin>", line 1, in <module>
ZeroDivisionError: int division or modulo by zero

>>> lst = [1,2,3]
>>> print(lst[3])
Traceback (most recent call last):
  File "<stdin>", line 1, in <module>
IndexError: list index out of range

>>> lst + 2
Traceback (most recent call last):
  File "<stdin>", line 1, in <module>
TypeError: can only concatenate list (not "int") to list
```

```
>>> lst.add
Traceback (most recent call last):
  File "<stdin>", line 1, in <module>
AttributeError: 'list' object has no attribute 'add'

>>> d = {'a': 'hello'}
>>> d['b']
Traceback (most recent call last):
  File "<stdin>", line 1, in <module>
KeyError: 'b'

>>> print(this_is_not_a_var)
Traceback (most recent call last):
  File "<stdin>", line 1, in <module>
NameError: name 'this_is_not_a_var' is not defined
```

Sometimes, these exceptions are indicators of something wrong in our program (in which case, we would go to the indicated line number and fix it), but they also occur in legitimate situations. A `ZeroDivisionError` error doesn't always mean we received an invalid input. It could also mean we have received a different input. The user may have entered a zero by mistake, or on purpose, or it may represent a legitimate value, such as an empty bank account or the age of a newborn child.

You may have noticed all the preceding built-in exceptions end with the name `Error`. In Python, the words `error` and `Exception` are used almost interchangeably. Errors are sometimes considered more dire than exceptions, but they are dealt with in exactly the same way. Indeed, all the error classes in the preceding example have `Exception` (which extends `BaseException`) as their superclass.

# Raising an exception

We'll get to responding to such exceptions in a minute, but first, let's discover what we should do if we're writing a program that needs to inform the user or a calling function that the inputs are invalid. We can use the exact same mechanism that Python uses. Here's a simple class that adds items to a list only if they are even numbered integers:

```
class EvenOnly(list):
    def append(self, integer):
        if not isinstance(integer, int):
            raise TypeError("Only integers can be added")
        if integer % 2:
            raise ValueError("Only even numbers can be added")
        super().append(integer)
```

This class extends the `list` built-in, as we discussed in `Chapter 16`, *Objects in Python*, and overrides the `append` method to check two conditions that ensure the item is an even integer. We first check whether the input is an instance of the `int` type, and then use the modulus operator to ensure it is divisible by two. If either of the two conditions is not met, the `raise` keyword causes an exception to occur. The `raise` keyword is followed by the object being raised as an exception. In the preceding example, two objects are constructed from the built-in `TypeError` and `ValueError` classes. The raised object could just as easily be an instance of a new `Exception` class we create ourselves (we'll see how shortly), an exception that was defined elsewhere, or even an `Exception` object that has been previously raised and handled.

If we test this class in the Python interpreter, we can see that it is outputting useful error information when exceptions occur, just as before:

```
>>> e = EvenOnly()
>>> e.append("a string")
Traceback (most recent call last):
  File "<stdin>", line 1, in <module>
  File "even_integers.py", line 7, in add
    raise TypeError("Only integers can be added")
TypeError: Only integers can be added

>>> e.append(3)
Traceback (most recent call last):
  File "<stdin>", line 1, in <module>
  File "even_integers.py", line 9, in add
    raise ValueError("Only even numbers can be added")
ValueError: Only even numbers can be added
>>> e.append(2)
```

 While this class is effective for demonstrating exceptions in action, it isn't very good at its job. It is still possible to get other values into the list using index notation or slice notation. This can all be avoided by overriding other appropriate methods, some of which are magic double-underscore methods.

# The effects of an exception

When an exception is raised, it appears to stop program execution immediately. Any lines that were supposed to run after the exception is raised are not executed, and unless the exception is dealt with, the program will exit with an error message. Take a look at this basic function:

```
def no_return():
    print("I am about to raise an exception")
    raise Exception("This is always raised")
    print("This line will never execute")
    return "I won't be returned"
```

If we execute this function, we see that the first `print` call is executed and then the exception is raised. The second `print` function call is never executed, nor is the `return` statement:

```
>>> no_return()
I am about to raise an exception
Traceback (most recent call last):
  File "<stdin>", line 1, in <module>
  File "exception_quits.py", line 3, in no_return
    raise Exception("This is always raised")
Exception: This is always raised
```

Furthermore, if we have a function that calls another function that raises an exception, nothing is executed in the first function after the point where the second function was called. Raising an exception stops all execution right up through the function call stack until it is either handled or forces the interpreter to exit. To demonstrate, let's add a second function that calls the earlier one:

```
def call_exceptor():
    print("call_exceptor starts here...")
    no_return()
    print("an exception was raised...")
    print("...so these lines don't run")
```

When we call this function, we see that the first `print` statement executes, as well as the first line in the `no_return` function. But once the exception is raised, nothing else executes:

```
>>> call_exceptor()
call_exceptor starts here...
I am about to raise an exception
Traceback (most recent call last):
  File "<stdin>", line 1, in <module>
  File "method_calls_excepting.py", line 9, in call_exceptor
    no_return()
  File "method_calls_excepting.py", line 3, in no_return
    raise Exception("This is always raised")
Exception: This is always raised
```

We'll soon see that when the interpreter is not actually taking a shortcut and exiting immediately, we can react to and deal with the exception inside either method. Indeed, exceptions can be handled at any level after they are initially raised.

Look at the exception's output (called a traceback) from bottom to top, and notice how both methods are listed. Inside `no_return`, the exception is initially raised. Then, just above that, we see that inside `call_exceptor`, that pesky `no_return` function was called and the exception *bubbled up* to the calling method. From there, it went up one more level to the main interpreter, which, not knowing what else to do with it, gave up and printed a traceback.

# Handling exceptions

Now let's look at the tail side of the exception coin. If we encounter an exception situation, how should our code react to or recover from it? We handle exceptions by wrapping any code that might throw one (whether it is exception code itself, or a call to any function or method that may have an exception raised inside it) inside a `try...except` clause. The most basic syntax looks like this:

```
try:
    no_return()
except:
    print("I caught an exception")
print("executed after the exception")
```

If we run this simple script using our existing `no_return` function—which, as we know very well, always throws an exception—we get this output:

```
I am about to raise an exception
I caught an exception
executed after the exception
```

The `no_return` function happily informs us that it is about to raise an exception, but we fooled it and caught the exception. Once caught, we were able to clean up after ourselves (in this case, by outputting that we were handling the situation), and continue on our way, with no interference from that offensive function. The remainder of the code in the `no_return` function still went unexecuted, but the code that called the function was able to recover and continue.

Note the indentation around `try` and `except`. The `try` clause wraps any code that might throw an exception. The `except` clause is then back on the same indentation level as the `try` line. Any code to handle the exception is indented after the `except` clause. Then normal code resumes at the original indentation level.

The problem with the preceding code is that it will catch any type of exception. What if we were writing some code that could raise both `TypeError` and `ZeroDivisionError`? We might want to catch `ZeroDivisionError`, but let `TypeError` propagate to the console. Can you guess the syntax?

Here's a rather silly function that does just that:

```
def funny_division(divider):
    try:
        return 100 / divider
    except ZeroDivisionError:
        return "Zero is not a good idea!"


print(funny_division(0))
print(funny_division(50.0))
print(funny_division("hello"))
```

The function is tested with the `print` statements that show it behaving as expected:

```
Zero is not a good idea!
2.0
Traceback (most recent call last):
  File "catch_specific_exception.py", line 9, in <module>
    print(funny_division("hello"))
  File "catch_specific_exception.py", line 3, in funny_division
    return 100 / divider
TypeError: unsupported operand type(s) for /: 'int' and 'str'.
```

The first line of output shows that if we enter 0, we get properly mocked. If we call with a valid number (note that it's not an integer, but it's still a valid divisor), it operates correctly. Yet if we enter a string (you were wondering how to get a TypeError, weren't you?), it fails with an exception. If we had used an empty except clause that didn't specify a ZeroDivisionError, it would have accused us of dividing by zero when we sent it a string, which is not a proper behavior at all.

> The *bare except* syntax is generally frowned upon, even if you really do want to catch all instances of an exception. Use the except Exception: syntax to explicitly catch all exception types. This tell the reader that you meant to catch exception objects and all subclasses of Exception. The bare except syntax is actually the same as using except BaseException:, which actually catches system-level exceptions that are very rare to intentionally want to catch, as we'll see in the next section. If you really do want to catch them, explicitly use except BaseException: so that anyone who reads your code knows that you didn't just forget to specify what kind of exception you wanted.

We can even catch two or more different exceptions and handle them with the same code. Here's an example that raises three different types of exception. It handles TypeError and ZeroDivisionError with the same exception handler, but it may also raise a ValueError error if you supply the number 13:

```python
def funny_division2(divider):
    try:
        if divider == 13:
            raise ValueError("13 is an unlucky number")
        return 100 / divider
    except (ZeroDivisionError, TypeError):
        return "Enter a number other than zero"


for val in (0, "hello", 50.0, 13):

    print("Testing {}:".format(val), end=" ")
    print(funny_division2(val))
```

The `for` loop at the bottom loops over several test inputs and prints the results. If you're wondering about that `end` argument in the `print` statement, it just turns the default trailing newline into a space so that it's joined with the output from the next line. Here's a run of the program:

```
Testing 0: Enter a number other than zero
Testing hello: Enter a number other than zero
Testing 50.0: 2.0
Testing 13: Traceback (most recent call last):
  File "catch_multiple_exceptions.py", line 11, in <module>
    print(funny_division2(val))
  File "catch_multiple_exceptions.py", line 4, in funny_division2
    raise ValueError("13 is an unlucky number")
ValueError: 13 is an unlucky number
```

The number `0` and the string are both caught by the `except` clause, and a suitable error message is printed. The exception from the number `13` is not caught because it is a `ValueError`, which was not included in the types of exceptions being handled. This is all well and good, but what if we want to catch different exceptions and do different things with them? Or maybe we want to do something with an exception and then allow it to continue to bubble up to the parent function, as if it had never been caught?

We don't need any new syntax to deal with these cases. It's possible to stack the `except` clauses, and only the first match will be executed. For the second question, the `raise` keyword, with no arguments, will re-raise the last exception if we're already inside an exception handler. Observe the following code:

```
def funny_division3(divider):
    try:
        if divider == 13:
            raise ValueError("13 is an unlucky number")
        return 100 / divider
    except ZeroDivisionError:
        return "Enter a number other than zero"
    except TypeError:
        return "Enter a numerical value"
    except ValueError:
        print("No, No, not 13!")
        raise
```

The last line re-raises the `ValueError` error, so after outputting `No, No, not 13!`, it will raise the exception again; we'll still get the original stack trace on the console.

If we stack exception clauses like we did in the preceding example, only the first matching clause will be run, even if more than one of them fits. How can more than one clause match? Remember that exceptions are objects, and can therefore be subclassed. As we'll see in the next section, most exceptions extend the `Exception` class (which is itself derived from `BaseException`). If we catch `Exception` before we catch `TypeError`, then only the `Exception` handler will be executed, because `TypeError` is an `Exception` by inheritance.

This can come in handy in cases where we want to handle some exceptions specifically, and then handle all remaining exceptions as a more general case. We can simply catch `Exception` after catching all the specific exceptions and handle the general case there.

Often, when we catch an exception, we need a reference to the `Exception` object itself. This most often happens when we define our own exceptions with custom arguments, but can also be relevant with standard exceptions. Most exception classes accept a set of arguments in their constructor, and we might want to access those attributes in the exception handler. If we define our own `Exception` class, we can even call custom methods on it when we catch it. The syntax for capturing an exception as a variable uses the `as` keyword:

```
try:
    raise ValueError("This is an argument")
except ValueError as e:
    print("The exception arguments were", e.args)
```

If we run this simple snippet, it prints out the string argument that we passed into `ValueError` upon initialization.

We've seen several variations on the syntax for handling exceptions, but we still don't know how to execute code regardless of whether or not an exception has occurred. We also can't specify code that should be executed **only** if an exception does **not** occur. Two more keywords, `finally` and `else`, can provide the missing pieces. Neither one takes any extra arguments. The following example randomly picks an exception to throw and raises it. Then some not-so-complicated exception handling code runs that illustrates the newly introduced syntax:

```
import random
some_exceptions = [ValueError, TypeError, IndexError, None]

try:
    choice = random.choice(some_exceptions)
    print("raising {}".format(choice))
    if choice:
```

```
        raise choice("An error")
except ValueError:
    print("Caught a ValueError")
except TypeError:
    print("Caught a TypeError")
except Exception as e:
    print("Caught some other error: %s" %
        ( e.__class__.__name__))
else:
    print("This code called if there is no exception")
finally:
    print("This cleanup code is always called")
```

If we run this example—which illustrates almost every conceivable exception handling scenario—a few times, we'll get different output each time, depending on which exception `random` chooses. Here are some example runs:

```
$ python finally_and_else.py
raising None
This code called if there is no exception
This cleanup code is always called

$ python finally_and_else.py
raising <class 'TypeError'>
Caught a TypeError
This cleanup code is always called
$ python finally_and_else.py
raising <class 'IndexError'>
Caught some other error: IndexError
This cleanup code is always called

$ python finally_and_else.py
raising <class 'ValueError'>
Caught a ValueError
This cleanup code is always called
```

Note how the `print` statement in the `finally` clause is executed no matter what happens. This is extremely useful when we need to perform certain tasks after our code has finished running (even if an exception has occurred). Some common examples include the following:

- Cleaning up an open database connection
- Closing an open file
- Sending a closing handshake over the network

The `finally` clause is also very important when we execute a `return` statement from inside a `try` clause. The `finally` handler will still be executed before the value is returned without executing any code following the `try...finally` clause.

Also, pay attention to the output when no exception is raised: both the `else` and the `finally` clauses are executed. The `else` clause may seem redundant, as the code that should be executed only when no exception is raised could just be placed after the entire `try...except` block. The difference is that the `else` block will not be executed if an exception is caught and handled. We'll see more on this when we discuss using exceptions as flow control later.

Any of the `except`, `else`, and `finally` clauses can be omitted after a `try` block (although `else` by itself is invalid). If you include more than one, the `except` clauses must come first, then the `else` clause, with the `finally` clause at the end. The order of the `except` clauses normally goes from most specific to most generic.

## The exception hierarchy

We've already seen several of the most common built-in exceptions, and you'll probably encounter the rest over the course of your regular Python development. As we noticed earlier, most exceptions are subclasses of the `Exception` class. But this is not true of all exceptions. `Exception` itself actually inherits from a class called `BaseException`. In fact, all exceptions must extend the `BaseException` class or one of its subclasses.

There are two key built-in the exception classes, `SystemExit` and `KeyboardInterrupt`, that derive directly from `BaseException` instead of `Exception`. The `SystemExit` exception is raised whenever the program exits naturally, typically because we called the `sys.exit` function somewhere in our code (for example, when the user selected an exit menu item, clicked the *Close* button on a window, or entered a command to shut down a server). The exception is designed to allow us to clean up code before the program ultimately exits. However, we generally don't need to handle it explicitly because cleanup code can happen inside a `finally` clause.

If we do handle it, we would normally re-raise the exception, since catching it would stop the program from exiting. There are, of course, situations where we might want to stop the program exiting; for example, if there are unsaved changes and we want to prompt the user if they really want to exit. Usually, if we handle SystemExit at all, it's because we want to do something special with it, or are anticipating it directly. We especially don't want it to be accidentally caught in generic clauses that catch all normal exceptions. This is why it derives directly from BaseException.

The KeyboardInterrupt exception is common in command-line programs. It is thrown when the user explicitly interrupts program execution with an OS-dependent key combination (normally, *Ctrl + C*). This is a standard way for the user to deliberately interrupt a running program, and like SystemExit, it should almost always respond by terminating the program. Also, like SystemExit, it should handle any cleanup tasks inside the finally blocks.

Here is a class diagram that fully illustrates the hierarchy:

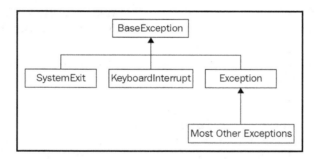

When we use the except: clause without specifying any type of exception, it will catch all subclasses of BaseException; which is to say, it will catch all exceptions, including the two special ones. Since we almost always want these to get special treatment, it is unwise to use the except: statement without arguments. If you want to catch all exceptions other than SystemExit and KeyboardInterrupt, explicitly catch Exception. Most Python developers assume that except: without a type is an error and will flag it in code review. If you really do want to catch everything, just explicitly use except BaseException:.

# Defining our own exceptions

Occasionally, when we want to raise an exception, we find that none of the built-in exceptions are suitable. Luckily, it's trivial to define new exceptions of our own. The name of the class is usually designed to communicate what went wrong, and we can provide arbitrary arguments in the initializer to include additional information.

All we have to do is inherit from the `Exception` class. We don't even have to add any content to the class! We can, of course, extend `BaseException` directly, but I have never encountered a use case where this would make sense.

Here's a simple exception we might use in a banking application:

```
class InvalidWithdrawal(Exception):
    pass

raise InvalidWithdrawal("You don't have $50 in your account")
```

The last line illustrates how to raise the newly defined exception. We are able to pass an arbitrary number of arguments into the exception. Often a string message is used, but any object that might be useful in a later exception handler can be stored. The `Exception.__init__` method is designed to accept any arguments and store them as a tuple in an attribute named `args`. This makes exceptions easier to define without needing to override `__init__`.

Of course, if we do want to customize the initializer, we are free to do so. Here's an exception whose initializer accepts the current balance and the amount the user wanted to withdraw. In addition, it adds a method to calculate how overdrawn the request was:

```
class InvalidWithdrawal(Exception):
    def __init__(self, balance, amount):
        super().__init__(f"account doesn't have ${amount}")
        self.amount = amount
        self.balance = balance

    def overage(self):
        return self.amount - self.balance

raise InvalidWithdrawal(25, 50)
```

The `raise` statement at the end illustrates how to construct this exception. As you can see, we can do anything with an exception that we would do with other objects.

Here's how we would handle an `InvalidWithdrawal` exception if one was raised:

```
try:
    raise InvalidWithdrawal(25, 50)
except InvalidWithdrawal as e:
    print("I'm sorry, but your withdrawal is "
            "more than your balance by "
            f"${e.overage()}")
```

Here we see a valid use of the `as` keyword. By convention, most Python coders name the exception `e` or the `ex` variable, although, as usual, you are free to call it `exception`, or `aunt_sally` if you prefer.

There are many reasons for defining our own exceptions. It is often useful to add information to the exception or log it in some way. But the utility of custom exceptions truly comes to light when creating a framework, library, or API that is intended for access by other programmers. In that case, be careful to ensure your code is raising exceptions that make sense to the client programmer. They should be easy to handle and clearly describe what went on. The client programmer should easily see how to fix the error (if it reflects a bug in their code) or handle the exception (if it's a situation they need to be made aware of).

Exceptions aren't exceptional. Novice programmers tend to think of exceptions as only useful for exceptional circumstances. However, the definition of exceptional circumstances can be vague and subject to interpretation. Consider the following two functions:

```
def divide_with_exception(number, divisor):
    try:
        print(f"{number} / {divisor} = {number / divisor}")
    except ZeroDivisionError:
        print("You can't divide by zero")

def divide_with_if(number, divisor):
    if divisor == 0:
        print("You can't divide by zero")
    else:
        print(f"{number} / {divisor} = {number / divisor}")
```

These two functions behave identically. If `divisor` is zero, an error message is printed; otherwise, a message printing the result of division is displayed. We could avoid `ZeroDivisionError` ever being thrown by testing for it with an `if` statement. Similarly, we can avoid `IndexError` by explicitly checking whether or not the parameter is within the confines of the list, and `KeyError` by checking whether the key is in a dictionary.

But we shouldn't do this. For one thing, we might write an `if` statement that checks whether or not the index is lower than the parameters of the list, but forget to check negative values.

 Remember, Python lists support negative indexing; $-1$ refers to the last element in the list.

Eventually, we would discover this and have to find all the places where we were checking code. But if we had simply caught `IndexError` and handled it, our code would just work.

Python programmers tend to follow a model of *ask forgiveness rather than permission*, which is to say, they execute code and then deal with anything that goes wrong. The alternative, to *look before you leap*, is generally less popular. There are a few reasons for this, but the main one is that it shouldn't be necessary to burn CPU cycles looking for an unusual situation that is not going to arise in the normal path through the code. Therefore, it is wise to use exceptions for exceptional circumstances, even if those circumstances are only a little bit exceptional. Taking this argument further, we can actually see that the exception syntax is also effective for flow control. Like an `if` statement, exceptions can be used for decision making, branching, and message passing.

Imagine an inventory application for a company that sells widgets and gadgets. When a customer makes a purchase, the item can either be available, in which case the item is removed from inventory and the number of items left is returned, or it might be out of stock. Now, being out of stock is a perfectly normal thing to happen in an inventory application. It is certainly not an exceptional circumstance. But what do we return if it's out of stock? A string saying out of stock? A negative number? In both cases, the calling method would have to check whether the return value is a positive integer or something else, to determine if it is out of stock. That seems a bit messy, especially if we forget to do it somewhere in our code.

Instead, we can raise OutOfStock and use the try statement to direct program flow control. Make sense? In addition, we want to make sure we don't sell the same item to two different customers, or sell an item that isn't in stock yet. One way to facilitate this is to lock each type of item to ensure only one person can update it at a time. The user must lock the item, manipulate the item (purchase, add stock, count items left...), and then unlock the item. Here's an incomplete Inventory example with docstrings that describes what some of the methods should do:

```python
class Inventory:
    def lock(self, item_type):
        """Select the type of item that is going to
        be manipulated. This method will lock the
        item so nobody else can manipulate the
        inventory until it's returned. This prevents
        selling the same item to two different
        customers."""
        pass

    def unlock(self, item_type):
        """Release the given type so that other
        customers can access it."""
        pass

    def purchase(self, item_type):
        """If the item is not locked, raise an
        exception. If the item_type does not exist,
        raise an exception. If the item is currently
        out of stock, raise an exception. If the item
        is available, subtract one item and return
        the number of items left."""
        pass
```

We could hand this object prototype to a developer and have them implement the methods to do exactly as they say while we work on the code that needs to make a purchase. We'll use Python's robust exception handling to consider different branches, depending on how the purchase was made:

```python
item_type = "widget"
inv = Inventory()
inv.lock(item_type)
try:
    num_left = inv.purchase(item_type)
except InvalidItemType:
    print("Sorry, we don't sell {}".format(item_type))
except OutOfStock:
    print("Sorry, that item is out of stock.")
else:
```

```
        print("Purchase complete. There are {num_left} {item_type}s left")
    finally:
        inv.unlock(item_type)
```

Pay attention to how all the possible exception handling clauses are used to ensure the correct actions happen at the correct time. Even though `OutOfStock` is not a terribly exceptional circumstance, we are able to use an exception to handle it suitably. This same code could be written with an `if...elif...else` structure, but it wouldn't be as easy to read or maintain.

We can also use exceptions to pass messages between different methods. For example, if we wanted to inform the customer as to what date the item is expected to be in stock again, we could ensure our `OutOfStock` object requires a `back_in_stock` parameter when it is constructed. Then, when we handle the exception, we can check that value and provide additional information to the customer. The information attached to the object can be easily passed between two different parts of the program. The exception could even provide a method that instructs the inventory object to reorder or backorder an item.

Using exceptions for flow control can make for some handy program designs. The important thing to take from this discussion is that exceptions are not a bad thing that we should try to avoid. Having an exception occur does not mean that you should have prevented this exceptional circumstance from happening. Rather, it is just a powerful way to communicate information between two sections of code that may not be directly calling each other.

# Case study

We've been looking at the use and handling of exceptions at a fairly low level of detail—syntax and definitions. This case study will help tie it all in with our previous chapters so we can see how exceptions are used in the larger context of objects, inheritance, and modules.

Today, we'll be designing a simple central authentication and authorization system. The entire system will be placed in one module, and other code will be able to query that module object for authentication and authorization purposes. We should admit, from the start, that we aren't security experts, and that the system we are designing may be full of security holes.

Our purpose is to study exceptions, not to secure a system. It will be sufficient, however, for a basic login and permission system that other code can interact with. Later, if that other code needs to be made more secure, we can have a security or cryptography expert review or rewrite our module, preferably without changing the API.

Authentication is the process of ensuring a user is really the person they say they are. We'll follow the lead of common web systems today, which use a username and private password combination. Other methods of authentication include voice recognition, fingerprint or retinal scanners, and identification cards.

Authorization, on the other hand, is all about determining whether a given (authenticated) user is permitted to perform a specific action. We'll create a basic permission list system that stores a list of the specific people allowed to perform each action.

In addition, we'll add some administrative features to allow new users to be added to the system. For brevity, we'll leave out editing of passwords or changing of permissions once they've been added, but these (highly necessary) features can certainly be added in the future.

There's a simple analysis; now let's proceed with design. We're obviously going to need a User class that stores the username and an encrypted password. This class will also allow a user to log in by checking whether a supplied password is valid. We probably won't need a Permission class, as those can just be strings mapped to a list of users using a dictionary. We should have a central Authenticator class that handles user management and logging in or out. The last piece of the puzzle is an Authorizor class that deals with permissions and checking whether a user can perform an activity. We'll provide a single instance of each of these classes in the auth module so that other modules can use this central mechanism for all their authentication and authorization needs. Of course, if they want to instantiate private instances of these classes, for non-central authorization activities, they are free to do so.

We'll also be defining several exceptions as we go along. We'll start with a special AuthException base class that accepts a username and optional user object as parameters; most of our self-defined exceptions will inherit from this one.

Let's build the `User` class first; it seems simple enough. A new user can be initialized with a username and password. The password will be stored encrypted to reduce the chances of its being stolen. We'll also need a `check_password` method to test whether a supplied password is the correct one. Here is the class in full:

```python
import hashlib


class User:
    def __init__(self, username, password):
        """Create a new user object. The password
        will be encrypted before storing."""
        self.username = username
        self.password = self._encrypt_pw(password)
        self.is_logged_in = False

    def _encrypt_pw(self, password):
        """Encrypt the password with the username and return
        the sha digest."""
        hash_string = self.username + password
        hash_string = hash_string.encode("utf8")
        return hashlib.sha256(hash_string).hexdigest()

    def check_password(self, password):
        """Return True if the password is valid for this
        user, false otherwise."""
        encrypted = self._encrypt_pw(password)
        return encrypted == self.password
```

Since the code for encrypting a password is required in both `__init__` and `check_password`, we pull it out to its own method. This way, it only needs to be changed in one place if someone realizes it is insecure and needs improvement. This class could easily be extended to include mandatory or optional personal details, such as names, contact information, and birth dates.

Before we write code to add users (which will happen in the as-yet undefined `Authenticator` class), we should examine some use cases. If all goes well, we can add a user with a username and password; the `User` object is created and inserted into a dictionary. But in what ways can all not go well? Well, clearly we don't want to add a user with a username that already exists in the dictionary.

If we did so, we'd overwrite an existing user's data and the new user might have access to that user's privileges. So, we'll need a `UsernameAlreadyExists` exception. Also, for security's sake, we should probably raise an exception if the password is too short. Both of these exceptions will extend `AuthException`, which we mentioned earlier. So, before writing the `Authenticator` class, let's define these three exception classes:

```python
class AuthException(Exception):
    def __init__(self, username, user=None):
        super().__init__(username, user)
        self.username = username
        self.user = user


class UsernameAlreadyExists(AuthException):
    pass


class PasswordTooShort(AuthException):
    pass
```

The `AuthException` requires a username and has an optional user parameter. This second parameter should be an instance of the `User` class associated with that username. The two specific exceptions we're defining simply need to inform the calling class of an exceptional circumstance, so we don't need to add any extra methods to them.

Now let's start on the `Authenticator` class. It can simply be a mapping of usernames to user objects, so we'll start with a dictionary in the initialization function. The method for adding a user needs to check the two conditions (password length and previously existing users) before creating a new `User` instance and adding it to the dictionary:

```python
class Authenticator:
    def __init__(self):
        """Construct an authenticator to manage
        users logging in and out."""
        self.users = {}

    def add_user(self, username, password):
        if username in self.users:
            raise UsernameAlreadyExists(username)
        if len(password) < 6:
            raise PasswordTooShort(username)
        self.users[username] = User(username, password)
```

We could, of course, extend the password validation to raise exceptions for passwords that are too easy to crack in other ways, if we desired. Now let's prepare the `login` method. If we weren't thinking about exceptions just now, we might just want the method to return `True` or `False`, depending on whether the login was successful or not. But we are thinking about exceptions, and this could be a good place to use them for a not-so-exceptional circumstance. We could raise different exceptions, for example, if the username does not exist or the password does not match. This will allow anyone trying to log a user in to elegantly handle the situation using a `try/except/else` clause. So, first we add these new exceptions:

```
class InvalidUsername(AuthException):
    pass

class InvalidPassword(AuthException):
    pass
```

Then we can define a simple `login` method to our `Authenticator` class that raises these exceptions if necessary. If not, it flags the `user` as logged in and returns the following:

```
def login(self, username, password):
    try:
        user = self.users[username]
    except KeyError:
        raise InvalidUsername(username)

    if not user.check_password(password):
        raise InvalidPassword(username, user)

    user.is_logged_in = True
    return True
```

Notice how `KeyError` is handled. This could have been handled using `if username not in self.users:` instead, but we chose to handle the exception directly. We end up eating up this first exception and raising a brand new one of our own that better suits the user-facing API.

We can also add a method to check whether a particular username is logged in. Deciding whether to use an exception here is trickier. Should we raise an exception if the username does not exist? Should we raise an exception if the user is not logged in?

To answer these questions, we need to think about how the method would be accessed. Most often, this method will be used to answer the yes/no question, *should I allow them access to <something>?* The answer will either be, *yes, the username is valid and they are logged in,* or *no, the username is not valid or they are not logged in.* Therefore, a Boolean return value is sufficient. There is no need to use exceptions here, just for the sake of using an exception:

```python
def is_logged_in(self, username):
    if username in self.users:
        return self.users[username].is_logged_in
    return False
```

Finally, we can add a default authenticator instance to our module so that the client code can access it easily using `auth.authenticator`:

```python
authenticator = Authenticator()
```

This line goes at the module level, outside any class definition, so the `authenticator` variable can be accessed as `auth.authenticator`. Now we can start on the `Authorizor` class, which maps permissions to users. The `Authorizor` class should not permit user access to a permission if they are not logged in, so they'll need a reference to a specific authenticator. We'll also need to set up the permission dictionary upon initialization:

```python
class Authorizor:
    def __init__(self, authenticator):
        self.authenticator = authenticator
        self.permissions = {}
```

Now we can write methods to add new permissions and to set up which users are associated with each permission:

```python
def add_permission(self, perm_name):
    '''Create a new permission that users
    can be added to'''
    try:
        perm_set = self.permissions[perm_name]
    except KeyError:
        self.permissions[perm_name] = set()
    else:
        raise PermissionError("Permission Exists")

def permit_user(self, perm_name, username):
    '''Grant the given permission to the user'''
    try:
        perm_set = self.permissions[perm_name]
```

```
        except KeyError:
            raise PermissionError("Permission does not exist")
        else:
            if username not in self.authenticator.users:
                raise InvalidUsername(username)
            perm_set.add(username)
```

The first method allows us to create a new permission, unless it already exists, in which case an exception is raised. The second allows us to add a username to a permission, unless either the permission or the username doesn't yet exist.

We use set instead of list for usernames, so that even if you grant a user permission more than once, the nature of sets means the user is only in the set once.

A PermissionError error is raised in both methods. This new error doesn't require a username, so we'll make it extend Exception directly, instead of our custom AuthException:

```
class PermissionError(Exception):
    pass
```

Finally, we can add a method to check whether a user has a specific permission or not. In order for them to be granted access, they have to be both logged into the authenticator and in the set of people who have been granted access to that privilege. If either of these conditions is unsatisfied, an exception is raised:

```
def check_permission(self, perm_name, username):
    if not self.authenticator.is_logged_in(username):
        raise NotLoggedInError(username)
    try:
        perm_set = self.permissions[perm_name]
    except KeyError:
        raise PermissionError("Permission does not exist")
    else:
        if username not in perm_set:
            raise NotPermittedError(username)
        else:
            return True
```

There are two new exceptions in here; they both take usernames, so we'll define them as subclasses of `AuthException`:

```
class NotLoggedInError(AuthException):
    pass

class NotPermittedError(AuthException):
    pass
```

Finally, we can add a default `authorizor` to go with our default authenticator:

```
authorizor = Authorizor(authenticator)
```

That completes a basic authentication/authorization system. We can test the system at the Python prompt, checking to see whether a user, `joe`, is permitted to do tasks in the paint department:

```
>>> import auth
>>> auth.authenticator.add_user("joe", "joepassword")
>>> auth.authorizor.add_permission("paint")
>>> auth.authorizor.check_permission("paint", "joe")
Traceback (most recent call last):
  File "<stdin>", line 1, in <module>
  File "auth.py", line 109, in check_permission
    raise NotLoggedInError(username)
auth.NotLoggedInError: joe
>>> auth.authenticator.is_logged_in("joe")
False
>>> auth.authenticator.login("joe", "joepassword")
True
>>> auth.authorizor.check_permission("paint", "joe")
Traceback (most recent call last):
  File "<stdin>", line 1, in <module>
  File "auth.py", line 116, in check_permission
    raise NotPermittedError(username)
auth.NotPermittedError: joe
>>> auth.authorizor.check_permission("mix", "joe")
Traceback (most recent call last):
  File "auth.py", line 111, in check_permission
    perm_set = self.permissions[perm_name]
KeyError: 'mix'

During handling of the above exception, another exception occurred:
Traceback (most recent call last):
  File "<stdin>", line 1, in <module>
  File "auth.py", line 113, in check_permission
    raise PermissionError("Permission does not exist")
auth.PermissionError: Permission does not exist
```

```
>>> auth.authorizor.permit_user("mix", "joe")
Traceback (most recent call last):
  File "auth.py", line 99, in permit_user
    perm_set = self.permissions[perm_name]
KeyError: 'mix'
During handling of the above exception, another exception occurred:

Traceback (most recent call last):
  File "<stdin>", line 1, in <module>
  File "auth.py", line 101, in permit_user
    raise PermissionError("Permission does not exist")
auth.PermissionError: Permission does not exist
>>> auth.authorizor.permit_user("paint", "joe")
>>> auth.authorizor.check_permission("paint", "joe")
True
```

While verbose, the preceding output shows all of our code and most of our exceptions in action, but to really understand the API we've defined, we should write some exception handling code that actually uses it. Here's a basic menu interface that allows certain users to change or test a program:

```
import auth

# Set up a test user and permission
auth.authenticator.add_user("joe", "joepassword")
auth.authorizor.add_permission("test program")
auth.authorizor.add_permission("change program")
auth.authorizor.permit_user("test program", "joe")


class Editor:
    def __init__(self):
        self.username = None
        self.menu_map = {
            "login": self.login,
            "test": self.test,
            "change": self.change,
            "quit": self.quit,
        }

    def login(self):
        logged_in = False
        while not logged_in:
            username = input("username: ")
            password = input("password: ")
            try:
                logged_in = auth.authenticator.login(username,
password)
```

```
            except auth.InvalidUsername:
                print("Sorry, that username does not exist")
            except auth.InvalidPassword:
                print("Sorry, incorrect password")
            else:
                self.username = username

    def is_permitted(self, permission):
        try:
            auth.authorizor.check_permission(permission,
self.username)
        except auth.NotLoggedInError as e:
            print("{} is not logged in".format(e.username))
            return False
        except auth.NotPermittedError as e:
            print("{} cannot {}".format(e.username, permission))
            return False
        else:
            return True

    def test(self):
        if self.is_permitted("test program"):
            print("Testing program now...")

    def change(self):
        if self.is_permitted("change program"):
            print("Changing program now...")

    def quit(self):
        raise SystemExit()

    def menu(self):
        try:
            answer = ""
            while True:
                print(
                    """
Please enter a command:
\tlogin\tLogin
\ttest\tTest the program
\tchange\tChange the program
\tquit\tQuit
"""
                )
                answer = input("enter a command: ").lower()
                try:
                    func = self.menu_map[answer]
                except KeyError:
```

```
                    print("{} is not a valid option".format(answer))
            else:
                    func()
    finally:
        print("Thank you for testing the auth module")


Editor().menu()
```

This rather long example is conceptually very simple. The is_permitted method is probably the most interesting; this is a mostly internal method that is called by both test and change to ensure the user is permitted access before continuing. Of course, those two methods are stubs, but we aren't writing an editor here; we're illustrating the use of exceptions and exception handlers by testing an authentication and authorization framework.

# Exercises

If you've never dealt with exceptions before, the first thing you need to do is look at any old Python code you've written and notice if there are places you should have been handling exceptions. How would you handle them? Do you need to handle them at all? Sometimes, letting the exception propagate to the console is the best way to communicate to the user, especially if the user is also the script's coder. Sometimes, you can recover from the error and allow the program to continue. Sometimes, you can only reformat the error into something the user can understand and display it to them.

Some common places to look are file I/O (is it possible your code will try to read a file that doesn't exist?), mathematical expressions (is it possible that a value you are dividing by is zero?), list indices (is the list empty?), and dictionaries (does the key exist?). Ask yourself whether you should ignore the problem, handle it by checking values first, or handle it with an exception. Pay special attention to areas where you might have used finally and else to ensure the correct code is executed under all conditions.

Now write some new code. Think of a program that requires authentication and authorization, and try writing some code that uses the `auth` module we built in the case study. Feel free to modify the module if it's not flexible enough. Try to handle all the exceptions in a sensible way. If you're having trouble coming up with something that requires authentication, try adding authorization to the Notepad example from `Chapter 16`, *Objects in Python*, or add authorization to the `auth` module itself—it's not a terribly useful module if just anybody can start adding permissions! Maybe require an administrator username and password before allowing privileges to be added or changed.

Finally, try to think of places in your code where you can raise exceptions. It can be in code you've written or are working on; or you can write a new project as an exercise. You'll probably have the best luck for designing a small framework or API that is meant to be used by other people; exceptions are a terrific communication tool between your code and someone else's. Remember to design and document any self-raised exceptions as part of the API, or they won't know whether or how to handle them!

# Summary

In this chapter, we went into the gritty details of raising, handling, defining, and manipulating exceptions. Exceptions are a powerful way to communicate unusual circumstances or error conditions without requiring a calling function to explicitly check return values. There are many built-in exceptions and raising them is trivially easy. There are several different syntaxes for handling different exception events.

In the next chapter, everything we've studied so far will come together as we discuss how object-oriented programming principles and structures should best be applied in Python applications.

# When to Use Object-Oriented Programming

**19**

In previous chapters, we've covered many of the defining features of object-oriented programming. We now know the principles and paradigms of object-oriented design, and we've covered the syntax of object-oriented programming in Python.

Yet, we don't know exactly how and, especially, when to utilize these principles and syntax in practice. In this chapter, we'll discuss some useful applications of the knowledge we've gained, looking at some new topics along the way:

- How to recognize objects
- Data and behaviors, once again
- Wrapping data behaviors using properties
- Restricting data using behaviors
- The Don't Repeat Yourself principle
- Recognizing repeated code

## Treat objects as objects

This may seem obvious; you should generally give separate objects in your problem domain a special class in your code. We've seen examples of this in the case studies in previous chapters: first, we identify objects in the problem, and then model their data and behaviors.

Identifying objects is a very important task in object-oriented analysis and programming. But it isn't always as easy as counting the nouns in short paragraphs that, frankly, I have constructed explicitly for that purpose. Remember, objects are things that have both data and behavior. If we are working only with data, we are often better off storing it in a list, set, dictionary, or other Python data structure. On the other hand, if we are working only with behavior, but no stored data, a simple function is more suitable.

An object, however, has both data and behavior. Proficient Python programmers use built-in data structures unless (or until) there is an obvious need to define a class. There is no reason to add an extra level of abstraction if it doesn't help organize our code. On the other hand, the *obvious* need is not always self-evident.

We can often start our Python programs by storing data in a few variables. As the program expands, we will later find that we are passing the same set of related variables to a set of functions. This is the time to think about grouping both variables and functions into a class. If we are designing a program to model polygons in two-dimensional space, we might start with each polygon represented as a list of points. The points would be modeled as two tuples $(x, y)$ describing where that point is located. This is all data, stored in a set of nested data structures (specifically, a list of tuples):

```
square = [(1,1), (1,2), (2,2), (2,1)]
```

Now, if we want to calculate the distance around the perimeter of the polygon, we need to sum the distances between each point. To do this, we need a function to calculate the distance between two points. Here are two such functions:

```
import math

def distance(p1, p2):
    return math.sqrt((p1[0]-p2[0])**2 + (p1[1]-p2[1])**2)

def perimeter(polygon):
    perimeter = 0
    points = polygon + [polygon[0]]
    for i in range(len(polygon)):
        perimeter += distance(points[i], points[i+1])
    return perimeter
```

Now, as object-oriented programmers, we clearly recognize that a `polygon` class could encapsulate the list of points (data) and the `perimeter` function (behavior). Further, a `point` class, such as we defined in `Chapter 16`, *Objects in Python*, might encapsulate the x and y coordinates and the `distance` method. The question is: is it valuable to do this?

For the previous code, maybe yes, maybe no. With our recent experience in object-oriented principles, we can write an object-oriented version in record time. Let's compare them as follows:

```python
class Point:
    def __init__(self, x, y):
        self.x = x
        self.y = y

    def distance(self, p2):
        return math.sqrt((self.x-p2.x)**2 + (self.y-p2.y)**2)

class Polygon:
    def __init__(self):
        self.vertices = []

    def add_point(self, point):
        self.vertices.append((point))

    def perimeter(self):
        perimeter = 0
        points = self.vertices + [self.vertices[0]]
        for i in range(len(self.vertices)):
            perimeter += points[i].distance(points[i+1])
        return perimeter
```

As we can see from the highlighted sections, there is twice as much code here as there was in our earlier version, although we could argue that the `add_point` method is not strictly necessary.

Now, to understand the differences a little better, let's compare the two APIs in use. Here's how to calculate the perimeter of a square using the object-oriented code:

```
>>> square = Polygon()
>>> square.add_point(Point(1,1))
>>> square.add_point(Point(1,2))
>>> square.add_point(Point(2,2))
>>> square.add_point(Point(2,1))
>>> square.perimeter()
4.0
```

That's fairly succinct and easy to read, you might think, but let's compare it to the function-based code:

```
>>> square = [(1,1), (1,2), (2,2), (2,1)]
>>> perimeter(square)
4.0
```

Hmm, maybe the object-oriented API isn't so compact! That said, I'd argue that it was easier to *read* than the functional example. How do we know what the list of tuples is supposed to represent in the second version? How do we remember what kind of object we're supposed to pass into the perimeter function? (a list of two tuples? That's not intuitive!) We would need a lot of documentation to explain how these functions should be used.

In contrast, the object-oriented code is relatively self-documenting. We just have to look at the list of methods and their parameters to know what the object does and how to use it. By the time we wrote all the documentation for the functional version, it would probably be longer than the object-oriented code.

Finally, code length is not a good indicator of code complexity. Some programmers get hung up on complicated *one liners* that do an incredible amount of work in one line of code. This can be a fun exercise, but the result is often unreadable, even to the original author the following day. Minimizing the amount of code can often make a program easier to read, but do not blindly assume this is the case.

Luckily, this trade-off isn't necessary. We can make the object-oriented `Polygon` API as easy to use as the functional implementation. All we have to do is alter our `Polygon` class so that it can be constructed with multiple points. Let's give it an initializer that accepts a list of `Point` objects. In fact, let's allow it to accept tuples too, and we can construct the `Point` objects ourselves, if needed:

```
def __init__(self, points=None):
    points = points if points else []
    self.vertices = []
    for point in points:
        if isinstance(point, tuple):
            point = Point(*point)
        self.vertices.append(point)
```

This initializer goes through the list and ensures that any tuples are converted to points. If the object is not a tuple, we leave it as is, assuming that it is either a `Point` object already, or an unknown duck-typed object that can act like a `Point` object.

 If you are experimenting with the above code, you could subclass `Polygon` and override the __init__ function instead of replacing the initializer or copying the `add_point` and `perimeter` methods.

Still, there's no clear winner between the object-oriented and more data-oriented versions of this code. They both do the same thing. If we have new functions that accept a polygon argument, such as `area(polygon)` or `point_in_polygon(polygon, x, y)`, the benefits of the object-oriented code become increasingly obvious. Likewise, if we add other attributes to the polygon, such as `color` or `texture`, it makes more and more sense to encapsulate that data into a single class.

The distinction is a design decision, but in general, the more important a set of data is, the more likely it is to have multiple functions specific to that data, and the more useful it is to use a class with attributes and methods instead.

When making this decision, it also pays to consider how the class will be used. If we're only trying to calculate the perimeter of one polygon in the context of a much greater problem, using a function will probably be quickest to code and easier to use *one time only*. On the other hand, if our program needs to manipulate numerous polygons in a wide variety of ways (calculating the perimeter, area, and intersection with other polygons, moving or scaling them, and so on), we have almost certainly identified an object; one that needs to be extremely versatile.

Additionally, pay attention to the interaction between objects. Look for inheritance relationships; inheritance is impossible to model elegantly without classes, so make sure to use them. Look for the other types of relationships we discussed in Chapter 15, *Object-Oriented Design*, association and composition. Composition can, technically, be modeled using only data structures; for example, we can have a list of dictionaries holding tuple values, but it is sometimes less complicated to create a few classes of objects, especially if there is behavior associated with the data.

 Don't rush to use an object just because you can use an object, but don't neglect to create a class when you need to use a class.

# Adding behaviors to class data with properties

Throughout this book, we've focused on the separation of behavior and data. This is very important in object-oriented programming, but we're about to see that, in Python, the distinction is uncannily blurry. Python is very good at blurring distinctions; it doesn't exactly help us to *think outside the box*. Rather, it teaches us to stop thinking about the box.

Before we get into the details, let's discuss some bad object-oriented theory. Many object-oriented languages teach us to never access attributes directly (Java is the most notorious). They insist that we write attribute access like this:

```
class Color:
    def __init__(self, rgb_value, name):
        self._rgb_value = rgb_value
        self._name = name

    def set_name(self, name):
        self._name = name
    def get_name(self):
        return self._name
```

The variables are prefixed with an underscore to suggest that they are private (other languages would actually force them to be private). Then, the `get` and `set` methods provide access to each variable. This class would be used in practice as follows:

```
>>> c = Color("#ff0000", "bright red")
>>> c.get_name()
'bright red'
>>> c.set_name("red")
>>> c.get_name()
'red'
```

This is not nearly as readable as the direct access version that Python favors:

```
class Color:
    def __init__(self, rgb_value, name):
        self.rgb_value = rgb_value
        self.name = name

c = Color("#ff0000", "bright red")
print(c.name)
c.name = "red"
print(c.name)
```

So, why would anyone insist upon the method-based syntax? Their reasoning is that, someday, we may want to add extra code when a value is set or retrieved. For example, we could decide to cache a value to avoid complex computations, or we might want to validate that a given value is a suitable input.

In code, for example, we could decide to change the `set_name()` method as follows:

```
def set_name(self, name):
    if not name:
        raise Exception("Invalid Name")
    self._name = name
```

Now, in Java and similar languages, if we had written our original code for direct attribute access, and then later changed it to a method like the preceding one, we'd have a problem: anyone who had written code that accessed the attribute directly would now have to access a method. If they didn't then change the access style from attribute access to a function call, their code will be broken.

The mantra in these languages is that we should never make public members private. This doesn't make much sense in Python since there isn't any real concept of private members!

Python gives us the `property` keyword to make methods that *look* like attributes. We can therefore write our code to use direct member access, and if we ever unexpectedly need to alter the implementation to do some calculation when getting or setting that attribute's value, we can do so without changing the interface. Let's see how it looks:

```python
class Color:
    def __init__(self, rgb_value, name):
        self.rgb_value = rgb_value
        self._name = name

    def _set_name(self, name):
        if not name:
            raise Exception("Invalid Name")
        self._name = name

    def _get_name(self):
        return self._name

    name = property(_get_name, _set_name)
```

Compared to the earlier class, we first change the `name` attribute into a (semi-)private _name attribute. Then, we add two more (semi-)private methods to get and set that variable, performing our validation when we set it.

Finally, we have the `property` declaration at the bottom. This is the Python magic. It creates a new attribute on the `Color` class called `name`, to replace the direct `name` attribute. It sets this attribute to be a **property**. Under the hood, `property` calls the two methods we just created whenever the value is accessed or changed. This new version of the `Color` class can be used exactly the same way as the earlier version, yet it now performs validation when we set the `name` attribute:

```python
>>> c = Color("#0000ff", "bright red")
>>> print(c.name)
bright red
>>> c.name = "red"
>>> print(c.name)
red
>>> c.name = ""
Traceback (most recent call last):
  File "<stdin>", line 1, in <module>
  File "setting_name_property.py", line 8, in _set_name
    raise Exception("Invalid Name")
```

**Exception: Invalid Name**

So, if we'd previously written code to access the name attribute, and then changed it to use our property-based object, the previous code would still work, unless it was sending an empty property value, which is the behavior we wanted to forbid in the first place. Success!

Bear in mind that, even with the name property, the previous code is not 100% safe. People can still access the _name attribute directly and set it to an empty string if they want to. But if they access a variable we've explicitly marked with an underscore to suggest it is private, they're the ones that have to deal with the consequences, not us.

# Properties in detail

Think of the property function as returning an object that proxies any requests to set or access the attribute value through the methods we have specified. The property built-in is like a constructor for such an object, and that object is set as the public-facing member for the given attribute.

This property constructor can actually accept two additional arguments, a delete function and a docstring for the property. The delete function is rarely supplied in practice, but it can be useful for logging the fact that a value has been deleted, or possibly to veto deleting if we have reason to do so. The docstring is just a string describing what the property does, no different from the docstrings we discussed in Chapter 16, *Objects in Python*. If we do not supply this parameter, the docstring will instead be copied from the docstring for the first argument: the getter method. Here is a silly example that states whenever any of the methods are called:

```python
class Silly:
    def _get_silly(self):
        print("You are getting silly")
        return self._silly

    def _set_silly(self, value):
        print("You are making silly {}".format(value))
        self._silly = value

    def _del_silly(self):
        print("Whoah, you killed silly!")
        del self._silly

    silly = property(_get_silly, _set_silly, _del_silly, "This is a
silly property")
```

If we actually use this class, it does indeed print out the correct strings when we ask it to:

```
>>> s = Silly()
>>> s.silly = "funny"
You are making silly funny
>>> s.silly
You are getting silly
'funny'
>>> del s.silly
Whoah, you killed silly!
```

Further, if we look at the help file for the `Silly` class (by issuing `help(Silly)` at the interpreter prompt), it shows us the custom docstring for our `silly` attribute:

```
Help on class Silly in module __main__:

class Silly(builtins.object)
 |  Data descriptors defined here:
 |
 |  __dict__
 |      dictionary for instance variables (if defined)
 |
 |  __weakref__
 |      list of weak references to the object (if defined)
 |
 |  silly
 |      This is a silly property
```

Once again, everything is working as we planned. In practice, properties are normally only defined with the first two parameters: the `getter` and `setter` functions. If we want to supply a docstring for a property, we can define it on the `getter` function; the property proxy will copy it into its own docstring. The `delete` function is often left empty because object attributes are so rarely deleted. If a coder does try to delete a property that doesn't have a `delete` function specified, it will raise an exception. Therefore, if there is a legitimate reason to delete our property, we should supply that function.

# Decorators – another way to create properties

If you've never used Python decorators before, you might want to skip this section and come back to it after we've discussed the decorator pattern in Chapter 22, *Python Design Patterns I*. However, you don't need to understand what's going on to use the decorator syntax in order to make property methods more readable.

The `property` function can be used with the decorator syntax to turn a `get` function into a `property` function, as follows:

```
class Foo:
    @property
    def foo(self):
        return "bar"
```

This applies the `property` function as a decorator, and is equivalent to the previous `foo = property(foo)` syntax. The main difference, from a readability perspective, is that we get to mark the `foo` function as a property at the top of the method, instead of after it is defined, where it can be easily overlooked. It also means we don't have to create private methods with underscore prefixes just to define a property.

Going one step further, we can specify a `setter` function for the new property as follows:

```
class Foo:
    @property
    def foo(self):
        return self._foo

    @foo.setter
    def foo(self, value):
        self._foo = value
```

This syntax looks pretty odd, although the intent is obvious. First, we decorate the `foo` method as a getter. Then, we decorate a second method with exactly the same name by applying the `setter` attribute of the originally decorated `foo` method! The `property` function returns an object; this object always comes with its own `setter` attribute, which can then be applied as a decorator to other functions. Using the same name for the get and set methods is not required, but it does help to group together the multiple methods that access one property.

We can also specify a `delete` function with `@foo.deleter`. We cannot specify a docstring using `property` decorators, so we need to rely on the property copying the docstring from the initial getter method. Here's our previous `Silly` class rewritten to use `property` as a decorator:

```
class Silly:
    @property
    def silly(self):
        "This is a silly property"
        print("You are getting silly")
        return self._silly
```

```
@silly.setter
def silly(self, value):
    print("You are making silly {}".format(value))
    self._silly = value

@silly.deleter
def silly(self):
    print("Whoah, you killed silly!")
    del self._silly
```

This class operates *exactly* the same as our earlier version, including the help text. You can use whichever syntax you feel is more readable and elegant.

# Deciding when to use properties

With the built-in property clouding the division between behavior and data, it can be confusing to know when to choose an attribute, or a method, or a property. The use case example we saw earlier is one of the most common uses of properties; we have some data on a class that we later want to add behavior to. There are also other factors to take into account when deciding to use a property.

Technically, in Python, data, properties, and methods are all attributes on a class. The fact that a method is callable does not distinguish it from other types of attributes; indeed, we'll see in `Chapter 20`, *Python Object-Oriented Shortcuts*, that it is possible to create normal objects that can be called like functions. We'll also discover that functions and methods are themselves normal objects.

The fact that methods are just callable attributes, and properties are just customizable attributes, can help us make this decision. Methods should typically represent actions; things that can be done to, or performed by, the object. When you call a method, even with only one argument, it should *do* something. Method names are generally verbs.

Once confirming that an attribute is not an action, we need to decide between standard data attributes and properties. In general, always use a standard attribute until you need to control access to that property in some way. In either case, your attribute is usually a noun. The only difference between an attribute and a property is that we can invoke custom actions automatically when a property is retrieved, set, or deleted.

Let's look at a more realistic example. A common need for custom behavior is caching a value that is difficult to calculate or expensive to look up (requiring, for example, a network request or database query). The goal is to store the value locally to avoid repeated calls to the expensive calculation.

We can do this with a custom getter on the property. The first time the value is retrieved, we perform the lookup or calculation. Then, we can locally cache the value as a private attribute on our object (or in dedicated caching software), and the next time the value is requested, we return the stored data. Here's how we might cache a web page:

```
from urllib.request import urlopen


class WebPage:
    def __init__(self, url):
        self.url = url
        self._content = None

    @property
    def content(self):
        if not self._content:
            print("Retrieving New Page...")
            self._content = urlopen(self.url).read()
        return self._content
```

We can test this code to see that the page is only retrieved once:

```
>>> import time
>>> webpage = WebPage("http://ccphillips.net/")
>>> now = time.time()
>>> content1 = webpage.content
Retrieving New Page...
>>> time.time() - now
22.43316888809204
>>> now = time.time()
>>> content2 = webpage.content
>>> time.time() - now
1.9266459941864014
>>> content2 == content1
True
```

I was on an awful satellite connection when I originally tested this code for the first version of this book back in 2010 and it took 20 seconds the first time I loaded the content. The second time, I got the result in 2 seconds (which is really just the amount of time it took to type the lines into the interpreter). On my more modern connection it looks as follows:

```
>>> webpage = WebPage("https://dusty.phillips.codes")
>>> import time
>>> now = time.time() ; content1 = webpage.content ; print(time.time()
 - now)
```

```
Retrieving New Page...
0.6236202716827393
>>> now = time.time() ; content2 = webpage.content ; print(time.time()
- now)
1.7881393432617188e-05M
```

It takes about 620 milliseconds to retrieve a page from my web host. From my laptop's RAM, it takes 0.018 milliseconds!

Custom getters are also useful for attributes that need to be calculated on the fly, based on other object attributes. For example, we might want to calculate the average for a list of integers:

```
class AverageList(list):
    @property
    def average(self):
        return sum(self) / len(self)
```

This very simple class inherits from `list`, so we get list-like behavior for free. We just add a property to the class, and hey presto, our list can have an average as follows:

```
>>> a = AverageList([1,2,3,4])
>>> a.average
2.5
```

Of course, we could have made this a method instead, but then we ought to call it `calculate_average()`, since methods represent actions. But a property called `average` is more suitable, and is both easier to type and easier to read.

Custom setters are useful for validation, as we've already seen, but they can also be used to proxy a value to another location. For example, we could add a content setter to the `WebPage` class that automatically logs into our web server and uploads a new page whenever the value is set.

# Manager objects

We've been focused on objects and their attributes and methods. Now, we'll take a look at designing higher-level objects; the kind of objects that manage other objects – the objects that tie everything together.

The difference between these objects and most of the previous examples is that the latter usually represent concrete ideas. Management objects are more like office managers; they don't do the actual *visible* work out on the floor, but without them, there would be no communication between departments and nobody would know what they are supposed to do (although, this can be true anyway if the organization is badly managed!). Analogously, the attributes on a management class tend to refer to other objects that do the *visible* work; the behaviors on such a class delegate to those other classes at the right time, and pass messages between them.

As an example, we'll write a program that does a find-and-replace action for text files stored in a compressed ZIP file. We'll need objects to represent the ZIP file and each individual text file (luckily, we don't have to write these classes, as they're available in the Python standard library). The manager object will be responsible for ensuring the following three steps occur in order:

1. Unzipping the compressed file
2. Performing the find-and-replace action
3. Zipping up the new files

The class is initialized with the `.zip` filename, and search and replace strings. We create a temporary directory to store the unzipped files in, so that the folder stays clean. The `pathlib` library helps out with file and directory manipulation. The interface should be pretty clear in the following example:

```
import sys
import shutil
import zipfile
from pathlib import Path

class ZipReplace:
    def __init__(self, filename, search_string, replace_string):
        self.filename = filename
        self.search_string = search_string
        self.replace_string = replace_string
        self.temp_directory = Path(f"unzipped-{filename}")
```

Then, we create an overall *manager* method for each of the three steps. This method delegates responsibility to other objects:

```
def zip_find_replace(self):
    self.unzip_files()
    self.find_replace()
    self.zip_files()
```

Obviously, we could do all three steps in one method, or indeed in one script, without ever creating an object. There are several advantages to separating the three steps:

- **Readability**: The code for each step is in a self-contained unit that is easy to read and understand. The method name describes what the method does, and less additional documentation is required to understand what is going on.
- **Extensibility**: If a subclass wanted to use compressed TAR files instead of ZIP files, it could override the zip and unzip methods without having to duplicate the find_replace method.
- **Partitioning**: An external class could create an instance of this class and call the find_replace method directly on some folder without having to zip the content.

The delegation method is the first in the following code; the rest of the methods are included for completeness:

```python
def unzip_files(self):
    self.temp_directory.mkdir()
    with zipfile.ZipFile(self.filename) as zip:
        zip.extractall(self.temp_directory)

def find_replace(self):
    for filename in self.temp_directory.iterdir():
        with filename.open() as file:
            contents = file.read()
        contents = contents.replace(self.search_string,
self.replace_string)
        with filename.open("w") as file:
            file.write(contents)

def zip_files(self):
    with zipfile.ZipFile(self.filename, "w") as file:
        for filename in self.temp_directory.iterdir():
            file.write(filename, filename.name)
    shutil.rmtree(self.temp_directory)


if __name__ == "__main__":
    ZipReplace(*sys.argv[1:4]).zip_find_replace()
```

For brevity, the code for zipping and unzipping files is sparsely documented. Our current focus is on object-oriented design; if you are interested in the inner details of the `zipfile` module, refer to the documentation in the standard library, either online or by typing `import zipfile ; help(zipfile)` into your interactive interpreter. Note that this toy example only searches the top-level files in a ZIP file; if there are any folders in the unzipped content, they will not be scanned, nor will any files inside those folders.

 If you are using a Python version older than 3.6, you will need to convert the path objects to strings before calling `extractall`, `rmtree`, and `file.write` on the `ZipFile` object.

The last two lines in the example allow us to run the program from the command line by passing the `zip` filename, the search string, and the replace string as arguments, as follows:

```
$python zipsearch.py hello.zip hello hi
```

Of course, this object does not have to be created from the command line; it could be imported from another module (to perform batch ZIP file processing), or accessed as part of a GUI interface or even a higher-level management object that knows where to get ZIP files (for example, to retrieve them from an FTP server or back them up to an external disk).

As programs become more and more complex, the objects being modeled become less and less like physical objects. Properties are other abstract objects, and methods are actions that change the state of those abstract objects. But at the heart of every object, no matter how complex, is a set of concrete data and well-defined behaviors.

# Removing duplicate code

Often, the code in management style classes such as `ZipReplace` is quite generic and can be applied in a variety of ways. It is possible to use either composition or inheritance to help keep this code in one place, thus eliminating duplicate code. Before we look at any examples of this, let's discuss a tiny bit of theory. Specifically, why is duplicate code a bad thing?

There are several reasons, but they all boil down to readability and maintainability. When we're writing a new piece of code that is similar to an earlier piece, the easiest thing to do is copy the old code and change whatever needs to be changed (variable names, logic, comments) to make it work in the new location. Alternatively, if we're writing new code that seems similar, but not identical, to code elsewhere in the project, it is often easier to write fresh code with similar behavior, rather than figuring out how to extract the overlapping functionality.

But as soon as someone has to read and understand the code and they come across duplicate blocks, they are faced with a dilemma. Code that might have appeared to make sense suddenly has to be understood. How is one section different from the other? How are they the same? Under what conditions is one section called? When do we call the other? You might argue that you're the only one reading your code, but if you don't touch that code for eight months, it will be as incomprehensible to you as it is to a fresh coder. When we're trying to read two similar pieces of code, we have to understand why they're different, as well as how they're different. This wastes the reader's time; code should always be written to be readable first.

I once had to try to understand someone's code that had three identical copies of the same 300 lines of very poorly written code. I had been working with the code for a month before I finally comprehended that the three *identical* versions were actually performing slightly different tax calculations. Some of the subtle differences were intentional, but there were also obvious areas where someone had updated a calculation in one function without updating the other two. The number of subtle, incomprehensible bugs in the code could not be counted. I eventually replaced all 900 lines with an easy-to-read function of 20 lines or so.

Reading such duplicate code can be tiresome, but code maintenance is even more tormenting. As the preceding story suggests, keeping two similar pieces of code up to date can be a nightmare. We have to remember to update both sections whenever we update one of them, and we have to remember how multiple sections differ so we can modify our changes when we are editing each of them. If we forget to update all sections, we will end up with extremely annoying bugs that usually manifest themselves as, *But I fixed that already, why is it still happening?*

The result is that people who are reading or maintaining our code have to spend astronomical amounts of time understanding and testing it compared to the time required to write it in a non-repetitive manner in the first place. It's even more frustrating when we are the ones doing the maintenance; we find ourselves saying, Why didn't I do this right the first time? The time we save by copying and pasting existing code is lost the very first time we have to maintain it. Code is both read and modified many more times and much more often than it is written. Comprehensible code should always be a priority.

This is why programmers, especially Python programmers (who tend to value elegant code more than average developers), follow what is known as the **Don't Repeat Yourself** (**DRY**) principle. DRY code is maintainable code. My advice for beginning programmers is to never use the copy-and-paste feature of their editor. To intermediate programmers, I suggest they think thrice before they hit *Ctrl + C*.

But what should we do instead of code duplication? The simplest solution is often to move the code into a function that accepts parameters to account for whatever parts are different. This isn't a terribly object-oriented solution, but it is frequently optimal.

For example, if we have two pieces of code that unzip a ZIP file into two different directories, we can easily replace it with a function that accepts a parameter for the directory to which it should be unzipped. This may make the function itself slightly more difficult to read, but a good function name and docstring can easily make up for that, and any code that invokes the function will be easier to read.

That's certainly enough theory! The moral of the story is: always make the effort to refactor your code to be easier to read instead of writing bad code that may seem easier to write.

# In practice

Let's explore two ways we can reuse existing code. After writing our code to replace strings in a ZIP file full of text files, we are later contracted to scale all the images in a ZIP file to 640 x 480. It looks like we could use a very similar paradigm to what we used in `ZipReplace`. Our first impulse might be to save a copy of that file and change the `find_replace` method to `scale_image` or something similar.

But, that's suboptimal. What if someday we want to change the `unzip` and `zip` methods to also open TAR files? Or maybe we'll want to use a guaranteed unique directory name for temporary files. In either case, we'd have to change it in two different places!

We'll start by demonstrating an inheritance-based solution to this problem. First, we'll modify our original `ZipReplace` class into a superclass for processing generic ZIP files:

```python
import sys
import shutil
import zipfile
from pathlib import Path


class ZipProcessor:
    def __init__(self, zipname):
        self.zipname = zipname
        self.temp_directory = Path(f"unzipped-{zipname[:-4]}")

    def process_zip(self):
        self.unzip_files()
        self.process_files()
        self.zip_files()

    def unzip_files(self):
        self.temp_directory.mkdir()
        with zipfile.ZipFile(self.zipname) as zip:
            zip.extractall(self.temp_directory)

    def zip_files(self):
        with zipfile.ZipFile(self.zipname, "w") as file:
            for filename in self.temp_directory.iterdir():
                file.write(filename, filename.name)
        shutil.rmtree(self.temp_directory)
```

We changed the `filename` property to `zipname` to avoid confusion with the `filename` local variables inside the various methods. This helps make the code more readable, even though it isn't actually a change in design.

We also dropped the two parameters to __init__ (search_string and replace_string) that were specific to ZipReplace. Then, we renamed the zip_find_replace method to process_zip and made it call an (as yet undefined) process_files method instead of find_replace; these name changes help demonstrate the more generalized nature of our new class. Notice that we have removed the find_replace method altogether; that code is specific to ZipReplace and has no business here.

This new ZipProcessor class doesn't actually define a process_files method. If we ran it directly, it would raise an exception. Because it isn't meant to run directly, we removed the main call at the bottom of the original script. We could make this an abstract base class in order to communicate that this method needs to be defined in a subclass, but I've left it out for brevity.

Now, before we move on to our image processing application, let's fix up our original zipsearch class to make use of this parent class, as follows:

```python
class ZipReplace(ZipProcessor):
    def __init__(self, filename, search_string, replace_string):
        super().__init__(filename)
        self.search_string = search_string
        self.replace_string = replace_string

    def process_files(self):
        """perform a search and replace on all files in the
        temporary directory"""
        for filename in self.temp_directory.iterdir():
            with filename.open() as file:
                contents = file.read()
            contents = contents.replace(self.search_string,
self.replace_string)
            with filename.open("w") as file:
                file.write(contents)
```

This code is shorter than the original version, since it inherits its ZIP processing abilities from the parent class. We first import the base class we just wrote and make ZipReplace extend that class. Then, we use super() to initialize the parent class. The find_replace method is still here, but we renamed it process_files so the parent class can call it from its management interface. Because this name isn't as descriptive as the old one, we added a docstring to describe what it is doing.

Now, that was quite a bit of work, considering that all we have now is a program that is functionally not different from the one we started with! But having done that work, it is now much easier for us to write other classes that operate on files in a ZIP archive, such as the (hypothetically requested) photo scaler. Further, if we ever want to improve or bug fix the zip functionality, we can do it for all subclasses at once by changing only the one ZipProcessor base class. Therefore maintenance will be much more effective.

See how simple it is now to create a photo scaling class that takes advantage of the ZipProcessor functionality:

```python
from PIL import Image

class ScaleZip(ZipProcessor):
    def process_files(self):
        '''Scale each image in the directory to 640x480'''
        for filename in self.temp_directory.iterdir():
            im = Image.open(str(filename))
            scaled = im.resize((640, 480))
            scaled.save(filename)

if __name__ == "__main__":
    ScaleZip(*sys.argv[1:4]).process_zip()
```

Look how simple this class is! All that work we did earlier paid off. All we do is open each file (assuming that it is an image; it will unceremoniously crash if a file cannot be opened or isn't an image), scale it, and save it back. The ZipProcessor class takes care of the zipping and unzipping without any extra work on our part.

# Case study

For this case study, we'll try to delve further into the question, When should I choose an object versus a built-in type? We'll be modeling a Document class that might be used in a text editor or word processor. What objects, functions, or properties should it have?

We might start with a str for the Document contents, but in Python, strings aren't mutable (able to be changed). Once a str is defined, it is forever. We can't insert a character into it or remove one without creating a brand new string object. That would be leaving a lot of str objects taking up memory until Python's garbage collector sees fit to clean up behind us.

So, instead of a string, we'll use a list of characters, which we can modify at will. In addition, we'll need to know the current cursor position within the list, and should probably also store a filename for the document.

 Real text editors use a binary tree-based data structure called a rope to model their document contents. This book's title isn't *Advanced Data Structures*, so if you're interested in learning more about this fascinating topic, you may want to search the web for *rope data structure*.

There are a lot of things we might want to do to a text document, including inserting, deleting, and selecting characters; cutting, copying, and, pasting the selection; and saving or closing the document. It looks like there are copious amounts of both data and behavior, so it makes sense to put all this stuff into its own Document class.

A pertinent question is: should this class be composed of a bunch of basic Python objects such as str filenames, int cursor positions, and a list of characters? Or should some or all of those things be specially defined objects in their own right? What about individual lines and characters? Do they need to have classes of their own?

We'll answer these questions as we go, but let's start with the simplest possible class first- Document  and see what it can do:

```python
class Document:
    def __init__(self):
        self.characters = []
        self.cursor = 0
        self.filename = ''

    def insert(self, character):
        self.characters.insert(self.cursor, character)
        self.cursor += 1

    def delete(self):
        del self.characters[self.cursor]

    def save(self):
        with open(self.filename, 'w') as f:
            f.write(''.join(self.characters))

    def forward(self):
        self.cursor += 1

    def back(self):
```

```
        self.cursor -= 1
```

This basic class allows us full control over editing a basic document. Have a look at it in action:

```
>>> doc = Document()
>>> doc.filename = "test_document"
>>> doc.insert('h')
>>> doc.insert('e')
>>> doc.insert('l')
>>> doc.insert('l')
>>> doc.insert('o')
>>> "".join(doc.characters)
'hello'
>>> doc.back()
>>> doc.delete()
>>> doc.insert('p')
>>> "".join(doc.characters)
'hellp'
```

It looks like it's working. We could connect a keyboard's letter and arrow keys to these methods and the document would track everything just fine.

But what if we want to connect more than just arrow keys. What if we want to connect the *Home* and *End* keys as well? We could add more methods to the Document class that search forward or backward for newline characters (a newline character, escaped as \n, represents the end of one line and the beginning of a new one) in the string and jump to them, but if we did that for every possible movement action (move by words, move by sentences, *Page Up*, *Page Down*, end of line, beginning of white space, and others), the class would be huge. Maybe it would be better to put those methods on a separate object. So, let's turn the Cursor attribute into an object that is aware of its position and can manipulate that position. We can move the forward and back methods to that class, and add a couple more for the Home and End keys, as follows:

```
class Cursor:
    def __init__(self, document):
        self.document = document
        self.position = 0

    def forward(self):
        self.position += 1

    def back(self):
        self.position -= 1
```

```
    def home(self):
        while self.document.characters[self.position - 1].character !=
"\n":
            self.position -= 1
            if self.position == 0:
                # Got to beginning of file before newline
                break

    def end(self):
        while (
            self.position < len(self.document.characters)
            and self.document.characters[self.position] != "\n"
        ):
            self.position += 1
```

This class takes the document as an initialization parameter so the methods have access to the content of the document's character list. It then provides simple methods for moving backward and forward, as before, and for moving to the home and end positions.

This code is not very safe. You can very easily move past the ending position, and if you try to go home on an empty file, it will crash. These examples are kept short to make them readable, but that doesn't mean they are defensive! You can improve the error checking of this code as an exercise; it might be a great opportunity to expand your exception-handling skills.

The Document class itself is hardly changed, except for removing the two methods that were moved to the Cursor class:

```
class Document:
    def __init__(self):
        self.characters = []
        self.cursor = Cursor(self)
        self.filename = ''

    def insert(self, character):
        self.characters.insert(self.cursor.position,
                character)
        self.cursor.forward()

    def delete(self):
        del self.characters[self.cursor.position]

    def save(self):
        with open(self.filename, "w") as f:
            f.write("".join(self.characters))
```

We just updated anything that accessed the old cursor integer to use the new object instead. We can now test that the `home` method is really moving to the newline character, as follows:

```
>>> d = Document()
>>> d.insert('h')
>>> d.insert('e')
>>> d.insert('l')
>>> d.insert('l')
>>> d.insert('o')
>>> d.insert('\n')
>>> d.insert('w')
>>> d.insert('o')
>>> d.insert('r')
>>> d.insert('l')
>>> d.insert('d')
>>> d.cursor.home()
>>> d.insert("*")
>>> print("".join(d.characters))
hello
*world
```

Now, since we've been using that string `join` function a lot (to concatenate the characters so we can see the actual document contents), we can add a property to the `Document` class to give us the complete string as follows:

```
@property
def string(self):
    return "".join(self.characters)
```

This makes our testing a little simpler:

```
>>> print(d.string)
hello
world
```

This framework is simple to extend, create and edit a complete plain text document (though it might be a bit time consuming!) Now, let's extend it to work for rich text; text that can have **bold**, <u>underlined</u>, or *italic* characters.

There are two ways we could process this. The first is to insert *fake* characters into our character list that act like instructions, such as *bold characters until you find a stop bold character*. The second is to add information to each character, indicating what formatting it should have. While the former method is more common in real editors, we'll implement the latter solution. To do that, we're obviously going to need a class for characters. This class will have an attribute representing the character, as well as three Boolean attributes representing whether it is *bold, italic, or underlined*.

Hmm, wait! Is this `Character` class going to have any methods? If not, maybe we should use one of the many Python data structures instead; a tuple or named tuple would probably be sufficient. Are there any actions that we would want to execute or invoke on a character?

Well, clearly, we might want to do things with characters, such as delete or copy them, but those are things that need to be handled at the `Document` level, since they are really modifying the list of characters. Are there things that need to be done to individual characters?

Actually, now that we're thinking about what a `Character` class actually **is**... what is it? Would it be safe to say that a `Character` class is a string? Maybe we should use an inheritance relationship here? Then we can take advantage of the numerous methods that `str` instances come with.

What sorts of methods are we talking about? There's `startswith`, `strip`, `find`, `lower`, and many more. Most of these methods expect to be working on strings that contain more than one character. In contrast, if `Character` were to subclass `str`, we'd probably be wise to override __init__ to raise an exception if a multi-character string were supplied. Since all those methods we'd get for free wouldn't really apply to our `Character` class, it seems we shouldn't use inheritance, after all.

This brings us back to our original question; should `Character` even be a class? There is a very important special method on the `object` class that we can take advantage of to represent our characters. This method, called __str__ (two underscores at each end, like __init__), is used in string-manipulation functions such as `print` and the `str` constructor to convert any class to a string. The default implementation does some boring stuff, such as printing the name of the module and class, and its address in memory. But if we override it, we can make it print whatever we like.

For our implementation, we could make it prefix characters with special characters to represent whether they are bold, italic, or underlined. So, we will create a class to represent a character, and here it is:

```
class Character:
    def __init__(self, character,
            bold=False, italic=False, underline=False):
        assert len(character) == 1
        self.character = character
        self.bold = bold
        self.italic = italic
        self.underline = underline

    def __str__(self):
        bold = "*" if self.bold else ''
        italic = "/" if self.italic else ''
        underline = "_" if self.underline else ''
        return bold + italic + underline + self.character
```

This class allows us to create characters and prefix them with a special character when the str() function is applied to them. Nothing too exciting there. We only have to make a few minor modifications to the Document and Cursor classes to work with this class. In the Document class, we add these two lines at the beginning of the insert method, as follows:

```
def insert(self, character):
    if not hasattr(character, 'character'):
        character = Character(character)
```

This is a rather strange bit of code. Its basic purpose is to check whether the character being passed in is a Character or a str. If it is a string, it is wrapped in a Character class so all objects in the list are Character objects. However, it is entirely possible that someone using our code would want to use a class that is neither a Character nor a string, using duck typing. If the object has a character attribute, we assume it is a Character-like object. But if it does not, we assume it is a str-like object and wrap it in Character. This helps the program take advantage of duck typing as well as polymorphism; as long as an object has a character attribute, it can be used in the Document class.

This generic check could be very useful. For example, if we wanted to make a programmer's editor with syntax highlighting, we'd need extra data on the character, such as what type of syntax token the character belongs to. Note that, if we are doing a lot of this kind of comparison, it's probably better to implement `Character` as an abstract base class with an appropriate __subclasshook__, as discussed in `Chapter 17`, *When Objects Are Alike*.

In addition, we need to modify the string property on `Document` to accept the new `Character` values. All we need to do is call `str()` on each character before we join it, as demonstrated in the following:

```
@property
def string(self):
    return "".join((str(c) for c in self.characters))
```

This code uses a generator expression, which we'll discuss in `Chapter 21`, *The Iterator Pattern*. It's a shortcut to perform a specific action on all the objects in a sequence.

Finally, we also need to check `Character.character`, instead of just the string character we were storing before, in the `home` and `end` functions when we're looking to see whether it matches a newline character, as demonstrated in the following:

```
def home(self):
    while self.document.characters[
            self.position-1].character != '\n':
        self.position -= 1
        if self.position == 0:
            # Got to beginning of file before newline
            break

def end(self):
    while self.position < len(
            self.document.characters) and \
            self.document.characters[
                    self.position
                    ].character != '\n':
        self.position += 1
```

This completes the formatting of characters. We can test it to see that it works as follows:

```
>>> d = Document()
>>> d.insert('h')
>>> d.insert('e')
>>> d.insert(Character('l', bold=True))
>>> d.insert(Character('l', bold=True))
>>> d.insert('o')
>>> d.insert('\n')
>>> d.insert(Character('w', italic=True))
>>> d.insert(Character('o', italic=True))
>>> d.insert(Character('r', underline=True))
>>> d.insert('l')
>>> d.insert('d')
>>> print(d.string)
he*l*lo
/w/o_rld
>>> d.cursor.home()
>>> d.delete()
>>> d.insert('W')
>>> print(d.string)
he*l*lo
W/o_rld
>>> d.characters[0].underline = True
>>> print(d.string)
_he*l*lo
W/o_rld
```

As expected, whenever we print the string, each bold character is preceded by a *
character, each italicized character by a / character, and each underlined character by
a _ character. All our functions seem to work, and we can modify characters in the list
after the fact. We have a working rich text document object that could be plugged into
a proper graphical user interface and hooked up with a keyboard for input and a
screen for output. Naturally, we'd want to display real *bold, italic, and underlined* fonts
in a UI, instead of using our __str__ method, but it was sufficient for the basic
testing we demanded of it.

# Exercises

We've looked at various ways that objects, data, and methods can interact with each other in an object-oriented Python program. As usual, your first thoughts should be how you can apply these principles to your own work. Do you have any messy scripts lying around that could be rewritten using an object-oriented manager? Look through some of your old code and look for methods that are not actions. If the name isn't a verb, try rewriting it as a property.

Think about code you've written in any language. Does it break the DRY principle? Is there any duplicate code? Did you copy and paste code? Did you write two versions of similar pieces of code because you didn't feel like understanding the original code? Go back over some of your recent code now and see whether you can refactor the duplicate code using inheritance or composition. Try to pick a project you're still interested in maintaining; not code so old that you never want to touch it again. That will help to keep you interested when you do the improvements!

Now, look back over some of the examples we looked at in this chapter. Start with the cached web page example that uses a property to cache the retrieved data. An obvious problem with this example is that the cache is never refreshed. Add a timeout to the property's getter, and only return the cached page if the page has been requested before the timeout has expired. You can use the `time` module (`time.time() - an_old_time` returns the number of seconds that have elapsed since `an_old_time`) to determine whether the cache has expired.

Also look at the inheritance-based `ZipProcessor`. It might be reasonable to use composition instead of inheritance here. Instead of extending the class in the `ZipReplace` and `ScaleZip` classes, you could pass instances of those classes into the `ZipProcessor` constructor and call them to do the processing part. Implement this.

Which version do you find easier to use? Which is more elegant? What is easier to read? These are subjective questions; the answer varies for each of us. Knowing the answer, however, is important. If you find you prefer inheritance over composition, you need to pay attention that you don't overuse inheritance in your daily coding. If you prefer composition, make sure you don't miss opportunities to create an elegant inheritance-based solution.

Finally, add some error handlers to the various classes we created in the case study. They should ensure single characters are entered, that you don't try to move the cursor past the end or beginning of the file, that you don't delete a character that doesn't exist, and that you don't save a file without a filename. Try to think of as many edge cases as you can, and account for them (thinking about edge cases is about 90% of a professional programmer's job!). Consider different ways to handle them; should you raise an exception when the user tries to move past the end of the file, or just stay on the last character?

In your daily coding, pay attention to the **copy** and **paste** commands. Every time you use them in your editor, consider whether it would be a good idea to improve your program's organization so that you only have one version of the code you are about to copy.

# Summary

In this chapter, we focused on identifying objects, especially objects that are not immediately apparent; objects that manage and control. Objects should have both data and behaviors, but properties can be used to blur the distinction between the two. The DRY principle is an important indicator of code quality, and inheritance and composition can be applied to reduce code duplication.

In the next chapter, we'll discuss how to integrate the object-oriented and not-so-object-oriented aspects of Python. Along the way, we'll discover that it's more object-oriented than it looks at first sight!

# 20
# Python Object-Oriented Shortcuts

There are many aspects of Python that appear more reminiscent of structural or functional programming than object-oriented programming. Although object-oriented programming has been the most visible paradigm of the past two decades, the old models have seen a recent resurgence. As with Python's data structures, most of these tools are syntactic sugar over an underlying object-oriented implementation; we can think of them as a further abstraction layer built on top of the (already abstracted) object-oriented paradigm. In this chapter, we'll be covering a grab bag of Python features that are not strictly object-oriented:

- Built-in functions that take care of common tasks in one call
- File I/O and context managers
- An alternative to method overloading
- Functions as objects

# Python built-in functions

There are numerous functions in Python that perform a task or calculate a result on certain types of objects without being methods on the underlying class. They usually abstract common calculations that apply to multiple types of classes. This is duck typing at its best; these functions accept objects that have certain attributes or methods, and are able to perform generic operations using those methods. We've used many of the built-in functions already, but let's quickly go through the important ones and pick up a few neat tricks along the way.

## The len() function

The simplest example is the `len()` function, which counts the number of items in some kind of container object, such as a dictionary or list. You've seen it before, demonstrated as follows::

```
>>> len([1,2,3,4])
4
```

You may wonder why these objects don't have a length property instead of having to call a function on them. Technically, they do. Most objects that `len()` will apply to have a method called `__len__()` that returns the same value. So `len(myobj)` seems to call `myobj.__len__()`.

Why should we use the `len()` function instead of the `__len__` method? Obviously, `__len__` is a special double-underscore method, suggesting that we shouldn't call it directly. There must be an explanation for this. The Python developers don't make such design decisions lightly.

The main reason is efficiency. When we call `__len__` on an object, the object has to look the method up in its namespace, and, if the special `__getattribute__` method (which is called every time an attribute or method on an object is accessed) is defined on that object, it has to be called as well. Furthermore, the `__getattribute__` for that particular method may have been written to do something nasty, such as refusing to give us access to special methods such as `__len__`! The `len()` function doesn't encounter any of this. It actually calls the `__len__` function on the underlying class, so `len(myobj)` maps to `MyObj.__len__(myobj)`.

Another reason is maintainability. In the future, Python developers may want to change len() so that it can calculate the length of objects that don't have __len__, for example, by counting the number of items returned in an iterator. They'll only have to change one function instead of countless __len__ methods in many objects across the board.

There is one other extremely important and often overlooked reason for len() being an external function: backward compatibility. This is often cited in articles as *for historical reasons*, which is a mildly dismissive phrase that an author will use to say something is the way it is because a mistake was made long ago and we're stuck with it. Strictly speaking, len() isn't a mistake, it's a design decision, but that decision was made in a less object-oriented time. It has stood the test of time and has some benefits, so do get used to it.

# Reversed

The reversed() function takes any sequence as input, and returns a copy of that sequence in reverse order. It is normally used in for loops when we want to loop over items from back to front.

Similar to len, reversed calls the __reversed__() function on the class for the parameter. If that method does not exist, reversed builds the reversed sequence itself using calls to __len__ and __getitem__, which are used to define a sequence. We only need to override __reversed__ if we want to somehow customize or optimize the process, as demonstrated in the following code:

```
normal_list = [1, 2, 3, 4, 5]


class CustomSequence:
    def __len__(self):
        return 5

    def __getitem__(self, index):
        return f"x{index}"


class FunkyBackwards:
    def __reversed__(self):
        return "BACKWARDS!"


for seq in normal_list, CustomSequence(), FunkyBackwards():
```

```
print(f"\n{seq.__class__.__name__}: ", end="")
for item in reversed(seq):
    print(item, end=", ")
```

The `for` loops at the end print reversed versions of a normal list, and instances of the two custom sequences. The output shows that `reversed` works on all three of them, but has very different results when we define __reversed__ ourselves:

```
list: 5, 4, 3, 2, 1,
CustomSequence: x4, x3, x2, x1, x0,
FunkyBackwards: B, A, C, K, W, A, R, D, S, !,
```

When we reverse `CustomSequence`, the __getitem__ method is called for each item, which just inserts an x before the index. For `FunkyBackwards`, the __reversed__ method returns a string, each character of which is output individually in the `for` loop.

 The preceding two classes aren't very good sequences, as they don't define a proper version of __iter__, so a forward `for` loop over them would never end.

# Enumerate

Sometimes, when we're looping over a container in a `for` loop, we want access to the index (the current position in the list) of the current item being processed. The `for` loop doesn't provide us with indexes, but the `enumerate` function gives us something better: it creates a sequence of tuples, where the first object in each tuple is the index and the second is the original item.

This is useful if we need to use index numbers directly. Consider some simple code that outputs each of the lines in a file with line numbers:

```
import sys

filename = sys.argv[1]

with open(filename) as file:
    for index, line in enumerate(file):
        print(f"{index+1}: {line}", end="")
```

Running this code using its own filename as the input file shows how it works:

```
1: import sys
2:
3: filename = sys.argv[1]
4:
5: with open(filename) as file:
6:     for index, line in enumerate(file):
7:         print(f"{index+1}: {line}", end="")
```

The `enumerate` function returns a sequence of tuples, our `for` loop splits each tuple into two values, and the `print` statement formats them together. It adds one to the index for each line number, since `enumerate`, like all sequences, is zero-based.

We've only touched on a few of the more important Python built-in functions. As you can see, many of them call into object-oriented concepts, while others subscribe to purely functional or procedural paradigms. There are numerous others in the standard library; some of the more interesting ones include the following:

- `all` and `any`, which accept an iterable object and return `True` if all, or any, of the items evaluate to true (such as a non-empty string or list, a non-zero number, an object that is not `None`, or the literal `True`).
- `eval`, `exec`, and `compile`, which execute string as code inside the interpreter. Be careful with these ones; they are not safe, so don't execute code an unknown user has supplied to you (in general, assume all unknown users are malicious, foolish, or both).
- `hasattr`, `getattr`, `setattr`, and `delattr`, which allow attributes on an object to be manipulated by their string names.
- `zip`, which takes two or more sequences and returns a new sequence of tuples, where each tuple contains a single value from each sequence.
- And many more! See the interpreter help documentation for each of the functions listed in `dir(__builtins__)`.

# File I/O

Our examples so far that have touched the filesystem have operated entirely on text files without much thought as to what is going on under the hood. Operating systems, however, actually represent files as a sequence of bytes, not text. Reading textual data from a file is a fairly involved process. Python, especially Python 3, takes care of most of this work for us behind the scenes. Aren't we lucky?!

The concept of files has been around since long before anyone coined the term *object-oriented programming*. However, Python has wrapped the interface that operating systems provide in a sweet abstraction that allows us to work with file (or file-like, vis-à-vis duck typing) objects.

The `open()` built-in function is used to open a file and return a file object. For reading text from a file, we only need to pass the name of the file into the function. The file will be opened for reading, and the bytes will be converted to text using the platform default encoding.

Of course, we don't always want to read files; often we want to write data to them! To open a file for writing, we need to pass a `mode` argument as the second positional argument, with a value of `"w"`:

```
contents = "Some file contents"
file = open("filename", "w")
file.write(contents)
file.close()
```

We could also supply the value `"a"` as a mode argument, to append to the end of the file, rather than completely overwriting existing file content.

These files with built-in wrappers for converting bytes to text are great, but it'd be awfully inconvenient if the file we wanted to open was an image, executable, or other binary file, wouldn't it?

To open a binary file, we modify the mode string to append `'b'`. So, `'wb'` would open a file for writing bytes, while `'rb'` allows us to read them. They will behave like text files, but without the automatic encoding of text to bytes. When we read such a file, it will return `bytes` objects instead of `str`, and when we write to it, it will fail if we try to pass a text object.

These mode strings for controlling how files are opened are rather cryptic and are neither Pythonic nor object-oriented. However, they are consistent with virtually every other programming language out there. File I/O is one of the fundamental jobs an operating system has to handle, and all programming languages have to talk to the operating system using the same system calls. Just be glad that Python returns a file object with useful methods instead of the integer that most major operating systems use to identify a file handle!

Once a file is opened for reading, we can call the `read`, `readline`, or `readlines` methods to get the contents of the file. The `read` method returns the entire contents of the file as a `str` or `bytes` object, depending on whether there is `'b'` in the mode. Be careful not to use this method without arguments on huge files. You don't want to find out what happens if you try to load that much data into memory!

It is also possible to read a fixed number of bytes from a file; we pass an integer argument to the `read` method, describing how many bytes we want to read. The next call to `read` will load the next sequence of bytes, and so on. We can do this inside a `while` loop to read the entire file in manageable chunks.

The `readline` method returns a single line from the file (where each line ends in a newline, a carriage return, or both, depending on the operating system on which the file was created). We can call it repeatedly to get additional lines. The plural `readlines` method returns a list of all the lines in the file. Like the `read` method, it's not safe to use on very large files. These two methods even work when the file is open in `bytes` mode, but it only makes sense if we are parsing text-like data that has newlines at reasonable positions. An image or audio file, for example, will not have newline characters in it (unless the newline byte happened to represent a certain pixel or sound), so applying `readline` wouldn't make sense.

For readability, and to avoid reading a large file into memory at once, it is often better to use a `for` loop directly on a file object. For text files, it will read each line, one at a time, and we can process it inside the loop body. For binary files, it's better to read fixed-sized chunks of data using the `read()` method, passing a parameter for the maximum number of bytes to read.

Writing to a file is just as easy; the `write` method on file objects writes a string (or bytes, for binary data) object to the file. It can be called repeatedly to write multiple strings, one after the other. The `writelines` method accepts a sequence of strings and writes each of the iterated values to the file. The `writelines` method does *not* append a new line after each item in the sequence. It is basically a poorly named convenience function to write the contents of a sequence of strings without having to explicitly iterate over it using a `for` loop.

Lastly, and I do mean lastly, we come to the `close` method. This method should be called when we are finished reading or writing the file, to ensure any buffered writes are written to the disk, that the file has been properly cleaned up, and that all resources associated with the file are released back to the operating system. Technically, this will happen automatically when the script exits, but it's better to be explicit and clean up after ourselves, especially in long-running processes.

# Placing it in context

The need to close files when we are finished with them can make our code quite ugly. Because an exception may occur at any time during file I/O, we ought to wrap all calls to a file in a try...finally clause. The file should be closed in the finally clause, regardless of whether I/O was successful. This isn't very Pythonic. Of course, there is a more elegant way to do it.

If we run dir on a file-like object, we see that it has two special methods named __enter__ and __exit__. These methods turn the file object into what is known as a **context manager**. Basically, if we use a special syntax called the with statement, these methods will be called before and after nested code is executed. On file objects, the __exit__ method ensures the file is closed, even if an exception is raised. We no longer have to explicitly manage the closing of the file. Here is what the with statement looks like in practice:

```
with open('filename') as file:
    for line in file:
        print(line, end='')
```

The open call returns a file object, which has __enter__ and __exit__ methods. The returned object is assigned to the variable named file by the as clause. We know the file will be closed when the code returns to the outer indentation level, and that this will happen even if an exception is raised.

The with statement is used in several places in the standard library, where start up or cleanup code needs to be executed. For example, the urlopen call returns an object that can be used in a with statement to clean up the socket when we're done. Locks in the threading module can automatically release the lock when the statement has been executed.

Most interestingly, because the with statement can apply to any object that has the appropriate special methods, we can use it in our own frameworks. For example, remember that strings are immutable, but sometimes you need to build a string from multiple parts. For efficiency, this is usually done by storing the component strings in a list and joining them at the end. Let's create a simple context manager that allows us to construct a sequence of characters and automatically convert it to a string upon exit:

```
class StringJoiner(list):
    def __enter__(self):
        return self
```

```
def __exit__(self, type, value, tb):
    self.result = "".join(self)
```

This code adds the two special methods required of a context manager to the `list` class it inherits from. The `__enter__` method performs any required setup code (in this case, there isn't any) and then returns the object that will be assigned to the variable after `as` in the `with` statement. Often, as we've done here, this is just the context manager object itself. The `__exit__` method accepts three arguments. In a normal situation, these are all given a value of `None`. However, if an exception occurs inside the `with` block, they will be set to values related to the type, value, and traceback for the exception. This allows the `__exit__` method to perform any cleanup code that may be required, even if an exception occurred. In our example, we take the irresponsible path and create a result string by joining the characters in the string, regardless of whether an exception was thrown.

While this is one of the simplest context managers we could write, and its usefulness is dubious, it does work with a `with` statement. Have a look at it in action:

```
import random, string
with StringJoiner() as joiner:
    for i in range(15):
        joiner.append(random.choice(string.ascii_letters))

print(joiner.result)
```

This code constructs a string of 15 random characters. It appends these to a `StringJoiner` using the `append` method it inherited from `list`. When the `with` statement goes out of scope (back to the outer indentation level), the `__exit__` method is called, and the `result` attribute becomes available on the joiner object. We then print this value to see a random string.

# An alternative to method overloading

One prominent feature of many object-oriented programming languages is a tool called **method overloading**. Method overloading simply refers to having multiple methods with the same name that accept different sets of arguments. In statically typed languages, this is useful if we want to have a method that accepts either an integer or a string, for example. In non-object-oriented languages, we might need two functions, called `add_s` and `add_i`, to accommodate such situations. In statically typed object-oriented languages, we'd need two methods, both called `add`, one that accepts strings, and one that accepts integers.

In Python, we've already seen that we only need one method, which accepts any type of object. It may have to do some testing on the object type (for example, if it is a string, convert it to an integer), but only one method is required.

However, method overloading is also useful when we want a method with the same name to accept different numbers or sets of arguments. For example, an email message method might come in two versions, one of which accepts an argument for the *from* email address. The other method might look up a default *from* email address instead. Python doesn't permit multiple methods with the same name, but it does provide a different, equally flexible, interface.

We've seen some of the possible ways to send arguments to methods and functions in previous examples, but now we'll cover all the details. The simplest function accepts no arguments. We probably don't need an example, but here's one for completeness:

```
def no_args():
    pass
```

And here's how it's called:

```
no_args()
```

A function that does accept arguments will provide the names of those arguments in a comma-separated list. Only the name of each argument needs to be supplied.

When calling the function, these positional arguments must be specified in order, and none can be missed or skipped. This is the most common way in which we've specified arguments in our previous examples:

```
def mandatory_args(x, y, z):
    pass
```

To call it, type the following::

```
mandatory_args("a string", a_variable, 5)
```

Any type of object can be passed as an argument: an object, a container, a primitive, even functions and classes. The preceding call shows a hardcoded string, an unknown variable, and an integer passed into the function.

# Default arguments

If we want to make an argument optional, rather than creating a second method with a different set of arguments, we can specify a default value in a single method, using an equals sign. If the calling code does not supply this argument, it will be assigned a default value. However, the calling code can still choose to override the default by passing in a different value. Often, a default value of None, or an empty string or list, is suitable.

Here's a function definition with default arguments:

```
def default_arguments(x, y, z, a="Some String", b=False):
    pass
```

The first three arguments are still mandatory and must be passed by the calling code. The last two parameters have default arguments supplied.

There are several ways we can call this function. We can supply all arguments in order, as though all the arguments were positional arguments, as can be seen in the following::

```
default_arguments("a string", variable, 8, "", True)
```

Alternatively, we can supply just the mandatory arguments in order, leaving the keyword arguments to be assigned their default values:

```
default_arguments("a longer string", some_variable, 14)
```

We can also use the equals sign syntax when calling a function to provide values in a different order, or to skip default values that we aren't interested in. For example, we can skip the first keyword arguments and supply the second one:

```
default_arguments("a string", variable, 14, b=True)
```

Surprisingly, we can even use the equals sign syntax to mix up the order of positional arguments, so long as all of them are supplied:

```
>>> default_arguments(y=1,z=2,x=3,a="hi")
3 1 2 hi False
```

You may occasionally find it useful to make a *keyword-only* argument, that is, an argument that must be supplied as a keyword argument. You can do that by placing a * before the keyword-only arguments:

```
def kw_only(x, y='defaultkw', *, a, b='only'):
    print(x, y, a, b)
```

This function has one positional argument, x, and three keyword arguments, y, a, and b. x and y are both mandatory, but a can only be passed as a keyword argument. y and b are both optional with default values, but if b is supplied, it can only be a keyword argument.

This function fails if you don't pass a:

```
>>> kw_only('x')
Traceback (most recent call last):
  File "<stdin>", line 1, in <module>
TypeError: kw_only() missing 1 required keyword-only argument: 'a'
```

It also fails if you pass a as a positional argument:

```
>>> kw_only('x', 'y', 'a')
Traceback (most recent call last):
  File "<stdin>", line 1, in <module>
TypeError: kw_only() takes from 1 to 2 positional arguments but 3 were
given
```

But you can pass a and b as keyword arguments:

```
>>> kw_only('x', a='a', b='b')
x defaultkw a b
```

With so many options, it may seem hard to pick one, but if you think of the positional arguments as an ordered list, and keyword arguments as sort of like a dictionary, you'll find that the correct layout tends to fall into place. If you need to require the caller to specify an argument, make it mandatory; if you have a sensible default, then make it a keyword argument. Choosing how to call the method normally takes care of itself, depending on which values need to be supplied, and which can be left at their defaults. Keyword-only arguments are relatively rare, but when the use case comes up, they can make for a more elegant API.

One thing to take note of with keyword arguments is that anything we provide as a default argument is evaluated when the function is first interpreted, not when it is called. This means we can't have dynamically generated default values. For example, the following code won't behave quite as expected:

```
number = 5
def funky_function(number=number):
    print(number)

number=6
funky_function(8)
funky_function()
```

```
print(number)
```

If we run this code, it outputs the number 8 first, but then it outputs the number 5 for
the call with no arguments. We had set the variable to the number 6, as evidenced by
the last line of output, but when the function is called, the number 5 is printed; the
default value was calculated when the function was defined, not when it was called.

This is tricky with empty containers such as lists, sets, and dictionaries. For example,
it is common to ask calling code to supply a list that our function is going to
manipulate, but the list is optional. We'd like to make an empty list as a default
argument. We can't do this; it will create only one list, when the code is first
constructed, demonstrated as follows::

```
//DON'T DO THIS
>>> def hello(b=[]):
...         b.append('a')
...         print(b)
...
>>> hello()
['a']
>>> hello()
['a', 'a']
```

Whoops, that's not quite what we expected! The usual way to get around this is to
make the default value `None`, and then use the `iargument = argument if
argument else []` idiom inside the method. Pay close attention!

# Variable argument lists

Default values alone do not allow us all the flexible benefits of method overloading.
One thing that makes Python really slick is the ability to write methods that accept an
arbitrary number of positional or keyword arguments without explicitly naming
them. We can also pass arbitrary lists and dictionaries into such functions.

For example, a function to accept a link or list of links and download the web pages
could use such variadic arguments, or **varargs**. Instead of accepting a single value
that is expected to be a list of links, we can accept an arbitrary number of arguments,
where each argument is a different link. We do this by specifying the * operator in the
function definition, as follows:

```
def get_pages(*links):
    for link in links:
        #download the link with urllib
        print(link)
```

The *links parameter says, *I'll accept any number of arguments and put them all in a list named* links. If we supply only one argument, it'll be a list with one element; if we supply no arguments, it'll be an empty list. Thus, all these function calls are valid:

```
get_pages()
get_pages('http://www.archlinux.org')
get_pages('http://www.archlinux.org',
        'http://ccphillips.net/')
```

We can also accept arbitrary keyword arguments. These arrive in the function as a dictionary. They are specified with two asterisks (as in **kwargs) in the function declaration. This tool is commonly used in configuration setups. The following class allows us to specify a set of options with default values:

```
class Options:
    default_options = {
            'port': 21,
            'host': 'localhost',
            'username': None,
            'password': None,
            'debug': False,
            }
    def __init__(self, **kwargs):
        self.options = dict(Options.default_options)
        self.options.update(kwargs)

    def __getitem__(self, key):
        return self.options[key]
```

All the interesting stuff in this class happens in the __init__ method. We have a dictionary of default options and values at the class level. The first thing the __init__ method does is make a copy of this dictionary. We do that instead of modifying the dictionary directly, in case we instantiate two separate sets of options. (Remember, class-level variables are shared between instances of the class.) Then, __init__ uses the update method on the new dictionary to change any non-default values to those supplied as keyword arguments. The __getitem__ method simply allows us to use the new class using indexing syntax. Here's a session demonstrating the class in action:

```
>>> options = Options(username="dusty", password="drowssap",
        debug=True)
>>> options['debug']
True
>>> options['port']
21
>>> options['username']
```

```
'dusty'
```

We're able to access our `options` instance using dictionary indexing syntax, and the dictionary includes both default values and the ones we set using keyword arguments.

The keyword argument syntax can be dangerous, as it may break the *explicit is better than implicit* rule. In the preceding example, it's possible to pass arbitrary keyword arguments to the `Options` initializer to represent options that don't exist in the default dictionary. This may not be a bad thing, depending on the purpose of the class, but it makes it hard for someone using the class to discover what valid options are available. It also makes it easy to enter a confusing typo (*Debug* instead of *debug*, for example) that adds two options where only one should have existed.

Keyword arguments are also very useful when we need to accept arbitrary arguments to pass to a second function, but we don't know what those arguments will be. We saw this in action in `Chapter 17`, *When Objects Are Alike*, when we were building support for multiple inheritance. We can, of course, combine the variable argument and variable keyword argument syntax in one function call, and we can use normal positional and default arguments as well. The following example is somewhat contrived, but demonstrates the four types in action:

```
import shutil
import os.path


def augmented_move(
    target_folder, *filenames, verbose=False, **specific
):
    """Move all filenames into the target_folder, allowing
    specific treatment of certain files."""

    def print_verbose(message, filename):
        """print the message only if verbose is enabled"""
        if verbose:
            print(message.format(filename))

    for filename in filenames:
        target_path = os.path.join(target_folder, filename)
        if filename in specific:
            if specific[filename] == "ignore":
                print_verbose("Ignoring {0}", filename)
            elif specific[filename] == "copy":
                print_verbose("Copying {0}", filename)
                shutil.copyfile(filename, target_path)
        else:
```

```
print_verbose("Moving {0}", filename)
shutil.move(filename, target_path)
```

This example processes an arbitrary list of files. The first argument is a target folder, and the default behavior is to move all remaining non-keyword argument files into that folder. Then there is a keyword-only argument, verbose, which tells us whether to print information on each file processed. Finally, we can supply a dictionary containing actions to perform on specific filenames; the default behavior is to move the file, but if a valid string action has been specified in the keyword arguments, it can be ignored or copied instead. Notice the ordering of the parameters in the function; first, the positional argument is specified, then the *filenames list, then any specific keyword-only arguments, and finally, a **specific dictionary to hold remaining keyword arguments.

We create an inner helper function, print_verbose, which will print messages only if the verbose key has been set. This function keeps code readable by encapsulating this functionality in a single location.

In common cases, assuming the files in question exist, this function could be called as follows:

```
>>> augmented_move("move_here", "one", "two")
```

This command would move the files one and two into the move_here directory, assuming they exist (there's no error checking or exception handling in the function, so it would fail spectacularly if the files or target directory didn't exist). The move would occur without any output, since verbose is False by default.

If we want to see the output, we can call it with the help of the following command:

```
>>> augmented_move("move_here", "three", verbose=True)
Moving three
```

This moves one file named three, and tells us what it's doing. Notice that it is impossible to specify verbose as a positional argument in this example; we must pass a keyword argument. Otherwise, Python would think it was another filename in the *filenames list.

If we want to copy or ignore some of the files in the list, instead of moving them, we can pass additional keyword arguments, as follows:

```
>>> augmented_move("move_here", "four", "five", "six",
        four="copy", five="ignore")
```

This will move the sixth file and copy the fourth, but won't display any output, since we didn't specify `verbose`. Of course, we can do that too, and keyword arguments can be supplied in any order, demonstrated as follows:

```
>>> augmented_move("move_here", "seven", "eight", "nine",
        seven="copy", verbose=True, eight="ignore")
Copying seven
Ignoring eight
Moving nine
```

# Unpacking arguments

There's one more nifty trick involving variable arguments and keyword arguments. We've used it in some of our previous examples, but it's never too late for an explanation. Given a list or dictionary of values, we can pass those values into a function as if they were normal positional or keyword arguments. Have a look at this code:

```
def show_args(arg1, arg2, arg3="THREE"):
    print(arg1, arg2, arg3)

some_args = range(3)
more_args = {
        "arg1": "ONE",
        "arg2": "TWO"}

print("Unpacking a sequence:", end=" ")

show_args(*some_args)
print("Unpacking a dict:", end=" ")

show_args(**more_args)
```

Here's what it looks like when we run it:

```
Unpacking a sequence: 0 1 2
Unpacking a dict: ONE TWO THREE
```

The function accepts three arguments, one of which has a default value. But when we have a list of three arguments, we can use the * operator inside a function call to unpack it into the three arguments. If we have a dictionary of arguments, we can use the ** syntax to unpack it as a collection of keyword arguments.

This is most often useful when mapping information that has been collected from user input or from an outside source (for example, an internet page or a text file) to a function or method call.

Remember our earlier example that used headers and lines in a text file to create a list of dictionaries with contact information? Instead of just adding the dictionaries to a list, we could use keyword unpacking to pass the arguments to the __init__ method on a specially built Contact object that accepts the same set of arguments. See if you can adapt the example to make this work.

This unpacking syntax can be used in some areas outside of function calls, too. The Options class earlier had an __init__ method that looked like this:

```python
def __init__(self, **kwargs):
    self.options = dict(Options.default_options)
    self.options.update(kwargs)
```

An even more succinct way to do this would be to unpack the two dictionaries like this:

```python
def __init__(self, **kwargs):
    self.options = {**Options.default_options, **kwargs}
```

Because the dictionaries are unpacked in order from left to right, the resulting dictionary will contain all the default options, with any of the kwarg options replacing some of the keys. Here's an example:

```python
>>> x = {'a': 1, 'b': 2}
>>> y = {'b': 11, 'c': 3}
>>> z = {**x, **y}
>>> z
{'a': 1, 'b': 11, 'c': 3}
```

# Functions are objects too

Programming languages that overemphasize object-oriented principles tend to frown on functions that are not methods. In such languages, you're expected to create an object to sort of wrap the single method involved. There are numerous situations where we'd like to pass around a small object that is simply called to perform an action. This is most frequently done in event-driven programming, such as graphical toolkits or asynchronous servers; we'll see some design patterns that use it in Chapter 22, *Python Design Patterns I*, and Chapter 23, *Python Design Patterns II*.

In Python, we don't need to wrap such methods in an object because functions already are objects! We can set attributes on functions (though this isn't a common activity), and we can pass them around to be called at a later date. They even have a few special properties that can be accessed directly. Here's yet another contrived example:

```python
def my_function():
    print("The Function Was Called")


my_function.description = "A silly function"


def second_function():
    print("The second was called")


second_function.description = "A sillier function."


def another_function(function):
    print("The description:", end=" ")
    print(function.description)
    print("The name:", end=" ")
    print(function.__name__)
    print("The class:", end=" ")
    print(function.__class__)
    print("Now I'll call the function passed in")
    function()


another_function(my_function)
another_function(second_function)
```

If we run this code, we can see that we were able to pass two different functions into our third function, and get different output for each one:

```
The description: A silly function
The name: my_function
The class: <class 'function'>
Now I'll call the function passed in
The Function Was Called
The description: A sillier function.
The name: second_function
The class: <class 'function'>
Now I'll call the function passed in
The second was called
```

We set an attribute on the function, named description (not very good descriptions, admittedly). We were also able to see the function's \_\_name\_\_ attribute, and to access its class, demonstrating that the function really is an object with attributes. Then, we called the function by using the callable syntax (the parentheses).

The fact that functions are top-level objects is most often used to pass them around to be executed at a later date, for example, when a certain condition has been satisfied. Let's build an event-driven timer that does just this:

```python
import datetime
import time


class TimedEvent:
    def __init__(self, endtime, callback):
        self.endtime = endtime
        self.callback = callback

    def ready(self):
        return self.endtime <= datetime.datetime.now()


class Timer:
    def __init__(self):
        self.events = []

    def call_after(self, delay, callback):
        end_time = datetime.datetime.now() + datetime.timedelta(
            seconds=delay
        )

        self.events.append(TimedEvent(end_time, callback))

    def run(self):
        while True:
            ready_events = (e for e in self.events if e.ready())
            for event in ready_events:
                event.callback(self)
                self.events.remove(event)
            time.sleep(0.5)
```

In production, this code should definitely have extra documentation using docstrings! The call_after method should at least mention that the delay parameter is in seconds, and that the callback function should accept one argument: the timer doing the calling.

We have two classes here. The `TimedEvent` class is not really meant to be accessed by other classes; all it does is store `endtime` and `callback`. We could even use a `tuple` or `namedtuple` here, but as it is convenient to give the object a behavior that tells us whether or not the event is ready to run, we use a class instead.

The `Timer` class simply stores a list of upcoming events. It has a `call_after` method to add a new event. This method accepts a `delay` parameter representing the number of seconds to wait before executing the callback, and the `callback` function itself: a function to be executed at the correct time. This `callback` function should accept one argument.

The `run` method is very simple; it uses a generator expression to filter out any events whose time has come, and executes them in order. The *timer* loop then continues indefinitely, so it has to be interrupted with a keyboard interrupt (*Ctrl + C*, or *Ctrl + Break*). We sleep for half a second after each iteration so as to not grind the system to a halt.

The important things to note here are the lines that touch callback functions. The function is passed around like any other object and the timer never knows or cares what the original name of the function is or where it was defined. When it's time to call the function, the timer simply applies the parenthesis syntax to the stored variable.

Here's a set of callbacks that test the timer:

```python
def format_time(message, *args):
    now = datetime.datetime.now()
    print(f"{now:%I:%M:%S}: {message}")


def one(timer):
    format_time("Called One")


def two(timer):
    format_time("Called Two")


def three(timer):
    format_time("Called Three")


class Repeater:
    def __init__(self):
        self.count = 0
```

```
        def repeater(self, timer):
            format_time(f"repeat {self.count}")
            self.count += 1
            timer.call_after(5, self.repeater)


timer = Timer()
timer.call_after(1, one)
timer.call_after(2, one)
timer.call_after(2, two)
timer.call_after(4, two)
timer.call_after(3, three)
timer.call_after(6, three)
repeater = Repeater()
timer.call_after(5, repeater.repeater)
format_time("Starting")
timer.run()
```

This example allows us to see how multiple callbacks interact with the timer. The first function is the `format_time` function. It uses the format string syntax to add the current time to the message; we'll read about them in the next chapter. Next, we create three simple callback methods that simply output the current time and a short message telling us which callback has been fired.

The `Repeater` class demonstrates that methods can be used as callbacks too, since they are really just functions that happen to be bound to an object. It also shows why the `timer` argument to the callback functions is useful: we can add a new timed event to the timer from inside a presently running callback. We then create a timer and add several events to it that are called after different amounts of time. Finally, we start the timer running; the output shows that events are run in the expected order:

```
02:53:35: Starting
02:53:36: Called One
02:53:37: Called One
02:53:37: Called Two
02:53:38: Called Three
02:53:39: Called Two
02:53:40: repeat 0
02:53:41: Called Three
02:53:45: repeat 1
02:53:50: repeat 2
02:53:55: repeat 3
02:54:00: repeat 4
```

Python 3.4 introduced a generic event loop architecture similar to this.

# Using functions as attributes

One of the interesting effects of functions being objects is that they can be set as callable attributes on other objects. It is possible to add or change a function to an instantiated object, demonstrated as follows:

```
class A:
    def print(self):
        print("my class is A")

def fake_print():
    print("my class is not A")

a = A()
a.print()
a.print = fake_print
a.print()
```

This code creates a very simple class with a `print` method that doesn't tell us anything we didn't know. Then, we create a new function that tells us something we don't believe.

When we call `print` on an instance of the A class, it behaves as expected. If we then set the `print` method to point at a new function, it tells us something different:

```
my class is A
my class is not A
```

It is also possible to replace methods on classes instead of objects, although, in that case, we have to add the `self` argument to the parameter list. This will change the method for all instances of that object, even ones that have already been instantiated. Obviously, replacing methods like this can be both dangerous and confusing to maintain. Somebody reading the code will see that a method has been called and look up that method on the original class. But the method on the original class is not the one that was called. Figuring out what really happened can become a tricky, frustrating debugging session.

It does have its uses though. Often, replacing or adding methods at runtime (called **monkey patching**) is used in automated testing. If testing a client-server application, we may not want to actually connect to the server while testing the client; this may result in accidental transfers of funds or embarrassing test emails being sent to real people. Instead, we can set up our test code to replace some of the key methods on the object that sends requests to the server so that it only records that the methods have been called.

Monkey-patching can also be used to fix bugs or add features in third-party code that we are interacting with, and does not behave quite the way we need it to. It should, however, be applied sparingly; it's almost always a *messy hack*. Sometimes, though, it is the only way to adapt an existing library to suit our needs.

# Callable objects

Just as functions are objects that can have attributes set on them, it is possible to create an object that can be called as though it were a function.

Any object can be made callable by simply giving it a \_\_call\_\_ method that accepts the required arguments. Let's make our Repeater class, from the timer example, a little easier to use by making it a callable, as follows:

```python
class Repeater:
    def __init__(self):
        self.count = 0

    def __call__(self, timer):
        format_time(f"repeat {self.count}")
        self.count += 1

        timer.call_after(5, self)

timer = Timer()

timer.call_after(5, Repeater())
format_time("{now}: Starting")
timer.run()
```

This example isn't much different from the earlier class; all we did was change the name of the repeater function to \_\_call\_\_ and pass the object itself as a callable. Note that, when we make the call_after call, we pass the argument Repeater(). Those two parentheses are creating a new instance of the class; they are not explicitly calling the class. This happens later, inside the timer. If we want to execute the \_\_call\_\_ method on a newly instantiated object, we'd use a rather odd syntax: Repeater()(). The first set of parentheses constructs the object; the second set executes the \_\_call\_\_ method. If we find ourselves doing this, we may not be using the correct abstraction. Only implement the \_\_call\_\_ function on an object if the object is meant to be treated like a function.

# Case study

To tie together some of the principles presented in this chapter, let's build a mailing list manager. The manager will keep track of email addresses categorized into named groups. When it's time to send a message, we can pick a group and send the message to all email addresses assigned to that group.

Now, before we start working on this project, we ought to have a safe way to test it, without sending emails to a bunch of real people. Luckily, Python has our back here; like the test HTTP server, it has a built-in **Simple Mail Transfer Protocol (SMTP)** server that we can instruct to capture any messages we send without actually sending them. We can run the server with the following command:

```
$python -m smtpd -n -c DebuggingServer localhost:1025
```

Running this command at command prompt will start an SMTP server running on port 1025 on the local machine. But we've instructed it to use the `DebuggingServer` class (this class comes with the built-in SMTP module), which, instead of sending mails to the intended recipients, simply prints them on the terminal screen as it receives them.

Now, before writing our mailing list, let's write some code that actually sends mail. Of course, Python supports this in the standard library, too, but it's a bit of an odd interface, so we'll write a new function to wrap it all cleanly, as can be seen in the following code snipet:

```python
import smtplib
from email.mime.text import MIMEText


def send_email(
    subject,
    message,
    from_addr,
    *to_addrs,
    host="localhost",
    port=1025,
    **headers
):

    email = MIMEText(message)
    email["Subject"] = subject
    email["From"] = from_addr
    for header, value in headers.items():
        email[header] = value
```

```
sender = smtplib.SMTP(host, port)
for addr in to_addrs:
    del email["To"]
    email["To"] = addr
    sender.sendmail(from_addr, addr, email.as_string())
sender.quit()
```

We won't cover the code inside this method too thoroughly; the documentation in the standard library can give you all the information you need to use the smtplib and email modules effectively.

We've used both variable argument and keyword argument syntax in the function call. The variable argument list allows us to supply a single string in the default case of having a single to address, as well as permitting multiple addresses to be supplied if required. Any extra keyword arguments are mapped to email headers. This is an exciting use of variable arguments and keyword arguments, but it's not really a great interface for the person calling the function. In fact, it makes many things the programmer will want to do impossible.

The headers passed into the function represent auxiliary headers that can be attached to a method. Such headers might include Reply-To, Return-Path, or *X-pretty-much-anything*. But in order to be a valid identifier in Python, a name cannot include the – character. In general, that character represents subtraction. So, it's not possible to call a function with Reply-To=my@email.com. As often happens, it appears we were too eager to use keyword arguments because they are a shiny new tool we just learned.

We'll have to change the argument to a normal dictionary; this will work because any string can be used as a key in a dictionary. By default, we'd want this dictionary to be empty, but we can't make the default parameter an empty dictionary. So, we'll have to make the default argument None, and then set up the dictionary at the beginning of the method, as follows:

```
def send_email(subject, message, from_addr, *to_addrs,
        host="localhost", port=1025, headers=None):

    headers = headers if headers else {}
```

If we have our debugging SMTP server running in one terminal, we can test this code in a Python interpreter:

```
>>> send_email("A model subject", "The message contents",
 "from@example.com", "to1@example.com", "to2@example.com")
```

Then, if we check the output from the debugging SMTP server, we get the following:

```
---------- MESSAGE FOLLOWS ----------
Content-Type: text/plain; charset="us-ascii"
MIME-Version: 1.0
Content-Transfer-Encoding: 7bit
Subject: A model subject
From: from@example.com
To: to1@example.com
X-Peer: 127.0.0.1

The message contents
------------ END MESSAGE ------------
---------- MESSAGE FOLLOWS ----------
Content-Type: text/plain; charset="us-ascii"
MIME-Version: 1.0
Content-Transfer-Encoding: 7bit
Subject: A model subject
From: from@example.com
To: to2@example.com
X-Peer: 127.0.0.1

The message contents
------------ END MESSAGE ------------
```

Excellent, it has *sent* our email to the two expected addresses with subject and message contents included. Now that we can send messages, let's work on the email group management system. We'll need an object that somehow matches email addresses with the groups they are in. Since this is a many-to-many relationship (any one email address can be in multiple groups; any one group can be associated with multiple email addresses), none of the data structures we've studied seem ideal. We could try a dictionary of group names matched to a list of associated email addresses, but that would duplicate email addresses. We could also try a dictionary of email addresses matched to groups, resulting in a duplication of groups. Neither seems optimal. For fun, let's try this latter version, even though intuition tells me the groups to email address solution would be more straightforward.

Since the values in our dictionary will always be collections of unique email addresses, we can store them in a `set` container. We can use `defaultdict` to ensure that there is always a `set` container available for each key, demonstrated as follows:

```python
from collections import defaultdict


class MailingList:
    """Manage groups of e-mail addresses for sending e-mails."""
```

```
def __init__(self):
    self.email_map = defaultdict(set)

def add_to_group(self, email, group):
    self.email_map[email].add(group)
```

Now, let's add a method that allows us to collect all the email addresses in one or more groups. This can be done by converting the list of groups to a set:

```
def emails_in_groups(self, *groups): groups = set(groups) emails =
set() for e, g in self.email_map.items(): if g & groups: emails.add(e)
return emails
```

First, look at what we're iterating over: `self.email_map.items()`. This method, of course, returns a tuple of key-value pairs for each item in the dictionary. The values are sets of strings representing the groups. We split these into two variables named e and g, short for email and groups. We add the email address to the set of return values only if the passed-in groups intersect with the email address groups. The `g&groups` syntax is a shortcut for `g.intersection(groups)`; the set class does this by implementing the special __and__ method to call `intersection`.

> This code could be made a wee bit more concise using a set comprehension, which we'll discuss in `Chapter 21`, *The Iterator Pattern*.

Now, with these building blocks, we can trivially add a method to our `MailingList` class that sends messages to specific groups:

```
def send_mailing(
    self, subject, message, from_addr, *groups, headers=None
):
    emails = self.emails_in_groups(*groups)
    send_email(
        subject, message, from_addr, *emails, headers=headers
    )
```

This function relies on variable argument lists. As input, it takes a list of groups as variable arguments. It gets the list of emails for the specified groups and passes those as variable arguments into `send_email`, along with other arguments that were passed into this method.

The program can be tested by ensuring that the SMTP debugging server is running in one command prompt, and, in a second prompt, loading the code using the following:

```
$python -i mailing_list.py
```

Create a `MailingList` object with the help of the following command:

```
>>> m = MailingList()
```

Then, create a few fake email addresses and groups, along the lines of:

```
>>> m.add_to_group("friend1@example.com", "friends")
>>> m.add_to_group("friend2@example.com", "friends")
>>> m.add_to_group("family1@example.com", "family")
>>> m.add_to_group("pro1@example.com", "professional")
```

Finally, use a command like this to send emails to specific groups:

```
>>> m.send_mailing("A Party",
"Friends and family only: a party", "me@example.com", "friends",
"family", headers={"Reply-To": "me2@example.com"})
```

Emails to each of the addresses in the specified groups should show up in the console on the SMTP server.

The mailing list works fine as it is, but it's kind of useless; as soon as we exit the program, our database of information is lost. Let's modify it to add a couple of methods to load and save the list of email groups from and to a file.

In general, when storing structured data on disk, it is a good idea to put a lot of thought into how it is stored. One of the reasons myriad database systems exist is that if someone else has put this thought into how data is stored, you don't have to. We'll be looking at some data serialization mechanisms in the next chapter, but for this example, let's keep it simple and go with the first solution that could possibly work.

The data format I have in mind is to store each email address followed by a space, followed by a comma-separated list of groups. This format seems reasonable, and we're going to go with it because data formatting isn't the topic of this chapter. However, to illustrate just why you need to think hard about how you format data on disk, let's highlight a few problems with the format.

First, the space character is technically legal in email addresses. Most email providers prohibit it (with good reason), but the specification defining email addresses says an email can contain a space if it is in quotation marks. If we are to use a space as a sentinel in our data format, we should technically be able to differentiate between that space and a space that is part of an email. We're going to pretend this isn't true, for simplicity's sake, but real-life data encoding is full of stupid issues like this.

Second, consider the comma-separated list of groups. What happens if someone decides to put a comma in a group name? If we decide to make commas illegal in group names, we should add validation to enforce such naming in our add_to_group method. For pedagogical clarity, we'll ignore this problem too. Finally, there are many security implications we need to consider: can someone get themselves into the wrong group by putting a fake comma in their email address? What does the parser do if it encounters an invalid file?

The takeaway from this discussion is to try to use a data storage method that has been field tested, rather than designing our own data serialization protocols. There are a ton of bizarre edge cases you might overlook, and it's better to use code that has already encountered and fixed those edge cases.

But forget that. Let's just write some basic code that uses an unhealthy dose of wishful thinking to pretend this simple data format is safe, demonstrated as follows:

```
email1@mydomain.com group1,group2
email2@mydomain.com group2,group3
```

The code to do this is as follows:

```python
def save(self):
    with open(self.data_file, "w") as file:
        for email, groups in self.email_map.items():
            file.write("{} {}\n".format(email, ",".join(groups)))

def load(self):
    self.email_map = defaultdict(set)
    with suppress(IOError):
        with open(self.data_file) as file:
            for line in file:
                email, groups = line.strip().split(" ")
                groups = set(groups.split(","))
                self.email_map[email] = groups
```

In the `save` method, we open the file in a context manager and write the file as a formatted string. Remember the newline character; Python doesn't add that for us. The `load` method first resets the dictionary (in case it contains data from a previous call to `load`). It adds a call to the standard library `suppress` context manager, available as `from contextlib import suppress`. This context manager catches any I/O Errors and ignores them. Not the best error handling, but it's prettier than try...finally...pass.

Then, the load method uses the `for...in` syntax, which loops over each line in the file. Again, the newline character is included in the line variable, so we have to call `.strip()` to take it off. We'll learn more about such string manipulation in the next chapter.

Before using these methods, we need to make sure the object has a `self.data_file` attribute, which can be done by modifying __init__ as follows:

```python
def __init__(self, data_file):
    self.data_file = data_file
    self.email_map = defaultdict(set)
```

We can test these two methods in the interpreter as follows:

```python
>>> m = MailingList('addresses.db')
>>> m.add_to_group('friend1@example.com', 'friends')
>>> m.add_to_group('family1@example.com', 'friends')
>>> m.add_to_group('family1@example.com', 'family')
>>> m.save()
```

The resulting `addresses.db` file contains the following lines, as expected:

```
friend1@example.com friends
family1@example.com friends,family
```

We can also load this data back into a `MailingList` object successfully:

```python
>>> m = MailingList('addresses.db')
>>> m.email_map
defaultdict(<class 'set'>, {})
>>> m.load()
>>> m.email_map
defaultdict(<class 'set'>, {'friend2@example.com': {'friends\n'},
'family1@example.com': {'family\n'}, 'friend1@example.com':
{'friends\n'}})
```

As you can see, I forgot to add the `load` command, and it might be easy to forget the `save` command as well. To make this a little easier for anyone who wants to use our `MailingList` API in their own code, let's provide the methods to support a context manager:

```python
def __enter__(self):
    self.load()
    return self

def __exit__(self, type, value, tb):
    self.save()
```

These simple methods just delegate their work to load and save, but we can now write code like this in the interactive interpreter and know that all the previously stored addresses were loaded on our behalf, and that the whole list will be saved to the file when we are done:

```python
>>> with MailingList('addresses.db') as ml:
...     ml.add_to_group('friend2@example.com', 'friends')
...     ml.send_mailing("What's up", "hey friends, how's it going",
'me@example.com',
    'friends')
```

# Exercises

If you haven't encountered the `with` statements and context managers before, I encourage you, as usual, to go through your old code, find all the places where you were opening files, and make sure they are safely closed using the `with` statement. Look for places to write your own context managers as well. Ugly or repetitive `try...finally` clauses are a good place to start, but you may find them useful any time you need to do before and/or after tasks in context.

You've probably used many of the basic built-in functions before now. We covered several of them, but didn't go into a great deal of detail. Play with `enumerate`, `zip`, `reversed`, `any`, and `all`, until you know you'll remember to use them when they are the right tool for the job. The `enumerate` function is especially important, because not using it results in some pretty ugly `while` loops.

Also explore some applications that pass functions around as callable objects, as well as using the __call__ method to make your own objects callable. You can get the same effect by attaching attributes to functions or by creating a __call__ method on an object. In which case would you use one syntax, and when would it be more suitable to use the other?

Our mailing list object could overwhelm an email server if there is a massive number of emails to be sent out. Try refactoring it so that you can use different send_email functions for different purposes. One such function could be the version we used here. A different version might put the emails in a queue to be sent by a server in a different thread or process. A third version could just output the data to the terminal, obviating the need for a dummy SMTP server. Can you construct the mailing list with a callback such that the send_mailing function uses whatever is passed in? It would default to the current version if no callback is supplied.

The relationship between arguments, keyword arguments, variable arguments, and variable keyword arguments can be a bit confusing. We saw how painfully they can interact when we covered multiple inheritance. Devise some other examples to see how they can work well together, as well as to understand when they don't.

# Summary

We covered a grab bag of topics in this chapter. Each represented an important non-object-oriented feature that is popular in Python. Just because we can use object-oriented principles does not always mean we should!

However, we also saw that Python typically implements such features by providing a syntax shortcut to traditional object-oriented syntax. Knowing the object-oriented principles underlying these tools allows us to use them more effectively in our own classes.

We discussed a series of built-in functions and file I/O operations. There are a whole bunch of different syntaxes available to us when calling functions with arguments, keyword arguments, and variable argument lists. Context managers are useful for the common pattern of sandwiching a piece of code between two method calls. Even functions are objects, and, conversely, any normal object can be made callable.

In the next chapter, we'll learn more about string and file manipulation, and even spend some time with one of the least object-oriented topics in the standard library: regular expressions.

# 21
# The Iterator Pattern

We've discussed how many of Python's built-ins and idioms seem, at first blush, to fly in the face of object-oriented principles, but are actually providing access to real objects under the hood. In this chapter, we'll discuss how the `for` loop, which seems so structured, is actually a lightweight wrapper around a set of object-oriented principles. We'll also see a variety of extensions to this syntax that automatically create even more types of object. We will cover the following topics:

- What design patterns are
- The iterator protocol—one of the most powerful design patterns
- List, set, and dictionary comprehensions
- Generators and coroutines

## Design patterns in brief

When engineers and architects decide to build a bridge, or a tower, or a building, they follow certain principles to ensure structural integrity. There are various possible designs for bridges (suspension and cantilever, for example), but if the engineer doesn't use one of the standard designs, and doesn't have a brilliant new design, it is likely the bridge he/she designs will collapse.

Design patterns are an attempt to bring this same formal definition for correctly designed structures to software engineering. There are many different design patterns to solve different general problems. Design patterns typically solve a specific common problem faced by developers in some specific situation. The design pattern is then a suggestion as to the ideal solution for that problem, in terms of object-oriented design.

Knowing a design pattern and choosing to use it in our software does not, however, guarantee that we are creating a *correct* solution. In 1907, the Québec Bridge (to this day, the longest cantilever bridge in the world) collapsed before construction was completed, because the engineers who designed it grossly underestimated the weight of the steel used to construct it. Similarly, in software development, we may incorrectly choose or apply a design pattern, and create software that *collapses* under normal operating situations or when stressed beyond its original design limits.

Any one design pattern proposes a set of objects interacting in a specific way to solve a general problem. The job of the programmer is to recognize when they are facing a specific version of such a problem, then to choose and adapt the general design in their precise needs.

In this chapter, we'll be covering the iterator design pattern. This pattern is so powerful and pervasive that the Python developers have provided multiple syntaxes to access the object-oriented principles underlying the pattern. We will be covering other design patterns in the next two chapters. Some of them have language support and some don't, but none of them is so intrinsically a part of the Python coder's daily life as the iterator pattern.

# Iterators

In typical design pattern parlance, an iterator is an object with a `next()` method and a `done()` method; the latter returns `True` if there are no items left in the sequence. In a programming language without built-in support for iterators, the iterator would be looped over like this:

```
while not iterator.done():
    item = iterator.next()
    # do something with the item
```

In Python, iteration is a special feature, so the method gets a special name, `__next__`. This method can be accessed using the `next(iterator)` built-in. Rather than a `done` method, Python's iterator protocol raises `StopIteration` to notify the loop that it has completed. Finally, we have the much more readable `foriteminiterator` syntax to actually access items in an iterator instead of messing around with a `while` loop. Let's look at these in more detail.

# The iterator protocol

The `Iterator` abstract base class, in the `collections.abc` module, defines the iterator protocol in Python. As mentioned, it must have a __next__ method that the `for` loop (and other features that support iteration) can call to get a new element from the sequence. In addition, every iterator must also fulfill the `Iterable` interface. Any class that provides an __iter__ method is iterable. That method must return an `Iterator` instance that will cover all the elements in that class.

This might sound a bit confusing, so have a look at the following example, but note that this is a very verbose way to solve this problem. It clearly explains iteration and the two protocols in question, but we'll be looking at several more readable ways to get this effect later in this chapter:

```python
class CapitalIterable:
    def __init__(self, string):
        self.string = string

    def __iter__(self):
        return CapitalIterator(self.string)


class CapitalIterator:
    def __init__(self, string):
        self.words = [w.capitalize() for w in string.split()]
        self.index = 0

    def __next__(self):
        if self.index == len(self.words):
            raise StopIteration()

        word = self.words[self.index]
        self.index += 1
        return word

    def __iter__(self):
        return self
```

This example defines an `CapitalIterable` class whose job is to loop over each of the words in a string and output them with the first letter capitalized. Most of the work of that iterable is passed to the `CapitalIterator` implementation. The canonical way to interact with this iterator is as follows:

```
>>> iterable = CapitalIterable('the quick brown fox jumps over the
lazy dog')
>>> iterator = iter(iterable)
>>> while True:
...     try:
...         print(next(iterator))
...     except StopIteration:
...         break
...
The
Quick
Brown
Fox
Jumps
Over
The
Lazy
Dog
```

This example first constructs an iterable and retrieves an iterator from it. The distinction may need explanation; the iterable is an object with elements that can be looped over. Normally, these elements can be looped over multiple times, maybe even at the same time or in overlapping code. The iterator, on the other hand, represents a specific location in that iterable; some of the items have been consumed and some have not. Two different iterators might be at different places in the list of words, but any one iterator can mark only one place.

Each time `next()` is called on the iterator, it returns another token from the iterable, in order. Eventually, the iterator will be exhausted (won't have any more elements to return), in which case `StopIteration` is raised, and we break out of the loop.

Of course, we already know a much simpler syntax for constructing an iterator from an iterable:

```
>>> for i in iterable:
...     print(i)
...
The
Quick
Brown
Fox
```

```
Jumps
Over
The
Lazy
Dog
```

As you can see, the `for` statement, in spite of not looking remotely object-oriented, is actually a shortcut to some obviously object-oriented design principles. Keep this in mind as we discuss comprehensions, as they, too, appear to be the polar opposite of an object-oriented tool. Yet, they use the exact same iteration protocol as `for` loops and are just another kind of shortcut.

# Comprehensions

Comprehensions are simple, but powerful, syntaxes that allow us to transform or filter an iterable object in as little as one line of code. The resultant object can be a perfectly normal list, set, or dictionary, or it can be a generator expression that can be efficiently consumed while keeping just one element in memory at a time.

## List comprehensions

List comprehensions are one of the most powerful tools in Python, so people tend to think of them as advanced. They're not. Indeed, I've taken the liberty of littering previous examples with comprehensions, assuming you would understand them. While it's true that advanced programmers use comprehensions a lot, it's not because they're advanced. It's because they're trivial, and handle some of the most common operations in software development.

Let's have a look at one of those common operations; namely, converting a list of items into a list of related items. Specifically, let's assume we just read a list of strings from a file, and now we want to convert it to a list of integers. We know every item in the list is an integer, and we want to do some activity (say, calculate an average) on those numbers. Here's one simple way to approach it:

```
input_strings = ["1", "5", "28", "131", "3"]

output_integers = []
for num in input_strings:
    output_integers.append(int(num))
```

This works fine and it's only three lines of code. If you aren't used to comprehensions, you may not even think it looks ugly! Now, look at the same code using a list comprehension:

```
input_strings = ["1", "5", "28", "131", "3"]
output_integers = [int(num) for num in input_strings]
```

We're down to one line and, importantly for performance, we've dropped an `append` method call for each item in the list. Overall, it's pretty easy to tell what's going on, even if you're not used to comprehension syntax.

The square brackets indicate, as always, that we're creating a list. Inside this list is a `for` loop that iterates over each item in the input sequence. The only thing that may be confusing is what's happening between the list's opening brace and the start of the `for` loop. Whatever happens here is applied to *each* of the items in the input list. The item in question is referenced by the `num` variable from the loop. So, it's calling the `int` function for each element and storing the resulting integer in the new list.

That's all there is to a basic list comprehension. Comprehensions are highly optimized C code; list comprehensions are far faster than `for` loops when looping over a large number of items. If readability alone isn't a convincing reason to use them as much as possible, speed should be.

nverting one list of items into a related list isn't the only thing we can do with a list prehension. We can also choose to exclude certain values by adding an `if` nent inside the comprehension. Have a look:

```
out_integers = [int(num) for num in input_strings if len(num) < 3]
```

different between this example and the previous one is the `if len(num) <`
extra code excludes any strings with more than two characters. The `if`
pplied to each element **before** the `int` function, so it's testing the length
e our input strings are all integers at heart, it excludes any number

ns are used to map input values to output values, applying a filter
lude or exclude any values that meet a specific condition.

Any iterable can be the input to a list comprehension. In other words, anything we can wrap in a `for` loop can also be placed inside a comprehension. For example, text files are iterable; each call to __next__ on the file's iterator will return one line of the file. We could load a tab-delimited file where the first line is a header row into a dictionary using the `zip` function:

```
import sys

filename = sys.argv[1]

with open(filename) as file:
    header = file.readline().strip().split("\t")
 contacts = [
 dict(
 zip(header, line.strip().split("\t")))
 for line in file
 ]

for contact in contacts:
    print("email: {email} -- {last}, {first}".format(**contact))
```

This time, I've added some whitespace to make it more readable (list comprehensions don't *have* to fit on one line). This example creates a list of dictionaries from the zipped header and split lines for each line in the file.

Er, what? Don't worry if that code or explanation doesn't make sense; it's confusing. One list comprehension is doing a pile of work here, and the code is hard to understand, read, and ultimately, maintain. This example shows that list comprehensions aren't always the best solution; most programmers would agree that a `for` loop would be more readable than this version.

Remember: the tools we are provided with should not be abused! Always pick the right tool for the job, which is always to write maintainable code.

# Set and dictionary comprehensions

Comprehensions aren't restricted to lists. We can use a similar syntax with braces to create sets and dictionaries as well. Let's start with sets. One way to create a set is to wrap a list comprehension in the `set()` constructor, which converts it to a set. But why waste memory on an intermediate list that gets discarded, when we can create a set directly?

Here's an example that uses a named tuple to model author/title/genre triads, and then retrieves a set of all the authors that write in a specific genre:

```
from collections import namedtuple

Book = namedtuple("Book", "author title genre")
books = [
    Book("Pratchett", "Nightwatch", "fantasy"),
    Book("Pratchett", "Thief Of Time", "fantasy"),
    Book("Le Guin", "The Dispossessed", "scifi"),
    Book("Le Guin", "A Wizard Of Earthsea", "fantasy"),
    Book("Turner", "The Thief", "fantasy"),
    Book("Phillips", "Preston Diamond", "western"),
    Book("Phillips", "Twice Upon A Time", "scifi"),
]

fantasy_authors = {b.author for b in books if b.genre == "fantasy"}
```

The highlighted set comprehension sure is short in comparison to the demo-data setup! If we were to use a list comprehension, of course, Terry Pratchett would have been listed twice. As it is, the nature of sets removes the duplicates, and we end up with the following:

```
>>> fantasy_authors
{'Turner', 'Pratchett', 'Le Guin'}
```

Still using braces, we can introduce a colon to create a dictionary comprehension. This converts a sequence into a dictionary using *key:value* pairs. For example, it may be useful to quickly look up the author or genre in a dictionary if we know the title. We can use a dictionary comprehension to map titles to `books` objects:

```
fantasy_titles = {b.title: b for b in books if b.genre == "fantasy"}
```

Now, we have a dictionary, and can look up books by title using the normal syntax.

In summary, comprehensions are not advanced Python, nor are they *non-object-oriented* tools that should be avoided. They are simply a more concise and optimized syntax for creating a list, set, or dictionary from an existing sequence.

# Generator expressions

Sometimes we want to process a new sequence without pulling a new list, set, or dictionary into system memory. If we're just looping over items one at a time, and don't actually care about having a complete container (such as a list or dictionary) created, creating that container is a waste of memory. When processing one item at a time, we only need the current object available in memory at any one moment. But when we create a container, all the objects have to be stored in that container before we start processing them.

For example, consider a program that processes log files. A very simple log might contain information in this format:

```
Jan 26, 2015 11:25:25 DEBUG This is a debugging message. Jan 26, 2015
11:25:36 INFO This is an information method. Jan 26, 2015 11:25:46
WARNING This is a warning. It could be serious. Jan 26, 2015 11:25:52
WARNING Another warning sent. Jan 26, 2015 11:25:59 INFO Here's some
information. Jan 26, 2015 11:26:13 DEBUG Debug messages are only
useful if you want to figure something out. Jan 26, 2015 11:26:32 INFO
Information is usually harmless, but helpful. Jan 26, 2015 11:26:40
WARNING Warnings should be heeded. Jan 26, 2015 11:26:54 WARNING Watch
for warnings.
```

Log files for popular web servers, databases, or email servers can contain many gigabytes of data (I once had to clean nearly 2 terabytes of logs off a misbehaving system). If we want to process each line in the log, we can't use a list comprehension; it would create a list containing every line in the file. This probably wouldn't fit in RAM and could bring the computer to its knees, depending on the operating system.

If we used a `for` loop on the log file, we could process one line at a time before reading the next one into memory. Wouldn't be nice if we could use comprehension syntax to get the same effect?

This is where generator expressions come in. They use the same syntax as comprehensions, but they don't create a final container object. To create a generator expression, wrap the comprehension in () instead of [] or {}.

The following code parses a log file in the previously presented format and outputs a new log file that contains only the WARNING lines:

```
import sys

inname = sys.argv[1]
outname = sys.argv[2]

with open(inname) as infile:
    with open(outname, "w") as outfile:
        warnings = (l for l in infile if 'WARNING' in l)
        for l in warnings:
            outfile.write(l)
```

This program takes the two filenames on the command line, uses a generator expression to filter out the warnings (in this case, it uses the if syntax and leaves the line unmodified), and then outputs the warnings to another file. If we run it on our sample file, the output looks like this:

```
Jan 26, 2015 11:25:46 WARNING This is a warning. It could be serious.
Jan 26, 2015 11:25:52 WARNING Another warning sent.
Jan 26, 2015 11:26:40 WARNING Warnings should be heeded.
Jan 26, 2015 11:26:54 WARNING Watch for warnings.
```

Of course, with such a short input file, we could have safely used a list comprehension, but if the file is millions of lines long, the generator expression will have a huge impact on both memory and speed.

 Wrapping a for expression in parenthesis creates a generator expression, not a tuple.

Generator expressions are frequently most useful inside function calls. For example, we can call sum, min, or max on a generator expression instead of a list, since these functions process one object at a time. We're only interested in the aggregate result, not any intermediate container.

In general, of the four options, a generator expression should be used whenever possible. If we don't actually need a list, set, or dictionary, but simply need to filter or convert items in a sequence, a generator expression will be most efficient. If we need to know the length of a list, or sort the result, remove duplicates, or create a dictionary, we'll have to use the comprehension syntax.

# Generators

Generator expressions are actually a sort of comprehension too; they compress the more advanced (this time it really is more advanced!) generator syntax into one line. The greater generator syntax looks even less object-oriented than anything we've seen, but we'll discover that once again, it is a simple syntax shortcut to create a kind of object.

Let's take the log file example a little further. If we want to delete the WARNING column from our output file (since it's redundant: this file contains only warnings), we have several options at various levels of readability. We can do it with a generator expression:

```
import sys

# generator expression
inname, outname = sys.argv[1:3]

with open(inname) as infile:
    with open(outname, "w") as outfile:
        warnings = (
            l.replace("\tWARNING", "") for l in infile if "WARNING" in
l
        )
        for l in warnings:
            outfile.write(l)
```

That's perfectly readable, though I wouldn't want to make the expression much more complicated than that. We could also do it with a normal `for` loop:

```
with open(inname) as infile:
    with open(outname, "w") as outfile:
        for l in infile:
            if "WARNING" in l:
                outfile.write(l.replace("\tWARNING", ""))
```

That's clearly maintainable, but so many levels of indent in so few lines is kind of ugly. More alarmingly, if we wanted to do something other than printing the lines out, we'd have to duplicate the looping and conditional code, too.

Now let's consider a truly object-oriented solution, without any shortcuts:

```
class WarningFilter:
    def __init__(self, insequence):
        self.insequence = insequence

    def __iter__(self):
        return self

    def __next__(self):
        l = self.insequence.readline()
        while l and "WARNING" not in l:
            l = self.insequence.readline()
        if not l:
            raise StopIteration
        return l.replace("\tWARNING", "")


with open(inname) as infile:
    with open(outname, "w") as outfile:
        filter = WarningFilter(infile)
        for l in filter:
            outfile.write(l)
```

No doubt about it: that is so ugly and difficult to read that you may not even be able to tell what's going on. We created an object that takes a file object as input, and provides a __next__ method like any iterator.

This __next__ method reads lines from the file, discarding them if they are not WARNING lines. When we encounter a WARNING line, we modify and return it. Then our for loop calls __next__ again to process the subsequent WARNING line. When we run out of lines, we raise StopIteration to tell the loop we're finished iterating. It's pretty ugly compared to the other examples, but it's also powerful; now that we have a class in our hands, we can do whatever we want with it.

With that background behind us, we finally get to see true generators in action. This next example does *exactly* the same thing as the previous one: it creates an object with a __next__ method that raises StopIteration when it's out of inputs:

```
def warnings_filter(insequence):
    for l in insequence:
        if "WARNING" in l:
            yield l.replace("\tWARNING", "")


with open(inname) as infile:
```

```
with open(outname, "w") as outfile:
    filter = warnings_filter(infile)
    for l in filter:
        outfile.write(l)
```

OK, that's pretty readable, maybe... at least it's short. But what on earth is going on here? It makes no sense whatsoever. And what is `yield`, anyway?

In fact, `yield` is the key to generators. When Python sees `yield` in a function, it takes that function and wraps it up in an object not unlike the one in our previous example. Think of the `yield` statement as similar to the `return` statement; it exits the function and returns a line. Unlike `return`, however, when the function is called again (via `next()`), it will start where it left off—on the line after the `yield` statement—instead of at the beginning of the function.

In this example, there is no line *after* the `yield` statement, so it jumps to the next iteration of the `for` loop. Since the `yield` statement is inside an `if` statement, it only yields lines that contain `WARNING`.

While it looks like this is just a function looping over the lines, it is actually creating a special type of object, a generator object:

```
>>> print(warnings_filter([]))
<generator object warnings_filter at 0xb728c6bc>
```

I passed an empty list into the function to act as an iterator. All the function does is create and return a generator object. That object has __iter__ and __next__ methods on it, just like the one we created in the previous example. (You can call the `dir` built-in function on it to confirm.) Whenever __next__ is called, the generator runs the function until it finds a `yield` statement. It then returns the value from `yield`, and the next time __next__ is called, it picks up where it left off.

This use of generators isn't that advanced, but if you don't realize the function is creating an object, it can seem like magic. This example was quite simple, but you can get really powerful effects by making multiple calls to `yield` in a single function; on each loop, the generator will simply pick up at the most recent `yield` and continue to the next one.

# Yield items from another iterable

Often, when we build a generator function, we end up in a situation where we want to yield data from another iterable object, possibly a list comprehension or generator expression we constructed inside the generator, or perhaps some external items that were passed into the function. This has always been possible by looping over the iterable and individually yielding each item. However, in Python version 3.3, the Python developers introduced a new syntax to make it a little more elegant.

Let's adapt the generator example a bit so that instead of accepting a sequence of lines, it accepts a filename. This would normally be frowned upon as it ties the object to a particular paradigm. When possible we should operate on iterators as input; this way the same function could be used regardless of whether the log lines came from a file, memory, or the web.

This version of the code illustrates that your generator can do some basic setup before yielding information from another iterable (in this case, a generator expression):

```
def warnings_filter(infilename):
    with open(infilename) as infile:
        yield from (
            l.replace("\tWARNING", "") for l in infile if "WARNING" in
l
        )


filter = warnings_filter(inname)
with open(outname, "w") as outfile:
    for l in filter:
        outfile.write(l)
```

This code combines the `for` loop from the previous example into a generator expression. Notice that this transformation didn't help anything; the previous example with a `for` loop was more readable.

So, let's consider an example that is more readable than its alternative. It can be useful to construct a generator that yields data from multiple other generators. The `itertools.chain` function, for example, yields data from iterables in sequence until they have all been exhausted. This can be implemented far too easily using the `yield from` syntax, so let's consider a classic computer science problem: walking a general tree.

A common implementation of the general tree data structure is a computer's filesystem. Let's model a few folders and files in a Unix filesystem so we can use `yield from` to walk them effectively:

```python
class File:
    def __init__(self, name):
        self.name = name


class Folder(File):
    def __init__(self, name):
        super().__init__(name)
        self.children = []


root = Folder("")
etc = Folder("etc")
root.children.append(etc)
etc.children.append(File("passwd"))
etc.children.append(File("groups"))
httpd = Folder("httpd")
etc.children.append(httpd)
httpd.children.append(File("http.conf"))
var = Folder("var")
root.children.append(var)
log = Folder("log")
var.children.append(log)
log.children.append(File("messages"))
log.children.append(File("kernel"))
```

This setup code looks like a lot of work, but in a real filesystem, it would be even more involved. We'd have to read data from the hard drive and structure it into the tree. Once in memory, however, the code that outputs every file in the filesystem is quite elegant:

```python
def walk(file):
    if isinstance(file, Folder):
        yield file.name + "/"
        for f in file.children:
            yield from walk(f)
    else:
        yield file.name
```

If this code encounters a directory, it recursively asks `walk()` to generate a list of all files subordinate to each of its children, and then yields all that data plus its own filename. In the simple case that it has encountered a normal file, it just yields that name.

As an aside, solving the preceding problem without using a generator is tricky enough that it is a common interview question. If you answer it as shown like this, be prepared for your interviewer to be both impressed and somewhat irritated that you answered it so easily. They will likely demand that you explain exactly what is going on. Of course, armed with the principles you've learned in this chapter, you won't have any problem. Good luck!

The `yield from` syntax is a useful shortcut when writing chained generators. It was added to the language for a different reason, to support coroutines. It is not used all that much anymore, however, because it's usage has been replaced with `async` and `await` syntax. We'll see examples of both in the next section.

# Coroutines

Coroutines are extremely powerful constructs that are often confused with generators. Many authors inappropriately describe coroutines as *generators with a bit of extra syntax*. This is an easy mistake to make, as, way back in Python 2.5, when coroutines were introduced, they were presented as *we added a* `send` *method to the generator syntax*. The difference is actually a lot more nuanced and will make more sense after you've seen a few examples.

Coroutines are pretty hard to understand. Outside the `asyncio` module, they are not used all that often in the wild. You can definitely skip this section and happily develop in Python for years without ever encountering coroutines. There are a couple of libraries that use coroutines extensively (mostly for concurrent or asynchronous programming), but they are normally written such that you can use coroutines without actually understanding how they work! So, if you get lost in this section, don't despair.

If I haven't scared you off, let's get started! Here's one of the simplest possible coroutines; it allows us to keep a running tally that can be increased by arbitrary values:

```
def tally():
    score = 0
    while True:
        increment = yield score
        score += increment
```

This code looks like black magic that couldn't possibly work, so let's prove it works before going into a line-by-line description. This simple object could be used by a scoring application for a baseball team. Separate tallies could be kept for each team, and their score could be incremented by the number of runs accumulated at the end of every half-innings. Look at this interactive session:

```
>>> white_sox = tally()
>>> blue_jays = tally()
>>> next(white_sox)
0
>>> next(blue_jays)
0
>>> white_sox.send(3)
3
>>> blue_jays.send(2)
2
>>> white_sox.send(2)
5
>>> blue_jays.send(4)
6
```

First, we construct two `tally` objects, one for each team. Yes, they look like functions, but as with the generator objects in the previous section, the fact that there is a `yield` statement inside the function tells Python to put a great deal of effort into turning the simple function into an object.

We then call `next()` on each of the coroutine objects. This does the same thing as calling next on any generator, which is to say, it executes each line of code until it encounters a `yield` statement, returns the value at that point, and then *pauses* until the next `next()` call.

So far, then, there's nothing new. But look back at the `yield` statement in our coroutine:

```
increment = yield score
```

Unlike with generators, this `yield` function looks like it's supposed to return a value and assign it to a variable. In fact, this is exactly what's happening. The coroutine is still paused at the `yield` statement and waiting to be activated again by another call to `next()`.

Except we don't call `next()`. As you see in the interactive session, we instead call to a method called `send()`. The `send()` method does *exactly* the same thing as `next()` except that in addition to advancing the generator to the next `yield` statement, it also allows you to pass in a value from outside the generator. This value is what gets assigned to the left side of the `yield` statement.

The thing that is really confusing for many people is the order in which this happens:

1. `yield` occurs and the generator pauses
2. `send()` occurs from outside the function and the generator wakes up
3. The value sent in is assigned to the left side of the `yield` statement
4. The generator continues processing until it encounters another `yield` statement

So, in this particular example, after we construct the coroutine and advance it to the `yield` statement with a single call to `next()`, each successive call to `send()` passes a value into the coroutine. We add this value to its score. Then we go back to the top of the `while` loop, and keep processing until we hit the `yield` statement. The `yield` statement returns a value, which becomes the return value of our most recent call to `send`. Don't miss that: like `next()`, the `send()` method does not just submit a value to the generator, it also returns the value from the upcoming `yield` statement. This is how we define the difference between a generator and a coroutine: a generator only produces values, while a coroutine can also consume them.

The behavior and syntax of `next(i)`, `i.__next__()`, and `i.send(value)` are rather unintuitive and frustrating. The first is a normal function, the second is a special method, and the last is a normal method. But all three do the same thing: advance the generator until it yields a value and pause. Further, the `next()` function and associated method can be replicated by calling `i.send(None)`. There is value to having two different method names here, since it helps the reader of our code easily see whether they are interacting with a coroutine or a generator. I just find the fact that in one case it's a function call and in the other it's a normal method somewhat irritating.

# Back to log parsing

Of course, the previous example could easily have been coded using a couple of integer variables and calling `x += increment` on them. Let's look at a second example where coroutines actually save us some code. This example is a somewhat simplified (for pedagogical reasons) version of a problem I had to solve while working at Facebook.

The Linux kernel log contains lines that look almost, but not quite entirely, unlike this:

```
unrelated log messages
sd 0:0:0:0 Attached Disk Drive
unrelated log messages
sd 0:0:0:0 (SERIAL=ZZ12345)
unrelated log messages
sd 0:0:0:0 [sda] Options
unrelated log messages
XFS ERROR [sda]
unrelated log messages
sd 2:0:0:1 Attached Disk Drive
unrelated log messages
sd 2:0:0:1 (SERIAL=ZZ67890)
unrelated log messages
sd 2:0:0:1 [sdb] Options
unrelated log messages
sd 3:0:1:8 Attached Disk Drive
unrelated log messages
sd 3:0:1:8 (SERIAL=WW11111)
unrelated log messages
sd 3:0:1:8 [sdc] Options
unrelated log messages
```

```
XFS ERROR [sdc]
unrelated log messages
```

There are a whole bunch of interspersed kernel log messages, some of which pertain to hard disks. The hard disk messages might be interspersed with other messages, but they occur in a predictable format and order. For each, a specific drive with a known serial number is associated with a bus identifier (such as 0:0:0:0). A block device identifier (such as sda) is also associated with that bus. Finally, if the drive has a corrupt filesystem, it might fail with an XFS error.

Now, given the preceding log file, the problem we need to solve is how to obtain the serial number of any drives that have XFS errors on them. This serial number might later be used by a data center technician to identify and replace the drive.

We know we can identify the individual lines using regular expressions, but we'll have to change the regular expressions as we loop through the lines, since we'll be looking for different things depending on what we found previously. The other difficult bit is that if we find an error string, the information about which bus contains that string as well as the serial number have already been processed. This can easily be solved by iterating through the lines of the file in reverse order.

Before you look at this example, be warned—the amount of code required for a coroutine-based solution is scarily small:

```python
import re


def match_regex(filename, regex):
    with open(filename) as file:
        lines = file.readlines()
    for line in reversed(lines):
        match = re.match(regex, line)
        if match:
            regex = yield match.groups()[0]


def get_serials(filename):
    ERROR_RE = "XFS ERROR (\[sd[a-z]\])"
    matcher = match_regex(filename, ERROR_RE)
    device = next(matcher)
    while True:
        try:
            bus = matcher.send(
                "(sd \S+) {}.*".format(re.escape(device))
            )
            serial = matcher.send("{} \(SERIAL=([^)]*)\)".format(bus))
```

```
            yield serial
                device = matcher.send(ERROR_RE)
            except StopIteration:
                matcher.close()
                return


    for serial_number in get_serials("EXAMPLE_LOG.log"):
        print(serial_number)
```

This code neatly divides the job into two separate tasks. The first task is to loop over all the lines and spit out any lines that match a given regular expression. The second task is to interact with the first task and give it guidance as to what regular expression it is supposed to be searching for at any given time.

Look at the `match_regex` coroutine first. Remember, it doesn't execute any code when it is constructed; rather, it just creates a coroutine object. Once constructed, someone outside the coroutine will eventually call `next()` to start the code running. Then it stores the state of two variables `filename` and `regex`. It then reads all the lines in the file and iterates over them in reverse. Each line is compared to the regular expression that was passed in until it finds a match. When the match is found, the coroutine yields the first group from the regular expression and waits.

At some point in the future, other code will send in a new regular expression to search for. Note that the coroutine never cares what regular expression it is trying to match; it's just looping over lines and comparing them to a regular expression. It's somebody else's responsibility to decide what regular expression to supply.

In this case, that somebody else is the `get_serials` generator. It doesn't care about the lines in the file; in fact, it isn't even aware of them. The first thing it does is create a `matcher` object from the `match_regex` coroutine constructor, giving it a default regular expression to search for. It advances the coroutine to its first `yield` and stores the value it returns. It then goes into a loop that instructs the `matcher` object to search for a bus ID based on the stored device ID, and then a serial number based on that bus ID.

It idly yields that serial number to the outside `for` loop before instructing the matcher to find another device ID and repeat the cycle.

Basically, the coroutine's job is to search for the next important line in the file, while the generator's (`get_serial`, which uses the `yield` syntax without assignment) job is to decide which line is important. The generator has information about this particular problem, such as what order lines will appear in the file.

---

**[ 573 ]**

The coroutine, on the other hand, could be plugged into any problem that required searching a file for given regular expressions.

# Closing coroutines and throwing exceptions

Normal generators signal their exit from inside by raising StopIteration. If we chain multiple generators together (for example, by iterating over one generator from inside another), the StopIteration exception will be propagated outward. Eventually, it will hit a for loop that will see the exception and know that it's time to exit the loop.

Even though they use a similar syntax, coroutines don't normally follow the iteration mechanism. Instead of pulling data through one until an exception is encountered, data is usually pushed into it (using send). The entity doing the pushing is normally the one in charge of telling the coroutine when it's finished. It does this by calling the close() method on the coroutine in question.

When called, the close() method will raise a GeneratorExit exception at the point the coroutine was waiting for a value to be sent in. It is normally good policy for coroutines to wrap their yield statements in a try...finally block so that any cleanup tasks (such as closing associated files or sockets) can be performed.

If we need to raise an exception inside a coroutine, we can use the throw() method in a similar way. It accepts an exception type with optional value and traceback arguments. The latter is useful when we encounter an exception in one coroutine and want to cause an exception to occur in an adjacent coroutine while maintaining the traceback.

The previous example could be written without coroutines and would be about equally readable. The truth is, correctly managing all the state between coroutines is pretty difficult, especially when you take things like context managers and exceptions into account. Luckily, the Python standard library contains a package called asyncio that can manage all of this for you. In general, I recommend you avoid using bare coroutines unless you are specifically coding for asyncio. The logging example could almost be considered an *anti-pattern*; a design pattern that should be avoided rather than embraced.

# The relationship between coroutines, generators, and functions

We've seen coroutines in action, so now let's go back to that discussion of how they are related to generators. In Python, as is so often the case, the distinction is quite blurry. In fact, all coroutines are generator objects, and authors often use the two terms interchangeably. Sometimes, they describe coroutines as a subset of generators (only generators that return values from yield are considered coroutines). This is technically true in Python, as we've seen in the previous sections.

However, in the greater sphere of theoretical computer science, coroutines are considered the more general principles, and generators are a specific type of coroutine. Further, normal functions are yet another distinct subset of coroutines.

A coroutine is a routine that can have data passed in at one or more points and get it out at one or more points. In Python, the point where data is passed in and out is the yield statement.

A function, or subroutine, is the simplest type of coroutine. You can pass data in at one point, and get data out at one other point when the function returns. While a function can have multiple return statements, only one of them can be called for any given invocation of the function.

Finally, a generator is a type of coroutine that can have data passed in at one point, but can pass data out at multiple points. In Python, the data would be passed out at a yield statement, but you can't pass data back in. If you called send, the data would be silently discarded.

So, in theory, generators are types of coroutines, functions are types of coroutines, and there are coroutines that are neither functions nor generators. That's simple enough, eh? So, why does it feel more complicated in Python?

In Python, generators and coroutines are both constructed using a syntax that **looks** like we are constructing a function. But the resulting object is not a function at all; it's a totally different kind of object. Functions are, of course, also objects. But they have a different interface; functions are callable and return values, generators have data pulled out using next (), and coroutines have data pushed in using send.

There is an alternate syntax for coroutines using the `async` and `await` keywords. The syntax makes it clearer that the code is a coroutine and further breaks the deceiving symmetry between coroutines and generators.

# Case study

One of the fields in which Python is the most popular these days is data science. In honor of that fact, let's implement a basic machine learning algorithm.

Machine learning is a huge topic, but the general idea is to make predictions or classifications about future data by using knowledge gained from past data. Uses of such algorithms abound, and data scientists are finding new ways to apply machine learning every day. Some important machine learning applications include computer vision (such as image classification or facial recognition), product recommendation, identifying spam, and self-driving cars.

So as not to digress into an entire book on machine learning, we'll look at a simpler problem: given an RGB color definition, what name would humans identify that color as?

There are more than 16 million colors in the standard RGB color space, and humans have come up with names for only a fraction of them. While there are thousands of names (some quite ridiculous; just go to any car dealership or paint store), let's build a classifier that attempts to divide the RGB space into the basic colors:

- Red
- Purple
- Blue
- Green
- Yellow
- Orange
- Gray
- Pink

(In my testing, I classified whitish and blackish colors as gray, and brownish colors as orange.)

The first thing we need is a dataset to train our algorithm on. In a production system, you might scrape a *list of colors* website or survey thousands of people. Instead, I created a simple application that renders a random color and asks the user to select one of the preceding eight options to classify it. I implemented it using `tkinter`, the user interface toolkit that ships with Python. I'm not going to go into the details of what this script does, but here it is in its entirety for completeness (it's a trifle long, so you may want to pull it from Packt's GitHub repository with the examples for this book instead of typing it in):

```python
import random
import tkinter as tk
import csv


class Application(tk.Frame):
    def __init__(self, master=None):
        super().__init__(master)
        self.grid(sticky="news")
        master.columnconfigure(0, weight=1)
        master.rowconfigure(0, weight=1)
        self.create_widgets()
        self.file = csv.writer(open("colors.csv", "a"))

    def create_color_button(self, label, column, row):
        button = tk.Button(
            self, command=lambda: self.click_color(label), text=label
        )
        button.grid(column=column, row=row, sticky="news")

    def random_color(self):
        r = random.randint(0, 255)
        g = random.randint(0, 255)
        b = random.randint(0, 255)

        return f"#{r:02x}{g:02x}{b:02x}"

    def create_widgets(self):
        self.color_box = tk.Label(
            self, bg=self.random_color(), width="30", height="15"
        )
        self.color_box.grid(
            column=0, columnspan=2, row=0, sticky="news"
        )
        self.create_color_button("Red", 0, 1)
        self.create_color_button("Purple", 1, 1)
        self.create_color_button("Blue", 0, 2)
        self.create_color_button("Green", 1, 2)
```

```
        self.create_color_button("Yellow", 0, 3)
        self.create_color_button("Orange", 1, 3)
        self.create_color_button("Pink", 0, 4)
        self.create_color_button("Grey", 1, 4)
        self.quit = tk.Button(
            self, text="Quit", command=root.destroy, bg="#ffaabb"
        )
        self.quit.grid(column=0, row=5, columnspan=2, sticky="news")

    def click_color(self, label):
        self.file.writerow([label, self.color_box["bg"]])
        self.color_box["bg"] = self.random_color()


root = tk.Tk()
app = Application(master=root)
app.mainloop()
```

 You can easily add more buttons for other colors if you like. You may get tripped up on the layout; the second and third argument to `create_color_button` represent the row and column of a two column grid that the button goes in. Once you have all your colors in place, you will want to move the **Quit** button to the last row.

For the purposes of this case study, the important thing to know about this application is the output. It creates a **Comma-Separated Value (CSV)** file named `colors.csv`. This file contains two CSVs: the label the user assigned to the color, and the hex RGB value for the color. Here's an example:

```
Green, #6edd13
Purple, #814faf
Yellow, #c7c26d
Orange, #61442c
Green, #67f496
Purple, #c757d5
Blue, #106a98
Pink, #d40491

 .
 .
 .

Blue, #a4bdfa
Green, #30882f
Pink, #f47aad
Green, #83ddb2
Grey, #baaec9
Grey, #8aa28d
Blue, #533eda
```

I made over 250 datapoints before I got bored and decided it was time to start machine learning on my dataset. My datapoints are shipped with the examples for this chapter if you would like to use it (nobody's ever told me I'm colorblind, so it should be somewhat reasonable).

We'll be implementing one of the simpler machine learning algorithms, referred to as *k-nearest neighbor*. This algorithm relies on some kind of *distance* calculation between points in the dataset (in our case, we can use a three-dimensional version of the Pythagorean theorem). Given a new datapoint, it finds a certain number (referred to as *k*, which is the *k* in *k-nearest*) of datapoints that are closest to it when measured by that distance calculation. Then it combines those datapoints in some way (an average might work for linear calculations; for our classification problem, we'll use the mode), and returns the result.

We won't go into too much detail about what the algorithm does; rather, we'll focus on some of the ways we can apply the iterator pattern or iterator protocol to this problem.

Let's now write a program that performs the following steps in order:

1. Load the sample data from the file and construct a model from it.
2. Generate 100 random colors.
3. Classify each color and output it to a file in the same format as the input.

The first step is a fairly simple generator that loads CSV data and converts it into a format that is amenable to our needs:

```
import csv

dataset_filename = "colors.csv"


def load_colors(filename):
    with open(filename) as dataset_file:
        lines = csv.reader(dataset_file)
        for line in lines:
            label, hex_color = line
            yield (hex_to_rgb(hex_color), label)
```

We haven't seen the `csv.reader` function before. It returns an iterator over the lines in the file. Each value returned by the iterator is a list of strings, as separated by commas. So, the line `Green,#6edd13` is returned as `["Green", "#6edd13"]`.

The `load_colors` generator then consumes that iterator, one line at a time, and yields a tuple of RGB values as well as the label. It is quite common for generators to be chained in this way, where one iterator calls another that calls another and so on. You may want to look at the `itertools` module in the Python Standard Library for a whole host of such ready-made generators waiting for you.

The RGB values in this case are tuples of integers between 0 and 255. The conversion from hex to RGB is a bit tricky, so we pulled it out into a separate function:

```
def hex_to_rgb(hex_color):
    return tuple(int(hex_color[i : i + 2], 16) for i in range(1, 6,
2))
```

This generator expression is doing a lot of work. It takes a string such as `"#12abfe"` as input and returns a tuple such as `(18, 171, 254)`. Let's break it down from back to front.

The `range` call will return the numbers `[1, 3, 5]`. These represent the indexes of the three color channels in the hex string. The index, `0`, is skipped, since it represents the character `"#"`, which we don't care about. For each of the three numbers, it extracts the two character string between `i` and `i+2`. For the preceding example string , that would be `12`, `ab`, and `fe`. Then it converts this string value to an integer. The `16` passed as the second argument to the `int` function tells the function to use base-16 (hexadecimal) instead of the usual base-10 (decimal) for the conversion.

Given how difficult the generator expression is to read, do you think it should have been represented in a different format? It could be created as a sequence of multiple generator expressions, for example, or be unrolled into a normal generator function with `yield` statements. Which would you prefer?

In this case, I am comfortable trusting the function name to explain what the ugly line of code is doing.

Now that we've loaded the *training data* (manually classified colors, we need some new data to test how well the algorithm is working. We can do this by generating a hundred random colors, each composed of three random numbers between 0 and 255.

There are so many ways this can be done:

- A list comprehension with a nested generator
  expression: `[tuple(randint(0,255) for c in range(3)) for r in range(100)]`

- A basic generator function
- A class that implements the __iter__ and __next__ protocols
- Push the data through a pipeline of coroutines
- Even just a basic `for` loop

The generator version seems to be most readable, so let's add that function to our program:

```
from random import randint

def generate_colors(count=100):
    for i in range(count):
        yield (randint(0, 255), randint(0, 255), randint(0, 255))
```

Notice how we parameterize the number of colors to generate. We can now reuse this function for other color-generating tasks in the future.

Now, before we do the classification step, we need a function to calculate the *distance* between two colors. Since it's possible to think of colors as being three dimensional (red, green, and blue could map to the *x*, *y*, and *z* axes, for example), let's use a little basic math:

```
def color_distance(color1, color2):
    channels = zip(color1, color2)
    sum_distance_squared = 0
    for c1, c2 in channels:
        sum_distance_squared += (c1 - c2) ** 2
    return sum_distance_squared
```

This is a pretty basic-looking function; it doesn't look like it's even using the iterator protocol. There's no `yield` function, no comprehensions. However, there is a `for` loop, and that call to the `zip` function is doing some real iteration as well (if you aren't familiar with it, `zip` yields tuples, each containing one element from each input iterator).

This distance calculation is the three-dimensional version of the Pythagorean theorem you may remember from school: $a^2 + b^2 = c^2$. Since we are using three dimensions, I guess it would actually be $a^2 + b^2 + c^2 = d^2$. The distance is technically the square root of $a^2 + b^2 + c^2$, but there isn't any need to perform the somewhat expensive `sqrt` calculation since the squared distances are all the same relative size to each other.

Now that we have some plumbing in place, let's do the actual k-nearest neighbor implementation. This routine can be thought of as consuming and combining the two generators we've already seen (`load_colors` and `generate_colors`):

```python
def nearest_neighbors(model_colors, target_colors, num_neighbors=5):
    model_colors = list(model_colors)

    for target in target_colors:
        distances = sorted(
            ((color_distance(c[0], target), c) for c in model_colors)
        )
        yield target, distances[:5]
```

We first convert the `model_colors` generator to a list because it has to be consumed multiple times, once for each of the `target_colors`. If we didn't do this, we would have to load the colors from the source file repeatedly, which would perform a lot of unnecessary disk reads.

The downside of this decision is that the entire list has to be stored in memory all at once. If we had a massive dataset that didn't fit in memory, it would actually be necessary to reload the generator from disk each time (though we'd actually be looking at different machine learning algorithms in that case).

The `nearest_neighbors` generator loops over each target color (a three-tuple, such as (255, 14, 168)) and calls the `color_distance` function on it inside a generator expression. The `sorted` call surrounding that generator expression then sorts the results by their first element, which is the distance. It is a complicated piece of code and isn't object-oriented at all. You may want to break it down into a normal `for` loop to ensure you understand what the generator expression is doing.

The `yield` statement is a bit less complicated. For each RGB three-tuple from the `target_colors` generator, it yields the target, and a list comprehension of the `num_neighbors` (that's the *k* in *k-nearest*, by the way. Many mathematicians and, by extension, data scientists, have a horrible tendency to use unintelligible one-letter variable names) closest colors.

The contents of each element in the list comprehension is an element from the `model_colors` generator; that is, a tuple of a tuple of three RGB values and the string name that was manually entered for that color. So, one element might look like this: ((104, 195, 77), 'Green'). The first thing I think when I see nested tuples like that is, *that is not the right datastructure*. The RGB color should probably be represented as a named tuple, and the two attributes should maybe go on a dataclass.

We can now add *another* generator to the chain to figure out what name we should give this target color:

```python
from collections import Counter

def name_colors(model_colors, target_colors, num_neighbors=5):
    for target, near in nearest_neighbors(
        model_colors, target_colors, num_neighbors=5
    ):
        print(target, near)
        name_guess = Counter(n[1] for n in near).most_common()[0][0]
        yield target, name_guess
```

This generator is unpacking the tuple returned by `nearest_neighbors` into the three-tuple target and the five nearest datapoints. It uses a `Counter` to find the name that appears most often among the colors that were returned. There is yet another generator expression in the `Counter` constructor; this one extracts the second element (the color name) from each datapoint. Then it yields a tuple RGB value and the guessed name. An example of the return value is `(91, 158, 250) Blue`.

We can write a function that accepts the output from the `name_colors` generator and writes it to a CSV file, with the RGB colors represented as hex values:

```python
def write_results(colors, filename="output.csv"):
    with open(filename, "w") as file:
        writer = csv.writer(file)
        for (r, g, b), name in colors:
            writer.writerow([name, f"#{r:02x}{g:02x}{b:02x}"])
```

This is a function, not a generator. It's consuming the generator in a `for` loop, but it's not yielding anything. It constructs a CSV writer and outputs rows of name, hex value (for example, `Purple`, `#7f5f95`) pairs for each of the target colors. The only thing that might be confusing in here is the contents of the format string. The `:02x` modifier used with each of the r,g, and b channels outputs the number as a zero-padded two-digit hexadecimal number.

Now all we have to do is connect these various generators and pipelines together, and kick off the process with a single function call:

```
def process_colors(dataset_filename="colors.csv"):
    model_colors = load_colors(dataset_filename)
    colors = name_colors(model_colors, generate_colors(), 5)
    write_results(colors)


if __name__ == "__main__":
    process_colors()
```

So, this function, unlike almost every other function we've defined, is a perfectly normal function without any `yield` statements or `for` loops. It doesn't do any iteration at all.

It does, however, construct three generators. Can you see all three?:

- `load_colors` returns a generator
- `generate_colors` returns a generator
- `name_guess` returns a generator

The `name_guess` generator consumes the first two generators. It, in turn, is then consumed by the `write_results` function.

I wrote a second Tkinter app to check the accuracy of the algorithm. It is similar to the first app, except it renders each color and the label associated with that color. Then you have to manually click **Yes** or **No** if the label matches the color. For my example data, I got around 95% accuracy. This could be improved by implementing the following:

- Adding more color names
- Adding more training data by manually classifying more colors
- Tweaking the value of `num_neighbors`
- Using a more advanced machine learning algorithm

Here's the code for the output checking app, though I recommend downloading the example code instead. This would be tedious to type in:

```python
import tkinter as tk
import csv


class Application(tk.Frame):
    def __init__(self, master=None):
        super().__init__(master)
        self.grid(sticky="news")
        master.columnconfigure(0, weight=1)
        master.rowconfigure(0, weight=1)
        self.csv_reader = csv.reader(open("output.csv"))
        self.create_widgets()
        self.total_count = 0
        self.right_count = 0

    def next_color(self):
        return next(self.csv_reader)

    def mk_grid(self, widget, column, row, columnspan=1):
        widget.grid(
            column=column, row=row, columnspan=columnspan,
sticky="news"
        )

    def create_widgets(self):
        color_text, color_bg = self.next_color()
        self.color_box = tk.Label(
            self, bg=color_bg, width="30", height="15"
        )
        self.mk_grid(self.color_box, 0, 0, 2)

        self.color_label = tk.Label(self, text=color_text, height="3")
        self.mk_grid(self.color_label, 0, 1, 2)

        self.no_button = tk.Button(
            self, command=self.count_next, text="No"
        )
        self.mk_grid(self.no_button, 0, 2)

        self.yes_button = tk.Button(
            self, command=self.count_yes, text="Yes"
        )
        self.mk_grid(self.yes_button, 1, 2)

        self.percent_accurate = tk.Label(self, height="3", text="0%")
```

```
            self.mk_grid(self.percent_accurate, 0, 3, 2)

            self.quit = tk.Button(
                self, text="Quit", command=root.destroy, bg="#ffaabb"
            )
            self.mk_grid(self.quit, 0, 4, 2)

    def count_yes(self):
        self.right_count += 1
        self.count_next()

    def count_next(self):
        self.total_count += 1
        percentage = self.right_count / self.total_count
        self.percent_accurate["text"] = f"{percentage:.0%}"
        try:
            color_text, color_bg = self.next_color()
        except StopIteration:
            color_text = "DONE"
            color_bg = "#ffffff"
            self.color_box["text"] = "DONE"
            self.yes_button["state"] = tk.DISABLED
            self.no_button["state"] = tk.DISABLED
        self.color_label["text"] = color_text
        self.color_box["bg"] = color_bg


root = tk.Tk()
app = Application(master=root)
app.mainloop()
```

You might be wondering, *what does any of this have to do with object-oriented programming? There isn't even one class in this code!*. In some ways, you'd be right; generators are not commonly considered object-oriented. However, the functions that create them return objects; in fact, you could think of those functions as constructors. The constructed object has an appropriate __next__() method. Basically, the generator syntax is a syntax shortcut for a particular kind of object that would be quite verbose to create without it.

# Exercises

If you don't use comprehensions in your daily coding very often, the first thing you should do is search through some existing code and find some for loops. See whether any of them can be trivially converted to a generator expression or a list, set, or dictionary comprehension.

Test the claim that list comprehensions are faster than for loops. This can be done with the built-in timeit module. Use the help documentation for the timeit.timeit function to find out how to use it. Basically, write two functions that do the same thing, one using a list comprehension, and one using a for loop to iterate over several thousand items. Pass each function into timeit.timeit, and compare the results. If you're feeling adventurous, compare generators and generator expressions as well. Testing code using timeit can become addictive, so bear in mind that code does not need to be hyperfast unless it's being executed an immense number of times, such as on a huge input list or file.

Play around with generator functions. Start with basic iterators that require multiple values (mathematical sequences are canonical examples; the Fibonacci sequence is overused if you can't think of anything better). Try some more advanced generators that do things such as take multiple input lists and somehow yield values that merge them. Generators can also be used on files; can you write a simple generator that shows lines that are identical in two files?

Coroutines abuse the iterator protocol but don't actually fulfill the iterator pattern. Can you build a non-coroutine version of the code that gets a serial number from a log file? Take an object-oriented approach so that you can store an additional state on a class. You'll learn a lot about coroutines if you can create an object that is a drop-in replacement for the existing coroutine.

The case study for this chapter has a lot of odd tuples of tuples being passed around that are hard to keep track of. See whether you can replace those return values with more object-oriented solutions. Also, experiment with moving some of the functions that share data (for example, model_colors and target_colors) into a class. That should reduce the number of arguments that have to be passed into most of the generators since they can look them up on self.

# Summary

In this chapter, we learned that design patterns are useful abstractions that provide best-practice solutions for common programming problems. We covered our first design pattern, the iterator, as well as numerous ways that Python uses and abuses this pattern for its own nefarious purposes. The original iterator pattern is extremely object-oriented, but it is also rather ugly and verbose to code around. However, Python's built-in syntax abstracts the ugliness away, leaving us with a clean interface to these object-oriented constructs.

Comprehensions and generator expressions can combine container construction with iteration in a single line. Generator objects can be constructed using the `yield` syntax. Coroutines look like generators on the outside but serve a much different purpose.

We'll cover several more design patterns in the next two chapters.

# 22
# Python Design Patterns I

In the previous chapter, we were briefly introduced to design patterns, and covered the iterator pattern, a pattern so useful and common that it has been abstracted into the core of the programming language itself. In this chapter, we'll be reviewing other common patterns, and how they are implemented in Python. As with iteration, Python often provides an alternative syntax to make working with such problems simpler. We will cover both the *traditional* design, and the Python version for these patterns.

In summary, we'll see:

- Numerous specific patterns
- A canonical implementation of each pattern in Python
- Python syntax to replace certain patterns

## The decorator pattern

The decorator pattern allows us to *wrap* an object that provides core functionality with other objects that alter this functionality. Any object that uses the decorated object will interact with it in exactly the same way as if it were undecorated (that is, the interface of the decorated object is identical to that of the core object).

There are two primary uses of the decorator pattern:

- Enhancing the response of a component as it sends data to a second component
- Supporting multiple optional behaviors

The second option is often a suitable alternative to multiple inheritance. We can construct a core object, and then create a decorator wrapping that core. Since the decorator object has the same interface as the core object, we can even wrap the new object in other decorators. Here's how it looks in a UML diagram:

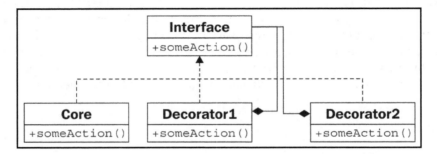

Here, **Core** and all the decorators implement a specific **Interface**. The decorators maintain a reference to another instance of that **Interface** via composition. When called, the decorator does some added processing before or after calling its wrapped interface. The wrapped object may be another decorator, or the core functionality. While multiple decorators may wrap each other, the object in the *center* of all those decorators provides the core functionality.

# A decorator example

Let's look at an example from network programming. We'll be using a TCP socket. The `socket.send()` method takes a string of input bytes and outputs them to the receiving socket at the other end. There are plenty of libraries that accept sockets and access this function to send data on the stream. Let's create such an object; it will be an interactive shell that waits for a connection from a client and then prompts the user for a string response:

```
import socket


def respond(client):
    response = input("Enter a value: ")
```

```
        client.send(bytes(response,  "utf8"))
        client.close()


server = socket.socket(socket.AF_INET,  socket.SOCK_STREAM)
server.bind(("localhost",  2401))
server.listen(1)
try:
    while True:
        client, addr = server.accept()
        respond(client)
finally:
    server.close()
```

The `respond` function accepts a `socket` parameter and prompts for data to be sent as a reply, then sends it. To use it, we construct a server socket and tell it to listen on port `2401` (I picked the port randomly) on the local computer. When a client connects, it calls the `respond` function, which requests data interactively and responds appropriately. The important thing to notice is that the `respond` function only cares about two methods of the socket interface: `send` and `close`.

To test this, we can write a very simple client that connects to the same port and outputs the response before exiting:

```
import socket

client = socket.socket(socket.AF_INET,  socket.SOCK_STREAM)
client.connect(("localhost",  2401))
print("Received: {0}".format(client.recv(1024)))
client.close()
```

To use these programs, follow these steps:

1. Start the server in one Terminal.
2. Open a second Terminal window and run the client.
3. At the **Enter a value:** prompt in the server window, type a value and press *Enter*.
4. The client will receive what you typed, print it to the console, and exit. Run the client a second time; the server will prompt for a second value.

The result will look something like this:

```
Terminal
(packt) dusty@localhost:~/code/Python-3-Object-Oriented-Programming-Third-Edition/Chapter 10: Design Patterns I
master $ python socket_decorator.py
Enter a value: 14
Sending b'14' to 127.0.0.1
Enter a value: 8
Sending b'8' to 127.0.0.1
Enter a value: 7
Sending b'7' to 127.0.0.1
```

```
Terminal
(3.6.5) dusty@localhost:~
 $ cd code/Python-3-Object-Oriented-Programming-Third-Edition/Chapter\ 10:\ Design\ Patterns\ I
(packt) dusty@localhost:~/code/Python-3-Object-Oriented-Programming-Third-Edition/Chapter 10: Design Patterns I
master $ python socket_client.py
Received: b'14'
(packt) dusty@localhost:~/code/Python-3-Object-Oriented-Programming-Third-Edition/Chapter 10: Design Patterns I
master $ python socket_client.py
Received: b'8'
(packt) dusty@localhost:~/code/Python-3-Object-Oriented-Programming-Third-Edition/Chapter 10: Design Patterns I
master $ python socket_client.py
Received: b'7'
(packt) dusty@localhost:~/code/Python-3-Object-Oriented-Programming-Third-Edition/Chapter 10: Design Patterns I
master $ []
```

Now, looking back at our server code, we see two sections. The `respond` function sends data into a `socket` object. The remaining script is responsible for creating that `socket` object. We'll create a pair of decorators that customize the socket behavior without having to extend or modify the socket itself.

Let's start with a *logging* decorator. This object outputs any data being sent to the server's console before it sends it to the client:

```python
class LogSocket:
    def __init__(self, socket):
        self.socket = socket

    def send(self, data):
        print(
            "Sending {0} to {1}".format(
                data, self.socket.getpeername()[0]
            )
        )
        self.socket.send(data)

    def close(self):
        self.socket.close()
```

This class decorates a `socket` object and presents the `send` and `close` interface to client sockets. A better decorator would also implement (and possibly customize) all of the remaining `socket` methods. It should properly implement all of the arguments to `send`, (which actually accepts an optional flags argument) as well, but let's keep our example simple. Whenever `send` is called on this object, it logs the output to the screen before sending data to the client using the original socket.

We only have to change one line in our original code to use this decorator. Instead of calling `respond` with the socket, we call it with a decorated socket:

```
respond(LogSocket(client))
```

While that's quite simple, we have to ask ourselves why we didn't just extend the `socket` class and override the `send` method. We could call `super().send` to do the actual sending, after we logged it. There is nothing wrong with this design either.

When faced with a choice between decorators and inheritance, we should only use decorators if we need to modify the object dynamically, according to some condition. For example, we may only want to enable the logging decorator if the server is currently in debugging mode. Decorators also beat multiple inheritance when we have more than one optional behavior. As an example, we can write a second decorator that compresses data using `gzip` compression whenever `send` is called:

```python
import gzip
from io import BytesIO


class GzipSocket:
    def __init__(self, socket):
        self.socket = socket

    def send(self, data):
        buf = BytesIO()
        zipfile = gzip.GzipFile(fileobj=buf, mode="w")
        zipfile.write(data)
        zipfile.close()
        self.socket.send(buf.getvalue())

    def close(self):
        self.socket.close()
```

The `send` method in this version compresses the incoming data before sending it on to the client.

Now that we have these two decorators, we can write code that dynamically switches between them when responding. This example is not complete, but it illustrates the logic we might follow to mix and match decorators:

```
client, addr = server.accept()
if log_send:
    client = LogSocket(client)
if client.getpeername()[0] in compress_hosts:
    client = GzipSocket(client)
respond(client)
```

This code checks a hypothetical configuration variable named log_send. If it's enabled, it wraps the socket in a LogSocket decorator. Similarly, it checks whether the client that has connected is in a list of addresses known to accept compressed content. If so, it wraps the client in a GzipSocket decorator. Notice that none, either, or both of the decorators may be enabled, depending on the configuration and connecting client. Try writing this using multiple inheritance and see how confused you get!

# Decorators in Python

The decorator pattern is useful in Python, but there are other options. For example, we may be able to use monkey-patching (for example, socket.socket.send = log_send) to get a similar effect. Single inheritance, where the *optional* calculations are done in one large method, could be an option, and multiple inheritance should not be written off just because it's not suitable for the specific example seen previously.

In Python, it is very common to use this pattern on functions. As we saw in a previous chapter, functions are objects too. In fact, function decoration is so common that Python provides a special syntax to make it easy to apply such decorators to functions.

For example, we can look at the logging example in a more general way. Instead of logging, only send calls on sockets; we may find it helpful to log all calls to certain functions or methods. The following example implements a decorator that does just this:

```
import time


def log_calls(func):
    def wrapper(*args, **kwargs):
```

```
            now = time.time()
            print(
                "Calling {0} with {1} and {2}".format(
                    func.__name__, args, kwargs
                )
            )
            return_value = func(*args, **kwargs)
            print(
                "Executed {0} in {1}ms".format(
                    func.__name__, time.time() - now
                )
            )
            return return_value

        return wrapper


def test1(a, b, c):
    print("\ttest1 called")


def test2(a, b):
    print("\ttest2 called")


def test3(a, b):
    print("\ttest3 called")
    time.sleep(1)


test1 = log_calls(test1)
test2 = log_calls(test2)
test3 = log_calls(test3)

test1(1, 2, 3)
test2(4, b=5)
test3(6, 7)
```

This decorator function is very similar to the example we explored earlier; in those cases, the decorator took a socket-like object and created a socket-like object. This time, our decorator takes a function object and returns a new function object. This code comprises three separate tasks:

- A function, `log_calls`, that accepts another function
- This function defines (internally) a new function, named `wrapper`, that does some extra work before calling the original function
- The inner function is returned from the outer function

Three sample functions demonstrate the decorator in use. The third one includes a `sleep` call to demonstrate the timing test. We pass each function into the decorator, which returns a new function. We assign this new function to the original variable name, effectively replacing the original function with a decorated one.

This syntax allows us to build up decorated function objects dynamically, just as we did with the socket example. If we don't replace the name, we can even keep decorated and non-decorated versions for different situations.

Typically, these decorators are general modifications that are applied permanently to different functions. In this situation, Python supports a special syntax to apply the decorator at the time the function is defined. We've already seen this syntax in a few places; now, let's understand how it works.

Instead of applying the decorator function after the method definition, we can use the `@decorator` syntax to do it all at once:

```
@log_calls
def test1(a,b,c):
    print("\ttest1 called")
```

The primary benefit of this syntax is that we can easily see that the function has been decorated whenever we read the function definition. If the decorator is applied later, someone reading the code may miss that the function has been altered at all. Answering a question like, *Why is my program logging function calls to the console?* can become much more difficult! However, the syntax can only be applied to functions we define, since we don't have access to the source code of other modules. If we need to decorate functions that are part of somebody else's third-party library, we have to use the earlier syntax.

There is more to the decorator syntax than we've seen here. We don't have room to cover the advanced topics here, so check the Python reference manual or other tutorials for more information. Decorators can be created as callable objects, not just functions that return functions. Classes can also be decorated; in that case, the decorator returns a new class instead of a new function. Finally, decorators can take arguments to customize them on a per-function basis.

# The observer pattern

The observer pattern is useful for state monitoring and event handling situations. This pattern allows a given object to be monitored by an unknown and dynamic group of *observer* objects.

Whenever a value on the core object changes, it lets all the observer objects know that a change has occurred, by calling an `update()` method. Each observer may be responsible for different tasks whenever the core object changes; the core object doesn't know or care what those tasks are, and the observers don't typically know or care what other observers are doing.

Here it is in UML:

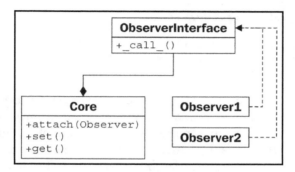

# An observer example

The observer pattern might be useful in a redundant backup system. We can write a core object that maintains certain values, and then have one or more observers create serialized copies of that object. These copies might be stored in a database, on a remote host, or in a local file, for example. Let's implement the core object using properties:

```python
class Inventory:
    def __init__(self):
        self.observers = []
        self._product = None
        self._quantity = 0

    def attach(self, observer):
        self.observers.append(observer)

    @property
    def product(self):
        return self._product

    @product.setter
    def product(self, value):
        self._product = value
```

```
        self._update_observers()

    @property
    def quantity(self):
        return self._quantity

    @quantity.setter
    def quantity(self, value):
        self._quantity = value
        self._update_observers()

    def _update_observers(self):
        for observer in self.observers:
            observer()
```

This object has two properties that, when set, call the _update_observers method on itself. All this method does is loop over any registered observers and let each know that something has changed. In this case, we call the observer object directly; the object will have to implement __call__ to process the update. This would not be possible in many object-oriented programming languages, but it's a useful shortcut in Python that can help make our code more readable.

Now let's implement a simple observer object; this one will just print out some state to the console:

```
class ConsoleObserver:
    def __init__(self, inventory):
        self.inventory = inventory

    def __call__(self):
        print(self.inventory.product)
        print(self.inventory.quantity)
```

There's nothing terribly exciting here; the observed object is set up in the initializer, and when the observer is called, we do *something*. We can test the observer in an interactive console:

```
>>> i = Inventory()
>>> c = ConsoleObserver(i)
>>> i.attach(c)
>>> i.product = "Widget"
Widget
0
>>> i.quantity = 5
Widget
5
```

After attaching the observer to the `Inventory` object, whenever we change one of the two observed properties, the observer is called and its action is invoked. We can even add two different observer instances:

```
>>> i = Inventory()
>>> c1 = ConsoleObserver(i)
>>> c2 = ConsoleObserver(i)
>>> i.attach(c1)
>>> i.attach(c2)
>>> i.product = "Gadget"
Gadget
0
Gadget
0
```

This time when we change the product, there are two sets of output, one for each observer. The key idea here is that we can easily add totally different types of observers that back up the data in a file, database, or internet application at the same time.

The observer pattern detaches the code being observed from the code doing the observing. If we were not using this pattern, we would have had to put code in each of the properties to handle the different cases that might come up; logging to the console, updating a database or file, and so on. The code for each of these tasks would all be mixed in with the observed object. Maintaining it would be a nightmare, and adding new monitoring functionality at a later date would be painful.

# The strategy pattern

The strategy pattern is a common demonstration of abstraction in object-oriented programming. The pattern implements different solutions to a single problem, each in a different object. The client code can then choose the most appropriate implementation dynamically at runtime.

Typically, different algorithms have different trade-offs; one might be faster than another, but uses a lot more memory, while a third algorithm may be most suitable when multiple CPUs are present or a distributed system is provided. Here is the strategy pattern in UML:

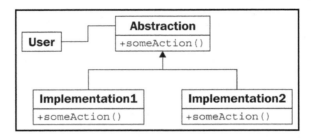

The **User** code connecting to the strategy pattern simply needs to know that it is dealing with the **Abstraction** interface. The actual implementation chosen performs the same task, but in different ways; either way, the interface is identical.

# A strategy example

The canonical example of the strategy pattern is sort routines; over the years, numerous algorithms have been invented for sorting a collection of objects; quick sort, merge sort, and heap sort are all fast sort algorithms with different features, each useful in its own right, depending on the size and type of inputs, how out of order they are, and the requirements of the system.

If we have client code that needs to sort a collection, we could pass it to an object with a `sort()` method. This object may be a `QuickSorter` or `MergeSorter` object, but the result will be the same in either case: a sorted list. The strategy used to do the sorting is abstracted from the calling code, making it modular and replaceable.

Of course, in Python, we typically just call the `sorted` function or `list.sort` method and trust that it will do the sorting in a near-optimal fashion. So, we really need to look at a better example.

Let's consider a desktop wallpaper manager. When an image is displayed on a desktop background, it can be adjusted to the screen size in different ways. For example, assuming the image is smaller than the screen, it can be tiled across the screen, centered on it, or scaled to fit.

There are other, more complicated, strategies that can be used as well, such as scaling to the maximum height or width, combining it with a solid, semi-transparent, or gradient background color, or other manipulations. While we may want to add these strategies later, let's start with the basic ones.

Our strategy objects take two inputs; the image to be displayed, and a tuple of the width and height of the screen. They each return a new image the size of the screen, with the image manipulated to fit according to the given strategy. You'll need to install the `pillow` module with `pip3 install pillow` for this example to work:

```python
from PIL import Image


class TiledStrategy:
    def make_background(self, img_file, desktop_size):
        in_img = Image.open(img_file)
        out_img = Image.new("RGB", desktop_size)
        num_tiles = [
            o // i + 1 for o, i in zip(out_img.size, in_img.size)
        ]
        for x in range(num_tiles[0]):
            for y in range(num_tiles[1]):
                out_img.paste(
                    in_img,
                    (
                        in_img.size[0] * x,
                        in_img.size[1] * y,
                        in_img.size[0] * (x + 1),
                        in_img.size[1] * (y + 1),
                    ),
                )
        return out_img


class CenteredStrategy:
    def make_background(self, img_file, desktop_size):
        in_img = Image.open(img_file)
        out_img = Image.new("RGB", desktop_size)
        left = (out_img.size[0] - in_img.size[0]) // 2
        top = (out_img.size[1] - in_img.size[1]) // 2
        out_img.paste(
            in_img,
            (left, top, left + in_img.size[0], top + in_img.size[1]),
        )
        return out_img
```

```
class ScaledStrategy:
    def make_background(self, img_file, desktop_size):
        in_img = Image.open(img_file)
        out_img = in_img.resize(desktop_size)
        return out_img
```

Here we have three strategies, each using `PIL` to perform their task. Individual strategies have a `make_background` method that accepts the same set of parameters. Once selected, the appropriate strategy can be called to create a correctly sized version of the desktop image. `TiledStrategy` loops over the number of input images that would fit in the width and height of the image and copies it into each location, repeatedly. `CenteredStrategy` figures out how much space needs to be left on the four edges of the image to center it. `ScaledStrategy` forces the image to the output size (ignoring aspect ratio).

Consider how switching between these options would be implemented without the strategy pattern. We'd need to put all the code inside one great big method and use an awkward `if` statement to select the expected one. Every time we wanted to add a new strategy, we'd have to make the method even more ungainly.

# Strategy in Python

The preceding canonical implementation of the strategy pattern, while very common in most object-oriented libraries, is rarely seen in Python programming.

These classes each represent objects that do nothing but provide a single function. We could just as easily call that function `__call__` and make the object callable directly. Since there is no other data associated with the object, we need do no more than create a set of top-level functions and pass them around as our strategies instead.

Opponents of design pattern philosophy will therefore say, *because Python has first-class functions, the strategy pattern is unnecessary*. In truth, Python's first-class functions allow us to implement the strategy pattern in a more straightforward way. Knowing the pattern exists can still help us choose a correct design for our program, but implement it using a more readable syntax. The strategy pattern, or a top-level function implementation of it, should be used when we need to allow client code or the end user to select from multiple implementations of the same interface.

# The state pattern

The state pattern is structurally similar to the strategy pattern, but its intent and purpose are very different. The goal of the state pattern is to represent state-transition systems: systems where it is obvious that an object can be in a specific state, and that certain activities may drive it to a different state.

To make this work, we need a manager, or context class that provides an interface for switching states. Internally, this class contains a pointer to the current state. Each state knows what other states it is allowed to be in and will transition to those states depending on actions invoked upon it.

So, we have two types of classes: the context class and multiple state classes. The context class maintains the current state, and forwards actions to the state classes. The state classes are typically hidden from any other objects that are calling the context; it acts like a black box that happens to perform state management internally. Here's how it looks in UML:

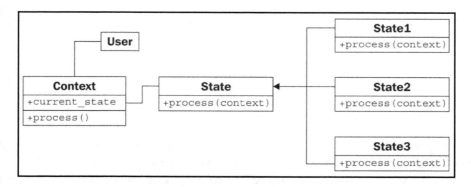

# A state example

To illustrate the state pattern, let's build an XML parsing tool. The context class will be the parser itself. It will take a string as input and place the tool in an initial parsing state. The various parsing states will eat characters, looking for a specific value, and when that value is found, change to a different state. The goal is to create a tree of node objects for each tag and its contents. To keep things manageable, we'll parse only a subset of XML – tags and tag names. We won't be able to handle attributes on tags. It will parse text content of tags, but won't attempt to parse *mixed* content, which has tags inside of text. Here is an example *simplified XML* file that we'll be able to parse:

```
<book>
    <author>Dusty Phillips</author>
    <publisher>Packt Publishing</publisher>
    <title>Python 3 Object Oriented Programming</title>
    <content>
        <chapter>
            <number>1</number>
            <title>Object Oriented Design</title>
        </chapter>
        <chapter>
            <number>2</number>
            <title>Objects In Python</title>
        </chapter>
    </content>
</book>
```

Before we look at the states and the parser, let's consider the output of this program. We know we want a tree of Node objects, but what does a Node look like? It will clearly need to know the name of the tag it is parsing, and since it's a tree, it should probably maintain a pointer to the parent node and a list of the node's children in order. Some nodes have a text value, but not all of them. Let's look at this Node class first:

```python
class Node:
    def __init__(self, tag_name, parent=None):
        self.parent = parent
        self.tag_name = tag_name
        self.children = []
        self.text = ""

    def __str__(self):
        if self.text:
            return self.tag_name + ": " + self.text
        else:
```

```
return self.tag_name
```

This class sets default attribute values upon initialization. The __str__ method is supplied to help visualize the tree structure when we're finished.

Now, looking at the example document, we need to consider what states our parser can be in. Clearly, it's going to start in a state where no nodes have yet been processed. We'll need a state for processing opening tags and closing tags. And when we're inside a tag with text contents, we'll have to process that as a separate state, too.

Switching states can be tricky; how do we know if the next node is an opening tag, a closing tag, or a text node? We could put a little logic in each state to work this out, but it actually makes more sense to create a new state whose sole purpose is figuring out which state we'll be switching to next. If we call this transition state **ChildNode**, we end up with the following states:

- `FirstTag`
- `ChildNode`
- `OpenTag`
- `CloseTag`
- `Text`

The **FirstTag** state will switch to **ChildNode**, which is responsible for deciding which of the other three states to switch to; when those states are finished, they'll switch back to **ChildNode**. The following state-transition diagram shows the available state changes:

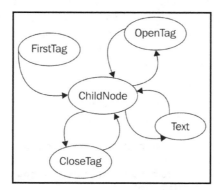

The states are responsible for taking *what's left of the string*, processing as much of it as they know what to do with, and then telling the parser to take care of the rest of it. Let's construct the `Parser` class first:

```
class Parser:
    def __init__(self, parse_string):
        self.parse_string = parse_string
        self.root = None
        self.current_node = None

        self.state = FirstTag()

    def process(self, remaining_string):
        remaining = self.state.process(remaining_string, self)
        if remaining:
            self.process(remaining)

    def start(self):
        self.process(self.parse_string)
```

The initializer sets up a few variables on the class that the individual states will access. The `parse_string` instance variable is the text that we are trying to parse. The `root` node is the *top* node in the XML structure. The `current_node` instance variable is the one that we are currently adding children to.

The important feature of this parser is the `process` method, which accepts the remaining string, and passes it off to the current state. The parser (the `self` argument) is also passed into the state's process method so that the state can manipulate it. The state is expected to return the remainder of the unparsed string when it is finished processing. The parser then recursively calls the `process` method on this remaining string to construct the rest of the tree.

Now let's have a look at the `FirstTag` state:

```
class FirstTag:
    def process(self, remaining_string, parser):
        i_start_tag = remaining_string.find("<")
        i_end_tag = remaining_string.find(">")
        tag_name = remaining_string[i_start_tag + 1 : i_end_tag]
        root = Node(tag_name)
        parser.root = parser.current_node = root
        parser.state = ChildNode()
        return remaining_string[i_end_tag + 1 :]
```

This state finds the index (the `i_` stands for index) of the opening and closing angle brackets on the first tag. You may think this state is unnecessary, since XML requires that there be no text before an opening tag. However, there may be whitespace that needs to be consumed; this is why we search for the opening angle bracket instead of assuming it is the first character in the document.

 Note that this code is assuming a valid input file. A proper implementation would be rigorously testing for invalid input, and would attempt to recover or display an extremely descriptive error message.

The method extracts the name of the tag and assigns it to the root node of the parser. It also assigns it to `current_node`, since that's the one we'll be adding children to next.

Then comes the important part: the method changes the current state on the parser object to a `ChildNode` state. It then returns the remainder of the string (after the opening tag) to allow it to be processed.

The `ChildNode` state, which seems quite complicated, turns out to require nothing but a simple conditional:

```
class ChildNode:
    def process(self, remaining_string, parser):
        stripped = remaining_string.strip()
        if stripped.startswith("</"):
            parser.state = CloseTag()
        elif stripped.startswith("<"):
            parser.state = OpenTag()
        else:
            parser.state = TextNode()
        return stripped
```

The `strip()` call removes whitespace from the string. Then the parser determines if the next item is an opening or closing tag, or a string of text. Depending on which possibility occurs, it sets the parser to a particular state, and then tells it to parse the remainder of the string.

The `OpenTag` state is similar to the `FirstTag` state, except that it adds the newly created node to the previous `current_node` object's `children` and sets it as the new `current_node`. It places the processor back in the `ChildNode` state before continuing:

```python
class OpenTag:
    def process(self, remaining_string, parser):
        i_start_tag = remaining_string.find("<")
        i_end_tag = remaining_string.find(">")
        tag_name = remaining_string[i_start_tag + 1 : i_end_tag]
        node = Node(tag_name, parser.current_node)
        parser.current_node.children.append(node)
        parser.current_node = node
        parser.state = ChildNode()
        return remaining_string[i_end_tag + 1 :]
```

The `CloseTag` state basically does the opposite; it sets the parser's `current_node` back to the parent node so any further children in the outside tag can be added to it:

```python
class CloseTag:
    def process(self, remaining_string, parser):
        i_start_tag = remaining_string.find("<")
        i_end_tag = remaining_string.find(">")
        assert remaining_string[i_start_tag + 1] == "/"
        tag_name = remaining_string[i_start_tag + 2 : i_end_tag]
        assert tag_name == parser.current_node.tag_name
        parser.current_node = parser.current_node.parent
        parser.state = ChildNode()
        return remaining_string[i_end_tag + 1 :].strip()
```

The two `assert` statements help ensure that the parse strings are consistent.

Finally, the `TextNode` state very simply extracts the text before the next close tag and sets it as a value on the current node:

```python
class TextNode:
    def process(self, remaining_string, parser):
        i_start_tag = remaining_string.find('<')
        text = remaining_string[:i_start_tag]
        parser.current_node.text = text
        parser.state = ChildNode()
        return remaining_string[i_start_tag:]
```

Now we just have to set up the initial state on the parser object we created. The initial state is a `FirstTag` object, so just add the following to the __init__ method:

```
self.state = FirstTag()
```

To test the class, let's add a main script that opens an file from the command line, parses it, and prints the nodes:

```
if __name__ == "__main__":
    import sys
    with open(sys.argv[1]) as file:
        contents = file.read()
        p = Parser(contents)
        p.start()

        nodes = [p.root]
        while nodes:
            node = nodes.pop(0)
            print(node)
            nodes = node.children + nodes
```

This code opens the file, loads the contents, and parses the result. Then it prints each node and its children in order. The __str__ method we originally added on the `node` class takes care of formatting the nodes for printing. If we run the script on the earlier example, it outputs the tree as follows:

```
book
author: Dusty Phillips
publisher: Packt Publishing
title: Python 3 Object Oriented Programming
content
chapter
number: 1
title: Object Oriented Design
chapter
number: 2
title: Objects In Python
```

Comparing this to the original simplified XML document tells us the parser is working.

# State versus strategy

The state pattern looks very similar to the strategy pattern; indeed, the UML diagrams for the two are identical. The implementation, too, is identical. We could even have written our states as first-class functions instead of wrapping them in objects, as was suggested for strategy.

While the two patterns have identical structures, they solve completely different problems. The strategy pattern is used to choose an algorithm at runtime; generally, only one of those algorithms is going to be chosen for a particular use case. The state pattern, on the other hand, is designed to allow switching between different states dynamically, as some process evolves. In code, the primary difference is that the strategy pattern is not typically aware of other strategy objects. In the state pattern, either the state or the context needs to know which other states that it can switch to.

# State transition as coroutines

The state pattern is the canonical object-oriented solution to state-transition problems. However, you can get a similar effect by constructing your objects as coroutines. Remember the regular expression log file parser we built in `Chapter 21`, *The Iterator Pattern*? That was a state-transition problem in disguise. The main difference between that implementation and one that defines all the objects (or functions) used in the state pattern is that the coroutine solution allows us to encode more of the boilerplate in language constructs. There are two implementations, but neither one is inherently better than the other. The state pattern is actually the only place I would consider using coroutines outside of `asyncio`.

# The singleton pattern

The singleton pattern is one of the most controversial patterns; many have accused it of being an *anti-pattern*, a pattern that should be avoided, not promoted. In Python, if someone is using the singleton pattern, they're almost certainly doing something wrong, probably because they're coming from a more restrictive programming language.

So, why discuss it at all? Singleton is one of the most famous of all design patterns. It is useful in overly object-oriented languages, and is a vital part of traditional object-oriented programming. More relevantly, the idea behind singleton is useful, even if we implement the concept in a totally different way in Python.

The basic idea behind the singleton pattern is to allow exactly one instance of a certain object to exist. Typically, this object is a sort of manager class like those we discussed in `Chapter 19`, *When to Use Object-Oriented Programming*. Such objects often need to be referenced by a wide variety of other objects, and passing references to the manager object around to the methods and constructors that need them can make code hard to read.

Instead, when a singleton is used, the separate objects request the single instance of the manager object from the class, so a reference to it need not to be passed around. The UML diagram doesn't fully describe it, but here it is for completeness:

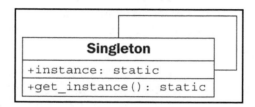

In most programming environments, singletons are enforced by making the constructor private (so no one can create additional instances of it), and then providing a static method to retrieve the single instance. This method creates a new instance the first time it is called, and then returns that same instance for all subsequent calls.

# Singleton implementation

Python doesn't have private constructors, but for this purpose, we can use the \_\_new\_\_ class method to ensure that only one instance is ever created:

```python
class OneOnly:
    _singleton = None
    def __new__(cls, *args, **kwargs):
        if not cls._singleton:
            cls._singleton = super(OneOnly, cls
                ).__new__(cls, *args, **kwargs)
        return cls._singleton
```

When \_\_new\_\_ is called, it normally constructs a new instance of that class. When we override it, we first check whether our singleton instance has been created; if not, we create it using a super call. Thus, whenever we call the constructor on OneOnly, we always get the exact same instance:

```
>>> o1 = OneOnly()
>>> o2 = OneOnly()
>>> o1 == o2
True
>>> o1
<__main__.OneOnly object at 0xb71c008c>
>>> o2
<__main__.OneOnly object at 0xb71c008c>
```

The two objects are equal and located at the same address; thus, they are the same object. This particular implementation isn't very transparent, since it's not obvious that a singleton object has been created. Whenever we call a constructor, we expect a new instance of that object; in this case, that contract is violated. Perhaps, good docstrings on the class could alleviate this problem if we really think we need a singleton.

But we don't need it. Python coders frown on forcing the users of their code into a specific mindset. We may think only one instance of a class will ever be required, but other programmers may have different ideas. Singletons can interfere with distributed computing, parallel programming, and automated testing, for example. In all those cases, it can be very useful to have multiple or alternative instances of a specific object, even though a *normal* operation may never require one.

# Module variables can mimic singletons

Normally, in Python, the singleton pattern can be sufficiently mimicked using module-level variables. It's not as *safe* as a singleton in that people could reassign those variables at any time, but as with the private variables we discussed in Chapter 16, *Objects in Python*, this is acceptable in Python. If someone has a valid reason to change those variables, why should we stop them? It also doesn't stop people from instantiating multiple instances of the object, but again, if they have a valid reason to do so, why interfere?

Ideally, we should give them a mechanism to get access to the *default singleton* value, while also allowing them to create other instances if they need them. While technically not a singleton at all, it provides the most Pythonic mechanism for singleton-like behavior.

To use module-level variables instead of a singleton, we instantiate an instance of the class after we've defined it. We can improve our state pattern to use singletons. Instead of creating a new object every time we change states, we can create a module-level variable that is always accessible:

```
class Node:
    def __init__(self, tag_name, parent=None):
        self.parent = parent
        self.tag_name = tag_name
        self.children = []
        self.text = ""

    def __str__(self):
        if self.text:
            return self.tag_name + ": " + self.text
        else:
            return self.tag_name


class FirstTag:
    def process(self, remaining_string, parser):
        i_start_tag = remaining_string.find("<")
        i_end_tag = remaining_string.find(">")
        tag_name = remaining_string[i_start_tag + 1 : i_end_tag]
        root = Node(tag_name)
        parser.root = parser.current_node = root
        parser.state = child_node
        return remaining_string[i_end_tag + 1 :]


class ChildNode:
    def process(self, remaining_string, parser):
        stripped = remaining_string.strip()
        if stripped.startswith("</"):
            parser.state = close_tag
        elif stripped.startswith("<"):
            parser.state = open_tag
        else:
            parser.state = text_node
        return stripped


class OpenTag:
    def process(self, remaining_string, parser):
        i_start_tag = remaining_string.find("<")
        i_end_tag = remaining_string.find(">")
        tag_name = remaining_string[i_start_tag + 1 : i_end_tag]
        node = Node(tag_name, parser.current_node)
        parser.current_node.children.append(node)
        parser.current_node = node
        parser.state = child_node
        return remaining_string[i_end_tag + 1 :]
```

```
class TextNode:
    def process(self, remaining_string, parser):
        i_start_tag = remaining_string.find("<")
        text = remaining_string[:i_start_tag]
        parser.current_node.text = text
        parser.state = child_node
        return remaining_string[i_start_tag:]


class CloseTag:
    def process(self, remaining_string, parser):
        i_start_tag = remaining_string.find("<")
        i_end_tag = remaining_string.find(">")
        assert remaining_string[i_start_tag + 1] == "/"
        tag_name = remaining_string[i_start_tag + 2 : i_end_tag]
        assert tag_name == parser.current_node.tag_name
        parser.current_node = parser.current_node.parent
        parser.state = child_node
        return remaining_string[i_end_tag + 1 :].strip()


first_tag = FirstTag()
child_node = ChildNode()
text_node = TextNode()
open_tag = OpenTag()
close_tag = CloseTag()
```

All we've done is create instances of the various state classes that can be reused. Notice how we can access these module variables inside the classes, even before the variables have been defined? This is because the code inside the classes is not executed until the method is called, and by this point, the entire module will have been defined.

The difference in this example is that instead of wasting memory creating a bunch of new instances that must be garbage collected, we are reusing a single state object for each state. Even if multiple parsers are running at once, only these state classes need to be used.

When we originally created the state-based parser, you may have wondered why we didn't pass the parser object to __init__ on each individual state, instead of passing it into the process method as we did. The state could then have been referenced as self.parser. This is a perfectly valid implementation of the state pattern, but it would not have allowed leveraging the singleton pattern. If the state objects maintain a reference to the parser, then they cannot be used simultaneously to reference other parsers.

Remember, these are two different patterns with different purposes; the fact that singleton's purpose may be useful for implementing the state pattern does not mean the two patterns are related.

# The template pattern

The template pattern is useful for removing duplicate code; it's intended to support the **Don't Repeat Yourself** principle we discussed in Chapter 19, *When to Use Object-Oriented Programming*. It is designed for situations where we have several different tasks to accomplish that have some, but not all, steps in common. The common steps are implemented in a base class, and the distinct steps are overridden in subclasses to provide custom behavior. In some ways, it's like a generalized strategy pattern, except similar sections of the algorithms are shared using a base class. Here it is in the UML format:

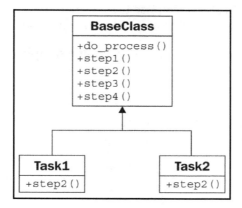

# A template example

Let's create a car sales reporter as an example. We can store records of sales in an SQLite database table. SQLite is a simple file-based database engine that allows us to store records using SQL syntax. Python includes SQLite in its standard library, so there are no extra modules required.

We have two common tasks we need to perform:

- Select all sales of new vehicles and output them to the screen in a comma-delimited format
- Output a comma-delimited list of all salespeople with their gross sales and save it to a file that can be imported to a spreadsheet

These seem like quite different tasks, but they have some common features. In both cases, we need to perform the following steps:

1. Connect to the database.
2. Construct a query for new vehicles or gross sales.
3. Issue the query.
4. Format the results into a comma-delimited string.
5. Output the data to a file or email.

The query construction and output steps are different for the two tasks, but the remaining steps are identical. We can use the template pattern to put the common steps in a base class, and the varying steps in two subclasses.

Before we start, let's create a database and put some sample data in it, using a few lines of SQL:

```python
import sqlite3

conn = sqlite3.connect("sales.db")

conn.execute(
    "CREATE TABLE Sales (salesperson text, "
    "amt currency, year integer, model text, new boolean)"
)
conn.execute(
    "INSERT INTO Sales values"
    " ('Tim', 16000, 2010, 'Honda Fit', 'true')"
)
conn.execute(
    "INSERT INTO Sales values"
    " ('Tim', 9000, 2006, 'Ford Focus', 'false')"
)
conn.execute(
    "INSERT INTO Sales values"
    " ('Gayle', 8000, 2004, 'Dodge Neon', 'false')"
)
conn.execute(
    "INSERT INTO Sales values"
```

```
        " ('Gayle', 28000, 2009, 'Ford Mustang', 'true')"
    )
    conn.execute(
        "INSERT INTO Sales values"
        " ('Gayle', 50000, 2010, 'Lincoln Navigator', 'true')"
    )
    conn.execute(
        "INSERT INTO Sales values"
        " ('Don', 20000, 2008, 'Toyota Prius', 'false')"
    )
    conn.commit()
    conn.close()
```

Hopefully, you can see what's going on here even if you don't know SQL; we've created a table to hold the data, and used six `insert` statements to add sales records. The data is stored in a file named `sales.db`. Now we have a sample we can work with in developing our template pattern.

Since we've already outlined the steps that the template has to perform, we can start by defining the base class that contains the steps. Each step gets its own method (to make it easy to selectively override any one step), and we have one more managerial method that calls the steps in turn. Without any method content, here's how it might look:

```
class QueryTemplate:
    def connect(self):
        pass

    def construct_query(self):
        pass

    def do_query(self):
        pass

    def format_results(self):
        pass

    def output_results(self):
        pass

    def process_format(self):
        self.connect()
        self.construct_query()
        self.do_query()
        self.format_results()
        self.output_results()
```

The `process_format` method is the primary method to be called by an outside client. It ensures each step is executed in order, but it does not care whether that step is implemented in this class or in a subclass. For our examples, we know that three methods are going to be identical between our two classes:

```python
import sqlite3

class QueryTemplate:
    def connect(self):
        self.conn = sqlite3.connect("sales.db")

    def construct_query(self):
        raise NotImplementedError()

    def do_query(self):
        results = self.conn.execute(self.query)
        self.results = results.fetchall()

    def format_results(self):
        output = []
        for row in self.results:
            row = [str(i) for i in row]
            output.append(", ".join(row))
        self.formatted_results = "\n".join(output)

    def output_results(self):
        raise NotImplementedError()
```

To help with implementing subclasses, the two methods that are not specified raise `NotImplementedError`. This is a common way to specify abstract interfaces in Python when abstract base classes seem too heavyweight. The methods could have empty implementations (with `pass`), or could be fully unspecified. Raising `NotImplementedError`, however, helps the programmer understand that the class is meant to be subclassed and these methods overridden. Empty methods or methods that do not exist are harder to identify as needing to be implemented and to debug if we forget to implement them.

Now we have a template class that takes care of the boring details, but is flexible enough to allow the execution and formatting of a wide variety of queries. The best part is, if we ever want to change our database engine from SQLite to another database engine (such as `py-postgresql`), we only have to do it here, in this template class, and we don't have to touch the two (or two hundred) subclasses we might have written.

Let's have a look at the concrete classes now:

```python
import datetime

class NewVehiclesQuery(QueryTemplate):
    def construct_query(self):
        self.query = "select * from Sales where new='true'"

    def output_results(self):
        print(self.formatted_results)


class UserGrossQuery(QueryTemplate):
    def construct_query(self):
        self.query = (
            "select salesperson, sum(amt) "
            + " from Sales group by salesperson"
        )

    def output_results(self):
        filename = "gross_sales_{0}".format(
            datetime.date.today().strftime("%Y%m%d")
        )
        with open(filename, "w") as outfile:
            outfile.write(self.formatted_results)
```

These two classes are actually pretty short, considering what they're doing: connecting to a database, executing a query, formatting the results, and outputting them. The superclass takes care of the repetitive work, but lets us easily specify those steps that vary between tasks. Further, we can also easily change steps that are provided in the base class. For example, if we wanted to output something other than a comma-delimited string (for example: an HTML report to be uploaded to a website), we can still override format_results.

# Exercises

While writing the examples for this chapter, I discovered that it can be very difficult, and extremely educational, to come up with good examples where specific design patterns should be used. Instead of going over current or old projects to see where you can apply these patterns, as I've suggested in previous chapters, think about the patterns and different situations where they might come up. Try to think outside your own experiences. If your current projects are in the banking business, consider how you'd apply these design patterns in a retail or point-of-sale application. If you normally write web applications, think about using design patterns while writing a compiler.

Look at the decorator pattern and come up with some good examples of when to apply it. Focus on the pattern itself, not the Python syntax we discussed. It's a bit more general than the actual pattern. The special syntax for decorators is, however, something you may want to look for places to apply in existing projects too.

What are some good areas to use the observer pattern? Why? Think about not only how you'd apply the pattern, but how you would implement the same task without using observer? What do you gain, or lose, by choosing to use it?

Consider the difference between the strategy and state patterns. Implementation-wise, they look very similar, yet they have different purposes. Can you think of cases where the patterns could be interchanged? Would it be reasonable to redesign a state-based system to use strategy instead, or vice versa? How different would the design actually be?

The template pattern is such an obvious application of inheritance to reduce duplicate code that you may have used it before, without knowing its name. Try to think of at least half a dozen different scenarios where it would be useful. If you can do this, you'll be finding places for it in your daily coding all the time.

# Summary

This chapter discussed several common design patterns in detail, with examples, UML diagrams, and a discussion of the differences between Python and statically typed object-oriented languages. The decorator pattern is often implemented using Python's more generic decorator syntax. The observer pattern is a useful way to decouple events from actions taken on those events. The strategy pattern allows different algorithms to be chosen to accomplish the same task. The state pattern looks similar, but is used instead to represent systems can move between different states using well-defined actions. The singleton pattern, popular in some statically typed languages, is almost always an anti-pattern in Python.

In the next chapter, we'll wrap up our discussion of design patterns.

# Python Design Patterns II

**23**

In this chapter, we will be introduced to several more design patterns. Once again, we'll cover the canonical examples as well as any common alternative implementations in Python. We'll be discussing the following:

- The adapter pattern
- The facade pattern
- Lazy initialization and the flyweight pattern
- The command pattern
- The abstract factory pattern
- The composition pattern

## The adapter pattern

Unlike most of the patterns we reviewed in the previous chapter, the adapter pattern is designed to interact with existing code. We would not design a brand new set of objects that implement the adapter pattern. Adapters are used to allow two preexisting objects to work together, even if their interfaces are not compatible. Like the display adapters that allow you to plug your Micro USB charging cable into a USB-C phone, an adapter object sits between two different interfaces, translating between them on the fly. The adapter object's sole purpose is to perform this translation. Adapting may entail a variety of tasks, such as converting arguments to a different format, rearranging the order of arguments, calling a differently named method, or supplying default arguments.

In structure, the adapter pattern is similar to a simplified decorator pattern. Decorators typically provide the same interface that they replace, whereas adapters map between two different interfaces. This is depicted in UML form in the following diagram:

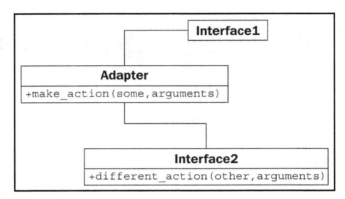

Here, **Interface1** is expecting to call a method called **make_action(some, arguments)**. We already have this perfect **Interface2** class that does everything we want (and to avoid duplication, we don't want to rewrite it!), but it provides a method called **different_action(other, arguments)** instead. The **Adapter** class implements the **make_action** interface and maps the arguments to the existing interface.

The advantage here is that the code that maps from one interface to another is all in one place. The alternative would be really ugly; we'd have to perform the translation in multiple places whenever we need to access this code.

For example, imagine we have the following preexisting class, which takes a string date in the format YYYY-MM-DD and calculates a person's age on that date:

```python
class AgeCalculator:
    def __init__(self, birthday):
        self.year, self.month, self.day = (
            int(x) for x in birthday.split("-")
        )

    def calculate_age(self, date):
        year, month, day = (int(x) for x in date.split("-"))
        age = year - self.year
        if (month, day) < (self.month, self.day):
            age -= 1
        return age
```

This is a pretty simple class that does what it's supposed to do. But we have to wonder what the programmer was thinking, using a specifically formatted string instead of using Python's incredibly useful built-in datetime library. As conscientious programmers who reuse code whenever possible, most of the programs we write will interact with datetime objects, not strings.

We have several options to address this scenario. We could rewrite the class to accept datetime objects, which would probably be more accurate anyway. But if this class had been provided by a third party and we don't know how to or can't change its internal structure, we need an alternative. We could use the class as it is, and whenever we want to calculate the age on a datetime.date object, we could call datetime.date.strftime('%Y-%m-%d') to convert it to the proper format. But that conversion would be happening in a lot of places, and worse, if we mistyped the %m as %M, it would give us the current minute instead of the month entered. Imagine if you wrote that in a dozen different places only to have to go back and change it when you realized your mistake. It's not maintainable code, and it breaks the DRY principle.

Instead, we can write an adapter that allows a normal date to be plugged into a normal AgeCalculator class, as shown in the following code:

```python
import datetime


class DateAgeAdapter:
    def _str_date(self, date):
        return date.strftime("%Y-%m-%d")

    def __init__(self, birthday):
        birthday = self._str_date(birthday)
        self.calculator = AgeCalculator(birthday)

    def get_age(self, date):
        date = self._str_date(date)
        return self.calculator.calculate_age(date)
```

This adapter converts datetime.date and datetime.time (they have the same interface to strftime) into a string that our original AgeCalculator can use. Now we can use the original code with our new interface. I changed the method signature to get_age to demonstrate that the calling interface may also be looking for a different method name, not just a different type of argument.

Creating a class as an adapter is the usual way to implement this pattern, but, as usual, there are other ways to do it in Python. Inheritance and multiple inheritance can be used to add functionality to a class. For example, we could add an adapter on the `date` class so that it works with the original `AgeCalculator` class, as follows:

```
import datetime
class AgeableDate(datetime.date):
    def split(self, char):
        return self.year, self.month, self.day
```

It's code like this that makes one wonder whether Python should even be legal. We have added a `split` method to our subclass that takes a single argument (which we ignore) and returns a tuple of year, month, and day. This works flawlessly with the original `AgeCalculator` class because the code calls `strip` on a specially formatted string, and `strip`, in that case, returns a tuple of year, month, and day. The `AgeCalculator` code only cares if `strip` exists and returns acceptable values; it doesn't care if we really passed in a string. The following code really works:

```
>>> bd = AgeableDate(1975, 6, 14)
>>> today = AgeableDate.today()
>>> today
AgeableDate(2015, 8, 4)
>>> a = AgeCalculator(bd)
>>> a.calculate_age(today)
40
```

It works but it's a stupid idea. In this particular instance, such an adapter would be hard to maintain. We'd soon forget why we needed to add a `strip` method to a `date` class. The method name is ambiguous. That can be the nature of adapters, but creating an adapter explicitly instead of using inheritance usually clarifies its purpose.

Instead of inheritance, we can sometimes also use monkey-patching to add a method to an existing class. It won't work with the `datetime` object, as it doesn't allow attributes to be added at runtime. In normal classes, however, we can just add a new method that provides the adapted interface that is required by calling code. Alternatively, we could extend or monkey-patch the `AgeCalculator` itself to replace the `calculate_age` method with something more amenable to our needs.

Finally, it is often possible to use a function as an adapter; this doesn't obviously fit the actual design of the adapter pattern, but if we recall that functions are essentially objects with a `__call__` method, it becomes an obvious adapter adaptation.

# The facade pattern

The facade pattern is designed to provide a simple interface to a complex system of components. For complex tasks, we may need to interact with these objects directly, but there is often a *typical* usage for the system for which these complicated interactions aren't necessary. The facade pattern allows us to define a new object that encapsulates this typical usage of the system. Any time we want access to common functionality, we can use the single object's simplified interface. If another part of the project needs access to more complicated functionality, it is still able to interact with the system directly. The UML diagram for the facade pattern is really dependent on the subsystem, but in a cloudy way, it looks like this:

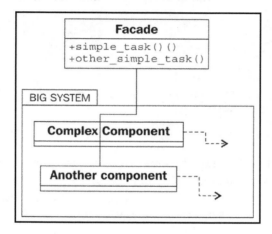

A facade is, in many ways, like an adapter. The primary difference is that a facade tries to abstract a simpler interface out of a complex one, while an adapter only tries to map one existing interface to another.

Let's write a simple facade for an email application. The low-level library for sending email in Python, as we saw in `Chapter 20`, *Python Object-Oriented Shortcuts*, is quite complicated. The two libraries for receiving messages are even worse.

It would be nice to have a simple class that allows us to send a single email, and list the emails currently in the inbox on an IMAP or POP3 connection. To keep our example short, we'll stick with IMAP and SMTP: two totally different subsystems that happen to deal with email. Our facade performs only two tasks: sending an email to a specific address, and checking the inbox on an IMAP connection. It makes some common assumptions about the connection, such as that the host for both SMTP and IMAP is at the same address, that the username and password for both is the same, and that they use standard ports. This covers the case for many email servers, but if a programmer needs more flexibility, they can always bypass the facade and access the two subsystems directly.

The class is initialized with the hostname of the email server, a username, and a password to log in:

```python
import smtplib
import imaplib

class EmailFacade:
    def __init__(self, host, username, password):
        self.host = host
        self.username = username
        self.password = password
```

The send_email method formats the email address and message, and sends it using smtplib. This isn't a complicated task, but it requires quite a bit of fiddling to massage the *natural* input parameters that are passed into the facade to the correct format to enable smtplib to send the message, as follows:

```python
def send_email(self, to_email, subject, message):
    if not "@" in self.username:
        from_email = "{0}@{1}".format(self.username, self.host)
    else:
        from_email = self.username
    message = (
        "From: {0}\r\n" "To: {1}\r\n" "Subject: {2}\r\n\r\n{3}"
    ).format(from_email, to_email, subject, message)

    smtp = smtplib.SMTP(self.host)
    smtp.login(self.username, self.password)
    smtp.sendmail(from_email, [to_email], message)
```

The if statement at the beginning of the method is catching whether or not the username is the entire *from* email address or just the part on the left-hand side of the @ symbol; different hosts treat the login details differently.

Finally, the code to get the messages currently in the inbox is a royal mess. The IMAP protocol is painfully over-engineered, and the `imaplib` standard library is only a thin layer over the protocol. But we get to simplify it, as follows:

```
def get_inbox(self):
    mailbox = imaplib.IMAP4(self.host)
    mailbox.login(
        bytes(self.username, "utf8"), bytes(self.password, "utf8")
    )
    mailbox.select()
    x, data = mailbox.search(None, "ALL")
    messages = []
    for num in data[0].split():
        x, message = mailbox.fetch(num, "(RFC822)")
        messages.append(message[0][1])
    return messages
```

Now, if we add all this together, we have a simple facade class that can send and receive messages in a fairly straightforward manner; much simpler than if we had to interact with these complex libraries directly.

Although it is rarely mentioned by name in the Python community, the facade pattern is an integral part of the Python ecosystem. Because Python emphasizes language readability, both the language and its libraries tend to provide easy-to-comprehend interfaces to complicated tasks. For example, `for` loops, `list` comprehensions, and generators are all facades into a more complicated iterator protocol. The `defaultdict` implementation is a facade that abstracts away annoying corner cases when a key doesn't exist in a dictionary. The third-party **requests** library is a powerful facade over less readable libraries for HTTP requests, which are themselves a facade over managing the text-based HTTP protocol yourself.

# The flyweight pattern

The flyweight pattern is a memory optimization pattern. Novice Python programmers tend to ignore memory optimization, assuming the built-in garbage collector will take care of them. This is usually perfectly acceptable, but when developing larger applications with many related objects, paying attention to memory concerns can have a huge payoff.

The flyweight pattern ensures that objects that share a state can use the same memory for that shared state. It is normally implemented only after a program has demonstrated memory problems. It may make sense to design an optimal configuration from the beginning in some situations, but bear in mind that premature optimization is the most effective way to create a program that is too complicated to maintain.

Let's have a look at the following UML diagram for the flyweight pattern:

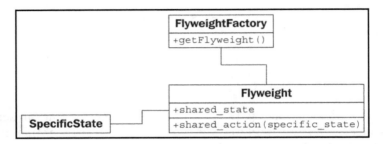

Each **Flyweight** has no specific state. Any time it needs to perform an operation on **SpecificState**, that state needs to be passed into the **Flyweight** by the calling code. Traditionally, the factory that returns a flyweight is a separate object; its purpose is to return a flyweight for a given key identifying that flyweight. It works like the singleton pattern we discussed in Chapter 22, *Python Design Patterns I*; if the flyweight exists, we return it; otherwise, we create a new one. In many languages, the factory is implemented, not as a separate object, but as a static method on the Flyweight class itself.

Think of an inventory system for car sales. Each individual car has a specific serial number and is a specific color. But most of the details about that car are the same for all cars of a particular model. For example, the Honda Fit DX model is a bare-bones car with few features. The LX model has A/C, tilt, cruise, and power windows and locks. The Sport model has fancy wheels, a USB charger, and a spoiler. Without the flyweight pattern, each individual car object would have to store a long list of which features it did and did not have. Considering the number of cars Honda sells in a year, this would add up to a huge amount of wasted memory.

Using the flyweight pattern, we can instead have shared objects for the list of features associated with a model, and then simply reference that model, along with a serial number and color, for individual vehicles. In Python, the flyweight factory is often implemented using that funky __new__ constructor, similar to what we did with the singleton pattern.

Unlike the singleton pattern, which only needs to return one instance of the class, we need to be able to return different instances depending on the keys. We could store the items in a dictionary and look them up based on the key. This solution is problematic, however, because the item will remain in memory as long as it is in the dictionary. If we sold out of LX model Fits, the Fit flyweight would no longer be necessary, yet it would still be in the dictionary. We could clean this up whenever we sell a car, but isn't that what a garbage collector is for?

We can solve this by taking advantage of Python's `weakref` module. This module provides a `WeakValueDictionary` object, which basically allows us to store items in a dictionary without the garbage collector caring about them. If a value is in a weak referenced dictionary and there are no other references to that object stored anywhere in the application (that is, we sold out of LX models), the garbage collector will eventually clean up for us.

Let's build the factory for our car flyweights first, as follows:

```python
import weakref


class CarModel:
    _models = weakref.WeakValueDictionary()

    def __new__(cls, model_name, *args, **kwargs):
        model = cls._models.get(model_name)
        if not model:
            model = super().__new__(cls)
            cls._models[model_name] = model

        return model
```

Basically, whenever we construct a new flyweight with a given name, we first look up that name in the weak referenced dictionary; if it exists, we return that model; if not, we create a new one. Either way, we know the __init__ method on the flyweight will be called every time, regardless of whether it is a new or existing object. Our __init__ method can therefore look like the following code snippet:

```python
    def __init__(
        self,
        model_name,
        air=False,
        tilt=False,
        cruise_control=False,
        power_locks=False,
        alloy_wheels=False,
```

```
            usb_charger=False,
    ):
        if not hasattr(self, "initted"):
            self.model_name = model_name
            self.air = air
            self.tilt = tilt
            self.cruise_control = cruise_control
            self.power_locks = power_locks
            self.alloy_wheels = alloy_wheels
            self.usb_charger = usb_charger
            self.initted = True
```

The `if` statement ensures that we only initialize the object the first time `__init__` is called. This means we can call the factory later with just the model name and get the same flyweight object back. However, because the flyweight will be garbage-collected if no external references to it exist, we must be careful not to accidentally create a new flyweight with null values.

Let's add a method to our flyweight that hypothetically looks up a serial number on a specific model of vehicle, and determines whether it has been involved in any accidents. This method needs access to the car's serial number, which varies from car to car; it cannot be stored with the flyweight. Therefore, this data must be passed into the method by the calling code, as follows:

```
def check_serial(self, serial_number):
    print(
        "Sorry, we are unable to check "
        "the serial number {0} on the {1} "
        "at this time".format(serial_number, self.model_name)
    )
```

We can define a class that stores the additional information, as well as a reference to the flyweight, as follows:

```
class Car:
    def __init__(self, model, color, serial):
        self.model = model
        self.color = color
        self.serial = serial

    def check_serial(self):
        return self.model.check_serial(self.serial)
```

We can also keep track of the available models, as well as the individual cars on the lot, as follows:

```
>>> dx = CarModel("FIT DX")
>>> lx = CarModel("FIT LX", air=True, cruise_control=True,
... power_locks=True, tilt=True)
>>> car1 = Car(dx, "blue", "12345")
>>> car2 = Car(dx, "black", "12346")
>>> car3 = Car(lx, "red", "12347")
```

Now, let's demonstrate the weak referencing at work in the following code snippet:

```
>>> id(lx)
3071620300
>>> del lx
>>> del car3
>>> import gc
>>> gc.collect()
0
>>> lx = CarModel("FIT LX", air=True, cruise_control=True,
... power_locks=True, tilt=True)
>>> id(lx)
3071576140
>>> lx = CarModel("FIT LX")
>>> id(lx)
3071576140
>>> lx.air
True
```

The id function tells us the unique identifier for an object. When we call it a second time, after deleting all references to the LX model and forcing garbage collection, we see that the ID has changed. The value in the CarModel __new__ factory dictionary was deleted and a fresh one was created. If we then try to construct a second CarModel instance, however, it returns the same object (the IDs are the same), and, even though we did not supply any arguments in the second call, the air variable is still set to True. This means the object was not initialized the second time, just as we designed.

Obviously, using the flyweight pattern is more complicated than just storing features on a single car class. When should we choose to use it? The flyweight pattern is designed for conserving memory; if we have hundreds of thousands of similar objects, combining similar properties into a flyweight can have an enormous impact on memory consumption.

It is common for programming solutions that optimize CPU, memory, or disk space to result in more complicated code than their unoptimized brethren. It is therefore important to weigh up the trade-offs when deciding between code maintainability and optimization. When choosing optimization, try to use patterns such as flyweight to ensure that the complexity introduced by optimization is confined to a single (well-documented) section of the code.

 If you have a lot of Python objects in one program, one of the quickest ways to save memory is through the use of __slots__. The __slots__ magic method is beyond the scope of this book, but there is plenty of information available if you check online. If you are still low on memory, flyweight may be a reasonable solution.

# The command pattern

The command pattern adds a level of abstraction between actions that must be done and the object that invokes those actions, normally at a later time. In the command pattern, client code creates a Command object that can be executed at a later date. This object knows about a receiver object that manages its own internal state when the command is executed on it. The Command object implements a specific interface (typically, it has an execute or do_action method, and also keeps track of any arguments required to perform the action. Finally, one or more Invoker objects execute the command at the correct time.

Here's the UML diagram:

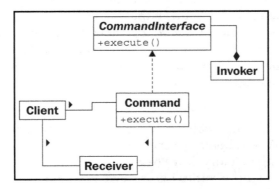

A common example of the command pattern is actions on a graphical window. Often, an action can be invoked by a menu item on the menu bar, a keyboard shortcut, a toolbar icon, or a context menu. These are all examples of `Invoker` objects. The actions that actually occur, such as `Exit`, `Save`, or `Copy`, are implementations of `CommandInterface`. A GUI window to receive exit, a document to receive save, and `ClipboardManager` to receive copy commands, are all examples of possible `Receivers`.

Let's implement a simple command pattern that provides commands for `Save` and `Exit` actions. We'll start with some modest receiver classes, themselves with the following code:

```python
import sys

class Window:
    def exit(self):
        sys.exit(0)

class Document:
    def __init__(self, filename):
        self.filename = filename
        self.contents = "This file cannot be modified"

    def save(self):
        with open(self.filename, 'w') as file:
            file.write(self.contents)
```

These mock classes model objects that would likely be doing a lot more in a working environment. The window would need to handle mouse movement and keyboard events, and the document would need to handle character insertion, deletion, and selection. But for our example, these two classes will do what we need.

Now let's define some invoker classes. These will model toolbar, menu, and keyboard events that can happen; again, they aren't actually hooked up to anything, but we can see how they are decoupled from the command, receiver, and client code in the following code snippet:

```python
class ToolbarButton:
    def __init__(self, name, iconname):
        self.name = name
        self.iconname = iconname

    def click(self):
        self.command.execute()
```

```
class MenuItem:
    def __init__(self, menu_name, menuitem_name):
        self.menu = menu_name
        self.item = menuitem_name

    def click(self):
        self.command.execute()


class KeyboardShortcut:
    def __init__(self, key, modifier):
        self.key = key
        self.modifier = modifier

    def keypress(self):
        self.command.execute()
```

Notice how the various action methods each call the execute method on their respective commands? This code doesn't show the command attribute being set on each object. They could be passed into the __init__ function, but because they may be changed (for example, with a customizable keybinding editor), it makes more sense to set the attributes on the objects afterwards.

Now, let's hook up the commands themselves with the following code:

```
class SaveCommand:
    def __init__(self, document):
        self.document = document

    def execute(self):
        self.document.save()


class ExitCommand:
    def __init__(self, window):
        self.window = window

    def execute(self):
        self.window.exit()
```

These commands are straightforward; they demonstrate the basic pattern, but it is important to note that we can store state and other information with the command if necessary. For example, if we had a command to insert a character, we could maintain state for the character currently being inserted.

Now all we have to do is hook up some client and test code to make the commands work. For basic testing, we can just include the following code at the end of the script:

```
window = Window()
document = Document("a_document.txt")
save = SaveCommand(document)
exit = ExitCommand(window)

save_button = ToolbarButton('save', 'save.png')
save_button.command = save
save_keystroke = KeyboardShortcut("s", "ctrl")
save_keystroke.command = save
exit_menu = MenuItem("File", "Exit")
exit_menu.command = exit
```

First, we create two receivers and two commands. Then, we create several of the available invokers and set the correct command on each of them. To test, we can use `python3-ifilename.py` and run code such as `exit_menu.click()`, which will end the program, or `save_keystroke.keystroke()`, which will save the fake file.

Unfortunately, the preceding examples do not feel terribly Pythonic. They have a lot of "boilerplate code" (code that does not accomplish anything, but only provides structure to the pattern), and the `Command` classes are all eerily similar to each other. Perhaps we could create a generic command object that takes a function as a callback?

In fact, why bother? Can we just use a function or method object for each command? Instead of an object with an `execute()` method, we can write a function and use that as the command directly. The following is a common paradigm for the command pattern in Python:

```
import sys


class Window:
    def exit(self):
        sys.exit(0)


class MenuItem:
    def click(self):
        self.command()


window = Window()
menu_item = MenuItem()
menu_item.command = window.exit
```

Now that looks a lot more like Python. At first glance, it looks like we've removed the command pattern altogether, and we've tightly connected the menu_item and Window classes. But if we look closer, we find there is no tight coupling at all. Any callable can be set up as the command on MenuItem, just as before. And the Window.exit method can be attached to any invoker. Most of the flexibility of the command pattern has been maintained. We have sacrificed complete decoupling for readability, but this code is, in my opinion, and that of many Python programmers, more maintainable than the fully abstracted version.

Of course, since we can add a __call__ method to any object, we aren't restricted to functions. The previous example is a useful shortcut when the method being called doesn't have to maintain state, but in more advanced usage, we can use the following code as well:

```python
class Document:
    def __init__(self, filename):
        self.filename = filename
        self.contents = "This file cannot be modified"

    def save(self):
        with open(self.filename, "w") as file:
            file.write(self.contents)


class KeyboardShortcut:
    def keypress(self):
        self.command()


class SaveCommand:
    def __init__(self, document):
        self.document = document

    def __call__(self):
        self.document.save()


document = Document("a_file.txt")
shortcut = KeyboardShortcut()
save_command = SaveCommand(document)
shortcut.command = save_command
```

Here, we have something that looks like the first command pattern, but a bit more idiomatic. As you can see, making the invoker call a callable instead of a `command` object with an execute method has not restricted us in any way. In fact, it's given us more flexibility. We can link to functions directly when that works, yet we can build a complete callable `command` object when the situation calls for it.

The command pattern is often extended to support undoable commands. For example, a text program may wrap each insertion in a separate command with not only an `execute` method, but also an `undo` method that will delete that insertion. A graphics program may wrap each drawing action (rectangle, line, freehand pixels, and so on) in a command that has an `undo` method that resets the pixels to their original state. In such cases, the decoupling of the command pattern is much more obviously useful, because each action has to maintain enough of its state to undo that action at a later date.

# The abstract factory pattern

The abstract factory pattern is normally used when we have multiple possible implementations of a system that depend on some configuration or platform issue. The calling code requests an object from the abstract factory, not knowing exactly what class of object will be returned. The underlying implementation returned may depend on a variety of factors, such as current locale, operating system, or local configuration.

Common examples of the abstract factory pattern include code for operating-system-independent toolkits, database backends, and country-specific formatters or calculators. An operating-system-independent GUI toolkit might use an abstract factory pattern that returns a set of WinForm widgets under Windows, Cocoa widgets under Mac, GTK widgets under Gnome, and QT widgets under KDE. Django provides an abstract factory that returns a set of object relational classes for interacting with a specific database backend (MySQL, PostgreSQL, SQLite, and others) depending on a configuration setting for the current site. If the application needs to be deployed in multiple places, each one can use a different database backend by changing only one configuration variable. Different countries have different systems for calculating taxes, subtotals, and totals on retail merchandise; an abstract factory can return a particular tax calculation object.

The UML class diagram for an abstract factory pattern is hard to understand without a specific example, so let's turn things around and create a concrete example first. In our example, we'll create a set of formatters that depend on a specific locale and help us format dates and currencies. There will be an abstract factory class that picks the specific factory, as well as a couple of example concrete factories, one for France and one for the USA. Each of these will create formatter objects for dates and times, which can be queried to format a specific value. This is depicted in the following diagram:

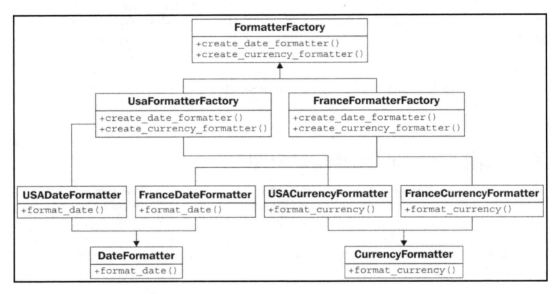

Comparing that image to the earlier, simpler text shows that a picture is not always worth a thousand words, especially considering we haven't even allowed for factory selection code here.

Of course, in Python, we don't have to implement any interface classes, so we can discard DateFormatter, CurrencyFormatter, and FormatterFactory. The formatting classes themselves are pretty straightforward, if verbose, shown here:

```
class FranceDateFormatter:
    def format_date(self, y, m, d):
        y, m, d = (str(x) for x in (y, m, d))
        y = "20" + y if len(y) == 2 else y
        m = "0" + m if len(m) == 1 else m
        d = "0" + d if len(d) == 1 else d
        return "{0}/{1}/{2}".format(d, m, y)
```

```
class USADateFormatter:
    def format_date(self, y, m, d):
        y, m, d = (str(x) for x in (y, m, d))
        y = "20" + y if len(y) == 2 else y
        m = "0" + m if len(m) == 1 else m
        d = "0" + d if len(d) == 1 else d
        return "{0}-{1}-{2}".format(m, d, y)


class FranceCurrencyFormatter:
    def format_currency(self, base, cents):
        base, cents = (str(x) for x in (base, cents))
        if len(cents) == 0:
            cents = "00"
        elif len(cents) == 1:
            cents = "0" + cents

        digits = []
        for i, c in enumerate(reversed(base)):
            if i and not i % 3:
                digits.append(" ")
            digits.append(c)
        base = "".join(reversed(digits))
        return "{0}€{1}".format(base, cents)


class USACurrencyFormatter:
    def format_currency(self, base, cents):
        base, cents = (str(x) for x in (base, cents))
        if len(cents) == 0:
            cents = "00"
        elif len(cents) == 1:
            cents = "0" + cents
        digits = []
        for i, c in enumerate(reversed(base)):
            if i and not i % 3:
                digits.append(",")
            digits.append(c)
        base = "".join(reversed(digits))
        return "${0}.{1}".format(base, cents)
```

These classes use some basic string manipulation to try to turn a variety of possible inputs (integers, strings of different lengths, and others) into the following formats:

|          | USA        | France      |
|----------|------------|-------------|
| Date     | mm-dd-yyyy | dd/mm/yyyy  |
| Currency | $14,500.50 | 14 500€50   |

There could obviously be more validation on the input in this code, but let's keep it simple for this example.

Now that we have the formatters set up, we just need to create the formatter factories, as follows:

```python
class USAFormatterFactory:
    def create_date_formatter(self):
        return USADateFormatter()

    def create_currency_formatter(self):
        return USACurrencyFormatter()


class FranceFormatterFactory:
    def create_date_formatter(self):
        return FranceDateFormatter()

    def create_currency_formatter(self):
        return FranceCurrencyFormatter()
```

Now we set up the code that picks the appropriate formatter. Since this is the kind of thing that only needs to be set up once, we could make it a singleton–except singletons aren't very useful in Python. Let's just make the current formatter a module-level variable instead:

```python
country_code = "US"
factory_map = {"US": USAFormatterFactory, "FR":
FranceFormatterFactory}
formatter_factory = factory_map.get(country_code)()
```

In this example, we hardcode the current country code; in practice, it would likely introspect the locale, the operating system, or a configuration file to choose the code. This example uses a dictionary to associate the country codes with factory classes. Then, we grab the correct class from the dictionary and instantiate it.

It is easy to see what needs to be done when we want to add support for more countries: create the new formatter classes and the abstract factory itself. Bear in mind that `Formatter` classes might be reused; for example, Canada formats its currency the same way as the USA, but its date format is more sensible than its Southern neighbor.

Abstract factories often return a singleton object, but this is not required. In our code, it's returning a new instance of each formatter every time it's called. There's no reason the formatters couldn't be stored as instance variables and the same instance returned for each factory.

Looking back at these examples, we see that, once again, there appears to be a lot of boilerplate code for factories that just doesn't feel necessary in Python. Often, the requirements that might call for an abstract factory can be more easily fulfilled by using a separate module for each factory type (for example: the USA and France), and then ensuring that the correct module is being accessed in a factory module. The package structure for such modules might look like this:

```
localize/
    __init__.py
    backends/
        __init__.py
        USA.py
        France.py
        ...
```

The trick is that __init__.py in the localize package can contain logic that redirects all requests to the correct backend. There are a variety of ways this might be done.

If we know that the backend is never going to change dynamically (that is, without a program restart), we can just put some if statements in __init__.py that check the current country code, and use the (normally unacceptable) from.backends.USAimport * syntax to import all variables from the appropriate backend. Or, we could import each of the backends and set a current_backend variable to point at a specific module, as follows:

```
from .backends import USA, France

if country_code == "US":
    current_backend = USA
```

Depending on which solution we choose, our client code would have to call either localize.format_date or localize.current_backend.format_date to get a date formatted in the current country's locale. The end result is much more Pythonic than the original abstract factory pattern and, in typical usage, is just as flexible.

# The composite pattern

The composite pattern allows complex tree-like structures to be built from simple components. These components, called composite objects, are able to behave sort of like a container and sort of like a variable, depending on whether they have child components. Composite objects are container objects, where the content may actually be another composite object.

Traditionally, each component in a composite object must be either a leaf node (that cannot contain other objects) or a composite node. The key is that both composite and leaf nodes can have the same interface. The following UML diagram is very simple:

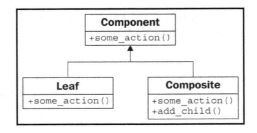

This simple pattern, however, allows us to create complex arrangements of elements, all of which satisfy the interface of the component object. The following diagram depicts a concrete instance of such a complicated arrangement:

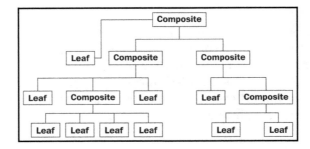

The composite pattern is commonly useful in file/folder-like trees. Regardless of whether a node in the tree is a normal file or a folder, it is still subject to operations such as moving, copying, or deleting the node. We can create a component interface that supports these operations, and then use a composite object to represent folders, and leaf nodes to represent normal files.

Of course, in Python, once again, we can take advantage of duck typing to implicitly provide the interface, so we only need to write two classes. Let's define these interfaces first in the following code:

```
class Folder:
    def __init__(self, name):
        self.name = name
        self.children = {}

    def add_child(self, child):
        pass
```

```
    def move(self, new_path):
        pass

    def copy(self, new_path):
        pass

    def delete(self):
        pass

class File:
    def __init__(self, name, contents):
        self.name = name
        self.contents = contents

    def move(self, new_path):
        pass

    def copy(self, new_path):
        pass

    def delete(self):
        pass
```

For each folder (composite) object, we maintain a dictionary of children. For many composite implementations, a list is sufficient, but in this case, a dictionary will be useful for looking up children by name. Our paths will be specified as node names separated by the / character, similar to paths in a Unix shell.

Thinking about the methods involved, we can see that moving or deleting a node behaves in a similar way, regardless of whether or not it is a file or folder node. Copying, however, has to do a recursive copy for folder nodes, while copying a file node is a trivial operation.

To take advantage of the similar operations, we can extract some of the common methods into a parent class. Let's take that discarded Component interface and change it to a base class with the following code:

```
class Component:
    def __init__(self, name):
        self.name = name

    def move(self, new_path):
        new_folder = get_path(new_path)
        del self.parent.children[self.name]
        new_folder.children[self.name] = self
        self.parent = new_folder
```

```
        def delete(self):
            del self.parent.children[self.name]


    class Folder(Component):
        def __init__(self, name):
            super().__init__(name)
            self.children = {}

        def add_child(self, child):
            pass

        def copy(self, new_path):
            pass


    class File(Component):
        def __init__(self, name, contents):
            super().__init__(name)
            self.contents = contents

        def copy(self, new_path):
            pass


    root = Folder("")


    def get_path(path):
        names = path.split("/")[1:]
        node = root
        for name in names:
            node = node.children[name]
        return node
```

We've created the move and delete methods on the Component class. Both of them access a mysterious parent variable that we haven't set yet. The move method uses a module-level get_path function that finds a node from a predefined root node, given a path. All files will be added to this root node or a child of that node. For the move method, the target should be an existing folder, or we'll get an error. As in many examples in technical books, error handling is woefully absent, to help focus on the principles under consideration.

Let's set up that mysterious `parent` variable in the folder's `add_child` method, as follows:

```
def add_child(self, child):
    child.parent = self
    self.children[child.name] = child
```

Well, that was easy enough. Let's see if our composite file hierarchy is working properly with the following code snippet:

```
$ python3 -i 1261_09_18_add_child.py

>>> folder1 = Folder('folder1')
>>> folder2 = Folder('folder2')
>>> root.add_child(folder1)
>>> root.add_child(folder2)
>>> folder11 = Folder('folder11')
>>> folder1.add_child(folder11)
>>> file111 = File('file111', 'contents')
>>> folder11.add_child(file111)
>>> file21 = File('file21', 'other contents')
>>> folder2.add_child(file21)
>>> folder2.children
{'file21': <__main__.File object at 0xb7220a4c>}
>>> folder2.move('/folder1/folder11')
>>> folder11.children
{'folder2': <__main__.Folder object at 0xb722080c>, 'file111':
<__main__.File object at
0xb72209ec>}
>>> file21.move('/folder1')
>>> folder1.children
{'file21': <__main__.File object at 0xb7220a4c>, 'folder11':
<__main__.Folder object at
0xb722084c>}
```

Yes, we can create folders, add folders to other folders, add files to folders, and move them around! What more could we ask for in a file hierarchy?

Well, we could ask for copying to be implemented, but to conserve trees, let's leave that as an exercise.

The composite pattern is extremely useful for a variety of tree-like structures, including GUI widget hierarchies, file hierarchies, tree sets, graphs, and HTML DOM. It can be a useful pattern in Python when implemented according to the traditional implementation, as in the example demonstrated earlier. Sometimes, if only a shallow tree is being created, we can get away with a list of lists or a dictionary of dictionaries, and do not need to implement custom component, leaf, and composite classes. Other times, we can get away with implementing only one composite class, and treating leaf and composite objects as a single class. Alternatively, Python's duck typing can make it easy to add other objects to a composite hierarchy, as long as they have the correct interface.

# Exercises

Before diving into exercises for each design pattern, take a moment to implement the `copy` method for the `File` and `Folder` objects in the previous section. The `File` method should be quite trivial; just create a new node with the same name and contents, and add it to the new parent folder. The `copy` method on `Folder` is quite a bit more complicated, as you first have to duplicate the folder, and then recursively copy each of its children to the new location. You can call the `copy()` method on the children indiscriminately, regardless of whether each is a file or a folder object. This will drive home just how powerful the composite pattern can be.

Now, as in the previous chapter, look at the patterns we've discussed and consider ideal places where you might implement them. You may want to apply the adapter pattern to existing code, as it is usually applicable when interfacing with existing libraries, rather than new code. How can you use an adapter to force two interfaces to interact with each other correctly?

Can you think of a system complex enough to justify using the facade pattern? Consider how facades are used in real-life situations, such as the driver-facing interface of a car, or the control panel in a factory. It is similar in software, except the users of the facade interface are other programmers, rather than people trained to use them. Are there complex systems in your latest project that could benefit from the facade pattern?

It's possible you don't have any huge, memory-consuming code that would benefit from the flyweight pattern, but can you think of situations where it might be useful? Anywhere that large amounts of overlapping data need to be processed, a flyweight is waiting to be used. Would it be useful in the banking industry? In web applications? At what point does adopting the flyweight pattern make sense? When is it overkill?

What about the command pattern? Can you think of any common (or better yet, uncommon) examples of places where the decoupling of action from invocation would be useful? Look at the programs you use on a daily basis and imagine how they are implemented internally. It's likely that many of them use the command pattern for one purpose or another.

The abstract factory pattern, or the somewhat more Pythonic derivatives we discussed, can be very useful for creating one-touch-configurable systems. Can you think of places where such systems are useful?

Finally, consider the composite pattern. There are tree-like structures all around us in programming; some of them, like our file hierarchy example, are blatant; others are fairly subtle. What situations might arise where the composite pattern would be useful? Can you think of places where you can use it in your own code? What if you adapted the pattern slightly; for example, to contain different types of leaf or composite nodes for different types of objects?

# Summary

In this chapter, we went into detail on several more design patterns, covering their canonical descriptions as well as alternatives for implementing them in Python, which is often more flexible and versatile than traditional object-oriented languages. The adapter pattern is useful for matching interfaces, while the facade pattern is suited to simplifying them. Flyweight is a complicated pattern and only useful if memory optimization is required. In Python, the command pattern is often more aptly implemented using first class functions as callbacks. Abstract factories allow runtime separation of implementations depending on configuration or system information. The composite pattern is used universally for tree-like structures.

In the next chapter, we'll discuss how important it is to test Python programs, and how to do it, focusing on object-oriented principles.

# 24
# Testing Object-Oriented Programs

Skilled Python programmers agree that testing is one of the most important aspects of software development. Even though this chapter is placed near the end of the book, it is not an afterthought; everything we have studied so far will help us when writing tests. In this chapter, we'll look at the following topics:

- The importance of unit testing and test-driven development
- The standard `unittest` module
- The `pytest` automated testing suite
- The `mock` module
- Code coverage
- Cross-platform testing with `tox`

## Why test?

Many programmers already know how important it is to test their code. If you're among them, feel free to skim this section. You'll find the next section–where we actually see how to create tests in Python–much more scintillating. If you're not convinced of the importance of testing, I promise that your code is broken, you just don't know it. Read on!

Some people argue that testing is more important in Python code because of its dynamic nature; compiled languages such as Java and C++ are occasionally thought to be somehow *safer* because they enforce type checking at compile time. However, Python tests rarely check types. They check values. They make sure that the right attributes have been set at the right time or that the sequence has the right length, order, and values. These higher-level concepts need to be tested in any language.

The real reason Python programmers test more than programmers of other languages is that it is so easy to test in Python!

But why test? Do we really need to test? What if we didn't test? To answer those questions, write a tic-tac-toe game from scratch without any testing at all. Don't run it until it is completely written, start to finish. Tic-tac-toe is fairly simple to implement if you make both players human players (no artificial intelligence). You don't even have to try to calculate who the winner is. Now run your program. And fix all the errors. How many were there? I recorded eight in my tic-tac-toe implementation, and I'm not sure I caught them all. Did you?

We need to test our code to make sure it works. Running the program, as we just did, and fixing the errors is one crude form of testing. Python's interactive interpreter and near-zero compile times makes it easy to write a few lines of code and run the program to make sure those lines are doing what is expected. But changing a few lines of code can affect parts of the program that we haven't realized will be influenced by the changes, and therefore neglect to test those parts. Furthermore, as a program grows, the number of paths that the interpreter can take through that code also grow, and it quickly becomes impossible to manually test all of them.

To handle this, we write automated tests. These are programs that automatically run certain inputs through other programs or parts of programs. We can run these test programs in seconds and cover far more potential input situations than one programmer would think to test every time they change something.

There are four main reasons to write tests:

- To ensure that code is working the way the developer thinks it should
- To ensure that code continues working when we make changes
- To ensure that the developer understood the requirements
- To ensure that the code we are writing has a maintainable interface

The first point really doesn't justify the time it takes to write a test; we can test the code directly in the interactive interpreter in the same time or less. But when we have to perform the same sequence of test actions multiple times, it takes less time to automate those steps once and then run them whenever necessary. It is a good idea to run tests every time we change code, whether it is during initial development or maintenance releases. When we have a comprehensive set of automated tests, we can run them after code changes and know that we didn't inadvertently break anything that was tested.

The last two of the preceding points are more interesting. When we write tests for code, it helps us design the API, interface, or pattern that code takes. Thus, if we misunderstood the requirements, writing a test can help highlight that misunderstanding. From the other side, if we're not certain how we want to design a class, we can write a test that interacts with that class so we have an idea of the most natural way to interface with it. In fact, it is often beneficial to write the tests before we write the code we are testing.

# Test-driven development

*Write tests first* is the mantra of test-driven development. Test-driven development takes the *untested code is broken code* concept one step further and suggests that only unwritten code should be untested. We don't write any code until we have written the tests that will prove it works. The first time we run a test it should fail, since the code hasn't been written. Then, we write the code that ensures the test passes, then write another test for the next segment of code.

Test-driven development is fun; it allows us to build little puzzles to solve. Then, we implement the code to solve those puzzles. Then, we make a more complicated puzzle, and we write code that solves the new puzzle without unsolving the previous one.

There are two goals to the test-driven methodology. The first is to ensure that tests really get written. It's so very easy, after we have written code, to say:

> *"Hmm, it seems to work. I don't have to write any tests for this. It was just a small change; nothing could have broken."*

If the test is already written before we write the code, we will know exactly when it works (because the test will pass), and we'll know in the future if it is ever broken by a change we or someone else has made.

Secondly, writing tests first forces us to consider exactly how the code will be used. It tells us what methods objects need to have and how attributes will be accessed. It helps us break up the initial problem into smaller, testable problems, and then to recombine the tested solutions into larger, also tested, solutions. Writing tests can thus become a part of the design process. Often, when we're writing a test for a new object, we discover anomalies in the design that force us to consider new aspects of the software.

As a concrete example, imagine writing code that uses an object-relational mapper to store object properties in a database. It is common to use an automatically assigned database ID in such objects. Our code might use this ID for various purposes. If we are writing a test for such code, before we write it, we may realize that our design is faulty because objects do not have IDs assigned until they have been saved to the database. If we want to manipulate an object without saving it in our test, it will highlight this problem before we have written code based on the faulty premise.

Testing makes software better. Writing tests before we release the software makes it better before the end user sees or purchases the buggy version (I have worked for companies that thrive on the *users can test it* philosophy; it's not a healthy business model). Writing tests before we write software makes it better the first time it is written.

# Unit testing

Let's start our exploration with Python's built-in test library. This library provides a common object-oriented interface for **unit tests**. Unit tests focus on testing the least amount of code possible in any one test. Each one tests a single unit of the total amount of available code.

The Python library for this is called, unsurprisingly, `unittest`. It provides several tools for creating and running unit tests, the most important being the `TestCase` class. This class provides a set of methods that allow us to compare values, set up tests, and clean up when they have finished.

When we want to write a set of unit tests for a specific task, we create a subclass of `TestCase` and write individual methods to do the actual testing. These methods must all start with the name `test`. When this convention is followed, the tests automatically run as part of the test process. Normally, the tests set some values on an object and then run a method, and use the built-in comparison methods to ensure that the right results were calculated. Here's a very simple example:

```python
import unittest


class CheckNumbers(unittest.TestCase):
    def test_int_float(self):
        self.assertEqual(1, 1.0)
```

```
if __name__ == "__main__":
    unittest.main()
```

This code simply subclasses the `TestCase` class and adds a method that calls the `TestCase.assertEqual` method. This method will either succeed or raise an exception, depending on whether the two parameters are equal. If we run this code, the `main` function from `unittest` will give us the following output:

```
.
----------------------------------------------------------------
Ran 1 test in 0.000s

OK
```

Did you know that floats and integers can be compared as equal? Let's add a failing test, as follows:

```
    def test_str_float(self):
        self.assertEqual(1, "1")
```

The output of this code is more sinister, as integers and strings are not considered equal:

```
.F
================================================================
FAIL: test_str_float (__main__.CheckNumbers)
----------------------------------------------------------------
Traceback (most recent call last):
  File "first_unittest.py", line 9, in test_str_float
    self.assertEqual(1, "1")
AssertionError: 1 != '1'


----------------------------------------------------------------
Ran 2 tests in 0.001s

FAILED (failures=1)
```

The dot on the first line indicates that the first test (the one we wrote before) passed successfully; the letter `F` after it shows that the second test failed. Then, at the end, it gives us some informative output telling us how and where the test failed, along with a summary of the number of failures.

We can have as many test methods on one `TestCase` class as we like. As long as the method name begins with `test`, the test runner will execute each one as a separate, isolated test. Each test should be completely independent of other tests. Results or calculations from a previous test should have no impact on the current test. The key to writing good unit tests is keeping each test method as short as possible, testing a small unit of code with each test case. If our code does not seem to naturally break up into such testable units, it's probably a sign that the code needs to be redesigned.

# Assertion methods

The general layout of a test case is to set certain variables to known values, run one or more functions, methods, or processes, and then *prove* that correct expected results were returned or calculated by using `TestCase` assertion methods.

There are a few different assertion methods available to confirm that specific results have been achieved. We just saw `assertEqual`, which will cause a test failure if the two parameters do not pass an equality check. The inverse, `assertNotEqual`, will fail if the two parameters do compare as equal. The `assertTrue` and `assertFalse` methods each accept a single expression, and fail if the expression does not pass an `if` test. These tests do not check for the Boolean values `True` or `False`. Rather, they test the same condition as though an `if` statement were used: `False`, `None`, `0`, or an empty list, dictionary, string, set, or tuple would pass a call to the `assertFalse` method. Nonzero numbers, containers with values in them, or the value `True` would succeed when calling the `assertTrue` method.

There is an `assertRaises` method that can be used to ensure that a specific function call raises a specific exception or, optionally, it can be used as a context manager to wrap inline code. The test passes if the code inside the `with` statement raises the proper exception; otherwise, it fails. The following code snippet is an example of both versions:

```
import unittest


def average(seq):
    return sum(seq) / len(seq)


class TestAverage(unittest.TestCase):
    def test_zero(self):
        self.assertRaises(ZeroDivisionError, average, [])
```

```
def test_with_zero(self):
    with self.assertRaises(ZeroDivisionError):
        average([])


if __name__ == "__main__":
    unittest.main()
```

The context manager allows us to write the code the way we would normally write it (by calling functions or executing code directly), rather than having to wrap the function call in another function call.

There are also several other assertion methods, summarized in the following table:

| Methods | Description |
| --- | --- |
| assertGreater<br>assertGreaterEqual<br>assertLess<br>assertLessEqual | Accept two comparable objects and ensure the named inequality holds. |
| assertIn<br>assertNotIn | Ensure an element is (or is not) an element in a container object. |
| assertIsNone<br>assertIsNotNone | Ensure an element is (or is not) the exact None value (but not another falsey value). |
| assertSameElements | Ensure two container objects have the same elements, ignoring the order. |
| assertSequenceEqualassertDictEqual<br>assertSetEqual<br>assertListEqual<br>assertTupleEqual | Ensure two containers have the same elements in the same order. If there's a failure, show a code difference comparing the two lists to see where they differ. The last four methods also test the type of the list. |

Each of the assertion methods accepts an optional argument named msg. If supplied, it is included in the error message if the assertion fails. This can be useful for clarifying what was expected or explaining where a bug may have occurred to cause the assertion to fail. I rarely use this syntax, however, preferring to use descriptive names for the test method instead.

# Reducing boilerplate and cleaning up

After writing a few small tests, we often find that we have to write the same setup code for several related tests. For example, the following `list` subclass has three methods for statistical calculations:

```python
from collections import defaultdict

class StatsList(list):
    def mean(self):
        return sum(self) / len(self)

    def median(self):
        if len(self) % 2:
            return self[int(len(self) / 2)]
        else:
            idx = int(len(self) / 2)
            return (self[idx] + self[idx-1]) / 2

    def mode(self):
        freqs = defaultdict(int)
        for item in self:
            freqs[item] += 1
        mode_freq = max(freqs.values())
        modes = []
        for item, value in freqs.items():
            if value == mode_freq:
                modes.append(item)
        return modes
```

Clearly, we're going to want to test situations with each of these three methods that have very similar inputs. We'll want to see what happens with empty lists, with lists containing non-numeric values, or with lists containing a normal dataset, for example. We can use the `setUp` method on the `TestCase` class to perform initialization for each test. This method accepts no arguments, and allows us to do arbitrary setup before each test is run. For example, we can test all three methods on identical lists of integers as follows:

```python
from stats import StatsList
import unittest


class TestValidInputs(unittest.TestCase):
    def setUp(self):
        self.stats = StatsList([1, 2, 2, 3, 3, 4])
```

```
    def test_mean(self):
        self.assertEqual(self.stats.mean(), 2.5)

    def test_median(self):
        self.assertEqual(self.stats.median(), 2.5)
        self.stats.append(4)
        self.assertEqual(self.stats.median(), 3)

    def test_mode(self):
        self.assertEqual(self.stats.mode(), [2, 3])
        self.stats.remove(2)
        self.assertEqual(self.stats.mode(), [3])


if __name__ == "__main__":
    unittest.main()
```

If we run this example, it indicates that all tests pass. Notice first that the setUp method is never explicitly called inside the three test_* methods. The test suite does this on our behalf. More importantly, notice how test_median alters the list, by adding an additional 4 to it, yet when the subsequent test_mode is called, the list has returned to the values specified in setUp. If it had not, there would be two fours in the list, and the mode method would have returned three values. This demonstrates that setUp is called individually before each test, ensuring the test class starts with a clean slate. Tests can be executed in any order, and the results of one test must never depend on any other tests.

In addition to the setUp method, TestCase offers a no-argument tearDown method, which can be used for cleaning up after each and every test on the class has run. This method is useful if cleanup requires anything other than letting an object be garbage collected.

For example, if we are testing code that does file I/O, our tests may create new files as a side effect of testing. The tearDown method can remove these files and ensure the system is in the same state it was before the tests ran. Test cases should never have side effects. In general, we group test methods into separate TestCase subclasses depending on what setup code they have in common. Several tests that require the same or similar setup will be placed in one class, while tests that require unrelated setup go in another class.

# Organizing and running tests

It doesn't take long for a collection of unit tests to grow very large and unwieldy. It can quickly become complicated to load and run all the tests at once. This is a primary goal of unit testing: trivially run all tests on our program and get a quick *yes or no* answer to the question, *did my recent changes break anything?*.

As with normal program code, we should divide our test classes into modules and packages that keep them organized. If you name each test module starting with the four characters *test*, there's an easy way to find and run them all. Python's `discover` module looks for any modules in the current folder or subfolders with names that start with `test`. If it finds any `TestCase` objects in these modules, the tests are executed. It's a painless way to ensure we don't miss running any tests. To use it, ensure your test modules are named `test_<something>.py` and then run the `python3-munittestdiscover` command.

Most Python programmers choose to put their tests in a separate package (usually named `tests/` alongside their source directory). This is not required, however. Sometimes it makes sense to put the test modules for different packages in a subpackage next to that package, for example.

# Ignoring broken tests

Sometimes, a test is known to fail, but we don't want the test suite to report the failure. This may be because a broken or unfinished feature has tests written, but we aren't currently focusing on improving it. More often, it happens because a feature is only available on a certain platform, Python version, or for advanced versions of a specific library. Python provides us with a few decorators to mark tests as expected to fail or to be skipped under known conditions.

These decorators are as follows:

- `expectedFailure()`
- `skip(reason)`
- `skipIf(condition, reason)`
- `skipUnless(condition, reason)`

These are applied using the Python decorator syntax. The first one accepts no arguments, and simply tells the test runner not to record the test as a failure when it fails. The `skip` method goes one step further and doesn't even bother to run the test. It expects a single string argument describing why the test was skipped. The other two decorators accept two arguments, one a Boolean expression that indicates whether or not the test should be run, and a similar description. In use, these three decorators might be applied as they are in the following code:

```python
import unittest
import sys


class SkipTests(unittest.TestCase):
    @unittest.expectedFailure
    def test_fails(self):
        self.assertEqual(False, True)

    @unittest.skip("Test is useless")
    def test_skip(self):
        self.assertEqual(False, True)

    @unittest.skipIf(sys.version_info.minor == 4, "broken on 3.4")
    def test_skipif(self):
        self.assertEqual(False, True)

    @unittest.skipUnless(
        sys.platform.startswith("linux"), "broken unless on linux"
    )
    def test_skipunless(self):
        self.assertEqual(False, True)


if __name__ == "__main__":
    unittest.main()
```

The first test fails, but it is reported as an expected failure; the second test is never run. The other two tests may or may not be run depending on the current Python version and operating system. On my Linux system, running Python 3.7, the output looks as follows:

```
xssF
======================================================================
FAIL: test_skipunless (__main__.SkipTests)
----------------------------------------------------------------------
Traceback (most recent call last):
  File "test_skipping.py", line 22, in test_skipunless
    self.assertEqual(False, True)
```

```
AssertionError: False != True


----------------------------------------------------------------
Ran 4 tests in 0.001s

FAILED (failures=1, skipped=2, expected failures=1)
```

The x on the first line indicates an expected failure; the two s characters represent skipped tests, and the F indicates a real failure, since the conditional to skipUnless was True on my system.

# Testing with pytest

The Python unittest module requires a lot of boilerplate code to set up and initialize tests. It is based on the very popular JUnit testing framework for Java. It even uses the same method names (you may have noticed they don't conform to the PEP-8 naming standard, which suggests snake_case rather than CamelCase to indicate a method name) and test layout. While this is effective for testing in Java, it's not necessarily the best design for Python testing. I actually find the unittest framework to be an excellent example of overusing object-oriented principles.

Because Python programmers like their code to be elegant and simple, other test frameworks have been developed, outside the standard library. Two of the more popular ones are pytest and nose. The former is more robust and has had Python 3 support for much longer, so we'll discuss it here.

Since pytest is not part of the standard library, you'll need to download and install it yourself. You can get it from the pytest home page at http://pytest.org/. The website has comprehensive installation instructions for a variety of interpreters and platforms, but you can usually get away with the more common Python package installer, pip. Just type pip install pytest on your command line and you'll be good to go.

pytest has a substantially different layout from the unittest module. It doesn't require test cases to be classes. Instead, it takes advantage of the fact that Python functions are objects, and allows any properly named function to behave like a test. Rather than providing a bunch of custom methods for asserting equality, it uses the assert statement to verify results. This makes tests more readable and maintainable.

When we run `pytest`, it starts in the current folder and searches for any modules or subpackages with names beginning with the characters `test_`. If any functions in this module also start with `test`, they will be executed as individual tests. Furthermore, if there are any classes in the module whose name starts with `Test`, any methods on that class that start with `test_` will also be executed in the test environment.

Using the following code, let's port the simplest possible `unittest` example we wrote earlier to `pytest`:

```
def test_int_float():
    assert 1 == 1.0
```

For the exact same test, we've written two lines of more readable code, in comparison to the six lines required in our first `unittest` example.

However, we are not forbidden from writing class-based tests. Classes can be useful for grouping related tests together or for tests that need to access related attributes or methods on the class. The following example shows an extended class with a passing and a failing test; we'll see that the error output is more comprehensive than that provided by the `unittest` module:

```
class TestNumbers:
    def test_int_float(self):
        assert 1 == 1.0

    def test_int_str(self):
        assert 1 == "1"
```

Notice that the class doesn't have to extend any special objects to be picked up as a test (although `pytest` will run standard `unittest` `TestCases` just fine). If we run `pytest <filename>`, the output looks as follows:

```
================================ test session starts
==============================
platform linux -- Python 3.7.0, pytest-3.8.0, py-1.6.0, pluggy-0.7.1
rootdir: /home/dusty/Py3OOP/Chapter 24: Testing Object-oriented
Programs, inifile:
collected 3 items

test_with_pytest.py ..F [100%]

==================================== FAILURES
====================================
_____ TestNumbers.test_int_str
_____
```

```
self = <test_with_pytest.TestNumbers object at 0x7fdb95e31390>

    def test_int_str(self):
>   assert 1 == "1"
E   AssertionError: assert 1 == '1'

test_with_pytest.py:10: AssertionError
======================= 1 failed, 2 passed in 0.03 seconds
========================
```

The output starts with some useful information about the platform and interpreter. This can be useful for sharing or discussing bugs across disparate systems. The third line tells us the name of the file being tested (if there are multiple test modules picked up, they will all be displayed), followed by the familiar .F we saw in the unittest module; the . character indicates a passing test, while the letter F demonstrates a failure.

After all tests have run, the error output for each of them is displayed. It presents a summary of local variables (there is only one in this example: the self parameter passed into the function), the source code where the error occurred, and a summary of the error message. In addition, if an exception other than an AssertionError is raised, pytest will present us with a complete traceback, including source code references.

By default, pytest suppresses output from print statements if the test is successful. This is useful for test debugging; when a test is failing, we can add print statements to the test to check the values of specific variables and attributes as the test runs. If the test fails, these values are output to help with diagnosis. However, once the test is successful, the print statement output is not displayed, and they are easily ignored. We don't have to *clean up* output by removing print statements. If the tests ever fail again, due to future changes, the debugging output will be immediately available.

# One way to do setup and cleanup

`pytest` supports setup and teardown methods similar to those used in `unittest`, but it provides even more flexibility. We'll discuss these briefly, since they are familiar, but they are not used as extensively as in the `unittest` module, as `pytest` provides us with a powerful fixtures facility, which we'll discuss in the next section.

If we are writing class-based tests, we can use two methods called `setup_method` and `teardown_method` in the same way that `setUp` and `tearDown` are called in `unittest`. They are called before and after each test method in the class to perform setup and cleanup duties. There is one difference from the `unittest` methods though. Both methods accept an argument: the function object representing the method being called.

In addition, `pytest` provides other setup and teardown functions to give us more control over when setup and cleanup code is executed. The `setup_class` and `teardown_class` methods are expected to be class methods; they accept a single argument (there is no `self` argument) representing the class in question. These methods are only run when the class is initiated rather than on each test run.

Finally, we have the `setup_module` and `teardown_module` functions, which are run immediately before and after all tests (in functions or classes) in that module. These can be useful for *one time* setup, such as creating a socket or database connection that will be used by all tests in the module. Be careful with this one, as it can accidentally introduce dependencies between tests if the object stores state that isn't correctly cleaned up between tests.

That short description doesn't do a great job of explaining exactly when these methods are called, so let's look at an example that illustrates exactly when it happens:

```
def setup_module(module):
    print("setting up MODULE {0}".format(module.__name__))


def teardown_module(module):
    print("tearing down MODULE {0}".format(module.__name__))


def test_a_function():
    print("RUNNING TEST FUNCTION")


class BaseTest:
```

```
        def setup_class(cls):
            print("setting up CLASS {0}".format(cls.__name__))

        def teardown_class(cls):
            print("tearing down CLASS {0}\n".format(cls.__name__))

        def setup_method(self, method):
            print("setting up METHOD {0}".format(method.__name__))

        def teardown_method(self, method):
            print("tearing down METHOD {0}".format(method.__name__))


    class TestClass1(BaseTest):
        def test_method_1(self):
            print("RUNNING METHOD 1-1")

        def test_method_2(self):
            print("RUNNING METHOD 1-2")


    class TestClass2(BaseTest):
        def test_method_1(self):
            print("RUNNING METHOD 2-1")

        def test_method_2(self):
            print("RUNNING METHOD 2-2")
```

The sole purpose of the BaseTest class is to extract four methods that are otherwise identical to the test classes, and use inheritance to reduce the amount of duplicate code. So, from the point of view of pytest, the two subclasses have not only two test methods each, but also two setup and two teardown methods (one at the class level, one at the method level).

If we run these tests using `pytest` with the `print` function output suppression disabled (by passing the `-s` or `--capture=no` flag), they show us when the various functions are called in relation to the tests themselves:

```
setup_teardown.py
setting up MODULE setup_teardown
RUNNING TEST FUNCTION
.setting up CLASS TestClass1
setting up METHOD test_method_1
RUNNING METHOD 1-1
.tearing down  METHOD test_method_1
setting up METHOD test_method_2
RUNNING METHOD 1-2
.tearing down  METHOD test_method_2
tearing down CLASS TestClass1
setting up CLASS TestClass2
setting up METHOD test_method_1
RUNNING METHOD 2-1
.tearing down  METHOD test_method_1
setting up METHOD test_method_2
RUNNING METHOD 2-2
.tearing down  METHOD test_method_2
tearing down CLASS TestClass2

tearing down MODULE setup_teardown
```

The setup and teardown methods for the module are executed at the beginning and end of the session. Then the lone module-level test function is run. Next, the setup method for the first class is executed, followed by the two tests for that class. These tests are each individually wrapped in separate `setup_method` and `teardown_method` calls. After the tests have executed, the teardown method on the class is called. The same sequence happens for the second class, before the `teardown_module` method is finally called, exactly once.

# A completely different way to set up variables

One of the most common uses for the various setup and teardown functions is to ensure certain class or module variables are available with a known value before each test method is run.

`pytest` offers a completely different way of doing this, using what are known as **fixtures**. Fixtures are basically named variables that are predefined in a test configuration file. This allows us to separate configuration from the execution of tests, and allows fixtures to be used across multiple classes and modules.

To use them, we add parameters to our test function. The names of the parameters are used to look up specific arguments in specially named functions. For example, if we wanted to test the `StatsList` class we used while demonstrating `unittest`, we would again want to repeatedly test a list of valid integers. But we can write our tests as follows instead of using a setup method:

```python
import pytest
from stats import StatsList


@pytest.fixture
def valid_stats():
    return StatsList([1, 2, 2, 3, 3, 4])


def test_mean(valid_stats):
    assert valid_stats.mean() == 2.5


def test_median(valid_stats):
    assert valid_stats.median() == 2.5
    valid_stats.append(4)
    assert valid_stats.median() == 3


def test_mode(valid_stats):
    assert valid_stats.mode() == [2, 3]
    valid_stats.remove(2)
    assert valid_stats.mode() == [3]
```

Each of the three test methods accepts a parameter named `valid_stats`; this parameter is created by calling the `valid_stats` function, which was decorated with `@pytest.fixture`.

Fixtures can do a lot more than return basic variables. A `request` object can be passed into the fixture factory to provide extremely useful methods and attributes to modify the funcarg's behavior. The `module`, `cls`, and `function` attributes allow us to see exactly which test is requesting the fixture. The `config` attribute allows us to check command-line arguments and a great deal of other configuration data.

If we implement the fixture as a generator, we can run cleanup code after each test is run. This provides the equivalent of a teardown method, except on a per-fixture basis. We can use it to clean up files, close connections, empty lists, or reset queues. For example, the following code tests the `os.mkdir` functionality by creating a temporary directory fixture:

```
import pytest
import tempfile
import shutil
import os.path


@pytest.fixture
def temp_dir(request):
    dir = tempfile.mkdtemp()
    print(dir)
    yield dir
    shutil.rmtree(dir)


def test_osfiles(temp_dir):
    os.mkdir(os.path.join(temp_dir, "a"))
    os.mkdir(os.path.join(temp_dir, "b"))
    dir_contents = os.listdir(temp_dir)
    assert len(dir_contents) == 2
    assert "a" in dir_contents
    assert "b" in dir_contents
```

The fixture creates a new empty temporary directory for files to be created in. It yields this for use in the test, but removes that directory (using `shutil.rmtree`, which recursively removes a directory and anything inside it) after the test has completed. The filesystem is then left in the same state in which it started.

We can pass a `scope` parameter to create a fixture that lasts longer than one test. This is useful when setting up an expensive operation that can be reused by multiple tests, as long as the resource reuse doesn't break the atomic or unit nature of the tests (so that one test does not rely on, and is not impacted by, a previous one). For example, if we were to test the following echo server, we may want to run only one instance of the server in a separate process, and then have multiple tests connect to that instance:

```
import socket

s = socket.socket(socket.AF_INET, socket.SOCK_STREAM)
s.setsockopt(socket.SOL_SOCKET, socket.SO_REUSEADDR, 1)
s.bind(('localhost',1028))
s.listen(1)

    while True:
        client, address = s.accept()
        data = client.recv(1024)
        client.send(data)
        client.close()
```

All this code does is listen on a specific port and wait for input from a client socket. When it receives input, it sends the same value back. To test this, we can start the server in a separate process and cache the result for use in multiple tests. Here's how the test code might look:

```
import subprocess
import socket
import time
import pytest


@pytest.fixture(scope="session")
def echoserver():
    print("loading server")
    p = subprocess.Popen(["python3", "echo_server.py"])
    time.sleep(1)
    yield p
    p.terminate()


@pytest.fixture
def clientsocket(request):
    s = socket.socket(socket.AF_INET, socket.SOCK_STREAM)
    s.connect(("localhost", 1028))
    yield s
    s.close()


def test_echo(echoserver, clientsocket):
    clientsocket.send(b"abc")
    assert clientsocket.recv(3) == b"abc"


def test_echo2(echoserver, clientsocket):
    clientsocket.send(b"def")
    assert clientsocket.recv(3) == b"def"
```

We've created two fixtures here. The first runs the echo server in a separate process, and yields the process object, cleaning it up when it's finished. The second instantiates a new socket object for each test, and closes the socket when the test has completed.

The first fixture is the one we're currently interested in. From the `scope="session"` keyword argument passed into the decorator's constructor, `pytest` knows that we only want this fixture to be initialized and terminated once for the duration of the unit test session.

The scope can be one of the strings `class`, `module`, `package`, or `session`. It determines just how long the argument will be cached. We set it to `session` in this example, so it is cached for the duration of the entire `pytest` run. The process will not be terminated or restarted until all tests have run. The `module` scope, of course, caches it only for tests in that module, and the `class` scope treats the object more like a normal class setup and teardown.

 At the time the third edition of this book went to print, the `package` scope was labeled experimental in `pytest`. Be careful with it, and they request that you supply bug reports.

# Skipping tests with pytest

As with the `unittest` module, it is frequently necessary to skip tests in `pytest`, for a similar variety of reasons: the code being tested hasn't been written yet, the test only runs on certain interpreters or operating systems, or the test is time-consuming and should only be run under certain circumstances.

We can skip tests at any point in our code, using the `pytest.skip` function. It accepts a single argument: a string describing why it has been skipped. This function can be called anywhere. If we call it inside a test function, the test will be skipped. If we call it at the module level, all the tests in that module will be skipped. If we call it inside a fixture, all tests that call that funcarg will be skipped.

Of course, in all these locations, it is often desirable to skip tests only if certain conditions are or are not met. Since we can execute the `skip` function at any place in Python code, we can execute it inside an `if` statement. So we may write a test that looks as follows:

```python
import sys
import pytest

def test_simple_skip():
    if sys.platform != "fakeos":
        pytest.skip("Test works only on fakeOS")
    fakeos.do_something_fake()
    assert fakeos.did_not_happen
```

That's some pretty silly code, really. There is no Python platform named `fakeos`, so this test will skip on all operating systems. It shows how we can skip conditionally, and since the `if` statement can check any valid conditional, we have a lot of power over when tests are skipped. Often, we check `sys.version_info` to check the Python interpreter version, `sys.platform` to check the operating system, or `some_library.__version__` to check whether we have a recent enough version of a given API.

Since skipping an individual test method or function based on a certain conditional is one of the most common uses of test skipping, `pytest` provides a convenience decorator that allows us to do this in one line. The decorator accepts a single string, which can contain any executable Python code that evaluates to a Boolean value. For example, the following test will only run on Python 3 or higher:

```python
@pytest.mark.skipif("sys.version_info <= (3,0)")
def test_python3():
    assert b"hello".decode() == "hello"
```

The `pytest.mark.xfail` decorator behaves similarly, except that it marks a test as expected to fail, similar to `unittest.expectedFailure()`. If the test is successful, it will be recorded as a failure. If it fails, it will be reported as expected behavior. In the case of `xfail`, the conditional argument is optional. If it is not supplied, the test will be marked as expected to fail under all conditions.

The `pytest` has a ton of other features besides those described here and the developers are constantly adding innovative new ways to make your testing experience more enjoyable. They have thorough documentation on their website at https://docs.pytest.org/.

The `pytest` can find and run tests defined using the standard `unittest` library in addition to its own testing infrastructure. This means that if you want to migrate from `unittest` to `pytest`, you don't have to rewrite all your old tests.

# Imitating expensive objects

Sometimes, we want to test code that requires an object be supplied that is either expensive or difficult to construct. In some cases, this may mean your API needs rethinking to have a more testable interface (which typically means a more usable interface). But we sometimes find ourselves writing test code that has a ton of boilerplate to set up objects that are only incidentally related to the code under test.

For example, imagine we have some code that keeps track of flight statuses in an external key-value store (such as redis or memcache), such that we can store the timestamp and the most recent status. A basic version of such code might look as follows:

```python
import datetime
import redis


class FlightStatusTracker:
    ALLOWED_STATUSES = {"CANCELLED", "DELAYED", "ON TIME"}

    def __init__(self):
        self.redis = redis.StrictRedis()

    def change_status(self, flight, status):
        status = status.upper()
        if status not in self.ALLOWED_STATUSES:
            raise ValueError("{} is not a valid
status".format(status))

        key = "flightno:{}".format(flight)
        value = "{}|{}".format(
            datetime.datetime.now().isoformat(), status
        )
        self.redis.set(key, value)
```

There are a lot of things we ought to test for that change_status method. We should check that it raises the appropriate error if a bad status is passed in. We need to ensure that it converts statuses to uppercase. We can see that the key and value have the correct formatting when the set() method is called on the redis object.

One thing we don't have to check in our unit tests, however, is that the redis object is properly storing the data. This is something that absolutely should be tested in integration or application testing, but at the unit test level, we can assume that the py-redis developers have tested their code and that this method does what we want it to. As a rule, unit tests should be self-contained and shouldn't rely on the existence of outside resources, such as a running Redis instance.

Instead, we only need to test that the set() method was called the appropriate number of times and with the appropriate arguments. We can use Mock() objects in our tests to replace the troublesome method with an object we can introspect. The following example illustrates the use of Mock:

```python
from flight_status_redis import FlightStatusTracker
from unittest.mock import Mock
import pytest


@pytest.fixture
def tracker():
    return FlightStatusTracker()


def test_mock_method(tracker):
    tracker.redis.set = Mock()
    with pytest.raises(ValueError) as ex:
        tracker.change_status("AC101", "lost")
    assert ex.value.args[0] == "LOST is not a valid status"
    assert tracker.redis.set.call_count == 0
```

This test, written using pytest syntax, asserts that the correct exception is raised when an inappropriate argument is passed in. In addition, it creates a Mock object for the set method and makes sure that it is never called. If it was, it would mean there was a bug in our exception handling code.

Simply replacing the method worked fine in this case, since the object being replaced was destroyed in the end. However, we often want to replace a function or method only for the duration of a test. For example, if we want to test the timestamp formatting in the Mock method, we need to know exactly what datetime.datetime.now() is going to return. However, this value changes from run to run. We need some way to pin it to a specific value so we can test it deterministically.

Temporarily setting a library function to a specific value is one of the few valid use cases for monkey-patching. The mock library provides a patch context manager that allows us to replace attributes on existing libraries with mock objects. When the context manager exits, the original attribute is automatically restored so as not to impact other test cases. Here's an example:

```python
import datetime
from unittest.mock import patch


def test_patch(tracker):
    tracker.redis.set = Mock()
    fake_now = datetime.datetime(2015, 4, 1)
    with patch("datetime.datetime") as dt:
        dt.now.return_value = fake_now
        tracker.change_status("AC102", "on time")
    dt.now.assert_called_once_with()
    tracker.redis.set.assert_called_once_with(
        "flightno:AC102", "2015-04-01T00:00:00|ON TIME"
    )
```

In the preceding example, we first construct a value called fake_now, which we will set as the return value of the datetime.datetime.now function. We have to construct this object before we patch datetime.datetime, because otherwise we'd be calling the patched now function before we constructed it.

The with statement invites the patch to replace the datetime.datetime module with a mock object, which is returned as the dt value. The neat thing about mock objects is that any time you access an attribute or method on that object, it returns another mock object. Thus, when we access dt.now, it gives us a new mock object. We set the return_value of that object to our fake_now object. Now, whenever the datetime.datetime.now function is called, it will return our object instead of a new mock object. But when the interpreter exits the context manager, the original datetime.datetime.now() functionality is restored.

After calling our change_status method with known values, we use the assert_called_once_with function of the Mock class to ensure that the now function was indeed called exactly once with no arguments. We then call it a second time to prove that the redis.set method was called with arguments that were formatted as we expected them to be.

Mocking dates so you can have deterministic test results is a common patching scenario. If you are in a situation where you are doing a lot of this, you might appreciate the `freezegun` and `pytest-freezegun` projects available in the Python Package Index.

The previous example is a good indication of how writing tests can guide our API design. The `FlightStatusTracker` object looks sensible at first glance; we construct a `redis` connection when the object is constructed, and we call into it when we need it. When we write tests for this code, however, we discover that even if we mock out that `self.redis` variable on a `FlightStatusTracker`, the `redis` connection still has to be constructed. This call actually fails if there is no Redis server running, and our tests also fail.

We could solve this problem by mocking out the `redis.StrictRedis` class to return a mock in a `setUp` method. A better idea, however, might be to rethink our implementation. Instead of constructing the `redis` instance inside __init__, perhaps we should allow the user to pass one in, as in the following example:

```
def __init__(self, redis_instance=None):
    self.redis = redis_instance if redis_instance else
redis.StrictRedis()
```

This allows us to pass a mock in when we are testing, so the `StrictRedis` method never gets constructed. Additionally, it allows any client code that talks to `FlightStatusTracker` to pass in their own `redis` instance. There are a variety of reasons they might want to do this: they may have already constructed one for other parts of their code; they may have created an optimized implementation of the `redis` API; perhaps they have one that logs metrics to their internal monitoring systems. By writing a unit test, we've uncovered a use case that makes our API more flexible from the start, rather than waiting for clients to demand we support their exotic needs.

This has been a brief introduction to the wonders of mocking code. Mocks are part of the standard `unittest` library since Python 3.3, but as you see from these examples, they can also be used with `pytest` and other libraries. Mocks have other more advanced features that you may need to take advantage of as your code gets more complicated. For example, you can use the `spec` argument to invite a mock to imitate an existing class so that it raises an error if code tries to access an attribute that does not exist on the imitated class. You can also construct mock methods that return different arguments each time they are called by passing a list as the `side_effect` argument. The `side_effect` parameter is quite versatile; you can also use it to execute arbitrary functions when the mock is called or to raise an exception.

In general, we should be quite stingy with mocks. If we find ourselves mocking out multiple elements in a given unit test, we may end up testing the mock framework rather than our real code. This serves no useful purpose whatsoever; after all, mocks are well-tested already! If our code is doing a lot of this, it's probably another sign that the API we are testing is poorly designed. Mocks should exist at the boundaries between the code under test and the libraries they interface with. If this isn't happening, we may need to change the API so that the boundaries are redrawn in a different place.

# How much testing is enough?

We've already established that untested code is broken code. But how can we tell how well our code is tested? How do we know how much of our code is actually being tested and how much is broken? The first question is the more important one, but it's hard to answer. Even if we know we have tested every line of code in our application, we do not know that we have tested it properly. For example, if we write a stats test that only checks what happens when we provide a list of integers, it may still fail spectacularly if used on a list of floats, strings, or self-made objects. The onus of designing complete test suites still lies with the programmer.

The second question—how much of our code is actually being tested—is easy to verify. **Code coverage** is an estimate of the number of lines of code that are executed by a program. If we know that number and the number of lines that are in the program, we can get an estimate of what percentage of the code was really tested, or covered. If we additionally have an indicator as to which lines were not tested, we can more easily write new tests to ensure those lines are less broken.

The most popular tool for testing code coverage is called, memorably enough, `coverage.py`. It can be installed like most other third-party libraries, using the `pip install coverage` command.

We don't have space to cover all the details of the coverage API, so we'll just look at a few typical examples. If we have a Python script that runs all our unit tests for us (for example, using `unittest.main`, `discover`, `pytest`, or a custom test runner), we can use the following command to perform a coverage analysis:

```
$coverage run coverage_unittest.py
```

This command will exit normally, but it creates a file named .coverage, which holds the data from the run. We can now use the coveragereport command to get an analysis of the code coverage:

```
$coverage report
```

The resulting output should be as follows:

| Name | Stmts | Exec | Cover |
|------|-------|------|-------|
| coverage_unittest | 7 | 7 | 100% |
| stats | 19 | 6 | 31% |
| TOTAL | 26 | 13 | 50% |

This basic report lists the files that were executed (our unit test and a module it imported). The number of lines of code in each file, and the number that were executed by the test are also listed. The two numbers are then combined to estimate the amount of code coverage. If we pass the −m option to the report command, it will additionally add a column that looks as follows:

```
Missing
----------
8-12, 15-23
```

The ranges of lines listed here identify lines in the stats module that were not executed during the test run.

The example we just ran the code coverage tool on uses the same stats module we created earlier in the chapter. However, it deliberately uses a single test that fails to test a lot of code in the file. Here's the test:

```
from stats import StatsList
import unittest

class TestMean(unittest.TestCase):
    def test_mean(self):
        self.assertEqual(StatsList([1,2,2,3,3,4]).mean(), 2.5)

if __name__ == "__main__":

    unittest.main()
```

This code doesn't test the median or mode functions, which correspond to the line numbers that the coverage output told us were missing.

The textual report provides sufficient information, but if we use the `coverage html` command, we can get an even more useful interactive HTML report, which we can view in a web browser. The web page even highlights which lines in the source code were and were not tested. Here's how it looks:

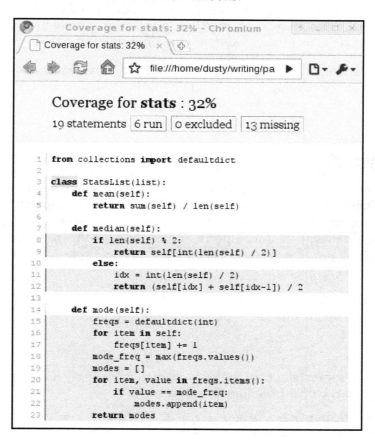

We can use the `coverage.py` module with `pytest` as well. We'll need to install the `pytest` plugin for code coverage, using `pip install pytest-coverage`. The plugin adds several command-line options to `pytest`, the most useful being `--cover-report`, which can be set to `html`, `report`, or `annotate` (the latter actually modifies the original source code to highlight any lines that were not covered).

Unfortunately, if we could somehow run a coverage report on this section of the chapter, we'd find that we have not covered most of what there is to know about code coverage! It is possible to use the coverage API to manage code coverage from within our own programs (or test suites), and `coverage.py` accepts numerous configuration options that we haven't touched on. We also haven't discussed the difference between statement coverage and branch coverage (the latter is much more useful, and the default in recent versions of `coverage.py`), or other styles of code coverage.

Bear in mind that while 100 percent code coverage is a lofty goal that we should all strive for, 100 percent coverage is not enough! Just because a statement was tested does not mean that it was tested properly for all possible inputs.

# Case study

Let's walk through test-driven development by writing a small, tested, cryptography application. Don't worry–you won't need to understand the mathematics behind complicated modern encryption algorithms such as AES or RSA. Instead, we'll be implementing a sixteenth-century algorithm known as the Vigenère cipher. The application simply needs to be able to encode and decode a message, given an encoding keyword, using this cipher.

 If you want a deep dive into how the RSA algorithm works, I wrote one on my blog at `https://dusty.phillips.codes/`.

First, we need to understand how the cipher works if we apply it manually (without a computer). We start with a table like the following one:

```
A B C D E F G H I J K L M N O P Q R S T U V W X Y Z
B C D E F G H I J K L M N O P Q R S T U V W X Y Z A
C D E F G H I J K L M N O P Q R S T U V W X Y Z A B
D E F G H I J K L M N O P Q R S T U V W X Y Z A B C
E F G H I J K L M N O P Q R S T U V W X Y Z A B C D
F G H I J K L M N O P Q R S T U V W X Y Z A B C D E
G H I J K L M N O P Q R S T U V W X Y Z A B C D E F
H I J K L M N O P Q R S T U V W X Y Z A B C D E F G
I J K L M N O P Q R S T U V W X Y Z A B C D E F G H
J K L M N O P Q R S T U V W X Y Z A B C D E F G H I
K L M N O P Q R S T U V W X Y Z A B C D E F G H I J
L M N O P Q R S T U V W X Y Z A B C D E F G H I J K
M N O P Q R S T U V W X Y Z A B C D E F G H I J K L
N O P Q R S T U V W X Y Z A B C D E F G H I J K L M
```

```
O P Q R S T U V W X Y Z A B C D E F G H I J K L M N
P Q R S T U V W X Y Z A B C D E F G H I J K L M N O
Q R S T U V W X Y Z A B C D E F G H I J K L M N O P
R S T U V W X Y Z A B C D E F G H I J K L M N O P Q
S T U V W X Y Z A B C D E F G H I J K L M N O P Q R
T U V W X Y Z A B C D E F G H I J K L M N O P Q R S
U V W X Y Z A B C D E F G H I J K L M N O P Q R S T
V W X Y Z A B C D E F G H I J K L M N O P Q R S T U
W X Y Z A B C D E F G H I J K L M N O P Q R S T U V
X Y Z A B C D E F G H I J K L M N O P Q R S T U V W
Y Z A B C D E F G H I J K L M N O P Q R S T U V W X
Z A B C D E F G H I J K L M N O P Q R S T U V W X Y
```

Given a keyword, TRAIN, we can encode the message ENCODED IN PYTHON as follows:

1. Repeat the keyword and message together, such that it is easy to map letters from one to the other:

```
E N C O D E D I N P Y T H O N
T R A I N T R A I N T R A I N
```

2. For each letter in the plaintext, find the row that begins with that letter in the table.
3. Find the column with the letter associated with the keyword letter for the chosen plaintext letter.
4. The encoded character is at the intersection of this row and column.

For example, the row starting with E intersects the column starting with T at character X. So, the first letter in the ciphertext is X. The row starting with N intersects the column starting with R at character E, leading to the ciphertext XE. C intersects A at C, and O intersects I at W. D and N map to Q, while E and T map to X. The full encoded message is XECWQXUIVCRKHWA.

Decoding follows the opposite procedure. First, find the row with the character for the shared keyword (the T row), then find the location in that row where the encoded character (the X) is located. The plaintext character is at the top of the column for that row (the E).

# Implementing it

Our program will need an `encode` method that takes a keyword and plaintext and returns the ciphertext, and a `decode` method that accepts a keyword and ciphertext and returns the original message.

But rather than just writing those methods, let's follow a test-driven development strategy. We'll be using `pytest` for our unit testing. We need an `encode` method, and we know what it has to do; let's write a test for that method first, as follows:

```
def test_encode():
    cipher = VigenereCipher("TRAIN")
    encoded = cipher.encode("ENCODEDINPYTHON")
    assert encoded == "XECWQXUIVCRKHWA"
```

This test fails, naturally, because we aren't importing a `VigenereCipher` class anywhere. Let's create a new module to hold that class.

Let's start with the following `VigenereCipher` class:

```
class VigenereCipher:
    def __init__(self, keyword):
        self.keyword = keyword

    def encode(self, plaintext):
        return "XECWQXUIVCRKHWA"
```

If we add a `fromvigenere_cipherimportVigenereCipher` line to the top of our test class and run `pytest`, the preceding test will pass! We've finished our first test-driven development cycle.

This may seem like a ridiculously silly thing to test, but it's actually verifying a lot. The first time I implemented it, I mispelled cipher as *cypher* in the class name. Even my basic unit test helped catch a bug. Even so, returning a hardcoded string is obviously not the most sensible implementation of a cipher class, so let's add a second test, as follows:

```
def test_encode_character():
    cipher = VigenereCipher("TRAIN")
    encoded = cipher.encode("E")
    assert encoded == "X"
```

Ah, now that test will fail. It looks like we're going to have to work harder. But I just thought of something: what if someone tries to encode a string with spaces or lowercase characters? Before we start implementing the encoding, let's add some tests for these cases, so we don't forget them. The expected behavior will be to remove spaces, and to convert lowercase letters to capitals, as follows:

```
def test_encode_spaces():
    cipher = VigenereCipher("TRAIN")
    encoded = cipher.encode("ENCODED IN PYTHON")
    assert encoded == "XECWQXUIVCRKHWA"

def test_encode_lowercase():
    cipher = VigenereCipher("TRain")
    encoded = cipher.encode("encoded in Python")
    assert encoded == "XECWQXUIVCRKHWA"
```

If we run the new test suite, we find that the new tests pass (they expect the same hardcoded string). But they ought to fail later if we forget to account for these cases.

Now that we have some test cases, let's think about how to implement our encoding algorithm. Writing code to use a table like we used in the earlier manual algorithm is possible, but seems complicated, considering that each row is just an alphabet rotated by an offset number of characters. It turns out (I asked Wikipedia) that we can use modular arithmetic to combine the characters instead of doing a table lookup.

Given plaintext and keyword characters, if we convert the two letters to their numerical values (according to their position in the alphabet, with A being 0 and Z being 25), add them together, and take the remainder mod 26, we get the ciphertext character! This is a straightforward calculation, but since it happens on a character-by-character basis, we should probably put it in its own function. Before we do that, then, we should write a test for the new function, as follows:

```
from vigenere_cipher import combine_character
def test_combine_character():
    assert combine_character("E", "T") == "X"
    assert combine_character("N", "R") == "E"
```

Now we can write the code to make this function work. In all honesty, I had to run the test several times before I got this function completely correct. First, I accidentally returned an integer, and then I forgot to shift the character back up to the normal ASCII scale from the zero-based scale. Having the test available made it easy to test and debug these errors. This is another bonus of test-driven development. The final, working version of the code looks like the following:

```
def combine_character(plain, keyword):
    plain = plain.upper()
    keyword = keyword.upper()
    plain_num = ord(plain) - ord('A')
    keyword_num = ord(keyword) - ord('A')
    return chr(ord('A') + (plain_num + keyword_num) % 26)
```

Now that `combine_characters` is tested, I thought we'd be ready to implement our `encode` function. However, the first thing we want inside that function is a repeating version of the keyword string that is as long as the plaintext. Let's implement a function for that first. Oops, I mean let's implement the test first, as follows:

```
def test_extend_keyword(): cipher = VigenereCipher("TRAIN") extended =
cipher.extend_keyword(16) assert extended == "TRAINTRAINTRAINT"
```

Before writing this test, I expected to write `extend_keyword` as a standalone function that accepted a keyword and an integer. But as I started drafting the test, I realized it made more sense to use it as a helper method on the `VigenereCipher` class so it could access the `self.keyword` attribute. This shows how test-driven development can help design more sensible APIs. The following is the method implementation:

```
def extend_keyword(self, number):
    repeats = number // len(self.keyword) + 1
    return (self.keyword * repeats)[:number]
```

Once again, this took a few runs of the test to get right. I ended up adding an amended copy of the test, one with fifteen and one with sixteen letters, to make sure it works if the integer division has an even number.

Now we're finally ready to write our `encode` method, as follows:

```
def encode(self, plaintext):
    cipher = []
    keyword = self.extend_keyword(len(plaintext))
    for p,k in zip(plaintext, keyword):
        cipher.append(combine_character(p,k))
    return "".join(cipher)
```

That looks correct. Our test suite should pass now, right?

Actually, if we run it, we'll find that two tests are still failing. The previously failing encode test is actually passing, but we totally forgot about the spaces and lowercase characters! It is a good thing we wrote those tests to remind us. We'll have to add the following line at the beginning of the method:

```
plaintext = plaintext.replace(" ", "").upper()
```

If we have an idea about a corner case in the middle of implementing something, we can create a test describing that idea. We don't even have to implement the test; we can just run `assert False` to remind us to implement it later. The failing test will never let us forget the corner case and it can't be ignored as easily as a ticket in an issue tracker. If it takes a while to get around to fixing the implementation, we can mark the test as an expected failure.

Now all the tests pass successfully. This chapter is pretty long, so we'll condense the examples for decoding. The following are a couple of tests:

```
def test_separate_character():
    assert separate_character("X", "T") == "E"
    assert separate_character("E", "R") == "N"


def test_decode():
    cipher = VigenereCipher("TRAIN")
    decoded = cipher.decode("XECWQXUIVCRKHWA")
    assert decoded == "ENCODEDINPYTHON"
```

And the following is the `separate_character` function:

```
def separate_character(cypher, keyword):
    cypher = cypher.upper()
    keyword = keyword.upper()
    cypher_num = ord(cypher) - ord('A')
    keyword_num = ord(keyword) - ord('A')
    return chr(ord('A') + (cypher_num - keyword_num) % 26)
```

Now we can add the `decode` method:

```
def decode(self, ciphertext):
    plain = []
    keyword = self.extend_keyword(len(ciphertext))
    for p,k in zip(ciphertext, keyword):
        plain.append(separate_character(p,k))
    return "".join(plain)
```

These methods have a lot of similarity to those used for encoding. The great thing about having all these tests written and passing is that we can now go back and modify our code, knowing it is still safely passing the tests. For example, if we replace our existing `encode` and `decode` methods with the following refactored methods, our tests still pass:

```
def _code(self, text, combine_func):
    text = text.replace(" ", "").upper()
    combined = []
    keyword = self.extend_keyword(len(text))
    for p,k in zip(text, keyword):
        combined.append(combine_func(p,k))
    return "".join(combined)

def encode(self, plaintext):
    return self._code(plaintext, combine_character)

def decode(self, ciphertext):
    return self._code(ciphertext, separate_character)
```

This is the final benefit of test-driven development, and the most important. Once the tests are written, we can improve our code as much as we like and be confident that our changes didn't break anything we have been testing for. Furthermore, we know exactly when our refactor is finished: when the tests all pass.

Of course, our tests may not comprehensively test everything we need them to; maintenance or code refactoring can still cause undiagnosed bugs that don't show up in testing. Automated tests are not foolproof. If bugs do occur, however, it is still possible to follow a test-driven plan, as follows:

1. Write a test (or multiple tests) that duplicates or *proves* that the bug in question is occurring. This will, of course, fail.

2. Then write the code to make the tests stop failing. If the tests were comprehensive, the bug will be fixed, and we will know if it ever happens again, as soon as we run the test suite.

Finally, we can try to determine how well our tests operate on this code. With the `pytest` coverage plugin installed, `pytest -coverage-report=report` tells us that our test suite has 100 percent code coverage. This is a great statistic, but we shouldn't get too cocky about it. Our code hasn't been tested when encoding messages that have numbers, and its behavior with such inputs is thus undefined.

# Exercises

Practice test-driven development. That is your first exercise. It's easier to do this if you're starting a new project, but if you have existing code you need to work on, you can start by writing tests for each new feature you implement. This can become frustrating as you become more enamored with automated tests. The old, untested code will start to feel rigid and tightly coupled, and will become uncomfortable to maintain; you'll start feeling like changes you make are breaking the code and you have no way of knowing, for lack of tests. But if you start small, adding tests to the code base improves it over time.

So, to get your feet wet with test-driven development, start a fresh project. Once you've started to appreciate the benefits (you will) and realize that the time spent writing tests is quickly regained in terms of more maintainable code, you'll want to start writing tests for existing code. This is when you should start doing it, not before. Writing tests for code that we *know* works is boring. It is hard to get interested in the project until you realize just how broken the code we thought was working really is.

Try writing the same set of tests using both the built-in `unittest` module and `pytest`. Which do you prefer? `unittest` is more similar to test frameworks in other languages, while `pytest` is arguably more Pythonic. Both allow us to write object-oriented tests and to test object-oriented programs with ease.

We used `pytest` in our case study, but we didn't touch on any features that wouldn't have been easily testable using `unittest`. Try adapting the tests to use test skipping or fixtures (an instance of `VignereCipher` would be helpful). Try the various setup and teardown methods, and compare their use to funcargs. Which feels more natural to you?

Try running a coverage report on the tests you've written. Did you miss testing any lines of code? Even if you have 100 percent coverage, have you tested all the possible inputs? If you're doing test-driven development, 100 percent coverage should follow quite naturally, as you will write a test before the code that satisfies that test. However, if writing tests for existing code, it is more likely that there will be edge conditions that go untested.

Think carefully about the values that are somehow different, such as the following, for example:

- Empty lists when you expect full ones
- Negative numbers, zero, one, or infinity compared to positive integers
- Floats that don't round to an exact decimal place
- Strings when you expected numerals
- Unicode strings when you expected ASCII
- The ubiquitous `None` value when you expected something meaningful

If your tests cover such edge cases, your code will be in good shape.

# Summary

We have finally covered the most important topic in Python programming: automated testing. Test-driven development is considered a best practice. The standard library `unittest` module provides a great out-of-the-box solution for testing, while the `pytest` framework has some more Pythonic syntaxes. Mocks can be used to emulate complex classes in our tests. Code coverage gives us an estimate of how much of our code is being run by our tests, but it does not tell us that we have tested the right things.

Thank you for reading Getting Started with Python. I hope you've enjoyed the ride and are eager to start implementing object-oriented software in all your future projects!

# Other Books You May Enjoy

If you enjoyed this book, you may be interested in these other books by Packt:

**Applied Data Science with Python and Jupyter**
Alex Galea

ISBN: 978-1-78995-817-1

- Get up and running with the Jupyter ecosystem
- Identify potential areas of investigation and perform exploratory data analysis
- Plan a machine learning classification strategy and train classification models
- Use validation curves and dimensionality reduction to tune and enhance your models
- Scrape tabular data from web pages and transform it into Pandas DataFrames
- Create interactive, web-friendly visualizations to clearly communicate your findings

**Python Data Science Essentials - Third Edition**
Alberto Boschetti, Luca Massaron

ISBN: 978-1-78953-786-4

- Set up your data science toolbox on Windows, Mac, and Linux
- Use the core machine learning methods offered by the scikit-learn library
- Manipulate, fix, and explore data to solve data science problems
- Learn advanced explorative and manipulative techniques to solve data operations
- Optimize your machine learning models for optimized performance
- Explore and cluster graphs, taking advantage of interconnections and links in your data

# Leave a review - let other readers know what you think

Please share your thoughts on this book with others by leaving a review on the site that you bought it from. If you purchased the book from Amazon, please leave us an honest review on this book's Amazon page. This is vital so that other potential readers can see and use your unbiased opinion to make purchasing decisions, we can understand what our customers think about our products, and our authors can see your feedback on the title that they have worked with Packt to create. It will only take a few minutes of your time, but is valuable to other potential customers, our authors, and Packt. Thank you!

# Index

Pythonic 42